SPARTA: NEW PERSPECTIVES

SPARTA
New Perspectives

Editors

Stephen Hodkinson

and

Anton Powell

Contributors

Paul Cartledge, Ephraim David, Jean Ducat, Thomas Figueira, Stephen Hodkinson, Noreen Humble, Nigel Kennell, Ellen Greenstein Millender, Massimo Nafissi, Anton Powell, Nicolas Richer, P.-J. Shaw, H.W. Singor, Hans van Wees

with translations from the French by Emma Stafford

The Classical Press of Wales

First published in hardback in 1999
This paperback edition 2009

The Classical Press of Wales
15 Rosehill Terrace, Swansea SA1 6JN
Tel: +44 (0)1792 458397
Fax: +44 (0)1792 464067
www.classicalpressofwales.co.uk

Distributor
Oxbow Books,
10 Hythe Bridge Street,
Oxford OX1 2EW
Tel: +44 (0)1865 241249
Fax: +44 (0)1865 794449

Distributor in the United States of America
The David Brown Book Co.
PO Box 511, Oakville, CT 06779
Tel: +1 (860) 945–9329
Fax: +1 (860) 945–9468

ISBN 978–1–905125–31–9

A catalogue record for this book is available from the British Library

Printed and bound in Great Britain by
CPI Antony Rowe, Chippenham and Eastbourne

To
Geoffrey de Ste. Croix

CONTENTS

INTRODUCTION

Stephen Hodkinson

This volume represents the fruits of the international conference on Spartan history held in Hay-on-Wye on 8–10 September 1997, jointly organised by the University of Wales Institute of Classics and Ancient History and by the University of Manchester Ancient History Seminar. The conference included scholars from four different continents and twelve countries: Australia, Canada, France, Germany, Greece, Israel, Italy, Japan, the Netherlands, Switzerland, the United Kingdom and the United States. It represents, to our knowledge, the first time that ancient historians from so many nationalities have gathered together for a conference devoted to Spartan history. Along with recent international conferences on Spartan and Lakonian art and archaeology (Palagia and Coulson (eds.) 1993; Cavanagh and Walker (eds.) 1998), it signals the notable resurgence of Spartan studies which has taken place around the world during the last generation.

It is in many respects appropriate that this first international conference on Spartan history should have been held in Britain. The preoccupation of British scholarship with ancient Sparta constitutes a notable sub-theme in the history of classical studies during the 20th century (cf. Cartledge 1998, 46–7). The efforts devoted by the British School at Athens from the 1900s onwards to excavation and survey within Sparta and Lakonia (Catling 1998) were matched, within the field of ancient history, by a remarkable dynasty of Oxford-based Sparta-watchers: Toynbee, Wade-Gery, Andrewes, Forrest, Jeffery, Holladay, and – above all – de Ste. Croix. It is a particular pleasure for us as editors to acknowledge the debt that the recent resurgence of Spartan historiography owes to Geoffrey de Ste. Croix, now in his 90th year, who gave his blessing to our conference but whose attendance was sadly prevented by ill-health. His penetrating analysis of the socio-economic basis of Spartan policy-making in *The Origins of the Peloponnesian War* (1972) revitalised the study of Spartan politics, which was then in danger of stagnating in the quagmire of controversy surrounding the infamous 'Great Rhētra', by demonstrating how much was to be gained from the underused classical evidence. On a more personal level, it was the breath of fresh air blown in by *OPW* that inspired Hodkinson as an undergraduate to turn to the study of Sparta. It was de Ste. Croix too who provided Powell in early career with much generous assistance and advice. Above all, however, his contribution has been tangible through his intellectual influence on the primary British historian of Sparta of the last twenty years, Paul Cartledge, whose own academic career began at Oxford.

However, to portray Spartan history-writing as a largely Oxford, or exclusively British, affair would be misleading. Powell's academic writing has been pursued from London and Wales. Hodkinson's study of Sparta began in the 'Manchester History School', from which Kathleen Chrimes' work on Sparta (1949) had emanated in an earlier generation. Most of Cartledge's career has been spent at Cambridge, for some years as colleague of Moses Finley, an American by birth and academic training, who supervised Hodkinson's early doctoral research. Finley's all-encompassing, revisionist essay on 'Sparta' (1968) continues to exercise a seminal influence over current approaches to classical Spartan society. Notably, it first appeared in a volume from a conference held in Paris. Indeed, modern Spartan studies have always been thoroughly international in character. The late 19th and early 20th centuries were marked by major contributions from Continental scholars: from Andreades, Stais and Tsountas in Greece; from Niccolini, Pareti and Solari in Italy; from Cavaignac, Jeanmaire, Ollier and Roussel in France; and from Ehrenberg, Kahrstedt, Niese and Wilamowitz in Germany. (I purposely omit works on Sparta distorted by their alignment with Nazi ideology.) As recent bibliographic surveys (Vagiakakos and Taïphakos 1975; Clauss 1983; Ducat 1983) amply attest, Spartan historiography in the second half of the twentieth century has extended well beyond the established Western European centres of classical learning to a truly world-wide academic community, with important works from scholars around the globe such as Andreev, Bockisch, Christou, Demakopoulou, Fuks, Furuyama, Hamilton, D.H. Kelly, Lotze, Oliva, Shimron, Starr, Steinhauer, Tigerstedt, Tsopanakis and Wolski.

It was in this internationalist context that we resolved to organise the present conference on Spartan history. Whereas Lakonian archaeologists are necessarily drawn together by collaborative enterprise and by the presence of their excavation sites, their survey areas and much of their study material in Greece itself, historians typically work solitarily and independently. The danger of pursuing our researches in parallel universes, of missing valuable interconnections, is ever-present. It therefore seemed to us important – and the time seemed ripe – to attempt to arrange a first international gathering of Spartan historians. Inevitably, there were certain restrictions. For sake of coherence, we resolved to focus upon the archaic to hellenistic periods, upon which most recent historical research has concentrated. Even within this time-span, restrictions of timetable and space limited the number of invitations we could issue. Our imperfect knowledge of the academic communities of certain countries also meant that some historians of Sparta became known to us only after the conference. Others were prevented from attending by alternative commitments or considerations of expense. We have attempted to remedy these deficiencies by inviting contributions for this volume from certain scholars who could not attend and from those who attended as non-speaking participants. Nevertheless, the scholars whose papers we publish here should not be regarded as representing an exhaustive list of important current historians of Sparta. We cordially invite communication from other interested scholars with a view to their inclusion in future conferences.

Despite these restrictions, the historians who gathered together in Hay constituted a significant sample of present Spartan historiography. Many were eminent scholars who knew one another's work but had never previously met. Others were younger scholars or postgraduate students whose participation we were especially keen to encourage. Since the purpose of the conference was internationalist in inspiration – to enable colleagues from different academic backgrounds to discuss and learn from each other's diverse work – we judged it inappropriate as organisers to impose a common theme, which would inevitably reflect our personal agendas and constrain the independent input of other colleagues, especially the fresh insights of younger scholars. Our only stipulation was that contributions should attempt to develop new perspectives on Spartan history which would point the way towards future research.

Diverse as the subjects of the papers were, they clustered around certain key areas of interest or types of approach which are reflected – albeit with many fruitful cross-currents – in the thematic groupings outlined below.

Spartiate institutions and society. Historical discussion of the Spartan polis has long concentrated upon the elite ruling body of Spartiate citizens. As several papers in this volume indicate, their institutions and society remain a central focus of much current analysis, with considerable scope for the re-evaluation of older approaches. The opening three papers deal with central institutions of Spartiate life:

political institutions, the public upbringing, and the common messes. Hans van Wees' contribution addresses an old problem involving the 'Great Rhētra', but applies a new perspective to free it from the quagmire mentioned above. His starting point is a text, the poem *Eunomia* ('Good Order') by the late-seventh-century poet Tyrtaios, which is usually thought to attest the Rhētra's creation of a new political order. Setting the poem within the context of popular discontent at the greed of leading citizens, he argues (through a new reconstruction of the text) that the *Eunomia* represents not a new politics but a conservative attempt to restore harmony by harnessing the religious power of Delphi to reassert the need for obedience to the established authorities. Taking the innovative step of disassociating poem and Rhētra, he suggests that their linkage arose only later in the context of fourth-century political controversies. The *Eunomia* and the Rhētra constituted two radically different responses to internal crisis, with the Rhētra representing a later, secular community agreement for political reform which would include the citizenry at large within the decision-making process. Tyrtaios' *Eunomia* is not the *eunomia* for which Sparta was famous in classical times (Hdt. 1.65). The Rhētra, in contrast, finds new life as part of the 'sixth-century revolution' (Finley 1968, 25) which created the classical Spartan social order.

Jean Ducat tackles a topic, the public upbringing, whose study is presently in a state of flux following Nigel Kennell's recent monograph (1995), which argued that observable transformations in its character in hellenistic and Roman times mean that much of the information in later sources does not constitute evidence for the upbringing of the classical period. Accepting and extending Kennell's argument through the observation that all our evidence takes the form not of descriptive accounts but of a succession of discourses, Ducat emphasises the 'private' aspects of the upbringing typically neglected in ancient accounts: the significant role of the family, its economic expense, and the features shared with Greek *paideia* elsewhere. Ducat's main subject, however, is the long-standing controversy regarding whether the upbringing – with all its associated elements, such as the age classes, pederasty and the upbringing of girls – derived from a set of tribal initiation rites or can be explained in terms of its contemporary pedagogical function of forming future citizens of a political community. Eschewing the frequently polarised character of past debate, he affirms the need to combine both anthropological and historical approaches. The classical upbringing, though thoroughly coherent, was an amalgam of both functional and 'non-functional' inherited elements.

The diversity of current approaches to Spartiate institutions is illustrated by Henk Singor's paper on another topic which has received much attention in recent years (Fisher 1989; Lavrencic 1993; Link 1998), the common messes or *syssitia*. Where Ducat analyses the underlying character of the upbringing, Singor's concern is to explore how recruitment to the messes operated in practice in the fifth century BC. Essential to such exploration, in the absence of clear evidence in the sources, is the exercise of thinking through the logic of the 'system'. Speculative though such exercises inevitably are, their great merit is their very specificity in making explicit assumptions about the working of institutions and their mutual interconnections which would otherwise remain clouded in generalities. In the case of the messes, the two key factors are their connection with the organisation of the basic unit of the army, the *enōmotia*, and the demographic constraints upon levels of recruitment, in so far as they can plausibly be deduced from the comparative evidence of Model Life Tables. Working from these starting-points, Singor detects the existence of a closely-regulated system whereby recruitment into specific *enōmotiai* and into larger regiments (*lochoi*) operated according to membership of Sparta's three Dorian 'tribes' (*phylai*) and five villages. A significant implication regarding the all-important pederastic relationships, which probably served as the basis for mess recruitment, is that a youth's choice in his selection of a boy was severely circumscribed and controlled. The image of a society which exercised quasi-totalitarian control over its citizens is thus brought sharply into focus.

The following two chapters treat aspects of this control which extended across diverse institutional contexts. Ten years ago an important study by Robert Parker (1989) outlined distinctive aspects of Sparta's religious practice and their relation to her society. Nicolas Richer's essay in this volume draws attention to one distinctive sphere of Spartan piety simply touched on by Parker: the various cults accorded to *pathēmata* – abstractions of physical states or dispositions which seize the body (such as Fear, Death, Laughter and Love) – which he suggests were significant religious manifestations of the innovatory spirit of archaic Sparta. Focusing upon the cult of *Aidōs* (deference), he examines the multiple guises in which it appears in Spartiate life and – in line with current approaches which view Greek religious phenomena not in isolation but as a system – its relation to the other *pathēmata* of *Phobos* (Fear) and *Gelōs* (Laughter). In some contexts *Aidōs* appears as a model for female behaviour as counterpart to the *Phobos* which governed male behaviour. More frequently, however, it is a characteristic virtue of Spartiate men: especially in military contexts, where it often distinguishes their behaviour from the *Phobos* felt by non-Spartiates, and in the upbringing where Spartiate teenage youths are said to possess more *Aidōs* than even virgins in the bridal chamber! In all these roles it formed part of the extensive psychological buttressing which the Spartan polis employed in support of the social order.

In the latest of a series of articles exploring the semiotics of communication in classical Sparta (David 1989a; 1989b; 1992) Ephraim David examines a further psychological buttress often ignored by historians: the polis' extensive use of silence as a mode of control, 'reducing...the communication process to the realm of the predictable'. Silence, he notes, was the essential complement to the Spartiates' famed laconic speech. It was enjoined on them in a variety of contexts: as part of the *Aidōs* expected of teenagers; by way of deference to the stated opinions of elders; to enforce secrecy and censorship; to stifle popular involvement in assembly debates; to restrict displays of grief during family bereavement. In these contexts silence reinforced the established hierarchy within the citizen body, privileging those (such as adults, elders, magistrates) to whom speech was permitted or those (such as deceased kings) for whom public lamentation was expected. In other contexts, as during the enforced intoxication of helots at the mess or through laconic responses to garrulous foreign ambassadors, it defined and distinguished Spartiates from non-Spartiates. More generally, the minimisation of speech enhanced the persuasive power of the striking visual images regularly employed by the Spartan authorities (cf. Powell 1989).

Spartans and the Outside World. The contrast drawn in certain classical writers between Spartan laconic speech and Athenian love of rhetoric reminds us that for contemporaries the relationship of Spartan praxis to that of other Greek poleis was a problematic issue. (Note in this volume Ellen Millender's discussion of Athenian ideological representations of empowered Spartan women.) Modern scholarship has often followed contemporaries in portraying Sparta as somewhat peculiar or exceptional, a polis isolated from wider Greek trends. Other recent studies, in contrast, have emphasised Sparta's thorough implication in broader Greek affairs (e.g. Herman 1987; Mitchell 1997, esp. 73–89) neatly encapsulated in Irad Malkin's telling phrase 'the Spartan Mediterranean' (1994). Several papers at the conference addressed, from various standpoints, questions relating to the relationship between the Spartiates and other Greeks, both inside and outside Spartan territory.

Hodkinson's investigation of how far Spartiates shared the general

Greek passion for engagement in the athletic *agōn* continues a long-term project (Hodkinson 1986; 1997a; 1998a; 1998b) to explore the complex manner in which apparently distinctive Spartan practices frequently reflect and exemplify trends observable elsewhere. Within their home territory Spartiate idiosyncrasy is evident in the prominence of team contests, in public athletics for girls, and in a certain disdain for boxing and the *pankration*. The evidence of private victory monuments and public victor lists shows, however, that Spartan citizens, both individually and collectively, accorded a high valuation to most forms of individual athletic competition. As regards participation in contests abroad, the much-highlighted decline of Spartiate athletic victories in the Olympic games was not the dramatic phenomenon normally assumed and was not unique to Sparta. Far from displaying a hostility to foreign athletics, the polis publicly commemorated the achievements of past victors. Policy towards contemporary victors was more circumspect: there were no material rewards, no public statues, no epinician odes; but victors were given a special military role in the king's bodyguard. Private Spartiate victory dedications at Olympia, though restrained in terms of monumentality, were advanced in the boastfulness of their commemorative inscriptions. In general, the well-known literary evidence – much of it late – consistently exaggerates Sparta's abstention from the athletic *agōn*. In contrast, the hitherto underexploited epigraphic evidence from both Sparta and Olympia displays the Spartiates' overt celebration of agonistic success.

One notable feature of this epigraphic record is the similarity between athletic inscriptions from Sparta itself and those from areas inhabited by the other free members of the Lakedaimonian polis, the *perioikoi*. This cultural *koinē* is apparent with other material artefacts too, such as the famous hero-reliefs (Hibler 1993; Salapata 1993) and the ΕΝ ΠΟΛΕΜΟΙ memorials for fallen warriors (*IG* V.i.701–10, 918, 921, 1124–5, 1320, 1591). Often neglected in past scholarship, the crucial role of the *perioikoi* in the classical period has recently received renewed attention from both archaeologists and historians through the Anglo-Dutch *Laconia Survey* and the work of the Copenhagen Polis Centre.[1] Nigel Kennell's paper in this volume extends this attention to a less well-known era, the second and first centuries BC, when the former perioikic communities were no longer dependent on Sparta but were independent poleis and had formed their own separate League of the Lakedaimonians. Inscriptions, especially from proxeny and other forms of honorific decrees, also form the backbone of Kennell's source material. They reveal that political life revolved largely around the individual poleis rather than the Lakedaimonian League, with the poleis maintaining their separate citizenships and levying import and export duties even on one another's citizens. Connected with this minimal degree of unity were the close ties which the poleis maintained with Sparta, adhering to her calendar and using her coins. This cultural influence, presumably an ongoing legacy of the classical cultural *koinē*, was augmented by informal socio-political influence. Frequent grants of proxeny decrees to Spartan citizens indicate the Lakedaimonian poleis' need for patrons in the region's most powerful city. One recalls the ties of clientship which wealthy classical Spartiate families probably established with aspiring protégés among the *perioikoi* (Hodkinson 1997b, 65).

Scholarly neglect of the *perioikoi* contrasts strongly with the controversies which, in modern times as in antiquity, have surrounded Sparta's servile population, the helots.[2] One vigorous debate concerns the extent of the threat posed to the Spartiate elite by the numerically superior helots. Were the helots mostly docile towards their Spartiate masters (Talbert 1989), 'a desirable commodity of which they wanted more' (Whitby 1994, 110)? Or a wolf held by the throat (Grundy 1911, 219), 'a potentially active human volcano' (de Ste. Croix 1972, 90) ever liable to erupt? If the latter, should helot efforts against their Spartiate masters be viewed as a class struggle (Cartledge 1987, 1991) or as a struggle for 'national' liberation? The prime obstacle to answering these questions is, as with all servile groups in antiquity, the extreme paucity of evidence from the helots' viewpoint – an issue especially acute with regard to the helots of Messenia, who successfully separated from Spartan control in 370/69 and thereafter maintained their independence. This Messenian perspective is currently the subject of specific archaeological focus through the work of the Pylos Regional Archaeological Project.[3]

Thomas Figueira's paper illuminates the questions of Messenian and helot identity via a new, historiographical approach which views the evidence of writers like Thucydides as testimony to contemporary ideological representations. He contextualises the emergence of Messenian ethnicity in the self-representations of the former rebels (from Lakonia as well as Messenia) of the great mid-fifth-century revolt, who were established by the Athenians as a free and autonomous community at Naupaktos and depicted themselves as the authentic citizens of a Messenian state. These self-representations received support from the official position of the Athenians in their imperial conflict with Sparta, which portrayed disaffected helots as a subjugated people fighting for their 'national' freedom rather than as a suppressed *dēmos* engaged in class struggle. The crucial obstacle to this latter approach was – as so often – the loyal support for Sparta provided by the bulk of the Lakedaimonian *dēmos*, the *perioikoi*. In contrast, Spartiate representations denied the existence of ethnic distinctions, portraying all helots as inhabitants of Lakōnikē. Helots who collaborated and received their freedom were treated, and viewed themselves – as the term *neodamōdeis* implies – as perioikic members of the *dēmos* of the Lakedaimonian polis. Both sets of representations were reflected in rival depictions of the events of 370/69, Messenian propaganda portraying them as a return from exile to refound the Messenian state, the Spartans as the liberation of their former slaves. What, however, of the existing helot inhabitants whose contribution was marginalised by both depictions? There are signs that already under Spartiate rule, faced with resistance to moves to grant them political rights, the region's inhabitants were themselves developing some sense of separate identity, based upon local cult and drawing upon folk memories of Messenian resistance to the Spartan conquest, which provided the basis for their subsequent participation in the independent polis of Messene.

The phenomenon of self-representation, including a purported helot connection, is also at issue in Massimo Nafissi's study of relations between Sparta and her colony, Taras, in southern Italy. The nature of that relationship was complex. Despite the contrasts drawn by some ancient writers between sober, austere Sparta and drunken, luxurious Taras, the two poleis maintained close political connections from the sixth to the late fourth centuries. Several of Taras' institutions bore a strong Spartan flavour, but it would be rash to assume that these resemblances shared a common chronological origin, still less that historically-attested Tarentine customs can be used to fill in gaps in our knowledge of early Sparta. The cult of Dionysos and the placename Satyrion for the Tarentine acropolis may suggest the importance of wine and banqueting in Spartan society at the time of the colony's foundation. But cults which hint more overtly at a Spartan connection are probably later creations designed to establish or reinforce contemporary links, as was the introduction of the ephorate attested at Taras and her colony Herakleia Lucana. Similarly, the divergent stories of Taras' foundation by the Spartan Partheniai are not reflections of the historical settlement, but later fictions which derive from classical political circumstances and present contrasting relations between the poleis. The account of Antiochos depicts the Partheniai as cowardly helots, implying the absence of ongoing ties; Ephorus' account highlights the Partheniai's courage and Spartan goodwill, implying a close contemporary relationship. The topic of her colonial relations – which, as Nafissi notes, were also claimed by other poleis – thus takes us to the heart of Sparta's thoroughgoing implication in the affairs of the classical Mediterranean world.

The final paper in this section, by P.-J. Shaw, also considers Spartan intervention abroad (against her arch-rival Argos) and returns us to Spartiate involvement in Messenia and the Olympic games – but from an even more unsettling historiographical perspective through which she questions the absolute dating conventionally assigned to archaic Greek history. The chronology of events in early Peloponnesian history is critically dependent upon post-classical Olympiad chronography. Yet clear discrepancies in Pausanias' account of Messenian history suggest the need for radical revision of established scholarly attributions of chronological values to numbered Olympiads. Evidence for the upward displacement of certain key events by some 43 Olympiads, or 172 years, prompts a substantial experiment in the global downward recalibration of early Olympiad 'dates'. The exercise produces some plausible synchronisms, including the resolution of several notorious Doppelgängers, and calls for a root-and-branch reconsideration of Sparta's historical development, with the Second Messenian war as an affair of the late archaic period and the infamous battle of Hysiai located *c.* 497 as a prelude to Sepeia. The potential implications are immense, including for several papers in the present volume: Nafissi's account of Spartan-Tarentine relations and Van Wees' account of political development would look very different with the foundation of Taras and Tyrtaios' *Eunomia* placed in the later sixth and early fifth centuries. A late archaic Chionis, dedicating his own victory monuments at Olympia and Sparta, would substantially revise Hodkinson's discussion of official attitudes and private behaviour regarding the celebration of athletic success. Complete exposition of this radical thesis in the author's Cardiff doctoral dissertation is keenly awaited.

Representations of Spartan society. As several of the above essays indicate, the study of Sparta is thoroughly complicated by the fact that the literary sources (almost all of them non-Spartan) were rarely, if ever, concerned to provide information about Sparta for its own sake. In the words of Oswyn Murray (1990, 9), 'it is portrayed by a succession of non-Spartan observers as an ideal construct, heavily contaminated with the usual anthropological failings, of emphasis on its otherness, its difference from the norm, and of its conformity to a system'. Indeed, several of the literary accounts are embedded in discourses marked by a high degree of ideological colouring which represent the character of Spartan society in ways which frequently involve considerable distortion or even invention, mostly with an overtly or implicitly idealising tendency. This phenomenon – known since François Ollier's epoch-making study (1933–43) as *le mirage spartiate* – creates, as Paul Cartledge notes, the major historiographical problem of how, from distorted evidence, we can assess the 'reality' under distortion. On the other hand, as he stresses, the mirage constitutes a significant historical phenomenon in its own right, a phenomenon which has left the enduring legacy in medieval and modern intellectual consciousness highlighted in Elizabeth Rawson's study of *The Spartan Tradition in European Thought* (1969).

In his chapter Cartledge undertakes a comparative examination of contemporary mirage and European tradition in the sphere of political thought, juxtaposing the intellectual idealisation of Sparta that arose within the circle of Socrates, which contained many upper-class Athenians disenchanted with their democratic system, with the laconism of the major modern political philosopher and advocate of direct participatory democracy, Jean-Jacques Rousseau. In discussing the Socratics, Cartledge acknowledges modern debate about their approach to Sparta. In the absence of any writings, the political views of Socrates himself must remain conjectural; but he was associated by Aristophanes with 'social laconism' and his remaining in Athens during the tyranny of the Thirty suggests his sympathy with a laconising oligarchy. Certainly, his pupil Xenophon has Socrates present Sparta as better than any other city. As for Xenophon's own views, despite his criticism of contemporary Sparta, Cartledge asserts a straightforward reading of his *Polity of the Lakedaimonians* as praise of the traditional Lykourgan system against those – most notably the followers of Leo Strauss – who interpret it as subtle criticism.[4] Similarly, he argues, although Plato was alert to Sparta's failings and open to other influences, many of the recommendations in his *Laws* resemble Spartan practice (cf. also Powell 1994). It is Rousseau, however, despite his proto-democratic stance, who emerges as the least critical advocate of the Spartan regime. Significantly, his knowledge of Sparta was derived not from the Socratics but from the moralising biographies of Plutarch, whose version is readily evident in Rousseau's emphasis upon Spartan austerity, civic morality and collectivising spirit, all stemming from the semi-divine lawgiver Lykourgos. For Rousseau Sparta served an essential function as affirmation of the practical possibility of his ideas of republican citizenship and the General Will. Between them the Socratics and Rousseau attest the critical importance of the Spartan mirage in the history of Utopian political thought.

One of the controversies discussed by Cartledge is taken up from a contrasting perspective by Noreen Humble in an essay which challenges scholarly readings of one particular aspect of the Spartan mirage: the view that classical writers regarded the quality of *sōphrosynē* (self-control, moderation) as a pre-eminently Spartan virtue. Focusing upon the writings of Xenophon, she argues that *sōphrosynē* is marginal to his account of Spartan education in the much-debated *Lak.Pol.*, a marginality that contrasts sharply with the virtue's centrality in his account of Persian education in the *Cyropaedia*. Indeed, throughout his writings Xenophon's sole unequivocal attribution of *sōphrosynē* to a Spartan is in his encomium of Agesilaos, where it was dictated by the genre; in so far as the association appears elsewhere he seems to distance himself from personal endorsement. In the *Lak.Pol.* the prime Spartan characteristic was the quality of *aidōs* (deference), which was instilled not by self-control but by fear of punishment – a conclusion which parallels Richer's account of the important roles played by the cults of *Aidōs* and *Phobos* (Fear). She, consequently, urges caution in regarding the *Lak.Pol.* as an uncritical idealisation of Spartan society, a thesis to be pursued across the breadth of Xenophon's writings in the forthcoming publication of her recent McMaster doctoral dissertation (1997). Her account thus forms part of a broader scholarly re-evaluation of Xenophon's *oeuvre* and political affiliations which is currently in progress.[5]

The final two papers in the volume examine, again from contrasting perspectives, ancient representations of another group of persons who, like the helots, were a source of ancient controversy: Spartan women. Here our source problems are multiplied by the fact that not only are the literary sources non-Spartan, they are also exclusively male. In the case of *classical* Spartan women there is the further problem – again as with the helots discussed by Figueira – that the sources largely derive from, or were influenced by, Sparta's imperial rival, Athens. In her recent Pennsylvania doctoral dissertation (1996) Ellen Millender drew attention to a major feature of the Spartan mirage which runs counter to the idealising tendencies discussed above: the negative 'barbarization' of Sparta in Athenian democratic ideology. Here she focuses on the role played by representations of Spartan women in the process of barbarization. The modern context for her study is the current vigorous debate about the position of women in Spartiate society. Scholars who portray Spartan women as unusually liberated or influential, Millender contends, pay insufficient attention to the bias of the fifth-century Athenocentric sources upon whom their views depend. These sources consistently portray Sparta (historical or mythical) in terms otherwise reserved for depictions of non-Greek societies, as a topsy-turvy world in which the women live free from normal restraints and dominate their menfolk. This was not simply a negative Athenian response to a somewhat freer female lifestyle and sexual mores. Other evidence attests male control over female marriage and other sexual relationships and indicates that female (semi-) nudity was part not of a liberated lifestyle but of a eugenic process of socialisation towards marriage; women's property rights probably gave them a measure of leverage in family affairs, but it is unlikely that men relinquished control. Athenian depictions of sexuality and gender roles played an essential role in Athens' self-definition vis-à-vis other poleis. The social order of the Athenian polis rested upon male control over female sexuality within the *oikos*, especially after the enactment of the citizenship law of 451/50 made citizenship rights dependent upon the status of both parents. Democratic ideology responded to consequent concerns about female transgressions by constructing women as secluded and quiescent. Conversely, and simultaneously, Sparta's replacement of Persia as Athens' main enemy stimulated the projection of barbarian-style images of the powerful Spartan woman which, in questioning the masculinity of Spartan men, bolstered Athens' claims to imperial hegemony.

Anton Powell's subject is the women of hellenistic Sparta who appear in prominent personal and political roles in Plutarch's account of the third-century revolution in his Lives of Agis and Kleomenes. Here the source material provides, not globalising claims about women in general or dramatised representations of archetypal Spartan females in tragedy and comedy, but purportedly historical accounts of the influence and actions of precise personages. Certainly, these stories require scrutiny for signs of distortion and invention. Plutarch, who has a taste for *exempla* of female virtue, has structured the lives to highlight the women in question, but is not known to invent entire episodes. The failings of his source, Phylarchos, are well known from the fierce, though probably biased, strictures of Polybius. His attested penchant for titillating tales of female assertiveness and death, his anti-Macedonian sympathies, not to mention the impossibility of first-hand reports of several incidents, argue for a sizeable fictional element. Yet certain events – the executions of two royal women – cannot be invention and Phylarchos also includes much plausible local detail. Could these tales of prominent female involvement derive from Spartan sources and reflect authentic local, perhaps even female-influenced, representations? Spartan precedents are suggestive: a tradition of moralising story-telling, including tales of (homo)sexual attachment and noble death; fourth-century accounts of feminine influence, including a politically-motivated female execution; sober evidence for increasing female property-ownership; the increasing exclusiveness of a wealthy (royal) elite, who were more likely to invest influence in their kinswomen than in impoverished male citizens. The immediate aftermath of the events related – post-Sellasian Sparta, denuded of male citizens, with a numerically-dominant but divided female population – would constitute a plausible context for dramatised self-representations of female political engagement.

The last paper thus brings us full-circle back to the realm of politics treated in the opening essay, but to a very different type of Spartan world. This introduction has attempted to convey a few of the common trends and themes which emerged from the various contributions, and also some of the contrasting approaches and points of disagreement which make Spartan historical studies a continuing source of lively and stimulating debate. Detailed reading of the contributions themselves will of course reveal many more parallels, nuances and divergences than can be touched on here. We should like, as organisers, to thank all the conference participants – whether represented in this volume or not – for the constructive and co-operative spirit of the conference which bore fruit, especially, in one session specifically set aside for an open forum on the future directions of Spartan studies. Underlying the many diverse ideas expressed was one common theme, the desire for increased future co-operation and communication: through future international Sparta conferences; through closer interaction with our colleagues in Lakonian archaeology, especially with colleagues in Greece; and through a proposal to establish a site devoted specifically to Sparta and Lakonia on the World Wide Web. On this last proposal, consultations are currently being extended to interested colleagues outside the conference and in other disciplines, with a view to the possible development of a network of websites within which – in keeping with the spirit of internationalism – colleagues could participate on an equal footing and communicate their research and/or teaching materials in the manner each person or institution chooses.[6]

Finally, this introduction would be incomplete without our expression of sincere thanks to certain specific persons and institutions who helped make the conference and this volume possible. We are especially grateful for generous financial assistance from the A.G. Leventis Foundation and from the University of Manchester Research Support Fund and Faculty of Arts Recurrent Grant for Research. Particular thanks are also due to Emma Stafford for her translation into English of the papers by Ducat and Richer.

Notes

[1] Cavanagh *et al.* 1996; Shipley 1992; 1997. The title of the 1995 British Museum conference, 'Sparta in Laconia' (Cavanagh and Walker (eds.) 1998), speaks volumes about current approaches.

[2] Cf., within recent years, disagreement over appropriate comparanda for helot economic exploitation (Hodkinson 1992; 2000; Cartledge 1993), and radical questioning of standard ideas concerning the collective character of helot servitude (Ducat 1990).

[3] Davis (ed.) 1998; Alcock forthcoming; Alcock *et al.* in prep.

[4] Strauss 1939; Higgins 1977; Proietti 1987.

[5] The thesis of Xenophon's partiality to Sparta in his *Hellenika* is challenged in Tuplin (1993); cf. his organisation of the first international conference on Xenophon ('The World of Xenophon') in Liverpool in July 1999.

[6] Any colleague who would be interested in participating in such a network and who has not yet been approached is cordially invited to contact the first-named editor by e-mail at:*Stephen.Hodkinson@man.ac.uk*

Bibliography

Alcock, S.E.

forthcoming 'The peculiar Book IV and the problem of the Messenian past', in S.E. Alcock and J. Elsner (eds.) *Pausanias: Travel and imagination in Roman Greece.*

Alcock, S.E., Berlin, A., Harrison, A., Heath, S. and Spencer, N.

in prep. 'The Pylos Regional Archaeological Project. Part IV: Historic Messenia, Geometric to Late Roman', *Hesperia.*

Cartledge, P.A.

1987 *Agesilaos and the Crisis of Classical Sparta*, London.

1991 'Richard Talbert's revision of the Spartan-helot struggle: a reply', *Historia* 40, 379–81.

1993 'Classical Greek agriculture: recent work and alternative views', *Journal of Peasant Studies* 21, 127–36.

1998 'City and *chora* in Sparta: archaic to Hellenistic', in Cavanagh and Walker (eds.) *Sparta in Laconia*, 39–47.

Catling, H.W.

1998 'The work of the British School at Athens at Sparta and in Laconia', in Cavanagh and Walker (eds.) *Sparta in Laconia*, 19–27.

Cavanagh, W., Crouwel, J., Catling R.W.V. and Shipley, G.
1996 *Continuity and Change in a Greek Rural Landscape: The Laconia Survey* II, Annual of the British School at Athens Supplementary Volume 27, London.

Cavanagh, W.G. and Walker, S.E.C. (eds.)
1998 *Sparta in Laconia: Proceedings of the 19th British Museum Classical Colloquium*, British School at Athens Studies 4, London.

Chrimes, K.M.T.
1949 *Ancient Sparta: A re-examination of the evidence*, Manchester. Second edn, 1952.

Clauss, M.
1983 *Sparta: eine Einführung in seine Geschichte und Zivilisation*, Munich.

David, E.
1989a 'Laughter in Spartan society', in Powell (ed.) *Classical Sparta*, 1–25.
1989b 'Dress in Spartan society', *Ancient World* 19, 3–13.
1992 'Sparta's social hair', *Eranos* 90, 11–21.

Davis, J. (ed.)
1998 *Sandy Pylos: an archaeological history from Nestor to Navarino*, Austin.

Ducat, J.
1983 'Sparte archaïque et classique: structures économiques, sociales, politiques (1965–1982)', *REG* 96, 195–225.
1990 *Les Hilotes*, Bulletin de Correspondance Hellénique, Supplementary Vol. XX, Paris.

Finley, M.I.
1968 'Sparta', in J.-P. Vernant (ed.) *Problèmes de la guerre en Grèce ancienne*, Paris 143–60 = *Economy and Society in Ancient Greece*, (eds.) B.D. Shaw and R.P. Saller, London 1981, 24–40 = *The Use and Abuse of History*, 2nd edn, London 1986, 161–78.

Fisher, N.R.E.
1989 'Drink, *hybris* and the promotion of harmony in Sparta', in Powell (ed.) *Classical Sparta*, 26–50.

Grundy, G.B.
1911 *Thucydides and the History of his Age*, Oxford. Reprinted with the addition of a second volume in 1948.

Herman, G.
1987 *Ritualised Friendship and the Greek City*, Cambridge.

Hibler, D.
1993 'The hero-reliefs of Lakonia: changes in form and function', in Palagia and Coulson (eds.) *Sculpture*, 199–204.

Higgins, W.E.
1977 *Xenophon the Athenian: The problem of the individual and the society of the polis*, Albany.

Hodkinson, S.
1986 'Land tenure and inheritance in classical Sparta'*CQ* n.s. 36, 378–406.
1992 'Sharecropping and Sparta's economic exploitation of the helots', in Sanders (ed.) ΦΙΛΟΛΑΚΟΝ, 123–34.

1997a 'The development of Spartan society and institutions in the archaic period', in L.G. Mitchell and P.J. Rhodes (eds.) *The Development of the Polis in Archaic Greece*, London and New York, 83–102.

1997b 'Servile and free dependants of the Spartan *oikos*', in M. Moggi and G. Cordiano (eds.) *Schiavi e Dipendenti nell'Ambito dell'Oikos e della Familia*, XXII Colloquio GIREA, Pisa, 45–71.

1998a 'Lakonian artistic production and the problem of Spartan austerity', in N. Fisher and H. van Wees (eds.) *Archaic Greece: New Approaches and New Evidence*, London, 93–117.

1998b 'Patterns of bronze dedications at Spartan sanctuaries, *c.* 650–350 BC: towards a quantified database of material and religious investment', in Cavanagh and Walker (eds.) *Sparta in Laconia*, 55–63.

2000 *Property and Wealth in Classical Sparta*, London.

Humble, N.M.

1997 'Xenophon's view of Sparta: a study of the *Anabasis*, *Hellenica* and *Respublica Lacedaemoniorum*', Diss. McMaster.

Kennell, N.M.

1995 *The Gymnasium of Virtue: Education and culture in ancient Sparta*, Chapel Hill and London.

Lavrencic, M.

1993 *Spartanische Küche: das Gemeinschaftsmahl der Männer in Sparta*, Vienna.

Link, S.

1998 '"Durch diese Tür geht kein Wort hinaus!" (Plut. Lyk. 12.8): Bürgergemeinschaft und Syssitien in Sparta', *Laverna* 9, 82–112.

Malkin, I.

1994 *Myth and Territory in the Spartan Mediterranean*, Cambridge.

Millender, E.G.

1996 '"The Teacher of Hellas": Athenian democratic ideology and the "barbarization" of Sparta in fifth-century Greek thought', Diss. Pennsylvania.

Mitchell, L.G.

1997 *Greeks Bearing Gifts: The public use of private relationships in the Greek world, 435–322* BC, Cambridge.

Murray, O.

1990 'Cities of reason', in O. Murray and S. Price (eds.) *The Greek City: from Homer to Alexander*, Oxford, 1–25.

Ollier, F.

1933–43 *Le mirage spartiate: étude sur l'idéalisation de Sparte dans l'antiquité grecque*, 2 vols., Paris. Reprinted in one volume, New York 1973.

Palagia O. and Coulson W. (eds.)

1993 *Sculpture from Arcadia and Laconia*, Oxford.

Parker, R.

1989 'Spartan religion', in Powell (ed.) *Classical Sparta*, 142–72.

Powell, A.

1989 'Mendacity and Sparta's use of the visual', in Powell (ed.) *Classical Sparta*, 173–92.

1994 'Plato and Sparta: modes of rule and of non-rational persuasion in the *Laws*', in A. Powell and S. Hodkinson (eds.) *The Shadow of Sparta*, London and New York, 273–321.

Powell, A. (ed.)
1989 *Classical Sparta: Techniques behind her success*, London.

Proietti, G.
1987 *Xenophon's Sparta: An introduction*, Leiden.

Rawson, E.
1969 *The Spartan Tradition in European Thought*, Oxford. Reprinted 1991.

Ste. Croix, G.E.M. de
1972 *The Origins of the Peloponnesian War*, London.

Salapata, G.
1993 'The Laconian hero-reliefs in the light of the terracotta plaques', in Palagia and Coulson (eds.) *Sculpture*, 189–97.

Sanders, J.M. (ed.)
1992 ΦΙΛΟΛΑΚΟΝ. *Lakonian Studies in honour of Hector Catling*, London.

Shipley, G.
1992 '*Perioikos*: the discovery of classical Lakonia', in Sanders (ed.) ΦΙΛΟΛΑΚΟΝ, 211–26.
1997 ' "The other Lakedaimonians": the dependent perioikic *poleis* of Laconia and Messenia', in M.H. Hansen (ed.) *The Polis as an Urban Centre and as a Political Community*, Acts of the Copenhagen Polis Centre Vol. 4, Copenhagen, 189–281.

Strauss, L.
1939 'The spirit of Sparta and the taste of Xenophon', *Social Research* 6, 502–36.

Talbert, R.J.A.
1989 'The role of the helots in the class struggle at Sparta', *Historia* 38, 22–40.

Tuplin, C.J.
1993 *The Failings of Empire: A reading of Xenophon Hellenica 2.3.11–7.5.27*, Historia Einzelschriften 76, Stuttgart.

Vagiakakos, D. and Taïphakos, I.G.
1975 'Λακωνικῆ Βιβλιογραφία', *Lakonikai Spoudai* 2, 417–87.

Whitby, M.
1994 'Two Shadows: images of Spartans and helots', in A. Powell and S. Hodkinson (eds.) *The Shadow of Sparta*, London and New York, 87–126.

Chapter 1

TYRTAEUS' *EUNOMIA*
Nothing to do with the Great Rhetra

Hans van Wees

Sparta was brought to the brink of civil war in the seventh century BC, during the Messenian revolt. 'This is clear from the poem by Tyrtaeus called *Eunomia*,' said Aristotle (*Politics* 1307a1; F 1 West). The fragments of this poem offer a rare glimpse of the politics and government of early Sparta, and are an invaluable corrective to the ancient myth that Sparta, ever since the reforms of Lycurgus in the early eighth century at the latest, had been the most stable and well-ordered city in Greece. Yet the evidence of *Eunomia* has not been exploited to the full.

With the exception of a scanty papyrus fragment, all we know of the poem comes from quotations in later authors, whose interpretations of the text have continued to dominate modern discussions. Since *Eunomia*'s ancient readers believed that Sparta's constitution had been created by Lycurgus long before Tyrtaeus' time, they were mainly interested in the poem as evidence for Lycurgus' legislation. Modern scholars, despite viewing stories about the deified lawgiver with all due scepticism, have followed suit. They have accepted the sources' claim that *Eunomia* made reference to Sparta's chief constitutional law, the Great Rhetra, and have concentrated on the question of what the poem tells us about the date of the law.[1] In doing so, scholars have drawn quite heavily on ancient conjectures about what Tyrtaeus implied in parts of the poem now lost.

In order to make fuller and better use of *Eunomia*, we need to deconstruct the interpretations imposed upon it in antiquity, and reconstruct what it meant to its original audience. A reassessment of the fragments in their contemporary context will show that the poem did not cite the Rhetra, and is likely to be older than this law. *Eunomia* will emerge, not as an appeal to keep faith with a formal constitution established by secular and political means, but as an example of a common seventh-century response to internal crisis: an attempt to restore harmony by reasserting the order sanctioned by the gods, through rituals, oracles, and songs.

Spartan greed and the seventh-century crisis

Aristotle cited Tyrtaeus' elegy as evidence for his thesis that civil wars break out 'when some are in great need while others enjoy affluence'. 'This happens especially in times of war,' he explained, 'and also occurred in Sparta during the Messenian War... Some people, crushed by the war, called for a redistribution of the land' (*Politics* 1306b36–7b2). Pausanias' travel guide informs us that the Spartans resolved to leave large tracts of land uncultivated so that the Messenians would not profit from their raids; that this caused a shortage of grain, and resentment among the owners of the abandoned land; and that Tyrtaeus managed to avert a civil war (4.18.2–3).

How much of this information came from *Eunomia* itself? Judging by what survives of other poetry in the same genre – especially the work of Solon, which also included an elegy on the subject of *eunomia*, 'good order' – Tyrtaeus' poem probably offered merely allusions to, rather than a full account of, the current situation. The details of Pausanias' scenario are thus likely to be later invention, stemming from an attempt to reconcile the evidence of Tyrtaeus with the legend of Lycurgus. Those who believed that Lycurgus had made a strictly equal division of land among all citizens[2] could only account for the inequality evident in Tyrtaeus by positing some such set of peculiar circumstances, unparalleled in the history of Greek warfare. Aristotle, too, may well have played up the effects of war to explain how Sparta's order could have suffered such disruption. All we can safely say is that *Eunomia* must have contained at least one allusion to demands for the redistribution of land. Even if it was no more explicit than Solon's remark that 'it did not please me that fine men should have the same share of the fertile soil of our country as the lower classes' (F 34.8–9 West), it must have been clear evidence of popular discontent at the inequality of wealth in Sparta.

Seventh- and sixth-century Laconian art reveals a society in which the elite engaged in all the forms of conspicuous consumption of wealth and leisure characteristic of archaic Greece. The poetry of Alcman reinforces that picture: a telling comment about the degree of social inequality in Sparta is the poet's description of himself as 'an omnivore' who needs no 'sweet confections' but loves pea-soup and 'looks for ordinary food, *like the common people*' (*damos*; F 17 Page).[3] Indeed, in Alcman's time Sparta appears to have had a reputation for attaching overriding importance to wealth. When Pindar, in the early fifth century, used the proverb 'a man is what he owns', [4] he called it 'the saying of the Argive' (*Isthmian* 2.9–11), but around 600 BC the same proverb was regarded as a saying of *Spartan* origin: 'Aristodemos, they say, once put it very effectively in Sparta: "A man is what he owns, and not a single poor man is noble or respected" ' (Alcaeus F 360 L–P). The earlier tradition of a Spartan society much concerned with the accumulation of wealth had, by Pindar's day, evidently given way to the legend of Lycurgan equality, so that a Spartan origin for the expression no longer seemed likely.[5]

Another proverb offers even better evidence for Spartan acquisitiveness:

> Greed will destroy Sparta, but nothing else
>
> Ἁ φιλοχρηματία Σπάρταν ὀλεῖ, ἄλλο δὲ οὐδέν

Most scholars agree that this hexameter verse is a proverb of classical date and irrelevant to archaic Sparta.[6] Yet it cannot be dismissed so easily.

Our sources all say that the proverb originated from a Delphic oracle, and they claim to know that the god delivered this oracle 'spontaneously' (Aristotle F 544 Rose), either to Lycurgus (Diodorus 7.12.6), or to the kings Alcamenes and Theopompus (Plutarch, *Moralia* 239f). A Delphic origin is possible in principle, since some famous oracular phrases did become proverbial,[7] but in practice it is excluded by the use of dialect in our verse. All of the several hundred preserved Delphic verse oracles, whether genuine or false, use a mixture of epic and Ionic language. Our verse is the only one to employ the long alpha of most other Greek dialects: it has the article *ha* (ἁ) instead of *hê* (ἡ) and speaks of *Sparta* (Σπάρτα) rather than *Spartē* (Σπάρτη).[8] An oracular response from Delphi – even a forged response – simply would not have been expressed in this way.

Given that our proverb takes the form of a complete hexameter line, it is unlikely that it was spontaneously generated by popular wisdom. Like so many other Greek proverbs, it must have been a snatch of archaic or classical poetry which entered the language in much the same way that phrases coined by Shakespeare became proverbial in English. Theognis' hexameter 'All excellence is contained in righteousness' (147), for instance, was cited as a proverb by Aristotle.[9] The question is: who could have composed hexameter poetry in this particular dialect? There are few candidates, since the language of epic or elegiac hexameter poetry did not normally feature the long alpha any more than Delphic responses did.[10] One select group of poets, however, could very well have composed our verse: Terpander and the other cithara-singers from Lesbos who are said to have been the most highly respected musical performers in seventh-century Sparta. We are told that they composed in hexameters, and the few lines which are cited – all attributed to Terpander – were written in a mixed dialect of which the long alpha is indeed a significant feature.[11]

The best way of explaining the language, metre, and content of the proverb, then, is to assume that it was originally composed by one of these cithara-singers as part of a poem warning a Spartan audience of the potentially destructive effects of greed. Since later sources insisted that the proverb was of oracular origin, one may further assume that the singer did not issue the warning in his own voice, but attributed it to a 'spontaneous' Delphic oracle. The attribution will have been vague enough to leave room for argument about whether this prophecy had been delivered to the lawgiver or to the kings. A very similar appeal to oracular authority appears in *Eunomia*, as we shall see, and the sentiment that a community might be destroyed by 'greed, but nothing else' is exactly paralleled in the opening lines of Solon's elegy on 'good order': 'Our polis, by Zeus' destiny and the will of the blessed immortal gods, will never be destroyed (οὔποτ' ὀλεῖται) ...but the townsmen themselves, in their folly, wish to ruin the great city for the sake of wealth (χρήμασι πειθόμενοι)' (F 4.1–6 West). In short, there is every reason to think that our line, long before it became a proverb, reflected tensions within archaic Sparta.

The calls for a redistribution of land alluded to in *Eunomia* must be seen in this light. The Messenian revolt may have aggravated the situation, but the main problem was surely the acquisitiveness hinted at in the warning of the 'oracle' and in the lament of Aristodemos. Intense competition for property, above all land, will have led to the concentration of resources 'in the hands of a few' (as Aristotle said about Athens, *Ath.Pol.* 2.2; 4.5), reducing the common people to such desperate straits that they rebelled.

According to tradition, poets played a remarkable role in containing the crisis. A story first mentioned obliquely by Plato claimed that Tyrtaeus was an Athenian who had been invited to Sparta at the command of an oracle, so that his songs might help the Spartans defeat the Messenians. The story goes on to say that Tyrtaeus had been lame and either mad or a schoolteacher, and had been picked as the man least likely to be of use to the Spartans. It has been argued that this tale was a fourth-century Athenian concoction aimed at undermining

Sparta's reputation.[12] However, if the Athenians had made up a story out of whole cloth, they would surely have dreamt up a less oblique way of embarrassing the Spartans; moreover, Tyrtaeus was not the only poet said to have come from abroad to play a prominent political role in Sparta. It is therefore likely that fourth-century Athenians merely elaborated an existing tradition that Tyrtaeus was an Athenian, adding some unflattering details about the poet so as to suggest that they had done everything possible to sabotage Sparta's conquest of Messenia. The basic story of a foreign singer brought in to deal with Sparta's problems must have originated in Sparta itself.

It was said that Terpander, too, had been invited to Sparta at the command of an oracle, in order to put an end to civil strife among the Spartans by means of his songs. The Spartan origin of this tradition seems guaranteed by the fact that the songs of Terpander were highly regarded and regularly performed in classical Sparta. [13] The same is true of a third poet, Thales (or Thaletas) from Gortyn in Crete, again invited to Sparta at the command of an oracle, and credited with ridding the city of the divisions created by civil war, through songs with 'texts encouraging obedience and harmony' and 'very orderly and soothing melodies and rhythms' (Plutarch, *Lycurgus* 4.2–3). Thales was known not only as a poet and inventor of the so-called 'Cretan rhythms' used in Spartan music, but also as an early lawgiver. [14] The classical native tradition, that Sparta's constitution was modelled on those of the Cretan cities, was probably based not only on general similarities, but also on the stories of Thales' visit. The early origin and importance of this tradition is put beyond doubt by the fact that another seventh-century poet, Polymnestus of Colophon, mentioned 'Thales of Gortyn' in 'verses about him composed for the Spartans'.[15]

The earliest Greek chronographical studies, which reconstructed the relative dates of famous poets, placed Terpander and Thales, like Tyrtaeus, in the seventh century BC. In the late fifth century, Hellanicus' *Victors at the Karneia* called Terpander the first such victor 'in the time of Midas', while Glaucus of Rhegium's *On the Ancient Poets and Musicians* placed Terpander before, and Thales after, Archilochus, but apparently close together in time. Terpander was given a range of seventh-century dates by subsequent generations of scholars.[16] One or two authors, however, moved him back to the time of Lycurgus, and credited him with 'setting to music the laws of the Spartans'.[17] Some later accounts of Thales, too, put his date back to make him a contemporary and associate of the lawgiver, while others denied that he had made laws, but credited him with ridding Sparta of a plague.[18] Once again, it seems, earlier tradition was transformed as the legend of Lycurgus took hold: surviving seventh-century songs urging the Spartans to restore order did not fit with the idea of a constitution which established perfect harmony at a much earlier date, so they were moved back in time or otherwise explained away.[19]

Originally, then, the Spartans believed that all three poets had come to their city at the behest of an oracle in the seventh century BC. From what we hear about the lost songs of Terpander and Thales, and from what we have of Tyrtaeus' *Eunomia*, the oracle about greed, and the proverbial wisdom of Aristodemos, we may conclude that at this time intense competition for land created in Sparta chronic civil unrest. Indeed, only such a history of conflict far into the seventh century can explain how Sparta acquired a reputation for having been 'most disorderly' (Herodotus 1.65) for a longer time than any other Greek state (Thucydides 1.18.1).

Kings and oracles: the fragments of *Eunomia*

What did Tyrtaeus tell the Spartans who demanded a redistribution of land? The first intelligible word in the first surviving fragment is 'prophe[cies]' (F 2.2 West) and the next is 'oracles' (F 2.4); a few lines later we have 'de[ar] to the gods...let us obey...closer in ori[gin]... since the son of Kronos, the husband of fair-garlanded Hera, Zeus himself gave this city to the Heraclids, with whom we came to the wide island of Pelops when we left behind windy Erineos' (F 2.9–15). Despite the gaps, the sense is fairly clear. The Spartans must obey their kings, the Heraclids, since their power is divinely sanctioned: not only are they 'closer in origin' and 'dear' to the gods, but Zeus himself gave them control over Sparta.[20] In this context, it seems likely that the 'oracles' referred to earlier also in some way supported the kings' right to rule.

The other fragment, which we know from quotations in Diodorus (7.12.6) and Plutarch (*Lycurgus* 6.10),[21] quotes the text of an oracle, presumably one of those already alluded to. The differences between the two quotations and interpretations, and the garbling of one of the verses, have inspired much debate and make it necessary to examine these texts in detail. In Diodorus, the oracle is introduced as follows:

> For thus spoke Apollo of the silver bow and golden hair,
> the lord who works from afar, from his rich shrine:

> Ὧδε γὰρ ἀργυρότοξος ἄναξ ἑκάεργος Ἀπόλλων
> χρυσοκόμης ἔχρη πίονος ἐξ ἀδύτου·

In Plutarch, however, the introductory couplet runs:

> Having listened to Phoebus, they brought home from Delphi
> prophecies of the god and words that will come true.
>
> Φοίβου ἀκούσαντες Πυθωνόθεν οἴκαδ' ἔνεικαν
> μαντείας τε θεοῦ καὶ τελέεντ' ἔπεα.

The two versions are linked to two different interpretations: according to Diodorus the oracle was received by Lycurgus,[22] but Plutarch thought that 'perhaps' the recipients were the kings Theopompus and Polydorus (6.9).

The majority of scholars prefer Plutarch's version, primarily because he drew on a reputable, scholarly authority, whereas Diodorus' ultimate source was a work of political propaganda which has been suspected of forging evidence. However, as I hope to show in the next section, these sources were not, after all, very different in their methods and reliability, despite having very different motives. When we judge the two versions without preconceptions about the trustworthiness of the sources from which they come, we find that there is no good reason to reject the authenticity of Diodorus' lines. Indeed, if any version is to be regarded as suspect, it ought to be Plutarch's.

It has been said that the verses in Diodorus, which use a string of epithets to describe Apollo, are too wordy and conventional to be genuine Tyrtaeus, and that they must have been made up by someone keen to remove the plural subject ('*they* brought home') in order to make the attribution to a single lawgiver, Lycurgus, more plausible.[23] But objections to the literary quality of the verses cannot stand, when an undisputed line of *Eunomia* is equally long-winded and conventional in speaking of 'the son of Kronos, husband of fair-garlanded Hera, Zeus' (F 2.12–13 West), while a forger would hardly have missed the opportunity to clinch his case by composing a couplet that actually *named* Lycurgus. A famous Delphic oracle cited by Herodotus (1.65) and two verses from the *Iliad* (6.130; 7.144) show four different ways of working 'Lykoörgos' into a hexameter. Since Diodorus' lines prove nothing either way concerning the oracle's recipient(s), and otherwise provide a perfectly suitable introduction to the oracle's text, we have no grounds for suspecting their authenticity.

Plutarch's version, on the other hand, with its plural subject, is exactly tailored to his argument that the oracle was given to two kings.[24] It is also worth noting that the transition between the statement that 'they brought back oracles' and the words of the oracle itself is quite abrupt. But there is no need to accuse Plutarch, or rather his sources, of forging these lines. It is much more likely that the couplet featured elsewhere in *Eunomia* and was linked directly with the oracle by a process of selective quotation. That is to say, Plutarch or his sources quoted a couplet which seemed to provide evidence that the kings, rather than Lycurgus, were its recipients, then skipped straight to the text of the oracle itself, omitting several intervening verses, including the actual, uninformative, introductory formula as given in Diodorus. The process is no different from the modern practice of editing quotations for brevity and relevance, except that ancient scholars did not use three dots (...) to mark the omissions.[25]

As it happens, the fragments of Solon reveal a couple of cases in which Plutarch does indeed present edited quotations while Diodorus offers fuller extracts. The correct texts of Solon's fragments 9 and 11 (West), it is generally accepted, are the six and eight lines, respectively, which appear in Diodorus (9.20.2). Each passage is coherent in itself, and each is confirmed by quotations in Diogenes Laertius (1.50, 51). Plutarch's *Solon*, by contrast, begins its version of fragment 11 with what in Diodorus is line 7 and continues with lines 5 and 6 (30.3), although the resulting text makes less sense and spoils the metre by juxtaposing two hexameters. Lines 1–4 are not cited until much later in the chapter (30.8). Even more cavalier is Plutarch's treatment of fragment 9. In Diodorus, the passage begins: 'Driving snow and hail come from a cloud, thunder comes from a bright bolt of lightning, and the ruin of a city comes from great men.' It continues with further warnings against 'monarchy'. In Plutarch (*Solon* 3.6), the same quotation purports to show that Solon's understanding of natural phenomena was 'simple and archaic', and runs as follows: 'Driving snow and hail come from a cloud, thunder comes from a bright bolt of lightning, and the sea is disturbed by the winds, but if no-one sets her in motion, she is the most righteous of all things' (F 12 West). Clearly, Plutarch or his source took out of context a passage in which images from the natural world served as political metaphors, and unscrupulously bolted it to another passage with a similar image – almost certainly also part of a political metaphor – in order to create the impression that Solon discoursed on physics in an amusingly quaint manner.

It is possible, then, that Plutarch and Diodorus do not offer one false and one genuine version of Tyrtaeus, but two different selections of genuine material from the same poem. Judged by his record in dealing with Solon's elegies, Plutarch is perhaps more likely than Diodorus to have given selective quotations. The contents of his opening lines – more abrupt and more geared towards the argument being pursued –

tend to confirm this. If both passages are genuine, the likelihood is, on balance, that Diodorus cited the actual verses introducing the oracle, and that Plutarch quoted his lines from another, earlier part of the poem.

Of the oracle itself, the first four verses appear in both sources, but the remaining four verses occur in Diodorus alone. They contain one line which has become garbled in transmission, and is here given in the corrupt, unmetrical version of the manuscript.

'Counsel is to begin with the divinely honoured kings,
who have the lovely city of Sparta in their care,
and with the ancient elders. Then the men of the people,
responding in turn to straight *rhētrai*
must say what is noble and do all that is just,
but no longer [?] plot [?] against this city [?].
Victory and power will attend the multitude of the people.'
For thus Phoebus declared to the city in these matters.

'ἄρχειν μὲν βουλῆς θεοτιμήτους βασιλῆας,
οἷσι μέλει Σπάρτης ἱμερόεσσα πόλις,
πρεσβυγενέας τε γέροντας· ἔπειτα δὲ δημότας ἄνδρας
εὐθείαις ῥήτραις ἀνταπαμειβομένους
μυθεῖσθαί τε τὰ καλὰ καὶ ἔρδειν πάντα δίκαια,
[?] μηδέ τι ἐπιβουλεύειν τῆιδε πόλει [?]
δήμου τε πλήθει νίκην καὶ κάρτος ἕπεσθαι.'
Φοῖβος γὰρ περὶ τῶν ὧδ' ἀνέφηνε πόλει.

Although some have wanted to reject the last four lines as another forgery, no real arguments against their authenticity have been adduced, and it is not at all clear in what way these lines would have served the purposes of a hypothetical forger. The most authoritative edition of the fragments accepts all four lines as genuine and is surely right to do so.[26]

In their attempts to interpret this oracle, and above all in restoring the garbled line, scholars have always looked at it in the light of the Great Rhetra. Since the Rhetra gives an active, if limited, political role to the popular assembly (see below), a similar role for the common people has been read into Tyrtaeus' poem. If one tries to understand and reconstruct *Eunomia* on its own terms, however, a different picture emerges.

The first question concerning the role of the popular assembly in the oracle is whether the people are supposed to 'respond in turn *to* straight *rhētrai*',[27] as the verse is translated here, which would mean that they respond to 'straight' decisions or proposals put before them by the kings and elders, or whether they are meant to 'respond in turn *with* straight *rhētrai*', as the verse is more commonly translated, which would mean that the people, in response to proposals, formulate 'straight' decisions. Both readings are grammatically possible, but the latter has been most widely adopted because it suggests a more active role for the assembly.[28]

Yet it would have been redundant for the oracle to say that the people's response should consist of formulating straight decisions, since it goes on to urge, in the next line, that their response must consist of saying and doing what is just and noble. The alternative interpretation, that it is the *rhētrai* put forward by the kings and elders which are 'straight', and that the people respond 'to' these, makes better sense. For one thing, instead of being redundant, the phrase would add something significant to the oracle. Secondly, the unique verb used for 'to respond *in turn*' (ἀνταπαμείβομαι) strongly suggests the idea that the people's response should match what has been presented to them, and this fits best if the oracle speaks of 'straight' proposals or decisions by the authorities, in response to which the assembly's words and deeds must be equally 'noble' and 'just'. Finally, in later Sparta, *rhētra* was indeed the technical term for a proposal put to an assembly or council.[29]

The oracle, then, not only says that the kings and elders must 'begin counsel', but assumes that the proposals which they bring before the assembly are always 'straight'. Since the people must reciprocate with words and deeds which are noble and just and therefore also 'straight', it follows that they are bound to agree with everything put to them. Tyrtaeus' point is, surely, that the authorities' proposals are *by definition* 'straight' and that the assembly must simply *accept* them: the people must speak and act as their rulers tell them to.[30]

This reading seriously affects our understanding of the next, corrupt line. The most widely accepted emendation reads: 'and not to give this city counsel [which is crooked]' (μηδέ τι βουλεύειν τῇιδε πόλει <σκολιόν>).[31] The addition of the word 'crooked' is based on Plutarch's opinion that the oracle cited by Tyrtaeus 'perhaps' echoed the so-called 'rider' to the Great Rhetra, which said 'If the people ask for something crooked (σκολιὰν) the elders and kings are to be rejecters' (*Lyc.* 6.7–10).[32] However, if Tyrtaeus' verse actually used the word 'crooked' just as the Rhetra did, one would expect Plutarch to have cited this line, which would have strongly supported his suggestion. Instead, his quotation stops abruptly, in mid-sentence, with the verse about 'responding to straight *rhētrai*'. Unless Plutarch, or his source, was quite inept in his use of evidence, he must have felt that the emphasis on 'straight' proposals was the clearest hint in Tyrtaeus' poem at the power to overrule 'crooked' decisions, and that the verses which followed added nothing more explicit. In other words, our corrupt line could hardly have contained a specific warning against 'crooked' decision-making.[33]

The context of the garbled verse suggests that it may have had a quite different meaning. Since the first five lines of the oracle said, politely, that the common people should simply *obey* their rulers, the first half of the next line may have reinforced this message in no uncertain terms: '*and not to counsel further*' (μηδ' ἔτι βουλεύειν).[34]

The second half of the line may have been connected with the next verse, promising 'victory and power' for 'the multitude of the people'. This promise has usually been understood in the light of a phrase in the Great Rhetra, itself garbled, which is restored to read: 'the people are to have the right to criticize, and power' (Plut. *Lyc.* 6.2). However, the combination '*victory* and power' suggests military success rather than political sovereignty. In Hesiod's *Theogony*, for example, Zeus says that the gods 'fight every day for victory and power' in the war against the Titans (647). Even better, an oracle which was supposed to have been delivered to the Messenians during their first war against Sparta promised them 'victory in the war, and power' (νίκην τοῦ πολέμου καὶ κράτος), if they sacrificed a virgin (Myron of Priene *FGrH* 106 F 9). It is admittedly possible to talk of 'victory' in assembly or debate, when one party 'defeats' a rival, but in the context of this poem, the implicit rivalry would be, not between peers, but between the people and their leaders. It is highly unlikely that the relation between the authorities and their subjects would be conceived of as antagonistic, especially in a poem which otherwise asserts the legitimacy of the kings, and in an oracle which emphasizes the need for obedience.

'Victory and power' must thus be taken in a military sense,[35] but it remains odd that they should be said to 'attend the multitude of the people'. I would suggest, therefore, that the last two words of the previous, corrupt line, 'this city', are to be taken as part of this clause, which then reads: 'Victory and power will attend this city and the multitude of the people'.[36] Tyrtaeus elsewhere uses a similar phrase connecting 'the city and the entire people'.[37] On this interpretation, the oracle promises that, for the common people, the reward for obedience to their leaders will be a share in the military success and power which the city as a whole will enjoy. In a poem addressing civil unrest at a time of war, Tyrtaeus could not have cited a more appropriate or convenient oracular pronouncement.

It may indeed have been the bluntness of these verses, in announcing that Sparta would enjoy power only if its citizens unquestioningly obeyed the authorities, which caused the corruption of the line. To later readers, a warning against conspiracy ('not to plot against this city') will have seemed more acceptable than a complete ban on discussion in the assembly for the sake of military success.[38]

If this interpretation is correct, the corrupt line would be most easily completed by inserting something before 'this city'. There is more than one way of producing a metrical verse, but among the possible supplements are ὥσθ' ἅμα, which would produce 'and not to counsel further, *so that* victory and power will attend [*both*] this city and the multitude of the people', and ἀλλ' αἰεὶ, 'and not to counsel further; *but always* victory and power will attend the city'. The latter would neatly mirror the prediction that the city would *never* be destroyed, so long as greed did not prevail.[39]

Eunomia thus included a ten-line passage, quoted by Diodorus, which paraphrased an oracle promising victory for Sparta if the common people obeyed their kings and Elders. This was preceded by two lines, quoted by Plutarch, stating that 'they' received 'oracles' from Delphi.

Did Tyrtaeus say who 'they' were? It is widely believed that he named Theopompus and Polydorus, on the assumption that Plutarch could have had no reason to link these kings with the oracle unless their names had been explicitly mentioned.[40] While it is true that Tyrtaeus referred to Theopompus by name elsewhere in his poetry (F 5.1 West), it is unlikely that he did so in *Eunomia*. If the oracle had been explicitly attributed to these kings, Plutarch and his sources would surely have wanted to strengthen their case by citing the relevant verse(s), as well as, or instead of, the vague lines which we now have. Not only that, but if Tyrtaeus had given the kings' names, Plutarch would hardly have been so cautious as to say that 'perhaps' (που) the oracle had something to do with them.

The uncertainty surrounding the recipients of the oracle is more easily understood if *Eunomia* expressed their identity quite vaguely. As we have seen, the other fragment of the poem exhorts the people to obey 'the Heraclids' as the legitimate rulers of Sparta (F 2.13 West), and there are several advantages in assuming that those who brought the oracles from Delphi were also identified only as 'the Heraclids'.[41] If so, one can see how it was feasible for some to argue that the Heraclids who received the oracle must have been two ruling kings, while others could claim that the phrase referred to Lycurgus, as a prominent member of one of the Heraclid dynasties. Neither side resorted to deliberate falsification: 'Heraclids' was simply vague enough to accommodate both views, and too vague to be worth quoting in support of either.

If the recipients of the oracles were identified merely as the Heraclids, two other puzzles may be solved as well. When Tyrtaeus told the Spartans to obey 'the Heraclids, with whom...we came to the broad island of Pelops' (F 2.13–15 West), he meant, no doubt, the kings whose *ancestors* brought them to the Peloponnese, but he could easily be misinterpreted as referring literally to the first descendants of Heracles to rule Sparta. If the poet then proceeded to speak of 'Heraclids' who received oracles, it would have seemed only logical to assume that these were the same first rulers. This misunderstanding would account for Hellanicus' unique view that the Spartan constitution was created, not by Lycurgus, but by Sparta's first kings, Eurysthenes and Procles (*FGrH* 4 F 116). He will have imagined that these were the recipients of this oracle describing the roles of the kings and the elders, key features of Sparta's constitution.[42]

The same misunderstanding would also account for the peculiar claims in Xenophon's *The Spartan Constitution* that Lycurgus lived at the time of the first kings (10.8), and went to Delphi, not alone, but 'with the most powerful men' (8.5). This will have been Xenophon's way of reconciling his belief that Lycurgus was the founder of all Sparta's institutions with the supposed evidence in Tyrtaeus that some of the most important of these institutions featured in an oracle given to a number of anonymous Heraclids of the first generation in Sparta.[43] In sum, it is most likely that *Eunomia* did indeed confine itself to vague references to 'the Heraclids': it is hard to see how such a wide variety of interpretations could have emerged if the poem had been any more explicit.

Tyrtaeus' poem thus exhorted the Spartans to be obedient to their rulers, because (a) the kings derived their legitimate authority from the gods, and (b) the kings had brought from Delphi oracles, one of which promised that obedience would ensure military success and power for the city.

This leaves us with two problems. If *Eunomia* merely attributed our oracle to 'the Heraclids', where did some ancient scholars get the idea that it had been given to Lycurgus, while others thought that it had been given to Theopompus and Polydorus? And if our oracle merely insisted on obedience to the established authorities, how did it come to be identified with the constitutional legislation of the Great Rhetra?

The answer to these questions lies in a long and heated political and scholarly controversy which began in the fourth century BC.

Kings and ephors: the use and abuse of *Eunomia*

The institution of the ephorate, classical Sparta's most powerful office, has in common with Tyrtaeus' oracle that it was variously attributed to Lycurgus and to Theopompus. This is no coincidence. It was the debate about the origins and legitimacy of the ephorate which led to divergent interpretations of *Eunomia* when the poem was dragged into the controversy as a supposedly key piece of evidence.

Sometime after being exiled in 395 BC for mishandling a military expedition (Xen. *Hell.* 3.5.25), the Spartan king Pausanias published a remarkable pamphlet on the constitution of his city. We know about this work because it was cited in Ephorus' *Histories*, in a passage paraphrased by Strabo. Amazed at Hellanicus' notion that the Spartan constitution was the creation of Eurysthenes and Procles rather than Lycurgus (see above), Ephorus countered, firstly, that it was Lycurgus, not these kings, who was worshipped as a god at Sparta, and, secondly, that

> Pausanias, having been driven out by the other [royal] family, the Eurypontids, in exile composed a discourse against the laws of Lycurgus, who belonged to the family which had deposed him, in which he also recounts the oracles which were given to him, contrary to the eulogies of most people.[44]

The precise text and the accuracy of Strabo's synopsis have been much debated; in particular, it has been argued that Pausanias' pamphlet was not 'a discourse against the laws of Lycurgus', but a discourse with the ironic title *Against the Laws of Lycurgus*, in which the author claimed that his *enemies* had offended against these (unimpeachable) laws. I shall follow Strabo in taking Pausanias as a rare critic of Lycurgus who disagreed with the standard eulogies – not only because this is a more straightforward reading of the text, but also because it makes better sense of the subsequent evolution of the debate in antiquity.[45] The details of interpretation, in any case, matter less than the general point, compatible with either view, that Pausanias adduced several 'oracles', among them both the oracle from *Eunomia* and the Great Rhetra, as evidence for Lycurgus' legislation, thereby sparking off a long controversy about the nature, meaning, and interrelation of these two texts.

Pausanias' pamphlet was a radical departure from classical Spartan tradition – and not only in being hostile to a lawgiver who was literally an object of worship. The king's account of Lycurgus differed on two points of fact from what Herodotus, only a generation earlier, presented as the view of 'the Spartans themselves': that the lawgiver was a member of the Agiad dynasty, i.e. Pausanias' *own* family, and that he had modelled his laws on those of Crete (1.65.6). Herodotus deserves to be taken seriously: he visited Sparta and was able to give distinct Spartan versions of several stories.[46] Pausanias thus abandoned native tradition when he dissociated his family from Lycurgus and argued that Sparta's constitution had been dictated by Delphic oracles, not Cretan models. In doing so, he did not simply re-invent history, but drew on an alternative tradition current outside Sparta (and conceivably among a minority within Sparta). Already in Herodotus' day, 'some' believed that Lycurgus derived his legislation from Delphic oracles (1.65.6), and earlier still the poet Simonides had spoken of Lycurgus as a member of the Eurypontid family (F 628 Page).

What could have driven Pausanias to take such an extreme, un-Spartan line? Aristotle tells us that 'Pausanias tried to abolish the ephorate' (*Politics* 1301b17–19), and the institution of 'the Elders and the ephors' is listed by Herodotus among Lycurgus' achievements (1.65.7). The simplest, most plausible inference is that a strong hostility to the ephorate, and an equally strong belief that Lycurgus created this institution, led Pausanias to disown the lawgiver by assigning him to the rival royal family, and to denounce the laws. In support of his rejection of the ephorate, Pausanias needed to appeal to an authority still higher than Lycurgus. Not even a king would have stood much chance of winning supporters for such a revolutionary cause if all he had to offer was his personal opinion. Hence Pausanias' recitation of oracles, remarked upon by Ephorus: he capitalized on the non-Spartan tradition that the ultimate source of Sparta's laws was the Delphic oracle, which allowed him to argue that the lawgiver had erred in not following Delphi's instructions to the letter and introducing the ephorate on his own initiative, without divine sanction.

It is highly probable that the excerpt from Diodorus' account of Lycurgus (7.12.1–8) includes the main evidence adduced by Pausanias. Diodorus was clearly drawing on Ephorus here, as so often,[47] and Ephorus, as we have seen, drew on Pausanias' pamphlet. Certainly, the oracular responses given by Diodorus, including the proverbial oracle about greed and the oracle from Tyrtaeus' *Eunomia*, would have supported Pausanias' case very nicely.

A first hexameter oracle served to establish that Lycurgus was indeed instructed by Delphi: it mentioned his name twice and said 'you have come searching for *eunomia*, and I will give you such as no other city on earth shall possess'. At least part of this oracle was current in the non-Spartan tradition before Pausanias wrote, and it suited his purposes admirably.[48]

The priestess allegedly proceeded to tell Lycurgus that the main aim of his legislation should be to ensure that 'some provide good leadership, and others obey' (Diod. 7.12.2; no. 217 Parke-Wormell). Asked for clarification, she uttered a second verse oracle, so vague that it would have been applicable to any state at any time, proclaiming that bravery and unity ensure a city's freedom, while cowardice and strife result in slavery (Diodorus, ibid.; no. 218 Parke-Wormell). By presenting this all-purpose oracle as an answer to the question *how* one should rule and obey, Pausanias may have used it to introduce his main concern: *who* should rule and *who* should obey. This is the question broached by a third hexameter oracle, not found in the excerpt, but closely linked with the previous oracular responses by a later source.

> For as long as you, abiding by the oracles, keep your promises and oaths and render justice to one another and to outsiders, behaving with respect for the elders in a holy and pure manner, and treating with reverence the sons of Tyndareus, Menelaos, and the other immortal heroes who in divine Sparta...[lacuna]...Thus far-seeing Zeus will take care of you.[49]

In itself, this oracle was little more specific than the previous one, except that it explicitly addressed Spartans: it simply encouraged decent behaviour, respect for authority, and piety towards local divinities. But it is easy to see how Pausanias might have used it to make a political point. The oracle demanded respect for the Elders and for the heroic predecessors of the kings (themselves heroized after death), yet it says nothing about Sparta's third great power, the board of ephors.[50]

Thus the ground would have been prepared for Pausanias' strongest evidence: the oracle from Tyrtaeus. As we have seen, Hellanicus appears already to have used Tyrtaeus' oracle in his discussion of the Spartan constitution. Pausanias' contribution to the debate will have been to insist that the poet's reference to 'the Heraclids' meant Lycurgus, and to point out that the oracle demanded obedience to the kings and elders alone. It made no mention of ephors, and its command that the people were 'not to counsel further' could be taken to deny any legitimacy to the ephors, who, unlike the Elders, were seen as representatives of the people.

The proverbial oracle about greed, which immediately preceded the quotation from Tyrtaeus in Diodorus, is not likely to have provided Pausanias with ammunition against Lycurgus or against the ephorate as an institution, but may have been fielded against the exiled king's personal enemies. It was claimed that overseas expansion after the Peloponnesian War brought an influx of wealth which ruined Sparta's unity and high moral standards. Pausanias may well have done much to propagate this view, since Spartan imperialism was associated particularly with his rivals, Lysander and Agesilaos.[51] By invoking an oracle against greed, the exiled king could suggest a parallel between his personal enemies and the lawgiver: just as Lycurgus had set up the ephorate in defiance of the Delphic oracle, so his descendant Agesilaos and others had defied the oracle in opening the floodgates to wealth; each time, Sparta had suffered.[52]

The pamphlet may have concluded with the same sentiment as the excerpt from Diodorus: 'Those who do not observe piety towards the divine are still less likely to observe justice towards men' (7.12.7).

The Great Rhetra does not feature in Diodorus, but it is tempting to assume that Pausanias did adduce it, too, in support of his arguments.[53] A Spartan king is more likely than most to have known the text of this archaic and obscure document, and the last sentence of the Rhetra ('if the people ask for something crooked, the elders and kings are to be rejecters') suited his polemic perfectly. It would have been odd if the king had *failed* to cite a law which granted him and the elders the authority to override decisions of the people, including the ephors. The Rhetra's absence from the excerpt and perhaps also from Diodorus' original, or even from Ephorus, on the other hand, is easily explained: much of the law was more difficult to understand and less relevant to the debate than Tyrtaeus' poem.

Pausanias' argument would have had to be that Lycurgus had ignored the instructions of the Rhetra, although this law, too, had come from Delphi. In support of this argument he is likely to have claimed that it was the Rhetra to which Tyrtaeus referred when he cited the oracle about obedience. Thus the link between our two sources was probably first forged.

A clever piecing together[54] of three oracles, two poems, and a law was not enough to discredit Lycurgus. Many sprang to his defence, and it may have been no more than a couple of years before another Spartan exile, Thibron, published his account of the Spartan constitution, possibly written in direct response to the king's pamphlet, and singled out by Aristotle for its admiring approach to the lawgiver. Pausanias does, however, seem to have set the terms for all subsequent debate.[55]

In the face of the evidence of the oracles, Tyrtaeus, and the Rhetra, three lines of defence remained open to Lycurgus' admirers.[56] They could reason that Lycurgus' institution of the ephorate somehow was not in breach of the oracles' commands, or they could argue that Lycurgus had not in fact created the ephorate, or again they could try to demonstrate that Lycurgus had not, after all, been given these oracles. Within two generations, each of these lines of argument had been formulated, and all three found a place in the works of Aristotle.

The first tack was taken by Xenophon in *The Spartan Constitution*. As a close friend of Pausanias' rival Agesilaos and a keen student of Sparta, he must have been aware of the pamphlet, and he appears to have taken on board its argument that Tyrtaeus' oracles were delivered to Lycurgus. As we have seen, Xenophon's idea that Lycurgus had lived in the time of the first kings is likely to be based on his interpretation of 'the Heraclids' in *Eunomia*. *The Spartan Constitution* has a lengthy discussion in chapter eight which seems odd and incoherent unless it is understood as an oblique polemic against Pausanias' views.

Xenophon ventured as his personal opinion that Lycurgus would not have given such great authority to the Spartan magistrates if he had not had the support of 'the most powerful people in the city' (8.1–2). He went on to argue that 'it is probable that these same people helped him also to set up the power of the ephorate, because they recognized that obedience is of the greatest importance in a city, army, or household' (8.3). Finally, after listing the powers of the ephors, he concluded:

> Lycurgus had many fine devices to make the citizens willing to obey the laws, and among the very finest, to my mind, was that he did not issue his laws to the masses until he had visited Delphi with the most powerful men, and had asked the god whether it would be more advantageous and better for Sparta to obey the laws which he himself had drawn up. Only when the reply came that it would be better in every way did he issue the laws, making it not only unlawful but sacrilegious to disobey the laws, which came from the Pythian oracle (8.5).

Xenophon thus defended the lawgiver by speculating that the institution of the ephorate must have been supported by everyone in Sparta, and that the oracles delivered to Lycurgus signalled general approval of what he had done. Delphi did not exclude the ephors, and Lycurgus, so far from disobeying the oracle, used its authority to ensure the obedience of others.

The key elements of this account – that the ephors were an integral part of the original constitution, which had been essentially Lycurgus' own work but fully ratified by Delphi – appeared also in Ephorus

(*FGrH* 70 F 149.18–19), who, in opposition to Pausanias' work, re-emphasized the Spartan tradition that Lycurgus drew on Cretan models (F 148.1, 10; 149.16–18). When Aristotle left it open whether the ephors' role as representatives of the people had resulted 'from the lawgiver's intention or from chance' (*Politics* 1270b19–20), noted that Lycurgus had visited Crete, and remarked upon Cretan parallels to the ephorate (1271b20–1272b1), he was clearly accommodating this line of thought. Part of Plutarch's picture of Lycurgus, too, derives from it: the future lawgiver got his ideas from Crete (among other places: *Lyc.* 4.1–6), then received encouragement from Delphi (5.3), then drafted his laws, and finally consulted Delphi again for ratification (29.3–4).[57]

On this interpretation, the oracles attributed by Pausanias to Lycurgus were essentially an elaborate, versified form of the 'yes' or 'no' answers a fourth-century questioner could expect when consulting Delphi on any course of action. While this approach had the advantage of 'normalizing' Lycurgus' relation to the oracle, it will have been obvious to many that the oracle in Tyrtaeus and the Rhetra did not sound as if they merely meant to say 'yes' to a proposed constitution, let alone a constitution which included the ephorate. Further lines of explanation had to be explored.

We first find an alternative account in Plato's *Laws*, around the middle of the fourth century, but it is alluded to in such an oblique manner that the theory must by then have been well known. Plato emphatically asserted that Lycurgus' laws were dictated by the Delphic oracle: he claimed that the Spartans regarded Apollo as their lawgiver (624a), spoke of 'the laws of Pythian Apollo which...Lycurgus enacted' (632d), and coined the phrase 'the Pythian lawgiver' (634a). Those who, like Plato, saw the oracle as formulating, rather than merely ratifying, law, were bound to give great weight to the precise wording of the responses and to concede that these left no room for ephors. Their solution was to argue that the ephors were introduced by what Plato calls a 'third saviour', after Apollo and Lycurgus (691d–692a; *Eighth Letter* 354b). Aristotle adopted this view as well, and gave the saviour a name: king Theopompus (*Politics* 1313a25–33). By the time the story reached Plutarch, it had further acquired a name for the first ephor, Elatus, and a date, 130 years after Lycurgus (*Lyc.* 7.1–2).

This second interpretation regards the introduction of the ephorate as a good thing. The power of the kings and Elders was too absolute and needed to be 'reined in', 'moderated', by the ephors. The result was a kingship which was less powerful but was thereby all the more durable, as Theopompus, according to anecdote, explained to his complaining wife.[58] Theopompus may have been chosen almost by default as the author of this important and necessary change to the constitution: he was the only king mentioned by name in Tyrtaeus, and a national hero for his conquest of Messenia (F 5 West). Among early kings, he had no serious competition.[59]

While this school of thought neatly accounted for the absence of ephors from the oracles, it had one awkward implication: the Delphic oracle had evidently dictated an imperfect constitution and somehow failed to foresee that the power of the kings and Elders would need checking. The third, and most radical, interpretation of the oracular evidence dealt with this unfortunate notion by arguing that neither the oracle in Tyrtaeus nor the full text of the Great Rhetra had been delivered to Lycurgus at all. This theory is only found in Plutarch, but he cites a work of Aristotle's, presumaby the lost *Spartan Constitution*, as his source for at least part of it.

The main prop for this thesis was, apparently, the curious contradiction between the last two clauses of the Rhetra. The Rhetra stipulated that regular assemblies should be held, and that 'the people are to have the right to criticize, and power'; yet the last clause countered: 'if the people ask for something crooked, the elders and kings are to be rejecters'. This ambivalence on the matter of sovereignty made it possible to argue that the last clause was a later addition to the original Rhetra as delivered to Lycurgus by Delphi (Plut. *Lyc.* 6.1–2, 8).[60] The 'original' Rhetra thus intended a constitution in which all played a part, but the people were sovereign; in other words, the Delphic oracle *did* foresee a constitution which had room for the ephors. Lycurgus' original constitution, with or without ephors, allowed sufficient power to the people's assembly. Neither the oracle nor the lawgiver could be faulted.

The blame for subsequent meddling with an in principle perfect constitution was laid instead at the door of the common people. A 'rider' curtailing popular sovereignty was made necessary, according to Plutarch, because the assembly began to arrogate too much power to itself (Plut. *Lyc.* 6.7). The oracle in *Eunomia*, urging the people to obey their rulers, echoed the supposed 'rider' rather than the 'original' Rhetra, and the obvious conclusion seemed to be that Tyrtaeus reported, not an oracle given to Lycurgus, but a later oracle which legitimated the actions of those who modified the constitution: 'they, too, persuaded the city that the god had ordained these things, as perhaps Tyrtaeus mentions' (*Lyc.* 6.9).

Again these hypothetical reforms and the associated oracles were attributed to Theopompus, this time in conjunction with his fellow-ruler Polydorus in order to account for Tyrtaeus' plurals ('they' and 'the Heraclids'). There need have been no firmer evidence for this theory than for the attribution of the ephorate to Theopompus, but it is quite likely that *Eunomia* said that the oracle had been given in time of war, as indeed the emphasis on 'victory' in its final line implies. To a classical audience, this would immediately have suggested the First Messenian War and therefore Theopompus and his colleague. The attribution of the oracle about greed to Theopompus and Alcamenes, Polydorus' father, might have been similarly based on an indication in the original poem that it had been delivered at the outbreak of a war: note its assurance that Sparta would not be destroyed (unless greed got the better of it). Theopompus and Alcamenes were believed to have reigned at the start of the First Messenian War; a few years later Polydorus succeeded (Pausanias 4.4.4, 5.9, 7.7).

As for the ultimate origin of this most ingenious and most satisfactory of the arguments constructed in defence of Lycurgus, we know that Aristotle, in his *Spartan Constitution*, expressed his admiration for the lawgiver by claiming that divine worship was not good enough for him (F 534 Rose), insisted on the Delphic origin of the Spartan constitution (F 535), gave a detailed explanation of the meaning of the Great Rhetra (F 536), and quoted the oracle about greed (F 544). There is thus every chance that Plutarch's entire discussion of the Rhetra and *Eunomia* is borrowed from the work of this philosopher. Aristotle may in turn have borrowed elsewhere, but he is as likely as anyone, and more likely than most, to have been the first to formulate this sophisticated argument. One can certainly see how it would have fitted his approach to Theopompus, the ephorate, and constitutional theory in general. On the one hand, Aristotle praised Theopompus for 'moderating' the power of the kings 'by, among other things, setting up the office of ephor' (*Politics* 1313a25–7). On the other hand, he saw the ephorate as a deeply flawed institution, which tended to be 'tyranny-like' (1265b35–41; 1270b6–35), and he must have felt uneasy about attributing it to Theopompus. By crediting the king with curbing the power of the assembly as well, however, the balance could be restored: Theopompus had not made Sparta more democratic or oligarchic, but steered it towards Aristotle's ideal 'middle' and 'moderate' constitution.

Such, I would suggest, were the outlines of the fourth-century debate which inspired different interpretations of, and quotations from, *Eunomia*, which gave rise to the idea that the Great Rhetra had been tampered with by the addition of a 'rider', and which established the view that Tyrtaeus paraphrased the Rhetra, whether in its original or in its modified form. No one forged poems or oracles, but everyone added to the debate by making reasoned, indeed scholarly, inferences from the evidence and offering imaginative reconstructions which varied with their political outlook. If we are to use the evidence for our own reconstruction of archaic Spartan history, however, we must strip away all this ancient theorizing and use only what is left: the text of the Great Rhetra, alleged 'rider' included, and a text of Eunomia which includes all the fragments quoted but makes no explicit reference either to Lycurgus or to Theopompus and Polydorus. Whether the connection between the law and the poem, probably made by Pausanias and modified by Aristotle, is tenable remains to be seen.

Oracles and laws: *Eunomia* and the Great Rhetra

The identification of Tyrtaeus' oracle with the Great Rhetra, generally accepted today, is of course only possible if the Great Rhetra was indeed an oracular text. There is good reason to think that it was not.

For one thing, it is not recognizably an oracle in form. The text reads[61]:

> Having built a temple for Zeus Syllanios and Athena Syllania, having made divisions tribe by tribe and *oba* by *oba*, having established thirty men, including the rulers, as Council of Elders, hold Apellai time after time [monthly?], between Babyka and Knakion. Thus propose and reject. The people are to have the right to criticize, and power. If the people ask for something crooked, the elders and rulers are to be rejecters.[62]

The Rhetra is in prose, whereas Delphic oracles are almost universally rendered in our literary sources as hexameter poems. Moreover, despite its somewhat obscure manner of expression, the Rhetra is not composed in the allusive and riddling style characteristic of so many oracular responses. We have very little reliable information on archaic oracles and these may have taken forms not transmitted to us, but, as things stand, nothing in the text of the Rhetra offers any indication of oracular origins.[63]

Plutarch, however, claimed that the document was indeed 'an oracle from Delphi...which they call a *rhētra*' (*Lyc.* 6.1), and that all Lycurgus' laws were called *rhētrai* 'as being oracles and issued by the god' (13.11). That we can attach no historical value to general claims about the Delphic origins of any of Lycurgus' laws will be clear by now, and Plutarch's notion that *rhētra* was a Spartan term for 'oracle' has no better foundation.

Elsewhere in Plutarch's work, a Spartan *rhētra* is a proposal put before the elders by the king (*Agis* 8.1; 9.1), or a law enacted on the initiative of an ephor (*Agis* 5.2), without even a hint of oracular consultation. We have seen how Tyrtaeus refers to proposals put by magistrates before the assembly as *rhētrai* (F 4.6 West). In Homer, in archaic inscriptions, and even in Xenophon, *rhētra* means an 'agreement' of some kind, whether a pact between individuals, a communal decision, a contract between community and individual, or a treaty between communities.[64] Photius' *Lexicon* offers three synonyms for 'agreements' as its definition of '*rhētrai*', but bows to Plutarch in making one exception: 'among the Spartans, a *rhētra* is a law of Lycurgus, as having been enacted on the basis of oracles'.

It is highly implausible that archaic Spartans used the word in a sense radically different not only from that current in classical Sparta, but also from the sense in which it was used by their contemporaries, including one of their own poets. The notion that *rhētra* ever meant 'oracle' must therefore be false. It may have been advanced by Pausanias to support his claim that Lycurgus disobeyed divine commands; more probably it was devised by some later author – perhaps Aristotle, or even Plutarch himself – trying to reconcile the secular term used by the Spartans with the supposed divine origin of their laws.[65]

The Great Rhetra was known as a *rhētra* because the Spartans regarded it as an 'agreement' made by the community, a law created by a secular, political process. The very use of the term *rhētra* by the Spartans thus vindicates Herodotus' assertion that, according to 'the Spartans themselves', their laws were not dictated by Delphi. If the Great Rhetra did not sound like an oracle, was not called an oracle, and, until the fourth century BC at least, was not believed to have any association with an oracle, it seems safe to conclude that it was not an oracle. And if it was not, it follows that the Delphic oracle in Tyrtaeus *cannot* be the Great Rhetra.[66]

Did Tyrtaeus' oracle at least *allude* to the arrangements set out in the Great Rhetra? May we infer from *Eunomia* that this constitutional law was already in existence, and that the oracle was intended to remind the Spartans to abide by the Rhetra's regulations? As the text of the poem has been most commonly restored, the position of 'the people' seems defined in a similar, and similarly ambiguous, manner: they are to 'respond' and have 'power', provided they make no 'crooked' plans. As the text has been restored and understood above, however, the similarities are superficial and the differences far more striking.

In *Eunomia*, the people are simply told to *obey* the kings and elders. Far from having a 'right to criticize', they are told 'not to counsel further', and the 'power' which they enjoy is not popular sovereignty but the supremacy of their city over its enemies. *Eunomia*'s description of Spartan government, in fact, has a distinctly Homeric ring to it. Just as in *Iliad* and *Odyssey* kings owe their authority directly to Zeus, who 'raises' them and gives them their sceptres, the kings of Sparta have received their territory from 'Zeus himself' and are 'divinely honoured'.[67] As in the epics, the kings and elders conduct their debates before assemblies, but the commoners who attend are apparently allowed to do no more than express approval by cheering or disapproval by remaining silent. In Homer, any who dare oppose the kings risk being beaten or bullied into submission.[68] Nothing in Tyrtaeus suggests that the Spartan people had a more active political role.

The Great Rhetra, on the other hand, presents a very different world. Far from being set apart by a divine right to rule, the kings are merely listed as two of the thirty members of the Council of Elders. This fixed membership of thirty is itself a new phenomenon: no number is specified in *Eunomia* or for the councils of elders in Homer. The law indicates that assemblies are to be held not only in a fixed location, but at regular intervals, something about which *Eunomia* says nothing, and which does not happen in Homer. Most importantly, the common people are granted a definite decision-making role: they are not confined to making a noise or keeping quiet, but are given the right to speak and vote on proposals put to them by the Council. Admittedly, their sovereignty is still qualified, and the magistrates can override 'crooked' popular demands, but their position as defined by the Rhetra is fundamentally different from their role in the Homeric world and, so far as one can tell, from their role in Tyrtaeus.[69]

Perhaps one might argue that Tyrtaeus, as a poet, drew on a Homeric vocabulary and style which obscured the constitutional realities of the day. Perhaps one might add that the privileges of the kings were greatest in war, when the political rights of ordinary Spartans were also most liable to erosion. But surely neither explanation will suffice. Tyrtaeus' reputation as a peacemaker does not suggest that he dealt with severe popular discontent by ignoring the people's established constitutional rights and telling them that unconditional obedience to the authorities was now required. Only in a society where all power had traditionally lain with kings and elders, where the common people had never had any formally established political role, would *Eunomia*'s blunt reassertions of royal power have had any chance of success. The formalization of the bodies and procedures of government, and the creation of a qualified popular sovereignty, must have taken place in

Sparta *after* Tyrtaeus' day; the Rhetra must *post*-date *Eunomia*.[70]

If Tyrtaeus' oracle was not the Great Rhetra, on what occasion and to what purpose *did* Delphi issue it? It cannot escape one's notice that the oracle was perfectly tailored to the circumstances in which Sparta found itself in Tyrtaeus' day: it urged obedience, at a time when there was serious popular unrest, and it promised 'victory', at a time when the Spartans were engaged in large-scale warfare against the Messenians. The obvious conclusion is that Delphi had *recently* delivered these oracles when consulted by Sparta during the Messenian Revolt. The anonymous 'Heraclids' who were said to have received this response from Delphi were therefore the same 'Heraclids' whose legitimacy the people were urged to accept elsewhere in the poem (F 2 West). They were the kings who reigned in Tyrtaeus' own day, but who were, we are told, never mentioned by name in his poems (Pausanias 4.15.2).[71] The original purpose of soliciting this oracle will thus have been the same as the purpose of broadcasting it through the medium of Tyrtaeus' poetry: countering popular discontent and calls for the redistribution of land by reasserting the legitimacy of the kings.[72]

Conclusion: *Eunomia*, the Great Rhetra, and state formation

Tyrtaeus' *Eunomia* is an example of the way in which the Spartan authorities typically responded to the seventh-century crisis attested in fragments of poetry and in the traditions about Terpander and Thales.[73] They would consult an oracle, which might offer in response a warning against greed, a reassertion of the legitimacy of the rulers, or the advice to invite an outsider to restore harmony by means of his songs. According to tradition, two major religious festivals, the Karneia and Gymnopaidiai, were instituted or reorganized to accommodate the performance of such songs, which in turn cited the oracles.[74] This kind of response to crisis has a parallel at Athens. Around 600 BC, Solon composed songs which, like those of Tyrtaeus, exhorted the Athenians to wage war on their neighbours while reflecting on the importance of 'good order' within the community; at the same time a Cretan religious expert, Epimenides, was brought in to end Athenian civil strife by means of purification rituals and the introduction of new sacrifices.[75]

This approach to conflict-resolution implied a notion that there was a fixed social and political order sanctioned by the gods, and that the best (or only) way to restore harmony was to face the discontents with reminders of the divinely sanctioned order, in the form of oracles, rituals, and songs. Such a strategy is fundamentally different from conflict-resolution through change, through secular social and political reform of the kind enacted by Solon's subsequent legislation and by the Great Rhetra. Hence, in their outlook on Spartan government, there is a stark contrast between Tyrtaeus' *Eunomia*, as it has been reconstructed here, and the Rhetra. In the poem, all emphasis is on royal power, granted by the gods and supported by oracular utterances. In the law, the focus of attention is the assembly, assigned a regular place and time to meet and granted formal (if not unqualified) sovereignty, by 'agreement' rather than divine command.

Religious and secular strategies for resolving conflict can coexist, as Athenian history shows: Epimenides' purification was preceded by Draco's legislation and followed by Solon's. Admonitory songs and written laws, too, can coexist, and indeed the distinction between them may be blurred: Solon is said to have attempted to put his laws into verse (as well as prose) and other early lawgivers are supposed to have done the same.[76] Yet it is likely that there was a gradual historical change. Classical Sparta and Athens did not rely on poets, and not primarily on religious means and justifications, to resolve internal problems; seventh-century Sparta did, and so did Athens, at least for a time, at the beginning of the sixth century.

Eunomia is the last-known of a series of attempts to effect community-wide reconciliations through songs and rituals which appealed to supernatural sanctions; the Great Rhetra, on the other hand, was known as the first and greatest of a series of laws designed to create order by means of reform, and through the exercise of secular power. If it is true, as has been argued here, that the Rhetra was formulated some time after *Eunomia* was composed, these two texts between them mark a transition to a new kind of political community, a key stage in the process of state formation, in late seventh- or early sixth-century Sparta.[77]

Acknowledgements

This paper was written at the Center for Hellenic Studies. It is significantly different from the version delivered at the Sparta conference, thanks to the helpful comments and suggestions of many of the participants, the editors, Kurt Raaflaub and Paola Ceccarelli. They have done much to improve this paper; its failings are the responsibility of the author.

Notes

[1] The connection between the poem and the law is 'unquestionable' for Nafissi 1991, 72–3, and for many before him: e.g. Busolt 1920, 46; Ehrenberg

1925, 33; Treu 1941, 32; Wade-Gery 1944, 3–4; Tigerstedt 1965, 56–7; West 1974, 185. Most recent scholarship simply takes the connection for granted. Two rare exceptions are Andrewes 1938, 96–101, and Den Boer 1954, 190–3, who argued that the oracle in *Eunomia* did not refer to the Rhetra; Andrewes subsequently recanted (Wade-Gery 1944, 3–4 n. 4: 'Captain Andrewes allows me to say he would withdraw this'; cf. Andrewes 1956, 73–7). Tyrtaeus is generally dated to the second half of the seventh century (e.g. Parker 1993; Nafissi 1991, 37), and all current theories about Spartan constitutional development accordingly date the Rhetra between *c.* 800 and 625 BC, making it the earliest known Greek law. (At the bottom end of this range, the Rhetra may be contemporary with the next earliest surviving law, in an inscription from Dreros of 650–25; Jeffery 1990, 315.1a) The view that the Rhetra is at the latest contemporary with Tyrtaeus has been dominant since the 1940s (Wade-Gery 1943, 1944; Chrimes 1949; Hammond 1950). Previously, some scholars dated the 'Lycurgan reforms' to *c.* 600 or 550 BC, after Tyrtaeus, and either regarded the Great Rhetra as a later forgery based on Tyrtaeus (Meyer 1892, 229–30) or the relevant fragments of *Eunomia* as later forgeries based on the Rhetra (Ehrenberg 1925, 33; retracted in 1927, 22). See n. 70 below.

[2] A myth current since the fourth century BC: Hodkinson 1986; 1989.

[3] On Alcman: Thommen 1996, 44–7; contra Ehrenberg 1933, 288–91; Janni 1965, 85–9. Important recent studies of archaic Spartan material culture: Hodkinson 1998 and Powell 1998 (and briefly already Starr 1965, 264–6).

[4] Called a proverb by Schol. ad Pindar *Isthmian* 2.17, and included in several ancient collections of proverbs: Leutsch and Schneidewin 1839, 173 (Zenobius 6.43), 377 (Gregory of Cyprus 3.98); Leutsch 1851, 226 (Macarius 8.85), 725 (Apostolius 18.32).

[5] The earliest surviving reference to Lycurgus is in Pindar's older contemporary Simonides (F 628 Page).

[6] It is cited as a proverb by Diodorus (7.12.6) and features as such in Leutsch and Schneidewin 1839, 39 (Zenobius 2.24), 201 (Diogenianus 2.36), 327 (Plutarch 43); Leutsch 1851, 150 (Macarius 2.68), 320, 452 (Apostolius 4.54b, 8.77). Other attestations: Aristotle F 544 Rose; Cicero, *De Officiis* 2.77; Plutarch, *Agis* 9; *Moralia* 239f; Clement of Alexandria, *Stromata* 4.5.24.5; Suda s.v. διειρωνόξενοι. A fourth-century origin was suspected by Meyer 1892, 226–7, because the verse fits Sparta's situation after the Peloponnesian war (so too Cartledge 1987, 403); however, Wilamowitz 1900, 108 n. 1, dated it to the fifth century, presumably because (as Fontenrose 1978, 84–5, points out) it was alluded to already in the 420s in Euripides' *Andromache* (which calls the Spartans 'bent on shameful gain', 451, and wishes 'may you be destroyed', 453; cf. schol. ad 446, and Poole 1994 on Euripides and Sparta) and perhaps in Aristophanes' *Peace* 623 (cf. schol ad 623a). Klinger 1929 and Tigerstedt 1965 are unusual in (rightly) regarding the proverb as evidence for the seventh century and (wrongly) attributing it to Tyrtaeus: see further n. 10 below.

[7] Examples are Fontenrose 1978, nos. Q26, 30, 88, 186. Since these proverbial phrases derive their meaning from the rest of the oracle, the oracles must have come first, the proverbs later. Fontenrose's notion (1978, 84–7) that the

proverbs came first and that the rest of the oracle was invented around them seems implausible.

8 See Parke and Wormell 1956, vol. 2, p. xxx; 1949, 139 n. 2, on the features of oracular language: surprisingly they do not comment on this exception (their no. 222). Pavese 1992, 285, nevertheless attributes our hexameter to an oracular response.

9 *Nicomachean Ethics* 1129b29; see schol. ad loc. which notes that the same proverb was also attributed to the poet Phocylides (F 17). Another example is Solon's 'As I grow old, I am constantly learning many things' (F 18 West), also called a proverb in the schol. ad [Plato], *Amat.* 133c, and cited as such in Leutsch and Schneidewin 1839, 58 (Zenobius 3.4), 229 (Diogenianus 3.80); Leutsch 1851, 65, 107 (Gregory of Cyprus 1.79, 2.69), 344 (Apostolius 5.40). The large proportion of Greek proverbs deriving from poems was noted by Crusius 1910, 64–6.

10 West 1974, 77, notes that of elegiac poets only Tyrtaeus, Theognis, and Solon 'occasionally allow features of their own dialects to show'. In the manuscript of the excerpt from Diodorus, the verse is immediately followed by a quotation from Tyrtaeus, which led Bergk (unlike all subsequent editors) to attribute it to Tyrtaeus (his F 3a.1). Tyrtaeus does have a few colloquial Doric forms (West 1974, 93, 104; Von Blumenthal 1942, 103–4), and also a few long alphas in some manuscripts (Prato 1968, 55 n. 215), but 'any Doricisms would be inadvertent lapses' (Adkins 1985, 67) and their emphatic presence in our line would be hard to explain for either Tyrtaeus or another elegiac poet (as Steinmetz 1969 pointed out).

11 See Gostoli 1990, xliii–xlvi, for the dialect of the verses attributed to Terpander; despite some manuscript variations, the use of the long alpha here is well attested: e.g. ἀοιδάν (F 4.2), αἰχμά (F 5.1), Δίκα (F 5.2 Gostoli). Another uncommon feature of our verse is the short scansion of ο before χρ in φιλοχρηματία, but there are parallels for this (West 1974, 114).

12 Plato, *Laws* 629a (without reference to the oracle; but see schol. ad loc.); Lycurgus, *Against Leocrates* 107; Philochorus *FGrH* 328 FF 215, 216; Kallisthenes *FGrH* 124 F 24; Diodorus 8.27, 36; Pausanias 4.15.6; Diogenes Laertius 2.43; Suda s.v. *Tyrtaios*; probably also Isocrates, *Archidamos* 31. Fisher 1994, 362–4, argues that the whole story is a fourth-century invention; Stibbe 1996, 89–96, accepts its historicity.

13 Terpander's story appears in Diodorus 8.28, and thus probably featured in Ephorus; it certainly featured in Aristotle's *Spartan Constitution* (F 545 Rose) as well as Herakleides' *Spartan Constitution* (7.5). Later sources: Philodemus, *De Musica* 1.30.31–5; 4: Col.19.4–20.7; [Plutarch], *De Musica* 1146b; Aelian *VH* 12.50; Zenobius 5.9; Suda s.v. μετὰ Λέσβιον ᾠδόν. Terpander's songs always highly regarded in Sparta: Plut. *Agis* 10.3; to be sung by Spartan citizens only: Plut. *Lyc.* 28.10.

14 Thales as inventor of 'Cretan rhythms' and lawgiver: Ephorus *FGrH* 70 F 149.16, 18–19; as lawgiver: Aristotle, *Pol.* 1274a26–31; as poet and lawgiver, creating harmony in Sparta: Plut. *Lyc.* 4.2–3; settles conflict in Sparta: Philodemus, *De Musica* 4, cols. 18.33–19.19 (which appears to refer to a 'boasting' dedication attributed to Thales, 19.1) and Plut. *Cum Princ. Phil.* 4.

His songs highly regarded in Sparta: Plut. *Agis* 10.3; cf. n. 74 below.

15 Pausanias 1.14.4. The early date of Polymnestus is guaranteed by the fact that he was mentioned *c.* 600 BC in the poetry of Alcman (F 145 Page). For the Spartan tradition of Cretan origins, see also below, pp. 15, 19.

16 Hellanicus *FGrH* 4 F 85b; Glaucus *FHG* II.23.2 and 24.4; Terpander's and Thaletas' close proximity in time follows from the list of musical reformers in Sparta given by [Plut.] *De Musica* 1134bc, which corresponds with Glaucus' fragments and in which Thaletas immediately succeeds Terpander, well before Polymnestus. Seventh-century dates: Phanias of Eresos ('later than Archilochus'; F 33 Wehrli); Parian Marble (645/4 BC); Eusebius, *Chronicle* (642/1 or 641/0). Terpander was also associated with the institution of the Karneia festival (see n. 74 below), which Sosibius (*FGrH* 595 F 3) dated to 676/72 BC. On the methods of Hellanicus and his contemporaries in compiling their chronographic works, see Möller, forthcoming. I would argue that both poets are historical figures (so Stibbe 1996, 89–96, contra Forrest 1963, 163–4; see also Oliva 1971, 115–17; Kiechle 1963, 193–202), who were 'mythologized' and given earlier dates in the fourth century, as set out below.

17 Hieronymus F 33 Wehrli; Clement of Alexandria, *Stromata* 1.16.78.5.

18 Lycurgus' contemporary: Ephorus *FGrH* 70 F 149.19; Aristotle, *Pol.* 1274a26–31 (noting the chronological problem); Plut. *Lyc.* 4.2–2; Diogenes Laertius 1.38. Plague: Pratinas F 713(iii) Page (in [Plut.] *De Musica* 1146b); Pausanias 1.14.4; Aelian *VH* 12.50 leaves both possibilities open.

19 Tyrtaeus could not be moved back due to his firm association with the Messenian revolt; Terpander's association with the first victory at the Karneia (see n. 74) may also have prevented a more widespread backdating of him to the time of Lycurgus.

20 West 1974, 184, suggests supplements along these lines.

21 Neither source attributes the quotation to *Eunomia*, and only Plutarch explicitly attributes it to Tyrtaeus, but it is generally agreed that it could hardly come from any other poem.

22 This is explicitly said only in a note in the margin of the manuscript (usually printed as part of the text in modern editions), but even if one were to ignore this as a gloss, the fragment features in the context of a series of oracles allegedly given to Lycurgus: see discussion in next section.

23 Andrewes 1938, 99; Wade-Gery 1944, 3, 5; Prato 1968, 66–7; West 1970, 151; 1974, 185–6; Nafissi 1991, 56, 73.

24 It is argued below that these kings were *not* actually named in the poem, and that the attribution to them was no less speculative than the attribution to Lycurgus.

25 So also (with or without lacuna between Plutarch's and Diodorus' couplets) Hudson-Williams 1926; Hammond 1950, 49; Tsopanakis 1954, 72–4; Oliver 1960, 40; Forrest 1968, 58.

26 Except for the garbled line, the text given is that of West 1992; for the arguments in support, see West 1970, 150–1; 1974, 184–6. The last four lines were rejected by Meyer 1892, 228–9; Andrewes 1938, 98–100; Treu 1941, 35–8; Prato 1968, 68–70, 150–3; Gentili and Prato 1979; Murray 1993, 169. Wade-Gery (1944, 3, 5) rejected only the last two lines. Nafissi (1991, 54, 56,

76) entertains doubts only about the last line, which is rightly defended as part of a ring composition by Adkins (1985, 69). It is perhaps worth noting that Wilamowitz hesitantly *preferred* Diodorus' version (1900, 109 n. 3).

[27] *Rhetra* covers both 'a form of words to which a number of people agree', i.e. a decision, and 'a form of words to which a number of people are asked to agree', i.e. a proposal (Wade-Gery 1944, 7); see further below.

[28] The possibilities are set out by Wade-Gery 1944, 1, 6 (who surprisingly claims that there is no significant difference between the two), and Prato 1968, 73. The choice is between taking εὐθείαις ῥήτραις as a true dative, as in e.g. Aeschylus, *Eumenides* 442 ('respond *to* all these questions') or as an instrumental dative (as in the common construction 'he responded *with* these words'). Those who reject the verses which follow in Diodorus are almost compelled to take the latter option, since otherwise the nature of the people's 'response' would be wholly unclear.

[29] For this meaning of *rhētra*, see Plutarch, *Agis* 5.3; 8.1; 9.1; Wade-Gery 1944, 7–8. In opting for this interpretation of the verse, I follow (*contra* most translators) Meyer 1892, 228, Ehrenberg 1925, 19–20, Treu 1941, 36, Bowra 1960, 45, and Nafissi 1991, 76 n. 189, who do not, however, offer reasons for their preference.

[30] Paraphrases such as 'replying to the proposals without distorting them' (Wade-Gery 1944, 6) take great liberties with the text to make it fit the conditions of the Great Rhetra.

[31] This emendation goes back to Bach's edition of Callinus, Tyrtaeus, and Asius (Leipzig 1831). Several other suggestions have been made (listed by Gentili and Prato 1979, ad F 14), but have found little acceptance. Wilamowitz 1884, 286, and Meyer 1892, 227, suggested that the line was meant to be in prose, and that no emendation was necessary.

[32] For this translation of the rider, see below, n. 62.

[33] Several scholars have claimed that Plutarch's quotation ends where it does because what followed was irrelevant to his argument about the Council of the Elders (Den Boer 1954, 189–91; Nafissi 1991, 77; Musti 1996, 280), but Plutarch was here concerned to prove that a rider was added, not merely that a Council was created. The implication for σκολιόν appears to have gone unnoticed.

[34] So also Hammond 1950, 48 (and despite their different emendations Den Boer 1954, 188–9, and Musti 1996, 262 (see n. 38), also conclude that the role of the people is essentially to obey). μηδ' is the first word of a line in Tyrtaeus F 11.3, 28; neither ἔτι nor βουλεύειν appears elsewhere in Tyrtaeus' fragments, but the former is common in Solon (FF 4.27; 13.24; 20.1; 27.1, 12, 15; and μηδ' ἔτι appears in Theognis 735), while the latter appears in Semonides (F 7.81) and Theognis (69, 633, 1052, 1089, 1101). For an explanation of the corruption, see below.

[35] Nafissi 1991, 77; Clauss 1983, 22; Den Boer 1954, 190–3. In favour of 'sovereignty' are e.g. Meyer 1892, 229; Lévy 1977, 100; Raaflaub 1993, 66; Thommen 1996, 39. Oliver 1960, 40, 43–5, argues that it means military victory and 'sovereignty' at the same time, which is difficult to accept.

[36] τῆιδε πόλει/δήμου τε πλήθει νίκην καὶ κάρτος ἕπεσθαι: taking τε as joining

the phrase 'multitude of the people' to what precedes it (as in Tyrtaeus F 10.23 West). Enjambment is not very common in early elegy (Prato 1968, 65; West 1974, 116), but it occurs at e.g. Tyrtaeus FF 5.4–5 and 9.16–17 West.

37 πόληϊ τε παντί τε δήμῳ, F 12.15 West (= *Iliad* 3.50).

38 The verb 'to plot' (ἐπιβουλεύειν) does not appear elsewhere in archaic poetry. Musti argues that it may have had an archaic meaning 'counsel in addition' (1996, 257–65); the effect of restoring this (and deleting ἔτι) would be the same as the reading proposed above.

39 ὥσθ' ἅμα is read by some in Theognis 264. ἅμα could either be taken with ἕπεσθαι, as commonly in Homer ('to attend *upon*'), or with τῇιδε πόλει δήμου τε πλήθει ('*both* this city and the multitude of the people'). ἀλλ' αἰεὶ appears e.g. in Theognis 32, 114. Clauses in Tyrtaeus rarely start in mid-verse (Adkins 1985, 71), but they do at FF 4.5, 10.27, 11.2 West.

40 See n. 23 above; also e.g. Murray 1993, 167–8. Forrest 1963, 159–60, perversely takes Plutarch's vagueness as evidence that Tyrtaeus was explicit. Steinmetz 1969, 69, even offers a supplement incorporating the names of the kings, as part of a highly unusual reconstruction of *Eunomia*, which is unconvincing mainly because it assumes that Tyrtaeus would have adopted the conventions of narrative epic in an exhortatory elegy and included the oracle twice: once as given by the god, and once as reported by messengers, the *Pythioi* (65–70).

41 Andrewes 1938, 99–100; Wade-Gery 1944, 2 (who also points out that Plutarch's opening lines then presumably followed soon after F 2 West); Parke and Wormell 1956, 90.

42 Andrewes 1938, 99–100.

43 Wade-Gery 1944, 5.

44 Strabo 8.5.5; Ephorus *FGrH* 70 F 118; Pausanias *FGrH* 582 T3. I have translated the text as established from a Vatican palimpsest and generally adopted since Ehrenberg (1925, 14) drew attention to it. Some scholars still have their doubts about the accuracy of these readings (David 1979, 96–7) and all are agreed that the text as transmitted is less than perfect. Various editors have suggested emendations, but the general sense seems clear enough, except that the last phrase, ἀπ' ἐγκωμίων πλείστων, translated here as '*contrary* to the eulogies of most people', is usually either emended or taken to mean that Pausanias took his list of oracles '*from* most eulogies' (so e.g. Ehrenberg 1925, 15). This, however, would be an odd thing to say (does it mean that Pausanias was very *thorough*, in scouring 'most' available sources for his pamphlet?), and it seems to me that ἀπό in the sense of 'away from, against' (LSJ s.v. I.3), as in Thucydides' 'contrary to human nature' (ἀπό τοῦ ἀνθρωπείου τρόπου, 1.76.2) makes far better sense in this context, reinforcing Ephorus' point (as I understand it, see below, with nn. 45, 46) that Pausanias was *opposed* to Lycurgus and yet accepted that it was he who had created Sparta's constitution.

45 My interpretation of Pausanias' arguments adds further detail to the reconstruction proposed by Nafissi 1991, 57–62 (see also Ehrenberg 1925, 14–17). David 1979 is the most recent and best exposition of the view that *Against The Laws of Lycurgus* was the title, but not the message of the pamphlet

(so too Tigerstedt 1965, 54, 111; Meyer 1892, 233–54); this is attractive insofar as it makes Pausanias less of an anomaly, but difficult to accept for the reasons given in n. 46, below.

[46] Herodotus visited the Spartan village of Pitana (3.55; cf. 9.53); he gave a Spartan version of the origin of the double kingship (6.52) and of Spartan hostilities against Samos (3.47). (On the ancient debate about relations between Sparta and Crete, see Nafissi 1984.) It is this Spartan tradition as reported by Herodotus which makes it hard to accept the views of David and others (see n. 45, above), which not only (1) put too much strain on Strabo's phrase 'a discourse against the laws of Lycurgus', but also (2) give Pausanias no plausible incentive to appeal to the non-Spartan (and/or Spartan minority) tradition of a Delphic origin of the constitution, since he could simply have appealed to the authority of the lawgiver himself; and (3) above all, cannot explain why Pausanias placed Lycurgus, traditionally supposed to be a member of his own family, in the family of his enemies (one would have to suppose that Strabo was seriously in error here). Why non-Spartans might have assumed that Spartan laws derived from the Delphic oracle is not difficult to see: the Spartans had a reputation for being even more concerned than the rest of the Greeks to act in accordance with oracular responses, and employed public officials, the *Pythioi*, whose sole task it was to seek Delphi's advice.

[47] Diodorus' dependence on Ephorus here is confirmed by the very close parallels between his exegesis of the meaning of the oracles (7.12.3–4) and Ephorus' interpretation of Lycurgus' reforms as summarized by Polybius (6.45.1 and 7–8; Ephorus *FGrH* 70 F 148)) and Strabo (10.4.16; Ephorus *FGrH* 70 F 149): the key point in both is the combination of bravery and unity, each useless without the other. Ephorus' attitude to Lycurgus was favourable, so he will have interpreted positively the material used in a hostile manner by Pausanias.

[48] Diodorus 7.12.1 (no. 216 Parke and Wormell). Herodotus cites the first four lines declaring Lycurgus a god (1.65.5; no. 29 Parke and Wormell): it has been assumed that the next two lines, speaking of *eunomia*, were added later (Meyer 1892, 223–4; Ehrenberg 1925, 12–13; Parke and Wormell 1956, 85–6), but it is possible that they were already in circulation as part of a non-Spartan version of the oracle, which Herodotus decided not to quote because it clashed with the native Spartan tradition. For Plutarch (*Lyc.* 5.4) the reference to *eunomia* was an integral part of 'that famous oracle' (see further Parke and Wormell, ad nos. 29 and 216).

[49] No. 220 Parke and Wormell, from Oinomaus as cited by Eusebius, *Praeparatio Evangelica* 5.27–8; attributed to Pausanias' pamphlet (and indeed believed to have been forged by, or on behalf of, the king: see below, n. 54) by Meyer 1892, 225–6; Nafissi 1991, 59–60.

[50] So Nafissi 1991, 59–60. On heroization of kings: Cartledge 1987, 335–43.

[51] See David 1979, 110–12; Cartledge 1987, 77–98. I should stress again that the fact that this oracle suited fourth-century circumstances very well does not mean that it was a fourth-century invention (see above n. 6). For what really happened to Sparta at the time, see Cartledge 1987, 405–12; Hodkinson 1989; 1993.

[52] There may have been an anti-ephor angle even here: Aristotle notes the large 'profits' and luxurious lifestyles of ephors (*Pol.* 1272a39–b1).

[53] So e.g. Tigerstedt 1965, 54; Lévy 1977, 88; David 1979, 112.

[54] I see no need to accuse Pausanias either of outright forgery (Busolt 1920, 47–52; Parke and Wormell 1956, 87–8; Nafissi 1991, 60), or of using recently invented oracles (Meyer 1892, 243), or of 'tampering' with his sources (Wade-Gery 1944, 5), or even of knowingly misconstruing the meaning of the texts which he cited (Wade-Gery 1944, 116). His sources were vague, and thus open to interpretation in support of his case; see also n. 56 below.

[55] Thibron: *FGrH* 581 (see Jacoby's commentary and notes ad loc. for the possible dates and circumstances of Thibron's work). The (negative) impact of Pausanias' pamphlet is stressed and convincingly reconstructed by Nafissi (1991, 62–71): my interpretation of developments in the subsequent debate about the origin of the ephors is almost identical to his (contra David 1979, 109–16). Nafissi does not, however, draw what are, for my purposes, the main conclusions: that this debate inspired the selective quoting which produced both Diodorus' and Plutarch's versions of Tyrtaeus, and that it brought about the (mis)identification of *Eunomia*'s oracle with the Rhetra.

[56] In theory, a fourth defence might have been to declare the evidence false, but there is no sign that anyone pursued this line – which supports the idea that Pausanias did not forge his material, but assembled it from known sources.

[57] The Cretan origin of Spartan law is also posited by the pseudo-Platonic *Minos* 318cd; the ephorate is also attributed to Lycurgus by Satyros (*FHG* III.162.8).

[58] Aristotle, *Pol.* 1313a28–33; Plutarch *Lyc.* 7.2. Another tradition claimed that Theopompus did not introduce the ephors as a necessary counterweight, but as his lowly assistants; it was later still that they began to acquire power (when Asteropus was ephor): this account appears in Plutarch's biography of Cleomenes and is likely to have been developed as part of this third-century king's propaganda against the ephors whom he assassinated in 227 BC (*Cleomenes* 7–10).

[59] There was something of a cult of his co-ruler, Polydorus (Pausanias 3.11.10; 3.12.3), but this was probably also largely a creation of third-century propaganda: Meyer 1892, 268 n. 1; Kennell 1995, 96.

[60] The seeming internal inconsistency of the Rhetra is suggested as the basis for this notion also by Wade-Gery 1943, 62, 115; 1944, 2; Bringmann 1975, 364; Nafissi 1991, 67–8; Murray 1993, 169; Thommen 1996, 34. Others attribute the notion of a 'rider' to a presumed explicit reference in Tyrtaeus to Theopompus and Polydorus, which was seen to be incompatible with the usual attribution of the Rhetra to Lycurgus; hence a separation of Theopompus' rider and Lycurgus' original law had to be invented: Kiechle 1963, 167–8; Forrest 1963, 165–6; Jones 1967, 31–3; West 1970, 151; 1974, 185–6. Most scholars accept that the last clause was not added later, but always part of the Rhetra, and that the notion of it being a 'rider' was a classical scholarly construct (see references in n. 70, under (1) and (2)), but some posit a genuinely separate origin for the rider (see references in n. 70, under (3), and also

Huxley 1962; Lévy 1977; Ogden 1994).

61 What follows is a translation of the text as emended by Wade-Gery 1943; 1944, 8–9 (and cf. Treu 1941, 32–5), except that (with e.g. Manfredini and Piccirilli 1980, 238; Ogden 1994, 85–6 n. 5) I have kept the mss. οὕτως, 'thus'. Wade-Gery's emendation of this word to τούτως, 'these', was meant to give a more central role to the Elders, to reflect Plutarch's claim that the Rhetra is 'about' them; that claim, however, was inspired by the fourth-century debate, and was not based on a close reading of the Rhetra, which clearly focuses on the role of the assembly (so e.g. Tigerstedt 1965, 54–5). Other emendations: e.g. Lévy 1977; Pavese 1992; Ogden 1994.

62 This last sentence (the 'rider') is usually translated as 'if the people formulate a crooked decision', or the like, which involves taking ἔροιτο as an unusual form of 'to say, speak, formulate', or emending it into something meaning 'choose' or 'decide' (see in detail Pavese 1992, 278–9; Ogden 1994, 88–9). This is based on Plutarch's claim that the people too often 'distorted... proposals by subtractions and additions' (*Lyc.* 6.7). It seems to me much simpler to suppose that Plutarch (or rather Aristotle) imposed on the Rhetra an anachronistic notion of how assemblies work, and that ἔροιτο really is what it seems to be, an optative of ἔρομαι 'ask (for)' (LSJ s.v., 2). The Rhetra is saying, then, that the people have (1) a right to *speak* ('criticize') in assembly, and (2) a right to *vote* on proposals ('power'). On the other hand, (3) the people cannot bring forward proposals of their own, but must put a request to the kings and elders ('ask for something'), who are entitled to turn it down if they deem it unacceptable ('crooked'). This fits perfectly well with what is known about Spartan procedures, and does not necessitate the kind of juggling with evidence from Aristotle indulged in by Wade-Gery 1943, 71–2. For Spartan decision-making, see Ruzé 1997, 129–240 (esp. 157–72 on the Rhetra); Andrewes 1966; Jones 1966.

63 Accordingly, Plutarch argues elsewhere that the Delphic oracle sometimes answered in prose: his only example is that of Lycurgus' *rhētrai* (*Mor.* 403e). Chrimes 1949, 477–89, Jeffery 1961, 145–7, and Forrest 1963, 179, argued that the Rhetra was a genuine 'prose oracle' (and Busolt 1920, 43, went so far as to say that the Rhetra was an oracle falsely called a Rhetra). Ehrenberg 1925, 39, and den Boer 1954, 158–9, defended the Rhetra's oracular nature despite acknowledging that it was not an oracle in form. Parker 1993, 59–60, Parke and Wormell 1956, 91, and Treu 1941, 40–2, point out that some sacred laws of Cyrene, also in prose, were attributed to the Delphic oracle by means of a prescript. This is in principle possible for the Rhetra, too, but here even the prescript is lacking. See n. 66 below.

64 Private pact: Homer, *Odyssey* 14.393. Communal decision: law of Chios (Jeffery 1990, 343.41 of *c.* 575–50 BC); laws of the Eleans (Jeffery 1990, 220.5 of *c.* 500, and 220.15 of *c.* 475–50; Van Effenterre and Ruzé 1994, no. 56 of *c.* 450); Xenophon, *Hellenica* 6.6.28. Treaties: Elis and Heraia (Jeffery 1990, 220.6 of *c.* 500); Anaitioi and Metapioi (Jeffery 1990, 220.12 of *c.* 475–50). Contract between community and individual: Onasilos with Stasikypros and the Idalians (Van Effenterre and Ruzé 1994, no. 31, of *c.* 470); Deukalion with Chaladrior (Van Effenterre and Ruzé 1994, no. 21 of *c.* 500–475). See the

discussions in Meyer (1892, 262–7, whose attempt to distinguish between 'treaty' and 'law' seems misguided: both are seen as 'agreements' by early Greeks) and Ehrenberg (1925, 18–22).

65 So too Meyer 1892, 230–3; Wade-Gery 1943, 62 n. 2; 1944, 6–8; West 1974, 185.

66 Unless one wishes to argue, with Meyer 1892, 230–3, that the verses were not composed by Tyrtaeus, but by some fourth-century forger. Wade-Gery 1944, 4, 114 tried to get around this difficulty by arguing that Tyrtaeus indeed referred to the Rhetra, but claimed that its provisions had earlier been 'enjoined' by 'an ancient oracle' found 'presumably in the Royal Archives'. Parke and Wormell 1956, 89, suggested that the Rhetra was 'the comment which might accompany a verse prophecy'. West 1974, 185, imagined that 'the passing of the law will have been immediately preceded by the publication of the oracle and justified by it... Perhaps [Tyrtaeus] went on to say "and the city decreed that it should be so".' All this is rather strained, and in any case tantamount to saying that the Spartans did, after all, believe in the Delphic origins of their constitution. Chrimes 1949, 475–7, noting this difficulty, goes so far as to suggest that the archaic Spartans *did* believe this, but had discarded that tradition by the time of Herodotus (only to pick it up again in the fourth century).

67 Divine support for Homeric kings: e.g. Mondi 1980; Van Wees 1999, 5–8.

68 On bullying in Homeric assemblies: Van Wees 1992, 33, 83–4, 95–6.

69 For this interpretation of the Rhetra's clauses, see above, n. 62. Andrewes was surely right to argue that the Rhetra's 'attitude to kings and constitution is more modern than that of the *Eunomia*' (1938, 101).

70 Earlier views that the Rhetra post-dated Tyrtaeus (which involved regarding our fragment of *Eunomia* as a forgery, see n. 1 above) were based on the argument that the Rhetra reflected a military organization (the 'obal' army) which did not yet exist in Tyrtaeus' time (when there was only a 'tribal' army), sometimes reinforced by the argument (now demolished by e.g. Hodkinson 1998 and Powell 1998) that political and social reform was reflected in a supposed radical change in Spartan material culture, *c.* 550. Wade-Gery (1944, 4, 115, 123) reasserted the view that *Eunomia* was genuine and that it did reflect the Rhetra; he made the two texts contemporary, but as a concession to the older view placed them both late in Tyrtaeus' career, after the Messenian revolt and after the introduction of the 'obal' army, *c.* 600 (despite Aristotle's assertion and the implication of the fragments that Tyrtaeus composed *Eunomia during* the war; Forrest 1963, 157, reports that Wade-Gery was later persuaded by his son to adopt an earlier date). Subsequently, scholars have adhered to one of three interpretations: (1) the Rhetra was enacted shortly before Tyrtaeus composed his poem and thus dates to *c.* 650–625 (e.g. Andrewes 1956, 73; Bowra 1960, 46; Bringmann 1975, 382–3; Cartledge 1979, 134–5; Hooker 1980, 130; Thommen 1996, 35–6), which suggests to many a connection with the Messenian Revolt; (2) the Rhetra was enacted somewhere between the late eighth century and about 650 (e.g. Forrest 1963, 166–70; 1968, 58; Starr 1965, 267–71; Jones 1966, 172; 1967, 31–3; West 1970, 151; 1974, 185–6; Welwei 1979, 442–5; Manfredini and

Piccirilli 1980, 243–4; Nafissi 1991, 73, 78; Murray 1993, 167–9; Musti 1996, 281; Osborne 1996, 178–9; Ruzé 1997, 143), a dating usually based on the association with Theopompus and Polydorus, or with the so-called hoplite reform, or both (Raaflaub 1993, 65, 68 n.130, accepts the date but not the association); (3) the 'rider' was enacted by Theopompus and Polydorus, and the rest of the Rhetra must therefore be earlier still (e.g. already Ehrenberg 1927, 22; also Den Boer 1954, 183; Oliver 1960, 53–66; Kiechle 1963, 167, 225), which dates it either *c.* 800 (if one links it with the ancient dates for Lycurgus: e.g. Chrimes 1949, 305–47, 413–18; Hammond 1950, 62; Pavese 1992, 280–2) or *c.* 725, if one links it with Sparta's conquest of Amyclae (e.g. Oliva 1971, 97–102; Parker 1993, 50–6). Unusual are Huxley (1962, 54–5: the 'rider' is contemporary with Tyrtaeus and the rest of the Rhetra dates to the reign of Theopompus); Lévy (1977, 102–3: some of the Rhetra dates to the eighth century, the rest to Theopompus, and the 'rider' to *after* Tyrtaeus); and Ogden (1994, 100–2: the 'rider' is *earlier* than the rest of the Rhetra; no dates specified). Tigerstedt 1965, 58–60, concludes that we cannot date the Rhetra beyond saying that 'it is older than Tyrtaeus'; Finley 1981, 26 n. 4, is content to date it somewhere before 600 BC (separating the Rhetra from the 'sixth-century revolution' in Spartan society); Clauss 1983, 116, refuses to discuss the Rhetra at all.

[71] That Aristotle, who knew the whole poem, felt able to attribute the oracle to the kings of the First Messenian War shows that Tyrtaeus expressed himself vaguely not only on the identity of the Heraclids but also on the circumstances under which they received the oracles.

[72] Similar themes occasionally feature in Tyrtaeus' other fragments. Descent from Herakles, support from Zeus: F 11.1–2; obedience to kings: F 19.11; perhaps also F 21.14–15 West.

[73] The stories about the Parthenioi and the Epeunaktoi (Nafissi 1991, 38–51) may also indicate internal division in early Sparta.

[74] Terpander was credited with 'the first organization of music' at Sparta, and Thales with 'the second' organization, the latter apparently a reference to the institution of the Gymnopaidiai: [Plutarch] *De Musica* 9.1134bc. Thales' songs continued to be performed at this festival: Sosibius *FGrH* 595 F 5. Terpander was associated with the (re)organization of the Karneia: Hellanicus *FGrH* 4 F 85a. Regular performances of the work of Tyrtaeus during military campaigns: Lycurgus, *Against Leocrates* 107; Philochorus *FGrH* 328 F 216 (Athenaeus 630c), but see Bowie 1986.

[75] Solon's elegy *Salamis* exhorted the Athenians to conquer this island (FF 1–3 West); before his reforms he composed at least one elegy on 'good order' (FF 4, 4abc West). For Epimenides (who was mythologized to an even greater extent than Terpander and Thales, see n. 16 above), see Manfredini and Piccirilli 1977, 153–62; Rhodes 1981, 81–4; Vernant 1982, 69–81. On the crisis in Athens (and elsewhere), see Van Wees 1999.

[76] Solon's versification of laws: F 31 West. For other poetic lawgivers, see Thomas 1995, 63.

[77] Vernant 1982, 69–81, sketches in outline a similar picture of a late-seventh-century transformation of Greek society at large: 'we can say that the

starting point of the crisis was economic; that initially it took the form of agitation that was both social and religious; but that…it finally led to the birth of a moral and political thought that was secular' (70–1).

Bibliography

Adkins, A.W.H.
1985 *Poetic Craft in the Early Greek Elegists*, Chicago.

Andrewes, A.
1938 'Eunomia', *CQ* 32, 89–102.
1956 *The Greek Tyrants*, London.
1966 'The government of classical Sparta', in *Ancient Society and Institutions. Studies presented to Victor Ehrenberg*. Oxford, 1–20.

Bowie, E.L.
1986 'Early Greek elegy, symposium and public festival', *JHS* 106, 13–35.

Bowra, C.M.
1960 *Early Greek Elegists*, Cambridge.

Bringmann, K.
1975 'Die Grosse Rhetra und die Entstehung des spartanischen Kosmos', *Historia* 24, 513–38 (cited from Christ 1986).

Busolt, G.
1920 *Griechische Staatskunde*, Munich.

Cartledge, P.A.
1979 *Sparta and Lakonia. A Regional History 1300–362* BC, London.
1987 *Agesilaos and the Crisis of Sparta*, London.

Chrimes, K.M.T.
1949 *Ancient Sparta. A Re-examination of the Evidence*, Manchester.

Christ, K. (ed.)
1986 *Sparta. Wege der Forschung, Bd. 622*, Darmstadt.

Clauss, M.
1983 *Sparta. Eine Einführung in seine Geschichte und Zivilisation*, Munich.

Crusius, O.
1910 *Paroemiographica. Textgeschichtliches zur alten Dichtung und Religion*, Munich.

David, E.
1979 'The pamphlet of Pausanias', *PdP* 34, 94–116.

Den Boer, W.
1954 *Laconian Studies*, Amsterdam.

Ehrenberg, V.
1925 *Neugründer des Staates. Ein Beitrag zur geschichte Spartas und Athens im VI. Jahrhundert*, Munich.
1927 'Der Gesetzgeber von Sparta', in *Epitymbion für H. Swoboda*, Reichenberg, 19–28.
1933 'Der Damos im archaischen Sparta', *Hermes* 68, 288–305.

Finley, M.I.
1981 'Sparta and Spartan society', in *Economy and Society in Ancient Greece*, London, 24–40.

Fisher, N.R.E.
1994 'Sparta re(de)valued', in A. Powell and S. Hodkinson (eds.) *The Shadow of Sparta*, London and New York, 347–400.
Fisher, N., and Van Wees, H. (eds.)
1998 *Archaic Greece: New Approaches and New Evidence*, London.
Fontenrose, J.
1978 *The Delphic Oracle*, Berkeley.
Forrest, W.G.
1963 'The date of the Lykourgan reforms at Sparta', *JHS* 70, 157–79.
1968 *A History of Sparta 950–192* BC, London.
Gentili, B., and Prato, C. (eds.)
1979 *Poetae Elegiaci. Pars prior*, Leipzig.
Gostoli, A. (ed.)
1990 *Terpander*, Rome.
Hammond, N.G.L.
1950 'The Lycurgean reform at Sparta', *JHS* 70, 42–64.
Hodkinson, S.
1986 'Land tenure and inheritance in classical Sparta', *CQ* 36, 378–406.
1989 'Inheritance, marriage and demography: perspectives upon the success and decline of classical Sparta', in A. Powell (ed.) *Classical Sparta. Techniques behind her success*, Norman and London, 79–121.
1993 'Warfare, wealth, and the crisis of Spartiate society', in J. Rich and G. Shipley (ed.) *War and Society in the Greek World*, London, 146–76.
1998 'Lakonian artistic production and the problem of Spartan austerity', in Fisher and van Wees (eds.) *Archaic Greece*, 93–117.
Hooker, J.T.
1980 *The Ancient Spartans*, London.
Hudson-Williams, T.
1926 *Early Greek Elegy*, Cardiff and London.
Huxley, G.L.
1962 *Early Sparta*, Cambridge, Mass.
Janni, P.
1965 *La cultura di Sparta arcaica. Ricerche I*, Rome.
Jeffery, L.H.
1961 'The pact of the first settlers at Cyrene', *Historia* 10, 139–47.
1990 *The Local Scripts of Archaic Greece. Revised edition with a supplement by A.W. Johnston* Oxford and New York.
Jones, A.H.M.
1966 'The Lycurgan Rhetra', in *Ancient Society and Institutions. Studies presented to Victor Ehrenberg*, Oxford, 165–75.
1967 *Sparta*, Oxford.
Kennell, N.M.
1995 *The Gymnasium of Virtue. Education and culture in ancient Sparta*, Chapel Hill and London.
Kiechle, F.
1963 *Lakonien und Sparta*, Munich.

Klinger, W.

1929 'Contribution à la reconstruction des fragments de Tyrtée', *Bulletin International de l'Académie Polonaise*, Cracow, 35–9.

Leutsch, E.L., and Schneidewin, F.G. (eds.)

1839 *Corpus Paroemiographorum Graecorum. Tomus I*, Göttingen.

Leutsch, E.L., (ed.)

1851 *Corpus Paroemiographorum Graecorum. Tomus II*, Göttingen.

Lévy, E.

1977 'La Grande Rhètra', *Ktèma* 2, 85–103.

Manfredini, M., and Piccirilli, L. (eds.)

1977 *Plutarco: La vita di Solone* (no place).

Manfredini, M., and Piccirilli, L. (eds.)

1980 *Plutarco: Le vite di Licurgo e di Numa* (no place).

Meyer, Ed.

1892 *Forschungen zur Alten Geschichte. Vol. I*, Halle.

Möller, A.

forthcoming 'The beginning of chronography: Hellanikos' *hiereiai*', in N. Luraghi (ed.) *Herodotus in Context.*

Mondi, R.

1980 '*Skeptoukhoi Basileis*. An argument for divine kingship in early Greece', *Arethusa* 13, 203–16.

Murray, O.

1993 *Early Greece. Second Edition*, Cambridge, Mass.

Musti, D.

1996 'Regole politiche a Sparta: Tirteo e la *Grande Rhetra*', *RdF* 124, 257–81.

Nafissi, M.

1984 'La controversia sulla prioritá fra le politeiai di Sparta e Creta: Eforo e Pausania', *Annali della Facoltà di Lettere e Filosofia dell' Università degli Studi di Perugia* 21, 345–66.

1991 *La nascita del kosmos. Studi sulla storia e la società di Sparta*, Perugia.

Ogden, D.

1994 'Crooked speech: the genesis of the Spartan Rhetra', *JHS* 114, 85–102.

Oliva, P.

1971 *Sparta and her Social Problems*, Amsterdam and Prague.

Oliver, J.H.

1960 *Demokratia, The Gods, And The Free World*, Baltimore.

Osborne, R.

1996 *Greece in the Making 1200–479* BC, London.

Parke, H.W., and Wormell, D.E.W.

1949 'Notes on Delphic oracles', *CQ* 43, 138–40.

1956 *The Delphic Oracle*, Oxford.

Parker, V.

1993 'Some dates in early Spartan history', *Klio* 75, 45–60.

Pavese, C.O.

1992 'La Rhetra di Licurgo', *RdF* 120, 260–85.

Poole, W.
1994 'Euripides and Sparta', in A. Powell and S. Hodkinson (eds.) *The Shadow of Sparta*, London, 1–33.

Powell, A.
1998 'Sixth-century Lakonian vase-painting: continuities and discontinuities with the "Lykourgan" ethos', in Fisher and van Wees (eds.) *Archaic Greece*, 119–46.

Prato, C. (ed.)
1968 *Tyrtaeus*, Rome.

Raaflaub, K.A.
1993 'The rise of the polis: Homer to Solon. The written sources', in M.H. Hansen (ed.) *The Ancient Greek City-State. Acts of the Copenhagen Polis Center, Vol. I*, Copenhagen, 41–105.

Rhodes, P.J.
1981 *A Commentary on the Aristotelian Athenaion Politeia*, Oxford.

Ruzé, F.
1997 *Délibération et pouvoir dans la cité grecque de Nestor à Socrate*, Paris

Starr, C.G.
1965 'The credibility of early Spartan history', *Historia* 14, 257–72.

Steinmetz, P.
1969 'Das Erwachen des geschichtlichen Bewusstseins in der Polis', in P. Steinmetz (ed.) *Politeia und Res Publica*, Wiesbaden, 52–78.

Stibbe, C.M.
1996 *Das andere Sparta*, Mainz.

Thomas, R.
1995 'Written in stone? Liberty, equality, orality, and the codification of law', *BICS* 40, 59–74.

Thommen, L.
1996 *Lakedaimonion Politeia. Die Entstehung der spartanischen Verfassung. Historia Einzelschriften 103*, Stuttgart.

Tigerstedt, E.N.
1965 *The Legend of Sparta in Classical Antiquity. Vol. I*, Lund.

Treu, M.
1941 'Der Schlusssatz der Grossen Rhetra', *Hermes* 76, 22–42.

Tsopanakis, A.G.
1954 *La Rhètre de Lycurgue. L'annexe. Tyrtée*, Thessaloniki.

Van Effenterre, H., and Ruzé, F.
1994 *Nomima. Recueil d'inscriptions politiques et juridiques de l'archaïsme grec. Vol. I*, Rome.

Van Wees, H.
1992 *Status Warriors. War, violence, and society in Homer and history*, Amsterdam.
1999 'The mafia of early Greece. Violent exploitation in the seventh and sixth centuries', in K. Hopwood (ed.) *Organized Crime in Antiquity*, London, 1–51.

Vernant, J.-P.
1982 *The Origins of Greek Thought*, Ithaca, N.Y.

Von Blumenthal, A.
1942 'Beobachtungen zu griechischen Texten IV', *Hermes* 77, 103–11.

Wade-Gery, H.T.
1943 'The Spartan Rhetra in Plutarch, *Lycurgus* VI A: Plutarch's text', *CQ* 37, 62–72.
1944 'The Spartan Rhetra in Plutarch, *Lycurgus* VI B: The Εὐνομία of Tyrtaeus; C: What is the Rhetra?', *CQ* 38, 1–9, 115–26.

Welwei, K.-W.
1979 'Die Spartanische Phylenordnung im Spiegel der Großen Rhetra und des Tyrtaios', *Gymnasium* 86, 178–96 (cited from Christ 1986).

West, M.L.
1970 Review of Prato 1968, *CR* 20, 149–51.
1974 *Studies in Greek Elegy and Iambus*, Berlin.
1992 *Iambi et Elegi Graeci. Editio Altera*, Oxford.

Wilamowitz-Moellendorff, U. von
1884 *Homerische Untersuchungen*, Berlin.
1900 *Die Textgeschichte der griechischen Lyriker*, Berlin.

Chapter 2

PERSPECTIVES ON SPARTAN EDUCATION IN THE CLASSICAL PERIOD

Jean Ducat

We have to remember that the education of children is a major anxiety for every society. Its principal aim is not to drum into them a certain quantity of knowledge thought to be basic, but to shape dissimilar individuals in order to make them conform to the collective norm; thus they can eventually be integrated into the social structure, and the latter can perpetuate itself in accordance with its self-appointed model, which is education's essential purpose. This is even more true for the Greek city: what characterises it is the rule of *Nomos*, but, in order to impose this norm on individuals, the State has only a very weak coercive power at its disposal; the social stability (*eunomia*) which is sought above all rests on a necessary consensus. This can only result from the interiorisation of the norm brought about by education. Of all Greek cities, Sparta is surely the one where education played the greatest role, because the model of the citizen was particularly demanding and exerted a very strong pressure on individuals; in particular, one of its principal missions was to make them as far as possible the same, which implied that the process should be identical for all. Education is, therefore, at the heart of Spartan ideology and practice. It has been considered as an essential part of the 'laws of Lycurgus', which means that it was in fact, and that it appeared to be, epitomising and gathering together in itself the whole Spartan *kosmos*.[1] This is why it is also at the centre of current debates on the way in which we should imagine the formation of this *kosmos* and its perpetuation.[2]

My intention here is obviously not to examine details of the classical *agōgē*;[3] I wish merely to sketch a perspective, a cavalier view in a way, by structuring the discussion around a problem which could be formulated thus: how should we conceive of the Spartan education system? But before tackling this, it is necessary to take stock of the constraints which the very nature of the evidence imposes: there would be no room for the current debate if the situation was different.

The principal accounts are those of Xenophon and Plutarch; without them we would know only scattered details. For education in the classical period Xenophon is obviously the major and incomparable source, as no one disputes; it is well known that he seems to have had personal reasons to know the system from inside. But his account is not in the least a description. From Xenophon we would know nothing, or next to nothing, on the annual age classes (if they existed at this point), on organisation, on the 'subjects taught'; impossible to extrapolate from him anything resembling a 'timetable'. The account is purely apologetic: it is less about praising than defending the Spartan educational system (this defensive attitude is very striking) on a certain number of points. What can be seen through his text, therefore, is the argumentation of Sparta's adversaries, which dictates his structure of listing successive answers. The formula 'other Greeks' recurs like a leitmotif: the central concept of this defence is in fact systematically to contrast Sparta's conduct in the matter of education with that of the other Greek cities.

Plutarch's account, in some respects, comes closer to being a description, but he remains rather vague on the organisational level; he too wishes above all to defend Lycurgus against the attacks of his critics. But what *agōgē* is he describing? He surely means to talk about the *agōgē* of times past ('of Lycurgus'), which for him is also the eternal *agōgē*. In fact his sources are spread over a wide time-span, from Xenophon to the late hellenistic period, and there is no doubt that he also knew the system which operated in his own time. He therefore risks having attributed to this 'eternal' education traits borrowed from every period. Must we, then, on principle give up using him to reconstruct the system of the classical period? Not necessarily: one of his main sources is Aristotle, who is anterior to the (probable) great reforms of the third century; but we must, as far as possible, only use him under the control of Xenophon (an excellent principle, but one which is not easy to put into practice).

The same problem is presented by our other 'late' sources, which are, on the one hand, scholia (on Strabo and 'Herodotus') on the system of age-classes, and, on the other, inscriptions of the hellenistic and especially Roman periods. To use these to reconstruct the *agōgē* of the classical period is in principle more than questionable, and seems even to have become near-impossible since the publication of Kennell's study. In sum, we have at our disposal a succession of discourses on the *agōgē* rather than real documentation. The result, distortions which seriously affect the picture we draw and disturb its perspectives. We should be alert to these.

1. One of the great originalities of the *agōgē* (emphasised by Xenophon and Plutarch, as well as by Aristotle, *Pol.* 8.1337a31–2) is the fact that it is obligatory, of the State, and so identical for everyone (further references below, p. 53). Nevertheless, in a general way, the domain of private life was very important at Sparta: Plato mentions this in his portrait of the 'timocratic man' (*Rep.* 8.548a), and Dionysius of Halicarnassus (20, extract 13.2 = 20.2) emphasises it in a manner rather surprising to us. We must therefore believe that, although our authors do not talk about it, the family also played an essential part in education. Firstly, it had complete responsibility for the boy up to the age of seven, which is no small matter, since this is the decisive period for the formation of personality. What happened afterwards? I might be tempted to take up an observation of Fustel de Coulanges,[4] 'children received a communal education; they nevertheless returned each evening to their paternal home', which attracted from Jeanmaire the retort: 'F. de C. has tried in vain to diminish the significance of this fact [the communal upbringing of the young] by affirming that children, brought up communally, continued to sleep under the paternal roof: the texts which he adduces [essentially Plutarch, *Agesilaus* 25–6] prove nothing of this, and, on the contrary, show us the young Spartiates sleeping rough [and he cites Plutarch *Lyc.* 16]'.[5] This is indeed what the texts 'show' us – the theoretical texts; but it is legitimate to doubt that children *always* slept out of doors, on *stibades*. Plutarch (for he, and he alone, is in question) is manifestly dramatising the *agōgē*, probably already dramatised itself in the Roman period, by presenting as an everyday practice something which was only certainly the case for brief 'stages'.

Plutarch, moreover, does not have the monopoly on dramatisation. Take the case of stealing: to read Xenophon you would believe that children were permanently forced to steal their food. Kennell (1995, 122–3) with good cause doubts that this was the case; he thinks that this practice only held force on the occasion of certain festivals; but the text which he adduces does not necessarily mean this, and I am rather inclined to think that stealing was imposed on children during 'stages' of life in isolation. Another detail demonstrates that the sources distort reality in representing the life of the young Spartiate as always excessively harsh and austere: glosses relating to the word *mothōnes* clearly imply that during the *agōgē* the citizen son was accompanied by a young helot who was at his personal service.[6]

Other texts, in fact, implicitly underline the role of the family; and especially, of the mother. Let us take the anonymous *Sayings of Spartan*

Women 9: 'When an Ionian woman was boasting about the luxury of one of her own garments [let it be understood: made by her; the whole scenario rests on this, in opposing the 'products' of two types of women], a Spartan woman, showing her four sons, all *kosmiōtatoi*, said: "Here are the products of a woman of substance" ' (Plut. *Mor.* 241d). I leave aside the ideology of the saying, weaving *versus teknopoiia*, the problem clearly being that of the woman's testing of her *aretē*. The point that I shall take up here is the following: to be called *kosmiōtatoi*, the boys are obviously more than seven years old, and, indeed, their ages are necessarily tiered; however, the mother presents them as her *own* products. The *Sayings of Spartan Women* in general show that the mother considers herself as having sole responsibility towards the city for the quality of her sons; many of them rest on the principle 'it is I who made you, but not for myself'. This explains the slightly strange formulation of Gorgo 5 (240e), *monai tiktomen andras* ('We alone produce men'); *andres* are not born fully-formed, and if their creation takes many years, it is the responsibility of the mother throughout.

It is more than probable, moreover, that, under the pressure of the myth of gynecocracy, the *Sayings* in their turn distort reality by exaggerating the role of the mother. I have difficulty imagining that the father, the Spartiate citizen, would have been absent from his home, as has been too often said, trusting Plutarch blindly, and would have been uninterested in the education of the son or sons who would replace him in the city one day. I imagine, on the contrary, that he followed the boy's performance in the *agōgē* with a passionate interest, and a text like the dedication of Damonon seems to me to point in this direction. Xenophon (*Lac.Pol.* 6.2) clearly confirms that it was indeed the father who was considered to have the principal responsibility for the education of his son. It is just that these aspects do not interest our authors, because they are a matter of common practice (so in *Lac.Pol.* 6.2); they only judge as worthy of being exhibited things particular to Sparta.

2. For the same reason they down-play or pass over in silence aspects of the *agōgē*, and they are numerous, which make it a *paideia*, an education of the usual Greek type (Xenophon calls it by no other name, as we have seen). First (for us), reading, writing, arithmetic. Certainly there is no lack of texts to down-play this. As far as reading and writing are concerned: *Dissoi Logoi* 2.10 (but the Spartans are not named, and the text also denies *mousikē*!); Isocrates 12 (*Panathenaicus*) 209 ('they do not even learn their letters'); Plutarch, *Lyc.* 16.10 ('they learn their letters as much as necessary', a formula which is not totally

negative; cf. *Inst.Lac.* 4, *Mor.* 237a). For arithmetic, Plato, *Hipp.Maj.* 285c ('many of them do not even know how to count, you might say'; Hippias is the speaker). It was obviously a commonplace, which confirms that the image of Spartan education current in the fourth century was in agreement on this point with that which Xenophon and Plutarch provide. As the contemporary enquiries of Cartledge and Boring have shown, this commonplace is far from reality.[7] Spartiates' basic instruction was at the level of that of other Greeks; the functioning of the city depended on it. How was it transmitted? No one talks about it, but I think that this part of education functioned at Sparta, as elsewhere, in a private manner.[8]

Next, self-expression. Plutarch himself insists on the fact that the Spartiates' mode of oral expression resulted from a long apprenticeship: 'They taught children to use a style of speech which combined piquancy with grace, and condensed much observation into a few words' (*Lyc.* 19.1). The two chapters 19 and 20 praise this manner of speaking, demonstrating, with examples, that it was completely the opposite of poor language, and that calculated brevity in fact highlighted the sense. All this smacks rather of hagiography; but the fact remains that there was something there which must have resembled Greek eloquence before the sophists, and that the Spartiates were anxious to preserve it as a kind of inheritance. This is not, in any case, a commonplace dating only from the imperial period: from Herodotus (3.46) on, 'laconism' is clearly proverbial, and, if Xenophon does not talk about its teaching, Plato (*Protagoras* 342d–e) gives it praise which, in contrast to his earlier remarks, seems to be lacking in irony, and Aristotle (fr. 611.13 Rose) specifies that it was inculcated 'from leaving the category of *paides*'.

Finally, *mousikē*, an amalgam encompassing music, singing, dance and poetry. At Sparta as in other cities it was the basis of education. As Plutarch says, 'They took no less care in teaching them poetry and singing than in making them learn to speak with accuracy and purity' (*Lyc.* 21.1). Music and singing were for the Spartiates an ancient inheritance which they were anxious to preserve: 'The Spartans, of all the Greeks, are those who have best guarded the art of music, because they have practised it a great deal, and because they have had many composers. Even now they have preserved their ancient songs and sing them with care and with art', writes Athenaeus at the beginning of the third century AD (14.632f), who, in order to demonstrate that this is an authentically ancient tradition, then cites in this connection a poet of the beginning of the fifth century, Pratinas of Phleious.

3. Equally misunderstood by the sources are the economic aspects of the *agōgē*. Let us take a particular case. We know that the Spartiates could lose their citizen-status through poverty. Their sons were then excluded from the *agōgē*; but was this because their fathers were no longer citizens, or because they were unable to meet the expenses which it entailed? The first answer seems to be so obvious as to render the second meaningless; but see how Phylarchus, an excellent author, defines the status of *mothakes*: 'Each child of citizen status, in accordance with his means, takes either one or two (and some even more) *syntrophoi*. Thus *mothakes* are free, though not Lacedaemonians, and they participate in the entire education' (81 F 43). It is Phylarchus himself who, by ὡς ἄν καὶ τὰ ἴδια ἐκποιῶσι ('in accordance with his means'), emphasises the *cost* of Spartiate public education. We could say, then, that the son of a disfranchised citizen was excluded from the *agōgē* both *by right* because his father was no longer a Spartiate, and *in practice* by lack of money. The expensive *agōgē* is something we might find surprising: does Xenophon not specify that the children had no shoes (2.3), wore few clothes (2.4), and received little food (2.5)? We can see that this presentation of the child's life is surely meant to be comparative; it must only concern certain periods or 'stages'. One of the major expenses, as for adults, was financing the *syssition*.[9] We can see in Xenophon 2.5 that there were children's *syssitia*, and that it was the leader of the group who was in charge of collecting individual contributions.[10]

In addition to these distortions, which are obvious, the sources for education at Sparta pose two general problems.

The chronological problem. On the face of it, Plutarch does not contradict Xenophon, and one might think that this was intentional; indeed, he takes up all the points treated by the latter. But he adds others to them, of which the most important is the organisational break at twelve years of age. In reality this system *replaces* in Plutarch the succession of phases *paides-paidiskoi-hebōntes* which structures Xenophon's exposition; he does not even mention the last two categories. As for the scholia, they present an entirely different system, with the names of year-classes after the age of fourteen. To what is this due? The thing which has convinced me once and for all that the *agōgē* changed over the course of the centuries is the study of flagellation. A profound transformation in this custom can be noted, from the stealing of offerings deposited on the altar of Orthia in the fourth century, with opposition and combat, to the whipping in due form of the Roman period, but also, it seems, an evolution can be seen within the Roman period itself.[11] I share Kennell's idea that the *agōgē* seems to have known three states; in inverse chronological order: that of the Roman period, attested from Cicero on; the probable reconstructions of the second half of the third century, with the reform of Cleomenes inspired by Sphairos of Borysthenes; the situation known by Xenophon. So instead of having, as is frequent, several images of the same reality, in the case of the *agōgē*, we have a single image of multiple and successive realities. This problem is obviously fundamental, and it is Kennell's achievement to have posed it clearly; from now on we can no longer be satisfied with a globalising discourse, treating the *agōgē* as an unchanging reality, or rather as an invariable ideal. We might, however, ask ourselves if we know enough about its different stages to produce an authentically historic discourse on the subject.

The problem of Spartan singularity. This is, as we have seen, Xenophon's main idea: some of his contemporaries were attacking the Spartans by pretending that they did nothing like other Greeks (which in fact essentially means the Athenians); to defend them, far from denying this difference, Xenophon claims it and systematically sings its praises. The common-sense reflections presented above have shown that for the period which interests us this difference concerns only one side of Spartiate education, the public and communal side, which in the end was perhaps not the most important. And further: if we take as example the stealing of offerings from the altar of Orthia, this ritual seems at first entirely original; but we know of two parallels for it in the Greek world. One, at Samos, can be read in Herodotus' account (3.48); the other, 'in Sicily', is only attested by the proverb ἁρπαγὰ Κοτυττίοις ('the Kotuttia stealing'). Nonetheless, even thus relativised, the originality of the Spartan educational system remains. It is this which we must try, if not to explain, at least to conceive. There are two approaches, one 'anthropological' and the other 'historical'; I would like to show that these need not be opposed, but combined.

Approaching the *agōgē* as the form taken in the classical period by a collection of tribal initiation rites is not the result of a recent fashion born of the vogue for 'human sciences'. This perspective was already that of Nilsson in 1912 and of Jeanmaire in 1913.[12] It found its most complete expression in the work of Brelich, *Paides e Parthenoi*;[13] having extracted a picture of the 'ideal type' of tribal initiations from the abundant ethnographic sources, he examines in turn every feature of the *agōgē* which seems to him to belong to this type. Here is a review of these features, which is no less critical for being brief; for the comparisons are not all equally valid.

1. The *agōgē*'s character as obligatory and identical for all is not explicitly formulated by Xenophon, but it is implicit throughout his account (the same goes for Plutarch). The duration of the *agōgē* is, however, exceptional; there certainly exist initiations which last as long, but not continuously. It would be a sort of initiation by degrees, but not by ranks (unless we take *hippeus* as a rank).

2. The system of age classes. Its existence is only attested by 'late' sources; Xenophon, as we have seen, knows only three large groups, which he calls *paides*, *paidiskoi* and *hebōntes*: these are the same sort of age categories as there were in all cities, and not properly age classes. I tend to think, however, that on this point too the hellenistic and Roman periods transformed things rather than radically innovating, and that the system described by the scholia to Strabo and 'Herodotus' (a system which Kennell thinks was the work of Cleomenes III) is the heir to an earlier system about which we are entirely ignorant, because Xenophon, given his particular purpose, has no reason to talk about it. I do not see how the classical *agōgē* could have functioned otherwise than by annual 'promotions'. It is, then, only the*names* we do not know.

3. Segregation. This feature is entirely typical of initiations: sojourn in the bush or at the margins of the settlement, usually surrounded by adults and including 'lessons'. In the *agōgē*, this practice is likewise only attested by 'late' and obscure texts: Hesychios' gloss on φούαξιρ, a term which appears in fact only to designate a period of retreat preparatory to the flagellation of the Roman period; Justin 3.3.6 and Plutarch, *Lyc.* 16.13–14, who express themselves as though this separation was permanent, which is impossible and in any case refuted by other passages. In the classical period the single attestation of a period of segregation is the (very allusive) 'description' by Plato of the *krypteia*, where it takes the form of a 'vagrancy'; but the *krypteia* only concerned *certain* selected young Spartiates.

4. Tests and other harsh treatment, sometimes going as far as torture, are equally one of the salient features of tribal initiations. If this is especially emphasised in Plutarch, in the form of the precarious and savage life which the young are made to lead, it is also present in Xenophon's treatise: no shoes, a single *himation* for the entire year (cf. Kennell 1995, 34), insufficient food. The whip plays a large role in education (2.2, *mastigophoroi*; 2.8. 2.10); its presentation as a punishment can be interpreted as a quite natural rationalisation.

5. Stealing. There are moments when, for initiands on retreat, or for the newly-initiated on their return, the customary social norms are either suspended or inverted: thus, they may or they must (there is in fact no sense in the distinction) engage in all sorts of thefts, rapine and extortion at the adults' expense. The practice of stealing is one of the things which Xenophon treats at greatest length, because it is this which he has the greatest difficulty in justifying. He interprets it as a preparation for war; for a better understanding of what he means, refer to *An.* 4.6.14–15, and especially *Cyr.* 1.6.31. Stealing recurs in the ritual at Orthia's altar: it is a component, copied from the *bōmolochia*, of a scenario which is meant to 'explain' the whip-lashes, and everything which Xenophon says about stealing in general conforms to the model offered by this ritual.

6. Combats. Xenophon only mentions them in connection with the *hebōntes* (4.6), and here it is a matter of *individual* fights (the same in Plutarch, in connection with children). The collective combat of Platanistas is only described by Pausanias (3.14.8–10); however, Plato's allusion, 'the systematic training in enduring suffering which we follow, in collective bare-handed combats' (*Laws* 1.633b7), refers either to Platanistas or to something which closely ressembles it. The practice of collective bare-handed combat is, then, attested in the classical *agōgē*.

7. Supervision. Tribal initiations are an important matter for the whole community. So all its members supervise the process, but often there are in addition specialised personnel (elders, sorcerers, etc). At Sparta this specialised personnel is represented by the *paidonomos* (Xenophon 2.2 and 10; 4.6), assisted by the *hebōntes mastigophoroi* (2.2). Selected eirens[14] play the role of team leaders (2.5 and 11). The ephors, too, intervene, by their frequent inspections of the *neoi*.[15] But every Spartiate felt responsible: 'Lycurgus gave each Spartiate the same authority over other men's children as over his own' (Xen. 6.1).

8. Pederasty appears to be one of the strong points of the anthropological approach. Certainly this practice is far from being peculiar to Sparta; but this is in no way an argument against its initiatory origins. At Sparta it has, in the presentation which Xenophon gives it (2.12–14), an almost institutional aspect, and it seems clear that it was imposed on young men by the social norm.

9. In search of a *rite de sortie* ('coming out rite'). Young Spartiate people participated in numerous city festivals, either separately from or beside other age categories. They were thus periodically 'shown' to the whole community, which makes a *rite de sortie* (of which 'demonstration' is one of the essential aspects) unnecessary. People have looked for

one, however: Brelich obviously leans towards the Gymnopaidia, but children do not figure alone in this, and it is only the boys; the same goes for the *Pompē Lydōn* which followed the ritual at the altar of Orthia. Personally, it is the Hyakinthia which seem to me to be the best candidate, if there must be one; but in any case none of these festivals can be placed with confidence at the very end of the process, as a true coming out rite would have to be.

The features common to the *agōgē* and to tribal initiations are too numerous to be simple coincidences. It is indeed not without reason that Brelich concluded that it was not a question of fragmentary survivals, but of an authentic *system* of tribal initiations, fulfilling perfectly its role of transformation and normalising the individual. But if this observation remains valid, we should not for all that accept it as a global explanation of the *agōgē*, insofar as only *certain aspects* of Spartan education have been subjected to the enquiry. This fragmentation hides the dynamic of the system, the thing which gives it its sense: its being the formation of a citizen. Comparison can seem pertinent for a particular feature, isolated from the system to which it belongs, and can turn out to be much less so when it is replaced in its context. To assimilate the *agōgē* totally to the practices of 'tribal' societies[16] would be to neglect the role of innovation brought by the development of the city in the archaic period.

Another observation would tend to temper our adherence to comparative interpretations: it is Plutarch's account, much more than Xenophon's, which supplies them with materials; Plutarch's *agōgē* is richer in rituals with a 'primitive' look, and because of this appears distinctly more 'savage'. Moreover, some details like the transformation of the whipping at Orthia's altar, the more extensive organisation of collective combats and the more evident existence of periods of separation, far from civilisation, suggest that effectively, at least on some points, by an archaising exaggeration which is patent, the *agōgē* of the Roman period was more savage and more brutal than that of the classical period. Nevertheless, we should not jump to conclusions. As we have just seen, Xenophon supplies an already-considerable number of elements; Plato and Aristotle stress the savagery of Spartan education. I think, therefore, that the gap between Xenophon and Plutarch is due less to the transformation of reality (after all, it is not the *agōgē* of the imperial period which Plutarch is describing) than to the differences of motives and nature which separate the two texts.

There is, though, an entirely different way of approaching Spartan education, without reference to any kind of model provided by ethnography: as an 'institution' of the city of Sparta, an institution which developed at the same time as the city and ended up as what we know from Xenophon.[17]

1. Some of the features retained in the comparative study can be explained *also*, and without doubt *better*, within a purely Spartan framework, by the wish to perpetuate the citizen body. Firstly, the fact that it is obligatory and identical for all. The *agōgē* is only relatively obligatory; to escape it (if such a thing was thinkable) would not entail any penal sanction. It is obligatory, precisely, in order to become a citizen: this is what the texts which formulate this obligation say explicitly (Teles, ap. Stobaeus 40.8; Plutarch, *Inst.Lac.* 21, *Mor.* 238e, and *Spartan Sayings* Anon. 54, *Mor.* 235b; Aelian, *VH* 12.43; Xen. 3.3 is not very clear). Teles and especially Aelian express themselves as if the *agōgē* (which, as we have seen, was open to the sons of non-citizens) was sufficient, but Phylarchos (81 F 43), on the subject of Lysander, is more precise, saying that one who had followed it *could* become a citizen. With this reservation, we can call the *agōgē* qualifying. If it is the same for all, this is because it intends to form identical citizens.

Age classes are a commonplace organisational principle in educational systems of all periods. More specifically, at Sparta they are the indispensable framework for creating group-solidarity and at the same time for creating the permanent competition which is the outstanding feature of the *agōgē*; this is why I think that, in one way or another, they must always have existed.

Supervision assumes forms adapted to the structures of the city and the formation of the citizen. It is exercised in the first place by magistrates, either specialised (the *paidonomos* with his assistants), or 'generalists' (the ephors). It takes a particular form, unknown in 'primitive' societies, and in close association with the Spartan concept of a homogeneous citizen body. This is not an exterior control, where an answer learnt and repeated in a mechanical manner would be acceptable: the questioning of a youth by the eiren (Plutarch, *Lyc.* 18.3–6) is meant also to probe his spirit and to ensure that the norm has truly been assimilated by him; there are techniques for this.[18] Another refinement is that of the 'supervisors supervised', which Hodkinson has analysed well. As for the principle of the authority of all citizens over the young, it has been re-thought in terms of civic ideology. Plutarch echoes this interpretation, which remains implicit in Xenophon (6.1): 'Lycurgus regarded children not as the exclusive property of their fathers, but rather as the common property of the city (κοινοὺς τῆς πόλεως)' (*Lyc.* 15.14); this is the justification for the whole of the *agōgē* as a public educational system.

Should pederastic relationships also be thought of in this context? Xenophon emphasises their pedagogic value (καλλίστην παιδείαν, 2.13), but this is pure ideology; moreover, as with the chastity of this type of love affair, what we have here is both a commonplace and a subject of eternal debate amongst the Greeks. The problem is different. In a study which has proved essential, Dover[19] maintains that it was only from the end of the seventh century and the beginning of the sixth that the practice of pederastic relationships is both attested and developed in Greece; but his method and its conclusion have been contested.[20] The development of pederasty and its institutionalisation have incontrovertible associations with two other major aspects of Greek civilisation in the course of the seventh century, the athletic life and the *symposium*;[21] but is this a chronological argument? I think we should not jump to conclusions, and I cannot accept either that pederasty was 'invented' at a specific period, or that the similarities between its practice at Sparta ('State' pederasty', of a kind) and that which is abundantly attested in tribal initiations, with its obligatory character and with supervision exercised over it, can be simply the result of chance. I persist, therefore, in believing in the initiatory origin of Greek pederasty, and that it developed by *fitting into* the social practices and the value-systems which came into being in the course of the seventh century.

2. Other features might appear alien to the spirit and the practice of initiations, and because of this are ignored by the anthropological approach. The most important is the omnipresence of competition: the *agōgē* is depicted as a perpetual *agōn*. Certainly ranked initiations exist, which may imply some selection, but nowhere do we see such a permanent and so minutely regulated a competition operating. Moreover, at Sparta, before election to the Gerousia, competition does not result in rank acquired once and for all.[22] It is, then, with one and the same movement that Spartan education both endeavours to render future citizens uniform, and seeks to extricate and create élites.

The texts relating to obligation (cited above p. 53) might make us think that this selection also involved the final outcome of the *agōgē*, in other words that one could 'fail', essentially by withdrawal: they use the verb ὑπομένειν, to say that anyone who does not 'endure' their tests does not become a citizen. It is doubtless for this reason that Kennell (1995, 133) claims that failure was not only possible but frequent in the *agōgē*. The trouble is that the continuation of his argument shows that he does not really have any facts at his disposal to back up this assertion; for what he names 'failures' are only cases where children were excluded from the public educational process by their status (he cites the *hypomeiones*), so they were excluded right from the start. The texts we have are theoretical texts, which set out a principle. I do not absolutely deny there may have been withdrawals from the *agōgē*, but I am convinced that this was a very rare and extreme case, and it is clear that in the classical period the Spartan State had no interest in refusing citizens. This does not mean that the *agōgē* was a formal process; but there was no 'selection by failure', and the aim was only to sort out the best youths, within promotions which in principle had to progress as a unit right up to the end.

Every State needs elites; Sparta more than any other, since the very principle of its government, which was at the same time the main line of its propaganda, was the tacit axiom according to which the government of the best was necessarily the best of governments. It was only necessary to insure that those to whom one was planning to entrust responsibilities truly merited it; for this it was necessary that no privilege was obtained permanently and that competition was constantly exercised. Even pederasty, as Cartledge has shown, plays a role in the formation of elites.[23]

Another characteristic pedagogic procedure of Spartan education is what I call 'active methods'. This consists of making those being educated themselves play an active role in their own education, something which results in a true appropriation of the norm, and at the same time allows a greater control of this appropriation. I do not mean to talk about the role played by some eirens as educators: it could in fact be said anyway that the newly-initiated frequently fulfil this function in initiations. I shall rather cite the following facts: the child-members of a group choose their leader themselves, who is either one of them (before the age of twelve, Plutarch, *Lyc.* 16.8), or an eiren (after twelve, *Lyc.* 17.2); in the children's *syssition*, the participants are invited to observe and criticise the behaviour of citizens in the city (*Lyc.* 18.3–4), and they are judged in this activity (18.5). Certainly this feature only appears in Plutarch, but I do not see why it should be the result of a late development; Xenophon 2.11 does not necessarily preclude election of the eiren.

3. The formation of *hebōntes* illustrates the principal aspects of the 'pedagogy' used by the Spartiates in order to form future citizens. Moreover, chapter 4 of the *Lac.Pol.* which discusses it, is, with its alternation between principles of education and practical applications,

one of the best structured chapters of the whole treatise, and the most focussed on its subject; it thus deserves a closer examination.[24]

The originality of the Spartan system is striking here. The educational process does not stop at the age of twenty. Taking up a formula of Cartledge (1987, 25) and giving it a different application, I shall say that what is aimed for is not physical maturity, but civic maturity. This puts youths between twenty and thirty in an ambiguous and paradoxical position. Physically they are considered to be adults: the proof is that they fight in the army. However, they are excluded from the *agora* – whatever this word means;[25] they cannot be magistrates (this can be inferred from Xenophon 4.7). Not only are they subject to inspection by the ephors (Agatharchides' text, cited above n. 16), but, according to Xenophon, they are not authorised to wear their hair long, which is very surprising for men who are already combatants, and some of them elite ones.[26] They are dependent on full adults: when, in the context of the competition which rules amongst them, they come to blows, 'anyone present' can put an end to the fight (Xenophon 4.6). However, as MacDowell has remarked, this dependence is limited:[27] if the *hebōn* does not obey, the adult cannot punish him, and neither can the *paidonomos* (which is logical, as he is no longer a *pais*); he must refer the matter to the ephors.

Of the probably very diverse activities of those he calls *hebōntes*, Xenophon wishes to draw attention to one thing alone: for him the period in question, a very long period, is one of trial. As §2 announces clearly, this takes the form of systematic competition. To believe Xenophon, it would not be a case of selecting an elite: competition had as its aim only to incite each to perfect himself as far as possible.[28] All the same, this author presents the institution of the *hippeis* as having no other end than this competition itself. In his eyes, then, this would not be a true institution, but simply the stakes of a competition pursued for itself. Everything turns on the selection procedure for the *hippeis*, which institutes a kind of role-play: the role of the chosen, the role of the rejected. The aim is to inculcate in the young man certain behavioural norms. Moreover, in a most surprising way – but in the end logical from the point of view of the State's interest as expressed in §2 and 5 – the behaviour inculcated in the loser was not passive acceptance of the decision of the authorities (embodied in the *hippagretēs* concerned), but, on the contrary, its permanent and unrelenting contestation, which entails the contestation of authority itself (something which would doubtless not have been possible if it was a 'real' institution). If nothing is ever acquired at Sparta, equally nothing is ever lost,

Xenophon seems to mean. We might naturally doubt the aptness of such a presentation of the *hippeis*, and indeed, on this point as often, the Xenophon of the *Hellenica* corrects the extreme thesis, with its apologetic aim, of the Xenophon of the *Lac.Pol.*: the account of the repression of Cinadon's conspiracy demonstrates that the *hippeis* were a completely real institution, and that the ephors could entrust them with missions of the highest importance.[29] This chapter 4, it is clear, is entirely governed by the ideology expounded in §2 and 5, but what Xenophon says about trial and competition is certainly true nonetheless. For the *hebōntes* the list of possible selections is long: to be chosen by the *hippagretēs*; eventually to be chosen *as hippagretēs*;[30] to be chosen for the *krypteia*; and, on leaving the age category, to be chosen as *agathoergos*. There could be no better preparation for the permanent competition which was civic life at Sparta.

It is, then, beyond doubt that Spartan education was narrowly and efficiently adapted to its aim, the formation of the citizen, and in order to achieve this the Spartiates had to develop a true pedagogy. But I do not think that this observation should lead us to consider the anthropological approach as irrelevant. There are some aspects of the *agōgē* which the latter 'explains' (we shall return to the meaning this word should be given), and which it alone 'explains'. We can test the same impression by looking at the education of girls.

Xenophon talks about the education of girls (1.3–4); he discusses it, indeed, *before* approaching the education of boys, because for him, as for Critias, the first point must be procreation (*teknopoiia*), and because this last is the only purpose which he attributes to female education. This is why the account of marriage is inserted between the education of girls and that of boys (1.5–10). Plutarch follows exactly the same order (education of girls, 14; marriage, 15) and his logic is the same.

Neither of these two accounts gives the reader the impression of being faced with a true *agōgē* comparable with that of the boys (moreover, the name never appears in connection with girls). There are no 'bands' for the girls (choirs take their place),[31] nor true age categories; it seems not to be a case of such a complete and structured system at all. There is however a female education, and to deprive Spartan culture of its feminine component would without doubt be seriously to mutilate it.

Nor can we assert that a uniform and obligatory State education existed for girls. The sources from the classical period, Euripides,

Critias and Xenophon, say nothing of such a thing.[32] Only a passage of Plato (*Laws* 7.806a1–2) can be interpreted in this sense: 'young girls obliged to live (ζῆν δεῖν) taking part in gymnastic exercises at the same time as in *mousikē*, while the women…'. But if the text does indeed talk of obligation, it does not clearly say that it was imposed on all; Plato means only to emphasise that those who follow the formation of *mousikē* must *also* follow physical training. It remains that the logic of the explanation (eugenic) given for this physical education, notably by Critias and Xenophon, only really functions if it was imposed on all girls.

1. 'Civic' education. As in other cities, the framework is the choir of young girls; it will suffice in this context to refer to the classic study of Calame, which the example of Alcman illustrates.[33] This teaching has three aims: to prepare the young girls to participate in the city's festivals; to inculcate in them its value-system; to make them into 'beautiful girls', future wives and mothers of citizens. This is why this side of female education can be designated 'civic': it is a matter of preparing young girls for their integration as women into the civic community. Every educational system supposes the control of results: this was exercised at the festivals, where the performances of young girls were appreciated by 'the public', that is the assembled city.[34]

2. The initiatory aspect. We know how, starting from the specific participation of young girls in certain festivals, Calame has reconstructed a kind of Spartan cursus of female initiations. There are phases of segregation in liminal sanctuaries, those of Artemis Limnatis and of Artemis Karyatis.[35] The coming out ritual is represented by the Hyakinthia festival;[36] it leads to marriage, the decisive passage for which the cult of Helen also prepares. The poems of Alcman witness the affective links which unite young girls with their older companions in the choir, and this homosexuality seems no less institutionalised than in the boys' *agōgē*. Calame concludes from this the existence of a cycle of female initiations, but this is not a complete and 'secular' system; as in other cities it takes the more commonplace form of religious rites performed by the young girls.

But the Spartan girl had another sphere of activity much remarked upon in antiquity, and which can be attached to the initiatory cycle: physical activities. Xenophon (1.4) talks about 'competitions in running and in strength', δρόμου καὶ ἴσχυος…ἀγῶνας. Exactly what disciplines are involved? Arrigoni[37] accepts Plutarch's list (*Lyc.* 14.3), wrestling, discus and javelin; but is this valid for the classical period? Wrestling, in any case, seems to be confirmed by Euripides' reference to palaestras (*Andr.* 599). But the practice of these athletic disciplines seems secondary and may only result from an imitation of the masculine programme. The oldest activity (already attested by Alcman's similes), and the most indicative of young girls, is running. Arrigoni proposes a distinction between two types of races: one taking place on the *dromos* of the Agora, in front of the public of the city, the young girls being clothed (it is to this that the bronze statuettes refer); the other would take place in the context of the cult of Helen, beside the Eurotas, without the public, the young girls being naked (this is what the famous passage of Theocritus evokes, 18.22–5). The initiatory value of the foot-race is well known; it is clearly attested on Crete for boys. For young girls, the Heraia at Olympia offer at the same time a parallel and, thanks to the detail of Pausanias' text describing it (5.16.2–3), a model.

The question which presents itself, then, is not that of knowing which choice to make between the anthropological and the historical approach: it is clear that we must combine them. The question is knowing what anthropology can teach the historian of the educational system at Sparta.

1. Brelich's conclusion – that tribal initiation rites observed at Sparta in the classical period are not a fragmented and fossilised survival, but constitute a living system, since their function subsists and continues to be perfectly fulfilled – remains entirely valid, but must be completed and refined. On the one hand, this function does not have the same meaning as in 'primitive' societies: here too it is a case of 'transforming' the child into a member belonging completely to the community, but the community in question is a political society, and what the child must be transformed into is either a citizen, or the wife of a citizen, future mother of citizens.

On the other hand we must distinguish two types of practice in the Spartan education system. Some, whether they are derived from initiations (obligatory and uniform character, supervision, collective authority) or whether they are of another nature (competition, 'active methods'), can be integrated perfectly into the ensemble which gives each its meaning; they are closely adapted to the formation of this very particular thing which is a Spartan citizen, they really work towards the realisation of this objective, and can because of this be considered as constituting a pedagogy.

Others do not have this pedagogic efficacity and can therefore appear to be survivals of an initiation system in an educational system to the functioning of which they could not logically contribute: segregation, 'harsh treatments', obligatory stealing, pederasty.[38] Naturally, the defenders of Sparta in antiquity were compelled to attribute a pedagogic usefulness to these practices too, and to this end their interpretation as training for war was greatly utilised, notably by Xenophon; but the competence of the latter in this area should not mask the fact that he is only making rationalising justifications.

2. It is naturally in connection with the second type of practice that ethnographic comparisons show their relevance most clearly. We could indeed be tempted to reserve them for this type, that is to explain everything that can be by the rational anxiety to form the citizen, and only to appeal to anthropology for the rest. But, on the one hand, this 'rest' is considerable; and above all, such an attempt to restrict the field of application of an initiatory model is bound to fail in its principal aim. In fact, if we are obliged to appeal to it in order to understand a single feature, this is enough to make it immediately valid in its totality.

3. Properly speaking, ethnographic parallels *explain nothing*. All they can do is to give meaning to certain behaviours by taking them out of the isolation which makes them unintelligible; or, more exactly, to show that in what the texts say on the subject *there is sense*. They also show in what direction the sense which thus manifests its presence points: not towards a pedagogical functionality of rational type, but towards another type of mentality, a mentality for which the transformation of the young person into the adult operates according to a logic which is very real, but which does not function like our rational and 'scientific' logic.

4. We are, then, led to attempt to understand this logic. At work in the *agōgē* we can distinguish two logics, a logic of testing and a logic of inversion; but, in reality, they are most often inseparable. This is what can be seen in the example of the practices of segregation. They come under the logic of inversion insofar as, in order to 'realise' the integration of the youth into the community, he is separated from it; more exactly, before being integrated, he is made to pass a phase where the opposite of integration is pushed to the extreme. They also come under the logic of the trial, since this separation spontaneously takes the form of a trial or a set of trials (the typical example being the *krypteia*).

Here are the features of the *agōgē* which come under the logic of the trial. Stealing: Xenophon (2.8; taken up by Plutarch, *Lyc.* 17.5–6) emphasises its trial character, and that failure is punished by the whip.

Combats between youths: Xenophon (4.2–6) for the *hebōntes*, and Plutarch (*Lyc.* 16.9) for the *paides*, describe precisely how they are provoked by adults or institutions, and the manner in which these same adults observe their outcome in order to draw conclusions about the aptitudes of the participants. In the same way the pederastic relationship is imposed by the system, and it allows judgement of the two partners (Xenophon 2.13; Plutarch, *Lyc.* 18.8). The *agōgē* is thus presented as a permanent trial.

The functioning of the logic of inversion has been demonstrated in connection with the *krypteia* by Vidal-Naquet, who applied Lévy-Strauss' conceptual system to the Greek domain; in fact it is at work in rites of passage in general (thus marriage at Sparta). The pederastic relationship is the most obvious of these practices of inversion, but the other features which have just been enumerated as relevant to the logic of the trial correspond at the same time to the logic of inversion. The obligation to steal constitutes another systematic subversion of a fundamental social norm. By encouraging physical confrontation the aggressiveness of the young is excited, when the end aimed for is the *sōphrosynē* of the citizen. Trials inflicted on the young man are very much counter-images of what adult life will be; they constitute a regression towards a pre- or anti-civic, uncivilised, existence, when this was not un-human: the absence of shoes, sparsity of clothing, dirtiness, sleeping on *stibades*, a vagrant and savage life.

5. To explain the *agōgē* would presuppose the ability to reconstruct the historical process which gave it birth; that is obviously impossible. Hypotheses must be based on the following observations:

Firstly, the *agōgē* constitutes an organic whole. It crowns the city's system and may seem because of this to have been instituted, in the form in which we know it, relatively 'late'. Everything depends on what we understand by that *for Sparta*. Is it the sixth century, as Finley thought, followed on this point by Kennell (1995, 146), whose formulation is particularly persuasive? Is it the seventh century, a period towards which those who consider that the social and institutional development of Sparta was remarkably precocious will perhaps lean? Other answers too remain possible, and the question must remain open.

Although very coherent, the *agōgē* is made up of two sides, each in the province of one of the two approaches we have presented. Some of the elements which make it up are not functional, and even appear anti-functional, in the pure logic of the formation of the citizen; ritual aspects are no less important in the education of girls. As soon as we recognise the existence of these non-functional elements, we are almost inevitably led to consider them as *anterior* to the institution of the *agōgē* proper, so if not as survivals, at least as an inheritance. Thus, for Cartledge,[39] what the anthropological approach clarifies is not the system of the classical period but its distant past. Someone as resolutely 'unitarian' as Kennell (1995, 146) can write: 'in the early sixth century, when preexisting rites of passage...came under the control of the Spartan state'. But where can these 'preexisting rites of passage' have come from?

Brelich considered their prehistoric origin as an obvious fact requiring neither explanation nor demonstration. Historians of Greek civilisation have been able to accept this theory only with the greatest scepticism: how indeed are we to believe that tribal initiation rites dating back to the Neolithic are supposed, in a reasonable state of preservation, to have traversed the successive periods of the Mycenaean palaces, their disappearance and the 'dark ages'? On the other hand, anthropologists now tell us that the idea of the permanence of tribal initiation rites, unchanged since prehistory, is illusory in the case of numerous 'primitive' societies, notably African ones, and that there are examples where these rites have in reality been activated (reactivated?) in response to the colonial phenomenon itself.[40] It is therefore possible that it was in the course of the structuration process which gave birth to the Greek city that initiation rituals were put in place by Greek societies, as a means of ensuring the coherence and durability of communities from now on conscious of their existence.[41] At Sparta, amongst these rites, some were later remodelled and reinterpreted according to the needs born of the city's development; others could, eventually, have disappeared; others again, although ill-adapted to the context in which they now found themselves, survived, although we cannot really say why. It seems to me that this transformation should be represented in the form of a slow and progressive maturation rather than the result of a 'revolution', so much so that the problem of the date at which the edifice received its final stone loses its interest.

Notes

[1] Finley 1968, 158: 'the *agoge* is...the one (element) which alone "makes" the Spartan system'.

[2] Nafissi 1991; for an account of these debates, about resolutely 'revisionist' positions, see Hodkinson 1997, especially pp. 97–8. On Spartan education the fundamental study is now Kennell 1995; the present article was conceived for the most part before I was able to consult this book, but I have taken account of it in what I hope is a reasonably complete manner.

[3] A word on this term. It is a fact that, as Kennell (1995, 113–14, 116) emphasises, the term *agōgē* to designate the education of boys at Sparta does not appear before the third century, with only Teles, moreover, being certain; but I do not think that we can draw a firm conclusion from this. If Xenophon uses παιδεία, it is because he generally avoids technical terms, and also because his context is that of a comparison with other cities. Plato (*Laws* 2.666e) puts into the mouth of the Athenian, addressing Megillus, metaphors belonging to the breeding and training of horses, which can be understood as allusions to the term itself (cf. ἀγωγὴ ἵππου, Xen. *Equ.* 6.4). In any case, if the term was unknown in the classical period, the institution was not: I mean that Xenophon, and Thucydides (2.39) before him, considered that the Spartans had a true educational *system*, different from that of Athens (Thucydides) and even those of all other cities (Xenophon). In general, Kennell too easily regards (it is even one of the mainstays of his method) the *absence* of a word, of a fact, of an institution, in literature before a certain date, as sufficient proof that the word or the fact did not exist then, even if the evidence has completely changed in nature in the meantime.

[4] *Nouvelles recherches sur quelques points d'Histoire*, ed. C. Jullian (1891) p. 70.

[5] Jeanmaire 1913, 130.

[6] Ducat 1990, 167–8.

[7] Cartledge 1978, 25–37; Boring 1978.

[8] In the same sense, Kennell 1995, 125–6 (who emphasises especially the role of the *erastēs*; but it is before the age for being an *erōmenos* that one learns to read and write).

[9] Kennell (1995, 133–4) is the only person so far to have considered this economic aspect of the *agōgē*; in this connection he quite rightly cites *Cyr.* 1.2.15, where the important word is ἀργοῦντας.

[10] This is if, in place of συμβουλεύειν which appears in the better manuscripts, we adopt the correction συμβολεύειν, proposed by F. Portus in 1596 and reproduced today by the majority of editors (Dindorf 1898, Ollier 1934, Marchant 1968). συμβολεύειν is a *hapax*, certainly, but reasonable, and the sense is much better.

[11] Ducat 1995, 347–58. Kennell too has noted this transformation, which he places in the period of Cleomenes. This example makes me think that the principal historic process was that of *modification*: later periods probably neither suppressed essential elements of the classical *agōgē*, nor created radically new structures, but were able to change names and modify practices, often in an archaising direction. Another example would be the change from *syntrophoi* to *kasen*.

[12] Nilsson 1912, Jeanmaire 1913.

[13] Brelich 1969, 'Iniziationi spartane', 113–207.

[14] Certainly, as Kennell (1995, 16–17) emphasises, this word is an emendation in the two passages; but does the text of the manuscripts really give an acceptable sense? In 2.5 the problem is complicated by that of συμβουλεύειν; in 2.11, I emphasize the parallel with Plutarch *Lyc.* 17.2.

[15] Agatharchides *FGH* 86 F 10. According to Müller and Jacoby, this text belonged to an account of the reform of Agis; cf. Aelian, *VH* 14.7. On

Agatharchides, see Alonso-Nuñez 1997.

16 Without going quite so far, Kennell seems to me to exaggerate the ritual aspect of the *agōgē*; as he constantly confuses the ritual and the religious, this distorts the image he gives.

17 The summary which follows can be filled out by Cartledge 1987 and 1992, and by Hodkinson 1983 (245–51) and 1997.

18 As interpreted by David (1989, 4–5), the Pedaretos anecdote would illustrate this type of control.

19 Dover 1978, 194–6.

20 Smit 1992–3.

21 Murray 1995, 230.

22 As the Pedaretos anecdote demonstrates, the *hippeis* were (at least formally) renewed each year. For the details of this competition I refer to the analyses of Cartledge and Hodkinson cited above (n. 17).

23 Cartledge 1981.

24 The commentary on this chapter in Ollier (1934, 34–6) is insufficiently critical.

25 Plut., *Lyc.* 25.1: οἱ μέν γε νεώτεροι τριάκοντ᾽ ἐτῶν τὸ παράπαν οὐ κατέβαινον ἐς ἀγοράν. There follows a phrase demonstrating that Plutarch interprets this word as signifying the market-place. I wonder whether this is not a case of an erroneous gloss (Plutarch's, or his source's), and whether in the original text behind this reference ἀγορά did not in fact signify the assembly of citizens (cf. Herodotus 6.58, and, perhaps, the Rhetra): the exclusion would then make better sense.

26 Xen. 11.3. Plutarch says the opposite (*Lyc.* 22.2); has he interpreted thus (wrongly, to judge by 4.7) ὑπὲρ τὴν ἡβητικὴν ἡλικίαν, as Kennell (1995, 207, n. 12) appears to think, or has usage changed? On hairstyle, cf. David 1992.

27 MacDowell 1986, 68. Kennell (1995, 118) remarks that at Athens too the position of citizens between twenty and thirty years of age is in some ways slightly inferior.

28 This is evidently a tendentious presentation; if necessary, a text like *Hell.* 5.4.32 would show that during this period of his life too the youth was judged and classed by the authorities, and that this would condition his future.

29 I do not mean the false mission to Aulon, where the *hippeis* chosen are supposed to be commanded by Cinadon, but the real one, the arrest of Cinadon, a mission where they had to act in an entirely autonomous manner.

30 αἱροῦνται τοίνυν αὐτῶν οἱ ἔφοροι ἐκ τῶν ἀκμαζόντων, §3. From this MacDowell (1986, 67) concludes reasonably that the *hippagretai* were chosen among the oldest of the *hebōntes*. If it is not emended (and no one has done so), this phrase refutes the interpretation Kennell (1995, 118 n. 12) gives of Xenophon's usage of ἀκμάζειν. It is, moreover, difficult to imagine any *hebōn* systematically contesting the decisions of citizens over the age of thirty.

31 It is wrongly, in my opinion, that the existence of female *agelai* is often deduced (e.g. Calame 1977, 372) from Pindar fr. 112, Λάκαινα παρθένων ἀγέλα; it is very improbable that the word would have a technical sense here. Furthermore, Kennell (1995, 108) even doubts that the word *agela* was ever used at Sparta to designate a troup of boys.

[32] Euripides, *Andromache* 595–601; Critias fr. 32 D–K.

[33] Calame 1977, 386–410.

[34] Thus, in the context of ceremonies where the girls judged the boys, Plutarch (*Lyc.* 14.6) makes a point of the extension of this public: 'All the citizens, including the kings and the elders, came together to watch these spectacles.'

[35] Calame 1977, 253–64 (Limnatis) and 264–76 (Karyatis).

[36] Calame 1977, 305–23.

[37] Arrigoni 1985, 65–95 and pls. 2–5.

[38] It is evidently not a coincidence if (with the exception of segregation) these are precisely the points on which Xenophon expands: these practices would have surprised and scandalised other Greeks because their purpose remained unintelligible.

[39] Cartledge 1987, 24–5.

[40] Kennell 1995, 143–6, with bibliography.

[41] Every society, every limited human group, in every period, may, in order to define and structure itself, 'secrete' initiation rituals, which are often remarkably true to the 'model'. Kennell (1995, 146) cites the age classes in gangs of youths on the streets of New York; I could cite other examples, like the hierarchy of ranks and titles among the 'climbers' (*grimpeurs*) of Fontainebleau and Saussois, or the age categories and rites of passage amongst the people who frequent the Catacombs of Paris, an eminently initiatory location. In every age, and every place, examples are countless.

Bibliography

Alonso-Nuñez, M.
1997 'Approaches to world history in the hellenistic period: Dicaearchus and Agatharchides', *Athenaeum* 85, 53–67.

Arrigoni, G.
1985 'Donne e sport nel mondo greco', in G. Arrigoni (ed.) *Le donne in Grecia*, Rome, 55–201.

Boring, T.A.
1978 *Literacy in Ancient Sparta, Mnemosyne* Suppl. 54, Leiden.

Brelich, A.
1969 *Paides e Parthenoi*, Rome.

Calame, C.
1977 *Les Choeurs de jeunes filles en Grèce archaïque* I, Rome.

Cartledge, P.A.
1978 'Literacy in the Spartan oligarchy', *Journal of Hellenic Studies* 98, 25–37.
1981 'The politics of Spartan pederasty', *Proceedings of the Cambridge Philological Society* 207, 17–30.
1987 *Agesilaos and the Crisis of Sparta*, London, ch. 3, pp. 23–33.
1992 'A Spartan education', in *Apodosis: Essays presented to Dr. W.W. Cruickshank*, London, 10–19.

David, E.
1989 'Laughter in Spartan society', in A. Powell (ed.) *Classical Sparta: Techniques behind her success*, London, 1–25.
1992 'Sparta's social hair', *Eranos* 90, 11–21.
Dover, K.J.
1989 *Greek Homosexuality*, Cambridge, Mass.
Ducat, J.
1990 *Les Hilotes, BCH* Suppl. 20, Paris.
1995 'Un rituel samien', *BCH* 119, 339–68.
Finley, M.I.
1968 'Sparta', in J.P. Vernant (ed.) *Problèmes de la Guerre en Grèce ancienne*, Paris and La Haye, 143–60.
Hodkinson, S.
1983 'Social order and the conflict of values in Classical Sparta', *Chiron* 13, 239–81.
1997 'The development of Spartan society and institutions in the archaic period', in P.J. Rhodes and L.G. Mitchell (eds.) *The Development of the Polis in Archaic Greece*, London, 83–102.
Jeanmaire, H.
1913 'La cryptie lacédémonienne', *REG* 26, 121–50.
Kennell, N.
1995 *The Gymnasium of Virtue*, Chapel Hill and London.
MacDowell, D.M.
1986 *Spartan Law*, Edinburgh.
Murray, O.
1995 *La Grèce à l'époque archaïque* [=1993 *Early Greece*, 2nd edn, London].
Nafissi, M.
1991 *La nascità del kosmos*, Naples.
Nilsson, M.P.
1912 'Die Grundlagen des Spartanischen Lebens', *Klio* 12, 308–40.
Ollier, F.
1934 *Xénophon, La République des Lacédémoniens*, Lyon and Paris.
Vidal-Naquet, P.
1981 'Le chasseur noir et l'origine de l'éphébie athénienne', in *Le chasseur noir*, Paris, 151–75.

Chapter 3

ADMISSION TO THE *SYSSITIA* IN FIFTH-CENTURY SPARTA

H.W. Singor

Herodotus ranged the *syssitia* alongside the ἐνωμοτίαι and the τριακάδες as the military institutions designed by Lycurgus (Hdt. 1.65.5). We need not doubt that the mid-fifth-century Spartans themselves saw their public messes mainly or primarily as organizations for war and had told the visitor from Halicarnassus accordingly. Plato has it that the *syssitia* had been invented for warfare (*Nomoi* 625d, 633a). Indeed, their synonym συσκήνια, 'tent-companies', clearly points to the army.[1] In a later source the units of the army in 371 are enumerated in descending order as: μόραι, λόχοι, ἐνωμοτίαι, and συσσίτια (Polyaen. 2.3.11). Likewise, the encamping troops of Agesilaus' army could be described as συσσίτια and στιβάδες.[2] In fact, the military function of the *syssitia* in classical Sparta is not in doubt.[3] In antiquity it was commonplace to speak of their double character of promoting frugality at home and courage on the battlefield (*Lak.Pol.* 5.2–3; Dion. Hal. 2.23.3; cf. Plut. *Lyk.* 10; 12.1) and to compare them with the clubs and messes which existed in Crete and elsewhere, a comparison that has even been extended in modern times to include institutions of non-Greek Indo-European provenance.[4]

In classical Sparta the συσσίτια were closely connected with the ἐνωμοτίαι, in such a manner that the character of the latter organizations depended in great measure on the composition of the former. The ἐνωμοτίαι were the backbone of Sparta's army organization and as such were probably as old as the all-hoplite army we meet in the classical sources. In the preserved fragments of Tyrtaeus there is no indication of the existence of ἐνωμοτίαι, and to my mind understandably so, for Tyrtaeus' Spartan army was not yet the all-hoplite army of later times.[5] In Thucydides and Xenophon, on the other hand, the *enōmotia* appears as the core unit of the army, consisting only of hoplites. At Mantinea in 418 BC it numbered 32 men at most (Thuc. 5.68.3), at Leuktra not more than 36 (Xen. *Hell.* 6.4.12, 17). In both cases there seems to be a connection between the strength of the *enōmotia* and the number of year-classes called up. In 418 the army had been fully mobilized at the outset, but after crossing into Arcadia 'the youngest and the oldest' troops, amounting to one-sixth of the army, were sent home (Thuc. 5.64.2–3). These almost certainly comprised the year-groups 18–19 and 55–59, together one-sixth of a total of 42 (from 18 up until 59 inclusive).[6] From the remaining 35 year-classes again 'older men' were left behind in the camp (Thuc. 5.72.3), so that the 32 men per *enōmotia* on the battlefield would have corresponded to 32 year-classes (20 up until 51 inclusive). For the army of the Leuktra campaign 35 year-classes had been called up (Xen. *Hell.* 6.4.17) and on the battlefield the *enōmotiai* were drawn up in three files of 'not more than twelve men' each (Xen. *Hell.* 6.4.12). It has been concluded from this, and I think rightly so, that the *enōmotia* consisted at least nominally of one man per year-class.[7]

An obvious objection to this is the demographic probability, or rather certainty, that in fifth-century Sparta, as in all ancient societies, there must have been considerably more 20-year-olds than, say, 40- or 50-year-olds. For the scheme of the *enōmotiai* to have worked, it must have been necessary to fill at least most of the vacancies that would inevitably open up in the older year-groups by extra recruits. But where could these have come from? In theory every year the 20-year-olds could have been assigned to the *enōmotiai* in such a way that after each *enōmotia* had received its yearly recruit, there would still be a surplus of 20-year-olds left to supplement the ranks of the older year-groups. I believe something of the kind did indeed occur. Apart from the *enōmotiai*, Sparta had an elite corps of 300 Hippeis, selected from the 20- to 30-year-olds.[8] On the battlefield of Mantinea in 418 BC they fought separately from the *lochoi* with their *enōmotiai* as a special guard around king Agis (Thuc. 5.72.4). According to *Lak.Pol.* 4.3 each year three bands of a hundred young men were selected by three so-called *Hippagretai* appointed by the ephors. A plausible suggestion is that in fact each year thirty Hippeis were picked from all the 20-year-olds to enter this corps, while at the same time those reaching the age of thirty would have to leave it.[9] Behind the short description in *Lak.Pol.* 4.3, then, there might be a formal enrolment of all Spartans coming of age into the κατάλογοι that would serve as musters for the mobilisation of the army: most young Spartans by far had their names entered into the musters for the regular army, while an elitist selection of thirty each year saw themselves registered on the lists of the Hippeis.[10] In any case, each year at most thirty ex-Hippeis but in reality less than that number, let us say on average twenty-five (as a result of casualties from whatever cause during their ten-years' service in that corps) must have been available to fill vacancies in the ranks of the *enōmotiai*. This would go some way at least towards bringing these units up to their nominal strength. Whether it would have been enough depends of course on the total number of *enōmotiai* that made up the Spartan army of the fifth century.

It is often assumed that at least in the beginning of the fifth century the Spartan army consisted of five all-Spartan λόχοι and that this organization gave way later to six mixed Spartan and Perioikic μόραι.[11] The latter army is mainly known from Xenophon's *Hellenika* and the *Lakedaimoniōn Politeia* attributed to Xenophon. Thucydides' description of the Spartan army at Mantinea in 418, listing seven *lochoi* of Spartans and of ex-Helots and not mentioning the *morai*, is usually taken to be defective or at least misleading. I must refrain here from discussing all the problems involved and restrict myself to stating merely that in my view there is no warrant for discarding Thucydides' evidence.[12] His seven *lochoi* at Mantinea can be interpreted as the five *lochoi* we also know from a fragment of Aristotle (F 541 Rose) to which were added two *lochoi* of ex-Helots. In all essentials this was also the army that had fought at Plataea in 479 (the 5000 Spartans there – according to Hdt. 9.10.1; 28.2 – seem to point to five *lochoi* – cf. Hdt. 9.53.2 – although the number of 5000 is almost certainly exaggerated). It was in my view only after 418 that the new organization of the *morai* was created. But for the argument I want to develop here it is of no consequence whether we take some date between 418 and 403 (the first mention of the *morai*: Xen. *Hell.* 2.4.31) or somewhere around 460 in the wake of the great earthquake and the helot revolt as the *terminus ante* for the existence of the army of five all-Spartan *lochoi*. In my opinion that army organization covered nearly the whole of the fifth century, but even if we place its end at around 460 it will throw some light on the connection between the *enōmotiai* and the *syssitia* in that earlier period, as I hope to show.[13]

According to Thucydides the *lochoi* in 418 consisted of 16 *enōmotiai* each, which in their turn were grouped into four *pentekostyes* (Thuc. 5.68.3). This organization is so neat – four *enōmotiai* constituting one *pentekostys*, four *pentekostyes* one lochos – that it could very well be the original organization. I find it at least hard to believe that when this army organization was created, the *lochoi* would have numbered five or more *pentekostyes* and seventeen or more *enōmotiai* each. The ratio 1 : 4 : 16 in my view must have been there from the start, that is from before

479 and probably from somewhere in the sixth century. This does not mean that in the whole period of its existence this army organization was stable as regards its total numbers. On the contrary, the number of Spartans could well have dropped – and almost certainly did so – over this period and the effects of that decline must have been seen by the gaps opening up in the ranks of the *enōmotiai* when drawn up for battle. At Mantinea in 418 the 32 year-classes did not yield exactly 32 men in the *enōmotia* but slightly less, on average 30 or 31, as we may assume from Thuc. 5.68.3.[14] However, when this organization was first established, Spartan numbers must have been sufficient to fill *all* places, or at least practically all, for had it been otherwise we would have to assume a deficient organization from its beginning! Be that as it may, I take Thucydides' description as the starting point for my argument and reckon with an army of five *lochoi* and eighty *enōmotiai* (sixteen in each *lochos*) together with a special force of 300 Hippeis from the adults under thirty.

To find out whether an army organization on the lines given above would have been possible I adduce here a hypothetical life table based on the model life tables from Coale-Demeny. In this model the various age-groups are divided as: (the total of 18+ being 100%):[15]

18 – 19:	6.7%
20 – 29:	29.7%
30 – 39:	25.0%
40 – 49:	18.0%
50 – 59:	11.9%
60 – :	8.7%

We can now list four tables: one (a) of the numbers of the various age-groups theoretically needed to fill all places in the army; a second one (b) of only the Hippeis and former Hippeis, starting with 30 Hippeis of the year-class 20; then (c) a table of the other Spartans who served in the *enōmotiai* from the age of twenty on, reckoning with exactly 80 men (the number of the *enōmotiai*) in the year-class 20; and finally (d) another such table reckoning with a little more than 80, say 90, men in the year-class 20:

a. *in theory:*	b. *(ex-)Hippeis:*	c. 80 *in* enom.*:*	d. *90 in* enom.*:*
20 – 29: 1100	20 – 29: 270	20 – 29: 720	20 – 29: 811
30 – 39: 800	30 – 39: 227	30 – 39: 606	30 – 39: 682
40 – 49: 800	40 – 49: 164	40 – 49: 436	40 – 49: 491
50 – 59: 800	50 – 59: 108	50 – 59: 288	50 – 59: 325

From these tables one may conclude that the system of one man per year-class in each *enōmotia* could hardly have worked if there were on average 80 men of the year-class 20 available each year for the 80 *enōmotiai* (table c.). For in that case in the age-group of 30–49 the numbers 1042 (606 + 436) together with 391 (227 + 164) of the former Hippeis make up 1433, which would be considerably less than the 1600 men required, let alone the vacancies left in the year-classes from 50 on. Reckoning with 90 men from the 20-year-olds entering the *enōmotiai* each year, the age-group of 30–49 would have 1173 + 391 former Hippeis = 1564 men. In this case the difference seems to be negligible. Admittedly, the gap between the numbers required and those realized on the battlefield might have been a little wider when we reckon with sick and infirm Spartans staying at home; on the other hand, the gap might be narrowed by the assumption that many or even most of the officers (from the enomotarch upwards) were in fact over 51 at Mantinea and so filled some of the open places in the year-groups below 51. Further, we have Thucydides' remark about the length of the files already referred to, from which it may be inferred that the *enōmotiai* at Mantinea did not in fact reach their theoretical strength of 32 men. For this reason I believe we are not entitled to suppose a much greater number than the 90 reckoned with here for the recruits of the *enōmotiai*; probably in 418 BC their number was already below 90. On the other hand, whenever this organization was established, the number of 20-year-olds must have been sufficient for this scheme to have worked without many gaps and was therefore presumably higher than 90. For the sake of my argument here I shall now reckon with 90 recruits for the *enōmotiai* together with 30 young Hippeis, that is with a total of 120 men in the year-class of the 20-year-olds.[16]

In this organization the *enōmotia*, then, had a 'paper strength' of 40 or 42 if one adds the 18- and 19-year-olds who sometimes, as initially in the Mantinea campaign, joined the army. The *syssitia* were smaller units than the *enōmotiai* and to judge from Thucydides' omission of them in his detailed description of the Spartan army one may conclude that the *syssitia* did not function as tactical units in battle, but as tent-companies in the camp, as indeed their synonym συσκήνια suggests. For the *syssition* we have two indications of size: 'about fifteen' (Plut. *Lyk.* 12.3) and 'ten' (Scholion on Plato, *Nomoi* 633a). Usually the latter indication is discarded, and to my mind rightly so.[17] One could argue also that Plutarch's evidence is suspect as being late and in a context which does not inspire immediate confidence (points to which I shall return at the end of this chapter). However, a number smaller than the nominal strength of the *enōmotia* is required and one that by multiplication would easily match the evidence on the size of the *enōmotia* that we have. I suggest that Plutarch's 'about fifteen' is right and that, consequently, three *syssitia* formed one *enōmotia*. Membership of the *syssitia* in classical Sparta was for life, so the 45 members of a given group of three *syssitia* must have sufficed to provide for one *enōmotia* of nominally 40 men from the age-groups up until 60.[18]

Although it is nowhere stated in our sources, the three *syssitia* forming one *enōmotia* in my view represented the three Dorian φυλαί of Sparta. In a well-known fragment of Tyrtaeus (F 19 West, 8) we hear of the three Dorian *phylai*, Hylleis, Dymanes, and Pamphyloi, engaged in warfare separately (χωρίς). Whether we have to think of three 'regiments', one from each of the *phylai*, or of an unknown number of smaller units, each recruited from members of the same *phylē*, is not clear. If the *syssitia* already existed then with the same military function as in the classical period they must have been homogeneous in belonging to one of the three *phylai*. However, the character of the *syssitia* or ἀνδρεῖα before, say, the mid-sixth century was surely not in all respects as we know it in the classical age and a specifically military function in this early period is, to say the least, not clear.[19] Nevertheless, the tradition of fighting in units on the basis of *phylē*-membership (referred to also in Nestor's advice to Agamemnon to draw up his men κατὰ φῦλα, κατὰ φρήτρας, *Iliad* 2.362) might very well have been preserved in fifth-century Sparta. We know that the three *phylai* still existed then, and that membership was, of course, hereditary. This is implied by Plutarch's story of the elders of each *phylē* examining the young-born males (*Lyk.* 16.1), whilst the three groups of a hundred men that form the special corps of the Hippeis (*Lak.Pol.* 4.3–6) also suggest selection on the basis of the *phylai*. But it is above all the character of the *syssition* and of the *enōmotia* that to my mind seems to point to the *phylai* as the organizing principle in the background.

The *phylē* was supposed to be a large 'family', or rather a kinship-group surpassing the natural family. However artificial its origin may have been, its image, so to speak, was one of solidarity based on real or supposed kinship. Now, one characteristic of the classical *syssition* was that its members were *not* related by family-ties. This we may conclude from Xenophon's remark that fathers, sons and brothers did not belong to the same *mora* (*Hell.* 4.5.10), so *a fortiori* they could not belong to the same *syssition* (this is probably corroborated by *Hell.* 5.4.27–28 where Kleonymos meets his lover Arkhidamos in the latter's *syssition* – here *philition* – for a conversation that should not be noticed by Arkhidamos' father Agesilaos). Instead, the*syssition* itself constituted for its members another 'family'. Here men of various ages met each other daily, while their real fathers, sons, and brothers were engaged elsewhere. Among themselves, the messmates were 'equals', albeit submitted to the authority of the eldest in their midst: a tight group, bound together by common experience and the solidarity that results from it (cf. Plut. *Lyk.* 12.5). As a 'substitute family' the *syssition* finds its place naturally in the even larger 'family' of the *phylē*. In both cases it was society or the state that authorized and enforced these bonds, and in the case of the *syssitia* by deliberately cutting across the real ties of kinship. The members of a given *syssition* simply had to belong to the same *phylē*, for different *phylai* in the bosom of such a group would, I believe, have been felt as self-contradictory.

To return to the ἐνωμοτία, this term means 'group bound together by oath' and so seems to recall the *con-iuratio* (or perhaps an hypothetical **in-iuratio*) of archaic Italy.[20] The *enōmotia*, then, refers to a group of warriors mutually bound by an oath. Why an oath? For members of the same family oath-swearing to ensure mutual help would have been unnatural and superfluous. On the same terms members of the artificial families and kinship-groups as were the *syssitia* and the *phylai* did not require oaths to be assured of mutual assistance. Belonging to a *syssition* or to a *phylē* was not the result of some solemn oath but membership of these organizations meant that one could reckon on the help and support of one's fellows as if they were one's natural family. On the other hand, between groups that were non-kin – however artificially kinship may have been defined – cooperation and mutual assistance were not at all self-evident. Here, these things had to be established by other means, i.e. by the swearing of an oath. The Spartan *enōmotia* is an illustration of this. As the basic tactical unit of the hoplite army it required a high degree of internal cohesion and solidarity. So, when members of three different *syssitia* were grouped together to form an *enōmotia*, it is precisely the oath that in my view points to the involvement of different *phylai*.

An *enōmotia*, then, seems to have been created by matching three *syssitia* from three *phylai*. We know that in the classical period a *syssition* comprised members of various ages up to over-sixty (*Lak.Pol.* 5.5, 7; Plut. *Lyk.* 12.5, 6; 26.4). Indeed, a mixing of different age-groups is said to have been the express purpose of the lawgiver Lycurgus (*Lak.Pol.* 5.5). Together, three *syssitia* would have covered most of the year-classes from twenty upwards and the combination of three *syssitia* would largely explain the peculiar make-up of the *enōmotiai*. These latter could never have *exactly* one man from every year-class from the age of twenty on, but by recruiting slightly more than ten men from the first ten year-classes (811 for 80 *enōmotiai* in table d. above) and by being reinforced, on average once in three years, by one of the former Hippeis of the age of thirty (on average 25 men to be divided over 80 *enōmotiai* each year) they went a long way towards having just as many men as there were year-classes mobilized, as I have tried to show above. Since in this reconstruction of the fifth-century military organization on average 120 young men reached the age of twenty each year, thirty of whom were enrolled among the Hippeis, the other ninety or so entering the *enōmotiai*, these latter units received, again on average, one fresh recruit each year, while each of the 240 *syssitia* would receive a new member every two years. Needless to say, this is a model: in reality the number of 20-year-olds will have fluctuated from year to year. In any case, we may now draw a first conclusion as to the recruitment of members for a *syssition*, viz. that only members of the same *phylē* could have been admitted to any *syssition*. This meant in practice that in our model a given *syssition* could not choose (if any choosing there was) from a pool of 120 potential candidates but from 40 at most.

Perhaps the possibilities of recruitment to the *syssitia* were restricted even further. For the eighty *enōmotiai* were grouped into five *lochoi* of sixteen *enōmotiai* each. These five *lochoi* had their own names, which strongly suggests that they were not regiments temporarily formed for a campaign but permanent organizations, in that respect perhaps not unlike the imperial Roman legions.[21] If that is correct, the distribution of the *enōmotiai* over the *lochoi* must have been permanent too, with the three *syssitia* that in combination made one *enōmotia* already permanently aligned to each other by means of an oath – whether taken once and for all at some moment in the past or being renewed from time to time (annually?), we do not know. In other words, here was a fixed organization in which every adult Spartan knew his place, from his *syssition* via his *enōmotia* to his *lochos*. This makes it highly improbable that these *lochoi* ever matched the villages or ὠβαί of classical Sparta. For the distribution of the Spartan population over these villages cannot realistically have been such as to produce *lochoi* of exactly the same number of men from each of the villages over the years. However, a permanent grouping together of *syssitia* and *enōmotiai* in particular *lochoi* could have had its effects on, or could have been influenced by, the real distribution of Spartan citizens over their villages. This was of course not necessarily the case, for the organization of the army could in theory very well have cut across the division of Sparta into villages. But we have the name of Messoagès or Mesoatès for one of the *lochoi* (n. 21 above), which recalls the name of the ὠβά Mesoa, and we have Herodotus' mention of a lochos from Pitana, another of the villages (Hdt. 9.53.2–3; 57.1). Admittedly, the existence of the latter is expressly denied by Thucydides (1.20.3), but that denial seems to me to affect the name of this particular *lochos* only, certainly not the existence of the *lochoi*, nor the principle that these regiments were somehow connected with the villages.

That connection could have taken various forms. Depending on the number of villages that together constituted the 'city' of Sparta, each of the five *lochoi* could have its commander and perhaps most or all of its officers from one particular village (the *lochagos* Amompharetos, mentioned by Herodotus, certainly was from Pitana). Or a Spartan village could have all or most of its citizens organized into one *lochos*, depending on whether their number was smaller or larger than the size of such a regiment. If there were five villages, shortages and surpluses of manpower could have been levelled out, and some of the villages could have matched the size of a *lochos* much more closely than others. This could also have been the case if the number of villages was only four: even so one or more *lochoi* could have come mainly or even wholly from a particular village. What I want to suggest is that whereas an exact correlation between *lochoi* and villages must have been impossible, some connection, no doubt stronger in one case than in another, could very well have existed. This is not at all certain, I hasten to add, but given the choice between such a rather imperfect connection or no connection at all, I would prefer the former possibility, considering the references to Mesoa and Pitana in relation to the *lochoi*. For the recruitment of the *enōmotiai* and thereby of the *syssitia* this would imply in some or perhaps in most cases a further restriction of choice, although it cannot be quantified. For where a given *lochos* would draw the bulk of its men from a particular village, most of the *enōmotiai* and thereby the *syssitia* concerned would by implication recruit their new members from that same village. This would not necessarily apply to all the *lochoi* and to the same extent, but in reconstructing the process by which a *syssition* kept up its membership we should in my view reckon with the possibility of further restriction on the basis of residence. The pool of possible candidates for admission to a given *syssition*, therefore, depending on the recruiting background of the *lochos* of which it formed part, could in practice be well under 40 and probably sometimes considerably so.[22]

Admission to the *syssitia* occurred at the age of twenty. But already before that age a young Spartan must have known to which *syssition* he would in future belong. For on some occasions the 18- and 19-year-olds were sent out with the army (as happened twice in 418, although in both cases they did not participate in the battle: Thuc. 5.64.3; 75.1). This suggests that they were then already assigned to the *enōmotiai* and so already knew into which *syssition* they would formally enter in one or two years' time. But how did a young Spartan of the age of 18 get into a *syssition* that would be formally 'his' two years later? It is hardly conceivable, in my view, that in the previous year, at the age of 17, he had been permitted to choose for himself from the pool of *syssitia* available. The whole authoritarian fabric of Spartan society speaks against such a freedom of choice for these young men. Instead, the choosing must have been done by the *syssitia*, not by the candidates. This selection was made even well before the boys reached the age of 18. For I believe that here Sparta's institutionalized pederasty operated, as some scholars have already suggested.[23]

At the age of twelve Spartan boys got lovers (ἐρασταί) from among the younger adults (Plut. *Lyk.* 17.1; cf. *Lak.Pol.* 2.13–14). I do not want to deal with the question of origins here – whether or not this practice arose from a ritual of initiation – or with the question whether this relationship in the fifth and fourth centuries always, or as a rule, had a sexual side to it. Suffice to say that in the classical period all Spartan boys were coached or tutored for at least some time by young men called their lovers and that this could and no doubt in many cases did imply a sexual relationship as well.[24] But sexual *mores* apart, it should be clear that Spartan pederasty played a major role in guiding the boys and young men through the various grades of the *paideia*, or what was later called the *agōgē*, and the, so to speak, undergraduate stage of adulthood. This was, moreover, the mechanism by which the *syssitia* recruited their membership.[25]

Since the relationship started when the boy as ἐρωμενός was twelve years old, it had to last at least till the boy would turn twenty and become a member of his lover's *syssition*. The lover for his part always was an adult but not yet in possession of all the rights of the *Homoioi* or 'Peers', i.e. he belonged to the age-group of the under-thirty.[26] We have to reckon, therefore, with a duration of eight years for this relationship, at the start of which the ἐρωμενός was twelve and the ἐραστής at least over twenty. No source mentioning his exact age, I venture the hypothesis that he was normally twenty-two. This would fit in well with the other evidence we have. For the eight years of the ἐρωμενός (from twelve to twenty) would correspond to the eight years of the ἐραστής (from twenty-two to thirty) in such a way that when the ἐρωμενός became a member of the *syssition* at age twenty, his lover would become a full *Homoios* at age thirty. In that case, both partners would never be in the same age-category before they both reached full citizen (*Homoios*) status. This would be in character with the tutorial or didactic side of this relationship. For even after the age of twenty, when the ἐρωμενός had become a member of the *syssition*, the relationship with his lover was not formally over. Since we hear that young men under thirty still had lovers (Plut. *Lyk.* 25.1) we may infer that the relationship went on – or at least did go on frequently – during the period that the younger partner was still in some respects 'under age'. This involves the further assumption that from the age of 22 to 30 a young man could very well be both the lover of a younger boy and at the same time still be the beloved of an adult man of thirty or older.[27]

If the *erastēs* was twenty-two when he chose an *erōmenos*, two years had passed since he himself had entered the *syssition* at age twenty. This means that a given *syssition* would normally associate with a future member (the *erōmenos* then aged twelve) every two years. In normal cases this implies a reinforcement of a *syssition* with a twenty-year-old once in two years. This inference is based on the age-limits twelve, twenty and thirty, given or implied by the sources, and on the hypothesis that one became an *erastēs* at age twenty-two. This accords well with the model of the fifth-century Spartan army outlined above, in which there were 80 *enōmotiai* comprising 240 *syssitia* and in which every year on average 120 young men would enter the army at age twenty, so that a given *syssition* would receive a new member normally every two years. In theory, then, the age-group 20–29 in an average *syssition* would number five men, but in reality in many cases only four, as a result of mortality over the years. On the basis of the model life table used here (above, n. 15) members of a *syssition* would be distributed over the various age-groups 20–29, 30–39, 40–49, 50–59, 60+ in numbers fluctuating around respectively 4, 4, 3, 2, 2. Of course, these numbers are too small to claim any accuracy, but at least they give an indication that an average of four members in the age-group 20–29 fits in with a total membership of 'about fifteen' for the *syssition* as a whole on the basis of Plut. *Lyk.* 12.3.

With the *syssitia* recruiting their new members in the way I believe they did, there usually must have been a problem with numbers, since the number of 12-year-olds (the potential *erōmenoi*) as a rule surpassed that of 22-year-olds (the *erastai*). In our model life table, 120 20-year-olds would correspond to 136 12-year-olds, 116 22-year-olds, and 99

30-year-olds.[28] How, then, could 116 *erastai* be matched with 136 potential *erōmenoi*? On this question there is no hint in our sources, as far as I can see. Yet, there must have been a solution to it, if the whole scheme of selection to the *syssitia* by way of the 12-year-old *erōmenoi* could have worked at all. Placing the moment of admission to the *syssitia* formally at age twenty but *de facto* at age twelve (when the *erōmenoi* would be introduced into the *syssitia* of their *erastai*) inevitably entailed a loss of would-be members over a period of eight years: from 136 to 120 in our model. Likewise, in the same period the average number of *erastai* would go down from 116 at age 22 to 99 at age thirty in the model used here. What I want to suggest is that these latter losses were of no consequence as regards the question raised above. For one could argue that as soon as a 12-year-old had been introduced to the *syssition* of his *erastēs* he had thereby become 'associated' with that *syssition* in such a way that, if the *erastēs* died before the *erōmenos* turned twenty, the latter would nevertheless stay on and become a member in due course without the close relationship with an *erastēs* most of his age-mates had. This is only an hypothesis, but to my mind not without some foundation.[29]

On the other hand, I believe the loss of life among the *erōmenoi* over the years from age 12 to 20 did have consequences as regards the recruitment to the *syssitia*. Let us suppose that as a rule every member of a *syssition* had to bring in one new member. By itself such a rule is not impossible: it is, for instance, the principle of *vir virum legere* by which sometimes bands of elitist warriors were selected in archaic Italy (cf. Livy 10.38.2). In the more modest context of the Spartan *syssitia* and the institutionalised pederasty that went with it, such a rule would have meant that the youngest member had the obligation to introduce a future candidate from among the boys of twelve at the first possible occasion, i.e. two years after he had become a member himself. This relationship was to last till the *erōmenos* had formally entered the *syssition* at age twenty and went on even after that moment till the younger partner had turned thirty, as we have seen. When at some moment the *erōmenos* died before the age of twenty, or rather twenty-two (see below n. 30), the *erastēs*, so to say, had failed in his duty to provide a new member. In that case, it is perfectly feasible that he would have to select a new *erōmenos* at the next occasion. For each *syssition* such an occasion occurred every two years. Most, by far, of the *erastai* would then be twenty-two, as I have suggested above, but a minority would be older: those former *erastai* who had lost their *erōmenoi* in the previous one or two years.

In the model life table I have used here, the number of 136 12-year-olds would drop to 120 20-year-olds and then be further reduced to 116 22-year-olds. The loss of 20 boys from one cohort over a period of ten years (from 136 to 116) would leave the same number of *erastai* without *erōmenoi* (except of course in those cases where both partners died). Of a given cohort of *erōmenoi* in this model on average two would be lost each year, each time bereaving an *erastēs* of his beloved and his *syssition* of a future member. If, as I presume, the bereft *erastai* again chose *erōmenoi* from the 12-year-olds, the problem of matching 136 boys with 116 young men would be largely solved. For in the ten years from the age of 12 to that of 22 on average 20 boys would be lost in every (!) cohort, which means that on average each year 20 young men would lose their *erōmenoi* and thus be obliged to start a new relationship in order to bring a new member into their *syssition*. In this way and in this static model the number of 116 22-year-olds would be enlarged by 20 older men to 136 and thus match the number of the 12-year-olds.[30]

This, I would like to stress, is a model based on my reconstruction of a fifth-century Spartan army of 80 *enōmotiai* divided into 240 *syssitia*, each of which on average took in one new member every two years, and on the use of a model life table. It is further based on two assumptions: first, that *erōmenoi* who lost their *erastai* would stay on in their respective *syssitia* and would not find new *erastai* to replace the lost ones, at least not in the 'institutionalised pederasty' with which we are concerned; second, that *erastai* who lost their *erōmenoi* would be obliged to find replacements among the 12-year-olds until the moment their *erōmenoi* had turned twenty-two and had themselves brought in new future candidates. This reconstruction has some further implications for the distribution of each cohort of *erōmenoi* over the *syssitia* which I would sketch only briefly here since they do not, in my opinion, invalidate the overall picture. If 136 *erastai* (116 aged 22, the others older) were matched with 136 *erōmenoi* aged 12, this would mean that in some *syssitia* there would be more than one erastes introducing a prospective member, let us say in 16 from a total of 120. After a period of eight years, the cohort of *erōmenoi* would be reduced to 120, but in a random way. The result would be that of the 120 *syssitia* concerned roughly eighty percent would receive one new member, some ten percent even two, but another ten percent none at all. The effects of this would be felt when these *erōmenoi* in their turn became *erastai* two years later: reinforced randomly by some twenty older *erastai* who had lost their *erōmenoi*, as I have suggested, they would after eight years bring in their new members, who would be spread even more unequally over the *syssitia*. At each turn the percentage of *syssitia* with just one new member would drop, whilst the percentages with two (or even three) members or with no new member at all would rise. This, however, would largely be remedied by the fact that this inbuilt unevenness affects only one 'line' of recruitment, bringing in fresh members every ten years. In practice, the *syssitia* recruited new members once in two years, so there were always several of such 'lines' operating. To a large extent the adverse effects of this way of recruiting would thereby be levelled out.

Another point that should be mentioned briefly is that the reconstruction sketched above is based on average numbers. Over a period of time on average the 'surplus' of 12-year-olds in respect to the number of *erastai* could have been compensated for in the way I suggested, but from year to year the numbers must have fluctuated. It is to be expected, therefore, that sometimes even when the older *erastai* who had lost their *erōmenoi* in the two years before were added to the number of 22-year-olds, the total number of *erastai* would fall below that of the 12-year-olds. Perhaps in such cases the 'recruiting' of *erastai* went up the age-grades to include men from thirty upwards who had lost their former *erōmenoi* (cf. above, n. 30). However, such cases will have been rare. The population of Sparta in the later fifth century declined, and perhaps that decline had set in already in the first half of that century. This enhances the probability, in my view, that instead of the number of potential *erōmenoi* surpassing that of the *erastai*, the number of the latter will more often have surpassed that of the young *erōmenoi*. What happened then, we do not know, but my guess is that in that case the older potential *erastēs* in search of a future candidate for his *syssition* would have preference over the 22-year-olds, so that some of the latter would have to wait for their turn two years later. To repeat, this is pure conjecture, for the whole mechanism of selecting the *erōmenoi* and thereby the candidates for the *syssitia* is nowhere in our sources described in any detail.

When it was the youngest member of a *syssition* who, at the age of 22, had to choose a potential future member who was at that time only twelve, it would be surprising to find that this selection was wholly a matter of free choice on the part of both parties or even of only the older lover. Keeping in mind that the latter at that age still could have *his* lover to guide him and naturally would be 'advised' by his other messmates, who were all older than he was, it is hard to escape the conclusion that the pederastic relationship more often than not must have been a pre-arranged affair. Possibly even years before the prospective *erōmenos* had the required age, various parties – the *erastēs* of the boy's future *erastēs* and their messmates, the families of the boy and of his eventual lover – would have agreed upon this relationship beforehand. One can easily imagine how in this way a certain continuity of membership among a particular group of families could be maintained.[31]

To sum up, the recruitment of new members to the *syssitia* was a selection process that started eight years in advance and was submitted to various practical rules and restrictions. In my reconstruction of the fifth-century army the 240 *syssitia* had a recruiting base of on average 120 20-year-olds or 136 12-year-olds. Each *syssition* received a new member normally once in two years. Since in my view membership was based on the three Dorian *phylai* the pool of possible candidates was at most some 45 12-year-olds. In many cases this pool might have been limited even further by rules of residence if, which is not unlikely in my opinion, the *lochoi* as permanent organizations were somehow connected with the distribution of the Spartans over their villages, although these villages and the five *lochoi* could never have exactly matched. In practice, then, for many *syssitia* the number of possible candidates might have fluctuated from the maximum 45 or 46 to well below that number, sometimes perhaps as low as about 10 or 12. Moreover, fathers, sons, and brothers did not share the same mess – and possibly this also applied to cousins and nephews – which limited the choice of candidates a little further. Finally, since the *erastēs* was the youngest member of his *syssition*, his selection of a future member was very probably often pre-arranged, guided and steered, perhaps sometimes more or less ordered, by his own lover and his other messmates, his family and the relatives of his *erōmenos*. All this left little room for free choice. On the part of the *erōmenos*, I suspect there was very little of it indeed. On the part of the *erastēs*, what freedom there was will have depended largely on his personal status and prestige, which in turn might have depended in great measure on the standing of his family.

One final matter requires a few comments. If admission to the *syssitia* in fifth-century Sparta was wholly or largely a pre-determined affair, what do we make, then, of Plutarch's description of the voting in the *syssition* on the candidacy of a prospective member? We are told that at such an occasion the servant of the mess (most probably a Helot) went round with a κάδδιχος (a vessel normally used for wine or water) on his head, and that each of the members of the *syssition* then silently cast into it his ἀπομαγδαλία (a piece of soft bread used for wiping one's hands). To signify approval of a candidate one left that piece just as it was, to signify disapproval one squeezed it first. Only one such piece was enough for the candidate not to be admitted, the term κεκαδδίχθαι serving as a synonym for being rejected (Plut. *Lyk.* 12.5–6). This is a strange story indeed and cannot be accepted as it stands.

In the first place, the idea of voting on the admission of new members seems to be foreign to the Spartan *syssitia*. Completion of the state-provided upbringing was the criterion of citizenship (*Lak.Pol.* 10.7; Plut. *Inst. Lac.* 21) and belonging to a *syssition* was its definition (Aristot. *Pol.* 1271a35; 1272a13–16). There is no mention of any further 'test' by means of a voting procedure in the transition from the official *paideia* to membership of the *syssitia*. In the second place, the voting system described points to a procedure normally used in the secret ballot current in democracies. The history of voting in ancient Greece went through the successive phases of 1: shouting (βοή), 2: hand-raising (χειροτονία) and 3: ballot-casting (ψηφοφορία), the latter procedure being reserved for cases in which a person ran the risk of being ostracized, being deprived of some status or position, or sentenced by jury vote. The use of leaves for ballots in Syracuse (in a kind of ostracism) and in Athens (the ἐκφυλλοφορία as the procedure for ejecting members from the Council) resembles to some extent the custom ascribed by Plutarch to the Spartan *syssitia*.[32] Against this background the use of the ἀπομαγδαλία in Sparta looks like being inspired by democratic procedures elsewhere and can hardly be older than the fourth century. Moreover, the parallels suggest a voting not on the admission of a new member but on the ejection of one who already belonged to the club. In any case, Plutarch mentions the strange verb κεκαδδίχθαι as a synonym for being rejected: apparently the procedure inspired a word for (r)ejection, not for admission.

All this should lead us to conclude that what Plutarch describes could possibly be a procedure for ejecting members from the *syssition*, *if* the procedure was historical at all and not the invention of some later writer on Spartan institutions that Plutarch has used as his source. We cannot be certain, I believe, but if we regard it as a historical procedure it most probably dates from the fourth century. By that time, ejections from the *syssitia* did indeed take place sometimes. Apart from the presumably rare cases of cowardice or some other misdemeanour, we may perhaps think of the *Hypomeiones* or Inferiors, most probably persons who because of their loss of income could no longer pay the required contributions and so had eventually to be dismissed from their *syssitia*. Be that as it may, with a procedure of admitting new members to a *syssition* Plutarch's description to my mind has nothing to do.

Notes

[1] *Lak.Pol.* 5.2; σύσκηνοι for the members: 5.4; 7.4; 9.4; 15.5. In *Hell.* 5.3.17 Xenophon uses συσσίτια but in 5.3.20 σύσκηνοι and the variant συσκήνια.

[2] Polyaen. 2.1.15. The distinction is not very clear. While the συσσίτια must have been companies of Spartans sleeping in their tents (the σύσκηνοι of Xenophon, see above note 1), the στιβάδες could refer to guards sleeping on 'mattresses' in the open, or, generally, to non-Spartiate troops.

[3] See also Hodkinson 1983, 258; Cartledge 1987, 151. As far as I can see, only Lazenby 1985, 13, denies the military function of the *syssitia* in the time of Xenophon. But the evidence cited above suggests that the *syssitia* were subdivisions in camp of larger units (i.e. the *enōmotiai*, see below).

[4] Cf. Aristot. *Pol.* 1271b 40—1272a 27. For the comparative approach see Murray 1983a, 195–9; 1983b, 257–72; 1990, 83–103; criticized by Van Wees 1995, 173, and Hodkinson 1997, 90–1. See further the literature in n. 19 below.

[5] Especially in F 11 West, the poet distinguishes between the heavy-armed in the first rank(s) and the light-armed troops following behind (see ll. 13, 35–8); elsewhere too hoplite-style warriors appear while mention is also made of stones (19.2, 19) and projectiles (11.28; 23.10). For a recent discussion of the Spartan army in Tyrtaeus see Nafissi 1991, 82–91. In my opinion this image of the battlefield reflects early hoplite fighting in which the heavy-armed go in front (the πρόμαχοι) and the lighter-armed troops (certainly not to be identified with only the younger troops, as Nafissi 1991, 88–9 rightly points out) follow behind; it is, in broad outlines, also the pattern of fighting in Callinus of Ephesus and in the *Iliad*; cf. Singor 1995.

[6] Also in Athens the 18- and 19-year-olds, who underwent some form of military training, were not normally called up for active duty; like the over-fifty (up until sixty) they formed a reserve force. In times of emergency, however, they too could be mobilised for a military campaign (Thuc. 1.105.4). In later fourth-century Athens the system of 42 year-classes was the basis for mobilisations of the citizen hoplite army, as described by Arist. *Athen.Pol.* 53.

[7] See e.g. Toynbee 1969, 368–71; Hodkinson 1983, 255; Lazenby 1985, 7, 12; Cartledge 1987, 41. At Leuktra the depth of the phalanx was 'not more than 12' (Xen. *Hell.* 6.4.12), which suggests that not all the files (three in each *enōmotia*) had exactly 12 men. Likewise, at Mantinea the depth was 'in general 8 men' (Thuc. 5.68.3), so that here too some of the files (of which there were four in each *enōmotia*) seem to have fallen short of that number. Cf. n. 14 below.

[8] *Lak.Pol.* 4.1–5 describes their recruitment from among the ἡβῶντες, the young adults who are still submitted to certain rules and restrictions and who owe obedience to older citizens (*Lak.Pol.* 4.6–7; cf. also Plut. *Lyk.* 15.3–4; 25.1 for the limited freedom of young adults). Since the Hippeis fought as a special

force in the army (Thuc. 5.72.4) they must have been 20 years old at least. Herodotus mentions men regularly (annually) leaving the corps (Hdt. 1.67.5). All this points to the year-classes 20 up until 29 inclusive as the group from which the Hippeis were selected. See also Lazenby 1985, 10–12 ('young men', but no ages mentioned); Cartledge 1987, 204 (the 20- to 30-year-olds); Nafissi 1991, 153–8.

[9] Hodkinson 1983, 249; Cartledge 1987, 204. This might very well have entailed the setting up each year of the complete καταλόγοι of the three bands of 'Knights', when also the names of those who died the previous year would have been erased. Needless to say, this is an assumption, but it would make the brief notice of the *Lak.Pol.* more understandable.

[10] *Lak.Pol.* 4.3 uses καταλέγει for drawing up the lists of the Hippeis; when it is stated that thereby also the reasons were given why they had been selected and why the others of their age-group had not, one could perhaps think of a full καταλόγος divided into two parts (Hippeis and non-Hippeis). The existence of such a *katalogos* in Sparta is to my knowledge otherwise unknown. In my paper on the Spartan army of the fifth century I have suggested that these thirty newly recruited Hippeis constituted the enigmatic τριακάδες mentioned by Hdt. 1.65.5. The three military institutions which had been devised by Lycurgus, according to Herodotus, would then relate to each other thus: at the age of twenty *all* Spartans formally became members of a *syssition*, *some* of them, a minority of thirty, formed the yearly *triēkas* of recruits to the Hippeis, while *the rest*, by far the majority, immediately entered into the *enōmotiai*: Singor 1999.

[11] See, among others, Toynbee 1969, 365–87; Hodkinson 1983, 255; Cartledge 1987, 40–2, 428–31; Lazenby, on the other hand, supposes the *morai* as all-Spartan regiments (including the so-called Hypomeiones) to have been the main army divisions already by the time of Plataea, for which I can see no evidence: Lazenby 1985, 14–20, 48–52.

[12] It is often thought that the great losses in population caused by the earthquake around 465 BC brought about a reorganization of the army in which the all-Spartan *lochoi* were replaced by mixed Spartan and Perioikic *morai* (see e.g. Hodkinson 1983, 255). In my opinion a population decline there certainly was, although less dramatic than is usually believed, for I can see no traces of an army reform on the lines suggested at such an early date. See Singor 1999.

[13] Indeed, not only for that earlier period, for I believe that the connection between *enōmotiai* and *syssitia* was maintained even when the five all-Spartan *lochoi* were replaced by six *morai* in which Spartans and Perioikoi were brigaded together. This change occurred in the superstructure of *lochoi* and *morai* above the level of the *enōmotiai*, as I hope to show elsewhere. Here I cannot go into all the problems of the *morai*-army, so I restrict myself to the period in which exclusively Spartan *lochoi* were the main army divisions.

[14] The commanders of the *lochoi* saw to it that the *enōmotiai* were drawn up 'on the whole' or 'in general' to a depth of eight. Since that was the normal depth for the hoplite phalanx in the fifth century (Pritchett 1971, 134 ff.) one may suspect that the *lochagoi* ordered a deployment into files of eight, and

seeing that the numbers were not sufficient everywhere had men from one *enōmotia* transferred to another, but even so not all the files could reach the required strength of eight men; per *enōmotia* on average one, sometimes two, must have had only seven men.

[15] Coale, Demeny, Vaughan 1983, 108 (Model West Males, mortality level 4). I follow the advice of the authors (p. 25) in using Model West for an otherwise practically unknown population, as did Hansen 1985, 9–13, for Athens, instead of Model South referred to by Figueira 1986, 168 n. 10. In Model South the distribution of the various age-groups is spread more evenly with a higher proportion of older people, whereas in Model West the younger age-groups are more heavily represented; for instance, the year-classes 20 to 30 comprise 29.7% of the adult population (18 +) in the model I have chosen as against 25.6% in the one used by Figueira. I believe, however, that the overall picture would not be radically different. Further, I have chosen the life table with growth rate 5.00 (½%), following Hansen. One could argue that for fifth-century Sparta the table with growth rate 0.00 would be more appropriate. In that case, the numbers would change only slightly (the percentages up to year-class 25 would be just a little lower, from 25 on just a little higher) but I do not believe that this would alter my argument in any substantial way.

[16] In my paper on the Spartan army at Mantinea I reckon with 85 men from the 20-year-olds entering the *enōmotiai*; this would perhaps accord best with the situation in 418 BC. In the earlier part of the fifth century their number surely must have been higher if *all* places (40 per *enōmotia*) had to be manned. The total number of 120 Spartans of the year-class 20 implies an adult male population (18 + ..) of 3636 men, or 3076 for the age-group 20 until 60, on the basis of the model life table used here.

[17] The number ten may very well have been derived from the king's mess when on campaign, consisting according to *Lak.Pol.*13.1 of ten persons: apart from the king, six polemarchs and three *homoioi*. These, however, formed a sort of general staff and not a normal *syssition*.

[18] Toynbee 1969, 369 (followed by Cartledge 1987, 41–2) suggested two *syssitia* constituting one *enōmotia*, but 17 or 18 men in the age-group 20 up until 55 (to form an *enōmotia* of 35 as would have been the case on Sphakteria in 425 BC according to Toynbee) seems to me to be too large; it would imply an average membership of the *syssitia* of well over twenty, for which there is in any case no testimony.

[19] For the *andreia* or *syssitia* of the early archaic Age see: Nafissi 1991, 173 ff.; Powell 1998, 119 ff.; Thommen 1996, 45–6; for the Homeric evidence: Van Wees 1995, 147 ff. (esp. 173–4); Rundin 1996, 179 ff.

[20] For the *coniuratio* see Tondo 1963, 13–19; for the *enōmotia* as 'eine gegenseitig eidlich verpflichtete Gemeinschaft': Siewert 1972, 58–9.

[21] The names of the *lochoi* are variously given as Edolos, Sinis, Arimas, Ploas, and Messoagès (Scholion on Ar. *Lys.* 452–4), or Aidolios, Sinis, Sarinas, Ploas, and Mesoatès (Scholion on Thuc. 4.8.9). The source seems to be Aristotle's lost *Lakedaimoniōn Politeia* (Arist. F 541 Rose). The comparison with the imperial legions is made by Kennell 1995, 167: Sinis and Sarinas as equivalent to *rapax* and *victrix*, whilst Ploas 'had a connection with the marines', with

Messoagès 'perhaps referring to the central unit of a Spartan battle formation'. I am not convinced by these explanations; there is no evidence for a fixed order into which the *lochoi* could have been lined up; while Ploas' name seems to be particularly odd, the name Aidolios or Edolos still remains obscure. For Kennell's argument that the villages or *ōbai* of Sparta numbered only four and consequently could never have matched the five *lochoi*, see below n. 22.

[22] Kennell has argued that Amyklai, usually seen as one of the five villages of classical Sparta, was in fact semi-autonomous till the end of the first century BC, so that classical Sparta was composed of four 'villages' only (Kennell 1995, 163–9). I find this rather doubtful. At least in 195 BC Amyklai was not among the Perioikic towns that gained independence from Sparta, so its 'semi-autonomous' status was probably not on a par with those of the Perioikoi. If the Amyklaioi in the fifth and fourth centuries formed some special category between the Spartans proper and the Perioikoi, there is no testimony to support this assumption. However, for my argument that there might have existed some connection between place of residence and recruitment into the *lochoi* – and consequently into the *enōmotiai* and *syssitia* – the question is of limited importance, since also five villages could never have exactly matched the five *lochoi*; on the other hand, some connection between *lochoi* and villages could have existed also when the latter numbered only four.

[23] In particular Cartledge 1981, 17–36; Hodkinson 1983, 245; Fisher 1989, 46 n. 37.

[24] For the thesis of an origin of this practice in initiation rites see: Bethe 1907, esp. 457–65; cf. Cartledge 1981, 23–7; Patzer 1982, 67–90. It is strongly criticized by Dover 1988, 115–33, followed by Hodkinson 1997, 90. Recently, Ogden 1996, 111–19 has tried to reaffirm the older thesis and to link Spartan institutionalized pederasty with homosexuality in a military context elsewhere, especially in Thebes and on Crete. To my mind, these parallels do indeed suggest that sexual consummation of the pederastic relationships in Sparta could have been a fairly normal thing, but they do not reveal anything about the *origin(s)* of this institution.

[25] See above, n. 23. This aspect, of course, involved 'the politics of Spartan pederasty': Cartledge 1981, 27–30.

[26] Plut. *Lyk.* 17.1 makes a distinction between the *neoi* as the lovers of the boys, and the older citizens. The age-group under 30 had to obey the older citizens, according to *Lak.Pol.* 4.6. It was probably the same young men who were not allowed to sleep at home (Plut. *Lyk.* 15.3–4), perhaps also those who did not yet consume the famous black soup (Plut. *Lyk.* 12.6).

[27] This 'chain of lovers' has already been proposed by Hodkinson 1983, 245–6.

[28] See n. 15 above. I have used Model West male, mortality level 4, growth rate 5.00. Males of age 12 would represent 2.15%, those of age 20 1.90%, of age 22 1.82%, and of age 30 1.57%. In the table based on growth rate 0.00 (one that fits a static population and so perhaps would be even more appropriate in the case of fifth-century Sparta) these percentages would be respectively 2.01, 1.85, 1.81, and 1.60. and the corresponding numbers would be

130, 120, 116, 104. In this case, the discrepancies would be smaller, but they would be there nevertheless.

[29] Plut. *Lyk.* 25.1, mentioning the group of adults under thirty, says that they did not visit the *agora* themselves but that their household needs were supplied by their relatives and their *erastai*. I wonder whether this could not mean for the individual Spartan concerned that it was *either* his relatives *or* his lover who provided for him in this way. If so, it could mean that some (probably most) of the under-thirty still had lovers, whilst others (in all probability a minority) had not and had to be taken care of by their relatives. So, after being admitted to a *syssition*, the death of his *erastēs* would not have changed the status of a young adult. Could this also not have been the case for the younger boys who, after being introduced into the *syssitia* of their lovers, would stay on there when their *erastai* died before they themselves had become members?

[30] This reconstruction leads to the assumption that bringing in a new member at the age of twenty could by itself sometimes not be good enough: when the latter died before he reached the age of twenty-two and in his turn could have introduced his *erōmenos*, the 'line of succession' would still be broken. This is why I presume that in such cases the *erastai*, although they could already have been 30 or 31, were still obliged to find another *erōmenos*. However, this must have been very exceptional.

[31] Cf. Cartledge 1981, 27 ff.

[32] Busolt-Swoboda 1920, 455.

Bibliography

Bethe, E.

1907 'Die dorische Knabenliebe. Ihre Ethik und ihre Idee', *Rheinisches Museum* 62, 438–75.

Busolt, G. and Swoboda, H.

1920 *Griechische Staatskunde I*, München.

Cartledge, P.A.

1981 'The politics of Spartan pederasty', *Proceedings of the Cambridge Philological Society* 27, 17–36.

1987 *Agesilaos and the Crisis of Sparta*, London and Baltimore.

Coale, A.J., Demeny, P. and Vaughan, B.

1983 *Regional Model Life Tables and Stable Populations*, New York.

Dover, K.J.

1988 'Greek homosexuality and initiation', in *idem*, *The Greeks and their Legacy*, London, 115–34.

Figueira, T.J.

1986 'Population patterns in late archaic and classical Sparta'*Transactions of the American Philological Association* 116, 165–213.

Fisher, N.R.E.

1989 'Drink, *hybris* and the promotion of harmony in Sparta', in A. Powell (ed.) *Classical Sparta: Techniques behind her success*, London, 26–50.

Hansen, M.H.
1985 *Demography and Democracy. The number of Athenian citizens in the fourth century BC*, Herning.

Hodkinson, S.
1983 'Social order and the conflict of values in classical Sparta', *Chiron* 13, 239–81.
1997 'The development of Spartan society and institutions in the archaic period', in L.G. Mitchell and P.J. Rhodes (eds.) *The Development of the* Polis *in Archaic Greece*, London, 83–102.

Kennell, N.G.
1995 *The Gymnasium of Virtue. Education and culture in ancient Sparta*, Chapel Hill.

Lazenby, J.F.
1985 *The Spartan Army*, Warminster.

Murray, O.
1983 'The Greek symposion in history', in E. Gabba (ed.) *Tria Corda. Scritti in onore di Arnaldo Momigliano*, Como, 257–72.
1983 'The symposion as social organization', in R. Hägg (ed.) *The Greek Renaissance of the Eighth Century BC. Tradition and innovation*, Stockholm, 195–9.

Murray, O. (ed.)
1990 *Sympotica. A symposium on the Symposion*, Oxford.

Nafissi, M.
1991 *La nascita del* Kosmos. *Studi sulla storia e la società di Sparta*, Perugia.

Ogden, D.
1996 'Homosexuality and warfare in Ancient Greece', in A.B. Lloyd (ed.) *Battle in Antiquity*, London, 107–78.

Patzer, H.
1992 *Die griechische Knabenliebe*, Wiesbaden.

Powell, A.
1998 'Sixth-century Lakonian vase-painting: continuities and discontinuities with the "Lykourgan" ethos', in N.R.E. Fisher and H. van Wees (eds.) *Archaic Greece: New approaches and new evidence*, London, 119–46.

Pritchett, W.K.
1971 *The Greek State at War I*, Berkeley.

Rundin, J.
1996 'A politics of eating: feasting in early Greek society', *American Journal of Philology* 117, 179–215.

Siewert, P.
1972 *Der Eid von Plataiai*, Munich.

Singor, H.W.
1995 '*Eni Prōtoisi Machesthai*: some remarks on the Iliadic image of the battlefield', in J.P. Crielaard (ed.) *Homeric Questions*, Amsterdam, 183–200.
1999 'The Spartan army at Mantinea and its organization in the fifth century BC', in W.M. Jongman and M. Kleijwegt (eds.) *Essays in*

Ancient History in Honour of H.W. Pleket forthcoming, Amsterdam.

Thommen, L.

1996 *Lakedaimoniōn Politeia. Die Entstehung der spartanischen Verfassung*, Stuttgart.

Tondo, S.

1963 'Il "sacramentum militiae" nell' ambiente culturale romano-italico', *Studia et Documenta Historiae et Iuris* 29, 1–123.

Toynbee, A.J.

1969 *Some Problems of Greek History*, Oxford.

Wees, H. van,

1995 'Princes at dinner: social event and social structure in Homer', in J.P. Crielaard (ed.) *Homeric Questions*, Amsterdam, 147–82.

Chapter 4

AIDŌS AT SPARTA

Nicolas Richer

Πολλὴν μὲν αἰδῶ, πολλὴν δὲ πειθὼ ἐκεῖ συμπαρεῖναι.
'There, great *aidōs* stands beside great obedience.'
Xenophon, *Constitution of the Lacedaemonians* 2.2

It has recently been emphasised once again that our sources for the history of Sparta are often too late for us to be able to trust them, especially as far as the archaic period is concerned.[1] Plutarch's *Life of Lycurgus*, in particular, without question presents us with a distorted vision of Spartan history.

When the astronomer examines the sky, he does not see it as it has ever been, but he sees it at a given time, 'as its different parts have been at *different periods*', since the light of different parts takes very variable amounts of time to reach us.[2] The same, *mutatis mutandis*, doubtless goes for the history of Sparta viewed through the *Life of Lycurgus*.

However, even if the accuracy of his synthesis leaves a great deal to be desired, in fact the *details* given by Plutarch are not generally products of the imagination first and foremost. In addition, we have at our disposal other images of Sparta apart from the *Life of Lycurgus*, and the comparison of facts supplied by our different sources can be enlightening, allowing us to approach 'what really happened', to recapitulate Ranke's expression. The sources on which we can reflect are both textual and archaeological in nature. These sources supply us with usable information even for the archaic period: Sparta was then characterised by a spirit of innovation which manifests itself especially in the spiritual, if not religious, sphere, by the place accorded in the Spartan spirit to *pathēmata*, to abstractions of physical states, of dispositions which seize the body.[3] The *pathēmata* which, according to our (very lacunose) sources, are explicitly recognised at Sparta are at least seven in number.

1. The παθήματα honoured at Sparta

Plutarch reports that during the *coup d'État* of Cleomenes III in 227, the ephor Agylaios, thought to be dead, managed to slip into a 'small room, which was a sanctuary of Fear' (εἴς τι δωμάτιον...μικρόν, ὃ Φόβου μὲν ἦν ἱερόν) and which must have been situated near the ephors' dining room (συσσίτιον).[4] This δωμάτιον may have been a room in the building where the ephors had their seat. Thus the sanctuary of Phobos appears to have been part of the *ephoreion*, and we may assume this was not due to chance.[5]

In connection with this story, Plutarch indicates that the Lacedaemonians have sanctuaries 'not only of Fear but also of Death, Laughter and of everything else which might befall them of this type' (καὶ τοιούτων ἄλλων παθημάτων ἱερά).[6] The existence of these cults indicates, according to David, that the Spartans were conscious of the mysterious power of these entities but not necessarily that they were submissive to them; rather, they would have made a continuous effort to use them in the interests of the city.[7]

The abstractions in question are the following:[8]

— Phobos, Fear (Plutarch, *Cleomenes* 9.1)

— Aidōs, Modesty or Reserve[9] (Xenophon, *Symposion* 8.35; Pausanias 3.20.10–11)

— Hypnos, Sleep (Pausanias 3.18.1)

— Thanatos, Death (Plutarch, *Cleomenes* 9.1 and Pausanias 3.18.1)

— Gelōs, Laughter (Sosibios, *FGrH* 595 F 19 *ap.* Plutarch, *Lycurgus* 25.4; Plutarch, *Cleomenes* 9.1)

— Erōs, Love (Sosicrates, *FHG* IV, p. 501 F 7 = *FGrH* 461 F 7, *ap.* Athenaeus 12.561e–f; in Lakonia, at Leuctra: cf. Pausanias 3.26.5)

— Limos, Hunger or Famine (Callisthenes, *FGrH* 124, F 13 *ap.* Athenaeus 10.452b; Polyaenus 2.15).[10]

2. Cult places and representations of the *pathēmata*

Thus, seven abstractions of psychological states with physical manifestations (Phobos, Aidōs, Gelōs, Erōs) or more generally of states of the body (Thanatos, Hypnos, Limos) are respected at Sparta and, if we may say so, deified there. David for his part[11] accepts 'the strange trinity Fear, Death and Laughter', but Plutarch[12] indicates the existence of ἱερά dedicated to them, as to everything which might befall them of this type (καὶ τοιούτων ἄλλων παθημάτων ἱερά), and the other *pathēmata* mentioned by our sources are Reserve, Sleep, Love and Hunger.

However, the ἱερά whose existence Plutarch mentions are not necessarily temples[13] but could more simply be places or objects consecrated to these entities.[14] In fact, except in the case of Phobos,[15] it does not seem

that these ἱερά can be understood with any certainty as being buildings:
— Limos is represented at the Amyklaion as a painted *gynaion*,[16] unless it was in the sanctuary of Athena Chalkioikos that a painting of Limos, in the form of a woman, was dedicated;[17]
— Gelōs is only known in the form of an *agalmation*;[18]
— Hypnos and Thanatos must have been represented in the form of *agalmata* near an *agalma* of Aphrodite Ambologera;[19]
— Aidōs is represented by an *agalma*;[20]
— Erōs for his part is worshipped at Leuctra in a cult building and a grove is dedicated to him (Ἐρωτός ἐστιν ἐν Λεύκτροις ναὸς καὶ ἄλσος),[21] but Wide,[22] following Furtwängler,[23] considers that this Erōs should be assimilated with an ancient god of nature and not a personification of love; if the two forms of Erōs are indeed distinct – which we might doubt – we have no information on the cult place of the properly Spartan Erōs; we know only that the kings sacrifice to Erōs before every military engagement.[24]

In the end, it seems that only Phobos certainly had a kind of temple; this might reflect his greater importance in the eyes of the Lacedaemonians.[25] This importance can be seen especially in the relationship which Phobos maintains with another *pathēma*, Aidōs, Reserve.

3. Aidōs

a) A feminine hypostasis of Phobos represented by an agalma?

Of all the personified abstractions of *pathēmata*, Aidōs is the only important one of feminine gender.[26] The fact deserves all the more attention, it seems to me, because – although the rule is far from being absolute – generally in Greece priests serve the cults of male divinities, priestesses those of female divinities.[27] Even if cult personnel are not universally of the same sex as all the worshippers and if, therefore, the latter may in this case be partly men, one could still be tempted *a priori* to see in Aidōs a form of Phobos for the use of women.[28] It is in this sense that Vernant[29] evokes the 'exaggerated, hyperfeminine [*aidōs*] of the *parthenos*'.[30]

Pausanias, it is true, does not mention a cult of Aidōs as such; he declares:[31]

> τὸ δὲ ἄγαλμα τῆς Αἰδοῦς τριάκοντά που στάδια ἀπέχον τῆς πόλεως Ἰκαρίου μὲν ἀνάθημα εἶναι, ποιηθῆναι δὲ ἐπὶ λόγῳ φασὶ τοιῷδε. ὅτ' ἔδωκεν Ὀδυσσεῖ Πηνελόπην γυναῖκα Ἰκάριος, ἐπειρᾶτο μὲν κατοικίσαι καὶ αὐτὸν Ὀδυσσέα ἐν Λακεδαίμονι, διαμαρτάνων δὲ ἐκείνου δεύτερα τὴν θυγατέρα ἱκέτευε καταμεῖναι καὶ ἐξορμωμένης ἐς Ἰθάκην ἐπακολουθῶν τῷ ἅρματι ἐδεῖτο. Ὀδυσσεὺς δὲ τέως μὲν ἠνείχετο, τέλος δὲ ἐκέλευε Πηνελόπην συνακολουθεῖν ἑκοῦσαν ἢ τὸν πατέρα ἑλομένην ἀναχωρεῖν ἐς Λακεδαίμονα. Καὶ

τὴν ἀποκρίνασθαί φασιν οὐδέν· ἐγκαλυψαμένης δὲ πρὸς τὸ ἐρώτημα, Ἰκάριος τὴν μὲν ἅτε δὴ συνιεὶς ὡς βούλεται ἀπιέναι μετὰ Ὀδυσσέως ἀφίησιν, ἄγαλμα δὲ ἀνέθηκεν Αἰδοῦς· ἐνταῦθα γὰρ τῆς ὁδοῦ προήκουσαν ἤδη τὴν Πηνελόπην λέγουσιν ἐγκαλύψασθαι.

The statue of Aidōs, some thirty stades from the city, is a dedication of Ikarios; it was made, they say, for the following reason. When Ikarios gave Penelope to Odysseus as wife, he tried to settle Odysseus himself in Lacedaemon; failing, he supplicated his daughter a second time to stay, and when she was departing for Ithaca he begged her, following the chariot. (11) Odysseus put up with this for a while, but in the end he ordered Penelope to follow him willingly or, if she preferred her father, to return to Lacedaemon. And, they say, she gave no reply, but when in answer she veiled herself, Ikarios, understanding that she wished to go with Odysseus, let her go, and he dedicated an image of Aidōs; this is in fact the place on the road which Penelope had reached, they say, when she veiled herself.

Thus, Pausanias indicates only the existence of, if not a statue, at least a sculpted offering (*agalma*) which was set up (*anathēma*), and Wide[32] points out that we are not certainly talking about a goddess here. Nevertheless, it is as the image of a divinity that Pausanias presents the *agalma*. To be more precise, he gives us to understand that it is Penelope's pose that inspired the representation of Aidōs: this statue should be imagined as representing Penelope in the attitude she adopted in response to her father's supplications: she covered her face (or rather her head) with a veil.

But the date at which Pausanias is writing, the second century AD, is late, and we might very well imagine that, its primary significance having been forgotten, the statue could have been reinterpreted,[33] especially from the characteristic gesture described by Pausanias.

Musti and Torelli[34] consider that the *aition* given by Pausanias could have been elaborated from popular traditions attached to a statue of a veiled woman, perhaps set up on a tomb. In addition, the traditional identification of the situation of this statue, near a cave, might allow us to establish a link between the name Aidōs and that of the subterranean Hades/Aidoneus, according to Wide's hypothesis.[35] The female statue of Aidōs would then be the vestige of a pre-existing cult of Hades.[36] This hypothesis, which, if we follow Wide, rests only on the phonetic proximity of the names,[37] could perhaps find a kind of confirmation in the field of Lakonian archaeology. Wide in fact even neglected[38] a reading, worthy of being retained, of the word ΑΙΔΕΥΣ (Hades), inscribed on a statue[39] which is itself generally associated with the male figures depicted on the Lakonian hero-reliefs.[40] Moreover, on these hero-reliefs, it is very often two figures that are represented, one male and the other female.[41]

These figures have been identified as being Hades and Demeter by Andronicos,[42] but Stibbe would rather see Dionysos and Demeter in them,[43] while Salapata considers that the original couple represented in this kind of depiction must have been Agamemnon and Alexandra/Cassandra.[44] Even if originally the sixth-century statue bearing the inscription ΑΙΔΕΥΣ did not represent Hades, it is possible, as Hibler suggests on the basis of the letter-forms,[45] that the denomination of the statue, ΑΙΔΕΥΣ, did not correspond to the first name of the character represented. But he might have taken this name when the statue was reinterpreted. Or indeed someone might have felt the need to inscribe the name Hades on the figure because he thought that this name was becoming forgotten. And we could propose that an analogous process might have applied to a statue representing this character's female *paredros*, who was also generally represented in relief and, in this case, eventually (but not necessarily) represented in the round. This *paredros* could have been the ΓΥΝΗ ΑΙΔΕΩΣ, the wife of Hades. Such a statue could easily have been interpreted as representing ΑΙΔΩΣ, Aidōs. For, as is strongly emphasised by Salapata, it is very probable that the type of representations known by the name 'Lakonian hero-reliefs' were endowed with a certain plasticity of meaning.[46] It is further highlighted by Hibler[47] that, on the hero reliefs of the sixth century, the female *paredros* of Hades (in Andronicos' interpretation) is precisely in the middle of veiling herself,[48] and such is the posture attributed, according to Pausanias, to the supposed representation of Penelope: the latter at least covers her head even if she does not veil her face.[49]

We could, then, propose, in line with what Wide suggested in 1893, that the statue which Pausanias said was a representation of Aidōs had originally represented the *paredros* of Hades. For the significance of the character of Aidōs would have been sufficient for a representation of the wife of Hades, established according to an iconographic formula attested in the sixth century, to have been able, at the latest in the time of Pausanias the Periegete but doubtless much earlier, to be reinterpreted as depicting Aidōs.

However, such an interpretation – and the details of its elaboration remain hypothetical[50] – is perhaps not absolutely compelling: Salapata[51] remarks that the absence of hero-reliefs in the great sanctuaries (of Athena Chalkioikos and Orthia, as at the Amyklaion) seems to indicate that the iconographic type of the so-called hero-reliefs was reserved for heroes; it could doubtless also serve to represent any anthropomorphic supernatural entity of minor importance, shall we say. It may, then, suffice to consider that Pausanias' text, bearing witness to the multiple interpretations to which a particular type of iconographic representation lends itself,[52] demonstrates the strength of the image of Aidōs in the Lakonian mentality even in the second century AD.[53] And Aidōs' significance must be ancient.

In fact, the *aition* recorded by Pausanias is remarkable: it specifies that Ikarios must have set up the monument to Aidōs once he understood the strength of the link uniting his daughter henceforth to Odysseus. Such an *aition*,[54] we may doubtless imagine, would have encouraged Spartan women to renounce their paternal family, the better to become integrated in that of their husband.[55] It is possible that the institution of a conjugal system[56] of this type[57] might have aroused the objections that Aristotle indicates when he mentions the vain efforts supposedly made by the law-giver of Lacedaemon to discipline women;[58] Aristotle deplores the lack of regulation of women (ἡ τῶν γυναικῶν ἄνεσις).[59]

If, as Cairns had clearly demonstrated,[60] Aidōs is an entity which, originally, must have governed men at least as much as women, the *aition* transmitted by Pausanias seems to indicate that Aidōs' power at Sparta could in principle have been exercised at least as much over women as over men. This is why, in Pausanias, we see Penelope veiling herself so as not to respond to entreaty in a manner which could have proved to be injurious (ἐγκαλυψαμένης δὲ πρὸς τὸ ἐρώτημα).[61] It is a gesture which expresses soberly the attitude inspired in a woman by Aidōs, understood as Reserve.[62] But for all that, women are not alone in having had their behaviour inspired by Aidōs – perhaps since the sixth century as attested by the Lakonian hero-reliefs, doubtless initially representing Cassandra.

b) Gelōs in the service of Aidōs. Demaratos ridiculed

The same gesture as that attributed to Penelope is also historically, in 491–86,[63] that of Demaratos interrogated *epi gelōti* (in order to make people laugh) by Leotychidas.[64] In order to examine this incident related by Herodotus, we have to bear in mind that Gelōs[65] is mentioned by Plutarch at the same time as Phobos[66] and that he is perhaps an 'accompanying' abstraction[67] (as Nike can accompany Athena, Erōs Aphrodite...), since he can be Fear's instrument: by fear of ridicule, a Spartiate remains within the norm. [68]

So, when Leotychidas wants, by recourse to Laughter, to underline sharply the current situation, which sees him ruling while Demaratos is no more than a magistrate,[69] the latter answers by assuming an attitude of Aidōs; he shows that he is a true Spartiate: not only is his response in the form of an apophthegm (he says that he has to his advantage the experience of magistrate and king, which Leotychidas does not), which is perhaps a way of trying to make people laugh in his turn (to invoke Gelōs?),[70] but in the end he displays his respect for Aidōs, whose gestural characteristic he adopts.[71] We could indeed see in this a play on the notions which ruled life at Sparta.[72]

Thus, even if the cult of Aidōs is not formally attested, the attitude of the statue seen by Pausanias seems to have corresponded to a reality of Spartan practice, at least in the example of male behaviour we have just seen. Aidōs inspires behaviour marked by silence but which is nonetheless significant of a very efficacious self-control, because this silence constitutes a response to an appeal.[73]

In the case of the offence inflicted on Demaratos, Aidōs seems able to concern the male sex too – such is the case already in the *Iliad*[74] – like the other *pathēmata*; in fact, the concept of Aidōs[75] is very close to that of Phobos.[76]

c) The respective places of Aidōs and Phobos among the pathēmata and their development

Plato[77] considers that 'a legislator and every man worthy of the name holds this[78] fear (φόβος) in the greatest esteem, calling it respect (αἰδώς)'. In terms of a plurisecular conceptual development the fourth-century Athenian philosopher thus underlines the great proximity, but also the difference, of the two concepts.[79]

It seems that the Spartans of the sixth century had already clearly distinguished the concepts. A saying attributed to Anaxandridas II,[80] Agiad king from *c.* 560 to 520, and father of Cleomenes I, says this: to someone who asked him 'the question why in their wars the Spartans confronted danger confidently, he replied, "Because we train ourselves, when life is at stake, to be inspired by *aidōs* and not, like others, by *phobos*" ' ("Οτι, ἔφη, αἰδεῖσθαι περὶ βίου μελετῶμεν, οὐχ ὥσπερ οἱ ἄλλοι φοβεῖσθαι). A saying similar to that of Anaxandridas is attributed to Polydoros, the seventh-century king: 'Having been asked the reason why the Spartans, in war, confronted danger with courage, he replied, "Because they have learnt to feel shame in front of their leaders, not to feel fear" ' ("Οτι, ἔφη, αἰδεῖσθαι τοὺς ἡγεμόνας ἔμαθον, οὐ φοβεῖσθαι).[81]

These passages show us that a difference, of which the Lacedaemonians were aware, exists between the two concepts. It seems that Aidōs could govern the behaviour of the Lacedaemonians while Phobos struck their enemies. One could perhaps almost see here an illustration of the agonistic character of the war waged by the Spartans: they acted under the governance of Reserve, while their enemies alone were supposed to be touched by Flight.[82] This idea is made explicit by Plutarch saying that the enemies of Sparta were all the more inclined to take to their heels because they knew that the Lacedaemonians would not pursue them far.[83]

A different idea appears, however, in the advice attributed by Diogenes Laertius to Chilon (supposed to have been ephor in 556/5).[84] In the middle of a whole series of precepts meant to govern internal social relationships at Sparta, we read: 'when one is strong, [one must] be gentle, in order to be respected rather than feared by one's neighbours' (ἰσχυρὸν ὄντα πρᾶον εἶναι, ὅπως οἱ πλησίον αἰδῶνται μᾶλλον ἢ φοβῶνται). The context indicates that Phobos can be considered as present at Sparta itself. The fact that, according to Anaxandridas, at a period slightly earlier than that of Chilon, Phobos concerns enemies tends to demonstrate that from now on Phobos takes on a double value at Sparta, concerned at the same time with enemies in war and with citizens in their daily life.

Moreover, another saying is attributed to Leonidas: μόνοι πρὸς τοὺς πολεμίους μάχονται οἱ τοὺς βασιλέας αἰδούμενοι [καὶ φοβούμενοι],[85] a text translated by Fuhrmann: [86] 'les seuls à se battre contre l'ennemi sont ceux qui ne veulent pas se déshonorer devant leurs rois' ('the only men who fight against the enemy are those who do not wish to be dishonoured before their kings'). In my opinion, more than human respect is in question, in this text as in that attributed to Polydoros, the respect the Spartans feel towards their kings, a respect which drove them to be killed in their service;[87] I share Fuhrmann's opinion, therefore, according to which 'the sentiment evoked differs precisely from fear',[88] but, in this light, I would rather translate Polydoros' saying: 'it is because they have learnt to surround their leaders with respect, not to be afraid'.[89] And I would rather understand Leonidas' saying: 'only those who respect their kings (and fear them) fight against their enemies'.[90]

It seems, then, that the sayings of Polydoros and Leonidas do not present the relationship between Aidōs and Phobos in the same way and that they do not afford Phobos the same role in Spartan military discipline; this could, however, be simply explained if we remember that Polydoros, endowed with an image of the king as friend of the people,[91] could not easily have the language of authority ascribed to him. But the same does not go for Leonidas; this is why, unlike Fuhrmann, I do not athetise the words καὶ φοβούμενοι attributed to Leonidas, 'an addition which the majority of the manuscripts present[92] and which – if we admit the attributions ascribed to the sayings transmitted by the *Moralia*[93] – seems to preserve a development of the idea of Phobos at Sparta: from the beginning of the fifth century, Phobos is present in the Lacedaemonian army in the same way as, according to the evidence of Chilon's saying, he is present in Spartan society[94] in the middle of the sixth century.

Henceforth Phobos is a power destined to ensure the cohesion of an army and not just an entity supposed to put the enemy to flight, and Aidōs, for her part, appears especially to be for internal usage at Sparta (an internal usage which has also become partly that of Phobos). It is in this spirit that in the classical period Aidōs, understood as Reserve, is often presented as a characteristic feature of Lacedaemonian behaviour. In Thucydides' rationalistic vocabulary, the Spartans find themselves reproached by their Corinthian allies, before the beginning of the Peloponnesian War, for being held back in their actions by the distrust (μηδέ…πιστεῦσαι) which they feel in the face of even the surest arguments.[95]

Moreover, if, as it seems, Phobos concerns especially men, Aidōs governs both men (see the behaviour of Demaratos at the beginning of the fifth century) and women. In this connection, if the cult dedicated to Aidōs did not always meet with the success among the female sex expected by its promoter (the 'lawgiver' mentioned by Aristotle;[96] should we understand Chilon[97] here?),[98] a statue representing a woman and called 'Aidōs' could have existed without a cult having been properly established.

In the *Constitution of the Lacedaemonians*, Xenophon stresses that education aims at inspiring great reserve (τὸ αἰδεῖσθαι ἰσχυρῶς ἐμφῦσαι)[99] in young boys,[100] and he makes explicit the idea of a competition between young boys and young girls in terms of *aidōs*; from this competition the young boys emerge victorious (αἰδημονεστέρους).[101]

Finally, whatever the moment when the statue mentioned by Pausanias was first said to represent Aidōs, this attribution demonstrates the duration of the significance accorded to this concept. The importance of Aidōs endured all the more because Aidōs seems to lend herself to a wide sphere of influence: in Homer, Riedinger[102] has in fact been able to distinguish clearly the αἰδώς felt before an individual from that felt before a group; and he concludes[103] that the existence of αἰδώς in these two forms shows that 'opinion largely took control of the behaviour' of individuals. At Sparta, we may imagine that one form might have been destined to concern women especially (whence the *aition* referring to Penelope) – but not only women if we judge by the example of Demaratos – while the other might have been supposed rather to govern combatants;[104] it is this second presentation which is given by Xenophon in the *Symposion*:[105] invoking the love-affairs that can unite Lacedaemonian soldiers, Socrates declares that, in order to avoid causing their *erastes* shame, the *eromenoi* have at heart to fight bravely in every circumstance: 'for it is not Absence-of-Aidōs but Aidōs which they consider as a goddess' (θεὰν γὰρ οὐ τὴν Ἀναίδειαν ἀλλὰ τὴν Αἰδῶ νομίζουσι).[106]

Aidōs had a wide sphere of influence at Sparta, then, in connection with both men and women, and the importance of the concept in Spartan customs (supervised by the ephors) appears clearly established. But the role of Phobos, for his part, appears more specifically masculine.

Founded on the Spartiates' particular sensitivity towards *pathēmata* – a sensitivity perhaps linked in part to the importance of the military at Sparta[107] – a cult of the *pathēmata* – at least of Phobos – could have been established at Sparta from the middle of the sixth century.[108] It is, moreover, very probable that even if the existence of cults dedicated to *pathēmata* is difficult to date precisely, the *hiera* mentioned by Plutarch[109] do imply the existence of a cult; and it is most probable that the very conceptualisation of an idea perceived as capable of influencing the behaviour of men only precedes by a little way the establishment of a cult in honour of this idea.[110]

The presence of a sanctuary of Phobos in the *ephoreion* on the one hand, and, on the other, the proximity of a representation of Hestia in the same *ephoreion*,[111] could doubtless demonstrate how Sparta made use of features known in other cities, like Athens, in her own way, giving them a particular meaning.[112]

So, the place of the *pathēmata* in the Spartan mentality sheds light on a passage of Plutarch:[113] the Lacedaemonians would have had a utilitarian apprenticeship in reading and writing, and 'all the rest of their instruction consisted in learning to obey well, to endure fatigue patiently and to conquer in battle'. The place granted to the *pathēmata* in this mentality founds the principle according to which 'All this [the Lacedaemonian system] was massively buttressed, psychologically and institutionally';[114] this is why viewing the life of Sparta from the point of view of the *pathēmata* allows us to read with relative coherence a certain number of (notably educational) practices and attitudes.

Notes

[1] See e.g. Hodkinson 1997. Stephen Hodkinson was kind enough to let me see this text before publication. I have profited from the remarks he and Anton Powell generously made on reading a first version of the present article: it is an agreeable duty for me to thank them.

[2] See C. Flammarion, *Les Terres du ciel*, Paris 1877, cited in *A la découverte de l'astronomie*, Paris, 1986, 91.

[3] On the different types of abstractions recognised by the Greeks and the classifications with which modern scholars have worked, see e.g. Shapiro 1976, 23–3 and 1993, 26. In her study of Phobos, Mactoux (1993) considers especially the role of Phobos, but gives little attention to the other *pathēmata*. She emphasises the 'close relationship between Phobos and the ephorate' (259) and invites us not 'to lose sight the bivalence of Phobos' (265–6), his active value (Terror or Rout) combining with his passive value (Fear): Plutarch's text 'constructs a plural Phobos' (271). For a more general account of the *pathēmata* at Sparta, see Richer 1998a, 217–33.

[4] *Cleomenes* 8.1–3. In my opinion, δωμάτιον here indicates a room rather than a building: cf. e.g. the prytany of Delos, one room of which (D) would have been 'the chapel containing the altar of Hestia' (Bruneau et Ducat 1983, 136). Δωμάτιον here is opposed to οἴκημα, the name of the room out of which Agylaios slips, and this term can equally designate part of a building, especially a dining room (see LSJ, s.v.), which is clearly the case here because the οἴκημα in question can be assimilated with the ephors' συσσίτιον, according to *Cleomenes* 8.1.

[5] Mactoux (1993, 280) considers that the 'privileged relationship [of Phobos] with the ephors [...can be seen...] in the spatial contiguity of the place where ephoric power was exercised and of the sanctuary'.

[6] *Cleomenes* 9.1. On the possibility that Plutarch's source here may be Sosibios, see David 1989, 2.

[7] David 1989, 2.

[8] If *pathēmata* are occasionally the objects of cult elsewhere in Greece, they do not seem to constitute a cult *system*, something which appears to be a specifically Lakonian feature (cf. *infra* n. 112). We are not here concerned with more conceptual abstractions such as Demos, Auxesia, Praxidike/Themis, Nemesis, Tyche, perhaps Nike (cf. Wide, s.v.): these other abstractions are not analogous to the *pathēmata*.

[9] Hani (1992, 61) points out that 'the word *aidōs* is nearly untranslatable, like all words of culture and civilisation which are pregnant, heavy with multiple and secondary senses, with resonances which are often inexpressible in conceptual terms'; the term contains ideas of fear, of honour and of respect. It is the richness of the concept which is the object of Cairns' study, *Aidōs* (1993).

[10] Although the *pathēma* Dipsa (Thirst) is not attested to my knowledge, her existence seems very probable to me: the story of Soos (presented as one of the first Eurypontids, between Prokles and Eurypon, by Pausanias 3.7.1) looks like the *aition* for the establishment of the cult of Dipsa: according to Plutarch, *Lycurgus* 2.1–3 and *Moralia* 232a, Soos, for having – alone of the troop he was commanding – been able to resist thirst, enabled Sparta to keep the territory

conquered from the Arcadians of Cleitor – and Plutarch explicitly takes the fact that Soos was the only one to have resisted thirst as a confirmation of his royalty; the anecdote appears as an illustration of the importance of controlling elementary physical needs. Thirst and hunger are moreover clearly associated, in a military context, for example in *Iliad* 19.166 (δίψά τε καὶ λιμός).

[11] David 1989, 12.

[12] *Cleomenes* 9.1.

[13] David mentions 'special sanctuaries', while Garland (1985, 59), referring to *Cleomenes* 9, declares that Sparta's temple to Death is unique ('Only once, at Sparta, do we hear of a temple being erected to him'). But in fact nothing indicates that there was a temple of Death. Mactoux (1993, 262–3) points out that 'the *hieron* of Phobos at Sparta is...in the current state of our knowledge, the only Greek sanctuary of Phobos'.

[14] See e.g. Rudhardt 1992, e.g. 23 and 26.

[15] Plutarch, *Cleomenes* 8.3–4.

[16] Callisthenes *ap.* Athenaeus 10.452a–b: γύναιον...διὰ γραφῆς ἀπομεμιμημένος Λιμὸς ἔχων γυναικὸς μορφήν ('*gynaion*... Hunger, represented by a painting, in the form of a woman').

[17] Polyaenus 2.15: ἀνακειμένη Λιμοῦ γραφή, γυνή...

[18] Plutarch, *Lycurgus* 25.4.

[19] Pausanias 3.18.1.

[20] Pausanias 3.20.10.

[21] Pausanias 3.25.5.

[22] Wide 1893, 252.

[23] 1884–6, 1343.

[24] According to Athenaeus 13.561e–f, 'The Lacedaemonians offer preliminary sacrifices to Erōs before the battle-line is drawn up, with the idea that safety and victory lies in the friendship of the men in line; and Sosikrates reports that the Cretans, having placed the most beautiful of the citizens in the lines, sacrifice via their intermediary to Erōs.'

[25] On Phobos at Sparta, see Mactoux 1993 and Richer 1998a, 219–24.

[26] On Aidōs, see Eckstein (1981, 351–3), who recalls Aidōs' nuances and the different associations she is subject to in literature. We can add to the bibliography, in addition to the references given by Nafissi (1991, 122), Riedinger 1980, Ferrari 1990, and Cairns' studies (1993, 1996a and b), as well as that of Lévy 1995. A particular case of abstraction is Limos, Hunger or Famine (unknown to Wide), who, according to Callisthenes (*FGrH* 124 F 13) cited by Athenaeus (10.452b), is represented in painting in the temple of Apollo at Amyclae in the form of a woman (Λιμὸς ἔχων γυναικὸς μορφήν) when the word is generally of masculine gender; according to Polyaenus (2.15), it is in the sanctuary of Athena Chalkioikos that a painting representing Limos had been dedicated, with the features of a woman, her hands tied behind her back (ἀνακειμένη Λιμοῦ γραφή, γυνή...τὼ χεῖρε ὀπίσω δεδεμένη). The procedure would be truly exceptional (cf. Shapiro 1976, 24 and 25 n. 38; 1993, 27 and n. 48) if Limos was never a feminine word, but this is in fact sometimes the case (cf. e.g. *Homeric Hymn to Demeter* 311; Aristophanes, *Acharnians* 743). On

the question of the gender of terms designating abstractions such as Limos or Eleos (Pity), see Stafford 1998.

[27] See e.g. Jost 1992, 105. On the altar of Aidōs on the Athenian Acropolis, cf. Pausanias 1.17.1 (and *KP* I, 1965 col. 154–5); Eustathius (*ad Iliadem* 10.451) specifies that the same altar was equally dedicated to Apheleia, Simplicity, Aidōs and Apheleia being characteristics of Athena; cf. also Hesychios s.v. Αἰδοῦς Βωμός, who mentions altars of Aidōs and of Philia on the Athenian Acropolis.

[28] Mactoux (1993, 271) considers that 'Phobos was just a denomination of *Aidōs*', 'a very ancient goddess' mentioned by Hesiod (*Works and Days* 200).

[29] 1990, 206.

[30] This form of *aidōs* is present at Sparta; it is indicated by Plutarch (*Lycurgus* 14.7) when he is talking about the young girls' gymnastic exercises and formulating a justificatory argument: he mentions their nudity which 'had nothing disgraceful about it, for modesty accompanied it, and wantonness was absent' (ἡ δὲ γύμνωσις τῶν παρθένων οὐδὲν αἰσχρὸν εἶχεν, αἰδοῦς μὲν παρούσης, ἀκρασίας δ' ἀπούσης). Plutarch may on this matter have been inspired (in a general way) by Xenophon (*Constitution of the Lacedaemonians* 3.5).

[31] Pausanias 3.20.10–11. A French translation of this text is given by Mactoux 1975, 2 n. 1.

[32] Wide 1893, 270.

[33] On such a hypothesis cf. Mactoux 1975, 211-12.

[34] Musti and Torelli 1991, ad loc.

[35] Wide 1893, 270.

[36] The cult of Hades is rarely attested elsewhere in Greece; it is known for example at Elis (Pausanias 6.25.2–3), in Triphylia (Strabo 8.3.14; p. 344); at Coroneia in Boeotia, Hades is associated with Athena (Strabo 9.2.29; p. 411); cf. Pausanias 2.35.9–10, on Klymenos who reigned underground and the *gēs chasma* at Hermione. On the entrance to the realm of Hades at Cape Taenaron in Lakonia, see e.g. Pindar, *Pythian* 4.79; Pausanias 3.25.5; other references, Wide 1893, 242–3.

[37] The weakness of the basis of this theory is pointed out by Ziehen 1929, col. 1456.

[38] Wide (1893, 4, 7, 243) retains only the reading ΔΕΥΣ (Zeus).

[39] Tod and Wace 1906, 72 and 195 (fig. 69; no. 600); *IG* V.1.214 (reading ẠΙΔΕΥΣ, in 1913).

[40] See Hibler 1992, 121, n. 28. La Genière (1986, 35–7 and fig. 5) would like to see a Cybele in the figure represented, because, according to her, 'nothing obliges us to close our eyes in front of the obviously female features of this statuette, in its heavy maturity, evocative of maternity' (cf. also La Genière 1993, 154–5 and fig. 1).

[41] The best known of these reliefs is that from Chrysapha (Berlin, Staat. Mus. 731), dating from the middle or third quarter of the sixth century; see e.g. Hooker 1980, fig. 39; Fitzhardinge 1980, 80 fig. 94; Nafissi 1991, pl. 7b; Rolley 1994, 238–40 and fig. 237.

[42] Andronicos 1956 (the statue bearing the inscription ΑΙΔΕΥΣ is reproduced p. 291 pl. 8).

43 Stibbe 1978. *Contra* Le Roy 1982, 282 n. 14.

44 Salapata 1993.

45 Hibler 1992, 121 n. 28; cf. also La Genière 1986, 35 and n. 43 (curiously, La Genière presents the reading ΔΕΥΣ (Treu, *Arch. Zeitung* 40, 1882, 76) as being more recent than the reading ΑΙΔΕΥΣ (Tod and Wace 1906, 72)). La Genière considers that the inscription 'can be dated at the earliest to the late fourth century' (1993, 154).

46 On the fact that the type of iconography in question has assumed different values over time, cf. Salapata 1993 and Hibler 1993. The vitality of the iconography under discussion is still attested in the hellenistic period: see Le Roy 1982.

47 Hibler 1992, 116, 119, 121.

48 It is exactly this gesture which led Schultz (1910, 98–9) to recognise in the Aidōs mentioned by Pausanias a *Demeter lugens*, Pausanias' description being susceptible of comparison with a passage in the *Homeric Hymn to Demeter* (v. 199) where the goddess pulls a veil across her face with her hand. In fact the Greek says 'the hands' (χερσί) and this gesture does not correspond to the Lakonian stelai, but 1) it might be a question of the poetic plural; 2) an Eleusinian text is not a Lakonian stele.

49 It is notable that, without comparing Pausanias' text on Aidōs with the Lakonian hero-reliefs, Salapata (1993, 190) mentions the '*anakalypsis* gesture' of the female *paredros* of the hero with the kantharos. We shall not concern ourselves here with the manner in which a gesture of unveiling has sometimes been interpreted as its opposite; on the problem see Andronicos 1956, 288–9; Cairns 1996b, 155 n. 32. On the gesture of unveiling by Persephone in front of her husband, see Chamoux 1953, 300 n. 4, but the metope of Temple E (so-called of Hera) of Selinous is interpreted in various ways: if it is not a '*Hierogamos* of Gargaros' (cf. *Iliad* 14.292–351), it is no more certain that it shows a *hierogamos* of Deo-Persephone and Dionysos-Hades (Picard 1939, 131 and fig. 64). Simon (1969, 54 and fig. 44) sees in the same representation the 'sacred marriage of Zeus and Hera' and compares it particularly with the representation of Hera Teleia presented on the Parthenon frieze (fig. 45); the gesture of unveiling is closely associated with marriage (p. 53). On Zeus Teleios and Hera Teleia, see Séchan and Lévêque 1966, 93 n. 87.

50 We could suggest that this reinterpretation was able to establish itself at least in part because of the existence of a fifth-century statue-type called 'Penelope', the name of the woman represented being certain (see Boardman 1985, 51 and figs. 24–6; cf. also Hausmann 1994 and Cairns 1996b, 155 and n. 37). If it is doubtful that the Lakonian statue called 'Penelope' was descended from this type of Attic origin (the original dated to *c.* 460), an *aition* like that recorded by Pausanias could have developed on the basis of the themes maintained by this type of statue. The reserve of which Boardman thinks when examining this type is naturally that of the wife patiently awaiting Odysseus' return and not that of a young woman who is renouncing her father in order to follow her husband. Nevertheless, this type is remarkable, as far as we are concerned, because of the fact that Penelope is represented with a veil on her head, her face being visible, as we also see the female faces in

the representations of the Lakonian hero-reliefs. We can add that a representation of the type known from the hero-reliefs, with its lower part removed, could easily have been interpreted as representing Odysseus and Penelope side by side in the body of a chariot, in accord with the representation suggested by Pausanias. However this may be, since the Lakonian hero-reliefs representing a couple all date at the latest to the first half of the fifth century (see Hibler 1993, 200–1), with the exception of one archaising sculpture (Sparta Museum no. 4), it is probable that the representation referred to by Pausanias can thus be dated as being from *c.* 450 at the latest (Salapata 1993, 190, remarks that the representation of the heroic couple continues after this date only on terracotta plaques).

[51] Salapata 1993, 194.

[52] Cf. Salapata 1993, 194.

[53] Hani (1992, 65) stresses that the name Aidōs given to a statue proves that Aidōs was honoured with a cult.

[54] On the Spartan nationality of Ikarios cf. Mactoux 1975, 203–6.

[55] Pausanias (3.15.11) describes as such a reinterpretation of another female statue, in cedarwood, representing Aphrodite under the name Morphō: the image was veiled and had fetters around its feet. Pausanias thinks childish the explanation given of this representation according to which Tyndareus wanted to avenge himself on the goddess for the shame of his daughters Helen and Clytaimnestra by making a statue and calling it Aphrodite, but he retains the first, more general, explanation provided, according to which the statue symbolised (cf. ἀφομοιοῦντα) the fidelity which wives owe to their husbands. In her analysis of the passage, Pirenne-Delforge (1994, 201) considers that 'the *aition* in question could refer to a strict regulation of the sexuality of girls, confined to the role of [wives] and mother[s]'.

[56] Plutarch speaks of the reserve and the order brought into marriage by Lycurgus (ἐπιστήσας αἰδῶ καὶ τάξιν, *Lycurgus* 15.11).

[57] On marriage *en bru* at Sparta, see Leduc 1991, 279–80. It is pointed out (ib. 269) that the archetype of the bride given *en bru* (*ktētē gunē*) is furnished by...Penelope.

[58] Aristotle, *Politics* 2.9.11, 1270a6–8. Cf. Plato, *Laws* 6, 781a and 7, 804e–805b. The reproach of this failure appears sufficiently serious to Plutarch for him to deny the lacuna in Lycurgus' work (*Lycurgus* 14.2), all the while contradicting himself elsewhere (*Numa* 25.5–9). On the links between the lack of regulation attributed to women and their facility to possess land, see Hodkinson 1986, 82–95, as well as Ducat 1983, who notes (165) the 'passionate background' of the Aristotelian reproach.

[59] Aristotle, *Politics* 2.9.5, 1269b12. Aristotle considers the importance of women in Lacedaemonian life in the fourth century, but the reproach which he addresses to the law-giver turns on a feature which in his understanding is structural. The Lacedaemonian practice, consisting in supervising women very little, is also pointed out by Hesychios (Λακωνικὸν τρόπον· ἥκιστα γὰρ φυλάττουσι Λάκωνες τὰς γυναῖκας). Ducat (1983, 161) considers that the theme of Spartan women's licence 'could well have their legal status as its real origin...and their activities in the economic field'.

[60] Cairns 1993, *passim*; cf. also Riedinger 1980 and Lévy 1995, especially 196–210.

[61] Pausanias 3.20.11.

[62] Cf. Helen in Homer, who, seized by 'gentle desire for her first husband' (*Iliad* 3.139–40), veils herself (καλυψαμένη, v.141) in order to cry (v.142), before declaring herself seized by reserve (αἰδοῖος, *Iliad* 3.172) in front of Priam, while invoking her tears (v.176).

[63] It is often admitted that Demaratos, king of Sparta deposed in 491 (Herodotus 6.67), could have fulfilled the functions of an ephor (see How and Wells 1912, ad loc., and Richer 1998, 526 n. 8).

[64] Herodotus 6.67: κατακαλυψάμενος, *katakalupsamenos* ('having covered his head'). Leotychidas wanted to make people laugh (ἐπι γέλωτι) at Demaratos' expense by posing him an insulting question through the medium of his servant (how does the position of magistrate [cf. τὸ ἄρχειν, *to archein*] feel after that of king?); it seems worthy of note that the only other occurrence of the same expression in the *Histories* appears at the moment where Herodotus recounts (9.82) how the Spartan Pausanias has a meal prepared in the Lakonian fashion in order to demonstrate the contrast between such a meal and the usual meal of the Medes 'who, having the means to live as' the spectators could see, had come to attack the Spartans in order to take away from them the little on which they lived. It is perhaps not too hazardous to imagine that the expression in question is picked up from Lakonian vocabulary and that this usage translates a social practice applied for religious reasons: one invokes Gelōs as one can also do when forging a γελοῖον, i.e., according to Delcourt (1957, 113–14), an object which 'obliges people to laugh' and leads to the breaking of an evil spell, a state of stupour or of passivity. A similar interpretation is allowed by Mactoux (1993, 287) who, while recalling the practices of aischrology, calls to minds 'the liberating laughter of the gods which resolves contradictions in situations of crisis'.

[65] On Laughter at Sparta and elsewhere, see Steuding 1890, Waser 1910, Vollkommer 1988. David (1989) notably envisages the different aspects of laughter (defensive, aggressive, expressing a sentiment of superiority, the wish to produce a reinforcement of the cohesion of those who laugh by excluding from their group the victims of laughter...); on the rationalisation which is characteristic of Plutarch's depictions, see David 1989, 2. It seems neat that Plutarch (*Cleomenes* 9.2) also rationalises Fear: see Epps 1933, 23–4: the author considers that the lengthy presentation of the place occupied by fear in the government of Sparta reveals Plutarch's embarrassment on this point which is unfavourable for Sparta's image.

[66] *Cleomenes* 9.1.

[67] In *Cleomenes* 9.1, Plutarch puts the *hiera* of Phobos, Thanatos and Gelōs on the same level, but elsewhere (*Lycurgus* 25.4), citing the Lakonian Sosibios (*FGrH* 595 F 19) who lived in the third century BC, he only speaks of a little statue of Laughter (τοῦ Γέλωτος ἀγαλμάτιον); I am inclined to think that this last, more precise, reference is worth retaining. Piccirilli (in Manfredini and Piccirilli 1980, 274) considers that the work of Sosibios from which Plutarch is drawing his information is the 'Περὶ τῶν ἐν Λακεδαίμονι θυσίων'; this opinion

is followed by David (1989, n. 5).

[68] We should not deny that, in certain cases, Laughter could be conceived at Sparta as a spontaneous manifestation of joy, as a moulded vase in the Louvre Museum shows (CA 2157), dating from *c.* 570 and in which a laughing face and a phallos are associated (Pasquier 1982, especially 289 (reproduction) and 304–6). But otherwise David (1989, 2, 14 and 17) points out that, as with the usage of terror (and of death), that of laughter served towards the consolidation of social order (and Mactoux 1993, 285, approves this opinion, which it would in fact be difficult to argue against). In fact, mockery seems fairly widespread at Sparta: the mockery of young girls criticises young men (Plutarch, *Lycurgus* 14.5) and other mockeries are exchanged between youths, and the importance of their role (they express a mutual control of individuals) is underlined by the attention which the older men pay to them (Plutarch, *Lycurgus* 17.1: 'the older men, for their part, watched [the young men] even more, often visiting the gymnasia and being present when they fought and exchanged taunts with one another' (μαχομένοις καὶ σκώπτουσιν ἀλλήλους)); men over thirty years of age would also embellish their conversations 'with pleasantries and jokes' (μετὰ παιδιᾶς καὶ γέλωτος) which helped warnings and criticisms pass by under a light banter' (Plutarch, *Lycurgus* 25.3). For a discussion of the concept of 'shame-culture' applied to Greece from Dodds onwards, see Cairns 1993, 27–47.

[69] I am all the more inclined to think that the function of archon exercised by Demaratos must have been the *ephoreia* because in this episode Demaratos is victim of Leotychidas' desire to make people laugh at his expense (ἐπὶ γέλωτι); to my thinking the episode would only have had more point in Spartan eyes if Demaratos had been, as ephor, individually or not, an official of the cult of Laughter. Whatever the case, David (1989, 16) points out that it is the fact of being made a laughing-stock, and not of being deposed, which decided Demaratos to go into exile; this indicates the importance of the torture that mockery could be at Sparta. Moreover, the way in which the Lacedaemonians tried to recapture Demaratos (Herodotus 6.70), the former king, when he went to consult Delphi – which kings consult – seems to indicate that the individual occupied an important place at Sparta at the time of his flight; it could also indicate that he was an ephor.

[70] In the absence of a spirit of repartee, a Spartiate who could not endure the mockery could ask for it to cease (Plutarch, *Lycurgus* 12.6–7).

[71] An attitude close to that of Demaratos is on two occasions that of Odysseus. When Demodokos sings, Odysseus veils his face, out of *aidōs*, to hide his tears (κάλυψε δὲ καλὰ πρόσωπα· | αἴδετο γάρ..., *Odyssey* 8, 85–6; καλυψάμενος, v. 92). Elsewhere Odysseus adopts an attitude indicating a state of caution, refusal to rush into things, when the winds carry him away after his companions have unleashed them close to Ithaca (*Odyssey* 10.53–5: 'wrapped in my cloak I lay on board (καλυψάμενος δ' ἐνὶ νηὶ | κείμην), while...my men lamented'. Cairns (1996b, 155) notes that in iconography Achilles lamenting the loss of Briseis and Ajax having failed to win the arms of Achilles are also represented with their faces veiled, a fact which would emphasise their anger: we might rather say that it is primarily (and not secondarily, as Cairns

suggests) a way of emphasising the humiliation felt by these characters. A comparison would perhaps also be possible between the attitude adopted by Demaratos and that eventually taken up by the Romans, covering the head when learning a misfortune (on the iconography of the Roman Pudicitia, see Cairns 1996b, 154 and n. 31).

[72] Parker (1989, n. 5) considers more simply that the point of the anecdote must be sought in the fact that the king Leotychidas is in possession of the power of *proedria* (Herodotus 6.57) while Demaratos is now deprived of it.

[73] And it seems possible to me to see an illustration of the power of Aidōs at Sparta in David's study 'Sparta and the power of silence' (this volume).

[74] Cf. the way in which his *aidōs* compels Hector to fight (*Iliad* 6.441–2 and the remarks of Cairns 1993, 79–83, where he points out that the hero must respond to the expectations of the society he lives in; cf. also Lévy 1995, 198 and n. 132).

[75] On the importance of Aidōs in the social psychology of Homeric heroes, see e.g. von Erffa 1937, Verdenius 1945, Lévy 1995.

[76] Plutarch seems very close to this position when he declares (*Cleomenes* 9.6) in connection with Phobos that an author (not specified) was right to say that 'where there is fear, there respect is also' (ἵνα γὰρ δέος, ἔνθα καὶ αἰδώς). For the nuance rendered by the verb αἰδεῖσθαι, see Plutarch *Moralia* 7e: δεῖ τοὺς θεοὺς σέβεσθαι, γονέας τιμᾶν, πρεσβυτέρους αἰδεῖσθαι ('we must revere the gods, honour our parents, respect our elders').

[77] *Laws* 1.647a.

[78] i.e. the fear of opinion, of δόξα.

[79] According to Thucydides (1.23.6) 'the truest cause' of the Peloponnesian War was the fear (*phobos*) inspired in the Spartans by the Athenians; further on, in the presentation of Spartan qualities placed by the same Thucydides in the mouth of king Archidamos (1.84.3), it is *aidōs* which appears, in company with *sōphrosynē* (1.84.1). Moreover, *aidōs* tends, in the fourth century, to be replaced by *sōphrosynē*, as Lévy (1995, 193 n. 98) points out when considering the differences between the myth of Protagoras and its commentary 'written in a less archaic language ' (Plato, *Protagoras* 322c–d, 323a–b and 329c). In the same sense, we can highlight that the only *pathēma* absent from the biography of Agesilaus written by Xenophon is precisely *aidōs*, while the individual is characterised by his *sōphrosynē* (*Agesilaus* 5.7 and cf. 11.10); cf. Richer 1998b, 24–6.

[80] Plutarch, *Moralia* 217a.

[81] Plutarch, *Moralia* 231e–f; translation inspired by that of Fuhrmann.

[82] For this is the primary sense of Phobos: 'After Homer, by a well known type of metonymy (the consequence for the antecedent) φοβεῖσθαι "to flee" acquired the sense "to be afraid" ' (Chantraine 1968–80, s.v. φέβομαι).

[83] Plutarch, *Lycurgus* 22.9–10 and *Moralia* 228f; cf. also e.g. Thucydides 5.73.4, Pausanias 4.8.11, Polyaenus 1.16.3. The principle might have been formulated by Cleomenes after the victory over the Argives at Sepeia (*Moralia* 224b): 'We would not want to wipe them out completely, so as to always have trainers available for our youth.' A similar saying is attributed to the ephors in unspecified circumstances (*Moralia* 233d). David (1989, n. 23) refers to other sayings characterised by the same spirit of superiority.

[84] Diogenes Laertius 1.70.
[85] Plutarch, *Moralia* 225d.
[86] Fuhrmann 1988.
[87] Cf. e.g. Herodotus 7.225 (for Leonidas at Thermopylae), Plutarch, *Agesilaos* 18.5 (for Agesilaos at Koroneia in 394), Xenophon, *Hellenica* 5.4.33 and 6.4.13–14, as well as Pausanias 9.13.10 (for Kleombrotos at Leuctra).
[88] Fuhrmann 1988, 331, n. 5.
[89] An ambiguity remains: are the soldiers frightened of the enemy or of their own leaders? The first response has simplicity and its natural character in its favour, and we could then consider that Pausanias' words (4.16.4) are marked by a scathing irony when he says of the Spartans engaged in the second Messenian war that they 'fled quite without reserve' (οὐχὶ σὺν αἰδοῖ φευγόντων): not only were they the victims of Phobos but they no longer even respected Aidōs; in Sophocles' *Ajax*, v. 1076 (the play was produced after 438), it is Phobos and Aidōs who maintain the discipline of a Lacedaemonian army. On Pausanias' partiality in favour of the Messenians, in the account he gives of the Messenian wars, see Auberger 1992. But the second possibility seems to me to be far from excluded: an analogous idea is made explicit in Herodotus (7.104) in the mouth of Demaratos speaking to Xerxes: the Lacedaemonians 'have a master, the law, of whom they stand in much greater awe than your subjects do of you' (ἔπεστι γάρ σφι δεσπότης νόμος, τὸν ὑποδειμαίνουσι πολλῷ ἔτι μᾶλλον ἢ οἱ σοὶ σέ). Naturally, this would suggest that fear of the leader is not absent from Sparta; this seems to be confirmed by the saying of Leonidas and also by the importance of the powers of the king commanding the army, attested by Herodotus 6.56, Xenophon, *Constitution of the Lacedaemonians* 13, and Aristotle who calls the king a *stratēgos autokratōr* (*Politics* 3.14.4, 1285a7–8). Carlier (1984, 257–65) clearly demonstrates the extent of the Lacedaemonian king's powers over his army on campaign.
[90] The same principle appears elsewhere: the Lacedaemonian *stratēgos* Klearchos, who died in 401, it was said, 'used to assert that the soldier must fear his leader more than the enemy' (καὶ λέγειν αὐτὸν ἔφασαν ὡς δέοι τὸν στρατιώτην φοβεῖσθαι μᾶλλον τὸν ἄρχοντα ἢ τοὺς πολεμίους), after Xenophon, *Anabasis* 2.6.10, and cf. 14.
[91] See, e.g., the fact that, according to Pausanias (3.11.10), the ephors used a seal with his image.
[92] Fuhrmann 1988, 331, n. 5. In support of his opinion, the editor of the CUF recalls also (p. 321, n. 3 ad p. 172) the existence of an anonymous maxim (similar in fact to that attributed to Chilon): Αἱροῦ μᾶλλον τοὺς συνόντας σοι αἰδεῖσθαί σε ἢ φοβεῖσθαι (*Gnomol. Byzant.* (Wachsmuth), 78): 'Prefer that those around you respect you than that they fear you' (my translation). But this is a theme susceptible of many variations.
[93] On the problem of the authenticity of the attributions ascribed to the Spartan sayings, see Tigerstedt 1974, 16–30. In this case, the differences in the formulations in question seem to me to preserve a probable development in the concepts known at Sparta.
[94] It is notable that Demaratos, asserting to Xerxes the fear that their master the law inspires in Lacedaemonians, says that they fear it like a *daimōn*

(δεσπότης νόμος, τὸν ὑποδειμαίνουσι), according to Herodotus 7.104. We might remember the fact that a lexically close term is found in a letter from Chilon to Periander, according to Diogenes Laertius 1.73: Chilon says that he considers fortunate (εὐδαιμονίζω) the tyrant who dies in his bed.

[95] Thucydides 1.69.2—71.4; here 70.3. On Spartan analysis of the Spartan temperament, see Demont 1990, 211–14.

[96] Above n. 58.

[97] On the problem of the Spartan 'law-giver' mentioned by Aristotle, see Richer 1998, 58–9.

[98] We will not stress the links between Aidōs and Dikē here; παρθένος γὰρ Αἰδοῦς Δίκη says Plato (*Laws* 12, 943e) referring to Hesiod (*Works and Days* 256–7); the myth of Protagoras also well emphasises the role of these two concepts in allowing the establishment of harmony and creative links of friendship within cities (Plato, *Protagoras* 322c–d). Perhaps Plato is remembering here the place attributed to Aidōs in Sparta for allowing *eunomia*. In the *Eumenides*, vv. 515–16, Aeschylus clearly places fear in relationship with justice.

[99] *Constitution of the Lacedaemonians* 3.4.

[100] And Xenophon takes up the idea, in his commentary (*Const. Lac.* 3.5), by the verb τὸ σωφρονεῖν; on the procedure see above n. 79.

[101] *Const. Lac.* 3.5.; cf. also *Const. Lac.* 2.10 in connection with *paides*.

[102] Riedinger 1980.

[103] Riedinger 1980, 78–9.

[104] Riedinger (1980, 66) points out that 'within the group of combatants there is also a reciprocal aidōs (*Il.* 5.531 = 15.561)' and he emphasises (p. 67) that in the *Odyssey* 'a womanly αἰδώς seems to appear (*Od.* 8.324, 18.184) and more particularly an αἰδώς of the wife (16.75), of the young girl (6.66), of the young man (3.14 and 24), even of the beggar (17.347, 352; cf. also 578)'.

[105] *Symposion* 8.35; my translation.

[106] It is not out of the question to think that it may be the same idea that Xenophon also mentions when, immediately before talking of the way in which the young boys are imbued with *aidōs*, he notes (*Const. Lac.* 3.3) that 'those who care (τοὺς κηδομένους) for each' watch that the *paidiskoi* are never despised for their conduct; cf. also, e.g., *Hellenika* 5.4.33.

[107] For many of the *pathēmata* have an obvious military importance, like Limos (and Dipsa if she exists) and Thanatos, as well as Erōs who rules relationships between combatants. Nevertheless, it is clear that the female sex must be subject at least to the rules of Aidōs and Erōs. Moreover, we read in Plutarch, *Moralia* 239c, 'the religious ceremonies were common to both girls and boys' (κόραις καὶ κόροις κοινὰ τὰ ἱερά).

[108] Cf. Richer 1998a, 230–2, and 1998b, 22–4.

[109] *Cleomenes* 9.1.

[110] Cf. Hani 1992.

[111] Pausanias 3.11.11.

[112] The Athenians, who worshipped the Hestia present in their Prytaneion (Pausanias 1.18.3), also knew Aidōs (Pausanias 1.17.1, and cf. above n. 27, but we do not have an Athenian equivalent to the *aition* related by Pausanias

3.20.10–11), Erōs (Pausanias 1.30.1, but it is not before battle, as far as we know, that the Athenians sacrificed to him), Hypnos and Thanatos (see e.g. Euphronios' krater dating from 515/10, which represents the carrying off of Sarpedon, Metropolitan Museum, New York 1972.11.10; on the history of the theme see e.g. Ramnoux 1986, 50 n. 29; a collection of Attic representations of Hypnos and Thanatos is analysed by Frontisi-Ducroux 1995, 81–94 and figs. 23–41; see also Sourvinou-Inwood 1995, 326–7); the Athenians also knew Limos, sometimes called Boulimos: beside the Athenian Prytaneion there was an area sacred to him (Zenobios 4.93; Diogenianos 6.13; Hesychios s.v.; *Anecdota Graeca* I p. 278, 4), the same *pathēma* being known by the inhabitants of Chaeroneia who practised his expulsion once a year (Plutarch, *Moralia* 693f). We do not know, however, of religious feeling at Athens towards Gelōs (apart from attaching comic drama to him?) or towards Phobos, the most important of the Spartan *pathēmata* (we could simply note the representations on some vases, where Phobos is generally represented as a chariot-driver: see Shapiro 1993, 208–15).

[113] *Lycurgus* 16.10; cf. also *Moralia* 237a. Plutarch may be inspired by Xenophon, *Const. Lac.* 2, where the education of children is described to a great extent from the point of view of the *pathēmata*: cf. Richer 1998a, 227.

[114] Finley 1986, p. 165.

Bibliography

Andronicos, M.

1956 ' Λακωνικά Ανάγλυφα ', Πελοποννησιακά I, 253–314.

Auberger, J.

1992 'Pausanias et les Messéniens: une histoire d'amour!' *REA* 94, 187–97.

Bailly, A. and Egger, E.

1963 *Dictionnaire grec-français*, rev. edn Séchan, L. and Chantraine, P., Paris.

Boardman, J.

1985 *Greek Sculpture. The Classical Period*, London.

Bruneau, Ph. and Ducat, J.

1983 *Guide de Délos*[3], Athens and Paris.

Cairns, D.L.

1993 *Aidōs. The psychology and ethics of honour and shame in ancient Greek literature*, Oxford.

1996a '*Hybris*, dishonour, and thinking big', *JHS* 116, 1–32 (critical review of Fisher 1992).

1996b 'Veiling, αἰδώς and a red-figure amphora by Phintias', *JHS* 116, 152–8.

Carlier, P.

1984 *La Royauté en Grèce avant Alexandre*, Strasbourg.

Cartledge, P.A.

1980 'The peculiar position of Sparta in the development of the Greek city-state', *Proceedings of the Royal Irish Academy* 80c.6, 91–108.

Chamoux, F.
1953 *Cyrène sous la monarchie des Battiades*, Paris.
Chantraine, P., et al.
1968–80 *Dictionnaire étymologique de la langue grecque*, Paris.
David, E.
1989 'Laughter in Spartan society', in A. Powell (ed.) *Classical Sparta: Techniques behind her success*, London, 1–25.
Delcourt, M.
1982 *Héphaistos ou la légende du magicien*, (Liège 1957) 2nd edn, Paris.
Demont, P.
1990 *La Cité grecque archaïque et classique et l'idéal de tranquillité*, Paris.
Ducat, J.
1983 'Le Citoyen et le sol à Sparte à l'époque classique', *Hommage à Maurice Bordes = Annales de la Faculté des Lettres et Sciences Humaines de Nice* 45, 143–66.
1990 *Les Hilotes, BCH* Suppl. 20, Paris.
Eckstein, F.
1981 s.v. 'Aidos', *LIMC* I, 351–3.
Epps, P.H.
1933 'Fear in Spartan character', *CPh* 28, 12–29.
Erffa, C.E. von
1937 ΑΙΔΩΣ *und verwandte Begriffe in ihrer Entwicklung von Homer bis Demokrit = Philologus* Suppl. 30.2.
Ferrari, G.
1990 'Figures of speech: the picture of *Aidos*', ΜΗΤΙΣ 5.1–2, 185–204
Finley, M.I.
1968 'Sparta', in J.-P. Vernant (ed.) *Problèmes de la Guerre en Grèce ancienne*, Paris and La Haye, 2nd edn 1985, 143–60; repr. 1981 as 'Sparta and Spartan Society', in *Economy and Society in Ancient Greece*, London, ch. 2. Also appears as 'Sparta', in *Use and Abuse of History*, London 1986, 161–77.
Fisher, N.R.E.
1992 *Hybris: A study in the values of honour and shame in Ancient Greece*, Warminster.
Fitzhardinge, L.F.
1980 *The Spartans*, London.
Fuhrmann, F.
1988 Plutarque, *Œuvres morales* III, Paris (CUF).
Frontisi-Ducroux, F.
1995 *Du Masque au Visage. Aspects de l'identité en Grèce ancienne*, Paris.
Furtwängler, A.
1884–6 s.v. 'Eros', in Roscher, *Ausführliches Lexikon der griechischen und römischen Mythologie*, Leipzig.
Garland, R.
1985 *The Greek Way of Death*, London.
Hani, J.
1980 'Aidôs personnifiée et sa portée réelle chez les Grecs', in J. Duchemin

(ed.) *Mythe et Personnification: travaux et mémoires (Actes du colloque du Grand Palais, Paris, 7–8 Mai 1977)*, Paris, 103–12. Text slightly modified as 'Les "abstractions personnifiées" et les origines du polythéisme', in *Mythes, rites et symboles*, Paris 1992, 61–72.

Hausmann, C.

1994 s.v. 'Penelope', *LIMC* VII, 291–5.

Hibler, D.

1992 'Three reliefs from Sparta', in J.M. Sanders (ed.) ΦΙΛΟΛΑΚΩΝ. *Lakonian Studies in honour of Hector Catling*, Athens, 115–22.

1993 'The Hero-Reliefs of Laconia: changes in form and function', in O. Palagia and W. Coulson (eds.) *Sculpture from Arcadia and Laconia*, Oxford, 199–204.

Hodkinson, S.

1986 'Land tenure and inheritance in Classical Sparta', *CQ* 80 = n.s. 36, 378–406.

1989 'Inheritance, marriage and demography: perspectives upon the success and decline of classical Sparta', in A. Powell (ed.) *Classical Sparta: Techniques behind her success*, London, 79–121.

1997 'The development of Spartan society and institutions in the archaic period', in P.J. Rhodes and L.G. Mitchell (eds.) *The Development of the Polis in Archaic Greece*, London, 83–102.

Hooker, J.T.

1980 *The Ancient Spartans*, London, Toronto and Melbourne.

How, W.W. and Wells, J.

1912 *A Commentary on Herodotus*, 2 vols., 2nd edn, Oxford.

Jost, M.

1992 *Aspects de la vie religieuse en Grèce du début du Ve siècle à la fin du IIIe siècle avant J.-C.*, Paris.

La Genière, J. de

1986 'Le culte de la mère des dieux dans le Péloponnèse', *CRAI*, 29–48.

1993 'Statuaire archaïque de la mère des dieux en Arcadie et en Laconie', in O. Palagia and W. Coulson (eds.) *Sculpture from Arcadia and Laconia*, Oxford, 153–8.

Le Roy, Ch.

1982 'Variation hellénistique sur un thème ancien: à propos d'un "relief héroique" de Gytheion', *Mélanges Metzger, RA*, 279–90.

Leduc, Cl.

1991 'Comment la donner en mariage? La mariée en pays grec (IXᵉ–IVᵉ s. av. J.-C.)', in G. Duby and M. Perrot (eds.) *Histoire des femmes* I (P. Schmitt Pantel ed.), Paris, ch. V.

Lévy, E.

1995 '*Arétè, Timè, Aidôs* et *Némésis*: le modèle homérique', *Ktèma* 20, 177–211.

Mactoux, M.-M.

1975 *Pénélope. Légende et mythe.* Annales littéraires de l'Université de Besançon, 175.

1993 'Phobos à Sparte', *RHR* 210.3, 259–304.

Manfredini, M. and Piccirilli, L.
1980 *Plutarco. Le Vite di Licurgo e di Numa*, Milan.
Musti, D. and Torelli, M.
1991 *Pausania. Guida della Grecia. Libro III. La Laconia*, Milan.
Nafissi, M.
1991 *La nascità del* kosmos. *Studi sulla storia e la società di Sparta*, Perugia.
Parker, R.
1989 'Spartan religion', in A. Powell (ed.) *Classical Sparta: Techniques behind her success*, London, 142–72.
Pasquier, A.
1982 'Deux objets laconiens méconnus au Musée du Louvre', *BCH* 106, 281–306.
Picard, Ch.
1939 *Manuel d'archéologie grecque* II, Paris.
Pirenne-Delforge, V.
1994 *L'Aphrodite grecque. Contribution à l'étude de ses cultes et de sa personnalité dans le panthéon archaïque et classique* (= *Kernos* Suppl. 4), Athens and Liège.
Ramnoux, C.
1986 *La Nuit et les enfants de la Nuit dans la tradition grecque*[2], Paris.
Richer, N.
1998a *Les Éphores. Études sur l'histoire et sur l'image de Sparte, VIIIe–IIIe siècle avant Jésus-Christ*, Paris.
1998b 'Des citoyens maîtres d'eux-mêmes: l'*eukosmon* de Sparte archaïque et classique', *Cahiers du Centre Gustave-Glotz* 9, 7–36.
Riedinger, J.-Cl.
1980 'Les deux αἰδώς chez Homère', *RPH* 54.1, 62–79.
Rolley, Cl.
1994 *La sculpture grecque. 1. Des origines au milieu du Ve siècle*, Paris.
Rudhardt, J.
1992 *Notions fondamentales de la pensée religieuse et actes constitutifs du culte dans la Grèce classique*, (Geneva 1958), 2nd edn, Paris.
Salapata, G.
1993 'The Lakonian hero reliefs in the light of the terracotta plaques', in O. Palagia and W. Coulson (eds.) *Sculpture from Arcadia and Laconia*, Oxford, 189–97.
Schultz, R.
1910 Αἰδώς, Diss. Rostock.
Séchan, L. and Lévêque, P.
1990 *Les grandes divinités de la Grèce*, (1966), 2nd edn, Paris.
Shapiro, H.A.
1976 *Personification of Abstract Concepts in Greek Art and Literature to the end of the fifth century* BC, Diss. Princeton. Revised 1993 as *Personifications in Greek Art: The representation of abstract concepts 600–400* BC, Zurich.
Simon, E.
1969 *Die Götter der Griechen*, Munich.

Sourvinou-Inwood, C.
1995 *'Reading' Greek Death to the end of the classical period*, Oxford.
Stafford, E.J.
1998 'Masculine values, feminine forms: on the gender of personified abstractions', in L. Foxhall and J. Salmon (eds.) *Thinking Men: Masculinity and its Self-Representation in the Classical Tradition*, London, 43–56.
Steuding, H.
1890 s.v. 'Gelos' in Roscher, *Ausführliches Lexikon der griechischen und römischen Mythologie* III, Leipzig, col. 1610–1.
Stibbe, C.
1978 'Dionysus auf dem Grabreliefs der Spartaner', in *Thiasos: sieben archäologische Arbeiten* (*Festschrift for Wolfgang Frommel*), Amsterdam, 6–26.
Tigerstedt, E.N.
1965–78 *The Legend of Sparta in Classical Antiquity*, Stockholm (I, 1965; II, 1974; III, 1978).
Tod, M.N. and Wace, A.J.B.
1906 *A Catalogue of the Sparta Museum*, Oxford.
Verdenius, W.J.
1945 'ΑΙΔΩΣ bei Homer', *Mnemosyne* 3rd series 12, 47–60.
Vernant, J.-P.
1990 *Figures, Idoles, Masques*, Paris.
Vollkommer, R.
1988 s.v. 'Gelos', in *LIMC* IV, 178–9.
Waser, O.
1910 s.v. 'Gelos (2)', in *RE* VIII.1, col. 1018–9.
Wide, S.
1973 *Lakonische Kulte*, (Leipzig 1893), 2nd edn, Darmstadt.
Ziehen, L.
1929 'Spartanische Kulte' = 'Sparta (Kulte)', in *RE* III.A, col. 1453–1525.

Chapter 5

SPARTA'S *KOSMOS* OF SILENCE

Ephraim David

A special interest in the anthropology of classical Sparta has led me to study various aspects of social life there, including the semiotics of communication, in particular non-verbal channels, such as dress, nudity, 'hair-behaviour' and laughter. This paper concentrates on another such channel, perhaps the most complex of them all, silence, in an attempt to decode its significance and assess its social and political functions.

The complex nature of silence is revealed *inter alia* by its power to convey an impressive range of diametrically opposed messages: e.g., consent/disapproval; respect/contempt; sympathy/antipathy; intimacy/alienation; politeness/rudeness.[1] Its ambiguity, opacity, subtlety and semiotic opulence have made silence the object of multi-disciplinary research: studies in linguistics, psychology, sociology and anthropology, communication, law, philosophy and literature have explored various perspectives. However, worshippers of Clio, perhaps in faithfulness to the basic logocentrism of her province, have usually, and regrettably so, shown indifference to the 'sounds of silence'.[2]

As far as Sparta is concerned, this silence about silence is all the more regrettable given the dominantly, almost exclusively, oral character of this face-to-face society and its famous aversion to wordiness. These traits are part of what, following Basil Bernstein and others,[3] may be described in sociolinguistic terms as a 'restricted code', marked by the predisposition for minimalizing verbal expression and reducing much of the communication process to the realm of the predictable. In Sparta the emergence of such a code was the result of complex, multidimensional processes which operated throughout the archaic period producing a *sui generis* social and political system identified as a *kosmos* (Hdt. 1.65.4).[4]

The taciturnity and terse style of the Spartans (the origin of the epithet 'laconic') are frequently contrasted in the sources with the love of speech displayed by the Athenians. A *locus classicus* is Perikles' funeral oration, where the Athenians are eulogized for believing, unlike the Spartans, that words are not an obstacle to action (Thuc. 2.40.2; cf. 1.69.2). Elsewhere in Thucydides (4.17.2) Spartan envoys remind an Athenian audience of the Laconian habit 'not to multiply words when brevity suffices'. The difference in attitude between the two *politeiai* towards verbal communication was presented by Plato, in the *Laws*, as a *communis opinio* in Greece: 'All the Greeks share the belief that where our own city is fond of discourse (φιλόλογος) and copious in it (πολύλογος), Lakedaimon is inclined to brachylogy (βραχύλογον)' (641e; cf. 721e). Such statements appear to encapsulate the contrast between a restricted and an elaborate code. However, as I shall try to show, for all its bearing on the restricted code, the manipulation of silence in classical Sparta was extremely elaborate and sophisticated.

The paper contains seven sections dealing synchronically with different aspects of silence, which often happen to intersect. Exemplification pertains mostly to the second half of the fifth and first half of the fourth centuries BC, the best documented period of Spartan history, and relies mainly on contemporary evidence, but in certain contexts there are also references to earlier and later periods, especially the early-classical and the early- to mid-hellenistic. The preference for a synchronic over a diachronic approach stems from the very nature of the subject: changes in mentality and communication habits tend to be much slower than in other domains (e.g., politics or economics),[5] particularly so in a restricted-code society.

Thus far the prelude. 'The rest is silence.'

1. Educational silences

The orientation towards the restricted code started with education. Manipulation of silence here was attested in the early fourth century by Xenophon in his *Lakedaimonion Politeia*. As an eye-witness and devoted admirer[6] he described how the ephebes used to walk in silence, their hands inside their cloaks, without looking around, keeping their eyes fixed on the ground: 'You would expect a stone statue to utter a sound sooner than them.'[7] When brought to the common messes (*syssitia*), they exhibited the same mute posture unless specifically asked to answer a question.[8] Xenophon's Laconizing inclinations should not impair the basic veracity of his testimony; its high value stems from the fact that no writer of non-Spartan origin in classical Greece was acquainted with Sparta as he was.

The group silence depicted by Xenophon may be compared to a mechanical and monolithic chorus. When operating as dominant vehicles of communication, both are typical of restricted codes or dogmatic systems, and contribute to the reinforcement of group solidarity. Thus, military groups habitually march either in silence or to repetitive chanting.[9] Spartan soldiers used to sing verses of Tyrtaios in marching.[10] Incidentally, the poet had recommended a technical method of keeping silent as a means of encouraging tenacity in battle: biting one's lip with his teeth – 'χεῖλος ὀδοῦσι δακών' (fr. 11.22 West). Exhortations before battle regularly took the form of war songs or the expression of shared beliefs in the futility of words, e.g., the self-reassurance that their training was worth more than all the words of the Athenians.[11]

Silence can be said to have been institutionalized in the educational process (the *agōgē*); the control over it was the focus of a comprehensive State supervision over verbal and nonverbal communication. As shown by the above passage from Xenophon's *Lak.Pol.*, the latter included *inter alia* body-language, posture, gazing behaviour and outward appearance – some of the most significant channels through which in a free and open society an individual is inclined and able to express his uniqueness. In the course of the upbringing as well as in adult life silence, like laconic speech and dress,[12] was a basic tool for discipline, self-restraint, uniformity and conformity. On the psychological level, one of the main reasons for this multi-purpose instrumentality is the very suppression of the self required by silence; on the sociological level, its integrative and authoritarian power. In a charming essay on garrulity, Plutarch remarked that 'those who have received an aristocratic and royal education learn first to be silent, and then to speak' (*Mor.* 506c). In a democratic education, one may infer, the order of things would be different... But in the Pythagorean school (which, in addition to philosophical and mathematical interests, had its own rules for a specific life-style) it was not: there a biennial to quinquennial silence was imposed on novices together with other elements reminiscent of Sparta, such as austerity, common messes and physical trials.[13]

The biblical dictum 'A time to keep silence, and a time to speak' (*Eccles.* 3.7) has a 'Spartan' parallel in the remark put by Euripides (*Orestes* 638–9) into Menelaos' mouth: 'Silence is sometimes better than speech and speech sometimes than silence.' The Spartan system of building up communication skills put a special emphasis on learning when, where, why and how not to talk, and the proper amount of talk versus silence. One anecdote contains an amusing flavour in referring to a criticism of a sophist (Hekataios) by some Spartans not for an excess of speech, but an abuse of silence – his constant speechlessness when a guest at their *syssition*; he was defended by a Spartan (Archidamidas), who reminded his comrades that 'he who knows how, knows also when to speak'.[14] Whether authentic or not, this and similar anecdotes suggest that even in Sparta in certain circumstances silence could be sufficiently problematic to require an explanation.[15]

Furthermore, silence was not the opposite of speech but the complement of laconic speech. Both were integral aspects of the overall linguistic austerity, typical of military style and defended by Plutarch through an analogy between the devastating results of excessive talking and excessive sex; the function of silence was to make the youths 'sententious and correct in their answers' (*Lyk.* 19.1–3; cf. *Mor.* 503b, 510e17). This hints at the meditative aspect of silence and its contribution to the improvement of speech performance. The process was encouraged by a pragmatically oriented catechism, which included questions of a formulaic repertoire, such as those an *eirēn* used to ask the boys under his supervision: 'who is the best man in the city?'; 'what is your opinion on this man's action?'[16]

Parenthetically, Spartan girls too must have undergone some similar exercises, though regrettably the sources are silent on this; but witness, for example, the *corpus* of sayings ascribed to Spartan women (most of them preserved in Plutarch, *Mor.* 240c–242d) which, regardless of authenticity, can be taken on the whole to presume a process of linguistic and ideological socialization. Moreover, *pace* Aristotle's assertion that they were completely neglected as part of the community (*Pol.* 1269b19–23; 1270a6–8), Spartan women, unlike their Athenian counterparts, were not supposed to keep silent, and starting from childhood were partly integrated in public life: recall, for instance, the maidens' habit of praising successful youths and mocking the 'failures', an activity which can hardly be envisaged without adequate preparation.[17]

Answering the above questions properly, by Spartan standards, could have implied something of an intellectual challenge, even if confined to rather limited horizons; it might have followed some moments of silence. The hesitative and over-cautious temperament of the Spartans must have affected the frequency and length of their psycholinguistic and interactive silences.[18] However, remaining silent at those questions, a reaction which might stem either from having nothing to say or timidity, was considered a disturbing symptom of phlegmatic mediocrity.[19] It is one of the multifaceted ambiguities of silence that its practitioner may be regarded as wise or stupid: 'Silence befits the wise; *a fortiori* the stupid' says a Talmudic maxim (cf. also *Proverbs* 17.28), matched by the well-known Latin dictum: '*si tacuisses, philosophus fuisses*' ('Had you kept silent, you would have been a philosopher').

For Spartan youths, though not considered a mark of wisdom, silence was still preferable to a wrong answer, for the latter entailed a violent reaction of the *eirēn*: a bite in the thumb of the non-entity.[20] One can imagine that the answer was deemed wrong in the extreme when contrary to basic values (e.g., presenting one of the 'failures' as the best citizen). The significantly oral, yet non-verbal, reaction, the ritual bite, was a powerfully silent reprimand of 'inappropriate' words by a decisive 'deed'. This didactic method was typical of the restricted code. So was the general habit of corporal punishment, sometimes inflicted on adults as well,[21] which led to one of Plato's main objections against Spartan education: its use of violence instead of persuasion.[22] In terms of communication this meant the preference for silence over words – the rule of silence.

In Plato's view, the type of person produced by such a system, the 'timocratic', was 'a lover of listening (φιλήκοον) but by no means a rhetorician (ῥητορικὸν δ' οὐδαμῶς)'.[23] However, at its best, the aphoristic style emerging from the combination of meditative silence and speech-exercises strongly impressed distinguished Greek intellectuals of different generations, including Plato himself.[24] After all, the mythical founder of the Spartan *kosmos* was aptly envisaged by his biographer as 'brief and sententious in his speech (βραχυλόγος καὶ ἀποφθεγματικός).'[25]

2. Deferential silences and gerontocracy

Despite criticism of Sparta in the *Republic* (as elsewhere), Plato's ideal State was intensely inspired by Spartan traits; one of them was the use of silence as a symbol of reverence for seniority: the duty of the youths to keep silent in the presence of their elders (425b). Plato adopted this together with another non-verbal convention of Spartan provenance, similarly gerontolatrous: giving up one's seat in favour of the aged.[26] Incidentally, according to a significant anecdote, nobody said a word against one of the younger men who, contrary to the norms, declined to offer his seat to Derkyllidas, at that time a distinguished general but a bachelor, explaining convincingly: 'You have produced no son who will rise to offer me his seat'.[27] *Se non è vero è ben trovato*... Such remarks were unanswerable: they could meet only with the silent approval of those present, including the humiliated victim. This reminds us of the obligation imposed on the 'tremblers' (τρέσαντες) to give up a seat even to a junior.[28] In this light, the anecdote becomes all the more relevant with respect to the humiliation involved as well as the silence of consent following it.

In Sparta normative silence was associated with the elders' priority and sometimes monopoly of speech not only during formal education but also later, as shown, for instance, by the fictitious discourse put by Isokrates into the mouth of Archidamos (Agesilaos' son). This opens with an apology for having dared despite his youth to offer advice to his elders. Nevertheless, he is made to challenge the norm imposing silence on the young in martial councils, on account of incompatibility with their tasks in war.[29]

Similar norms are attested in anthropological studies of folk-traditional societies: among the Abkasians (in the Caucasus), the Yakuti (Siberia), the Chippewa and Creek tribes of North America, the Kikuyu and Kamba (Kenya) and the Australian Dieri, the young usually remain silent when their elders speak in council.[30]

Although certainly relevant for an ethnography of silence, such analogies must be treated with caution, since the society of classical Sparta was not genuinely archaic or folk-traditional, but pseudo-archaic: the centrality of the family and the tribe, and the subordination of the individual to their interest, as interpreted by the elders – the basic traits of a folk-traditional gerontocracy – had been replaced by the centrality of the State and its omnipotent authority over its citizens, in a word, by *étatisme*. Here reverence for seniority (as for official authority) was needed by the State as a conservative tool to guarantee continuity and conformity. Silence was a moderating factor on the juvenile tendency towards innovations and recalcitrance; also on juvenile aggressiveness which, although in certain respects strongly encouraged, could be seriously detrimental to social harmony if left unchecked. Thus, while youths were taught to jest and to endure jesting, if someone could bear it no longer he had only to ask and the jester ceased.[31] The limitation of jesting could also serve for the protection of the young against abuses of teasing by older Spartans. In all these cases the imposed cessation of speaking became a significant component of a conflict-avoidance strategy, which was given priority even over the training in endurance.

3. Socio-ritual silences: the ideal and the counter-ideal

Teaching endurance was also a major objective of certain pseudo-archaic rites, which had been artificially preserved but adapted to new functions, as illustrated by the flagellation at the altar of Artemis Orthia. Originally a fertility rite (or other chthonic cult), this was adapted to the function of teaching endurance and thereby associated with toughness, self-assertion and non-verbal behaviour: according to Xenophon, for the ephebes it was a great honour to endure pain when scourged by a rival team in the course of attempting to steal cheeses from the altar.[32] Significant parallels offered by anthropological research stress the importance of enduring a flagellation test in silence.[33] So do some later texts, notably certain passages in Cicero referring to a ritual whipping (at the shrine of Orthia), which appears to have been closely associated with the above although the stealing element and, with it, the agonistic aspect of the trial disappeared.[34] There is a tradition according to which the youths were whipped there in the nude[35] – a tantalizing piece of evidence in view of the parallelism between nudity and silence as channels of communication reducing *ad limitem* (or *ad nihil*) dress and speech.[36] Note, by the way, the combined application of these channels in the ephors' regular inspection (every ten days) of the taciturn ephebes in the nude.[37] Ritual nudity was accompanied by choral chanting, as the proper substitute for choral silence, at the *Gymnopaidiai* festival as well as at its wintry parody designed for the exemplary humiliation of obstinate bachelors.[38]

Silence was also a factor in consolidating the Spartan ideal against a counter-ideal, often embodied by the helots. [39] Thus, one is tempted to associate and contrast the flagellation ritual with the annual beating of the helots attested by the early-hellenistic historian Myron – a non-verbal reminder of their servile status:[40] this ceremony can be plausibly interpreted as a parody of the Orthia beatings.[41] The contrast between the helots' natural reaction (cries of pain) and the tough endurance of the ephebes could have provided the Spartans with a reassuring proof of their superiority.

Silence versus garrulity must also have been part of the anti-alcoholic demonstration they used to show the younger generation at the *syssitia* by intoxicating helots with wine.[42] Logorrhoea, like ridiculous laughter, is a common symptom of drunkenness.[43] Thus the difference between moderate and excessive drinking could be revealed among other means by the sober smiles and dignified (if mocking) silence of the spectators as opposed to the unrestrained laughter and garrulity of the 'actors'. The Spartans' solidarity and sensation of superiority were likely to be animated by a double contempt: for habits regarded as base by their code (such as drunkenness and garrulity) as well as for those who served to exemplify vice – the helots. These must have usually been treated with an intimidating silence of scorn and exclusion which, like despotic brachylogy, is typical of the attitude to a servile class (cf. Demetrios, *On Style*, 7). However, volitional silence, accompanied by a façade of docility, is known as a strategy of passive resistance among the oppressed.[44] If this applied to the helots as well, intoxication with wine was liable to break their resistance, deprive them of their silence and make them appear in this respect as dissimilar as possible to their masters.

For the Spartans there was no graver deviation from the ideal code than cowardice in battle. Silence of exclusion could be used as a sanction; although not mentioned explicitly in the sources concerned with the 'tremblers', this was inflicted in the case of Aristodemos, nicknamed 'Trembler' for surviving Thermopylai (ophthalmia had prevented him from taking part in the battle). According to Herodotos the sanctions he faced, leading him to seek death in war at his first opportunity, included an embargo on speech: no Spartan would speak to him.[45] Thus, silence was not only a major channel of communication but also, as could be expected in a face-to-face society, an efficient means of excommunication.

4. Cryptic, deceptive and xenophobic silences

Returning from the silence of exclusion to that of inclusion, an important aspect is provided once more by the *syssitia*: the promotion of *esprit de corps* through secrecy. The *syssitoi* were reminded of their obligation for strict confidentiality by the eldest member, who indicated the topographical dimension of silence in the sense of secrecy by pointing to the doors and proclaiming time and again: 'Through these not a word goes out.'[46] This order should remind us that in the intimate atmosphere of these 'clubs', the Spartans tended to be more talkative than in other public contexts.[47] Sometimes, however, cohesive talk, like laughter (another promoter of group solidarity frequently present at the messes),[48] could be replaced by cohesive (and coercive) silence: new members were co-opted by a peculiar voting procedure (requiring *unanimity*), which reportedly had to take place *in silence*.[49]

Silence was needed for practical purposes in the case of stealing food, a significant test of the upbringing, as well as in military operations and hunting, two of the most important activities in Sparta;[50] also in helot hunting, as the *krypteia* has often, and accurately, been described. Originally another rite of passage meant to test endurance and resourcefulness, this pseudo-archaic institution was preserved in classical Sparta, but was assigned as one of its main functions the policing and terrorizing of the helots.[51] Fear must frequently have led many among these to keep a self-protective silence lest they be targeted by the select *kryptoi*. The isolation of the latter and the necessity of hiding and profiting from the element of surprise (typical of hunting) presupposed a functional silence, coupled by the conspirative and complicitous silence which enveloped the entire affair. As in some other initiation rites, silence not only protected the mysterious character of the activity, but also provided its condition and context. Secrecy could be maintained through a conspiracy of silence even in the case of a massacre, such as that of the two thousand helots who had been promised freedom: '...no one ever knew how each of them perished' (Thuc. 4.80).[52]

In this case, as in many others, secrecy and silence were allied with deception. This holds true with respect to the efficient suppression of rebellions, such as the conspiracy of Kinadon (note especially the method used for his arrest).[53] Here secretive silence, always vital for a conspiracy, was broken by an informer; his name is not mentioned by Xenophon, our main source: for obvious reasons the Spartan authorities were interested in keeping such data strictly secret. To deceive successfully, Spartan individuals entrusted with a secret had to know how to hold their tongue. This could be explicitly included in an order, like that given to those who had brought the news of the Arginousai defeat to sail away in silence speaking to no one and to return later proclaiming a glorious victory;[54] silence and deception were tools of a delaying information strategy aimed at temporarily protecting the soldiers' morale.

The device of burying problematic information in silence, through secrecy and censorship, was perfectly consistent with Spartan mentality. Recall, for example, regardless of strict authenticity, the tradition (derived from Ephoros) concerning the fate of the speech Lysander commissioned from a logographer, Kleon of Halikarnassos, in support of a revolution: never used, it is reported to have been discovered only after his death by Agesilaos, who was persuaded by the expedient advice to inter it in silence.[55]

The cryptic character of Spartan society was closely associated with its notorious xenophobia; foreigners' questions about State affairs, particularly if probing into military matters, were normally greeted with suspicious reserve.[56] (When security was not at stake, it could be easier to get information.) The reserved attitude to foreigners is universally known as one of the typical reactions to diversity.[57] Much like laughter, silence can often serve as a defensive-aggressive tool, whose operation is particularly efficient in semi-closed or parochial societies, like the Spartan. Here silence (or laconic style), combined with a peculiar kind of humour, helped in consolidating an ideal as opposed to a counter-ideal; it is repeatedly presented in the sources as an arrogant and jocular antidote to alien prolixity: 'Report that you [the foreign envoy] found it hard to stop speaking and we to listen.'[58] Perhaps the best-known example is Herodotos' story on the Spartans' self-confessed inability to cope with the long speech of the Samian delegation on account of forgetting the beginning and being therefore unable to understand the conclusion.[59] Even Antalkidas (famous particularly for his role in diplomacy) could be credited with a very undiplomatic way of 'encouraging' a lecturer who was about to read an encomium on Herakles – a rhetorical question (typically philistine) pointing to the futility of words: 'Who says anything against him?'[60]

Some of these apophthegms seem to owe their wide circulation to the Cynics, who recognized in Sparta's restricted code certain features in line with their ideal *paideia* and life-style. (Sometimes they appear to have exaggerated and distorted the reality in order to adapt it as far as possible to their tenets.) Simplicity of dress, sometimes to the point of nudity, rough and terse speech, often pushed to the limit of monosyllabic brevity or silence, had a very special appeal for those eccentric philosophers,[61] as an integral part of the 'virile' medium which they presented in sharp contrast to the 'effeminate' and verbose character of the elaborate code embodied in Athens: 'the men's apartment and the women's'[62] ...The Cynics tended to ignore that some of the basic elements associated in Sparta with the above traits, such as *étatisme* and militarism, were completely foreign to their cosmopolitan and (in many respects) apolitical minds.

5. Political silences

Aristotle's definition of man as a political animal is based on the ability to speak (*Pol.* 1253a 8–18), which distinguishes humans from other animals. But the faculty of speech inevitably implies that of silence as well: human silence has a special significance as an integral part of the speech process, all the more special in a sociocultural system so openly hostile to verbosity as that developed by Sparta. Here, this hostility could sometimes serve as an antidote to rhetoric in political debate, as shown, for instance, by Thucydides' account of the confrontation preceding the outbreak of the Peloponnesian War; Sthenelaidas' brief speech, which won the day, typically opened with the arrogant *cliché*: 'The long speeches of the Athenians I do not understand.'[63] However, here, as in other cases where differences of opinion within the ruling elite arose, the decision of the Assembly followed a rhetorical debate, and this in itself (let alone the political and diplomatic necessity of addressing non-Spartans in persuasive discourse) presupposed the need of adequate rhetorical competence, based on talent as well as a certain training, even if far from the sophisticated education of Athenian politicians (frequently designated as *rhētores*). As already mentioned, when in need of a persuasive speech for promoting his political schemes, even a prominent politician of Lysander's calibre is reported to have solicited the services of a foreign expert. Thucydides' depiction of Brasidas (4.84.2) as an able speaker, *for a Spartan*, sharply epitomizes the issue. So does Plato's portrayal of the 'timocratic' man as definitely not an outstanding speaker, 'not basing his claim to office on speech proficiency (οὐκ ἀπὸ τοῦ λέγειν ἀξιῶν ἄρχειν) or anything of that sort...' (*Rep*. 548e–549a). The implicit contrast with Athens cannot be missed. Could this antithesis have occasionally led Athenian sources to exaggerate in their depiction of the Spartans' linguistic behaviour? Although the possibility cannot be excluded, one should bear in mind that the difference between the two cities in this respect is consistent with our evidence on their distinctive patterns of culture and public life.

As is well known, the character of the Spartan Assembly was extremely different from that of the Athenian, *inter alia* because the normal speech conduct of its members, excepting kings, *gerontes*, ephors and possibly some others, consisted of either silence or voting acclamation, i.e. not individual but choral modes of expressing the *vox populi* (one of them non-vocal, the other vocal, even vociferant). Both channels present a levelling element consonant with the ideological implications of the term defining citizens as 'similars' (ὅμοιοι). Moreover, on the psychological level, shouting could have offered compensation for keeping silent most of the time, thereby providing the 'silent majority' with the illusion of active participation and equal right of speech (ἰσηγορία), all the more so as this method of voting allowed for certain nuances in the expression of opinion (through volume variability). Thus, silence and shouting were in line with the dominantly oligarchic character of the 'mixed constitution' – a basic catchphrase of the Spartan '*mirage*'.[64]

Worthy of special note is the electoral function of silence alongside shouting: the passing in silence through the Assembly (one by one) of the socially privileged candidates for the *gerousia* to be assessed by a secluded panel according to the loudness of popular acclamation.[65] Acoustically, this amounted to a mixture of silence and rhythmically variable noise. Furthermore, the *gerousia*'s right to veto 'crooked' decisions of the Assembly[66] can be viewed among other perspectives as the triumph of silence over discussion, and an additional aspect of the link between silence, gerontarchy and oligarchy.

Silence could also be manipulated as an alternative to discussion in mass communication – political debates within the Assembly. This is the eloquent power of silence – 'by their silence they cry aloud' ('*cum tacent, clamant*') in Cicero's oxymoronic utterance (*Cat.* 1.8.21). Witness the 'un*parl*iamentary' way in which the Assembly adopted its decision to dispatch Kleombrotos' army on the mission which ended at Leuktra in irremediable disaster. The attempt of Prothoos to plead for a more prudent course of action had been regarded by his fellow-citizens as mere nonsense, as Xenophon put it: 'ἡ δ' ἐκκλησία ἀκούσασα ταῦτα ἐκεῖνον μὲν φλυαρεῖν ἡγήσατο' (*Hell.* 6.4.3). It is a pity that he did not elaborate on what had actually happened there. However, since no deliberation is recorded (in spite of Xenophon's habit to report, even briefly, public debates), the most plausible interpretation of what went on is that Prothoos' proposal was not rejected through verbal arguments, but remained a *vox clamantis in deserto*, a desert of mocking silence, presumably accompanied (or preceded) by other nonverbal channels: scornful gestures, restlessness and malicious laughter were likely to be encouraged by leading politicians to silence a non-conformist voice. Given their contagious nature, these channels could be effectively manipulated among the gregarious Spartans even more than elsewhere.

The Athenian *ekklēsia* could also be temporarily paralysed by an overwhelming silence: recall Demosthenes' dramatic depiction of the urgent meeting convened at the news of Philip's invasion of Elateia.[67] This, however, was an exceptional case of consternation, confusion and helplessness, not a manipulated silence devised as a substitute for discussion. What strikes one most about Spartan silences is their intentional and manipulative character, typical of a directed and controlled communication – a 'tyranny of silence'.

The comprehensive system of control itself used to operate in silence. As a vital constituent, much of the ephors' 'tyrannic' power was based on silent inspection; punitive reaction, when deemed appropriate, could come immediately or at a later stage. The latter possibility was in force with respect to the two ephors who used to accompany a king in military campaigns watching his actions, with the threatening option of eventual prosecution on his return.[68] In the case of Pausanias the regent, the ephors' suspicion led to a detective investigation, which was carried out in silence. Later, when the ephors were about to arrest him, Pausanias managed to read their intention on the face of one of them, while another, out of personal friendship, even went as far as using a covert nod to warn him (Thuc. 1.134.1). Since the historian could get these details, directly or indirectly, only from Spartan informants, the episode supplies additional evidence for the importance attached to the dexterity of using silence and other non-verbal channels in coping with critical situations.[69] Silence structured communication also in the case of political protocol as, for instance, in the norm obliging all citizens, with the significant exception of the ephors, to rise from their seats when a king appeared in public.[70]

For all their proverbial discipline and law-abidingness, there were Spartans who declined to appear in court when summoned. Thus, in 395 BC King Pausanias adopted this form of 'silent pleading' and was condemned to death *in absentia* (Xen. *Hell.* 3.5.25). In Sparta, however, such 'forensic silence' did not entail instant conviction, as it did in Athens; as shown by the Sphodrias affair, a trial could proceed nevertheless and even terminate in acquittal. Facing a capital charge for his miserable initiative, the attempt to seize the Piraeus (378 BC), Sphodrias was acquitted *in absentia*. The episode provides an interesting case of silence manipulation in the sphere of a family relationship, yet closely associated with other domains as well (pederasty, the administration of justice and politics). Xenophon relates that Sphodrias' son, Kleonymos, asked Archidamos, his lover, to interfere in order to persuade his father Agesilaos to vote, despite his predictable stand, for acquittal. The ensuing 'dialogue' is a masterpiece of Spartan discourse:

> ...then he [Archidamos] arose at dawn and kept watch, so that his father should not leave the house without his notice. But when he saw him going out...if anyone among the citizens was present, he gave way to allow them to converse with Agesilaos, and again if it was a foreigner, he did the same; he even made way for any one of the servants...Finally, when Agesilaos came back from the Eurotas...Archidamos went away without even having come near him. On the following day he also acted in the very same way. And Agesilaos, while he suspected for what reason he kept going to and fro with him, nevertheless asked no question...
> (*Hell.* 5.4.28–9; cf. Plut. *Ages.* 25.3)

Xenophon's source was most probably one of the 'interlocutors' – his friend, Agesilaos; note that the historian was familiar with minute details, including manipulation of time and space (chronemics and proxemics). Archidamos' silence appears to have been part of a delaying and conflict-avoidance strategy meant to prepare the ground for a positive answer to a request that had every chance of meeting with a prompt and definitive refusal had it been made directly. This holds true even if Agesilaos' eventual change of mind was motivated mainly by political, not personal, considerations. The Sphodrias affair provides an appropriate link between political and emotional silences.

6. Emotional silences

Given the taciturn disposition of the Spartans and the high status of reticence in their mentality, the universal tendency to look for refuge in silence in states of embarrassment, intense joy or sadness, anger and despair[71] must have been extremely pronounced among them. Let us examine some cases, on the individual as well as on the communal level.

To start with the latter, one of the most dramatic examples is the reaction to the news of Leuktra, as reported by Xenophon, possibly an eye-witness: the ephors' distress, their decision not to interrupt the Gymnopaedic celebration but to leave the chorus to finish its performance, their care to give the names of the dead to their families coupled with an explicit order to the women not to make any outcry, but 'to bear the suffering in *silence* (σιγῇ τὸ πάθος φέρειν)'; on the following day the bright and cheerful countenance of those whose relatives had fallen and the gloomy and downcast appearance of the others, less fortunate...[72] (Note that the instruction to suffer in silence was deemed superfluous for the men.) Even allowing for a measure of exaggeration in Xenophon's account, we are faced with an example as to how a functional silence, meant to control emotions and to keep order, could assume the dimensions of an intensively expressive silence[73] which, accompanied by other non-verbal channels, structured and dominated for a while the whole fabric of civic communication.

An additional, and more humane, illustration of the Spartans' gregarious and taciturn behaviour (also documented *inter alios* by Xenophon) is provided by their reaction to the news of Archidamos' victory over the Arcadians and Argives (with no casualties on the Spartan side) in the so-called 'Tearless Battle' (368 BC), which ironically turned out to be anything but tearless; for, on receiving the news, Agesilaos, the *gerontes* and the ephors are reported to have shed tears of joy, and to have infected all the public with their weeping[74] – a sort of probouleutic lachrymation silently adopted by the 'Assembly'. This Byronic way of receiving the news, in silence and tears, can be understood in the light of the fresh memory and traumatic impact of Leuktra.

Turning to individual examples, an amusing case is offered by the Paidaretos anecdote: a young man reported to have intrigued the ephors by looking content and smiling after having failed to be selected for a prestigious *corps d'élite* (the 300 *hippeis*); invited to explain his *prima facie* improperly cheerful physiognomy, he expressed satisfaction at the realization that the State had 300 citizens better than himself.[75] The combination of silence and smiling, although typical of certain psychological states of embarrassment, evoked the suspicion of the ephors as a defying attitude ('dumb insolence'?); therefore the suspect had to be deprived of his 'right to remain silent'. Whether authentic or not, the anecdote is illustrative of Spartan mentality. Extremely sensitive as they were to various aspects of face-behaviour, the Spartans could not tolerate a joyful expression on behalf of those who according to their code had nothing to be proud of: thus, the 'tremblers' were forbidden to show themselves in public with a cheerful countenance.[76] The unusual sensitivity to this channel must have been associated with the practice of silence, which provides the face with the priority, and sometimes monopoly, of 'speech'.

When conditioned by disturbing emotions (sadness, frustration, anger and despair), silence can become depressive and, as such, the prelude to extreme or destructive reactions. This is an ominous and explosive silence. A relevant example is provided by Demaratos' reaction, after being deposed, when mocked by Leotychidas. After a brief and enigmatic reply, he is reported (by Herodotos) to have covered his head with his cloak, so as to avoid being seen, using silence both as self-retreat and as vehicle of that deep hostility which eventually ended in defection:[77] 'The silence and the fury'...

Silence is not always a safe antidote to harm (*pace* Aesch. *Agam*. 548), certainly not self-inflicted harm. Psychological states of the above spectrum could lead to suicide, in Sparta even more than elsewhere, among other factors because of the very tendency prevalent in this honour/shame society[78] to refrain from speaking and to look for refuge in silence. The paradigmatic story of Lykourgos' decision to starve himself to death[79] could provide inspiration and moral support. The list of Spartan suicides includes persons of different standing and historical contexts, among them prominent politicians, kings, generals, office-holders or ex-magistrates, as well as some anonymous youths and women (heroes of dubious stories) who, taken captive, preferred to commit suicide rather than perform menial tasks.[80] Worthy of note here is also the theatrically silent threat of Chilonis to hang herself if her former husband, Kleonymos, succeeded in returning home with Pyrrhus' support.[81] In addition to the recorded cases, we might expect many others among those whose conditions of life had become intolerable, particularly the 'tremblers'. Xenophon's remark (*Lak.Pol.* 9.6) that death was preferable to their ignominious existence (which is usually interpreted only in the sense of falling in battle to prevent becoming a 'trembler') may refer to suicide as well. Despite all this, with the exception of what sometimes amounted to 'suicidal conduct' in war, self-killing does not appear to have become a distinct cultural or religious pattern in the Spartan tradition[82] as, *mutatis mutandis,* it has, for example, in the Japanese, where silence also enjoys a highly privileged rank.

7. Cultural and religious silences

The linguistic aspect of the restricted code was closely associated with other sociocultural aspects, such as the legal, as illustrated by a maxim explaining the paucity of laws: 'those who use few words have need of but few laws'(Plut. *Mor*. 232c (1); cf. 189f (1); *Lyk*. 20.2). Not only few, but also brief and usually non-written,[83] one might add.

Moreover, those who use few words will make do with only a few official documents, a few literary genres (lyric or elegiac poetry and the pamphlet are the only specimens as far as pre-hellenistic Sparta is concerned), a different kind of art, a minimalist type of clothing (a kind of uniform) [84] – in short, a restricted code in many sectors of culture. These, however, did not include music and dance, which flourished there in the service of State purposes (educational, social and military). Nor did they include the use of inscriptions: in this field, especially in dedicatory inscriptions commemorating individual prowess, Sparta appears to have been quite similar to Athens, at least until the middle of the fifth century.[85] Could the use of inscriptions by Spartans have expressed, at the level of the unconscious, the search for an alternative to speech and literature?

Be that as it may, the absence of a developed form of drama can be viewed as a symptom of the restricted code and the relative 'silence of the muses'. There is a tradition (preserved in Plutarch, *Mor.* 239b 33) trying to explain: the Spartans would not tolerate either tragedy or comedy so as to prevent criticism, both serious and jocular, of their laws – a sort of overall, self-imposed, pseudo-primitive censorship (cf. Plato, *Laws*, 634 d–e). This, however, should not mislead us into concluding that they had no drama at all: there was a theatre in Sparta,[86] and while it functioned as a place where certain festivals, such as the *Gymnopaidiai*, were celebrated, it also appears to have staged some rudimentary productions, especially of comic type. The character of Spartan comedy is best revealed by the antiquarian Sosibios, the first Laconian scholar, through some edifying examples: the imitation of persons stealing fruit, old men leaning on sticks or a foreign doctor 'talking in the manner portrayed by Alexis',[87] i.e. trying unsuccessfully to imitate the local Doric accent. (One can imagine that the Spartans were able to detect a foreign 'accent' even in the silence of outsiders.) Some comic patterns included obscene dances. Sosibios reports that the performers were called δεικηλισταί, a term explained as 'maskers or mummers'.[88]

The major function of silence in these performances can be associated with the Spartans' high appreciation for the *visual*: silence helps in structuring communication when nonverbal and visual aspects assume a dominant role in a sociocultural interaction.[89] Theatrical effects could be intensified by the use of masks, such as those discovered by excavations at the sanctuary of Orthia, most of which belong to the sixth century BC. They are of several standard types, but can roughly be classified in two main categories – 'ideal' and 'grotesque'.[90] What matters most for our subject is that the masks of the ideal type have their mouth shut or only slightly open, whereas most of the others have their mouth open[91] – an iconographic aspect of the status held by silence in Spartan mentality (*Figs*. 1 and 2).[92]

Within ancient religious practice silence had an important function in concealing mystery rites as well as creating a proper medium for worship. The latter is a universal element in the history of religion.[93] In Sparta the presence of silence, sometimes possibly accompanied by nudity, at various rites of passage discussed above (such as the Orthia flagellations) must have preserved a religious significance even after their transformation and adaptation to new functions. A peculiar example of a Spartan ritual with an archaic (or pseudo-archaic) flavour, in which silence is reported to have been absolutely mandatory, is known to us owing to its late revival (or invention) and political manipulation by the supporters of Agis IV: the custom of the ephors periodically (every ninth year) to gaze at the stars *in silence* in order to make sure that the kings had committed no religious offence.[94] In such augural circumstances silence was a necessary context of communication between human inquiry and divine revelation, 'the privileged channel through which the gods transmit their will'.[95] Divination played a central role in Spartan religion,[96] and silence must have been an indispensable medium.

As in many other societies of different times and places, in Sparta too abstinence from speech was frequently imperative in stressing the solemnity of the ritual, especially in funeral ceremonies.[97] Here,

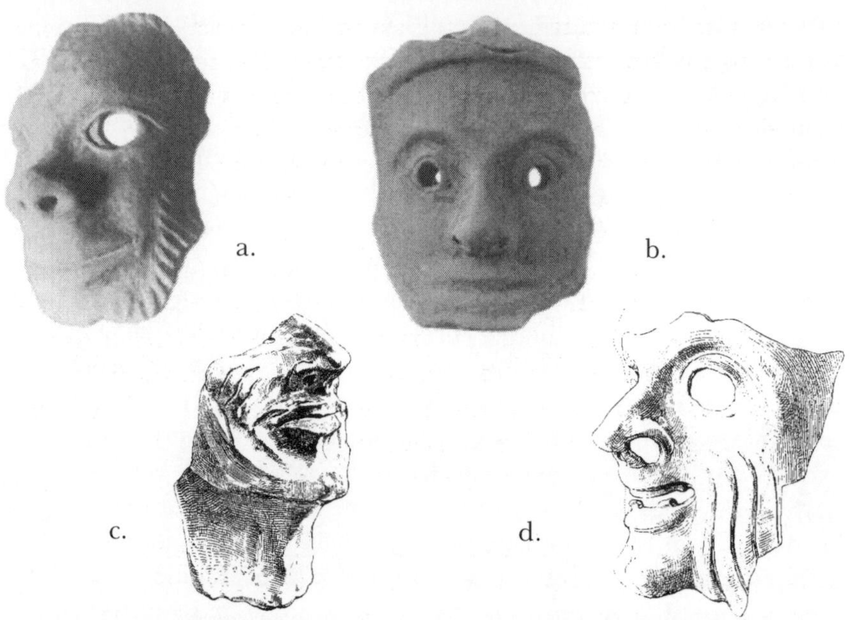

Fig. 1 (a–d): 'ideal' masks – mouths shut or slightly open (Dickins 1929, Pls. LIV 2, 4; LV 1, 2).

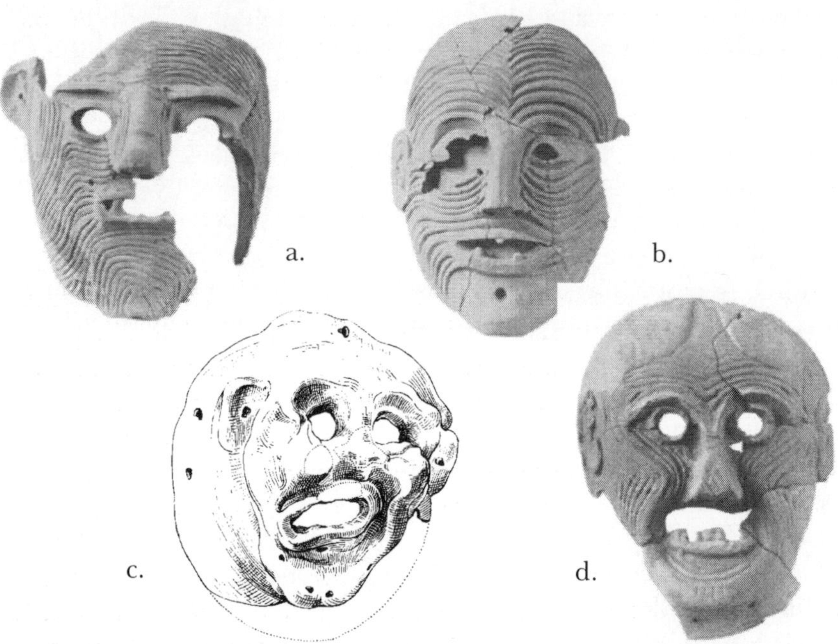

Fig. 2 (a–d): 'grotesque' masks – mouths open (Dickins 1929, Pls. LIX 1; LXI 1; LVIII 3; XLVII 1).

however, public mourning, with the exception of ritual lamentations over a king's death, was officially suppressed.[98] The sensation of fear and reverence when confronted with death is universally accompanied by silence. We are told that the Spartans paid tribute to Phobos because they believed that their polity was chiefly maintained by fear.[99] This could be expected with respect to silence as well.

It is therefore somewhat disappointing not to find in the Spartan pantheon a female divinity of Silence (Siga)[100] keeping company with male symbolic divinities, such as Fear, Laughter (Gelos), Sleep (Hypnos) and Death (Thanatos),[101] who had their special cult there. Nevertheless, this absence is mitigated by the close links which, one way or another, associate 'gracious silence'[102] with these symbolic powers (natural consorts in a supernatural polyandry?).

Symphony of silence

Like other channels of communication, silence was manipulated in classical Sparta in the service of the State with an impressive degree of perseverance and sophistication. The acquisition of proper silence habits by its citizens was the concern of the State. So was the question of *when, where, why, how* and *to what extent* one should speak or remain silent depending on social class, status, official rank, age, gender and circumstances. The Spartans had an exceptionally developed awareness of the multidimensional power condensed in silence: its integrative, authoritarian, conservative, intimidating, suppressive, disciplinary, derisive, ostracizing, mediating, conspirative, deceptive and other manipulative capacities.

Silence was thus associated with some of the basic traits and trends of the Spartan *kosmos*: its pseudo-archaic character and deliberately restricted code, based on homogeneity, monotony, conformism and propensity for formulaic modes of communication; its rigid discipline and need for obedience; the strictly hierarchical outlook on the one hand and levelling inclinations on the other; the dominantly oligarchic and totalitarian character of the 'mixed constitution'; the profound respect for seniority and official authority; the obsessive protection of social order and harmony through conflict-avoidance strategies; the attempt to build up an ideal ethos on the basis of a counter-ideal; the high appreciation for the visual and the concrete; the strong predilection for secrecy, deceptiveness and xenophobia; the orientation towards self-restraint and control over emotions in what may ultimately be seen as an abortive attempt to alter human nature.

In line with certain remarks of prominent Athenian intellectuals,

Thucydides and Plato among them, it is justifiable to conceive the impressive dissimilarities of education, way of life, culture, mentality and political regime between their own city and Sparta in terms of *communication*: the Athenian democracy can be viewed as the realm of the words; Sparta as the dominion of silence – a *sigocracy*.

Acknowledgements

I am grateful to the participants at Clyro, Hay-on-Wye, for their comments. Special thanks are due to Anton Powell and Steve Hodkinson.

Notes

[1] Cf. Dinouart 1771 (repr. 1987), 69; Walker 1985, 56: 'the Janus-like nature of silence'.

2 For remarkable exceptions see, e.g., Nagel/Vecchi 1984; Burke 1993, 123–41.

[3] Bernstein 1971, 77, 134–6, 146–8 and *passim*; Douglas 1973; with reference to Sparta: Fisher 1989, 38; Parker 1989, 162, 172, n. 100.

[4] e.g. Nafissi 1991; for a brief survey: Hodkinson 1997.

[5] See, e.g., Le Goff 1974, esp. 81; cf. the criticism of Gismondi 1985, which does not affect the validity of the concept concerning the unequal speed of change in different 'sectors of history'.

[6] The interpretation of the *Lak.Pol.* as a sarcastic criticism of Sparta has been convincingly refuted: e.g., Tigerstedt 1965, 161–9, 458–64 (esp. 464, n. 530); cf. Cartledge in this volume. For Xenophon and Sparta: *idem* 1987, 55–66.

[7] *Lak.Pol.* 3.4–5; cf. Plut. *Mor.* 237d 10. The strict silence ascribed by Aristophanes to the Athenian youths under the 'old education' (*Clouds*, 961 ff.) is reminiscent of Sparta; note that it is accompanied by other Spartan traits, such as self-restraint, simplicity, nudity and an austere diet (see also below, nn. 26, 37); cf. Brelich 1969, 125, 129.

[8] Xen. *Lak.Pol.* 3.5; cf. Plut. *Lyk.* 12.6. For children and silence in a historical perspective: Nagel/Vecchi 1984, 741–4; Burke 1993, 132.

[9] For similarities between the two channels, cf. Bruneau 1973, 19–20.

[10] Athen. 14. 630F; cf. Powell 1994, 302–7.

[11] Thuc. 5.69.2; for Sparta and the *res/verba* dichotomy, cf. Ion of Chios, fr. 63 Snell, *TrGF*, with Rawson 1969, 19; Cozzo 1991, 1374 ff.

[12] Cozzo, ibid., stresses the ideologically cohesive and conservative aspects of '*laconicità*'. Cf. Francis 1991–93 (focusing on Spartan speeches in Thucydides), and below, esp. nn. 16, 24, 25, 58–60. For dress: below, n. 84.

[13] Aul. Gell. 1.9.1–5; Diog. Laert. 8.10; Iambl. *Vit. Pyth.* 68, 72, 94; cf. Casel 1919, 30–5; 54–5. For Sparta and the Pythagoreans: Ollier 1933, 197–206; Powell 1994, 282–3.

[14] Plut. *Lyk.* 20.3; *Mor.* 218b 2; except for the youths, constant silence was

incompatible with the norms of speech behaviour obtaining at the *syssitia*: see below, section 4 and n. 47.

[15] Cf. Plut. *Mor.* 220a (4): the insulting question, reportedly addressed to Demaratos, whether his silence in council had been due to stupidity or lack of words, and the aphoristic reply: 'A stupid man would not be able to hold his tongue.'

[16] Plut. *Lyk.* 18.3; (cf. Xen. *Lak.Pol.* 5.6: subjects of discussion at the *syssitia*; also Herakl. Lembos, *Exc. Pol.* 374.13 Dilts, for exercises in brachylogy starting from childhood). When Plutarch's sources remain unknown, his reliability can be assessed by criteria of plausibility, inner coherence and compatibility with other available evidence. For Plutarch and Spartan history: e.g., Tigerstedt 1974, 230–64; 509–37; MacDowell 1986, 17–22.

[17] Plut. *Lyk.* 14.3–6. On their education see, e.g., Xen. *Lak.Pol.* 1.4; Plat. *Protag.* 342d; *Laws*, 806a; cf. Cartledge 1981, 90–3. For decent Athenian women being expected to keep silent: Pomeroy 1994, 269–70, 272; Ormand 1996, 38, 41, 57–62.

[18] e.g. Thuc. 1.69.2–4; 8.96.5; cf. Hodkinson 1983, 265–8; Francis 1991–93, with a special emphasis on Thucydides' portrayal of Alkidas.

[19] Plut. *Lyk.* 18.4. On timidity and silence: Kurzon 1995, 55–60, with a taxonomy of silence based on the intentional/unintentional dichotomy; cf. *idem* 1998, 25–50. For psycholinguistic and interactive silences: Bruneau 1973, 17–46.

[20] Plut. *Lyk.* 18.5; cf. Den Boer 1954, 274–81.

[21] e.g. Xen. *Hell.* 3.1.9 – Derkyllidas (below, n. 27) was made to stand holding his shield (it is not specified for how long).

[22] *Rep.* 548b; cf. Arist. *Pol.* 1338b.

[23] *Rep.* 548e; cf. *Hipp. Mai.* 284c–286a. But the Spartans were not always good listeners: see nn. 58–60. Sparta as the prototype of 'timocracy': *Rep.* 544c, 545a; cf. Arist. *Pol.* 1316a18–23.

[24] *Protag.* 342d–e, 343b; cf., e.g., Thuc. 4.40.2; Arist. *Rhet.* 1394b 35; Herakl. Lembos, *Exc. Pol.* 373.13 Dilts; fr. com. adesp. 417–19 Edmonds; Demetr. *On Style*, 7–8, 241–2; Plut. *Lyk.* 20; *Ages.* 14.4; *Apophth. Lak. passim*; Sextus Emp. *Adv. Math.* 2.21.

[25] Plut. *Lyk.* 19.6; cf. Diog. Laert. 1.72 for Chilon as βραχυλόγος and the laconic style as 'Chilonean'. On the face of it, a verse of Alkman (Ael. Arist. *Or.* 45.32 = 152 Calame) appears to suggest the existence of a different attitude towards verbal communication in the poet's day by applying the 'name' 'Loquacious' (?) (Πολλαλέγων) to a man (*vis-à-vis* 'All-enjoying' (?) (Πασιχάρηα) to a woman). However, since the very meaning of the names is controversial (cf. Calame 1983, 565–6) and the context obscure, it would be hazardous to draw conclusions from this fragment.

[26] *Rep.* 425b; for Sparta: David 1991, 64–6, with evidence. Cf. Aristoph. *Clouds*, 993, with n. 7 above. For Plato's *Laws*, Sparta and gerontocracy: Powell 1994, 274–84.

[27] Plut. *Lyk.* 15.3; *Mor.* 227f (14). On Derkyllidas: Poralla/(Bradford) 1985, 44–5 (s.v.); cf. Cartledge 1987, 210–12, 322–3, 355–6.

[28] Xen. *Lak.Pol.* 9.5; for the 'tremblers': below, n. 45.

[29] Isokr. *Archid.* 1–6; cf. also Lys. 16. 20.

[30] Simmons 1945, 54 –5, 60, 114–18; Jamin 1977, 60–4.

[31] Plut. *Lyk.* 12.6–7 (cf. *Mor.* 631f), most probably based on Aristotle's lost *Lak.Pol.*; cf. Herakl. Lembos, *Exc. Pol.* 373.13 Dilts.

[32] Xen. *Lak.Pol.* 2.9; cf. Plato, *Laws*, 633b; see also below, n. 34. (For a new interpretation of the metamorphosis undergone by this ritual, see Powell 1998, 130–4.) Cf. the anecdote about a 'lover' being fined on account of a contemptible sound, presumably a cry of pain, his boyfriend had let slip in fighting: Plut. *Lyk.* 18.8.

[33] e.g., the puberty rites of the Tucano Indios of South America: Scarpi 1987, 31, 34; cf. Brelich 1969, 34, 80; Jamin 1977, 65–7.

[34] Cic. *Tusc.* 2.34, 46; 5.77; cf. Bonnechère 1993, 11–22; Kennell 1995, 79–80, 149–61, with further evidence. Juvenile ability to endure pain in silence has become a commonplace in the folklore of Spartan 'mythology': cf. Rawson 1969, 88, 202 n. 2, 252, 355, 364.

[35] Lucian, *Anacharsis*, 38; cf. Powell 1998, 131 Fig. 4, 134, for whipping and nudity (in another context) on a Laconian vase dedicated at the shrine of Orthia.

[36] Cf. Bauman 1983, 84–94 for nudity and silence among the Quakers in seventeenth-century England.

[37] Agatharchides *ap.* Athen. 12. 550c–d = Jacoby, *FGrH* 86 F 10. On nudity and silence, cf. Aristoph. *Clouds*, 963–5, with n. 7 above.

[38] For the *Gymnopaidiai*: Kennell 1995, 65–9, with evidence; for the parody: Plut. *Lyk.* 15.2.

[39] Building up an ideal on a counter-ideal: Devereux 1965, 18–44; Ducat 1974, 1455–8.

[40] *ap.* Athen. 14. 657c–d = Jacoby, *FGrH* 106 F 2.

[41] Cf. Ducat 1974, 1458.

[42] Plut. *Lyk.* 28.8; *Demetr.* 1.5; *Mor.* 239a (30), 455e; Clem. Alex. *Pedagogue* 3.41.5; Diog. Laert. 1.103; cf. Fisher 1989, 34.

[43] As aptly observed by Plutarch: *Mor.* 503e–504b; cf. also Plato, *Laws*, 671c. For drunkenness and laughter: David 1989a, 6.

[44] Cf. Houston/Kramarae 1991, 394–5 (with the example of African-American slaves); Ettin 1994, 176–8.

[45] Hdt. 7.231; for the 'tremblers': Xen. *Lak.Pol.* 9.4–6; Plut. *Ages.* 30.2–4. The social sanction of silence would have been exacerbated, by way of contrast, by the nagging that Xenophon (ibid. 9.5) implies the coward to have got from his womenfolk for their lack of suitors.

[46] Plut. *Lyk.* 12.8; *Mor.* 236f(1); 697e; here the warning is addressed to young and foreign visitors.

[47] With the possible exception of the public halls (λέσχαι), where the elderly appear to have spent much of their time in talking: Plut. *Lyk.* 25.2–3; cf. David 1991, 97–8. For talk at the *syssitia* see, e.g., Fisher 1989, esp. 38, 48, n. 66.

[48] See David 1989a, 5–7.

[49] Plut. *Lyk.* 12.9.

[50] For stealing food: Xen. *Lak.Pol.* 2.7–8; Herakl. Lembos, *Exc. Pol.* 373.13 Dilts; Plut. *Lyk.* 17.3. In military operations silence helped in hiding from the

enemy, supported discipline and the efficient transmission of orders: e.g., Thuc. 2.89.9; Xen. *Hell.* 4.3.17; cf. *Lak.Pol.* 11.5–8; Plut. *Lys.* 10.1; for the martial power of silence, cf. Xen. *Anab.* 1.8.11; silence and hunting: Jamin 1977, 15–43; also below, n. 97. On the importance of hunting in Spartan society and consciousness: David 1993.

51 Aristotle *ap.* Plut. *Lyk.* 28. 2–5 (= fr. 538 Rose); Herakl. Lembos, *Exc. Pol.* 373.10 Dilts (= 611.10 Rose); cf. Lévy 1988, 245–52; Ducat 1990, 123–4, with bibliography.

52 I am not persuaded by recent scepticism: e.g., Whitby 1994, 97–100, 117–19, with further literature.

53 Xen. *Hell.* 3.3.8–11; cf., e.g., Sartori 1991, 492, 506–9.

54 Xen. *Hell.* 1.6.36–37; cf. Powell 1989, 178–90; Lewis 1996, 59.

55 Diod. 14.13.8; Plut. *Lys.* 25.1, 30.3; *Ages.* 20.3–5; *Mor.* 212c; cf. Bommelaer 1981, 224–5 and n. 123.

56 e.g. Thuc. 5.68.2, 74.3; periodic expulsion of foreigners: Thuc. 2.39.1; Xen. *Lak.Pol.* 14.4; Plut. *Lyk.* 27.7–9; *Agis*, 10.3. But the Spartans' attitude to *xenoi* was more complex: see, e.g., Hodkinson 1983, 276–78; *idem* 1994, 211–12; Thommen 1996, 145–6.

57 Basso 1973, 143–5; Bruneau 1973, 32–3.

58 Plut. *Mor.* 232e (2); cf., e.g., 216a (15), 224f (3), 229c (8), e (13).

59 Hdt. 3.46 (The story goes that the Samians' attempt to comply and minimize verbality met with another lesson in brevity); cf., e.g., Thuc. 1.86.1 (below). For an extreme case, in which total silence is reported to have been the Spartans' reply see, for what it is worth, Paus. 4.5.7.

60 Plut. *Mor.* 192c (3), 217d (5).

61 For similarities between some Cynic, esp. Diogenian, norms of education and those of the Spartans: Diog. Laert. 6.27, 31 (cf. Xen. loc. cit. above, n. 7); Dudley 1967, 33–4, 87–8; Rawson 1969, 86–7; Tigerstedt 1974, 36. On the Cynics' attitude to Sparta: ibid. 30–41.

62 Diog. Laert. 6.59. For manliness and brachylogy, cf. Powell 1988, 235–6.

63 Thuc. 1.86.1, with Francis 1991–93, 203–5.

64 For oligarchic traits of the Spartan Assembly see, e.g., Cartledge 1987, 129–32; *idem* 1996, 180–1. The 'mixed constitution' and the mirage: e.g., Rawson 1969, 59, 69, 73, 83–4 and *passim*.

65 Plut. *Lyk.* 26.3–5 (probably based on Arist. *Lak.Pol.*); Aristotle regarded the system as 'childish' (*Pol.* 1271a 10), an epithet by which he 'complimented' the method of electing ephors as well (1270b 28); but see Flaig 1993.

66 Plut. *Lyk.* 6.7–8 and 6.10; cf. Diod. 7.12.6 = Tyrt. fr. 4.5–6 West.

67 Dem. 18.170; on a previous occasion Demosthenes himself had been ridiculed by Aischines (2.35) for speechlessness *vis-à-vis* Philip.

68 The ephors' powers as 'tyrannic': Xen. *Lak.Pol.* 8.4; Plat. *Laws*, 712d; Arist. *Pol.* 1265b40, 1270b15; punishment on the spot: Xen. ibid.; the two ephors accompanying a king in campaigns: ibid. 13.5; *Hell.* 2.4.36. On the general supervision over military commanders: Hodkinson 1983, 268 and n. 83, with evidence; over punishments in the *agōgē*: Plut. *Lyk.* 18.6–7.

69 Cf., for what it is worth, the tradition (probably derived from Ephoros) on the sinisterly silent way Pausanias' mother suggested how to deal with her son

by placing a brick against the doors of the sanctuary in which he had taken refuge: Diod. 11.45.6; Nepos, *Paus.* 5.3; Polyain. 8.51. The use of a nonverbal signal, a peculiar cap (κυνέη or πῖλος Λακωνικός), in mass communication at Sparta is attested for as early as the late eighth century BC, with respect to the *Partheniai* episode: David 1992, 18–19 and nn. 42–4, with evidence.

[70] Xen. *Lak.Pol.* 15.6; cf. Herakl. Lembos, *Exc. Pol.* 373.10 Dilts; cf. Plut. *Ages.* 4.5 for standing up in the presence of the ephors as one of Agesilaos' political gimmicks.

[71] Cf. Rutherford 1996, 1406–7 for examples from classical (esp. Greek) literature.

[72] Xen. *Hell.* 6.4.16; (cf. ibid. 4.5.10); Plut. *Ages.* 29.4–7, with Shipley 1997, 328. The official suppression of public mourning in Sparta: below and n. 98. Reactions ascribed to Spartan mothers in similar circumstances: Nafissi 1991, 299–300 and nn. 94–8, 307, n. 131.

[73] For the distinction between functional and expressive silences: Bock 1976, 285–94.

[74] Xen. *Hell.* 7.1.32; Diod. 15.72.3; Plut. *Ages.* 33.6–8.

[75] Plut. *Mor.* 231b (3); cf. *Mor.* 191f; *Lyk.* 25.6. On Paidaretos = Pedaritos (e.g. Thuc. 8.28), see Poralla/(Bradford) 1985, 104 (s.v.); Cartledge 1987, 92, 145, 205, 288.

[76] Xen. *Lak.Pol.* 9.5. Such inappropriate behaviour was treated with another non-verbal channel, beating (ibid.)

[77] Hdt. 6.67.3; cf. Lateiner 1987, 93, 115; also Richer in this volume. Turning to hellenistic Sparta, the Phylarchean tradition presents another confrontation between a king and the previous holder of his throne: Leonidas II, restored king, *vis-à-vis* his usurping son-in-law Kleombrotos, by that time a suppliant in a sanctuary, looking 'perplexed and silent' (Plut. *Agis*, 17.1); but the details of this scene may derive from Phylarchos' tendency to dramatize. This also holds true for the silent 'dialogue' between Kleomenes III and his mother: Plut. *Kleom.* 22.4–5.

[78] The Spartans' obsession with honour: Lendon 1997.

[79] e.g. Ephoros *ap.* Ael. *Var. Hist.* 13.23 = Jacoby, *FGrH* 70 F 175; Plut. *Lyk.* 29.8; cf. (Manfredini)/Piccirilli 1980, 284–5.

[80] For Kleomenes: Hdt. 6.75 (cf. the sceptical approach of Griffiths 1989: 60–1); Pantites: Hdt. 7.232; Timokrates: Thuc. 2.92.3; Gylippos (?): Athen. 6. 234a; Antalkidas: Plut. *Artax.* 22.6–7; Therykion: Plut. *Kleom.* 31.4–12; Kleomenes III and his associates (but first he argued against Therykion's suggestion to commit suicide): ibid. 31. 8–11, 37; note that Plutarch (Phylarchos?) was explicit about Therykion's silence after Kleomenes' reply and before the suicide. Cf. Lewis 1977, 30, n. 27; van Hooff 1990, 89, 110–11, 193. For unnamed Spartans: Sen. *Ep. Mor.* 77.14; Plut. *Mor.* 234b–c (38); 242d (30). For silence as the prelude of suicide or disaster in Greek tragedy see, e.g., Soph. *Oed. Tyr.* 1075; *Antig.* 1251, 1256.

[81] Plut. *Pyrrh.* 27.5: presented as holding a halter about her neck; cf. the verbal threat of her granddaughter and namesake: Plut. *Agis*, 17.7.

[82] The priority of the collective over the individual in Spartan mentality (cf. in the context of suicide esp. Plut. *Kleom.* 31.10) and the pressure of

oliganthropy must have been among the main factors working against such a trend.

[83] Plut. *Lyk*. 13.1–4; *Mor*. 221b (1); 227b (8); cf. Plat. *Laws*, 721e, 793a–b; cf. Cartledge 1978, 35–6; Boring 1979, 24–31; (Manfredini)/Piccirilli 1980, 254–5; Whitley 1997, 648–9.

[84] For dearth of documents see, e.g., Cartledge 1978, 35–7; the absence of epinician poetry: Hodkinson in this volume; plastic art: cf. Hodkinson 1998; dress: David 1989b, 3–13.

[85] Whitley 1997, 645–9; cf. Hodkinson in this volume. For music and dance: e.g. Powell 1994, 302–6; Rahe 1994, 129–33, 301, nn. 72–9, 302, n. 96. But, as observed, choral music could be a monotonous equivalent of silence.

[86] The Spartan theatre: Hdt. 6.67; Aristoxenos *ap*. Athen. 14. 631c = F 108 Wehrli; Polykrates *ap*. Athen. 4. 139e = Jacoby, *FGrH* 588 F 1; Plut. *Ages*. 29.3; Paus. 3.14.1; cf. Bulle 1937, 271 ff.

[87] Sosibios *ap*. Athen. 14. 621d–e = Jacoby, *FGrH* 595 F 7, with Jacoby's commentary, IIIb, 649 and Breitholtz 1960, 115–21; for Alexis, cf. Arnott 1996, 430–2.

[88] *ap*. Athen. 14. 621e–f = Jacoby, *FGrH* 595 F 7; cf. Suda, *s.v*. 'Sosibius' = Jacoby, *FGrH* 595 T 1 and Hesych. s.v. 'δεικηλισταί'. For the obscene dances: David 1989a, 7–9, with evidence.

[89] Saville-Troike 1985, 11; Jaworsky 1993, 168; Sparta and the visual: Powell 1989, 173–92.

[90] Dickins 1929, 163–86; cf. David 1989a, 11–12; 22, nn. 60–4.

[91] Dickins 1929, 163–86 and pls. XLVII 1–3, XLVIII 3, XLIX 2, LVII 2, LVIII 3, LIX 1, 4, LXI 1, 2, LXII 1 (for the grotesque); pls. LI 3, LIII 1, 3, LIV 1–4, LV 1, 2 (for the ideal); see illustrations, figs. 1 and 2.

[92] Masks could have been produced not only by *perioikoi* but also by Spartiates who, at least during the archaic period, were not debarred from manual crafts: Cartledge 1976, 115–19.

[93] e.g. Scarpi 1987, 21–40; Szuchewycz 1997, 239–60.

[94] Plut. *Agis*, 11.4–5.

[95] Scarpi 1987, 25.

[96] Cf. Hodkinson 1983, 273–6; Parker 1989, 154–61; Powell 1994, 288–91.

[97] The 'solemn, holy and mysterious character of silence': Plut. *Mor*. 510e (17); cf. 505f. Ritual silence *vis-à-vis* death accompanies also sacrificial ceremonies; Sansone (1988, 86) looks for the origin in the hunters' practice of maintaining lengthy silences.

[98] Plut. *Mor*. 238d; on a similar prohibition in Lokris: Herakl. Lembos, *Exc. Pol*. 383.60 Dilts; cf. Nafissi 1991, 285–6. Legislation interfering with women's funeral laments: Ormand 1996, 41, n. 16, 58–9.

[99] Plut. *Kleom*. 9.2; on Fear and the ephors, see Richer in this volume.

[100] The divine personification of silence: Höfer 1965, 817. Silence was honoured with the name of a street in Elis – ἡ ἀγυιὰ Σιωπῆς (Paus. 6.23.8), and recently also with an entry in the *OCD*^{3} (above, n. 71).

[101] Plut. *Kleom*. 9.1; Paus. 3.18.1; cf. David 1989a, 1–2, 17–18.

[102] As the protagonist addresses his wife in Shakespeare, *Coriolanus*, II.i.194.

Bibliography

Arnott, W.G.

1996 *Alexis: The Fragments. A Commentary*, Cambridge.

Basso, K.H.

1973 'Il silenzio nella cultura degli Apache occidentali', in P. Giglioli (ed.) *Linguaggio e società*, Bologna, 139–58.

Bauman, R.

1983 *Let Your Words Be Few*, Cambridge.

Bernstein, B.

1971 *Class, Codes and Control*, London.

Bock, Ph.K.

1976 'I think but dare not speak', *Journal of Anthropological Research* 32, 285–94.

Bommelaer, J.-F.

1981 *Lysandre de Sparte*, Paris.

Bonnechère, P.

1993 'Orthia et la flagellation des éphèbes spartiates', *Kernos* 6, 11–22.

Boring, T.A.

1979 *Literacy in Ancient Sparta*, Leiden.

Breitholz, L.

1960 *Die dorische Farce*, Uppsala.

Brelich, A.

1969 *Paides e Parthenoi*, Rome.

Bruneau, T.G.

1973 'Communicative Silences', *Journal of Communication* 23, 17–46.

Bulle, H.

1937 *Das Theater zu Sparta*, Munich.

Burke, P.

1993 *The Art of Conversation*, Cambridge.

Calame, C.

1983 *Alcman*, Rome.

Cartledge. P.A.

1976 'Did Spartan citizens ever practise a manual tekhne?', *LCM* 1, 115–19.

1978 'Literacy in the Spartan oligarchy', *JHS* 98, 25–37.

1981 'Spartan wives: liberation or licence?', *CQ* 31, 84–105.

1987 *Agesilaos and the Crisis of Sparta*, London.

1996 'Comparatively equal', in J. Ober and Ch. Hedrick (eds.)*Demokratia*, Princeton, 175–85.

Casel, O.

1919 *De philosophorum graecorum silentio mystico*, Giessen.

Cozzo, A.

1991 'Note sulla condotta linguistica degli Spartani', in *Studi di filologia classica...G. Monaco*, Palermo, IV, 1371–8.

David, E.

1989a 'Laughter in Spartan society', in A. Powell (ed.) *Classical Sparta*, London, 1–25.

1989b 'Dress in Spartan society', *AncW* 19, 3–13.
1991 *Old Age in Sparta*, Amsterdam.
1992 'Sparta's social hair', *Eranos* 90, 11–21.
1993 'Hunting in Spartan society and consciousness', *EMC/CV* 37, 393–414.

Den Boer, W.
1954 *Laconian Studies*, Amsterdam.

Devereux, G.
1965 'La psychoanalyse et l'histoire', *Annales ESC* 20, 18–44.

Dickins, G.
1929 'Terracotta Masks', in R.M. Dawkins (ed.) *The Sanctuary of Artemis Orthia, JHS* suppl. 5, 163–86.

Dilts, M.R.
1971 *Heraclidis Lembi Excerpta Politiarum*, Durham, North Carolina.

Dinouart, J.A.T. (Abbé)
1771 (1987) *L'Art de se taire*, Grenoble.

Douglas, M.
1973 *Natural Symbols*, Harmondsworth.

Ducat, J.
1974 'Le mépris des hilotes', *Annales ESC* 30, 1451–64.
1990 *Les hilotes*, *BCH* suppl. 20, Paris.

Dudley, D.R.
1967 *A History of Cynicism*, Hildesheim.

Edmonds, J.M.
1961 *The Fragments of Attic Comedy* IIIA, Leiden.

Ettin, A.V.
1994 *Speaking Silences*, Charlottesville and London.

Fisher, N.R.E.
1989 'Drink, hybris and the promotion of social harmony in Sparta', in A. Powell (ed.) *Classical Sparta*, London, 26–50.

Flaig, E.
1993 'Die spartanische Abstimmung nach der Lautstärke', *Historia* 42, 139–60.

Francis, E.D.
1991–93 'Brachylogia Laconica', *BICS* 38, 198–212.

Gismondi, M.A.
1985 ' "The Gift of Theory": a critique of the *histoire des mentalités*', *Social History* 10, 211–30.

Griffiths, A.
1989 'Was Kleomenes mad?', in A. Powell (ed.) *Classical Sparta*, London, 51–78.

Hodkinson, S.
1983 'Social order and the conflict of values in classical Sparta', *Chiron* 13, 239–81.
1994 ' "Blind Ploutos"? Contemporary images of the role of wealth in classical Sparta', in A. Powell and S. Hodkinson (eds.) *Shadow of Sparta*, London and New York, 183–222.

1997 'The development of Spartan society and institutions in the archaic period', in L.G. Mitchell and P.J. Rhodes (eds.) *The Development of the Polis*, London and New York, 83–102.
1998 'Lakonian artistic production and the problem of Spartan austerity', in N. Fisher and H. van Wees (eds.)*Archaic Greece*, London, 93–117.

Höfer, O.
1965 'Siga', 'Sige', in Roscher *Lexikon* IV, Hildesheim.

Hooff, A.J. L. van
1990 *From Autothanasia to Suicide. Self-killing in Classical Antiquity*, London and New York.

Houston, M. and Kramarae, Ch.
1991 'Speaking from silence', *Discourse and Society* 2.4, 387–99.

Jacoby, F.
1955–1962 *Fragmente der griechischen Historiker* IIA–B;III b, Leiden.

Jamin, J.
1977 *Les lois du silence*, Paris.

Jaworski, A.
1993 *Power of Silence*, Newbury Park.

Kennell, N.G.
1995 *The Gymnasium of Virtue*, Chapel Hill and London.

Kurzon, D.
1995 'The right of silence', *Journal of Pragmatics* 23, 55–69.
1998 *Discourse of Silence*, Amsterdam and Philadelphia.

Lateiner, D.
1987 'Nonverbal communication in the *Histories* of Herodotus', *Arethusa* 20, 83–119.

Le Goff, J.
1974 'Les mentalités: une histoire ambigue', in J. Le Goff and P. Nora, *Faire de l'histoire* III, Paris, 76–90.

Lendon, J. E.
1997 'Spartan Honor', in C.D. Hamilton and P. Krentz (eds.) *Polis and Polemos. Essays...Donald Kagan*, Claremont, 105–26.

Lévy, E.
1988 'La kryptie et ses contradictions', *Ktema* 13, 245–52.

Lewis, D.M.
1977 *Sparta and Persia*, Leiden.

Lewis, S.
1996 *News and Society in the Greek Polis*, Chapel Hill and London.

Link, S.
1994 *Der Kosmos Sparta*, Darmstadt.

MacDowell, D.M.
1986 *Spartan Law*, Edinburgh.

Manfredini, M. and Piccirilli, L. (commentary by Piccirilli)
1980 *Plutarco, Le vite di Licurgo e di Numa*, Milan.

Nafissi, M.
1991 *La Nascita del Kosmos*, Naples.

Nagel, S. and Vecchi, S.
1984 'Il bambino, la parola, il silenzio nella cultura medievale', *Quaderni Storici* 19, 719–63.
Ollier, F.
1933–43 *Le mirage spartiate* I–II, Paris.
Ormand, K.
1996 'Silent by convention? Sophokles' Tekmessa', *AJPh* 117, 37–64.
Parker, R.
1989 'Spartan religion', in A. Powell (ed.) *Classical Sparta*, London, 142–72.
Pomeroy, S.B.
1994 *Xenophon, Oeconomicus. A Social and Historical Commentary*, Oxford.
Poralla, P.
1913 (1985) *Prosopographie der Lakedaimonier*, Diss. Breslau (revised by A.S. Bradford).
Powell, A.
1988 *Athens and Sparta*, London.
1989 'Mendacity and Sparta's use of the visual', in A. Powell (ed.) *Classical Sparta*, London, 173–92.
1994 'Plato and Sparta', in A. Powell and S. Hodkinson (eds.) *The Shadow of Sparta*, London and New York, 273–321.
1998 'Sixth-century Lakonian vase-painting', in N. Fisher and H. van Wees (eds.) *Archaic Greece*, London, 119–46.
Rahe, P.A.
1994 *Republics Ancient and Modern* I, Chapel Hill and London.
Rawson, E.
1969 *The Spartan Tradition in European Thought*, Oxford.
Rose, V.
1886 (1967) *Aristotelis qui ferebantur Librorum Fragmenta*, Leipzig.
Rutherford, R.B.
1996 'Silence', in *OCD*[3], Oxford.
Sansone, D.
1988 *Greek Athletics and the Genesis of Sport*, Berkeley and Los Angeles.
Sartori, F.
1991 'Il "pragma" di Cinadone', in E.Olshausen and H. Sonnabend (eds.) *Stuttgarter Kolloquium zur historischen Geographie des Altertums*, Bonn, 487–514.
Saville-Troike, M.
1985 'The place of silence in an integrated theory of communication', in D. Tannen and Saville-Troike (eds.) *Perspectives of Silence*, Norwood, 3–18.
Scarpi, P.
1987 'The eloquence of silence', in M.G. Ciani (ed.) *Regions of Silence*, Amsterdam, 19–40.
Shipley, D.R.
1997 *A Commentary on Plutarch's Life of Agesilaos*, Oxford.

Snell, B. (ed.)
1986 *Tragicorum Graecorum Fragmenta* I, Göttingen.
Szwchewycz, B.
1997 'Silence in ritual communication', in A. Jaworski (ed.) *Silence*, Berlin and New York, 239–60.
Thommen, L.
1996 *Lakedaimonion Politeia*, Stuttgart.
Tigerstedt, E.N.
1965–1974 *The Legend of Sparta in Classical Antiquity* I–II, Lund and Uppsala.
Walker, A.G.
1985 'The two faces of silence', in D. Tannen and Saville-Troike (eds.) *Perspectives on Silence*, Norwood, 55–76.
Wehrli, F.
1967 *Die Schule des Aristoteles* II, Basel and Stuttgart.
Whitby, M.
1994 'Two shadows: images of Spartans and helots', in A. Powell and S. Hodkinson (eds.) *Shadow of Sparta*, London and New York, 87–126.
Whitley, J.
1997 'Cretan laws and Cretan literacy', *AJA* 101, 635–61.

Chapter 6

AN AGONISTIC CULTURE?

Athletic competition in archaic and classical Spartan society

Stephen Hodkinson

During the archaic period the passion for engagement in the *agōn* (or 'contest'), which was a defining characteristic of Greek culture, came to focus above all upon the sphere of athletic competition. As Oswyn Murray (1993, 202) has noted, 'Greek society is the first to exhibit the cult of the sportsman.' Correct as Murray's observation is, one must be cautious about using modern terms like 'sportsman' and 'sport', since they might be taken to imply notions of fair play and honourable defeat which were utterly alien to the 'winner-takes-all' spirit of the Greek athletic *agōn*. Greek athletic contests were serious business in which honour and reputation were exalted by victory or dashed by defeat. The potential rewards were great: some home cities accorded their victorious athletes symbolic and material prizes such as triumphal entries, statues, money and, sometimes, military commands. Such was the importance of athletic success as a determinant of status that it became a central preoccupation of aspiring individuals, not least among the aristocratic elite. The four Sacred or 'Crown' games – at Olympia, Delphi, the Isthmus of Corinth and Nemea – were developed into an integrated circuit during the sixth century in response to the demand for an ongoing arena in which athletes could achieve glory of panhellenic dimensions. This panhellenic circuit was backed up by numerous local games of lesser importance but no less fiercely contested.

The question I want to raise in this chapter is to what extent this preoccupation with the athletic *agōn* applied also in Sparta, the polis often regarded as different from other Greek states. Certainly, Aristotle believed that the Spartans had avoided the error of other poleis who had produced in their children an athletic habit which was detrimental to their bodily development (*Politics* 1338b9–13). Some modern scholars have interpreted this cautionary attitude as a thoroughgoing disdain for athletics. According to Michael Poliakoff (1987, 101), 'Spartan disaffection with sport started early; the state reduced its role in civic life and developed new "utilitarian" events atypical of the rest of the Greek world.' Aristotle, however, is not saying that Spartiate youths abstained from athletics, simply that athletics did not dominate their activities or bodily formation. Indeed, there is no doubt that Spartan citizens of the archaic and classical periods did participate in the athletic *agōn*. The question raised by Aristotle's comments is rather to what extent the singular character of the Spartan polis modified the character of that participation. What role did participation in athletic contests play within Spartiate society?

Complete coverage of this large subject is impossible within the limits of this volume. Hence I shall exclude here direct coverage of equestrian contests, and especially chariot racing, which were an important part of Greek athletics and played a major role in Spartiate society.[1] I shall concentrate my attention on those athletic contests which necessarily involved personal participation; in equestrian events the horse- or chariot-owner did not normally compete in person. (For convenience, I shall use the term 'athletic(s)' in the modern sense, to exclude equestrian events.) My discussion falls into two parts: I shall look first at athletic competition within Sparta's home territory; I shall then consider Spartiate participation in contests abroad, especially at the Olympic games.

Competition within Spartan home territory

Team or individual competition?

Regarding contests within Spartan territory, there is one obvious sign of Spartan idiosyncrasy: namely, the significant role of team contests, which were not normally prominent within Greek agonistic activity. One such team game was the *sphaireis* contest, whose importance is indicated by the fact that Xenophon (*Lak.Pol.* 9.5) includes it with the common messes, wrestling bouts and choruses among significant activities from which cowards were excluded.[2] The *sphaireis* contest was an activity for adult males; but Xenophon also mentions a team contest specifically for boys at the sanctuary of Artemis Orthia in which certain youths attempted to steal cheeses from the altar, which was defended by a team who drove them off with whips (*Lak.Pol.* 2.8–9; cf. Plato *Laws* 633b–c). Both the *sphaireis* contest and the whipping of boys at the altar of Artemis also appear in the evidence for Roman Sparta, but by that time the functions of both were considerably transformed.[3] These team contests can be related to special features of Spartiate society, especially the group coordination and competitive solidarity upon which Spartan military and social cohesion depended.

This picture of a state which placed less emphasis upon individual competition might appear to be confirmed by the late seventh-century Spartan poet Tyrtaios (fr. 12.1–9):

> I would not rate a man worth mention or account
> (τ' ἂν μνησαίμην οὔτ' ἐν λόγῳ ἄνδρα τιθείμην)
> for skill in running or wrestling,
> not even if he had a Cyclops' size and strength
> or outstripped in the race the Thracian Boreas
> or if he matched Tithonos in good looks
> or Midas and Kinyras in his wealth
> or outshone Pelops in his kingliness
> or had Adrastos' gift of honeyed speech
> and every virtue, save a warrior's might...

Tyrtaios gives priority to military prowess over athletic skill and other personal attributes on grounds of its value to the community. As he later indicates, the athletic attributes of speed and strength gain their proper value only through their use in the phalanx (ll. 16–17, 21–2). The passage, in the words of one recent interpreter, displays an 'obsessive concern with non-individuality' (Tarkow 1983, 55 and 61) which seems overtly inimical to the practice of individual competition. The poems of Tyrtaios were frequently recited in Sparta in later centuries and the sentiments they expressed exercised a continuing influence over the society's values. Nevertheless, we should not over-interpret this perceived depreciation of athletic prowess. Tyrtaios is not dismissing athletic ability outright, simply arguing that he would not value an athlete who did not also demonstrate military prowess.

Moreover, although Tyrtaios' poems undoubtedly contributed to one strand of classical Spartan thought, his prescriptive views were never an uncontested or complete statement of Spartiate attitudes. This is indicated for Tyrtaios' own day by the very fact that he thought athleticism needed devaluing for a Spartiate audience. The classical evidence (Xen. *Lak.Pol.* 4.2–6; 10.1–3), moreover, indicates that the lives of Spartan citizens from youth to old age included various forms of individual competition.[4] Prominent among these were athletic contests. As we have seen, individual wrestling bouts are named as an important activity of adult male citizens. Athletic competition was also important within the Spartan public upbringing. According to Xenophon (*Lak.Pol.* 1.4), the female upbringing included contests of speed and strength parallel to those for males. His statement presupposes the importance of athletic contests in the boys' upbringing, a point reinforced by Pausanias' reference (3.14.6) to the young men practising running in the Dromos racecourse by the river Eurotas, a stadium which probably went back to classical times (Delorme 1969, 72–4).

Female athletic competition

It is the prescription of athletic contests for girls, however, which is most unusual (cf. Arrigoni 1985, esp. 65–95). Xenophon's statement lacks detail regarding the precise contests involved. According to Plutarch (*Lyk.* 14.2), following here – as so often – the hellenistic *Apophthegmata Lakonika* (*Mor.* 227d), they consisted of 'running and wrestling and throwing the discus and javelin'.[5] Doubts about the reliability of this information, at least as regards the archaic and classical periods, are raised, however, by the fact that the passage from the *Apoph. Lak.* claims that one purpose of this training was that the women 'might be able to fight for themselves, their children and the country', a purpose which – even if true of later periods – could never have been envisaged before the unprecedented and unexpected enemy invasion of Lakonia in 370/69. Note the comments of Plato (*Laws* 805e–806b) that Spartan girls were unfitted for warfare, despite their engagement in gymnastics. Indeed, of the contests claimed by Plutarch and the *Apophthegmata Lakonika*, only running and wrestling are specifically attested in the late archaic or classical evidence. The running Spartan girl is depicted in four sixth-century Lakonian bronze figurines from Sparta, Dodona and Prizren.[6] Three of these girls wear a short, less than knee-length, *chitōn*; two of them pull the hem further up the leg for ease of movement (PLATE 1). This state of dress led the sixth-century poet Ibykos to dub Spartan girls as 'thigh-showers' (fr. 339, Davies, *ap.* Plut. *Comp. Lyk.-Num.* 3.3). Running and wrestling – and naked thighs – are highlighted in Peleus' abusive comments on Spartan women

PLATE 1. Bronze figurine of Spartan running girl from Prizren; *c.* 540 BC (photograph courtesy of British Museum, Bronzes 208).

in Euripides' *Andromachē* (595–601). Pausanias (3.13.7) too details a contemporary foot race involving a female group, the Dionysiades, which Calame (1977, I.333) traces back to the archaic period. The passage from the *Andromachē* is sometimes interpreted (e.g. by Cartledge 1981, 91) as signifying that the girls actually wrestled with the boys; but all Euripides really says is that they shared the same racetracks and palaistras. This is confirmed by other sources, such as by the lines the hellenistic poet Theokritos (18.22–5) puts into the mouths of a group of Spartan girls: 'we, as all her age mates, who run the same racecourse and oil ourselves down like men alongside the bathing pools of the Eurotas'. Not even writers from the Roman period (Propertius 3.14; Ovid, *Heroides* 16.149–52; Plut. *Lyk.* 15.1), who might be expected to develop any hint of mixed athletics, make any reference to the point. What the sources are agreed on is that the girls' athletics were conducted side by side with the boys in full public view. Neither was this an occasional activity. Female athletic participation was grounded in regular outdoor exercise, as is emphasised in the portrayal of the Spartan Lampito in Aristophanes' *Lysistrata* (81–2).

Female athletic competition was of course officially prescribed not for its own sake but for achieving physical fitness for procreation, as part of the Spartiate girl's curriculum for marriage (Xen. *Lak.Pol.* 1.4; Stewart 1997, 108–16). Participation may have involved only unmarried girls and not married women, perhaps not even those of child-bearing age.[7] It was therefore only a circumscribed version of agonistic activity. Nevertheless, performance in such public contests presumably did make a real difference to the reputation and eligibility of the participants; and it constituted a greater degree of engagement in the *agōn* than was available to women in other classical Greek states. Not that female athletic contests were completely unknown elsewhere in Greece. The girls' foot races at the festival of Hera at Olympia noted by Pausanias (5.16.2–4) probably originated in the archaic period.[8] (It is unclear whether or not the contests were restricted to girls from Elis.) Fifth-century vases from the sanctuary of Artemis at Brauron suggest that foot races formed part of the rituals of the resident pubescent girls (Scanlon 1988, 186; Kahil 1977). Spartan practice, however, appears unique in the incorporation of girls' athletic competition not just into religious ritual but as a regular part of their upbringing, in its extension to all girls of citizen households, and in the public character of the activity, practised not in rural sanctuaries like Olympia and Brauron but at the very centre of the Spartan polis.[9] That these singular phenomena developed under state auspices indicates that there was no necessary opposition between athletic contests and the ethos of the Spartan polis.

Dedications by athletic victors

Epigraphic and archaeological evidence from the late archaic and classical periods demonstrates the existence of a range of athletic contests within Spartan territory which were typically Greek in the predominance of contests of individual prowess. The clearest indication comes from the inscription on the well-known marble stēlē dedicated in the sanctuary of Athena Chalkioikos on the Spartan acropolis in which a certain Damonon celebrates the equestrian and athletic victories achieved by himself and his son Enymakratidas (PLATE 2).[10] The inscription mentions no fewer than nine different Lakonian festivals at which these victories were achieved, indicating a veritable circuit of local games held at various locations in Sparta itself, Lakonia and Eastern Messenia.[11] Previous studies have focused largely upon Damonon's equestrian victories; but he also boasts that in his youth he gained eleven running victories: six in the *stadion* (a sprint over one stade, about 200 metres) and five in the *diaulos* race (a race over two stades). Due to breaks in the inscription (evident in PLATE 2), the list of Enymakratidas' victories is incomplete; but the surviving text records eleven,

PLATE 2. Two parts of an inscribed marble victory stēlē dedicated by Damonon to Athena on the Spartan acropolis; shortly before or after the Peloponnesian war (Sparta Museum 440; reproduced with permission of the British School at Athens).

five in the stade, two in the *diaulos* and four in the *dolichos* (long race). Of these, at least one is labelled as a boys' race, though the majority seem to be adult races. The inscription paints a remarkable picture of a father and son apparently dedicated to agonistic pursuits in both boyhood and manhood. The most remarkable fact, however, is that Damonon was able to advertise these individual achievements on the acropolis of Sparta in the sanctuary of the guardian deity of the polis, to whom the stēlē was dedicated.

Damonon was by no means the only athlete to advertise his victories. The significance of individual athletic activity as a preoccupation of Spartan citizens is indicated by a range of extant votive offerings made by successful athletes from the sixth and fifth centuries. Some are 'raw' offerings of items actually used in the athletic competition, such as a jumping-weight or discus; others are 'converted' offerings, such as a bronze figurine or a marble stēlē listing the athlete's victories.[12] This last, the athletic victory list, has been termed 'a peculiarly Laconian form of dedication', a distinctive manifestation of 'Spartan pride in athletic achievement' (Whitley 1998, 647).

Several of these offerings come from unknown locations in Sparta itself, such as a bronze figurine of an athlete dated 520–500 and two late-sixth-century marble stelai which record the victories achieved by their respective dedicators. These stelai – the first dedicated by a certain [G]laukat[ias], the other a dedication to Karneios by a certain Aiglatas, who records his multiple victories in the *dolichos* and in another event called the *makros* – share a distinctive visual feature.[13] The lettering of both texts is placed between guidelines which curve round at the end of each line so that they resemble the appearance of a race-track and the letters follow the course as it would have been run (Aupert 1980; cf. Jeffery 1990, 192). The dedication of Aiglatas' stēlē to Karneios suggests a connection with the annual festival of the Karneia, which presumably contained athletic contests in addition to the musical *agōn* attested by literary evidence (Athen. 635e–f). The incorporation of athletics into this major festival is further testimony to their central role in Spartiate life.

It is likewise significant that those votive offerings of known provenance cluster around two Spartan sanctuaries: Athena Chalkioikos on the acropolis and the sanctuary of Apollo at Amyklai.[14] On the acropolis some of the earliest extant offerings are relatively modest: two inscribed marble jumping weights, one dedicated by a certain Kleocha[res] around 550–525, the other by one Paitiadas in the early fifth century (Plate 3). Both relate to the long jump, which formed

PLATE 3. Inscribed marble jumping-weight from the Spartan acropolis, dedicated by Paitiadas to Athena; early fifth century (reproduced with permission of the British School at Athens).

part of the pentathlon.[15] The other offerings are more monumental. A late-sixth-century marble stēlē, which once bore a separate capital, bears an incomplete inscription recording an unknown athlete's multiple victories in the *dolichos*.[16] Another marble stēlē of similar date (PLATE 4), whose inscription was originally thought to be a 'Hymn to Athena', is now interpreted as another athletic dedication. The so-called 'Hymn' inscribed vertically on one side is apparently a dedicatory victory couplet, with the victories being recorded in the fragmentary inscriptions on the two flanking sides.[17] From the early fifth century, a long inscription on a white marble block from nearby Magoula 'reads like a verse-dedication to Athena from yet another

PLATE 4. Three sides of a marble stēlē from the Spartan acropolis, bearing a dedicatory couplet to Athena, flanked by lists of victories; late sixth century (Sparta Museum; reproduced with permission of the British School at Athens).

athlete' (Jeffery 1990, 192) and may well also derive from the Chalkioikos sanctuary.[18] The Damonon stēlē, which itself includes a dedicatory couplet, seems therefore to follow an established tradition of monumental athletic offerings at the sanctuary.[19]

The extant offerings at the Amyklaion contrast with those at Athena Chalkioikos in their marked focus on the discus event, which – like the long jump – was not an event in its own right but merely a discipline within the pentathlon. The earliest offering is an inscribed bronze discus dated (loosely) to the sixth century.[20] This is followed, *c.* 520–500, by a bronze figurine of a discus thrower (Plate 5).[21] Then, from *c.* 475, there survives a fragmentary inscribed and sculpted stone stēlē bearing a life-size frontal relief of a discus thrower, a unique form of representation among the surviving offerings (Plate 6).[22]

Several features of these votive offerings deserve attention. First, the changing nature of the dedications at the Amyklaion accords with general developments in the character of Greek votive offerings during the later sixth and fifth centuries: the increasing monumentality of dedications, the shift from 'raw' to 'converted' offerings (which is evident also at Athena Chalkioikos), and the growing trend towards representation of the person of the athlete himself. In these respects the evolving patterns of Spartiate athletic offerings reflect and exemplify those taking place throughout the Greek world. Secondly, the employment of skilled craftsmanship or of expensive materials, such as bronze and marble, for several of the dedications demonstrates a substantial expenditure of resources which is strong testimony to their social significance. Thirdly, although the surviving sample is small, the evident degree of differentiation between the character of dedications at

Plate 5. Bronze figurine of discus thrower from the Amyklaion; *c.* 520–500 BC (photograph Musée du Louvre, Br. 118; M. and P. Chuzeville)

PLATE 6. Fragmentary inscribed and sculpted stone stēlē from the Amyklaion, bearing a life-size relief of a discus thrower; *c.* 475 BC (Sparta Museum; photograph courtesy of Deutsches Archäologisches Institut, Athens).

Athena Chalkioikos and at the Amyklaion indicates a level of specialisation which suggests that the extant examples are merely the tip of what was originally a much larger iceberg of Spartiate victory offerings.

The suggestion that Spartiate athletic votive offerings shared common trends with those elsewhere in Greece receives support from the fact that they are paralleled in sanctuaries in other parts of Lakonia, including areas remote from Sparta where the dedicators are unlikely to have been Spartiates. The sixth-century discus from the Amyklaion is matched by a similar mid-sixth-century dedication by a certain Melas at the sanctuary of Apollo Pythaios at Thornax (mod. Kosmas).[23] The stone jumping-weights from Athena Chalkioikos are paralleled by finds, not only from the state sanctuary of Zeus Messapios at Tsakona (Catling 1990, 32), but also further afield, from Aigiai, near Gytheion (Vonias 1985). The Spartiate stelai recording running victories find their counterpart in a fragmentary fifth-century inscription from Geronthrai (mod. Geraki) listing an athlete's victories in the *stadion*, *diaulos*, *dolichos*, *pente dolichos* and the hoplite race.[24]

Public recognition of athletic success

Athletic success was not merely celebrated privately by the victor; it was also recognised by the Spartan polis. Its communal significance is demonstrated by evidence that lists of athletic victors were officially preserved and kept on public display. In the fifth century Hellanikos of Lesbos was able to compile a list of victors in the Karneian games (Athen. 635e–f). Jeffery has suggested that two fragmentary, late-sixth-century inscribed lists of names from the precinct of Athena Chalkioikos are public victory records of the sort upon which Hellanikos may have drawn. (Notably, these lists are paralleled by two lists of comparable date from perioikic Geronthrai.)[25] Further evidence for public display of these lists may be detectable in a change of presentation within the Damonon inscription. Throughout most of the text Damonon lumps together victories won at given festivals in different years. Even when he itemizes victories won within a single year, they are given without indication of date, not even when he once mentions separately victories gained at different annual meetings of the Lithesian games (ll. 54–6; 59–61). In the final section (ll. 67–95), however, the manner of listing changes: here Damonon itemizes each individual victory under the eponymous ephor in whose year of office the victory was won. The explanation, Jeffery suggests, is that 'in the earlier period...the official method of recording the victories merely recorded the victors' names in a simple list; but that during Damonon's later life...it became the official practice to cite the ephor's name at the head of the annual list of victors' (1990, 196). If this is correct, the presence of the eponymous ephor's name would provide definitive confirmation of the public recognition accorded to victorious athletes. Indeed, if a recent hypothesis is accepted, such recognition went one stage further, in the form of the donation of prizes, for it has been suggested that the cone-lidded amphoras which appear on certain reliefs of the Dioskouroi were the Lakonian equivalent of the similarly-shaped Panathenaic prize amphoras, a hypothesis made more plausible by the connections between the Dioskouroi and the Dromos racecourse at Sparta.[26]

The problem of boxing and the pankration

A substantial body of evidence suggests, then, that Spartan citizens both individually and collectively accorded a high valuation to various forms of athletic competition. There may, however, have been certain exceptions. According to some hellenistic and Roman sources, Spartiates were prohibited from participating in two events, boxing and the *pankration* (a kind of all-in wrestling in which only biting and gouging were prohibited), on the grounds that the result was determined by one contestant signalling his submission, a practice incompatible with the Spartan ethic of not conceding defeat during combat.[27]

Was this prohibition an authentic classical measure or merely part of the Spartan mirage? In contrast to the prohibitionist view, one tradition from the Roman Imperial period links Sparta with the invention of boxing (Philostratos, *Gymnastikos* 9). Other traditions, which first appear in the first century BC, refer to Spartan practice of the *pankration* – including a distinctive version which permitted biting and gouging – and even participation by Spartan women.[28] These late traditions, however, inspire little confidence, especially as references to the *pankration* may be influenced by its practice in Roman Sparta.[29] The prohibitionist tradition does at least go back a little earlier, to the revolutionary period of the late third century BC, whose influence is evident in the Lykourgan sayings in the *Apophthegmata Lakonika* (Tigerstedt 1965–78, ii.85), where the alleged prohibition is first attested.

Other evidence is equally controversial. Contemporary evidence for contests at Sparta itself might initially seem to contradict the idea of prohibition. Xenophon (*Lak.Pol.* 4.6), describing the activities of the Spartiate youths, the *hēbōntes*, uses the verb *pykteuein* ('to box'). Plato (*Protagoras* 342b–c; *Gorgias* 515e) has Sokrates characterise lakonophile Athenians as sporting cauliflower ears and wrapping on boxing thongs (*himantes*) in imitation of Spartan practice. Xenophon's reference, however, is not to proper individual boxing contests, but to informal scuffles, including group fights, which broke out unpredictably between those selected and rejected for membership of the *hippeis* (4.3–6). Similarly, if the *sphaireis* contests were boxing matches, as some suppose, they too were undoubtedly group affairs. As for Plato's evidence, current understanding of the development of the Spartan mirage within Athenian philolakonian circles suggests that their boxing activities are perhaps better interpreted as a translation of these Spartiate practices into an eminently Athenian context rather than as direct reflections of individual boxing contests in contemporary Sparta.[30]

One argument in favour of the claimed prohibition is the absence of boxing and the *pankration* from extant victory dedications in Lakonia. Against this, it might be noted that dedications for wrestling are also absent, despite its prominence in Spartiate life. The parallel, however, is not quite exact, since wrestling was part of the pentathlon for which dedications do survive, though the absence of direct commemoration is peculiar. Spartiate boxers and pankratiasts are also apparently absent from the standard list of Olympic victors compiled by Moretti (1957, 1970, 1992), though this too is a matter of controversy. According to the third-century AD writer Diogenes Laertius (1.72–3; cf. *Palatine Anthology* 7.88), citing the hellenistic writer Hermippos (fr. 14 Müller), the mid-sixth-century ephor Chilon died while applauding his son's Olympic boxing victory. Moretti (1957, no. 1024) dismissed this story as legendary invention, a view which has recently been challenged by Crowther (1990). Other writers (Pliny, *NH* 7.119; Tertullian, *De anim.* 52) who give the same account of Chilon's death, however, do not specify the event won by his son.[31] Hence some doubt must persist about this supposed boxing victory. Even if its authenticity is accepted, there remains the absence of *pankration* victories and the fact that Sparta's record in Olympic boxing would still lag behind her record in other major athletic events, in each of which at least three Spartiate victories are recorded.[32] The early date of the supposed boxing victory, moreover, would not preclude the possibility that a ban was imposed subsequently in the late sixth or early fifth century.

Although no single category of evidence in this controversy is ultimately decisive, cumulatively its overall trend suggests that, whether formally banned or not, neither boxing nor the *pankration* played a significant role in Spartiate life. It may not be excessive to conclude, in Crowther's words (1990, 201), that 'boxing and the pancration in competition were clearly not encouraged by the Spartan state'. Was this discouragement particular to Sparta? Certainly, Spartans are not the only ones portrayed as hostile to these contests.[33] Alexander the Great reportedly despised all athletes and never offered prizes for boxing and the *pankration* (Plut. *Alex.* 4.6). The Theban general Epaminondas is said to have told his troops on campaign to impress the enemy by wrestling and exercising with weaponry, but warned his fellow citizens when at home to avoid the *palaistra* (Nepos, *Epam.* 5.4; Plut. *Mor.* 192c–d; 788a). Although the Achaean general Philopoimen showed early promise as a wrestler, he purposely shunned all athletics, against his friends' advice, and banned them from his army as injurious to the training and bodily condition of a soldier (Plut. *Philopoimen* 3.2–4). The sources for these views are late, but the belief that athletic training and skills were useless for war is attested already in classical sources (Euripides, *Autolykos*, fr. 282 N; Plato, *Republic* 403e–404b; *Laws* 796a–b).

This comparative evidence shares generic features with the perceived Spartan ethic, though it differs in some of its particulars. First, the views expressed are those of individual commanders, in opposition to common opinion within their respective states – even Alexander's view is contrasted with that of his father Philip II – whereas the Spartan discouragement of boxing and the *pankration* was the general policy of the polis. Secondly, although those two events were singled out for opprobrium by Alexander, and there is some limited sympathy for running and wrestling, the general attitude expressed is critical of all athletics in a manner not attested in the Spartan evidence. Hence the reported Spartan objection to boxing and the *pankration*, the requirement to indicate submission, does not appear. The main criticism, in contrast, is the poverty of athletics as physical and technical training for war. Here there is some common ground with the Spartan approach, which – as noted earlier through the evidence of Aristotle – prevented the growth of an athletic habit detrimental to proper bodily development. The difference is that, unlike other states, the Spartiates possessed an in-built corrective to the impact of athletics, in the all-round physical and military training provided within the compulsory public upbringing and way of life. For classical Spartans, therefore, overt blanket criticism of all athletics was unnecessary. Note the contrast with the general depreciation of athletics in the poem of Tyrtaios, who was writing before the emergence of these institutions.

Similarly, the generalised polemic of the non-Spartan commanders cited above is explicable in the absence of systematic public military training in their native states. In the case of the Thebans, there is evidence that at the time of Epaminondas in the early fourth century they were moving in the direction of the Spartan system through their creation of the publicly maintained 'Sacred Band' (Plut. *Pelopidas* 18–19). Aristotle's comments (*Pol.* 1338b25–9) that, whereas the Spartans had previously been alone in their laborious exercises, they had now fallen behind others in both gymnastic and military contests, also imply that Boiotia's military success over Sparta in the early fourth century was founded on a Spartan-style prioritisation of all-round physical and military training, which would tie in with Epaminondas' warning to avoid the *palaistra*. On the relationship between warfare and athletics, therefore, the particulars of the reputed Spartan attitude to athletics – discouraging participation in certain events without being in principle hostile to athletics as such – were singular and more closely defined than elsewhere, in keeping with the more advanced and systematic nature of their public military training. The grounds for that attitude and the practices that went with it, however, were things which other Greeks – most notably military commanders – could appreciate and even attempt to emulate.

Spartiate participation in athletic competition abroad

The limits of the evidence

In considering Spartiate involvement in athletic contests abroad, one can again point to respects in which its character was affected by the particular nature of Spartan society. Above all, the compulsory public way of life precluded any Spartiate from pursuing the itinerant career of a professional athlete, such as that of Theogenes of Thasos with his reported total of some 1,200–1,400 victories (*Syll.*[3] 64a; Plut. *Mor.* 811e; Paus. 6.11.5). The Spartiate way of life, however, did not prevent citizens from competing at specific festivals outside Sparta.

Unfortunately, our understanding of the implications, however, is limited by the paucity of evidence, except for that relating to the Olympic games. We have no information about Spartiate non-equestrian victors at the other 'Crown' games at Delphi, Nemea and the Isthmus. The sanctuaries of Athena Chalkioikos and the Menelaion have produced tens of fragments of prize amphoras from the Panathenaic games at Athens; but only seven of the amphoras have been individually published and only one dated.[34] Of these seven only three are diagnostic and all show chariot-racing rather than athletic scenes. The value of athletic prizes at the Panathenaia – for adult competitors, from 12 to 100 *metrētai* of olive oil contained in an equivalent number of Panathenaic amphoras (Young 1984, 119–23, 186–7) – means that the inadequate publication of the amphoras is particularly unfortunate in depriving us of an opportunity to form some assessment of the material implications of Spartiate athletic participation abroad. Only through the evidence from the Olympic games, which provided no material rewards, can we seriously pursue the questions posed at the start of this paper.

Official attitudes and the decline of Spartiate athletic victors

What was the Spartan attitude towards the participation of its citizens in Olympic competition? How did such participation interact with the demands of the classical Spartan social order? The answers to these questions have been a matter of some controversy. The ultimate source of debate is the record of Spartiate victories at the Olympic games (*Fig.* 1). It is frequently claimed that Spartiate athletic victories – which, according to ancient victor lists, were numerous in the seventh century – declined from around 550 BC. This decline is usually linked with the beginning of Spartiate chariot-race victories, with rich Spartiates portrayed as turning their attention from athletics to chariot racing (e.g. Ste. Croix 1972, 354–5).

Before discussing this question, one must acknowledge recent debates concerning the authenticity of the traditional date of 776 BC for the foundation of the Olympic games. Some scholars would now downdate the start of the Olympics to *c.* 700 BC (Mallwitz 1988), some even to the early sixth century (Peiser 1990). This latter reconstruction would reject the authenticity of the early victor list, including the run of Spartiate seventh-century athletic victories. It could therefore be that the supposed decline of Spartiate athletic victories is a mere chimaera.

Even if we take the victor list at its face value, however (at least from the later seventh century onwards), the picture of a dramatic mid-

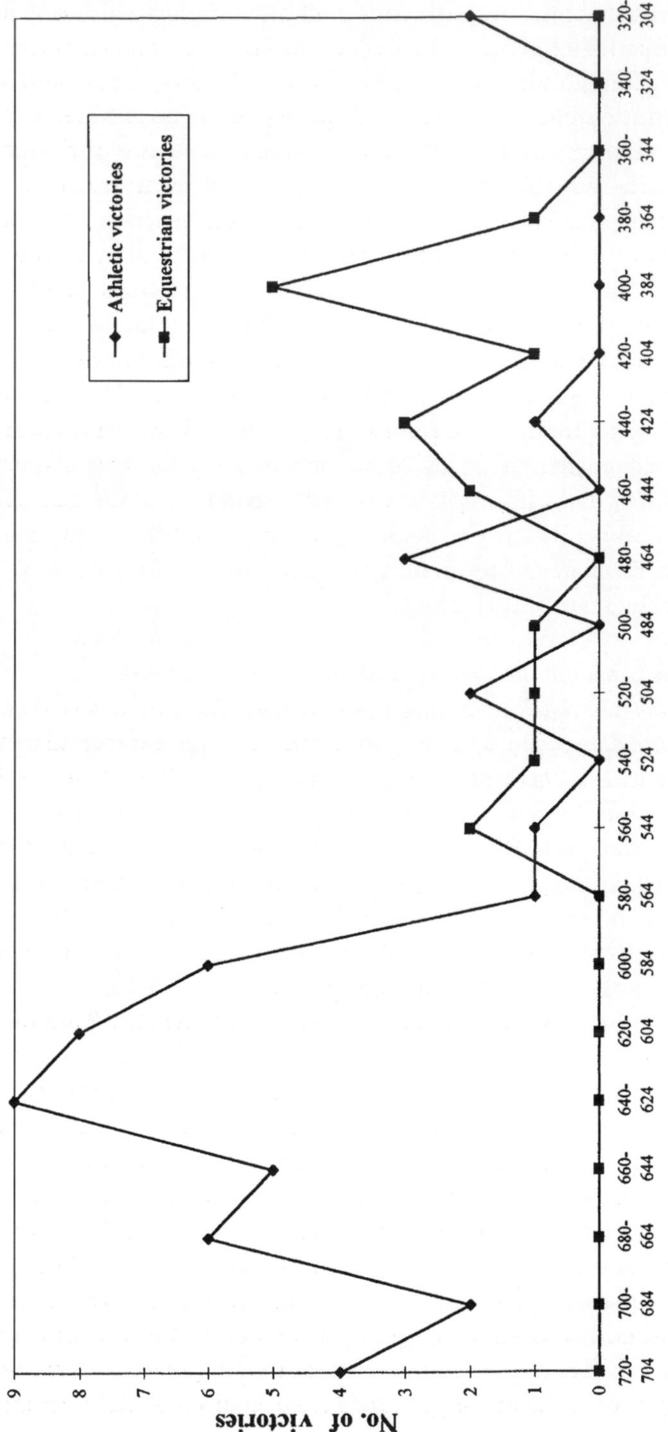

Fig. 1. Spartiate Olympic victories.

sixth-century shift from athletics to chariot-racing will not hold water. As is evident from *Fig.* 1, the decline in athletic victories started somewhat earlier, in the 580s or 570s (Powell 1998, 139); and the real concentration of chariot victories did not occur until the later fifth and early fourth centuries (Hodkinson 1989, 97). In the period from 550 to 450, in fact, Sparta had as many victories in athletics (five in number) as in chariot racing. That athletic success still possessed greater prestige as late as the early fifth century is suggested by the fact that Polypeithes, a Spartiate chariot victor (perhaps in 484) set up a representation not of himself but of his father Kalliteles, who was a wrestling victor (perhaps in 508).[35] A reversal of values *is* evident later in the century, when Anaxandros, another chariot victor (possibly in 428) with an athletic ancestor, dedicated his own statue, giving his grandfather's pentathlon victory merely a mention in his victory inscription (Paus. 6.1.7); but this cannot explain the decline of athletic victories in the early sixth century which was at best only marginally connected with developments in chariot racing.

The timing of the decline might suggest a connection with the remodelling of Spartan society which many scholars place in the late seventh and early sixth centuries. But, if so, what is the precise nature of the connection? Some scholars (e.g. Hönle 1972, 131–5) view the decline as an unintended by-product of a lifestyle concentrating upon military fitness rather than the full-time, specialized training for particular events which was being undertaken by a growing number of athletes elsewhere (cf. Pleket 1974). Others attribute it to a direct hostility of the new militarily-oriented regime towards athletic competition (e.g. Nafissi 1991, 167–9). I would agree that there was some conscious policy behind the avoidance of specialisation. The poetry of Tyrtaios shows that the depreciation of athletic prowess was one strand of Spartan thought. Moreover, certain hellenistic sources ascribe to Sparta the attitude that victorious death in battle was superior to Olympic success, and that a victory achieved through courage or might was worth more than one gained through superior *technē* – hence, it is claimed, the Spartans' refusal to appoint wrestling trainers.[36]

This evidence should not, however, be over-interpreted. First, it is far from clear that specialised athletic training was a significant feature of Greek athletics at the period when Spartan victories declined in the early sixth century. A range of evidence (literary references to athletic specialisation and dietary changes, evidence for the emergence of athletic coaches and the incidence of multiple victories suggestive of specificity of training) suggests that specialised athletic training took hold properly only in the fifth century (Serwint 1987, 27–38). Secondly, even if the late passages cited above do reflect the genuine voice of classical Sparta, they do not indicate a deliberate reduction of athletic activity. Indeed, one passage is a Spartan victory epigram and two of the others are excuses for defeats by foreign competitors! The rhetoric suggests, rather, an ideological stance that Spartans would compete, but according to their own value system. The Olympic victor list, we should remember, is precisely that and nothing more. The decline in athletic victors does not necessarily imply a decline in Spartiate participation or in their desire to win. Indeed, the strident use of their value system as excuse for defeat suggests a deep sensitivity to their relative lack of Olympic success.

Neither was there any insuperable conflict between the demands – in terms of the expenditure of time and energy – of athletic participation at Olympia and those of the Spartiate public way of life. Roman sources (Paus. 5.24.9; Philostratos, *Vita Apollonii* 5.43) indicate that in their day adult competitors had to swear that they had been in full training for ten months and that all competitors, both men and boys, had to reside at Olympia for a month's training before the games. Most scholars believe that these regulations went back to earlier periods (Crowther 1991), although there is no definite proof. In theory, the Spartiate way of life required regular, if not daily, attendance at the mess (Plut. *Lyk.* 12.2) or in the upbringing. In practice, the life of adult Spartiates was probably not so tightly controlled: citizens might be absent from Sparta for shorter or longer periods for various personal reasons: supervising distant estates, visiting foreign sanctuaries or cultivating ties of *xenia*. A month's absence, predictable quadrennially, for a limited number of men and boys could presumably be accommodated within the system. The ten-month training period might appear to conflict with Sparta's official rhetoric against specialised preparation; but it did not apply to boys, and it may have been designed not so much to dictate a particular training regime as simply to ensure that competitors were fully fit. The public way of life, with its provision for wrestling contests, team games and regular hunting on foot (Xen. *Lak.Pol.* 5.7; cf. 5.3, 6.3) would have enabled most Spartiate competitors to satisfy that criterion without difficulty.

In any case, it would be mistaken to consider the decline in Spartiate athletic victories purely in terms of internal social change or to imagine that the decline in Spartiate victories was unique. At least two major external developments were at work. First, there were greater numbers of competitors from an enlarging circle of Greek states, as there developed in the early sixth century a regular circuit of games in response to a growing demand for occasions at which aspiring individuals could gain symbolic capital for use in the increasingly competitive power struggles within their home poleis. It is probably no mere chance that the start of the decline in Spartiate victories in the 570s coincided with the establishment of the circuit of 'Crown' games. Secondly, there was the concerted effort of the western Greek poleis, led by Kroton, to appropriate Olympic success by offering significant material and symbolic rewards to athletes, including outside recruits, who were victorious under their name (Xenophanes, fr. 2.1–9, West, *ap*. Athen. 137e; Young 1984, 131–41; Kyle 1996, 115–16). Between 588 and 488 Kroton, after achieving only one victory in the seventh century, gained no fewer than 20 out of 40 recorded victories in running and wrestling. Sparta was not the only state affected: Athens won at least six athletic victories in the seventh century, but none is recorded thereafter until 472 BC. The Spartans' lack of response to the growth of athletic rewards was extreme, as we shall see; but this should not be confused with aversion to Olympic success. In fact Sparta's record of three running and wrestling victories in the period of Kroton's dominance was actually better than that of any other polis, including those which had followed the Krotoniate path.

Public commemoration of past Olympic success

It is clear, moreover, that even in the period when her Olympic victories were few, Sparta never abandoned the general Greek view that such victories brought honour to the polis. In the early fifth century the Spartans erected public monuments to commemorate the achievements of several Olympic victors from earlier centuries. The Athenian sculptor Myron (*fl. c.* 470–440) was commissioned to produce a statue of a seventh-century athlete, the multiple running victor Chionis (Paus. 6.13.2). Chionis' statue, along with a stēlē recording his victories, was placed at Olympia next to the statue of the seven-times victor of the 480s, Astylos of Syracuse.[37] This was an overt mark of political rivalry which is surely related to the dispute between Sparta and Syracuse over leadership of the Greek forces in 480 (Hdt. 7.158–60).[38] Another stēlē listing Chionis' victories was erected in Sparta near the tombs of the Agiad kings (Paus. 3.14.3). The youth Eutelidas, winner of the boys' wrestling and pentathlon in 628, was another seventh-century Spartiate victor officially honoured in this period with a statue at Olympia (Paus. 6.15.8).[39] Still more notable, however, are the cases of Hipposthenes and his son Hetoimokles, who between them were said to have won 11 Olympic wrestling victories from the 630s to the 580s. Whereas the statues of Chionis and Eutelidas were erected at Olympia, Hetoimokles was given a statue in Sparta itself (Paus. 3.13.9). The honours given to Hipposthenes were even more extraordinary, as we learn from Pausanias (3.15.7): 'nearby is a temple (ναός) of Hipposthenes, who won so many victories in wrestling; they worship (σέβουσι) Hipposthenes, in accordance with an oracle, paying him honours as to Poseidon'.

The cult of Hipposthenes is clearly a somewhat different phenomenon from the erection of his son's statue; and this concurs with the fact that, though remembered as father and son, their respective statue and shrine stood at different locations within the polis. Sparta's cult of Hipposthenes indeed fits into a wider pattern of the heroization or divinization of Olympic victors which occurred in a number of poleis during the fifth century.[40] This phenomenon presents two salient common features. The first is that the persons so honoured were a mixture of victors only recently deceased and victors from earlier centuries. The sources' accounts (which relate and intermingle in varying degrees information of historical and symbolic authenticity) indicate that they were all controversial figures, in whom there was an imbalance in the *kudos*, or magical potency, which derived from their Olympic victory: 'those athletes become heroes who possess a superabundance of *kudos* or who suffered in life from a dearth of proper honours in response to their *kudos*' (Kurke 1993, 151). The fact that for Hipposthenes Pausanias provides no aetiological explanation, no legend concerning any controversial personal circumstances or grounds for divinization such as he provides for other heroised victors, may reflect Spartan control of disturbing information; or it may signify that he was simply a notable figure from the past whom fifth-century Spartans perceived as not having received sufficient recognition.

The second common feature is that the poleis in which this phenomenon occurred were all cities faced with crises, whether from external threat or internal *stasis* (Bohringer 1979). Through the recuperation of such exceptional personalities – possessors of magical potency, but also themselves embodiments of tension – the poleis in question acted on a symbolic plane both to express and, if not to resolve, at least to efface the manifestations of the crisis. The early fifth century was for Sparta a times of several major crises – the problems with Kleomenes and Pausanias, the Persian invasion, revolts in Arkadia, the 'Great Earthquake' of *c*. 465 BC which caused heavy destruction and loss of life, and the ensuing helot revolt – all of which were sufficiently severe to have prompted the extraordinary response of Hipposthenes' divinization.[41] We shall never know the precise circumstances for certain; but there are certain indications which suggest that perhaps the most probable occasion was the combined crisis of the 465 earthquake and subsequent major helot revolt of 464–460. Note that Hipposthenes was given honours as to the god Poseidon, who in Sparta was worshipped as the 'Earthholder', the preserver against earthquakes (Cartledge 1976). The Spartans themselves ascribed the earthquake to their murder of helot suppliants at the sanctuary of Poseidon at Tainaron (Thuc. 1.128). It was amidst the chaos, destruction and heavy loss of Spartiate lives caused by the earthquake that the helots seized the opportunity to mount their dangerous and long-lasting revolt. Given Poseidon's close connection with both earthquake and revolt, it is tempting to suggest that in calling upon the magical potency of Hipposthenes and harnessing it to the worship of Poseidon the Spartans were attempting to restore their good relations with the god in order to defeat the helots on the religious plane.[42] It is also relevant that Hipposthenes' cult, like those of several other victors, is said to have been a response to the command of an oracle. One is reminded of other occasions in fifth-century Spartan history – the burial of Pausanias the Regent and the recall of the exiled King Pleistoanax (Thuc. 1.134; 5.16) – when the Spartans restored unhonoured individuals to their rightful place to avert the disastrous consequences of an oracular curse.

Public treatment of contemporary Olympic victors

Although the polis honoured certain past Olympic victors, with living victors it was more circumspect. Its policy is best illustrated by comparison with other poleis. As intimated above, a number of other poleis offered citizenship to outside athletic recruits or material prizes to their own victorious athletes. Xenophanes (fr. 2, West, ll. 1–9) implies that in the later sixth century many poleis provided other privileges too, such as free meals at public expense and front-row seats at state spectacles.[43] Fifth-century sources attest further privileges: public celebration of the victor's homecoming and the erection of his statue in his home polis.[44] None of these things is attested in Sparta. The Spartiates' citizen ranks remained notoriously closed. When they did, exceptionally, offer citizenship to the seer Teisamenos, it was for the prospect of military victories; they had ignored him while he pursued Olympic success (Hdt. 9.33–5). Spartan athletic victors received no prizes or privileges in everyday civic life. Public subsidies of food and permanent front-row seats were a privilege of the kings (Hdt. 6.57), and a prerogative probably reserved to them alone. As we shall see, the one privilege which *was* given to Olympic victors was to serve the kings in a special way, not to be treated as their equal. For this reason too there were no statues of living victors such as would raise them above the level of the established leadership.[45]

In denying these various rewards Spartan policy might seem to represent the antithesis of practice elsewhere. The contrast, however, should not be exaggerated. First, it is uncertain whether there were no public celebrations at all of Spartan athletic success. We simply do not know what typically happened on the homecoming of an Olympic victor. Whilst we may imagine that his welcome was more subdued than in other poleis, can we realistically believe that he simply entered the polis as any other citizen returning from abroad? Secondly, Xenophanes' criticism of the privileges given to victorious athletes and his more general prioritisation of civic achievements over those of athletics (ll. 15–22) show that Sparta's reaction to athletic achievement was not unparalleled in Greek thought. And perhaps not even inconceivable in practice: although Athens did offer prizes, Solon is said by one – admittedly late – source to have limited their value on the grounds that athletic victors were less deserving than orphans of fallen warriors (Diog. Laert. 1.55; cf. Diod. 9.2.5; Plut. *Solon* 23.3). Thirdly, we should be wary of assuming that every polis but Sparta necessarily offered all the incentives and rewards detailed above. Much of the literary evidence relates particularly to the 'colonial' poleis of Magna Graecia, for whom athletic success was a vital means of establishing their pedigrees; and, while several poleis in the Greek homeland undoubtedly followed their example, there are other poleis for whom our evidence is as mute as it is for Sparta.

There was, moreover, one significant mark of recognition which the Spartan polis did give to its athletic victors, a privilege which illustrates that its policy towards Olympic success was at once distinctive and yet based upon attitudes not qualitatively different from those of other Greeks. Asked what he had gained from his victory after he had refused bribes to lose, a Spartiate Olympic wrestler is said to have replied, "I shall stand in front of my king when I fight our enemies" (Plut. *Lyk.* 22.4; cf. *Mor.* 639e). In one sense, this honorific reward of fighting in the king's bodyguard is closely linked to Sparta's singular military system of values. Yet, as Leslie Kurke (1993, 133) has noted, Spartan practice accords here with the general Greek belief in the talismanic power of victors at the Crown games. The difference – as with so many aspects of Spartan society – lies partly in the Spartans' institutionalisation of this general belief into a matter of systematic practice, partly in their careful harnessing of the athletic victor's talismanic authority in support of, rather than as a challenge to, the established hierarchy.

This latter point can be further exemplified with reference to the participation of Olympic victors in special enterprises such as military or colonial expeditions. In other states their talismanic power made Olympic victors ideal persons for the leadership of such expeditions (Kurke 1993, 136–7). Note, for example, the case of Phrynon, leader of the Athenian expedition to Sigeion (Diog. Laert. 1.74; Strabo 599–600); or Miltiades, oikist for the Dolonkoi in the Thracian Chersonese (Hdt. 6.34–8). In such hazardous enterprises the command of someone favoured with success in games held at a religious festival could be thought to provide some guarantee of divine support. For Sparta too Olympic victors were an important part of colonial enterprises; but the Spartan representation of their role seems to have portrayed them as special helpers rather than leaders. According to local tradition (Pausanias 3.14.3), the Spartan victor Chionis was said to have helped Battos of Thera in the foundation of Kyrene and subjugation of the native Libyans. Likewise, the colonial expedition of Dorieus, half-brother of King Kleomenes I, received help from the Krotoniate victor, Philippos; but his role is distinguished by Herodotus, drawing upon Spartan sources, from those of Dorieus' four Spartiate co-founders (5.46–7). From the Spartan viewpoint, apparently, athletic victors were special auxiliaries, but not marked out for supreme command.

As in life, so in death. We know the name of one Spartan Olympic victor who fought in the bodyguard of his king: a certain Lakrates, who died in King Pausanias' expedition to Athens in 403 BC.

> And there died Chairon and Thibrachos, both polemarchs, and Lakrates the Olympic victor, and the other Lakedaimonians who lie buried in front of the city gate in the Kerameikos. (Xen. *Hell.* 2.4.33)

The level of Lakrates' prestige is shown by the fact that Xenophon singles out his name for special mention alongside those of the polemarchs, holders of the highest military office under the king.[46] It seems likely, moreover, that he received a special place in the impressive collective tomb for the Lakedaimonian dead to which Xenophon refers (Van Hook 1932; Willemsen 1977). On excavation the tomb was found to contain 13 skeletons placed in three chambers. The central chamber contained only three bodies, which were laid out with greater care than the five bodies in each of the two flanking chambers. The probable identity of the select trio, in view of Xenophon's remarks, is the two polemarchs and the Olympic victor. Lakrates' honours in burial were thus special, though no greater than those of the polemarchs who were explicitly subordinates of the king. In the inscription on the front of the tomb monument, moreover, the names of the polemarchs came first, as they do in Xenophon's account.[47]

The limits on private victory commemorations inside Sparta

A similar picture emerges from the evidence of private funerary monuments located within Spartan home territory. Compared with most other Greek states, the erection of commemorative inscriptions by the kin of deceased Spartiates was subject to strict control. Unlike in other poleis, the success of a deceased Spartan Olympic victor could not be commemorated for its own sake. The only men entitled to commemorative inscriptions were those who had died in war.[48] There survive, dating from the fifth century onwards, a number of undecorated, roughly-worked stelai commemorating such fallen warriors.[49] Most bear a simple inscription stating just the name of the deceased followed by the words ΕΝ (or ΕΜ) ΠΟΛΕΜΟΙ (or ΠΟΛΕΜΩΙ), i.e. 'X. [died] in battle'. One inscription, however, carries the name of two deceased warriors, the first of whom is described as ΕΥΡΥΑΔΗΣ ΟΛΥΜΠΙΟΝΙΚΑΣ, 'Euryades the Olympic victor'.[50] So the Olympic success of a fallen warrior could be recorded on his commemorative stēlē alongside the record of his death in battle. As in the case of Lakrates, the fallen Olympic victor was commemorated within the same framework as other citizens who died in battle, rather than in a separate extraordinary manner such as was reserved for Spartan kings (Hdt. 6.58). But his athletic success was a cause for additional commemoration beyond that of other fallen warriors.

With the case of private funerary monuments we have begun to move beyond privileges which were solely in the gift of the Spartan polis into the realm of personal and family celebration of Olympic success. Even here, as we have seen, there were official limitations upon private celebrations. State policy and institutions seem indeed to have precluded another major form of personal celebration known from other poleis: the *epinikion* or victory ode. The *epinikion* was a poem 'written on commission for victors at athletic games and usually performed at the site of the games or at the victor's home in the context of a victory celebration'. Despite recent controversy, it seems that the initial performance was usually 'by a chorus of his fellow citizens before an audience that would include many of his countrymen'.[51] Sometimes this performance might even coincide with an official polis festival (Bernadini 1992, 969). Subsequently, however, the ode 'was chiefly reperformed at symposia, sung by a solo singer who accompanied himself on the lyre'. That such symposiastic evocations of the victory would often lead on to further celebrations in the form of the *kōmos* (an outdoor processionary revel) is envisaged in several epinician texts.[52] The content of epinician often focused not just upon the individual victor but also upon his family background and lineage. Its origins are obscure. Some scholars have suggested that early forms of the genre can be detected in surviving fragments of the poet Ibykos shortly before the middle of the sixth century (Barron 1984, 19–22; Jenner 1986; Bernadini 1992, 969–71). Certainly, between around 520 and the 440s, in the hands of the major epinician poets, Simonides, Bacchylides and Pindar, it was a primary method by which the most prominent victors in the Crown games sought to immortalize their success. Its wide diffusion is shown by the fact that the 40 or so epinician odes in the Pindaric corpus alone were commissioned for victors from no fewer than 16 different states, including several Peloponnesian poleis.

With one possible exception, there are, however, no known epinicians for Spartiate victors. The potential exception is one of the aforementioned poems of Ibykos which, it has been argued, celebrates a Spartiate running and wrestling victor at the games at Sikyon.[53] After this, however, the record is blank. True, there are relatively few known Spartiate victors in the Crown games during the period of Simonides, Bacchylides and Pindar. But there were some; and since all three poets wrote other works for a Spartan audience,[54] the absence of epinician odes looks like a phenomenon of Spartan society. At one level, the explanation surely lies in the essentially public and paideutic role of music within Spartan society and in the state's control over occasions at which epinician odes might otherwise have been sung. Choral singing was undoubtedly a major feature of Spartiate life: 'the cicada is a Spartan, eager for a chorus', wrote the late archaic playwright Pratinas of Phleious (fr. 709, Page, *ap.* Athen. 633a). But our extant evidence, at least for the classical period, suggests that Spartan choruses were thoroughly state-controlled affairs, in which all citizens were expected to participate, often collectively in their age classes, in roles structured hierarchically to reflect and define their status.[55] The attested content of choral songs at state festivals reinforced approved behavioural norms of military valour and civic conformity. Such festivals clearly had no room for individual celebration, let alone for the advertisement of family lineage. It may be that the sources, with their overriding emphasis upon the phenomenon of social order, provide only a partial account of the range of choral occasions; but it is hard to avoid the conclusion that the use of choral song, especially with a privately organised choir, to immortalize individual athletic success would have been highly anomalous.

Similar considerations apply to sympotic reperformance of the *epinikion*, without which the victor's fame would be short lived (Morgan 1993, 10). Music was undoubtedly part of the luxurious *symposia* and *kōmoi* depicted on archaic Lakonian pottery (Powell 1998, 122–3); but solo singing is completely absent from the sources' accounts of the practices of classical Spartan non-royal *syssitia*, which placed less emphasis on the stage of drinking, when musical performance typically took place, than did symposia elsewhere.[56] Ewen Bowie (1990) has, it is true, argued for a continuing sympotic tradition in classical Sparta, in order to explain late-fourth-century evidence for the competitive individual singing of the poems of Tyrtaios in the royal *syssition* on campaign (Philochoros, *FGrH* 328 F 216; Lykourgos, *Against Leokrates* 107). But, even if one can extrapolate such performances beyond their immediate royal and military context to the mass of ordinary *syssitia* in Sparta, the sentiments expressed in Tyrtaian martial elegy, with (*inter alia*) its overt depreciation of athletic prowess, were hardly conducive to positive reception of the ideology of athletic glory expressed in the epinician ode.[57] Indeed, the very organisation and ethos of the Spartan messes – with their military connections, their composition cutting across family and generational ties, their ethic of collective solidarity, and their control of drunkenness and hybristic behaviour – were a hostile environment for the solo reperformance of epinician and its associated komastic victory celebrations.

Behind the factors so far adduced lies the fundamental point that the rise of epinician seems to have represented an attempted revival of the very social forces which the Spartans' recent transformation of their society – their 'sixth-century revolution' – had been designed to escape. Kurke (1991, 258–9) has suggested that 'the impetus behind epinikian performance represents a kind of counterrevolution on the part of the aristocracy. Constrained by sumptuary legislation, the aristocracy uses epinikion as a new outlet for prestige displays' of the kind that many sixth-century poleis had been seeking to control. The local Spartan context for these general developments is, unfortunately, obscure; but the suggestion that one Spartiate victor may have led the way in the rise of epinician indicates the possibility that prestige displays of victory celebration may once have been commonplace in 'pre-revolution' Sparta. For classical Sparta such displays would have been dangerous affairs. As Plato (*Laws* 802a) was later to warn, in a comment which has been linked to Spartiate practice (Powell 1994, 294), 'It is unsafe to honour those still living with encomia and hymns'. At all events, the absence of epinician in the later sixth– and early fifth–century is a mark of the success of the Spartan revolution in eradicating such displays in a manner that many other poleis could not.

Private commemorations of victory at Olympia

At home the Spartan citizen body could clearly control the forms through which their Olympic victors expressed their prestige. A further sign of this is that, among all the extant votive offerings made at Spartan sanctuaries by athletic victors at local games during the sixth or fifth centuries, there survives not a single commemoration of a contemporary Olympic victory. Only in the fourth century does the picture change, first in the sphere of chariot racing, then in the last quarter of the century with the inscribed stēlē set up, probably at the Amyklaion, by Deinosthenes, the stade victor of 316.[58] There was, however, a location outside Sparta which was available for such commemoration: the sanctuary at Olympia itself. Did Spartiate Olympic victors take advantage of this external location to advertise their victories in a manner they apparently did not, or could not, within Sparta itself?

Some victors clearly did. From the late archaic period there survive two inscribed stone jumping weights dedicated by pentathletes which parallel those of similar date at the sanctuary of Athena Chalkioikos. The first bears merely the name of its dedicator, a certain Koiris. The inscription on the second, dedicated by Akmatidas, Olympic victor in perhaps 500 BC, is altogether more self-congratulatory (PLATE 7). Akmatidas boasts that he gained his victory ἀσσκονικτεί, 'dust-free': that is, without participating in the final discipline, the wrestling, signifying either that his opponents had defaulted through fear or that his victories in the first four disciplines rendered the final discipline unnecessary.[59] Aside from these offerings, we know of no other dedications or commemorative monuments set up in person by Spartan athletic (as opposed to equestrian) victors until the final quarter of the fourth century when Deinosthenes and Seleadas erected personal statues to celebrate their respective successes in the stade race of 316 and wrestling contest of 308.[60] As noted earlier, however, at least two

PLATE 7. Jumping weight dedicated by Akmatidas, Olympic pentathlon victor. The inscription reads: 'Akmatidas the Lakedaimonian dedicated [this], winning the five dust-free', *c.* 500 BC (Olympia Museum; photograph courtesy of Deutsches Archäologisches Institut, Athens).

athletic victors were commemorated by their descendants who won victories in the Olympic four-horse chariot race. Either a statue or a relief of Kalliteles the wrestling victor was erected a generation later, in the early fifth century, by his son Polypeithes (Paus. 6.16.6).[61] In the later fifth century Anaxandros included in the inscription on his statue-base a reference to his paternal grandfather's victory in the pentathlon (Paus. 6.1.7).[62]

From a comparative perspective, this record of Olympic commemoration may not look impressive in terms of either numbers or precocity. At the time when Akmatidas, Kalliteles and Anaxandros' grandfather won their victories in the late sixth century some Olympic athletic victors had already begun to erect their own statues (Lattimore 1987). None of the Spartiate victors participated in this new trend. One reason for Spartiate reluctance to advance from the modest, 'raw' votive offerings of Akmatidas and Koiris to the grandiose athletic statue may be that from their very onset such statues (unlike those of equestrian victors) were regarded not just as victory dedications but as honorific representations of the person of the athlete, with the potential to attract reverence and cult (Lattimore 1987, esp. 248–9). The erection of such a statue to a citizen at the very height of his success would have been a danger to the Spartiate social order. There is uncertainty, as we have seen, about the form of the monument which Polypeithes erected for his father Kalliteles; but even if Kalliteles' representation was a statue, rather than merely a relief, one wonders whether he was still alive at the time or whether it was possible only because he was already dead.

From a more narrowly Spartan perspective, however, the record appears less restrained. The comparative paucity of attested Spartiate commemorations is hardly significant in view of the small number of known athletic victors, especially given the accidents of survival in both the archaeological and literary record. The offerings of Koiris and Akmatidas perform on a panhellenic stage a comparable self-advertisement to similar contemporary local dedications at the Amyklaion. The implications of the representation of Kalliteles are obscured by the uncertainty regarding its nature and whether he was then alive or dead. If a statue, however, the fact that it was commissioned – whether posthumously or not – in the same period as those of the more distant victors Chionis and Eutelidas may suggest a degree of competitive emulation between family and state. If merely a relief, it nevertheless parallels the early-fifth-century sculpted relief of the discus-thrower from the Amyklaion. This parallel development of local and panhellenic, of state and private, forms of commemoration suggests an element of official restraint upon Olympic celebrations, but also an attempt by Spartiate victors and their families to exploit the boundaries of the permissible to the fullest extent.

Even from a comparative perspective, one can exaggerate the reticence of Spartiate victory monuments. Although a few Olympic victors from other poleis did dedicate their own statues at the time of the late-sixth-century Spartiate victories, they were still very much the exception. A significant increase in the number of such statues did not take place until after the Persian wars. Even then, many athletic victors from a range of Greek poleis were never commemorated by statues, and several who were so commemorated did not receive their statues until some time after their victories, some not until after their death (Amandry 1957). Spartiate practice was therefore neither as unusual nor as backward as it first appears. Moreover, there is one sphere in which Spartiate commemorations of Olympic success led the way in the search for athletic renown: namely, in the content of their inscriptions. Recent work has emphasized the manner in which the inscriptions of panhellenic victors often attempted to add a 'surplus-value' to their success by emphasizing some special feature which gave it extra distinction (Pleket 1975, 79). Spartiate inscriptions exemplify this tendency to a high degree. The monuments of the chariot-race victors, Polypeithes and Anaxandros, evidently included inscriptions detailing the victories of their athletic ancestors. There was clearly significant additional symbolic capital to be gained from adding to their own victories the advertisement of their ancestors' success. So too, Akmatidas was concerned to stress that his was no mere Olympic pentathlon victory, but one achieved in the most superior manner, 'dust-free'. The fact that Akmatidas is the earliest recorded Greek athlete to advertise this claim and that Polypeithes is among the first attested victors to erect an inscribed monument to his father's success shows that in their employment of commemorative inscriptions Spartiate victors were ahead of the game.[63]

An agonistic culture

In this exploration of Spartiate participation in the athletic *agōn* we have witnessed both a number of local peculiarities in the character of Spartiate athletic competition and a marked degree of official control over privileges for Olympic victors and the forms of their victory celebration. Yet, despite these restrictions, the sphere of the victory inscription remained – as we have seen – one arena in which Spartiate athletes could exploit their successes, both at home and abroad, in the quest for recognition and prestige. This conclusion is indeed not merely valid for Spartiate athletics, but has a wider application throughout Spartiate life. As James Whitley's recent comparative study of Athenian, Spartan and Cretan inscriptions has shown (1998, 645–9), Spartiate athletic victory dedications form part of a broad corpus of extant dedicatory inscriptions which dominate the epigraphic record of archaic and early classical Sparta. Two striking points deserve emphasis. The first is the homogeneity of this corpus: Spartiate victory inscriptions are not anomalous but typical of other dedicatory inscriptions as a whole in their near-universal advertisement of the personal name of the dedicator. Hence, for all the restrictions to which they were subject, Spartiate methods of celebrating athletic success in the sixth and fifth centuries appear broadly in tune with the overall tenor of Spartan society in its commemoration and communication of individual achievement. The second point is the remarkable similarity of Spartiate dedicatory inscriptions to those from contemporary

Athens in 'the tendency evident in both Athenian and Spartan society to use inscriptions to make a public display of personal prowess' (Whitley 1998, 647). Paradoxically, therefore, it is in the sphere of writing and communication, the one aspect of Spartiate society which is most often dismissed as culturally impoverished, that we can see most clearly the connections between Spartiate participation in the athletic *agōn* and the competitive character of Greek society. In this fundamental sense, Spartiate society can be said truly to have shared in the agonistic culture which was the common currency of the archaic and classical Greek world.

Acknowledgements

This article was researched and written during my tenure of a Nuffield Foundation Social Science Research Fellowship and an award under the Research Leave Scheme of the British Academy Humanities Research Board. Earlier versions have been given in Torino, Atlanta, Newcastle and Manchester, as well as at Hay-on-Wye. I am grateful to those seminar audiences for their comments, to Robin Osborne and Tim Cornell for helpful criticism of an earlier draft and to Mark Golden for bibliographic references and an advance sight of part of his recent book (Golden 1998). Although I am not unsympathetic to P.-J. Shaw's suggestions (ch. 10, this volume) for a revised chronology of archaic Greece, I have for the purposes of this paper retained the standard chronological framework familiar to students of the period.

Notes

[1] On the significance of chariot racing in Spartiate society, Hodkinson 1989, 96–100; Nafissi 1991, 153–72.

[2] The nature of the *sphaireis* contest is uncertain. Most scholars see it as a ball game (e.g. Ollier 1934, 49; Kennell 1995, 38–40); for claims that ballplaying was a Spartan invention, Athenaios *Deipnosophistai* 14e; cf. Lucian *Anacharsis* 38. Some view it as a form of boxing, drawing upon references to a boxing glove called the *sphaira* (Poliakoff 1987, 73 and 173 n. 7, with refs.).

[3] The *sphaireis* contest had become 'a type of graduation ceremony, marking the transition from ephebe to adult', the cheese-stealing contest a simple test of individual endurance (Kennell 1995, 40, 71–9). Roman sources (Cicero *Tusculan Disputations* 5.27.77; Pausanias 3.14.8–10, 20.2 and 8; Lucian *Anacharsis* 38) mention another team contest: following preliminary ceremonies connected with Apollo, Achilles, Herakles and Lykourgos, two teams of youths attempted to drive each other off an artificial island at the Platanistas ('Plane-tree Grove'). There is no classical evidence for the contest; and the artificial landscape and antiquarian evocation of divine and heroic beings, including ancestral figures from the Spartan past, suggest a hellenistic or Roman origin.

[4] Note the fourth-century inscribed marble stēlē, dedicated by a certain Arexippos at the sanctuary of Artemis Orthia, which contains grooves for five iron sickles commemorating his multiple victories in the 'gatherings of boys' (*IG* V.1.255; Woodward 1929, no. 1; *CEG* II.821). This dedication is a forerunner of the large number of similar hellenistic and Roman dedications for victories in the *paidikos agōn*.

[5] For wrestling, cf. also Cic. *Tusc.* 2.15, ¶36 and the scholiast to Juvenal 4.53. According to Propertius (3.14.1–20), Spartan girls engaged not only in wrestling and ball and hoop games, but also in the *pankration*, boxing, hunting and warfare. This fantastical account, which subsequently asserts Spartan acceptance of adultery, is merely wishful erotic idealisation by way of antithesis to the perceived inaccessibility of Roman girls.

[6] Herfort-Koch 1986, K 48–50 (respectively, Sparta Mus. 3305; Athens National Mus., Carapanos Coll. 24; British Mus., Bronzes 208); De Ridder 1894, no. 171 (Paris, Louvre 171). My list differs from that of Scanlon (1988, 214 n. 62), in the inclusion of the Louvre bronze and the exclusion of Delphi Mus. 3072 and Palermo, Mus. Nazionale 8265, neither of which is judged Lakonian by Herfort-Koch (1986, 29). All these figurines were probably ornaments of large bronze vessels.

[7] So Plato, *Laws* 833c–d, possibly following Spartan practice. Kritias, fr. 32, Diels-Kranz (*ap.* Clement *Miscellanies* 6.9), recommends in his prose *Polity of the Lakedaimonians* that ἡ μήτηρ τοῦ παιδίου τοῦ μέλλοντος should grow physically strong and take exercise. It is unclear whether he means a woman already pregnant or simply a girl who will one day be a mother.

[8] Serwint 1993, 404–6. Scanlon (1984) suggests that they were initiated under the influence of Spartan female athletics.

[9] Although the *arkteia* at Brauron was perceived as a rite ideally performed by all Athenian girls, in practice its participants were a (sizeable) representative sample (Sourvinou-Inwood 1988, 75 n. 61, 111–17).

[10] *IG* V.1.213; Jeffery 1990, 201 no. 52; *CEG* I.378. Its exact date is uncertain, but it seems to belong after *c.* 450 BC, either sometime before or shortly after the Peloponnesian war (Jeffery 1988; cf. 1990, 196–7 with 201 no. 52; 448). For a translation, Sweet 1987, 145–6.

[11] For further athletic locations, see Livy 34.27 and Pausanias 3.14.6 on Dromos at Sparta; also *IG* V.1.1120, with Bingen 1958, on the festival of Hekatombaion at Geronthrai.

[12] On the distinction between 'raw' and 'converted' offerings, cf. Snodgrass 1989/90, 291: 'a "raw" dedication is an unmodified object of real, secular use… By contrast, a statue or statuette…is a *conversion* of a part of his or her wealth…and in most cases it has been produced for the specific purpose of dedication'.

[13] Bronze figurine: *BSA* 28 (1926/27) 85 fig. 1; Herfort-Koch 1986, K 121, Taf. 16.3 (Cambridge, Fitzwilliam Mus. GR 11–1928). Stēlē of [G]laukat[ias]: *IG* V.1.720; Jeffery 1990, 200 no. 31; *CEG* I.376. Stēlē of Aiglatas: *IG* V.1.222; Lazzarini 1976, 299 no. 849; Jeffery 1990, 199 no. 22; *CEG* I.374.

[14] Jeffery 1990, 194 n. 5 suggests that a fragmentary later sixth-century stēlē from Artemis Orthia (201 no. 41; Woodward 1929, 354 no. 139a–c) and an

even more fragmentary text found at Mystra (210 no. 42; *IG* V.1.2 = Sparta Mus. 599) may also be victory monuments.

[15] Dedication of Kleocha[res]: *IG* V.1.216; *BSA* 14 (1907/8) 137; Lazzarini 1976, 296 no. 831; Jeffery 1990, 199 no. 21, with p. 448; of Paitiadas: *BSA* 27 (1925/26) 251–2; Lazzarini 1976, 296 no. 830.

[16] *BSA* 27 (1925/26) 249–50; Lazzarini 1976, 299 no. 850; Jeffery 1990, 200 no. 28. It appears to bear similar race-track guidelines to the stēlē of Glaukatias above.

[17] *BSA* 29 (1927/28) 45–8; Jeffery 1990, 192, 199 no. 23; *CEG* I.375.

[18] *IG* V.1.238; Jeffery 1990, 195, 201 no. 48; *CEG* I.377 (Sparta Mus. 611).

[19] Cf. two other possible athletic dedications from the site: (i) a bronze figurine of a running male, *c.* 550–525, which once decorated a larger object, possibly a tripod: *BSA* 28 (1926/27) 83 pl. 9.3; Herfort-Koch 1986, K 109, Taf. 15,4 (Athens National Mus. 15893); (ii) a male bronze figurine, 500–475, sometimes interpreted as a javelin thrower, sometimes as a trumpeter: *BSA* 13 (1906/07) 146 no. 1, fig. 3; Lamb 1969, 150 pl. 56c; Thomas 1981, 47 pl. 20, 2; Steinhauer n.d., 30 fig. 7 (Sparta Mus. 2019). This latter figurine is doubly difficult to interpret, since it seems that the currently bent position of the figurine's right arm is not original.

[20] Lazzarini 1976, 296 no. 834 (Athens, National Mus. 8618).

[21] Herfort-Koch 1986, K 122, Taf. 16.7 (Paris, Louvre, Bronze 118).

[22] *SEG* xi.696; Jeffery 1990, 195 and 201 no. 51. Von Massow (1926) identified this stēlē with that bearing the likeness of Ainetos, the Olympic pentathlete, seen by Pausanias (3.18.7); but there are no grounds for this in the details of relief or inscription (which seems to refer to multiple victories). Note also a fragment of another victory inscription, probably from a stēlē (Buschor and Von Massow 1927, 61, fig. in text; Jeffery 1990, 193 n. 4).

[23] Lazzarini 1976, 296 no. 835; Jeffery 1990, 199 no. 14; *SEG* XI.890 (Private coll.).

[24] *BSA* 11 (1904/05) 108–11; *IG* V.1.1120; Bingen 1958. Note also three figurines (respectively, from Monemvasia, Phoiniki and eastern Messenia – or possibly Arcadia: Herfort-Koch 1986, K 114, 115 and 118) which may represent either javelin-throwers or warriors with spears.

[25] Athena Chalkioikos lists: *SEG* XI.638 and *IG* V.1.357; Jeffery 1990, 60, 195, 201 nos. 44 and 47. Geronthrai lists: *IG* V.1.1133–4; Jeffery 1990, 201 nos. 45 and 46.

[26] Sanders 1992, 206–7, with reference to Sparta Museum nos. 575 and 613. Cf. the Dioskouroi 'starters' at the beginning of the Dromos racecourse and the presence nearby of their sanctuary and of a trophy purportedly set up by Polydeukes (Paus. 3.14.6–7).

[27] *Apophthegmata Lakonika*, Lykourgos no. 23 (= Plut. *Mor.* 228d); *Sayings of Kings and Commanders*, Lykourgos no. 4 (= *Mor.* 189e); Seneca, *De Beneficiis* 5.3; Plut. *Lykourgos* 19.4; Philostratos, *Gymnastikos* 9 and 58.

[28] Propertius 3.14.8; Lucian, *Symp.* 19; Philostratos, *Imag.* 2.6.3.

[29] *IG* V.1.658 = *CIG* 1421; *IG* V.1.669 = *CIG* 1428; *IG* V.1.670.

[30] Compare how the restriction of Spartiate youths to one cloak per year (Xen. *Lak.Pol.* 2.4; cf. Kennell 1995, 32–4) was distorted into the lakonophile

practice of purposely wearing tattered cloaks (Demosthenes 54.34).

31 Herodotus' account (1.59) of Chilon's advice to Hippokrates at the Olympic festival mentions no victory; but no conclusion can be drawn from this.

32 Cf. the table of Spartiate Olympic victories in Crowther 1990, 202.

33 I owe the following references to a forthcoming paper by Tim Cornell, 'On war and games in the ancient world', to be published in T.B. Allen and T.J. Cornell (eds.) *Warfare and Games*.

34 *BSA* 13 (1906/7) 150–3; 14 (1907/8) 145; 15 (1908/9) 114; Catling 1976/7, 41. The dated amphora is from *c.* 525–500 BC, Leagros Group (Brandt 1978, no. 72).

35 Paus. 6.16.6. Pausanias' description of this monument has led to dispute concerning its nature. He states: 'here too is dedicated a small chariot of Polypeithes the Lakonian and on the same stēlē Kalliteles, the father of Polypeithes, a wrestler' (ἅρμα οὐ μέγα...καὶ ἐπὶ στήλης τῆς αὐτῆς Καλλιτέλης...). Most scholars view the monument as a form of pillar bearing a free-standing miniature chariot and lifesize statue (cf., most recently, Herrmann 1988, 172 no. 170). Amandry (1957, 66 and 68 n. 22), however, believes that Kalliteles was represented not by a statue but by a sculpted relief. His view is based upon the argument of Guillon (1936, 216–27) that the word 'stēlē' in Pausanias always refers to a stone bearing a relief, never to a statue. It is true that the vast majority of Pausanias' 50 or so uses appear to bear this meaning. The question, however, is whether we should expect complete uniformity of usage in all remaining cases (1.44.5; 6.13.10; 6.16.6; 8.34.6) where the form of monument is less certain. The other difficulty with this view is that Pausanias' initial reference to Polypeithes' chariot is more suggestive of a free-standing object than a relief (cf. Lévêque 1946, 137); yet the chariot and representation of Kalliteles must have been of the same form, since they were on the same stēlē.

36 *Apophthegmata Lakonika*, Anon. nos. 27 and 72 = Plut. *Mor.* 233e and 236e; *Lakainōn Apophthegmata*, Anon. no. 21 = *Mor.* 242a–b; *Palatine Anthology* 16.1.

37 Pausanias' account mentions both statue and stēlē, but he was confused by apparent discrepancies in their dates. He comments rightly that the stēlē must be a subsequent dedication by the Lakedaimonian state rather than by Chionis himself, since it refers to the introduction of the hoplite race which took place in 520 BC. He mistakenly believed, however, that the victor statue next to the stēlē must have been dedicated by the athlete himself and therefore, as the work of Myron, could not be a statue of Chionis.

38 The Spartans' engagement in this rivalry is further signified by Pausanias' statement (3.14.3) regarding Chionis' victories that the hoplite race did not exist in his time. As Moretti (1957 nos. 42–3) notes, this reads like a Spartan commentary on one feature of Astylos' success (his Olympic hoplite race victory of 480) which Chionis did not share. On the uncertainty regarding the exact number of Chionis' victories, six or seven, Moretti 1957, no. 40.

39 Some scholars (e.g. Hyde 1921, 333) think that Eutelidas' statue was contemporary with his victory, on the strength of Pausanias' comment that the statue was ancient and its inscription dim with age. Yet this would contradict his explicit statement (6.18.7) that the first athletes commemorated by

statues belonged to the 59th and 61st Olympiads, i.e. 544 and 536 BC. Moreover, Pausanias' normal practice is to point out statues not made of bronze; but he makes no comment upon the material of Eutelidas' statue. This too indicates a later date, since lifesize bronze statues became technically possible only in the second half of the sixth century. A *terminus ante quem* is apparently indicated by the original placing of the statue in the area later occupied by the temple of Zeus which was completed in 457 (Hyde 1921, 346). On its classical date, cf. also Amandry 1957, 68 n. 21.

[40] References to previous work in Kurke 1993, 161 n. 68.

[41] According to Kurke (1993, 153), the phenomenon was also symptomatic of a more general fifth-century crisis in Greece, which prompted a beleaguered aristocracy to attempt to renew their power through Olympic success. This theory, however, is dubious, owing to the strictly limited number of poleis in which athletic heroization or divinization is attested. Full criticism of her suggestion (1993, 162–3 n. 87) that in Sparta 'kings and certain aristocrats' engaged in chariot racing by way of opposition to 'the encroaching power of the Ephorate' must await a subsequent occasion.

[42] Note the comparable case of the conspiracy of Kinadon (Xen. *Hell.* 3.3.4–11), in which the 'struggle' against the enemies surrounding the Spartiates was fought first through repeated sacrifices to the gods who avert evil and grant safety.

[43] Free meals are also attested on Keos (*IG* XII.5.1060), Paros (*IG* XII.5.274, 281, 289) and at Athens (*IG* I^2.77, the Prytaneion decree, from the 430s or 420s).

[44] Celebratory homecomings: Pindar, *Nem.* 2.25, 4.78–9; *Ol.* 11.15; *Pyth.* 8.85–7. Statues in home polis: Lattimore 1987, 249–50.

[45] This subordination of athletic victors to the state establishment is graphically illustrated by the contrast between the Spartans' and Athenians' treatment of the multiple panhellenic victor Dorieus of Rhodes and Thurii. When Dorieus, then their enemy, was captured by the Athenians, the latter released him unharmed out of pity and respect. When the Spartans captured him in changed political circumstances, they had him executed (Xen. *Hell.* 1.5.19; Paus. 6.7.4–7 = Androtion, *FGrH* 342 F 46).

[46] There is no reason to follow the argument of Willemsen (1977) that Lakrates was not a Spartan but should be identified with an Athenian athlete found buried 50 m from the Lakedaimonian monument. Xenophon's words identify him clearly as a Lakedaimonian buried in their collective tomb.

[47] Only the opening part of the retrograde inscription survives. Two names survive complete: 'THIBRAKOS POLEMARCHOS' and 'CHAIRON POLEMARCHOS' (note the different order from that in Xenophon and the divergent spellings of Thibrakos/Thibrachos), followed by the initial letter of a third name. This letter is normally read as 'M'; but this reading is challenged by Pritchett (1974–91, IV.134 n. 123), who sees 'only two joining diagonal strokes as for the upper part of an alpha, delta, or lambda'. Hence the third name might be that of Lakrates, though this is uncertain.

[48] *Instituta Laconica* no. 18 = Plut. *Mor.* 238d; Plut. *Lyk.* 27.1–2. This literary evidence is supported by the absence of archaeological evidence for funerary

inscriptions and by the evidence of the ΕΝ ΠΟΛΕΜΟΙ inscriptions discussed in the main text.

[49] *IG* V.i.701–10, 918, 921, 1124–5, 1320, 1591; Papanikolaou 1976; one unpublished stēlē for a certain Gorgopas in the Sparta Museum.

[50] *IG* V.i.708, perhaps dating to the third century BC (Tod and Wace 1906, no. 509).

[51] Quotations from Kurke 1991, 3 and 5.

[52] Quotation from Morgan (1993, 11), who provides a convenient summary of recent debates, reaffirmation of the traditional view that the initial context for the performance of (Pindaric) epinician involved choral rather than solo singing, and discussion of the relationship between epinician and the *kōmos*.

[53] Ibykos (S 166), as interpreted by Barron 1984, 20–1.

[54] Simonides fr. 531, Campbell, ap. Diod. 11.11.6; fr. XXII(b); Bacchylides, fr. 20, Campbell; Pindar, frs. 112 and 199, Maehler, *ap*. Athen. 631c and Plut. *Lyk*. 21.4, respectively.

[55] Parker 1989, 149; Xen. *Lak.Pol*. 9.5; *Ages*. 2.17; *Hell*. 6.4.16; Plut. *Lyk*. 14.3, 21.1–2; *Mor*. 149a, 208d–e, 219e; Athen. 555c.

[56] Only in a fragment of the early fifth century poet Ion of Chios (fr. 27 West; cf. West 1985), which may relate to the entertainment of foreign visitors in the Spartan royal mess, is there mention of song and dance.

[57] Similarly, the collective singing of the paean to Poseidon (Xen. *Hell*. 4.7.4), again on campaign, offers no hint of solo performance.

[58] Paus. 6.18.8; cf. also the reference to it in a partner stēlē at Olympia (*IvO* no. 171). This monument had, admittedly, been preceded earlier in the century by commemorations of chariot racing victories: *IG* V.1.235 = *BSA* 15 (1908/9) 86–7; Paus. 3.15.1; 17.6.

[59] Dedication of Koiris: Lazzarini 1976, no. 833; Jeffery 1990, 202 no. 63 (date sometime in the sixth century). Dedication of Akmatidas: Moretti 1957, no. 160; Ebert 1972, no. 9; Lazzarini 1976, no. 832; *CEG* I.372; Jeffery 1990, 199 no. 20, 448 (various dates have been proposed between *c*. 530 and the early fifth century).

[60] Deinosthenes: Paus. 6.16.6, plus the stēlē referenced in n. 58; Seleadas: Paus. 6.16.8.

[61] On the dispute concerning the form of the monument, n. 35 above.

[62] Some scholars (e.g. Moretti 1957, no. 160) suggest that the grandfather in question was the aforementioned Akmatidas, but there is no evidence for this guess. Pausanias does not give the victor's name.

[63] On sons commemorating their fathers' success, Amandry 1957, 66–68. All are later than Polypeithes, with the possible exception of Theopompos (I) of Erea (victor in 484 and 480: Moretti 1957, nos. 189 and 200), although it may be that the latter's statue and that of his father Damaretos were both erected only later in the century by their son and grandson, Theopompos II (Moretti 1957, nos. 313 and 317; Paus. 6.10.4–5).

Bibliography

Amandry, P.
1957 'A propos de Polyclète: statues d'Olympioniques et carrière de sculpteurs', in K. Schauenburg (ed.) *Charites: Studien zum Altertumswissenschaft*, Bonn, 63–87.

Arrigoni, G.
1985 'Donne e sport nel mondo greco: religione e società', in G. Arrigoni (ed.) *Le Donne in Grecia*, Bari, 55–201.

Aupert, P.
1980 'Athletica I: Épigraphie archaïque et morphologie des stades anciens', *BCH* 104, 309–15.

Barron, J.P.
1984 'Ibycus: *Gorgias* and other poems', *BICS* 31, 13–24.

Bernadini, P.A.
1992 'La storia dell'epinicio: aspetti socio-economici', *Studi Italiani di Filologia Classica*, ser. 3, 10, 965–79.

Bingen, J.
1958 'ΤΡΙΕΤΙΡΗΣ (*IG* V 1, 1120)', *AC* 27, 105–7.

Bohringer, F.
1979 'Cultes d'athlètes en Grèce classique: propos politiques, discours mythiques', *REA* 81, 5–18.

Bowie, E.
1990 '*Miles Ludens*: the problem of martial exhortation in early Greek elegy', in O. Murray (ed.) *Sympotica*, Oxford, 221–9.

Brandt, J.R.
1978 'Archaeologia Panathenaica I: Panathenaic prize-amphorae from the sixth century BC', *Acta ad archaeologiam et artium historiam pertinentia* 8, 1–24.

Buschor, E. and Von Massow W.
1927 'Vom Amyklaion', *AM* 52, 1–85.

Calame, C.
1977 *Les Choeurs de Jeunes Filles en Grèce Archaïque*, 2 vols., Rome.

Cartledge, P.A.
1976 'Seismicity in Spartan society', *LCM* 1, 25–8.
1981 'Spartan wives: liberation or licence?', *CQ* n.s. 31, 84–105.

Catling, H.W.
1976/7 'Excavations at the Menelaion, Sparta, 1973–76', *JHS*, *AR* 23, 24–42.
1990 'A sanctuary of Zeus Messapios: excavations at Aphyssou, Tsakona, 1989', *BSA* 85, 15–35.

Crowther, N.B.
1990 'A Spartan Olympic boxing champion', *AC* 59, 198–202.
1991 'The Olympic training period', *Nikephoros* 4, 161–6.

De Ridder, A.
1894 *Catalogue des Bronzes de la Société Archéologique d'Athènes*, Bibliothèque des Écoles Françaises d'Athènes et de Rome, fasc. 69, Paris.

Delorme, J.
1969 *Gymnasion*, Paris.

Ebert, J.
1972 *Griechische Epigramme auf Sieger an Gymnischen und Hippischen Agonen*, Berlin.
Golden, M.
1998 *Sport and Society in Ancient Greece*, Cambridge.
Guillon, P.
1936 'La stèle d'Agamédès (Paus., IX,37,7)', *RPh* 3ème sér., 10, 209–35.
Hamilton, R.
1996 'Panathenaic amphoras: the other side', in Neils (ed.)*Worshipping Athena*, 137–62.
Herrmann, H.-V.
1988 'Die Siegerstatuen von Olympia', *Nikephoros* 1, 119–83.
Herfort-Koch, M.
1986 *Archaische Bronzeplastik Lakoniens*, Boreas: Münstersche Beiträge zur Archäologie, Beiheft 4, Münster.
Hodkinson, S.
1989 'Inheritance, marriage and demography: perspectives upon the success and decline of classical Sparta' in Powell (ed.)*Classical Sparta*, 79–121.
Hönle, A.
1972 *Olympia in der Politik der griechischen Staatenwelt*, Bebenhausen (originally, Diss. Tübingen 1968).
Hyde, W.W.
1921 *Olympic Victor Monuments and Greek Athletic Art*, Washington.
Jeffery, L.H.
1988 'The development of Lakonian lettering: a reconsideration', *BSA* 83, 179–81.
1990 *The Local Scripts of Archaic Greece*, revised ed., with a supplement by A.W. Johnston, Oxford.
Jenner, E.A.B.
1986 'Further speculations on Ibycus and the epinician ode: S 220, S 176, and the "Bellerophon Ode" ', *BICS* 33, 59–66.
Kahil, L.
1977 'L'Artémis de Brauron: rites et mystère', *Antike Kunst* 20, 86–98.
Kennell, N.M.
1995 *The Gymnasium of Virtue: Education and culture in ancient Sparta*, Chapel Hill and London.
Kurke, L.
1991 *The Traffic in Praise: Pindar and the poetics of social economy*, Ithaca and London.
1993 'The economy of *kudos*', in C. Dougherty and L. Kurke (eds.) *Cultural Poetics in Archaic Greece*, Cambridge, 131–63.
Kyle, D.G.
1996 'Gifts and glory: Panathenaic and other Greek athletic prizes', in Neils (ed.) *Worshipping Athena*, 106–36.
Lamb, W.W.
1969 *Ancient Greek and Roman Bronzes*, Chicago; reprint with additions of

original 1929 edition.
Lattimore, S.
1987 'The nature of early Greek victor statues', in S.J. Bandy (ed.) *Coroebus Triumphs: the Alliance of Sports and the Arts*, San Diego, 245–56.
Lazzarini, M.L.
1976 *Le Formule delle Dediche Votive nella Grecia Arcaica*, Atti della Accademia Nazionale dei Lincei, Memorie. Classe di Scienze morali, stor. e filol. 19, Rome, 45–354.
Lévêque, P.
1946 'Les consécrations de chars dans le sanctuaire d'Olympie', *RA* 6ème sér. 25, 129–38.
Mallwitz, A.
1988 'Cult and competition locations at Olympia', in Raschke (ed.) *The Archaeology of the Olympics*, 79–109.
Moretti, L.
1957 *Olympionikai, i Vincitori negli Antichi Agoni Olimpici*, Atti della Accademia Nazionale dei Lincei, Memorie. Classe di Scienze morali, stor. e filol., ser. 8, vol. 8, fasc. 2, Rome, 53–198.
1970 'Supplemento al catalogo degli Olympionikai', *Klio* 52, 295–303.
1992 'Nuovo supplemento al catalogo degli Olympionikai', in W. Coulson and H. Kyrieleis (eds.) *Proceedings of an International Symposium on the Olympic Games*, Athens, 119–28.
Morgan, K.A.
1993 'Pindar the professional and the rhetoric of the ΚΩΜΟΣ', *CPh* 88, 1–15.
Murray, O.
1993 *Early Greece*, 2nd edn, London.
Nafissi, M.
1991 *La Nascita del Kosmos: Studi sulla Storia e la Società di Sparta*, Naples.
Neils J. (ed.)
1996 *Worshipping Athena: Panathenaia and Parthenon*, Madison, Wisconsin and London.
Ollier, F.
1934 *Xénophon, La République des Lacédémoniens*, Lyon. Repr. New York 1979.
Papanikolaou, A.D.
1976–7 ' Ἐπιτύμβιον ἐξ ἀρχαίας Σελλασίας ', *Athena* 76, 202–4.
Parker, R.
1989 'Spartan religion', in Powell (ed.) *Classical Sparta*, 142–72.
Peiser, B.
1990 'The crime of Hippias of Elis: zur Kontroverse um die Olympionikenliste', *Stadion* 16, 37–65.
Pleket, H.W.
1974 'Zur Sociologie des antiken Sports', *MNIR* 36, 57–87.
1975 'Games, prizes, athletes and ideology', *Stadion* 1, 49–89.

Poliakoff, M.B.

1987 *Combat Sports in the Ancient World*, New Haven and London.

Powell, A.

1994 'Plato and Sparta: modes of rule and of non-rational persuasion in the *Laws*', in A. Powell and S. Hodkinson (eds.) *The Shadow of Sparta*, London and New York, 273–321.

1998 'Sixth-century Lakonian vase-painting: continuities and discontinuities with the 'Lykourgan' ethos', in N. Fisher and H. van Wees (eds.) *Archaic Greece: New Approaches and New Evidence*, London and Oakville, Conn., 119–46.

Powell, A. (ed.)

1989 *Classical Sparta: Techniques behind her success*, London.

Pritchett, W.K.

1974–91 *The Greek State at War*, 5 vols, Berkeley and Los Angeles.

Raschke, W.J. (ed.)

1988 *The Archaeology of the Olympics*, Madison, Wisconsin.

Ste. Croix, G.E.M. de

1972 *The Origins of the Peloponnesian War*, London.

Sanders, J.M.

1992 'The early Lakonian Dioskouroi reliefs', in J.M. Sanders (ed.) ΦΙΛΟΛΑΚΩΝ: *Lakonian Studies in honour of Hector Catling*, London, 205–10.

Scanlon, T.F.

1984 'The footrace of the Heraia at Olympia', *Ancient World* 8, 77–90.

1988 '*Virgineum gymnasium*: Spartan females and early Greek athletics', in Raschke (ed.) *The Archaeology of the Olympics*, 185–216.

Serwint, N.J.

1987 'Greek Athletic Sculpture from the fifth and fourth centuries BC: an iconographic study', Diss. Princeton.

1993 'The female athletic costume at the Heraia and prenuptial initiation rites', *AJA* 97, 403–22.

Snodgrass, A.M.

1989/90 'The economics of dedication at Greek sanctuaries', in *Anathema: Regime delle Offerte e Vita dei Santuari nel Mediterraneo Antico*, special issue of *Scienze dell'Antichità* 3–4, 287–94.

Sourvinou-Inwood, C.

1988 *Studies in Girls' Transitions: Aspects of the Arkteia and Age Representation in Attic Iconography*, Athens.

Steinhauer, G.

n.d. *Museum of Sparta*, Athens.

Stewart, A.F.

1997 *Art, Desire, and the Body in Ancient Greece*, Cambridge.

Sweet, W.E.

1987 *Sport and Recreation in Ancient Greece: a sourcebook*, New York and Oxford.

Tarkow, T.A.

1983 'Tyrtaios 9D: the role of poetry in the new Sparta', *AC* 52, 48–69.

Thomas, R.
1981 *Athletenstatuetten der Spätarchaik und des Strengen Stils*, Rome.
Tigerstedt, E.N.
1965–78 *The Legend of Sparta in Classical Antiquity*, 3 vols., Stockholm, Göteborg and Uppsala.
Tod, M.N. and Wace, A.J.B.
1906 *A Catalogue of the Sparta Museum*, Oxford.
Van Hook, L.
1932 'On the Lacedaemonians buried in the Kerameikos', *AJA* 36, 290–2.
Von Massow, W.
1926 'Die Stele des Ainetos in Amyklai', *AM* 51, 41–7.
Vonias, Z.I.
1985 ' Ενεπίγραφος αλτήρας Αιγιών ', *Athens Annals of Archaeology* 18, 246–53 (German summary, 'Sprunggewicht mit Inschrift aus Aigiai', 253).
West, M.L.
1985 'Ion of Chios', *BICS* 32, 71–8.
Whitley, J.
1998 'Cretan laws and Cretan literacy', *AJA* 101, 635–61.
Willemsen, F.
1977 'Zu den Lakedämoniergraben im Kerameikos', *AM* 92, 117–57.
Woodward, A.M.
1929 'Inscriptions', in R.M. Dawkins (ed.) *The Sanctuary of Artemis Orthia at Sparta*, London, 285–377.
Young, D.C.
1984 *The Olympic Myth of Greek Amateur Athletics*, Chicago.

Chapter 7

FROM *PERIOIKOI* TO *POLEIS*

The Laconian cities in the late hellenistic period

Nigel M. Kennell

Over the past few years, more and more light has been shed on the history of later Sparta. An important aspect of that history, however, still lies in obscurity – the fate of the former perioecic towns that came to form the League of Lacedaemonians in the second century BC and its successor in the following century, the League of Eleutherolaconians. There is, of course, a valid reason for this neglect, the appalling lack of evidence, even in comparison with that available for late hellenistic and Roman Sparta.[1] Nevertheless, such a dearth is nothing new for historians of Laconia and, in the case of the Lacedaemonian League, the little that survives can be valuable when placed in a broader context of late hellenistic constitutional and social history. The major questions concerning the League of Lacedaemonians – the date of its beginning and the nature of its end, or, to be more precise, its metamorphosis into the Eleutherolaconian League – have been treated before, notably by André Aymard and Kathleen Chrimes, and exhaustively by David Martin in his 1975 Princeton dissertation.[2] The present evidence still cannot support any radical new appraisals that diverge significantly from the consensus of their conclusions. Nonetheless, there is some scope for an examination of the League and its relations with the former ruling power in the last two centuries before our era, when Sparta was definitively stripped of any institutional uniqueness and the perioecic communities developed into fully-fledged *poleis*.

Before the second century BC no perioecic history can be recovered. Based on the few scattered references an outline has been drawn of relatively complex societies in the fifth and fourth centuries BC, with the sort of social stratification found in most Greek cities. Far from simply supplying artisans and tradesmen for the Spartiates, perioecic towns are now seen as little different from other small communities outside Laconia, with a hoplite class, landowners, tradesmen, workers, and slaves.[3] This social structure, in conjunction with whatever administrative institutions the perioeci possessed, would have made the transition from being dependencies of Sparta to being independent *poleis* all the easier. That at least some of the perioeci in the classical period desired either liberation from Spartan control or a more equal relationship is shown by the supposed perioecic sympathy for the designs of Cinadon and the rebellion of many perioeci during the Theban invasion of Laconia after Leuctra.[4] But in the end the perioeci remained loyal.

The 'normalization' of Spartan life during the third century must have had an effect on the perioecic towns. Both Agis and Cleomenes attempted to bring perioeci into the Spartan mainstream by proposing to distribute *klaroi* among them, although life on the periphery does not seem to have been unprofitable. An Aetolian raid after the fall of Agis targeted perioecic communities in southern Laconia and carried off 50,000 slaves as booty.[5] Though doubtless exaggerated, the number of captives does indicate a level of wealth that drew Aetolian attention. As Sparta's influence declined further in the later years of the century, so the perioecic communities passed in and out of her control.[6] A final settlement, however, would only come with Roman intervention in the next century.

195 BC was as disastrous a year for Sparta as that of Leuctra, almost two centuries before in 371. As the territorial losses in Leuctra's wake reduced Sparta from a great power to a 'second-rate provincial squabbler' (in the words of Paul Cartledge), so the partitioning of Laconia itself following the Roman defeat of Nabis put paid to all of the ambitions the Spartans evidently had of regaining their earlier position.[7] Sparta's loss was the perioeci's gain, as the vast bulk of the lands detached from Sparta's control never reverted to her for any appreciable period of time. The settlement that saw the separation of the so-called 'maritime cities' (*maritimae civitates*) of Laconia came after a brief but decisive war.[8] This clash, between a determined Nabis and the Romans, who represented the conservative interests of his nervous neighbors, was an inevitable consequence of Flamininus' declaration of Greece's freedom at the Isthmian games in 196. Although the Romans had effectively recognized Spartan suzerainty over the city of Argos before that date, their very public new policy statement fitted awkwardly with the continued occupation of a Greek city by a foreign power. Quickly bringing Greek opinion into line, Titus Quinctius Flamininus was soon at the head of a huge allied invasion force making its way toward Sparta by land and sea.[9]

While Titus himself besieged the capital, his brother Lucius dealt with the coastal cities. As Livy puts it, the towns of the seacoast came over to him, 'partly of their own free will, partly through fear and force'.[10] Gythium was a harder nut to crack: only after a siege sustained with the aid of king Eumenes of Pergamum and a Rhodian fleet did Laconia's most important seaport surrender to Roman arms.[11] The fall of Gythium induced Nabis to sue for peace, and after some discussion on the Roman side terms were dictated. Spartan forces were to withdraw from Argos; the ships Nabis had confiscated from the maritime cities were to be returned and he was to possess in the future no more than two *lembi*, a measure effectively aimed at destroying Sparta's naval capability; he was to stay out of Crete; and he was to evacuate all garrisons from all the cities which he himself had restored and which had handed themselves and their chattels over 'into the trust and sovereignty of the Roman people' (*in fidem ac dicionem populi Romani*).[12]

Research into the precise legal significance to the Romans of the various forms of surrender (*deditio in fidem, in dicionem*, etc.) has consumed small forests without significantly improving on Badian's minimalist approach of forty years ago.[13] Luckily, such jurisprudential subtleties are of no real concern in this instance: in the eyes of the Greeks as well as the Romans, the maritime cities were clearly under Flamininus' control, who could do with them as he wished. What precise measures the Roman commander did take in 195 constitutes the central question in the problem of the Lacedaemonian League's foundation date.

Livy provides some partial aid: on two subsequent occasions when Sparta threatened the maritime cities, he says that Titus placed the cities under the guardianship of the Achaean League. In describing Nabis' attempts in 193 to subvert the coastal cities, Livy says that 'the duty of guarding all the coastal Laconians (*omnium maritimorum Laconum tuendorum*) had been mandated to the Achaeans by Titus Quinctius'.[14] When the Spartans attacked the Laconian city of Las in 189, the Achaeans viewed this as a violation of the treaty of 195, 'since Titus Quinctius and the Romans had handed the strongholds (*castella*) and towns of the Laconian shore to the trust and safekeeping of the Achaeans (*in fidem Achaeorum tutelamque*)'.[15] Despite the apparent precision of Livy's terminology, especially in the second passage, I think it is a mistake to see the relationship between the Laconian towns and the Achaean League in terms of Roman conventions. Any such connection between independent Greek entities would surely be shaped by the norms governing Greek interstate affairs, not Roman law. *Fides ac tutela* here must represent the rendering into Latin of a Greek concept.

Protectorates like the one exercised by the Achaeans were not unknown in the hellenistic world. The city of Chersonesus in the Crimea, although originally autonomous, was forced by the incursions of the surrounding tribes to put itself under the protection of Mithradates Eupator of Pontus, to choose him as *prostatēs,* in the words of Strabo; on Crete, Itanus was under the protectorate (*prostasia*) of Ptolemy Philometor, while the federation (*koinon*) of Cretan cities had elected Philip V of Macedon as the island's single *prostatēs*.[16] There can be little doubt that, in Greek eyes, the Achaeans held the *prostasia* of the Laconian cities.[17] Thus, when those cities felt themselves in danger from Sparta, they sent to the Achaean League, not to Rome, for armed intervention on their behalf.[18] This accords with the view of Niccolini and Aymard that the coastal towns enjoyed control over their internal affairs, while the Achaean League had a monopoly on all foreign relations.[19] As Aymard goes on to point out, there is no reason to believe, as Swoboda did, that the Achaean League went so far as actually to annexe the Laconian towns without allowing them to participate in League affairs; in fact, the evidence tells against it.[20] When, in a senatorial reply to an Achaean embassy in 183, reference is made to the territories the Achaean League gained thanks to the Romans – Sparta, Corinth, and Argos – the Laconian towns are not among them.[21]

It may perhaps be possible to gain a fairly clear picture of the nature of the relationship between the Achaeans and the former perioecic settlements, but the answer to another, more pressing question is not so forthcoming. Did the Laconian towns form a League immediately upon being separated from Sparta in 195, or was the League created later, in 146? The sources are certainly scanty and, to make matters worse, confused and contradictory as well. Both Strabo and Pausanias mention the liberation from Spartan rule of Laconian towns and a League of Eleutherolaconians.[22] Of the two, Pausanias is clearly describing the creation of the actual Eleutherolaconian League under Augustus, whereas the passage in Strabo is less straightforward.

Immediately after telling of the fate of C. Julius Eurycles, ruler of Sparta under Augustus, Strabo says,

> it happened that the Eleutherolaconians also got some sort of constitutional arrangement (*tina taxin politeias*), since (or 'when') the perioeci, the others and especially the helots, had gone over first to the Romans, while Sparta was under a tyranny.

Despite the reference to Eleutherolaconians and the immediate context, it must be admitted, virtually no one believes that Strabo is referring to the transformation of the League of Lacedaemonians into the Eleutherolaconian League, which took place under Augustus.[23] The appearance of helots, perioeci, and a tyranny all point back to the time of Nabis, as does the passage's larger context, for the brief description of the fall of Eurycles is itself an aside within a longer account of the development of the Spartan constitution until 146 BC, which concludes after this statement with the names of its putative founders. Moreover, just before the Eurycles passage, Strabo has already alluded to Nabis' tyranny in telling of Spartan opposition to generals sent by the Romans, which was a result of their civil affairs being badly run under a tyrant at that time (*turanneuomenoi tote kai politeuomenoi mochtherōs*). A mere ten lines later, he uses the same middle form of *turanneuein* to characterize Sparta's government at the time the perioeci received 'some sort of constitution'. Allowing for a confusion in nomenclature, Strabo undoubtedly associated the formation of the Lacedaemonian League with the settlement of Flamininus in 195.

Admittedly, this argument from word usage is hardly decisive. However, a passage in Livy, while not enough to confirm this reconstruction, may afford some support. When the Spartans occupied Las, one of the former perioecic towns, in 189 'terror overran the whole sea coast, and all the strongholds and towns as well as the exiles who had dwellings there, jointly sent representatives to the Achaeans'.[24] At the very least, Livy's words attest to the perioecic towns' acting all together in a matter of common interest. Although hardly showing that the coastal towns had already formed a league, the passage does illustrate that in the years following their separation from Sparta, the conditions were favorable for a league to coalesce. For my part, I believe that Strabo was right in connecting the birth of the League to the defeat of Nabis in 195, but I would not go so far as to date the creation of the League of Lacedaemonians to that year precisely.

Strabo himself is vague concerning the form the League took at first. 'Some sort of constitutional arrangement' (*tina taxin politeias*) seems to indicate that he, or his source, saw something unusual in it. I think that what he means here is something less than the ordinary form of federal government that would have been familiar from the Achaean and Aetolian Leagues. And, as there is no reason to believe that the Romans, or the Achaeans for that matter, imposed a federal structure on the cities immediately after they became independent of Sparta, it is attractive to think the Laconian towns gradually discovered a common identity which resulted in the formation over several decades of a loose confederation of states.

That thought, of course, must for the present remain sheer speculation. We can be reasonably sure, though, that Sparta was not a member of this confederation, whatever form it took. K.M.T. Chrimes argued on the basis of coin types that the League of Lacedaemonians included Sparta and supplied priests for its common sanctuary of Apollo Hyperteleates at Asopus.[25] However, in a decree emanating from the League itself, probably in the early first century BC, a Spartan was appointed to the honorary post of *proxenos* to look after the interests of visitors from the League to Sparta – proof that Sparta was not part of the League.[26] That Spartan priests are attested at a League shrine merely points to the enduring sacral ties of a pan-Laconian cult. Spartan religious officials are also attested later in connection with the communities of Helos and Pleiae in the southeastern part of Laconia, although Marchetti has recently argued in the case of Helos that the epigraphically attested name actually refers to part of the Spartan agora.[27] Nevertheless, the ties between the cities of the League and the former ruling power were extremely close, though at times rather fraught. During the later second and first centuries BC, several towns cultivated proxeny links with Sparta. Cotyrta, Geronthrae, and Gythium all had one or more Spartan proxenoi.[28] In the 70s, a time of economic hardship for the city, Gythium honored a Spartan doctor, Damiadas, who stayed on after the term of his contract with the city had expired, treating his patients at no charge.[29]

Despite the intimate connections between the League and its more eminent neighbor, there is no reason to think that any city of the League of Lacedaemonians or its successor, the League of Eleutherolaconians, shared Sparta's privilege of being a *civitas libera*. Strabo is unambiguous on this point.[30] He says that the privilege of being free and contributing nothing apart from 'friendly services' had been bestowed on 'those who came to occupy Laconia' (*hoi de kataschontes tēn Lakōnikēn*) who had enjoyed good government early in their history by turning it over to Lycurgus, and who had subsequently become the masters of the Greeks by land and by sea only to see their leadership pass to the Thebans and then the Macedonians – in other words, the Spartans themselves. Surprisingly, on no grounds whatsoever, some have taken this statement to include the ex-perioecic cities, particularly Gythium.[31] The question, though, may now be a literally academic one as regards the second century BC, if Robert Kallet-Marx's view of Greece's constitutional situation after the Achaean war is correct.[32] For he argues that the cities of Greece did not come directly under the Roman *imperium* at that time: rather the Roman province of

Achaea took its final shape as a result of a much more incremental and gradual process than has heretofore been realized.[33] Whatever the accuracy of Kallet-Marx's picture (and I admit to favoring it), there is no reason to think that the League of Lacedaemonians or its constituent cities enjoyed any of the privileges the Romans granted the Spartans.[34]

In general, amicable relations between Sparta and the former subject cities of Laconia seem to have been the rule. They appear to have continued through the imperial period, even surviving the regime of Eurycles at Sparta, notorious for his opportunistic meddling in affairs beyond his borders.[35] By way of illustration, to stretch the chronological bounds of this volume a little, and leap to the reign of Claudius, the wealthy Gytheate woman Phaenia Aromation evidently counted on Sparta to safeguard the provisions of her will.[36] The Spartan presence inevitably had a profound influence on the shape and functioning of the League and its member cities. For example, if Alan Samuel's supposition is correct, the Laconian cities even kept the Spartan calendar.[37] And it seems more than likely that, after Sparta began minting her own coins again after 48 BC, the League cities used Spartan coinage as well.[38]

Examples of a single coin of the League of Lacedaemonians have been known since the time of Foucart.[39] On the obverse is a bust identified as that of the goddess Roma; on the reverse, which is encircled by a victory wreath, a figure of Artemis stands facing left, in a *chitoniskos* and boots, with a quiver on her shoulder and a cypress branch in her hand.[40] More helpful is the reverse legend, 'Federation of Lacedaemonians. Kyparissia' (*KOI(non) (tōn) LAKE(daimoniōn) KUPARISSIA)*, which the numismatist Head thought identified a festival coinage. In literary sources, Kyparissia appears only in Pausanias as an epithet of the Athena worshiped in two cities called Asopus, one in Messenia and one in Laconia.[41] Luckily, a third-century inscription from the shrine of Apollo Hyperteleates near Laconian Asopus solves the problem by referring to a priest of Apollo and Agrotera Kypharissia – Apollo and Artemis.[42] This is the basis of the *communis opinio* that the coin bears witness to a festival of the Lacedaemonian League held at or near one of the League's two major cult sites, the other being the shrine of Poseidon at Tainaron.

Twenty years ago, Suzanne Grunauer-von Hoerschelmann, in her indispensable *Die Münzprägung der Lakedaimonier*, brought to light another League coin, with the head of Apollo on the obverse and an eagle beside the League's title on the reverse.[43] Although comparison of the two series of coins is difficult because there are only two examples of the new coin extant, she thought it conceivable that the weight of the Apollo coin was half that of the Artemis. It is attractive to speculate that the two series were issued jointly by the League in connection with a festival of Artemis held at the sanctuary of Apollo Hyperteleates, especially since they both carry the monogram or abbreviation, *TI–KA*. These still-mysterious letters might even indicate that the coins were actually minted by Sparta for the League, because the last two letters appear on Grunauer-von Hoerschelmann's Spartan Group XVI Series 6 in precisely the same form of ligature, that is, with the alpha formed by the branches of the kappa.[44] Whatever the likelihood of such coincidence, the eagle on the reverse of the Apollo coin closely recalls a Spartan reverse type that Grunauer-von Hoerschelmann dates between *c.* 43 and 31 BC and shows that the cultural influence of Sparta was strong enough for the League, at the very least, to model types for the few coins it issued upon those of its former masters.[45]

In much the same way as the turbulence of the later hellenistic period left traces in the composition and nomenclature of the public institutions at Sparta, the League's constitution, like those of its individual member cities, shows the marks of history. In those towns with any evidence for how they governed themselves, Spartan-style (or, to be more precise, Dorian) institutions are to be found. There are ephors in Gerenia, Hippola, Caenepolis, Pyrrichus, Cotyrta, Epidaurus Limera, Geronthrae, and Gythium.[46] As Chrimes pointed out, it would be rash to consider these ephorates as direct imitations of a purely Spartan institution, since the ephorate is attested in a great many Dorian cities throughout the Greek world.[47] Similarly, Gythium celebrated the characteristic Dorian festival of Apollo, the Apellai; in two decrees the assembly is described as having passed a bill in the '*megalai apellai*'.[48] As de Ste. Croix noticed, this implies that the *ekklesia* at Gythium, like its Spartan counterpart, usually met during festivals of Apollo.[49] Only three honorific decrees tell us anything about its competence during the last decades of the hellenistic period. Despite the banality of the honors involved – grants of priesthoods of Apollo for two citizens who had repaired the temple at their own expense, proxeny to the Spartan doctor Damiadas, and honors for the notorious brothers Cloatii – a certain few features do stand out upon closer scrutiny.[50]

The three decrees under examination were all passed within a short period of time. Probably no more than about ten years or so separate *IG* V.1.1144, the earliest, from 1146, the latest in the series, which was passed in 71/70 BC. As for *IG* V.1.1145, it dates from 73/2. The good fortune of their relative contemporaneity allows us to assume that the differences in these documents reflect variations from current practice and not changes that developed in the course of time. In *IG* V.1.1144 and 1146, both passed *en tais megalais apellais*, extraordinary honors are given. In 1144, Philemon and his son Theoxenos are made priests and given possession of the shrine of Apollo in perpetuity as recompense for repairing it; not only do they and their descendants become the priests and owners of the shrine itself, but they also receive all the honors and privileges due to hereditary priests, as well as control over all affairs of the shrine and its estates (lines 21–33). In 1146, the *damos* confirms the privileges of the Cloatii, who are already proxenoi, and grants them the additional honor of being publicly invited by the ephors to sit in the *proedria* with them at any set of games the city holds. In contrast, *IG* V.1.1145, which contains no mention of the Great *Apellai*, records a run-of-the-mill grant of proxeny to one Damiadas, with the normal right to own land and a house, including 'all the privileges and honors that the city grants to other proxenoi and benefactors' (lines 42–4). From this we may deduce that the *damos* sat in the Great *Apellai* when the granting of extraordinary honors was on the agenda.

Two other elements distinguish the decrees passed at the Great *Apellai*: the site of the erection of the *stelai* and the source of finance for their erection. To address the second point, only in the two decrees passed in the Great *Apellai* are public funds explicitly earmarked for their recording and display (*IG* V.1.1144, line 36; 1146, lines 55–6). The absence of any such provision in the decree for Damiadas requires us to assume that private citizens paid for the inscription and erection of that stele. Such private funding was the rule rather than the exception in the later hellenistic and Roman periods, especially when it came to the erection of statues. In Sparta, for example, the vast majority of honorific bases record the names of the individuals who financed the statues that once stood upon them.[51] At Oenoanda, the city granted the leader of the winning team in the torch race the honors of a decree and a statue, if he paid for it; if not, the victorious captain was to be 'satisfied with the honor of a decree'.[52] That a record was made of Gythium's financial contribution merely for the erection of two marble stelai in the sanctuary of Apollo confirms the precarious state of the civic finances in the 70s BC, while at the same time showing the importance attached to the two decrees.

As to the placement of the inscriptions, both *IG* V.1.1144 and 1146 were to be set up in the sanctuary of Apollo, located beside the agora, whereas 1145 was to be placed in the most conspicuous spot in the agora itself.[53] Although the reasons for placing a decree that honors benefactors of Apollo in the god's own shrine are obvious, as in the case of 1144, they are less so in the case of a decree honoring money-lenders. The explanation may be that official acts of the *ekklesia* sitting during the Great *Apellai* were usually displayed in the grounds of Apollo's shrine.

The Dorian bedrock upon which the public institutions of the Laconian cities rested can best be seen at Gythium, where the epigraphical evidence is the most plentiful. Outside Gythium, there is little to go on besides the use of a doricising form of the Greek vernacular language *(koinē)* in the inscriptions and the tendency to erect honorific decrees in temples of Apollo, as, for example, at Geronthrae, which had its own, and at those towns near the sanctuary of Apollo Hyperteleates.[54]

The League of Lacedaemonians was not ambitious in its dealings with foreign cities: of the thirteen proxeny decrees from the League and its members in which the home city of the honorand is preserved, only one grant went to recipients beyond the old boundaries of Laconia. These men, from Carystus and Eretria, were rewarded for representing Geronthrae in a dispute before the *koinon* of Lacedaemonians.[55] In two other disputes, non-Laconian tribunals were used: when the Gytheates brought their dispute over repayment of a loan to the Cloatii to an Athenian board, and when Zarax and Epidaurus Limera went before a tribunal of Tenians.[56] This is the sum total of surviving epigraphical evidence for the League's contact with cities beyond its immediate environs.

Among the remaining proxeny decrees, over half, that is seven out of twelve, are grants to Spartans.[57] As we would expect, the Laconian cities still felt the need for someone to represent their interests in the region's most important city. The honors mentioned explicitly in the texts invariably include the right to possess land and a dwelling (*gās kai oikiās enktēsis*), very often freedom from arbitrary seizure of property (*asylia*) and exemption from taxes and/or duties (*ateleia*), and sometimes the privilege of *epinomia*, the right to graze flocks without charge on the common.[58] The rarely-attested privilege of *epigamia*, the right to legal marriage with citizens, appears once, as does the ancient complement to *asylia*, *asphaleia* (security).[59] The granting of these thoroughly traditional privileges in the last century before this era by newly-independent cities, at a time when modern accounts have supposed Greek civic institutions to have been moribund, attests to those very institutions' continuing vitality.

Two proxeny decrees have survived that emanated from the League itself, but only one preserves any appreciable amount of information. It is a decree granting proxeny to a Spartan along with the right to own land and a dwelling, grazing rights, exemption from duties and unwarranted seizure.[60] Such league proxenics are known from elsewhere in Greece and were, assuredly, a greater honor than a proxeny granted by a single city.[61] In these two documents, the Lacedaemonian League granted privileges that were valid in all its member cities. These grants of privileges to outsiders are, ironically, almost the only extant testimony for the League actually acting like a League as we tend to think of one, as a confederation of cities having certain laws and rights in common. Admittedly, Geronthrae's dispute with its neighbor seems to have been heard by the *koinon* acting as a court, but such judicial activity was not peculiar to Leagues.[62] But apart from what seems to be a rather vestigial federal administrative structure, the cities of the League dealt with one another as more-or-less independent entities. Thus, among the honors that were bestowed on proxenoi from other member cities were exemption from import and export duties (*ateleia*) and the enjoyment of citizen rights (*isopoliteia*). Had the members of the League 'enjoyed full sympolity in their relationships with each other', as Martin inexplicably supposed, such grants would have been meaningless.[63] The situation must have resembled what Christian Marek argued for the case of the Boeotian League, a federation within which citizens in each of its constituent cities did not automatically enjoy unrestricted rights in every other member state.[64]

As I have just mentioned, the Lacedaemonian League does not appear to have had a very complex bureaucracy. There was an annual eponymous magistrate (*stratēgos*) whose title obviously derives from the Achaean League and who is mentioned in decrees from Lacedaemonian cities.[65] There was a treasurer (*tamias*) attested in two League proxeny decrees, who was to arrange for the documents' inscription and erection at the League's religious center, the sanctuary of Poseidon on Cape Taenarum.[66] One other official, the *presbys* of the *ethnos*, who was perhaps a priest, is attested in a sepulchral inscription at Hippola on the Mani peninsula.[67] No other posts are known. However, the existence of a treasurer implies a League treasury, though Martin's contention that it was funded by import and export duties rests on pure speculation.[68] Pausanias does mention something he calls a *synedrion* of the Eleutherolaconians which, as the Lacedaemonian League's successor, apparently retained all of its predecessor's governmental apparatus.[69] But, as Kallet-Marx points out, Pausanias habitually uses this word to mean 'league' rather than 'league council', so we cannot retroject his usage into the hellenistic period to become evidence that the Lacedaemonian League possessed a league council (*synedrion*) in the Achaean style.[70] Nonetheless, some sort of representative assembly or council must have met at Taenarum to pass these decrees.

Apart from this institution, there is little reason to think that the administrative apparatus was very large. Unusually for members of a Greek league, individual cities appear to have levied their own import and export duties, even on goods coming from other member states. That, at least, is implied by the grants of *ateleia* given by League cities to proxenoi from other League cities. Furthermore, no League officials other than those known from the late hellenistic period are attested later, after its transformation into the League of Eleutherolaconians. All this suggests that the League's structure, its *politeia*, was always rather loose and, in consequence, that Strabo's reference to its taking on 'some sort of *politeia*' had contemporary force.

Other evidence, less direct in nature, also exists for the looseness of the Lacedaemonian League's federal ties. In his analysis of the Achaean League after 146 BC, Thomas Schwertfeger drew attention to a statue base at Olympia erected by the *koinon* of the Achaeans in honor of the propraetor Quintus Ancharius.[71] This same Ancharius also appears in the famous inscription from Gythium honoring the Roman businessmen Nemerius and Marcus Cloatius for their 'help' during the harsh decade of the 70s BC, when the city struggled under the weight of Roman requisitions for the anti-piracy campaign of Marcus Antonius Creticus.[72] Ancharius came to Gythium in 73/2 as the last in a string of Roman officials demanding supplies. The inscription describes the process as follows: 'And when Gaius Gallius requisitioned grain and Quintus Ancharius clothing from this city of ours according to the allotted share, they (i.e. the brothers Cloatii) brought to bear their whole zeal and generosity (*philotimia*) for this city of ours and petitioned that our city might not make a contribution, but be relieved, in which they were successful, and we did not make a contribution.'[73]

Fundamental to Schwertfeger's interpretation of Achaean-Roman relations is Accame's insight that the erection of the statue at Olympia for Ancharius was probably an expression of gratitude for his moderation in executing the orders for requisitions in the cities of the Achaean League. He builds on it by observing that Ancharius received his honors not from those cities individually, but from the League as a whole, from which he then concludes that, even in the first century BC, the Achaean League as a body rather than individual cities, was responsible to Rome in matters of monetary or material contributions.

The Gythium inscription tells a different story: at no point in the saga of the Cloatii's sometimes rapacious involvement in the city's financial affairs is there any mention of the Lacedaemonian League. The reference to the city's 'allotted share' of the requisitions imposed by Ancharius implies that other cities were approached, but, in view of the Olympia statue base, the demands were obviously not confined to Laconia alone, and were almost certainly made of every city in the Peloponnese.

Accordingly, if Schwertfeger is right, the Romans dealt with Gythium and the cities of the Achaean League in quite different ways. In Achaea they worked through an intermediary, the League itself, but Gythium they approached directly with no reference to the Lacedaemonian League, The logical conclusion is that the Lacedaemonian League did not operate as a corporate entity in the same manner as the Achaean League. Besides its absence from dealings with the ruling power, we have seen already that the League lacked a consistent federal coinage, that there was no unencumbered right of land ownership throughout the League, that the cities levied duties on goods traveling within Laconia, and that there were no communal citizenship rights. In other words, the Lacedaemonian League seems to have been a perfectly normal loose confederation of a very common type under the Romans, the religious league. The contemporary Boeotian League, for instance, was chiefly concerned with the upkeep of sanctuaries and the celebration of festivals, as were the majority of Greek leagues at the time.[74] The slender file of testimonia for the Lacedaemonian League is not incompatible with the hypothesis that its main functions were religious: the single known coin issue commemorates a festival, league decrees were set up at sanctuaries, and one of the three known league officials seems to have been a priest. To be sure, the evidence is far from conclusive, yet we can reasonably expect a minor *koinon* such as the Laconian cities formed under the Roman aegis to be of this sort. The Achaean and Thessalian Leagues were the exceptions, not the rule.

Whether the League performed a mainly religious function or not, weaker federal ties would have made the domination of individual cities by Spartan interests all that much easier. This domination reached its height in the last decades of the first century BC, when the cities of Laconia fell under the sway of the Spartan hegemon, Gaius Julius Eurycles. Contrary to all the Spartan stereotypes, Eurycles was a seafaring entrepreneur. More precisely, he came from a family of pirates or buccaneers whose base may have been on the island of Cythera. Lachares, his father, had been a man of importance, whom the *boulē* and *dēmos* of Athens honored as benefactor and whom Marc Antony had ordered executed for piracy.[75] Chrimes noticed that this charge perhaps hid Lachares' harassment of Antony's grain ships from Egypt.[76] His son therefore committed himself to Octavian's side in the ensuing conflict and brought a fleet to his aid at the battle of Actium. In gratitude, Octavian gave the city the presidency of the new Actian games at Nicopolis and handsomely rewarded Eurycles, granting him Roman citizenship, installing him in power at Sparta and extending his control to encompass the whole of Laconia.[77]

Eurycles cast the net of his ambition wide. Not only Laconia, which was already under his suzerainty, but cities like Epidaurus and Megalopolis also experienced his generosity. Even Athens felt it politic to honor the hegemon of Sparta, his son, and the *dēmos* of the Lacedaemonians.[78] Within Laconia itself, his relations with the communities of Roman businessmen were close: the Roman '*negotiatores* in the cities of Laconia' (which may have included Sparta) erected a statue in Gythium to him as their benefactor and another at Boeae in conjunction with the city.[79] In addition to being the largest city in the region after Sparta and the port through which most of the products of the Eurotas valley were exported, Gythium's main resource was in the Laconian gulf, namely murex, the shellfish that was the essential ingredient in purple dye. This would have attracted such traders in luxury goods as the family of Phaenia Aromation, the Claudian benefactress. Doubtless, Gythium's Roman community was sizable and continued to be at least as influential in the early Empire as it had been during the time of the Cloatii. At Boeae, the impetus to honor Eurycles probably came from the Romans too, since the inscription on the statue base observes Roman onomastic practice when referring to him.[80] Contrast the form of his name in the inscription from Asopus, where Eurycles made the traditional gesture of setting up a fund to pay for the civic gymnasium's supply of oil. The prominence of *negotiatores* in Gythium and Boeae and their implicit presence in the other Laconian cities should encourage us to take seriously the allegations made by the historian Josephus that Eurycles, after sowing dissent and discord at the court of Herod the Great in Judaea, returned home and 'filled Achaia with civil strife and stripped the cities.'[81] If Josephus were referring to some sort of financial oppression of the cities under his hegemony, the Roman businessmen might well have seen an opportunity of profiting from any increased exactions.[82] This would also give some point to Pausanias' characterization of Spartan control of the other Laconian cities as 'slavery' (*douleia*).[83]

Antony Spawforth has recently expressed doubt that Eurycles actually did extort money from the cities of Greece on the grounds that it 'is not supported by the epigraphical evidence, which presents him...as a benefactor of the Peloponnese', but this is hardly reason enough to reject Josephus.[84] For example, Eurycles' near-contemporary, Nicias the tyrant of Cos, was so hated that his tomb was desecrated after his death, but statues and other stones were dedicated during his regime to the ancestral gods 'for the safety of Nicias, son of the people, patriot, hero, benefactor of the city.'[85] Epigraphical praises, then, should often be taken with a grain of salt. Similarly, the statues erected by the Roman *negotiatores* in Laconia might not have been prompted so much by an unfeigned regard for the Spartan *hēgemōn* as by a desire to appease the man whose fleet had, until recently, prowled the waters off Gythium and who now, thanks to Augustus, held the island of Cythera as his personal fief.[86] Whatever the feelings of people in the cities of the Lacedaemonian League (and they are irrecoverable), Eurycles certainly had enemies among the old Spartan aristocracy who wished to see the upstart put in his place. To this end they twice brought him to trial before the Emperor, first probably in 22/1, during Augustus' visit to Greece, and, with more success, at a date between 7 and 2 BC.[87] An anecdote in Plutarch's *Moralia*, which has long proved puzzling, can shed some light on the trial's proceedings with the help of an inscription found in, of all places, Macedonia.

> When one of Eurycles' accusers in an unrestrained and intemperate harangue even went so far as to say something like this, 'Caesar, if this doesn't appear important to you, order him to read Thucydides' seventh for me.' [Augustus] became angry and ordered his arrest. But upon learning that the man descended from the family of Brasidas, he summoned him back and freed him after a moderate remonstrance.[88]

The Plutarchean vignette reveals quite clearly the animosity of the established families of Sparta for the new man encouraged by the emperor and, although some have assigned it to Eurycles' second trial, nothing precludes it from originating at the first. The descendant of Brasidas almost certainly belonged to the same family as the later epigraphically-attested men named Tiberius Claudius Brasidas who were especially prominent in the later first and second centuries AD. The reference to Thucydides' seventh book is striking but has been considered either unclear, 'unfortunately incomprehensible', or even 'nonsensical'. Of course, it is none of these.[89]

Bowersock saw that the reference here must be to the seventh book of the ancient thirteen-book edition of Thucydides, which comprised

Book 4 chapters 78–135 of the present edition, but he went no further than to state that Eurycles' accuser 'invoked...Thucydides' account of his great ancestor'.[90] But more can be said. Much of this section of the *History* is taken up with accounts of Brasidas' campaigns in Thrace and the Chalcidic peninsula in 424 BC, with a prominent place given to a speech by Brasidas to the people of Acanthus on the Chaldidice in which he attempts to persuade them to the Spartan side. Thucydides puts a reworking of the old Spartan policy of opposition to unconstitutional rule (*turannōn katalusis*) into his mouth, and Augustus would not have been pleased to hear such passages as this:[91]

> I have not come here to take sides in your internal affairs, and I do not think that I should be giving you real freedom if I were to take no notice of your own constitution and were to enslave either the many to the few or the few to the many. That would be even worse than being governed by foreigners.

Brasidas' descendant was thus alluding to what he regarded as a betrayal of Sparta's traditional opposition to tyranny, which Augustus would have justifiably seen as a jibe at his support of Eurycles.

A new inscription assigned by its editor to Anthemous, another town on the Chalcidic peninsula, may help account for the Spartan's choice of quotation.[92] In it, the city honors as a hero a certain Lycurgus the Spartan, son of Brasidas. Dated on the basis of letter forms to about 100 BC, it attests to continued connections between the Spartan family and the cities on the Chaldidice, perhaps in the form of property ownership. In the historically self-conscious atmosphere of the late hellenistic period, the relations between the descendants of Brasidas and these cities were no doubt articulated in terms of the activity of the Spartans' classical ancestor in the region, with Thucydides' account effectively enjoying canonical status. It would have been natural, then, for the Spartan advocate to have resorted to this particular passage to bolster his case against Eurycles.

Returning to the topic from this rather lengthy excursus, Eurycles' fall from favor in the last decade of the first century BC meant the 'liberation' of the Laconian cities. As Pausanias put it, 'the emperor Augustus freed [them] from bondage when they were subject to the Lacedaemonians in Sparta'.[93] In return for this, the city of Gythium honored Augustus and Tiberius for restoring the city's 'ancient freedom' and Augustus received the same title as Flamininus, 'Liberating Saviour' (*Sōtēr Eleutherios*). [94] All agree that the League now took on its new name as the League of Free Laconians, probably to emphasize the cities' newly-won independence from Sparta.[95] On the other hand,

Sparta may have obtained control of the little port of Cardamyle on the Messenian Gulf to compensate partly for the loss of Gythium, although it is inconceivable that the vast majority of Spartan, as well as Laconian, goods did not continue to pass through the nearer, larger port. The memory of Eurycles was soon rehabilitated and his family's influence over all of Laconia restored, even though Sparta apparently never ruled the whole region again.

The League of Lacedaemonians was never 'important' or 'significant'; only briefly did it cross the main stage of history. The cities of Laconia had the misfortune, or perhaps the good luck, to gain their independence when the once-great powers of Greece had been eclipsed by Rome. Nonetheless, the fleeting glimpses afforded us by the evidence show the League and its members energetically involved in the life of the late hellenistic and Roman world to the fullest extent of their admittedly modest capacities. Much information has been lost–on the governmental structures, on cults, and on civic culture in general. The meagerness of the evidence and the comments of both Strabo and Pausanias on the depopulation of the region might be thought to indicate a continuing decline in the region's prosperity, but that can hardly be true. Rural abandonment and loss of political autonomy by smaller centers is not an infallible indicator of economic conditions. For the cities of the Lacedaemonian League, the resources of Laconia, particularly the luxury goods prized by the Romans, must have been the backbone of the trade that enabled them to exist and even, I believe, flourish. In this context, it is at least ironic and perhaps even significant, that no inscription of more than local interest, strictly speaking, has come from post-classical Sparta, whereas the towns of the Lacedaemonian and Eleutherolaconian Leagues have furnished several of prime importance to ancient history: the Cloatii decree, vital for the understanding of the activities of Roman *negotiatores*; the sacred law of Gythium, again indispensable for clarifying the development of Roman imperial cult; and most significantly, the many fragments of Diocletian's price edict found at Geronthrae, Gythium, and Boeae. The only way for modern scholarship to learn more about these cities and communities scattered about the coast and interior of Laconia, however, is through a full-scale excavation of a perioecic site. Unless that increasingly unlikely event should occur, we are left with these few scraps and shards of knowledge to reconstruct the political evolution of a Laconia at last released from Sparta's domination.

Notes

[1] This situation does not seem likely to change in the foreseeable future, as the disappointing results of the Laconian survey regarding the hellenistic and Roman periods make clear: W. Cavanagh et al. 1996, 91–110, 199–211.

[2] Aymard 1938; Chrimes 1949, 435–41; Martin 1975.

[3] The question of the perioeci was profitably rephrased by Ridley 1974, and taken up and elaborated by Cartledge 1979, 178–85. The archaeological evidence forms the basis for Shipley1992.

[4] Cinadon: X. *Hell.* 3.3.6., on which see now Lazenby 1997. Rebellion: X. *Hell.* 6.5.25–26; 6.5.32; 7.2.2.

[5] Plut. *Cleom.* 18.3.

[6] On the period between Cleomenes and Nabis, see Cartledge and Spawforth 1989, 59–67.

[7] Cartledge and Spawforth 1989, 3.

[8] Livy 34.35.5; 34.36.2; cf. 35.13.2; 38.31.2.

[9] Livy 34.22.4–26.14.

[10] Livy 34.29.1.

[11] Livy 34.29.1–13.

[12] Livy 34.35.3–11.

[13] Badian1958, 6–9.

[14] Livy 35.13.2.

[15] Livy 38.31.2.

[16] Strabo 7.4.3 C308; cf. *IOS* 2nd edn, I.349; *ICret.* 3 p. 96 no. 9, line 107; Polyb. 7.11.9.

[17] On *prostasia*, see Schaeffer 1960, esp. 1300–1301; Ferrary 1988, 118.

[18] Livy 35.13.3; 38.30.9.

[19] Niccolini 1914, 131; Aymard 1938, 252–3.

[20] Swoboda 1912, 21.

[21] Polyb. 23.9.13.

[22] Strabo 8.5.5 C366; Paus. 3.21.6.

[23] Martin 1975, 461–4.

[24] Livy 38.30.9.

[25] Chrimes 1949, 436–9.

[26] *IG* V.1.1226.

[27] *IG* V.1.497, 602; Cartledge and Spawforth 1989, 137; Marchetti and Kolotsas 1995, 211–14.

[28] Cotyrta: *IG* V.1.961, 965, 966; Geronthrae: *IG* V.1.1112, 1113; Gythium: *IG* V.1.1145, *SEG* 2 (1924) 160.

[29] *IG* V.1.1145.

[30] Strabo 8.5.5 C365.

[31] e.g. Martin 1975, 452–3. Accame 1946, 160, thought that the League was attached, like other non-free cities, to the province of Macedonia.

[32] Kallet-Marx 1995, 59–65.

[33] Habicht 1997, 267 n. 14, takes the opposite view.

[34] Kallet-Marx 1995, 48, argues that grants of freedom right after 146 did not imply exemption from a bordering province, but rather implied freedom from interference by Roman magistrates.

[35] For Eurycles' activities, see Bowersock 1965, 1984 and my discussion below. As between all Greek neighbors, there were the usual disputes, e.g. *IG* V.1.37a.

[36] *SEG* 13 (1956) 258, lines 25–38.

[37] Samuel 1972, 93.

[38] Grunauer-von Hoerschelmann 1978, 57–9.

[39] Grunauer-von Hoerschelmann 1978, Table 18, XXIII, nos. 1 and 2.

[40] Grunauer-von Hoerschelmann 1978, 59–62.

[41] Paus. 3.22.9; 4.36.7.

[42] *IG* V.1.977.

[43] Grunauer-von Hoerschelmann 1978, Table 18, XXIV, no. 1.

[44] Grunauer-von Hoerschelmann 1978, Table 11, no. 89.

[45] The League coins are too few and too insecurely dated for any meaningful comparison of their weights with those of Spartan coins. On a possible relationship between the weights of Spartan denominations and the coinage issued between 49–28 BC by the prefect of the Roman fleet, see Grunauer-von Hoerschelmann 1978, 51.

[46] *IG* V.1.1336, *SEG* 11.948 (Gerenia); *IG* V.1.1336 (Hippola); *IG* V.1.1240, 1241 (both third century AD) (Caenepolis); *IG* V.1.1281, 1282 (Pyrrichus); *IG* V.1.961, 962, 965, 966 (Cotyrta); *IG* V.1.931, 932 (Epidaurus Limera); *IG* V.1.1110, 1111, 1114 (Geronthrae); *IG* V.1.1144, 1146 (Gythium).

[47] Chrimes 1949, 283–4.

[48] *IG* V.1.1140, line 20; 1146, lines 40–41.

[49] On the name of the Spartan assembly, see de Ste. Croix 1972, 347. The assembly at Gythium was also called the*ekklēsia*: *SEG* 11 (1954) 923, lines 12–14.

[50] Priests: *IG* V.1.1144, lines 20–36; Damiadas: *IG* V.1.1145, lines 44–42; Cloatii: *IG* V.1.1146, lines 40–56.

[51] e.g. *IG* V.1.464, 466, 479, 483.

[52] Wörrle 1988, 10, lines 66–8.

[53] The site of the Apollo temple: *IG* V.1.1144.

[54] *IG* V.1.1110, 1111, 1113 (Geronthrae).

[55] *IG* V.1.1111.

[56] *IG* V.1.1145 (Gythium); cf. Migeotte 1984, 95; *IG* V.1.931 (Zarax, Epidaurus Limera): cf. Ager 1996, 221–3, no. 80.

[57] *IG* V.1.961, 965, 966 (Cotyrta); *IG* V.1.1112, 1113 (Geronthrae); *IG* V.1.1145, 1533 (Gythium); *IG* V.1.1226 (*koinon*).

[58] On *epinomia*, see Marek 1984, 147–50.

[59] See Marek 1984, 155, 159.

[60] *IG* V.1.1226.

[61] See Marek 1984, 126.

[62] Cf. Ager 1996, 223–6, no. 81.

[63] *IG* V.1.962 (Cotyrta), 1312 (Thalamae), 1336 (Gerenia); Martin 1975, 477.

[64] Marek 1984, 123–6.

[65] Geronthrae: *IG* V.1.1110, lines 12–13; 1111, lines 35–36. Gythium: *IG* V.1.1145, line 45.

[66] *IG* V.1.1226, 1227.

[67] *IG* V.1.1280; Weil 1876, 163.

[68] Martin 1984, 477.
[69] Paus. 3.26.8.
[70] Kallet-Marx 1995, 76 n. 75.
[71] *InsOly* 328; Schwertfeger 1974, 73–4.
[72] On the Cloatii's role, see Migeotte 1984, 90–6.
[73] *IG* V.1.1146, lines 25–29. For this meaning of *philotimia*, see Robert 1989, 46–47, 101.
[74] Schachter 1981, 124–5.
[75] *IG* 2^2 3885; Plut. *Ant.* 67.3.
[76] Chrimes 1949, 180.
[77] Cartledge and Spawforth 1989, 97–101.
[78] Cartledge and Spawforth 1989, 103.
[79] *SEG* 11 (1954) 924 (Gythium); Michaud 1971, 888 (Boiae).
[80] Michaud 1971, 888: the *negotiatores* honor him as *Gaion Ioulion Euryklē Lacharous huion* (i.e. *Gaius Julius Eurycles Lacharis filius*). At Asopus (*IG* V.1.970), where the city honored him for setting up a fund to pay for the civic gymnasium's supply of oil, Eurycles' names lacks the filiation normal in Roman nomenclature.
[81] Jos. *BJ* 1.531; Bowersock 1984, 169–88.
[82] LeRoy 1978, 265.
[83] Paus. 3.21.6.
[84] Cartledge and Spawforth 1989, 101.
[85] Ath. 5.54; Paton and Hicks 1891, nos. 76–80.
[86] Cythera: DC 54.7.2.
[87] Bowersock 1961, 113–15.
[88] Plut. *Moralia* 207F.
[89] Kjellberg 1921, 57 n. 3; Oliver 1953, 955 n. 8.
[90] Bowersock 1965, 105 and n. 5.
[91] Thuc. 4.86.4–5.
[92] Hatzopoulos and Loukopoulou 1992, 53, no. A8 (Anthemous). Date: 'vers le début du Ier siècle'.
[93] Paus. 3.21.6.
[94] *IG* V.1.1160; *SEG* 11 (1954) 923.
[95] Kennell 1985, 25–7.

Bibliography

Accame, S.
1946 *Il dominio romano in Grecia dalla guerra acaica ad Augusto*, Rome.

Ager, S. L.
1996 *Interstate Arbitration in the Greek World 337–90 BC*, Berkeley and London.

Aymard, A.
1938 *Les Premiers rapports de Rome et de la Confédération achaienne*, Bibliothèque des universités de Midi 22, Bordeaux and Paris.

Badian, E.
1958 *Foreign Clientelae 264–70 BC*, Oxford.

Bowersock, G.W.
1961 'Eurycles of Sparta,' *JRS* 51, 111–18.
1965 *Augustus and the Greek World,* Oxford.
1984 'Augustus and the East; the problem of the succession,' in F. Millar and E. Segal eds, *Caesar Augustus: Seven Aspects,* Oxford.

Cartledge, P.A.
1979 *Sparta and Laconia,* London.

Cartledge P.A. and Spawforth, A.
1989 *Hellenistic and Roman Sparta. A tale of two cities,* London and New York.

Cavanagh,W.J., Crouwell, R., Catling,W.V. and Shipley, G.
1996 *Continuity and Change in a Greek Rural Landscape,* vol. 2, *The Archaeological Data, ABSA* Supplementary vol. 27, London.

Chrimes, K.M.T.
1949 *Ancient Sparta: A re-examination of the evidence,* Manchester.

de Ste. Croix, G.E.M.
1972 *The Origins of the Peloponnesian War,* Ithaca.

Ferrary, J.-L.
1988 *Philhellénisme et impérialisme: Aspects idéologiques de la conquête romaine du monde hellénistique*, BEFAR 271, Rome and Paris.

Grunauer-von Hoerschelmann, S.
1978 *Die Münzprägung der Lakedaimonier*, AMuGS 7, Berlin.

Habicht, C.
1997 *Athens from Alexander to Antony,* Trans. D. L. Schneider, Cambridge Mass.

Hatzopoulos M. and Loukopoulou, L.
1992 *Recherches sur les marches orientales des Temenides (Anthemonte–Kalindoia),* Part I, Meletemata 2, Athens and Paris.

Kallet-Marx, R.
1995 *Hegemony to Empire. The development of Roman* Imperium *in the East from 148 to 62 BC,* Berkeley, Los Angeles, and Oxford.

Kennell, N.M.
1985 *The Public Institutions of Roman Sparta,* Diss. Toronto.

Kjellberg, E.
1921 'C. Iulius Eurykles,' *Klio* 17, 49–58.

Lazenby, J. F.
1997 'The Conspiracy of Kinadon Reconsidered,' *Athenaeum* 85, 437–49.

LeRoy, Chr.
1978 'Richesse et exploitation en Laconie au 1er siècle av. J.-C.' *Ktema* 3, 261–66.

Marchetti P. and Kolotsas, K.
1995 *Le nymphée de l'agora d'Argos. Fouille, étude architecturale et historique,* Études peloponnésiennes 11, Paris.

Marek, C.
1984 *Die Proxenie,* Europäische Hochschulschriften Reihe 3: Geschichte und ihre Hilfswissenschaften, Bd. 213, Frankfurt am Main.

Martin, D.G.
1975 *Greek Leagues in the Later Second and First Centuries BC*, Diss. Princeton.
Michaud, J.P.
1971 'Chronique des fouilles et découvertes archéologique en Grèce en 1970 et 1971', *BCH* 95, 803–1067.
Migeotte, L.
1984 *L'emprunt public dans les cités grecques. Recueil des documents et analyse critique*, Quebec and Paris.
Niccolini, G.
1914 *La confederazioni achea,* Pavia.
Oliver, J.H.
1953 *The Ruling Power,* Transactions of the American Philosophical Society, n.s. 43.4, Philadelphia.
Paton, W.R. and Hicks, E.L.
1891 *The Inscriptions of Cos,* Oxford.
Ridley, R. T.
1974 'The Economic Activities of the Perioikoi,' *Mnemosyne* 27, 281–92.
Robert, L. and J.
1989 *Claros I. Décrets hellénistiques,* Fasc. 1, Paris.
Samuel, A.E.
1972 *Greek and Roman Chronology,* Handbuch der Altertumswissenschaft 1.7, Munich.
Schachter, A.
1981 *The Cults of Boeotia,* vol. 1, London.
Schaeffer, H.
1960 '*prostatēs*,' *RE* Supp. 9, 1287–1304.
Schwertfeger,T.
1974 *Der achaïsche Bund von 146 bis 27 v. Chr.*, Vestigia Beiträge zur alten Geschichte, Bd. 19, Munich.
Shipley, G.
1992 '*Perioikos:* The discovery of classical Laconia,' in J. M. Sanders (ed.) *PHILOLAKON. Laconian Studies in Honour of Hector Catling,* London.
Swoboda, H.
1912 'Studien zu den griechischen Bunden 3. Die Stadte im achäischen Bunde,' *Klio* 12, 17–50.
Weil, R.
1876 'Aus Lakonien,' *MDAI(A)* 1, 163.
Wörrle, M.
1988 *Stadt und Fest im kaiserzeitliche Kleinasien,* Vestigia Beiträge zur alten Geschichte, Bd. 39, Munich.

Chapter 8

THE EVOLUTION OF THE MESSENIAN IDENTITY

Thomas J. Figueira

The actual unfolding of events can exercise a peculiar tyranny over scholars. Ancient historians regularly lecture on the nature of archaic and classical Spartan military primacy, including its basis in the rents and services of the Helots. The Helots are customarily (and rightly) portrayed as a marginalized class of dependent agricultural laborers, the lowest stratum of Spartan society. The same authorities in due course analyze the fall of Sparta from its candidacy for panhellenic hegemony. In the midst of that treatment, the significance of the loss to Sparta of the region of Messenia and the Helots living there finds its place, as does the ensuing resistance of the new city-state of Messene to Spartan reconquest. The evolution of the Helots, however, from *déclassé* members of Spartan society to persons proclaiming another civil and social identity altogether was not an inevitable progression. My discussion will explore the emergence of the Messenian identity as it was constructed through the dynamic interplay of mythological, historical, and religious tradition with the contemporary political and military situation. Fifth-century representation of and by those Helots disaffected from Spartan authority was strongly conditioned by the perspectives on the Spartan state and society adopted in Athens, the only external power to whom appeals for help (or protests against it) were practicable. Thus we shall find ourselves reverting repeatedly to the vital testimony of Athenian witnesses not only to the forward march of events in *Lakōnikē* (i.e., Spartan territory) but also to the attitudes assumed in response by the historical actors.

I. Thucydides on Helot dissidents

Consequently, there can be no better place to start our investigation of the development of the Messenian identity than with a most prominent Attic witness on Peloponnesian politics, the historian Thucydides. Let us start with a remark in his discussion of the Great Revolt of 465/4

(Thuc. 1.101.2):

> ...σεισμοῦ, ἐν ᾧ καὶ οἱ Εἵλωτες αὐτοῖς καὶ τῶν περιοίκων Θουριᾶταί τε καὶ Αἰθαιῆς ἐς Ἰθώμην ἀπέστησαν. πλεῖστοι δὲ τῶν Εἱλώτων ἐγένοντο οἱ τῶν παλαιῶν Μεσσηνίων τότε δουλωθέντων ἀπόγονοι· ᾗ καὶ Μεσσήνιοι ἐκλήθησαν οἱ πάντες.

> ...of the earthquake, during which the Helots and the Thouriatai and the Aithaies of the Perioeci decamped in revolt to Ithome. The majority of the Helots were the descendants of the ancient Messenians enslaved earlier. Therefore they were all called Messenians.

The derivation of the majority of the Helots from the ancient Messenians and their denomination as 'Messenians' appears a straightforward observation, superficially non-problematical, but is in fact fraught with ramifications when its implications are unraveled. It helps to note at the start that Thucydides is not making a point about the primarily Messenian character of the rebels in practical terms, but is observing that the Helot rebels were perceived as 'Messenian'.[1]

We may continue with his statement that the majority of Helots were descended from the ancient Messenians. This is a side topic for us, not for exploration in detail, as it belongs to Laconian and Messenian demography rather than to identity formation in the classical period. Thucydides may be merely reflecting contemporary knowledge that the majority of Spartiate allotments were Messenian and with them were associated a proportionate number of attached Helot laborers.[2] It would be an understandable extrapolation to see archaic Messenians as the ancestors of those working the land in that region. Yet a fifth-century observer could hardly do other than speculate here. The pre-conquest Messenians may not have been the actual biological antecedents of the majority of the Helot workforce. Spartan conquest and its subsequent re-imposition and extension had been accompanied, according to tradition, by substantial Messenian flight overseas (see note 36 below). Before the creation of Spartan alliances with the Arcadians, Messenian borders were porous to flight by non-compliant Helots. The creation and allocation of *klāroi* (Spartan landholdings) in Messenia may have seen transfers of Helots from Laconia. That development would account for the homogenization of separate dependent populations and their linguistic and cultural convergence with other Spartan classes. Furthermore, the availability of Messenian land for settlement by dependent laborers might have been a factor in the hypothetical quiescence of the Helots during the sixth century.[3]

It is specifically from the qualifier 'Messenian' for the totality of the Helots that complexities begin to emerge. Given that the conquest of

Messenia was so prominent a threshold in Spartan tradition, the application of the term Messenian to the entire servile class seems counterintuitive. Moreover, on several occasions, Thucydides provides equally emphatic balancing of his earlier generalization. Before the climactic battle at Syracuse, he provides an enumeration of the allies on either side. Here he deftly interweaves observations on *syngeneia* ('affinity'), dialect and customs, self-interest, and constraint (7.57.8).[4]

> καὶ οἱ Μεσσήνιοι νῦν καλούμενοι ἐκ Ναυπάκτου καὶ ἐκ Πύλου τότε ὑπ' Ἀθηναίων ἐχομένης ἐς τὸν πόλεμον παρελήφθησαν.
>
> And the Messenians, as they are now called, from Naupactus and from Pylos, which was then being occupied by the Athenians, were taken along for the campaign.

Tellingly, it is 'the Messenians as they are now called' or 'the now so-called Messenians' who feature among Attic allies, persons who do not derive from occupied Messenia but from Naupactus and Pylos. Thus, despite the aforestated generality of the epithet 'Messenians' to denote Helots, the term is *marked* in this setting. Also note how in another context Thucydides conditions the claim that Messenia was the *patris* ('fatherland') of the raiders from Pylos by calling them 'Messenians from Naupactus' (4.41.2).[5] Therefore, from the perspective of these passages, the denomination 'Messenian' appears considerably more ideologically determined and less naively reflective of a panhellenic consensus.[6]

For Thucydides, the capacity of the Messenian raiders to damage Spartan interests is owed to their ability as natives to exploit the Messenian site of Pylos and to their sharing a common dialect, their being *homophōnoi* to the Spartans (4.4.3, 4.41.2 (note 5)).[7] Thucydides observes elsewhere how the common possession of a Greek dialect can confer advantages or disadvantages on the battlefield. For instance, Demosthenes exploits Doric-speaking Messenians to launch a surprise attack on the Akarnanians (Thuc. 3.112.4). In contrast, the singing of the *paian* in Doric by the Argives and Messenians in the midst of the storming of the Epipolai at Syracuse confounds the Athenian army (7.44.6). While a less pervasive mode of linguistic affinity is invoked by noting the common possession of the Doric dialect, the term *homophōnoi* connotes the most emphatic manifestation of such affinity.[8] Here an equivalence of language signifies the common possession of a constellation of social behaviors. The Messenians who infiltrated *Lakōnikē* at the behest of the Athenians could mimic, it seems, both Spartan masters *and* dependents.

The equation of Messenians and Helots in the initial Thucydidean formulation parallels the self-understanding both of the rebels of the Great Revolt (usually dated to 464) and of a later community at Naupactus in west Lokris that was formed by escapees from that rebellion. They consistently represent themselves as the government and army of a Messenian state. The emergence of this pattern of nomenclature is obscure, owing to the controversial attribution of inscribed documents from the era of the Great Revolt and of the first Peloponnesian War with the Athenians (459–46). Spear-butts that denominate their dedicants as 'Methanioi' have been found at Olympia and at the sanctuary of Apollo Korythos near Korone in Messenia itself.[9] While alternatives to the rebel Messenians for the identity of the dedicators of both objects are viable, they cannot preserve the elegance of a single aetiology for such similar dedications.[10] The Olympian dedication is explicit on the origin of the spoils from the Lakedaimonioi (i.e., the Spartan state). The inscription at the Messenian shrine of Apollo is damaged, so that the identity of the defeated is unclear. Recent editors have restored ...ἀπ'] | Αθαναί[ον..., '...from Athenians ...', which suggests spoils taken from Attic auxiliaries aiding Sparta under the command of Kimon in the 460s. Yet the alternative ... | 'Αθάναι..., 'to Athena' is possible, despite the placement of the dedication in a sanctuary of Apollo.[11] Notwithstanding the archaic appearance of their lettering, both inscriptions ought to be downdated from *c.* 500–475 to after 465.

The community of fugitives from Messenia established by the Athenians at Naupactus continued this pattern of self-representation. G. Daux has reconstructed a long low base at Delphi with an early inscription of the Messenians (Μεσ]σάνιο).[12] He opts to associate this grand dedication with Messenian operations against Akarnania and Oiniadai *c.* 455 (Paus. 5.26.1, cf. 4.25.1–10; Thuc. 1.111.3). It may also be possible, however, that this monument – in a manner difficult to reconstruct at present – commemorated retrospectively the achievements of the rebels of the Great Revolt. Another related document is an inscription, which has remained unpublished for many years, containing arrangements for the joint occupation of Naupactus by the Mesanioi, that is, Messenian fugitives, and the Naupaktioi, presumably local Lokrians.[13] Accordingly, the Messenians appear to have been careful to distinguish themselves from the other inhabitants of Naupactus (cf. Meiggs-Lewis #13). They did not want their identity as Messenians lost through submergence within the new community.

Subsequently, the Messenians at Naupactus (along with the Naupactians themselves) dedicate as 'Messenioi' at Olympia and Delphi.[14]

The Olympian inscription accompanied a statue of *Nikē*, the goddess of military victory, by the sculptor Paionios. The mid-century context, involving the Messenian victories in Akarnania and Oiniadai, that is suggested by our source Pausanias is too early when one considers likely dates for the sculptor. Thus the Messenians themselves ought to be trusted in their connecting the statue with their contribution to the capture by the Athenians of the Spartan soldiers at Sphakteria in 425 (Paus. 5.26.1; cf. Thuc. 4.32.2–3, 36.1–3). The occasion for the Delphic dedication cannot be the same, since the name of the defeated began with Καλ- (perhaps Kalydon or, less preferably, Kallion in Aitolia). A context during the Archidamian War (431–21) is also to be preferred over mid-century for this occasion. The surviving dossier of documentation attests a virtual *blitzkrieg* of self-assertion by the Messenians spanning about a generation from *c.* 460.

The same system of presentation belongs to the Athenian official position, as is also amply substantiated in Thucydides. Fugitive Helots seem to constitute the legitimate government of Messenia in Athenian eyes. Even from the first days of their habitation at Naupactus, Thucydides implies that the Messenians had a formal alliance with Athens.[15] The Messenians in Naupactus later send forces to Pylos as though to their homeland (Thuc. 4.41.2). In military actions, they interact with the Athenians rather like other allies, providing troops and cooperating with Attic generals. Moreover, the goddess Athena Polias is prominent in the arrangements made by the Messenian refugees at Naupactus. To honor this patroness of the Athenians was to align oneself with Attic claims to hegemony. The relevant parallel is the contemporary creation of a Samian cult of Athena Polias, a gesture of solidarity made by another allied community.[16] The Messenians in Naupactus stand in the catalogue of Attic allies from the beginning of the Peloponnesian War and they have already been seen in the battle order in Sicily (Thuc. 2.9.4, 7.57.8). The devoted and energetic service of these Messenians is so well attested in Thucydides that we cannot linger to discuss their activities in detail.[17]

It is worth pausing for a moment to observe that there would have been Helots from Laconia, the home region of the Spartans, among those whom the Athenians established at Naupactus and who subsequently called themselves Messenians. Some of the Helots who rose in Laconia, like those who had downed tools and contemplated storming Sparta itself before being checked by King Arkhidamos, will have made their way to Messenia, and others may well have eventually joined the diehards at Mt. Ithome.[18] During the years of rebellion, some Helots from Laconia, attending Spartiates (or first-class citizens) on campaign, were probably themselves not immune to the lure of desertion. Once the community at Naupactus was created, restive Laconian Helots would have been attracted to it. Another source of recruits from the Laconian Helots could have been desertions as well as captures by the Athenians during military actions of the First Peloponnesian War, starting from the operations of Tolmides.[19] These Laconians among the rebels and defectors do indeed appear to have been true 'invisible men' when the self-references of Messenian dissidents and their appreciation by their Attic patrons are considered.[20]

Thus the dependent population of Sparta appears in Thucydides under two discrete styles of reference. As just noted, they are Messenians when acting as allies of the Athenians. In contrast, they are Helots in the contexts that involve their social and political status *vis-à-vis* the Spartiates and the Lakedaimonian state. As the object of machinations by Pausanias, they are Helots (Thuc. 1.132.4–5). When that entanglement stimulates an effort by a group of fugitive dependents at self-protection through suppliancy at the sanctuary of Poseidon at Tainaron, the persons taking refuge (later deceived and massacred by the Spartan government) are described as Helots (1.128.1). The rebels are normally referred to as Helots in their Great Revolt, during which the Athenians and others were called to give help to Sparta.[21] They are Helots when they decamp from their duties.[22] In a variety of military settings, Thucydides remarks on the Helots deployed with Spartan forces.[23] When Thucydides focuses on the pervasiveness of the Spartan concern for their security, unsurprisingly 'the Helots' become the subject of a famous *dictum* (Thuc. 4.80.3).

There is, however, a single revealing instance in the text of Thucydides where the two categories intermingle (Thuc. 5.35.6–7). Its difficulty of interpretation helps to reveal the unfeasibility of a single perspective on the identity of the Helots, be it the Attic/Messenian viewpoint, that all Helot defectors were participants in a Messenian political community, or the Spartan vision of a unitary Helot servile class. Our analysis will be helped, however, if the reference is contextualized first. After the Peace of Nikias, the status of Pylos, the main Athenian base on Spartan territory, was controversial. The Spartans had no realistic expectation of an Attic evacuation of Pylos because they could not hand back the Attic colony of Amphipolis in Thrace in the face of local resistance. Hence the continued presence at Pylos of an Athenian garrison could not reasonably be challenged. Nonetheless, the Spartans were concerned about the composition of that garrison, preferring Athenian citizens. Interestingly, the alternative was not a garrison of the Messenians from Naupactus, presumably because they had retired homeward at the end of hostilities (cf. Thuc. 5.56.2). Instead, the Spartans were requesting the withdrawal from Pylos of Μεσσηνίους καὶ τοὺς ἄλλους Εἱλωτάς τε καὶ ὅσοι ηὐτομολήκεσαν ἐκ τῆς Λακωνικῆς, 'Messenians and the other Helots and anyone who had run away from *Lakōnikē* [Spartan territory]' (Thuc. 5.35.7).

Apparently, these persons could not simply be sent to Naupactus in order to join the body of Messenians established there. Either that community could not sustain them or some agreement with the resident Lokrians precluded this option. Thus the Athenians were forced to find another suitable refuge, seeking a site within the region under their influence where the government was prepared to harbor a group of fugitives without levying its own demands on them. Krania on the island of Kephallenia was the eventual choice. These latest fugitives from *Lakōnikē* – Thucydides' Messenians, Helots, and deserters – had to accept a condition of virtually permanent mobilization. Thucydides' 'catch-all' terminology reflected the group's composite nature and provisory identity. Notwithstanding the Athenian willingness to consider all those liberating themselves from Spartan control as *ipso facto* citizens of a Messenian polity, those evacuated from Pylos could not be presented diplomatically as a Messenian community. In this passage, Thucydides was reporting negotiations between Sparta and Athens, and such interchanges required formulations that merged discrepant identifications of the persons in question.[24]

Thucydidean terminology can be juxtaposed and contrasted with the usage of Ephorus, as reflected in Diodorus Siculus. In Diodorus, those who are disaffected and contemplating revolt in the early 460s are 'Helots and Messenians' (11.63.4); 'Messenians with Helots' prepare a direct attack on Sparta (11.64.1); and 'Helots and Messenians' accept Spartan terms (11.84.8). Do Helots plus Messenians here equal rebels? Or is it that Helots who are Messenians equal rebels? Or could Helots and Messenian Perioeci equal rebels? None of these constructions is entirely satisfactory analytically. Such terminological compromise helped Diodorus into confusion about the terms of the withdrawal of the rebels from Mt. Ithome. The truth is almost certainly what is reported by Thucydides (1.103.1): rebels with their families received safe conduct to depart *Lakōnikē,* but if subsequently captured on Spartan territory they were liable to enslavement. Diodorus, however, seems to report that only Messenians withdrew from Ithome under truce and were established at Naupactus by the Athenians, while the Spartans punished those of the Helots who were responsible for the revolt (11.84.7–8).

Ephorus apparently identified the players during the Great Revolt with the benefit of the perspective provided by the successful foundation of Messene in the fourth century, where local historiography proclaimed that a submerged Messenian polity had always opposed the Spartans. In contrast, Ephoran terminology for the Peloponnesian War (as reflected again in Diodorus) follows the same pattern observed in Thucydides: Helots are Helots from the Spartan perspective and Messenians from the Attic/Messenian perspective.[25] For the Ionian/Dekeleian War, the same pattern continues, which suggests that Ephorus may have drawn on one of the historians who continued the narrative of Thucydides.[26]

The system of nomenclature applied to the rebellious Helots in Thucydides is also remarkable for the references that it does not activate. Messenian collaborators in Thucydides are never *phugades* 'fugitives', although they fully met the criteria for such a classification: flight from their homeland, ideological dissidence, and collaboration with Attic policy.[27] Unlike other groups that aligned themselves with the Athenians during the fifth century, the Helots are never the *dēmos* or the *plēthos* of *Lakōnikē* in Thucydides. Hence the Athenians eschewed their customary tactic against oligarchic adversaries like the Aiginetans or Boiotians, namely promoting the interests of a group that could be portrayed as the legitimate and sovereign *dēmos* that was being victimized by an unjust elite. On occasion, the Athenians even incorporated deracinated representatives of such a *dēmos* into their own body politic, sometimes through supplication, and so inherited a right to ownership of or hegemony over the community in question.[28]

Although such claims should not be taken at face value, the project of discrediting the Spartans by treating the Helots as a segment of a suppressed Laconian *dēmos* was viable. It was not utilized in written polemics of Attic provenience until the fourth century, however, when changes in the balance of classes may have encouraged observers to believe that some Perioeci might align with the Helots.[29] Outside fourth-century Attica, the polemical possibilities of this approach are also indicated by a tradition preserved in Ephorus that describes an early Heraclid Laconia where the Perioeci had *isotimia* ('equality of civil rights') under Spartan hegemony and Helotage did not yet exist. King Agis, the son of Eurysthenes, is claimed to have violated this dispensation, first extracting contributions from the Perioeci and then reducing the Perioeci of Elos (or Helos) to dependent status (as Helots) when they resisted (Ephorus *FGH* 70 F 117). The issue of *oliganthropy* ('shortage of manpower') that was so salient for fourth-century Spartans is a circumstance invoked here to account for the original condition of *isotimia*.

We might hypothesize accordingly that this portrait of heroic Laconia had the early fourth-century king Agesilaus II (of the line of Agis) as its target, perhaps envisaging him as the main prop of the *status quo* at Sparta. By his period, warfare, 'family planning', and downward social mobility had diminished the Spartiate or full citizen class. Discontented Perioeci and Hypomeiones ('Inferiors'), members of groups now shouldering increased military burdens, appeared to be more likely dissidents. Instead of the fifth-century Attic strategy of crippling Spartan military power by occupying Messenian bases and reducing the Helot labor force, a fourth-century anti-Spartan strategy could contemplate social revolution. Then, with property redistributed and access to decision-making widened, the new Laconia might well have become less inclined to meddle abroad, such as intervening in central Greece against Thebes or acting on behalf of oligarchy in the Aegean. Even barring that upheaval in policy, the new regime would have been much less capable of projecting military force over distance, having become an Argos, perhaps writ a bit larger, but no longer a Lysandrian or Agesilean panhellenic power. Thus the Ephoran vision of prehistoric Laconia underwrites early fourth-century partisanship.

Lest the distinction between the Helots as Laconian *dēmos* and as Messenian *politai* be considered merely word-juggling, it is worth noting that it exactly parallels the two ways of envisaging the separation of Messenia from Spartan control by the Thebans. This was either a liberation or a return from exile and a refoundation of the city-state of Messene.[30] The prominence of the latter terminological system within the descriptions of Epaminondas' founding of Messene is notable in a portrayal of what was essentially a strike from without, supported by only the slightest local contribution. For example, the term *kathodos* ('return') itself appears seven times in book 4 of Pausanias to describe the establishment of Messene amid a rich deployment of other language connoting return and refoundation.[31] Diodorus, reflecting what may have been the treatment of Ephorus or Theopompus, portrays the creation of Messene as a standard colonial refoundation with the appropriate vocabulary of depopulation and resettlement (D.S. 15.66.1, 6). The same idea is attested in the Latin of Cornelius Nepos (*Epam.* 8.5; *Pelop.* 4.3).[32] Thus the interpretation by fourth-century and later historiography of Epaminondas' campaign in

Messenia had its conceptual roots in fifth-century self-representations of the Messenians themselves.

There is another note of dissonance between Attic nomenclature regarding their Helot sympathizers and patterns of reference toward groups similarly sponsored. Naupactus was envisaged by the Athenians rather uniquely: alone of the locations that the Athenians caused to be settled during the fifth-century hegemony, Naupactus does not elicit the terminology of an *apoikia* ('colony').[33] Indeed the Messenian escapees from Spartan retribution were situationally equivalent to others who had been bested in political infighting, so that they were available for recruitment in Attic projects of colonization.[34] For the same reasons of policy, Messenians at Naupactus are never identified as *epoikoi* ('reinforcing colonists' or 'secondary settlers'), although that appellation would have satisfied expectations established by Athenian practice elsewhere.[35] Rather a Messenian community was sheltered at Naupactus, whose colonial status was suppressed conceptually and rhetorically.

Both the Helot fugitives themselves and the Athenians espoused their cause as members of a *polis* whose territory had been occupied by an aggressor, although its primordial rights were not thereby abrogated, and also as a people maintaining its communal identity without incorporation into another polity. The main group of disaffected Messenians and their Athenian patrons did not conceptualize their efforts against the Laconian social order as a 'class struggle'. Rather than as a submerged caste, the dissidents perceived themselves as a subjugated *polis* or *ethnos*. Theirs was a struggle of 'national liberation', if one chooses to select a modern slogan.

Subsequently, Messenian tradition made much of the fugitives from various bouts of archaic hostilities with the Spartans who had fled to the Peloponnesian enemies of Sparta or had supposedly helped to colonize Rhegion and Zancle/Messana, the Greek colonies that straddled the Strait of Messina between Italy and Sicily.[36] The integration of earlier Messenian fugitives into their host communities is not excluded by the *Messeniaka*, the Messenian local histories that are reflected in the account of Pausanias. Even so, the Messenians in Arcadia and Italy are implicitly held by the *Messeniaka* to retain some essential elements of their identity, although we may suspect considerable anachronism concerning such early refugees. In contrast, the Messenians of Naupactus and Kephallenia did truly attempt to preserve their cohesion after the Athenian defeat in the Peloponnesian War and their expulsion from their homes in exile.[37] Their efforts affected the manner in which the *Messeniaka* treated the aspirations and fate of those who had fled Messenia centuries before.

II. Laconian readings

Naturally, the Spartan vision of the Helot identity could not be a mirror image of the Attic/Messenian conceptualization. The Spartans were ever aware of the economic importance of the conquest of Messenia and its inhabitants. Spartan oral tradition was incorporated into later Laconian historiography and Peripatetic constitutional treatises; its contents thus survive in scattered references. The various self-serving rationales for Spartan ownership of Messenia were based on a list of alleged grievances against the Messenians, such as the malfeasance of Kresphontes during the original Heraclid division of the Peloponnesus; assaults on Spartan maidens in ritual settings; and the assassination of the Spartan king Teleklos.[38] Hence the Spartans had no incentive to efface from memory the Messenian origins of many of their Helots. Nevertheless, the issue of the Helots as Messenians played no practical role in their day-to-day exploitation. In the socialization by which the Spartiates endeavored to inculcate into the Helots their inferior status, it is noteworthy that elaborated *ethnic* symbolism was not included.[39] Moreover, the various theories offered for the origin of Helotage agree that it originated in Laconia before the conquest of Messenia, and, even for the Laconian Helots, outright conquest was only one of several alternative modes in which the inception of their status was visualized. The accounts of its origin in fact exhibit motifs that tend to exemplify historical features of the Helot status. Thus, justifications of Helotage and of ownership of Messenia run along separate tracks of signification.

Concomitantly, the Spartans and those Helots prepared to comply with their wishes naturally did not concede that the totality of the Lakedaimonian dependent population was classifiable as 'Messenian'. Nor does it appear that the Spartans envisaged even a segment of the Helot population as constituting a separate political community. Their attitude seems well put in a formulation of Isocrates in one of his more Laconizing moments in the remarks he attributes to Spartan King Arkhidamos III. He has this Spartan leader take pains to rebut the very idea of a refounded Messenian community. Messene was not a community of true Messenians but an aggregation of Spartan Helot rebels (*Archidamus* [6] 28; cf. 87–8).

> Καὶ εἰ μὲν τοὺς ὡς ἀληθῶς Μεσσηνίους κατῆγον, ἠδίκουν μὲν ἄν, ὅμως δ' εὐλογωτέρως ἂν εἰς ἡμᾶς ἐξημάρτανον· νῦν δὲ τοὺς Εἵλωτας ὁμόρους ἡμῖν

παρακατοικίζουσιν, ὥστε μὴ τοῦτ' εἶναι χαλεπώτατον, εἰ τῆς χώρας στερησόμεθα παρὰ τὸ δίκαιον, ἀλλ' εἰ τοὺς δούλους τοὺς ἡμετέρους ἐποψόμεθα κυρίους αὐτῆς ὄντας.

And if they were leading back those who were truly Messenians, they would be doing wrong, but nevertheless committing a misdeed against us with a fairer-seeming motive. Yet now in fact they establish as a neighboring population Helots so that this becomes the most grievous thing, not if we will be deprived of territory contrary to justice, but if we will look upon our *douloi* [slaves] as masters of it.

Furthermore, the practice of liberating Helots from their dependency after or on behalf of military service entails that the Helots in question and the Spartans authorizing and administering the process perceived these recruits as Lakedaimonian.[40] Such persons' community was hardly an alien, Messenian one. After the experiments with those carrying supplies to Sphakteria and with the Helots enlisted for service with Brasidas, liberated Helots were denominated Neodamodeis, where the *dāmos* ('people') in question is obviously that of the Lakedaimonioi.[41] Their subsequent settlement in Triphylia seems to have approximated a perioecic establishment (Thuc. 5.34.1). Those Helots accepting this service clearly aspired to an amelioration of their condition within the Spartan order and not the alternative represented by a Messenian state. If any of them considered themselves defectors from an enslaved Messenian *ethnos*, they did a good job disguising this attitude both from their opponents in battle and from our informants.

In a notorious and controversial anecdote, Thucydides tells us of the savagery of the Spartans toward the Helots who had responded to a proclamation of freedom for those who had achieved *aristeia* ('excellence') in Spartan military service (Thuc. 4.80.3–4).[42] The chronology of the episode is murky indeed. Is it to be dated to the Archidamian War and its aftermath (suggested by the placement of the notice) or is Thucydides digressing about an earlier incident? One detail, however, draws our particular attention: the 2000 adjudged worthy were crowned and made a circuit of Laconian *hiera* ('sanctuaries'). This progress is certainly evocative of their celebration of their newly acquired status in the Laconian ritual settings that they already appreciated as being their own, not those of a foreign *polis*. Yet the Spartan authorities and the honored Helots had vastly disparate intentions. The former were marking out for elimination those who had presumptively defied their inherited sociopolitical roles by responding and the latter were naively seeking individual betterment. Nevertheless, both masters and Helots acted out their intentions within the framework of the Spartan community. The actions of the Helots so honored have no rationale at all within the history of a community that was consciously Messenian, possessing its own religious traditions.

The manner in which 'liberated' or 'naturalized' Helots conformed to the expectations held of Spartan soldiers and of perioecic citizens underlines the possession of a common culture by all elements of Spartan society (just as demonstrated by the common dialect). Various modes of overt behavior were subsumed within this same social matrix. Although the Helots manifested or played out the servile version of Laconian behavior, one marked by dependent labor, stigmatization, and marginality, they had equally internalized the other modes. During the Theban invasion of *Lakōnikē* in 370, some captured Helots refused the requests of the invaders to perform the poetry of Terpander, Alcman, and Spendon because their masters forbade such renditions (Plut. *Lyc.* 28.5). In doing so, they showed themselves, at least for the moment, faithful to the traditional demarcation between the Helot and Spartiate modes of behavior. Nevertheless, by their answer, they indicate that they knew the prohibited poems. Thus, had they been able to overcome their internalization of their masters' wishes, they might have offered their own performance of the Spartan civic regime of song. Concomitantly, liberated Helots readily adopted the identity of perioecic Laconians.

One might suggest systematic differences between the Messenian and the Laconian Helots to account for the two systems of reference that have been outlined above. For example, Laconian Helots could have been disproportionately represented among the Helot attendants of Spartan hoplites, or among the Helots who personally waited upon Spartiates, or among those enlisted as Neodamodeis – to mention just a few conjectures. Equally, those who had achieved *aristeia* in Spartan service and responded to governmental proclamation might have been (just conceivably) exclusively Laconian Helots. Such hypotheses, not *prima facie* unreasonable, are in the first place quite unsubstantiated. That no contemporary witness ever identifies an individual as a Laconian Helot or a Messenian Helot might be put down to an absence of interest in the lives of individuals who were far removed from the levers of power. Yet the absence of characterizing or global commentary is more troubling, if one believes that so salient a differentiation existed between the Helots of the two regions. It is left to observe that any such real distinctions that did exist were less interesting to Thucydides and his contemporaries – even the Spartans – than were the representations that have been outlined above.[43]

The lack of differentiation of Helots between the two regions and between Helots who derived from different linguistic and ethnic backgrounds within the regions may be owed to a mixing of the historical elements of the Helot class. Along with the settlement of Messenia from Laconia, personal service, attendance in the messes, and labor on non-allotted land may have contributed to homogenizing the Helots. Ordinary responsibilities often brought male Helots to Sparta itself. Helots from rural *Lakōnikē* presumably made up many of the 4000 persons in the Spartan *agora* at any typical moment (as the would-be insurrectionist Cinadon noted: Xen. *HG* 3.3.5), as there were hardly that many Helots working local fields.

Because of the stratification of classes in Spartan society, its caste-like structure, cultural homogenization did not necessarily lead to general integration, but paradoxically provided an opportunity for polarization. Fifth-century Helots could define their present affinity to other Helots as a facet of their Messenian character rather than as a result of assimilation. Thus, instead of reflecting genealogy, feeling 'Messenian' or identifying oneself as 'Messenian' appears to be inversely correlated with the degree of psychological compliance with the Spartan government and with the Spartiates as a social class. Individuals with the same apparatus of social behaviors made conscious decisions about their future affiliations, with the result that final statuses as radically different as a Messenian hoplite living at Naupactus and a hoplite of the *Neodamōdeis* living at Lepreon could be reached from the same point of departure.

Nonetheless, it would be fallacious to treat self-identification as Messenian as the only radical alternative to acquiescence in an inferior status. It is necessary to remember that the Spartan social order did not maintain stability without weathering serious challenges. There were those among the Spartans themselves who were prepared to consider changes transcending piecemeal, individual amelioration in status. Pausanias, the victor of Plateia, was accused of wishing to offer the Helots political rights.[44] This charge and the related accusation of Medism were not merely judicial 'exhibits' that illustrated the desperate gambits of a hybristic and thwarted personality. Rapprochement with the Great King and reform of the institution of Helotage were both reasonable maneuvers preparatory to an anticipated conflict with Athens. Hence his Helot collaborators need not be considered mere dupes or even rebels. Instead some of them may have comprised the group of Helots who later became suppliants at the sanctuary of Poseidon at Tainaron (just as earlier had the Argilian servitor and agent of Pausanias).[45] They presumably hoped to achieve a pardon or some measure of satisfaction of their grievances or aspirations through that supplication. Traditionally, the sanctuary of Poseidon may have been consecrated space within which Helots could find respite from masters whose behavior was transgressive and there receive a mediated reconciliation. That expectation was unfulfilled, perhaps because the government perceived these suppliants as state enemies and not merely as individuals who had abandoned their duties. Hence they were lured out with guarantees and executed. Taking refuge in a Laconian sanctuary, and an isolated one at that, may in itself be significant. From Tainaron, after all, it might well have been possible for some or all of them to escape Laconia altogether.

Another figure who challenged the Spartan status quo was Cinadon, whose conspiracy was unmasked around 399 (Xen. *HG* 3.3.4–11; Arist. *Pol.* 1306b34–6; Polyaen. 2.14.1; Max. Tyr. 35.8c).[46] His misstep was describing the prospects of his plot to a prospective recruit, who played the informer. Unfortunately, Cinadon's aspirations are only known through the self-interested version that his enemies passed along to Xenophon. Nonetheless, his accounting of the 4,000 men in the Spartan agora as Helots, Perioeci, and Hypomeiones who would 'eat the Spartiates raw', while it might smack of hyperbole, has no suggestion that he was anticipating a rising on behalf of an independent Messenia. Cinadon, apparently a Hypomeion ('Inferior') himself, described his aim as 'to be inferior to no one at Sparta'. Coming from an individual of ability to whom state officers could confide an important and delicate mission despite his status, that quote may well be genuine, as it does little to enhance the official position regarding the episode. Thus, these conspirators probably sought a more egalitarian Sparta in which the class of Homoioi would be augmented through a redefinition of status boundaries, and perhaps a community possessing liberalized rules for future social mobility. In particular, the Hypomeiones probably sought the promulgation of legislation compensating for or insuring against the loss of status through impoverishment.

III. Building the Messenian identity

How then are we to explain these two visions of the Helots, one as subjugated aliens and the other as more intimate enemies? The classical Helots emerge as linguistically and culturally homogeneous with the Spartiates and Perioeci but inhibited from full-scale expression of that culture through the exclusivity of Spartiate behavior patterns.

Whatever had been the institutional order of eighth- and seventh-century Messenia, little seems to have survived. The continuities and discontinuities will be explored shortly.[47] The institutional high ground within *Lakōnikē* was occupied by the Spartiates, whose social identity ramified and deepened. One is bound to be skeptical that the Helots thoroughly or regularly internalized the degraded *persona* that was a mirror image of the Spartiate self-vision, despite any outward manifestations of compliance. Nonetheless, they had no regime of song, no rich ritual calendar, and no maturational and agonistic organization of time to set against the dominant ideology. They assimilated tacitly the Spartiate ideology because it was enacted before them as spectators. Hence, the Neodamodeis were excellent soldiers, and save for Cinadon's perhaps fanciful portrayal, remained loyal and true members of the Laconian state and society. Their whole lives had been spent as understudies.

In contrast, in the social performance of their identity, Helot dissidents within *Lakōnikē* confronted a blank canvas of social manifestation. Our best evidence for their *modus operandi* in creating an identity as Messenians is twofold. There is first the account in Pausanias, book 4, that is drawn from Messenian historiography, the *Messeniaka*, including the history of Myron of Priene and the historical epic of Rhianus of Bene (cf. *FGH* 106, 265), and secondly, the evidence from Messenian cults. In both cases, modern scholars face the formidable task of establishing a stratigraphy of signification. The Messenian self-portrayal was finally realized by the independent city-state of the fourth century and hellenistic period. The path for authors of the *Messeniaka* was blazed by fourth-century historians like Callisthenes, since we know from his references to the Messenian hero Aristomenes, the treason of Aristokrates, and the battle of the Great Trench that he was viewing Boiotian policy toward Messenia against the background of an emerging Messenian historical consciousness.[48] The first stages of the process in the fifth century, however, are shrouded from us. Especially problematic is the critical issue of the relative contributions of the fugitive community at Naupactus and of the Helots in *Lakōnikē*.

The deficiencies of the accounts of Myron and Rhianus were recognized and elaborated upon by nineteenth-century German historiographical scholarship.[49] We need pause only briefly for some general observations. There is a pervasive geographical vagueness. A frail chronological framework is hung with a series of anachronistic military encounters that do not add up to a realistic conquest or reconquest of Messenia. The whole portrait of the war follows a pattern that might be called the 'invincible losers' in that the Messenians outfight the Spartans in every detailed episode, but are defeated because of factors extraneous to their *aretē*. The wavering of our sources between the figure of Aristomenes as an eighth-century or seventh-century fighter is beyond being merely unsettling. Even if we choose to ignore the most extreme interpretation, that Rhianus placed Aristomenes in an early fifth-century Helot revolt, it is likely that later personalities and events infiltrated his treatment of a supposed Second Messenian War.[50] For instance, his technique for trumping Herodotus was to reshape the Herodotean events involving the tyrant of Rhegion, Anaxilas, and the city of Zankle/Messana in Sicily (cf. Hdt. 6.23.2–24.1, 7.164.1).[51] Rhianus presented a disturbingly similar version to the Herodotean events in the form of precedents or foreshadowings involving an earlier homonym of the tyrant. Presumably, these archaic happenstances were partially re-enacted by the historical Anaxilas in the early fifth century.

What the self-proclaimed Messenians within or without *Lakōnikē* during the fifth century had to work with was relatively meager. Eventually, the *Messeniaka* could draw upon the traditions derived from the experiences of Messenian refugees of the archaic period like those established in Italy. This material, however, could only become available extensively once a body of Messenians existed as a community. The Messenians of Naupactus may well have started to collect and utilize colonial traditions. Of the other Greeks outside *Lakōnikē*, the Helots had the most contact with the Arcadians. Thus, it is hardly surprising that the figure of Aristokrates of Orchomenos, who was so prominent not only in the collective memory of his own people but also in other Peloponnesian political traditions, plays the essential role of arch-villain not only in Callisthenes but also in the *Messeniaka* (Paus. 4.17.2–7, 22.3–7).[52] The Helots were also good listeners: some of the names and events enshrined in the *Messeniaka* were derived from Spartan poetry and storytelling, refracted by the perspective of their victims. One suspects, for example, that the significance of the Battle of the Great Trench may be owed to Spartan tradition as exemplified by a Tyrtaean elegy, of which fragments have now been found on an Oxyrhynchus papyrus (*POxy* 47, #3317).[53] The papyrus is terribly fragmentary, but mentions the Spartiates, Argives, walls, a trench, and several classes of combatants.

These Helots who would be Messenians also drew on oral tradition, but it is doubtful that recollection subsumed much accurate history. Here above all, there was that all-important myth-historical amalgam,

Aristomenes, whose adventures constitute a veritable catalogue of folk motifs.[54] Fittingly, he is as elusive chronologically as Lycurgus, and any genuine historical presence has been massively overlaid with distortions and accretions.[55] All this material, however, was scarcely enough to integrate a political community and it amounted to little of propaganda value in the context of fifth-century constitutional thought, for it built no bridges to the most likely sponsors of the dissident Helots, the Athenians.

Religious tradition and ritual seem to have been more significant vectors in the creation of a Messenian identity in its earlier stages of development. The survival of a mystery cult at Andania is perhaps the most prominent example of this process.[56] The place of Andania in Messenian tradition was enormous. It was supposedly the capital of pre-Dorian Messenia and the home of the later hero Aristomenes (cf. Paus. 4.14.7). Although the genealogy of the pre-Dorian kings of Messenia may be derivative from Spartan mythology, Messena was the local heroine after whom the land was believed to have been named, and she reigned from Andania (Paus. 4.1.1–3, 5–9; 3.9).[57] The *Messeniaka* claimed that Messena was also the recipient of mysteries conveyed to Andania from Eleusis. A number of contentions are embedded in this idea. First, it supports the claim that the Athenians were the first to be granted the practical and ritual capacity for cultivating grain. Second, it implies that the Messenian mysteries derived not only from ancient traditions but also from the non-Dorian cult of the autochthonous Athenians. The treatment in the *Messeniaka* of the Andanian mysteries resonates in the same key as various aspects of Athenian imperial ideology, such as claiming to possess an ancient and especially holy communal fire, levying *aparkhai* from the Greeks for the Eleusinian cult, and requiring Attic subject allies to honor Athens as their mother city.

Furthermore, the supposed links between Eleusis and Messenia did not terminate with the inauguration of the Andanian cult. After the first conquest of Messenia, cult personnel from Andania (said to be associated with the Great Goddesses) supposedly took refuge at Eleusis (Paus. 4.14.1). That motif amounts to a mythological precedent for the harboring of refugees by democratic Athens. Much as the Greeks had summoned the Aiakidai to give supermundane succor against the Persians at Salamis (cf. Hdt. 8.63, 83.1, 84.2; cf. 5.80.2), the Messenians called the cult personnel of the Great Goddesses back from Eleusis to offer support during later struggles against the Spartans (Paus. 4.15.7, 16.2). As opposed to other allies expected to offer actual assistance, the celebrants were non-participants, performing the symbolic role of witnessing the righteousness of Messenian resistance.

The mysteries at Andania do in fact seem to have existed during the years of Spartan control over Messenia. The underlying structure of the cult, as revealed by the famous inscription of 92/1 BC, shows the persistence of elements inherited from the Spartan hegemony (*IG* V.1 #1390 = *LSCG* #65).[58] An anecdote is told by Pausanias, presumably out of the *Messeniaka*, that speaks of a renewal of the cult under the auspices of Epaminondas, assisted by the Argive general Epiteles (Paus. 4.26.6, 33.5). Epiteles was directed by a dream to dig up an urn containing a document of tin foil that was written by none other than Aristomenes himself. It contained the pristine, uncontaminated provisions for the cult of the mysteries (Paus. 4.26.7–8). That seems to imply that the mysteries had been conducted in the period before independence in a form that was held as 'tainted' on account of Laconian observances. Concomitantly, these years during the 360s were also the most likely juncture for the infiltration of features from Boiotian cult, such as the veneration of the *Megaloi Theoi* ('Great Gods').[59]

The date of the introduction of the cult of Demeter and eventually of her daughter Kore (who was equated with Andanian Hagne: Paus. 4.33.4) is less transparent (*LSCG* #65.30–3, 68). It is important for us to consider the question, as it bears on the collaboration of Helots and Athenians in creating a Messenian identity. Methapos, a late reformer at Andania who was probably a member of the Attic *genos* of the Lykomidai, attributed the cult role of the Eleusinian goddesses to the Attic hero Lykos, son of Pandion, in a statuary inscription he erected in the cult place of his *genos* (Paus. 4.1.7–9). The Attic Lykos could thus be considered the eponym of a sacred oak grove of Lykos at Andania (cf. Rhianus *FGH* 265 F 45). By his own inscribed statement, Methapos emphasized Demeter and Kore in his cult reform at Andania, apparently raising the goddesses to the status of *Megalai Theai* ('Great Goddesses').[60] Perhaps he wished them to stand on a level with the Boiotian *Megaloi Theoi*. The Great Goddesses were preeminent in the Roman imperial era cult, as indicated by Pausanias (4.33.5; cf.14.1, 27.6).

An Athenian of the Lykomidai was welcome as a religious authority at Andania because of an earlier connection of the cult with the *genos* that probably derived from the fifth century. A hymn about the Eleusinian mysteries seems to have mentioned the derivation of the Messenian mysteries from Eleusis. The hymn was inserted into the *corpus* of the poet Musaeus under the sponsorship of the Lykomid *genos*, probably not later than the third quarter of the fifth century

(Paus. 4.1.5; cf. 1.22.7).[61] That shows that the polemics linking Andania and Eleusis, and thereby Messenian 'nationalism' and Attic populism, were current in the Pentekontaetia. It was also claimed that predictions of Lykos, the son of Pandion, vouched for the re-establishment of Messene if a secret object was protected (Paus. 4.20.4).[62] That pronouncement appears designed to sponsor rebel Messenian claims as well as raising the spirits of the other enemies of the Spartans. One cannot refrain from mentioning here that active member of the Lykomidai and adversary of the Spartans during the 470s and 460s, Themistokles (note Plut. *Them.* 1.4, 15.3).

The large question remains unanswered whether Eleusinian Demeter became associated ritually with the gods of the Andanian mysteries only after the refoundation of Messene as a reflection of the earlier Lykomid advocacy. Or had the Helots and Messenian Perioeci who were worshipping at Andania already begun to honor Eleusinian Demeter (or a local Demeter as Eleusinian Demeter) during their years of subjugation? There may be an indication in favor of the latter hypothesis in the account of the sacrifices that were performed at the foundation of Messene. Pausanias reports that Epaminondas and the Thebans sacrificed to Dionysos and Apollo Ismenios, the Argives to Hera Argeia and Zeus Nemeios, and the Messanioi to Zeus Ithomatas and the Dioskouroi. The *hiereis* of the Great Goddesses, however, sacrificed to them and to Kaukon, the founding hero of the mysteries (Paus. 4.27.6). That may indicate that the Eleusinian goddesses and Kaukon had their own cult personnel even before the foundation of Messene. While the Laconian cult personnel, such as the priestess of Apollo Karneios, would not have been a party to the founding sacrifices of the *polis* of Messene, these 'Eleusinian' priests cooperated.[63] Were they perhaps cult personnel drawn from Perioeci living in Messenia? It is also notable in this regard how Isocrates has his Arkhidamos inveigh against the blasphemies of the newly established Messenians through their *aparkhai* and sacrifices in cults that were properly Spartan (*Archid.* [6] 96).

In the account of Pausanias on the Aristomenean war, the role of the Andanian repatriates from Eleusis is to balance the intervention of Tyrtaeus, whom the *Messeniaka* treat as an Attic poet officially sent to the aid of the Spartans (Paus. 4.15.6, 16.2). Let us pause to observe how little sense an Attic Tyrtaeus makes in archaic poetics and performance, but how eloquently the tradition speaks in terms of fifth-century polemics.[64] This Ionic-speaking, immigrant Tyrtaeus implicates Athens in the suppression of Messenian freedom, especially when he was considered an auxiliary officially dispatched by the Athenian state. He provided an archaic precedent for fifth-century Athenian commitments to come to aid Sparta if the *douleia* rose against their masters. Such a stipulation was enshrined in the Attic-Spartan alliance of 421 (Thuc. 5.23.3), and may well have been the provision of the oaths of the Hellenic League that justified the request(s) to which Kimon responded. The creators of the Messenian past had to counteract this tradition, presumably because it was too well established to deny outright, by putting the Athenian action down to a mistake, an Athenian underestimation of the ability of their lame, didactic poet (Paus. 4.15.6). Both the Eleusinian connection with Andania and the Attic derivation of Tyrtaeus are gambits in a fifth-century polemical battle waged by Spartans and self-proclaimed Messenians and their respective Attic sympathizers for the support of the Athenians.

Not only does the comparison with the treatment of Tyrtaeus support the fifth century for the provenience of the Eleusinian connection with Andanian myth, but a number of other details of Messenian myth also indicate fifth-century polemics. While the heroine Messena was unknown in archaic mythological poetry, she appears to have been discussed by Hellanicus.[65] Her myth is a product of the Pentekontaetia, because we need to differentiate her from the female heroine and patroness portrayed on the earlier coins of Sicilian Messana.[66] In addition, the mythology about the founder of Dorian Messenia, Kresphontes, presents him as a particularly suitable figure for fifth-century anti-Spartan polemics. He had united pre-Dorians and Dorians in early Heraclid Messenia on terms of *isonomia* ('equality of law') and had been killed by oligarchs on account of his democratic tendencies.[67] And this version might have been presented in a play of Euripides entitled *Cresphontes* that was staged in the late 420s.[68] Thus, witnesses like Hellanicus and Euripides represent an Attic/Ionic reflection of Messenian mythopoiesis, in the creation or mediation of which the Messenians of Naupactus were probably involved.

Many details in the *Messeniaka* recall the Peloponnesian War and are also to be traced to the Messenians at Naupactus, who were so deeply committed to service in that conflict. For instance, a seventh-century Messenian connection with Kephallenia would be hardly worth concocting except when the Helot rebels were based on the island during the Peloponnesian War and its immediate aftermath. The plague that damages Messenian prospects against the Spartans in the Aristomenean conflict is an analogue to the great plague of the early Archidamian War. Other specific items in the *Messeniaka* arguably reflect the same war, as archaic Messenian experiences have been made to parallel those of fifth-century Athenians.[69]

The foregoing remarks sketch a historical process (beginning in the fifth century and continuing into the early fourth century) through which disaffected Helots, both in *Lakōnikē* and abroad at Naupactus, opted to create an ethnic identity that drew on folk memories of Messenian resistance which were pervaded by motifs fashioned from wish fulfillment. This evolution utilized an inversion of Spartan oral and poetic traditions. These approaches were alloyed with a sacralized, agrarian populism that certainly reshaped myth and possibly infiltrated cult practices. For early fifth-century peasants who lacked a literate political culture and who had little exposure to the operation, let alone the theoretical underpinnings, of civic life, this line of development for the Messenian identity was a good option.

An alternative would have been a program of thorough reform of Spartan institutions. We are unfortunately too well conditioned by the actual progression of events to envisage easily what course such changes might have taken. That mental exercise is, however, not for this essay, where it is more important to perceive that the formulation of such a program had to come from the Spartiates themselves. After the fall of Pausanias and the massacre at Tainaron (in 469–67?), the outward manifestation of dissatisfaction with the *status quo* may have seemed suicidal. Until the downfall of imperial Athens, disaffected Helots in *Lakōnikē* would have to become rebels and not revolutionaries.

IV. The Athenian factor

One readily notes our debt to Athenian testimony for the myths that supported the Messenian identity. Why then did the Attic championing of the interests of the Messenians assume the ideological coloration that it presents? A beginning at answering that question can be made if we consider a pivotal incident for fifth-century relations between Sparta and Athens, namely the dismissal of the Athenians from service in Messenia in 462.[70] Our sources, which are heavily dependent on Thucydides through various intermediaries, are unanimous about the anger and dishonor experienced by the Athenians. Yet, an impression gained from some modern discussion is that the Spartans were merely diplomatically obtuse, as though Kimon could not predict the result of his dismissal and communicate that anxiety. Is it not more likely that the Spartans acted deliberately, with full knowledge of the potential for estrangement from the Athenians? In that case, they possessed solid reasons in their minds for fearing the alternative of allowing Attic forces to remain in Messenia, however much Athenian outrage may genuinely reflect a sense of innocence.

Thucydides says that the Spartans feared the Athenian *tolmēron* ('daring') and *neōteropoiia* ('habit of innovation'), believing the Athenians were *allophulous* ('alien') (1.102.3).[71] The Athenians might be persuaded by the rebels on Ithome to *neōterizein* ('innovate').[72] Innovation is coupled here with the idea of a switch in Attic sympathy over to the rebels. As so often in static military contexts, fraternization had occurred between rebels and Athenians on the slopes of Mt. Ithome. Thucydides is using the terminology of revolution, denoting changes either in the basic terms of an alliance or in constitutional arrangements.[73] The parallel passages regarding Sparta envisage radical change in social structure activated by and through the Helots.

'Culture shock' is undoubtedly a trite phrase, but may do some justice here to the mutual reactions of Spartans and Athenians in Messenia. The Athenians were probably responding to a treaty commitment from the Hellenic League binding them to help in suppressing the Spartan *douleia*. On the basis of their own experience of the institution of chattel slavery, ordinary Athenian hoplites would not necessarily have expected a homogeneous, Greek body of rebels whom they (moreover) could not easily differentiate from their Spartan allies and hosts. The intensity of the Attic reaction to dismissal may indicate that the Athenians were not consciously trying to overturn the Spartan government. Even after the dismissal, the ostracism of Kimon, and the Ephialtic reforms, the Athenians were restrained in their policy toward Sparta. They received as allies past Medizing states, hitherto out-of-bounds, and upheld the Megarians against the Corinthians, who had taken advantage of the distraction of Sparta to victimize their erstwhile allies. Hostilities then ensued, probably on the initiative of Corinth and its Peloponnesian allies, whereupon Athens launched a preemptive strike on Aigina. For the moment, the Athenians did nothing to abet the Messenians at Mt. Ithome.

Thus, it is improbable that the Spartans had been afraid that the Athenians at Ithome would change sides in order to support militarily an independent Messenia. Rather, the Attic *stratēgoi* may have judged that the Spartans, even with allied assistance, would not be able to capture the rebels by main force, a prognosis borne out by the eventual result years later. In that case, individual Athenians may have thought that some compromise better suited the interests of all parties (Messenians, Spartans, and their allies). Were the Spartiates not then in a similar constitutional situation to other privileged classes in the states of the Delian League who had to be 'helped' by the Athenians toward a rapprochement with their *dēmos* ('common people')? In the face of Attic flexibility – an alien Ionian quality – concerning Laconian institutional arrangements, the Spartans were dismayed at this 'fresh take' on what were to them the fundamental features of the time-sanctioned, Lycurgan dispensation.

It is unfortunately an unanswerable query whether the mythological and religious contentions outlined above played any role in winning Attic sympathy or whether that particular common ground was only staked out after the Helot fugitives reached Naupactus. Nonetheless, the rebels had not yet become definitively the subjugated Messenians in the eyes of the Athenians serving with Kimon in *Lakōnikē*.

Once the Spartans ventured north of the isthmus in the campaign that eventuated in the battle at Tanagra, Athenian policy toward Sparta hardened.[74] Not only did the former friends actually meet on the battlefield, but the very presence of the Spartans in eastern Boiotia had also been intended to destabilize Athens by giving an opportunity for anti-democratic intrigues.[75] Tolmides then made his expedition against *Lakōnikē*, a manifest riposte to Tanagra.[76] The sequence of events by which the rebels of Mt. Ithome came to be established at Naupactus is hard to establish (cf. Thuc. 1.103.1–3).[77] Tolmides' expedition was admirably designed to relieve pressure on the besieged at Mt. Ithome, even if he was in fact too late to offer any military assistance. The Spartans in turn did well to reach terms with the rebels when they did, before the new willingness of the Athenians to strike directly at *Lakōnikē* became a factor. Subsequently, the rebels may have settled on terms with the Spartans secure in the knowledge that they would survive as a community under Attic patronage and not be compelled to scatter as bands of exiles. As Diodorus states (11.84.7), Tolmides himself probably occupied Naupactus, possibly with the acquiescence of some locals (the later Naupaktioi who fused with the Messenians). Tolmides' attempts to ensure the control of various strategic points north and north-west of the Peloponnesus may have been planned with the Messenian fugitives in mind as a garrisoning force. Thucydides states that *ekhthos* ('enmity') was the Athenian motivation (1.103.3).

Thereafter, the dichotomous pattern of reference, familiar to us from Thucydides, asserts itself. In the terms of the safe conduct from Mt. Ithome, we discern Spartan persistence in viewing their adversaries as runaway Helots (Thuc 1.103.2–3). The Delphic oracle authorizing the negotiations speaks of releasing the suppliant of Zeus Ithomatas, treating the rebels as exploited Helots who had fled their masters to sanctuary. The parallel with the earlier group of suppliants at Tainaron is striking. The provision that captured returnees would become the chattel slaves of their captors looks ahead to making disposition for individual troublemakers rather than confronting companies of raiders in collaboration with the Athenians. The expatriates for their part would soon style themselves the 'Messenians'.

Afterwards, Athenian appreciation of the Helot issue remained stable. If Sparta chose to fight Athens, the Athenians would enlist Helots as Messenian allies. Implicitly, they would also seek a settlement that would accommodate their Messenian allies as a *polis* within *Lakōnikē*, presumably with the scale of that occupation open to the play of events. The Athenians avoided the more substantial challenge to the Spartan constitution that a call for the liberation of the Laconian *dēmos* constituted. Not only would that have been an invitation to an open-ended conflict, but the loyalty of the Perioeci to the prevailing regime rendered such a *démarche* less attractive as propaganda. As seen in the Peace of Nicias and the alliance with Sparta thereafter, the Athenians could stop agitating at will. They could even readily agree to assist the Spartans against their slaves. Everyone who had not voted with his feet and joined the Messenians during the Archidamian War had characterized himself as a Helot, not a Messenian. For the Athenians, to be Messenian was to resist Sparta and avow affiliation with Athens, in one sense the mother-city of the most important cult of heroic-age Messenia.

Those Helots in *Lakōnikē* dissatisfied with their dependent and servile status found an identity that was viably constructed out of the folk traditions and religious customs that were a common possession of a cross section of their class and were easily communicable. Out of homogeneity with the Spartiates, they achieved differentiation. The Messenian community at Naupactus that grew up under Athenian auspices exhibited extraordinary cohesion and considerable military skills. They positioned themselves admirably to profit from an Attic victory over, or a standoff with, the Spartans that they would do so much to realize. If their Attic patrons could not consummate that victory, no one can attribute responsibility to the Messenian exiles.

Notes

1 Cf. Ducat 1990, 138, 143.

2 See Figueira 1984, 101–2.

3 Among the powerful incentives that must be assumed for the scale and

duration of Spartan efforts to subjugate Messenia may be the non-availability of additional *klārotic* or allotted land in Laconia (at least, under then current rules of land tenure and organization of labor). The same circumstances might have engendered demographic restrictions affecting procreation and family size for late seventh- and sixth-century Laconian Helots. The flight of Messenian resisters cleared territory for allotment (see note 36 below). That the Spartans established emigrants from the Argolid at Asine and Mothone indicates a policy of peroecic colonization on vacated territory (Paus. 4.14.3, 35.2; cf. 2.36.4–5; 3.7.4; 4.24.4, 27.8). The allocation of vacant farm land for *klāroi* in Messenia helped to relieve demographic limitations on Laconian Helots, as the Spartan regime could offer young males an opportunity to form their own households earlier and with more productive potential. Their compliance under the Spartan social order was the price paid for these material advantages.

[4] Note Figueira 1993, 260–4.

[5] Thuc. 4.41.2:

τῆς δὲ Πύλου φυλακὴν κατεστήσαντο, καὶ οἱ ἐκ τῆς Ναυπάκτου Μεσσήνιοι ὡς ἐς πατρίδα ταύτην (ἔστι γὰρ ἡ Πύλος τῆς Μεσσηνίδος ποτὲ οὔσης γῆς) πέμψαντες σφῶν αὐτῶν τοὺς ἐπιτηδειοτάτους ἐλῄζοντό τε τὴν Λακωνικὴν καὶ πλεῖστα ἔβλαπτον ὁμόφωνοι ὄντες.

('[the Athenians] established a garrison over Pylos, and the Messenians from Naupactus as though against this land as *patris* [fatherland] (for Pylos is a part of the land that was once Messenian), sending out the most suitable of themselves, ravaged *Lakōnikē* and did the greatest harm, being *homophōnoi*.')

[6] Treating polemical nomenclature as cultural classification is particularly unhelpful for understanding the Helots/Messenians during the Peloponnesian war. Thuc. 4.41.2 (see note 5) encouraged A.W. Gomme to observe: 'it is possible that there was little love lost between the Messenians, who were Dorians and had probably themselves oppressed the native population after the Dorian occupation of the Peloponnese, and the rest of the Helots…' (*HCT* 3, 481). Not only does this commentary embroider freely on Thucydides, but it causes Gomme to underplay the crucial point in 4.41.3 about the impact of the raids from Pylos. Similarly, he offers on 4.3.3 (see note 7) 'We must conclude that not all the Helots by any means, perhaps, after the last revolt, only a small minority, were of Dorian speech; and those of non-Dorian origin could still apparently be distinguished by their dialect' (*HCT* 3, 440).

[7] Thuc. 4.3.3:

…καὶ τοὺς Μεσσηνίους οἰκείους ὄντας αὐτῷ τὸ ἀρχαῖον καὶ ὁμοφώνους τοῖς Λακεδαιμονίοις πλεῖστ' ἂν βλάπτειν ἐξ αὐτοῦ ὁρμωμένους, καὶ βεβαίους ἅμα τοῦ χωρίου φύλακας ἔσεσθαι.

('[and the appreciation of Attic general Demosthenes was that] the Messenians, being familiar as natives to it [Pylos] from antiquity and being *homophōnoi* to the Lakedaimonians, would do the greatest harm setting out from there [Pylos], and they would be at the same time steadfast guardians of the place [Pylos].')

[8] On the common possession of a dialect, in general, see Morpurgo Davies 1987.

[9] *LSAG2* 177 attributes the Olympian dedication to Argive Methana (on #4, p. 182 with bibliography), but the dedication at the sanctuary of Apollo Korythos is hesitantly linked with the peroecic community of Messenian Mothone or Methone (pp. 203–4 on #3, p. 206).

[10] In seeking parallels for the orthography of name Μεθανιοι on the spear-butts, Bauslaugh 1990 adduces for its comparable phonetic treatment the expression καθάλαθαν 'at sea' in line 7 of the Spartan treaty with the Erxadieis (Meiggs-Lewis #67*bis*). A similar argument was made by Fordyce W. Mitchel in a talk at the Institute for Advanced Study, Princeton, in October 1979.

[11] Another spear-butt in the same sanctuary is silent on its dedicants, but describes itself as 'sacred of Apollo' (*LSAG2* #10, p. 206).

[12] Daux 1937, 67–72. See also *LSAG2* 205 on #8, p. 206.

[13] Mastrokostas 1964, 295; Mattheou 1983, 84; Figueira 1991, 200; Lewis *CAH2* 5, 117–18.

[14] Olympia: *IG* V, 1 #1568 = Meiggs-Lewis #74 (pp. 223–4). Note Harder 1954, 192–8; Hölscher 1974. Delphi: *SIG3* 81 = *FdD* 3, 4, 1, #1. See Bousquet 1961, 69–71; Jacquemin and Laroche 1982, 191–204. See also *LSAG2* 204–5 on #12–13, p. 206.

[15] Thuc. 1.103.4 as interpreted by Pritchett 1995, 78–81.

[16] The cult is attested by the inscribed *horoi* ('boundary stones') (*IG* I^3 1492–9 with Barron 1964, 35–7, 43).

[17] Thuc. 2.25.3–5: the Messenians aid an Athenian *periplous* that attacks Pheia in Elis; 2.90.1–6: the *peza* 'infantry' of the Messenians cooperates with Phormio's squadron at Naupactus; 2.102.1: 400 Messenian hoplites assist Phormio in Akarnania; 3.75.1, 81.2: 500 Messenian hoplites serve with Attic general Nikostratos on Corcyra; 3.94.3, 95.1–2, 97.1, 98.1: Demosthenes is induced by the Messenians to make an Aitolian campaign in which they participate; 3.107–8: service at the Battle of Olpai under Demosthenes; 3.112.4: operating under Demosthenes against Ambrakia; 4.3.3: Demosthenes envisages the potential for the Messenians to raid from Pylos; 4.9.1–2: a small Messenian force helps in the fortification of Pylos; 4.32.2–3, 36.1–3: Messenians help to overcome the Spartans at Sphakteria; 4.41.2: Messenians from Naupactus raid *Lakōnikē*; 5.35.6–7: Athenians withdraw Messenians and Helots from Pylos and settle some in Kephallenia; 5.56.2–3: Messenians and Helots return from Krania on Kephallenia to Pylos to resume raiding; 7.31.2: Demosthenes visits the Ionian Islands for reinforcements for Sicily, summons Messenian troops from Naupactus and visits Alyzia and Anaktorion, points apparently garrisoned by the Messenians; 7.57.8: Messenians in Attic forces at Syracuse.

[18] For the Helot attack on Sparta: D.S. 11.63.4–64.1; Plut. *Cimon* 16.6–7. One proximate source is Ephorus' account of the Great Revolt. Although it might be questioned for its over-dramatization in detail, some hostile activity by the Laconian Helots probably provided the historical basis for any elaboration.

[19] The raids on Boiai and Kythera: Paus. 1.27.5; ΣAesch. 2.75; the burning of the naval base at Gytheion: Thuc. 1.108.5; D.S. 11.84.6; and his movement(s) inland: Aesch. 2.75.

[20] After the outbreak of the Peloponnesian War, sustained hostilities

probably brought Laconian Helots into the ranks of the 'Messenians', i.e., the fugitives to the Attic fort on Cape Malea (Xen. *HG* 1.1.18; cf. D.S. 13.64.7). One might counter, however, that the character of the community at Naupactus was well established by then as that of the Messenioi in exile.

[21] Thuc. 1.101.2, 2.27.2, 3.54.5, 4.56.2.

[22] Thuc. 4.41.3, 5.14.3, 7.26.2.

[23] Thuc. 4.8.9 (hoplites' attendants); 4.26.5 (offered freedom for conveying supplies to Sphakteria); 4.80.3–4 (freedom for services in war); 4.80.2, 80.5–81.1 (Brasideioi enlisted); 5.34.1 (Brasideioi and Neodamodeis); 5.57.1 (pandemic levy); 5.64.1–2 (pandemic levy); 7.19.3 (Neodamodeis).

[24] Subsequently, when the Athenians needed to counteract a Spartan move at Epidauros and to reassure the Argives of their commitment to their alliance, they moved these Messenians and Helots from Kephallenia back to Pylos (Thuc. 5.56.2).

[25] Messenians: D.S. 12.42.5, 60.1–3, 63.5; cf. 12.44.3, 61.1. Helots: 12.67.4–5 (~ Thuc. 4.80.2–81.1); 12.76.1 (Brasideioi).

[26] D.S. 13.48.6, 64.5–7; 14.34.3–6.

[27] Compare Thuc. 4.66.1, 76.2–3; 6.7.3, 12.1, 19.1, 43, 64.1; 7.57.8; cf. 5.83.3, 115.1; 6.7.1.

[28] For the Aiginetans, compare: Figueira 1991, 83–4, 105; 1993, 131, 193, 277–8.

[29] A passage (12.178) in a famous denunciation of Spartan domestic policy in Isocrates, *Panathenaicus* (of 342–39), paragraphs 176–81 (cf. 231–44), is illustrative.

> ...ἀλλὰ παρὰ σφίσιν μὲν αὐτοῖς ἰσονομίαν καταστῆσαι καὶ δημοκρατίαν τοιαύτην οἵαν περ χρὴ τοὺς μέλλοντας ἅπαντα τὸν χρόνον ὁμονοήσειν, τὸν δὲ δῆμον περιοίκους ποιήσασθαι, καταδουλωσαμένους αὐτῶν τὰς ψυχὰς οὐδὲν ἧττον ἢ τὰς τῶν οἰκετῶν·
>
> ('...but establish *isonomia* [equality before the laws] for themselves and *dēmokratia* of such sort that behoves those intending to be of a common mind for all time, but make of the *dēmos* Perioeci, enslaving their souls not any less than the souls of their *oiketai* [household slaves = Helots].')

[30] See Asheri 1983.

[31] *Kathodos*: Paus. 4.20.4, 26.3*bis*, 27.4*bis*, 27.8, 29.4. Refoundation of Messene: Paus. 4.26.6, 28.4–7.

[32] *Epam.* 8.5: Messene restituta; *Pelop.* 4.3: Messena celerius restitueretur.

[33] See Figueira 1991, 199–200; cf. 22–3.

[34] Parallel groups were the Plataians who were settled at Skione (Thuc. 5.32.1; D.S. 12.76.3) or various contingents of Peloponnesian dissidents at Thourioi (D.S. 12.10.7, 11.3).

[35] For example at Poteidaia (Thuc. 2.70.4; *IG* I^3 62.8; 514; cf. D.S. 12.46.7) or in the Chersonese (Plut. *Per.* 19.1; cf. 11.5). See Figueira 1991, 14–30, 35–9.

[36] Paus. 4.14.1: Sikyon, Argos, areas of Arcadia, and Eleusis; 4.23.1–10: refugees, mainly from Pylos and Mothone to Italy, with some staying behind in Arcadia; 4.24.2–3: Aristomenes to Rhodes.

[37] Epaminondas would find reinforcements for his refounded Messene from the descendants of those expelled from Naupactus and Kephallenia,

who had themselves been enlisted as colonists in Cyrene and for Tyndaris in Sicily, the latter group by Dionysios of Syracuse (D.S. 14.78.5–6; Paus. 4.26.2–3, 5).

[38] Strikingly, Spartan justifications have descended to us as encapsulations within Messenian historiography. The *Messeniaka* preserved Spartan justifications for the subjugation and Messenian ripostes, as reflected in Paus. 4.3.4–6; 4.4.4–5.3.

[39] See, in general, Ducat 1974.

[40] Compare Cozzoli 1978.

[41] Hesych. s.v. δαμώδεις, δ 214 Latte; νεοδαμώδεις, ν 314; ΣThuc. 5.34.1; Poll. 3.83; Myron *FGH* 106 F 1; cf. Xen. *HG* 3.3.6; Dio Chrys. *Or*. 36.38. See Willetts 1954; Welwei 1974, 142–58.

[42] See most, recently, Jordan 1990.

[43] Hence it is a paradox fathered by the retrospective nature of surviving, subsequent, accounts that Pausanias envisioned the fifth-century rebels as Messenians. He was not drawing on some lost demography of classical *Lakōnikē*. Rather, as the surviving author most affected by Messenian historiography, he equated rebels with Messenians *per se*. In a parallel fashion, Xenophon has the Spartans, faced with the prospect of pro-Theban Messene, remind the Athenians in 370 of earlier aid when they 'were besieged by the Messenians' in order to get military assistance (*HG* 6.5.33).

[44] Thuc. 1.132.4; Nepos *Paus*. 3.6; cf. Aris. *Pol*. 1307a1–5. See Lotze 1970, 271–4; Lazenby 1975, 246–8; Wolski 1979.

[45] Thuc. 1.128.1; Paus. 4.24.5–6; ΣArist. *Ach*. 510a–c; Ael. *VH* 6.7; cf., on the flight of the Argilian, Thuc. 1.133; D.S. 11.45.4–5; Nepos *Paus*. 4.4. Note Cartledge 1979, 214. The supplication and the massacre may perhaps be dated to 469/8 and 468/7, if these events headed the narrative of the Helot revolt in Atthidography (observe ΣArist. *Lys*. 1144; D.S. 11.63.1).

[46] See David 1979; Cartledge 1987, 164–5; Sartori 1991.

[47] Virtually as I was completing the revisions for this piece, I received a most provocative prospectus titled, *Gefährdete Identität. Bewahrung und Konstruktion kollektiver Identität in Messenien von den dark ages bis zum Hellenismus*, from Dr Nino Luraghi of the Seminar für Alte Geschichte, Universität Freiburg. Dr Luraghi outlines therein a significant research project on the historical consciousness of the Messenians that I believe all interested in this presentation will await with anticipation.

[48] Callisthenes *FGH* 124 F 23 = Polyb. 4.33.2–9. A similar impact of Messenian polemics could perhaps be hypothesized for Theopompus but for the bad luck of preservation. His *Hellenika* discussed the origin of Helots, including the Messenians (*FGH* 115 F 13 from book 7 *re* 399). His *Thaumasia* noted the capture of Messene (F 70, 71). Book 31 of his *Philippika* (*re* Philip's alliance with Messene) digressed on Spartan losses in the Second Messenian War and the origin of the *epeunaktoi*, a category of freed Helots (F 171, cf. F 172, 383). For Ephorus, see the discussion below.

[49] See, more recently, Schwartz 1937, Pearson 1962, Wade-Gery 1966, which, along with Jacoby's treatment in *FGH*, are helpful for earlier bibliography.

[50] *FGH* 265 F 38–46. Note Wade-Gery 1966.

[51] Paus. 4.23.6–10; cf. Strabo 6.1.6 C257–9. See Cordiano 1991.

[52] See, e.g., Figueira 1993, 29–30.

[53] Coles and Haslam 1980, 1–6. Note also Tausend 1993. For the relationship of the account of Pausanias to Tyrtaeus, cf. Pritchett 1985, 1–31; 1991, 179–81.

[54] See also Shero 1938.

[55] Yet, his preeminent status was assured even before Leuktra, where Epaminondas supposedly displayed his shield in a trophy (Paus. 4.22.4–6).

[56] Hero cults at Mycenaean burial sites may provide another mechanism for Messenian identity formation within Messenia itself, most prominently seen at the *tholos* at Nichoria but attested elsewhere. See Coulson 1983; Antonaccio 1995, 70–102. Yet, care must be exercised against concluding too readily that such cults were a means for the preservation of pre-conquest communality. The efflorescence of the Nichoria cult in the late fifth century raises the issue of the role of the Messenians at Naupactus in stimulating such ritual activity.

[57] See Deshours 1993.

[58] See Sokolowski 1969, 120–34. The role of the cult of Apollo Karneios and his priestess (lines 7, 97) shows the subordination of the Andanian cult to an important Spartan state cult. The liberated Messenians added a priest of the mysteries and developed over time a large cultic personnel, while either establishing a new priestess of Hagne beside a naturalized Karneian priestess or equating the priestess of the mysteries with the Karneian priestess (lines 28–9, 96–7).

[59] The gods of the mysteries were equated with the *Megaloi Theoi* (lines 34, 68–9), who presumably also equal the Boiotian Kabeiroi.

[60] Cf. Hippolyt. *Ref. Omn. Haeres.* 5.20.5, p. 194.25–7 Marcovich, for worship of the goddesses by the Lykomidai.

[61] The spurious works attributed to Musaeus are of varied provenance and time of composition. Different sub-corpora, defined by genre, achieved fixation at differing dates. For example, various versions of the oracles of Musaeus were circulating as early as the 480s and throughout the fifth century (Hdt. 8.96.2, 9.43.2; Soph. fr. 1116 Radt; Arist. *Ranae* 1032–3; cf. Plato *Prot.* 316d; Paus. 10.12.11; see also Thuc. 2.8.2, 5.26.3). That the collection of the hymns was relatively early is indicated by Pausanias, who rejected the authenticity of the hymns save for this very Lykomid hymn (Paus. 1.22.7). Strikingly, he offers as an alternative author for the remaining hymns an early authority indeed, Onomacritus. Onomacritus was active in the entourage of the Peisistratid Hipparchus, probably during the 520s, where he was detected by Lasus of Hermione interpolating a corpus of Musaean oracles (n.b.) and punished with banishment (Hdt. 7.6.3). Moreover, the Lykomid hymn presumably established the status of Musaeus as the father of the Eleusinian hero Eumolpos (cf. Andron *FGH* 10 F 13; Philochorus *FGH* 328 F 208). That link is illustrated explicitly on a late fifth-century *pelike* of the Meidias Painter (Beazley, *ARV2* 1313, #7) and may have been noted in Euripides, *Erechtheus*, a play of 422, fr. 65.100–1 Austin. See West 1983, 39–44; Graf 1974, 13–21, 168 with n. 50.

[62] That the oracles of Bakis too supposedly predicted the restoration of the Messenians is another indication of an Athenian connection (Paus. 4.27.4), given the importance of this figure in archaic Attic *manteia*, where Peisistratos was called Bakis (*Suda* s.v. Βάκις, B 47 Adler ~ ΣArist. *Birds* 962 with

Theopompus *FGH* 115 F 77).

[63] For this explanation to be cogent, the late cult title of *Megalai Theai* for Demeter and Kore would have to be applied anachronistically and retrospectively by Pausanias.

[64] On an Attic Tyrtaeus: Plato *Laws* 629a with scholia; D.S. 8.36; *Suda* s.v. Τυρταῖος, τ 1206 Adler; cf. Philochorus *FGH* 328 F 216.

[65] Note ΣEur. *Or.* 932.

[66] See Deshours 1993, 47–9.

[67] Ephorus *FGH* 70 F 116; Nic. Dam. *FGH* 90 F 31; Paus. 4.3.6–8. There are traces of a philo-Spartan version of the same myth in which the Spartans restore the sons of Kresphontes (Isoc. 6.22–23; cf. Plato *Laws* 692b). The Attic/Messenian variant may be its inversion. In general, see Harder 1985, 1–12.

[68] Euripides, *Kresphontes*: fr. 449–59 Nauck. See Harder 1985, 27–45 for full testimonia and fragments.

[69] Peloponnesian War analogies: exhaustion of funds on garrisons, desertion of slaves, and plague: 4.9.1, cf. 4.11.1; siege and famine: 4.13.5; Kephallenia used for coastal raids: 4.23.5, cf. 4.20.8; the Messenian office of *stratēgos autokratōr*: 4.13.5, 15.4; Spartans enlist Helot soldiers: 4.11.1; 4.16.6; Aristokrates compared to Adeimantos at Aigospotamoi: 4.17.3; coastal raids on Laconia and Messenia: 4.18.1–2; some Lepreates side with Sparta: 4.15.8.

[70] Thuc. 1.102.3–4; Plut. *Cimon* 17.3; D.S. 11.64.2–3; Paus. 1.29.8–9, 4.24.6–7; Just. 3.6.3–4. For the revolt: Buonocore 1982. For the Athenians at Ithome, contrast Papantoniou 1951, French 1955, Cole 1974. For our purposes, we may ignore the possible first expedition of Kimon (Plut. *Cimon* 16.8–17.2; cf. Arist. *Lys*. 1137–44 with scholia). It is uncertain whether this first expedition reached Laconia, let alone Mt. Ithome.

[71] For *allophulos*, compare Thuc. 1.2.4. Strikingly, the remaining appearances are in speeches: 4.64.4, 4.86.5, 4.92.3, 6.9.1, 6.23.2.

[72] Atthidographic intermediation may be responsible for *neōter-* terminology in Plut. *Cimon* 17.3, Paus. 4.24.6.

[73] Symmachic change: 2.73.3, 3.4.4, 3.11.1, 3.72.1, 4.51, 4.108.3. Constitutional change: 1.115.2, 2.3.1, 3.75.5, 3.79.1, 3.82.1, 4.76.5, 8.70.1, 8.73.1; cf. 7.87.1 for a change in the bodily 'constitution'. Constitutional or symmachic change: 1.58.1 (Poteidaia); 1.97.1 (Attic allies); 3.66.2 (Plataia). Structural change at Sparta: 4.41.3, 4.80.2, 5.14.3. Term *neōteropoios*: 1.70.2 (Corinthians on the Attic character).

[74] See Lewis 1981.

[75] Thuc. 1.107.4, 6; cf. Plut. *Cimon* 17.4–7, *Per.* 10–13.

[76] For recent discussion, see Badian 1993, 89–96; Pritchett 1995, 61–81.

[77] No emendation of Thuc. 1.103.1 and a ten-year war, starting from 465/4, is still the best option. See Reece 1962; Lewis *CAH*^{2} 5, 110, 500.

Bibliography

Antonaccio, C.M.

1995 *An Archaeology of Ancestors: Tomb cult and hero cult in early Greece*, Lanham.

Asheri, D.

1983 'La diaspora e il ritorno dei Messeni', in E. Gabba (ed.) *Tria Corda: Scritti in onore di Arnaldo Momigliano,* Como, 27–42.

Badian, E

1993 *From Plataea to Potidaea,* Baltimore.

Barron, J.P.

1964 'Religious propaganda of the Delian League', *JHS* 84, 35–48.

Bauslaugh, R.A.

1990 'Messenian dialect and dedications of the "Methanioi" ', *Hesperia* 59, 661–8.

Beazley, J.D.

1963 *Attic Red-Figure Vase-Painters 2*, Oxford = *ARW2*.

Bousquet, J.

1961 'Inscriptions de Delphes', *BCH* 85, 69–97.

Buonocore, M.

1982 'Ricerche sulla terza guerra Messenica', *Migra* 8, 57–123.

Cartledge, P.A.

1979 *Sparta and Lakonia: A regional history,* London.

1987 *Agesilaus and the Crisis of Sparta,* London.

Cole, J.R.

1974 'Cimon's dismissal, Ephialtes' revolution and the Peloponnesian Wars', *GRBS* 15, 1369–85.

Coles, R.A. and Haslam, M.W.

1980 *The Oxyrhynchus Papyri 46,* London.

Cordiono, G.

1991 'Strabone ed i Messeni di Reggio', *Hesperia* 2, 63–77.

Coulson, W.D.E. with Wilkie, N.

1983 'The site and environs', in W.A. McDonald, W.D.E. Coulson, and J. Rosser, *Excavations at Nichoria in Southwest Greece: Volume III, Dark Age and Byzantine occupation,* Minnesota, 332–9.

Cozzoli, U.

1978 'Sparta e l'affrancamento degli iloti nel V e nel IV secolo', *Migra* 6, 213–32.

Daux, G.

1937 'Inscriptions et monuments archaïques de Delphes', *BCH* 61, 57–78.

David, E.

1979 'The conspiracy of Cinadon', *Athenaeum* 57, 239–59.

Deshours, N.

1993 'La légende et la culte de Messènè ou comment forger l'identité d'une cité', *REG* 106, 39–60.

Ducat, J.

1974 'Le mépris des Hilotes', *Annales* 30, 1451–64.

1990 *Les Hilotes, BCH* Supp. 20, Paris.

Figueira, T.J.

1984 'Mess contributions and subsistence at Sparta', *TAPA* 114, 87–100.

1991 *Athens and Aigina in the Age of Imperial Colonization,* Baltimore.

1993 *Excursions in Epichoric History,* Lanham, Maryland.

French, A.
1955 'The Spartan earthquake', *G&R*^{2} 2, 108–18.
Graf, F.
1974 *Eleusis und die orphische Dichtung Athens in vorhellenistischer Zeit*, Berlin and NewYork.
Harder, A.
1985 *Euripides' Kresphontes and Archelaos,* Leiden.
Harder, R.
1954 'Paionios und Grophon: Zwei Bildhauerinschriften', in R. Lullies (ed.) *Neue Beiträge zur Klassischen Alterumswissenschaft: Festschriftum 60. Geburtstag von Bernhard Schweitzer,* Stuttgart.
Hölscher, T.
1974 'Die Nike der Messenier und Naupaktier in Olympia', *JDAI* 89, 70–111.
Jacquemin, A, and Laroche, D.
1982 'Notes sur trois piliers delphiques', *BCH* 106, 191–218.
Jordan, B.
1990 'The ceremony of the Helots in Thucydides', *AC* 59, 37–69.
Lazenby, J.F.
1975 'Pausanias, son of Kleombrotos', *Hermes* 103, 235–51.
Lewis, D.M.
1981 'The origins of the First Peloponnesian War', in G.S. Shrimpton and D.J. McCargar (eds.) *Classical Contributions: Studies in honour of Malcolm Francis McGregor,* Locust Valley, N.Y., 71–8.
Lotze, D.
1970 'Selbstbewusstsein und Machtpolitik: Bemerkungen zur machtpolitischen Interpretation spartanischen Verhaltens in den Jahren 479–477 v. Chr.', *Klio* 52, 255–75.
LSAG2 = L.H. Jeffery
1990 *The Local Scripts of Archaic Greece*, rev. by A.W. Johnston, Oxford.
Mastrokostas, E.
1964 ' Ναύπακτος ', *AD* 19 B' 2, 294.
Mattheou, A.P.
1983 ' 19 χρόνια ', *Horos* 1, 84.
Morpurgo Davies, A.
1987 'The Greek notion of dialect', *Verbum* 10, 7–28.
Papantoniou, G.A.
1951 'Once or Twice?', *AJP* 72, 176–81.
Pearson, L.
1962 'The pseudo-history of Messenia and its authors', *Historia* 11, 397–426.
Pritchett, W.K.
1985 *Studies in Greek Topography: Part V,* Berkeley and Los Angeles.
1991 *Studies in Greek Topography: Part VII,* Amsterdam.
1995 *Thucydides' Pentekontaetia and Other Essays*, Amsterdam.
Reece, D.W.
1962 'The date of the fall of Ithome', *JHS* 82, 1962.

Sartori, F.
1991 'Il "pragma" di Cinadone', *Stuttgarter Kolloquium zur Historischen Geographie des Altertums: 2, 1984 und 3, 1987*, Bonn, 487–514.

Schwartz, E.
1937 'Die Messenische Geschichte bei Pausanias', *Philologus* 92, 19–46.

Shero, L.R.
1938 'Aristomenes the Messenian', *TAPA* 49, 500–31.

Sokolowski, F.
1969 *Lois sacrées des cités grecques,* Paris = *LSCG.*

Tausend, K.
1993 'Argos und der Tyrtaiospapyrus P.Oxy. XLVII 3316', *Tyche* 8, 197–201.

Wade-Gery, H.T.
1966 'The "Rhianos-Hypothesis" ', in *Ancient Society and Institutions: Studies presented to Victor Ehrenberg on his 75th birthday,* Oxford, 289–302.

Welwei, K.W.
1974 *Unfreie im antiken Kriegsdienst I, Athen und Sparta,* Wiesbaden.

West, M.L.
1983 *The Orphic Poems,* Oxford.

Willetts, R.F.
1954 'The Neodamodeis', *CP* 49, 27–32.

Wolski, J.
1979 'Les hilotes et la question de Pausanias, régent de Sparte', in *Schiavitù. manomissione e classi dipendenti nel mondo antico,* Rome, 7–33.

Chapter 9

FROM SPARTA TO TARAS

Nomima, ktiseis and relationships between colony and mother city

Massimo Nafissi

In a well-known passage of Plato's *Laws*, the Lacedaemonian Megillus compares some customs of Sparta, Athens and Taras. In Sparta wine is to be drunk in absolute moderation, infringers are severely punished and not even the Feast of Dionysus may serve as an excuse. After recalling the Athenian Dionysia, Megillus says: 'even at our colony of Taras I saw the whole city drunk at the Dionysia. But with us no such thing is possible' (*Leg.* 1.637 b). It was a common assumption that mother cities and colonies had the same *nomoi* ('customs'). Plato perhaps regarded the Tarentines' drinking habits as an exception to the rule, but that Sparta's and Taras' *nomoi* were very different was often stressed by later writers. Rivalry with Rome, betrayal in the Hannibalic war and democratic excesses shaped the image of Taras. Authors of the Roman age often depict the city as cowardly and lascivious, addicted to unrestrained drinking, with a mob fed every day at public expense.[1]

Callimachus (fr. 617 Pf.) once praised Tarentines' prowess, recalling their Herculean lineage with words which echo Tyrtaeus' Ἡρακλῆος γὰρ ἀνικήτου γένος ἐστέ (fr. 8.1 G.-P.: 'You are of the lineage of the invincible Heracles'). In this he likened Tarentines to the Spartans.[2] Virgil recalled Callimachus' lines, but he threw doubt upon the Herculean origins of Taras: 'Hinc sinus Herculei, si vera est fama, Tarenti | cernitur' (*Aen.* 3.551: 'Hence the Herculean, if true the tale, Tarentum's Gulf is sighted'). The passage puzzled modern interpreters; but in Servius (ad loc.) we can find the correct explanation. Virgil had raised doubts ('si vera est fama') on the Herculean origins of Taras, 'in quo molles et luxuriosi nascuntur' ('where people grow unmanly and lascivious). Tarentines did not preserve the virtues of their mythical stock. Someone found a reason for this, too. Everything is, again, to be explained through origins, this time through the *ktisis*.

Eustathius (*Comm. Dion. Perieg.* 376) relates that the founders of Taras, the Partheniae, were rightly expelled from their home. His source followed mainly Ephorus' account,[3] adding the following detail: 'The Partheniae, because they were not educated lawfully and bravely according to the Lycurgan laws, conducted their lives in a completely different manner from good citizens. After nineteen years and after conquering Messene, the Spartans who had fought the war came back home. They found the city in a bad state and drove out the Partheniae.' What kind of city could the Partheniae found?

The Sparta-Taras topic extends far beyond this footnote to the *mirage spartiate*. After an introductory sketch of the political and military relations between Sparta and Taras and of the role of the Spartan origins in Tarentine policy and political culture, I shall select two main topics and examine the Spartan *nomima* ('customs') and the foundation story of Taras. I will concentrate my attention on their role and their significance in the relations between Sparta and Taras and in the archaic history of the metropolis.

1.

Herodotus offers probably the first evidence of an awareness of the Spartan origins of Taras and possibly of their effect upon external relations. The historian records the *philia* ('friendship') between Taras and Cnidus, which was according to him a colony of Sparta (3.138.2). The rich imports of Laconian pottery during the late seventh and the sixth century are probably an earlier trace of Taras' Spartan origin.[4] Before the end of the sixth century Tarentine coins show types clearly related to the foundation story of the city.[5] In fact political relationships between Sparta and Taras are well known, although evidence is as usual rare.[6] We have no epigraphical or literary evidence about mutual citizen rights, or other privileges granted to the citizens of the two *poleis*, or about regulations on religious matters, such as admission of individuals to the sacrifices in each city or requirement of the colony to offer a tribute to the deities of the metropolis.[7] In the late fifth century Taras stressed its Laconian lineage, which in turn seems to have affected the city's politics. The foundation of Heraclea Lucana by Taras (433/2), together with the political changes in Thurii, stopped Athenian ambitions for a while in the Ionian area.[8] The very name of the colony is noteworthy, but above all we must remember that the newborn Heraclea had ephors as eponymous magistrates.[9] In the Peloponnesian War, Taras did not help the besieged Syracuse, but in 411 BC sent its ships as far as the Aegean sea to support Sparta.[10]

In the fourth century *syngeneia* ('kinship') carried a great weight in Taras' choice of *condottieri* to lead her military campaigns. The first of them was Archidamus III of Sparta (344/3–338). In the following years Taras turned to the Molossian king Alexander (d. 330). But then, after supporting the Sicilian venture of King Acrotatus in 315, Taras went back in 303 to get further help from the Spartan Cleonymus.[11] In the late fourth century Laconian descent was a cornerstone of Tarentine self-consciousness and the city's policy made use of it. I shall recall just two examples. Strabo makes clear that the traditions about the Spartan origins of the Samnites were spread by and in the interest of Taras (5.4.12). During the Samnitic wars Tarentines were using Laconian kinship to fortify the Italic block against Rome.[12] The *peri nomou kai dikaiosynēs*, a work ascribed to the Tarentine Pythagorean philosopher and political leader Archytas, but written in the age of the *condottieri*, shows that from Taras – as from elsewhere – people looked to Sparta as a model of a mixed constitution.[13]

2.

Whatever some ancient writers thought, Taras' political and religious institutions, not to say script and dialect, had a very strong Laconian flavour.[14]

A list of Tarentine deities illustrates the point well. Athena was almost certainly the guardian goddess of Taras, as she was of Sparta. The Tarentines also, like the Spartans, honoured Apollo Hyacinthus, Apollo Carneus and the Dioscuri. Gaia, Aphrodite Basilis, Artemis Corythalia and Artemis Agrotera also have Laconian counterparts.[15] All this need not surprise us, because Polybius (8.33.8–9), while mentioning a river in the *chōra* of Taras, the Galaesus, says that it was also called Eurotas and adds that many places at Taras had Spartan names. This Spartan landscape included Apollo Hyacinthus' tomb, which stood on a hill outside the city, as did its Laconian counterpart.

In the case of widely-practised panhellenic cults, some proof of the distinctive Laconian character of the Tarentine religion might be useful. But our evidence sometimes is too scanty: we know that the Tarentines honoured some gods who were major deities in the Spartan pantheon, but we are not in a position to detect the possible Laconian flavour of the colonial cults. Such are the cases of Zeus[16] or Poseidon. Poseidon, father of the eponymous Taras, was surely favoured because of the maritime bent of the town, but it is a fact that the mythological and antiquarian learning of the polis used the god to reaffirm its ties with Sparta. Gold coins of the second half of the fourth century depict the young Taras suppliant before an enthroned Poseidon: their connection with the Tarentines' use of Spartan *condottieri* is clear.[17] Anyway, this *use* of Poseidon's character proceeds more from his parental role, well suited to express the ideal relationships between mother city and colony,[18] than from a specific Laconian connotation, though such, of course, he had.[19]

In as far as the colonists' horizon of experience was strictly related to the socio-cultural context from which they moved, colonies were similar to their mother cities. Studies of Greek colonization rightly include the systematic comparison between the customs of colony and metropolis.[20] However, since the evidence is often late and scanty, it is very dangerous to assume that every institutional correspondence between metropolis and colony goes back to the original foundation. The immediate assumption of a primary derivation underestimates the common features of the religion of the Greek cities and the power their leading classes had to modify or create political and religious institutions.[21]

Furthermore, the active relations with the metropolis and the actual role of the origins in the politics, society and culture of the colony fostered the old *patria* ('ancestral customs') as well as recent borrowings. I would suggest that such borrowings are especially likely in the case of the public institutions of Spartan colonies, because of the peculiar position of Sparta in Greek politics and the fascination produced by its Lycurgan political system.

At Taranto an inscription painted on a Chian amphora of the beginning of the third century BC, bearing as date the name of an eponymous ephor, has recently been found.[22] If we accept that the eponym is, as likely, a Tarentine official, we have here the first evidence of this office at Taras. Ephors have long been known in Heraclea Lucana,[23] Thera and Cyrene, as well as in other cities of Cyrenaica and in the minor Laconian *poleis* during the hellenistic and Roman age.[24] The newly discovered text may seem to corroborate the view of many scholars, that the ephorate was introduced from Sparta to Thera and Taras and then to Cyrene and Heraclea when each city was founded.[25] But I doubt that many scholars would subscribe to the opinion that Sparta already had ephors when Thera was founded.[26] Ephors could very well be introduced *ex novo* in classical times. In Messene they were probably established in 369.[27] We can assume that this office was introduced in Thera and Cyrene as a result of independent political developments in two cities very conscious of their Laconian descent. The ephors of Heraclea, founded in 433/2, could suggest, but do not prove, their pre-existence at Taras. Unfortunately, we do not have much information about Taras' institutions. We know from Aristotle that a moderate aristocratic constitution preceded the classical democracy, which was founded *c.* 470–60 BC and still flourished in Archytas' day; it is particularly unfortunate that we lack information about this earlier regime, because the philosopher termed it a *politeia*, the same word he used to classify the Spartan one.[28] In these circumstances I would not exclude the possibility of a later introduction of the ephorate in Taras.

As for the cults, the ones that are a focus of collective identity or are very important for social and political life are likely to be of ancient derivation from the *mētropolis*. More liable to be late creations are the minor cults[29] or rituals which hint consciously and overtly at the *mētropolis* and its heroic past. I will try to clarify this point with an example. At Taras the Atridae shared heroic honours with the Aeacidae, Tydidae and Laertiadae, while the Agamemnonidae received separately, and on another day, divine honours. I have suggested elsewhere that these rituals originated in the alliance of Taras with the Molossian king, the Aeacid Alexander, and its aftermath.[30] The *enagismoi* ('heroic sacrifices') for the homeric heroes and their descendants were instituted to set the Trojan War as a precedent for a war to be waged on the barbarians of Apulia, whose ancestors were believed to have killed Diomedes (Tydidae). The alliance between Taras (Atridae) and Alexander (Aeacidae), apparently involved Corcyra (which, according to ancient tradition, largely benefited from a stop of Diomedes, during the hero's last journey to the West) and the Ionian islands (Laertiadae). When the alliance between Taras and Alexander collapsed,[31] Taras bestowed emphatic new honours on the hero responsible for the death of the Aeacid Neoptolemus, Orestes (Agamemnonidae). Through myth and ritual the city made specific symbolic statements on its relations with the king. The cults of the Atridae and the Agamemnonidae in Taras are, therefore, not a direct offspring of Spartan cults for Agamemnon and Cassandra, Menelaus and Orestes. It is not only to cults that the point is relevant. Ephorate was also introduced in the Spartan 'colonies' as a symbol of the Spartan *eunomia*. Some of the Spartan place-names at Taras to which Polybius refers could have also been a late creation, because they express very directly Laconian self-consciousness.[32] This should not be the case, of course, with Apollo Hyacinthus' tomb, because of its religious and social significance.

On the other hand, it is quite natural that in the course of time Taras and Sparta became two very different cities. The most evident differences are perhaps to be seen in the Dionysiac cult and in the banqueting customs. As already stated, Sparta was looked upon as the city of moderation, of sobriety. Its traditional laws imposed strict limitations on the use of wine, and most modern scholars consider Dionysus' role of little significance in the Laconian city.[33] Taras, however, was well known for an indulgence in drinking that was not merely limited to the feasts of Dionysus.[34] No doubt the ancient sources indulge in topical aspects, but there is the fact that no evidence leads us to believe that the Tarentines were obliged, as the Spartans were, to participate in common meals, to pay a fixed tribute mainly in kind and to eat traditional foods, such as the ill-famed black broth.[35] In the Spartan common messes the usual Greek distinction of the meal into the two stages of consumption of food and wine (*deipnon* and *symposion*, respectively) came to be blurred by the growing cultural, social and practical importance of the *epaikla*, the extra contributions offered especially by the well-off Spartans.[36] Authors of the classic and hellenistic age (and their Laconian informers) perceived the second half of the Spartan meal, when *epaikla* were offered, not as a *symposion*, but as an additional meal, although it was certainly derived from the *symposion*. In the heart of the archaic age a vase-type for *symposia* was created, the κρατὴρ Λακωνικός ('Laconian mixing-bowl'),[37] in whose name and in whose wide diffusion and imitation one just might see a clue to the rising of the Spartan mirage: admiration for the common messes of the Spartan citizens as a typical custom of the new leading power in Greece is likely to have contributed to the renown of the Laconian mixing-bowl. I would be cautious about using its creation and development in order to date the transformation of the Spartan dining customs:[38] austerity did not stop the drinking of wine in Sparta and the sympotic functions of the so-called *epaikla* were never completely uprooted. Nonetheless, the favour which the crater met seems to imply a different perception of this part of the meal, more akin to the one which Alcman and the Laconian vase-painters convey. On the other hand, Taras' civic identity had the mark of Dionysus. This is made clear not only by the evidence for his cult.[39] The foundation oracle quoted by Antiochus names a place called Satyrion: 'I have given you Satyrion and Taras, a rich country to dwell...' (Parke-Wormell 1956, I p. 72). Another foundation oracle, which is recalled by Diodorus, makes clear that Satyrion was the acropolis of Taras.[40] Such a Greek name was very likely given to the acropolis by the settlers and seems to me to imply self-identification with the Satyrs.[41] There was a statue of a Satyr in the *prytaneum* at Taras, still much revered in Cicero's time.[42] The name the colonists gave to the city acropolis may help us to understand why Tarentines chose the banqueter as their ideal image of the citizen, on the terracottas which by the thousand fill Taranto's votive deposits from the late sixth century to the end of the fourth century BC.[43] The place-name Satyrion hints at the importance of Dionysus, wine and banquet in the Spartan society at the time of the foundation of Taras. In this way, it seems, we can trace a common background to religious and social institutions which experienced very diverging developments.[44]

I think we may perceive many of these diverging developments. In Taras, as in every Greek city, the stages of the young people's growth were marked with religious solemnities. We meet Spartan gods (Apollo Hyacinthus and Carneus, Artemis Corythalia), but we have no evidence of the severe and militaristic overtones of the rituals in which Spartan youth showed its physical and moral virtues to the citizens. Does the difference result from the evolution of Tarentine society? Was Taras' culture *more modern* than the one of Sparta? Or was the Sparta the colonists knew *more ancient* than the Sparta we are better acquainted with? Or both?

The same difficulties arise with political institutions. I have suggested that the ephorate was not an 'original' office at Taras. On the other hand, Herodotus remembers a *basileus* (3.162.2), Aristophilides, who ruled at Taras in late archaic times; many scholars have considered him a tyrant, but the opposite view that Taras had traditional *basileis* – as Sparta, Thera and Cyrene did – cannot be disproved. One could think of him as a king whose *timai* and powers were consistent with a *politeia* as defined by Aristotle.[45] One might also add that Aphrodite Basilis and the Dioscuri have some royal connotation.[46]

It is clear that in considering the customs of a colony we have to take into account the chronology of the colonial foundation and the history of the metropolis.[47] It would be very dangerous, however, to use the Tarentine customs of Spartan origin to confirm what we presume had been the course of Spartan history. Vicious circles (cf. the ephorate), inferences *ex silentio* and lack of evidence would be the main flaws in our argument.

3.

Many of the customs we have reviewed probably contributed to the Tarentines' deep awareness of their Laconian descent. But in this respect the *ktisis* ('foundation story') and the oikist cult surpassed them by far. The latter was obviously a main focus of the memories of the city's origins. One might suggest that the different honours paid to the oikist by the *polis* at different times were related to the role of the mother city in the colony's consciousness and that they might sometimes reflect their contemporary relations. The Spartan oikist of Taras, Phalanthus, had a 'rival' in the eponymous hero, Taras, believed to be a son of Poseidon and devoid of Phalanthus' strong ties with Sparta. But, as evidence is scanty, the history of Phalanthus' and Taras' cults can be outlined only in a very hypothetical way. Since, furthermore, I have discussed it elsewhere I shall now put aside this point and concentrate my attention on the foundation story.[48]

The foundation stories were not 'historical' reflections of the actual facts of the settling, but a fiction based on the actions, characters and times of the *histoire événementielle*. As Claude Calame points out, foundation stories are in between what we call myth and history.[49] This ambiguous position is very clear in the studies of the last decades. Scholars of colonial praxis and institutions and historians of the archaic Age often rely, I fear, too much on their details. Research on the literary and cultural aspects of the foundation stories (including the stories of an undoubtedly legendary nature), studies on the themes of civic identity and ideology, on the culture of the Greek *poleis* in hellenistic and Roman times, usually have a more prudent approach.[50] In fact, as stories about beginnings, the foundation stories oriented the judgement of listeners and readers about the communities involved in the story.[51] First of all, of course, they remembered the very special ties of kinship which join colony and mother city; however, they were not a simple genealogical tree, but precise stories. Now these narratives often emphasize respect for, or violation of, ethical principles and human and divine laws, as well as noble or base social origins and prowess or cowardice; they also recall panhellenic ideals and fights against the barbarians, ancient kindnesses (*euergesiai*) or offences, and they make clear whether the settlers possess their land by a good right and with oracular sanction. It is these details that determine the opinion of readers and listeners and are obviously relevant for the foundation stories that revolve around the vicissitudes of bastard sons and unintentional murders, two sets of stories to which much attention has been recently paid.[52] I would stress the ethical point, which gives the chance to explain the colonists' departure without putting any sort of blame on them. The pragmatic function made the actual content of the foundation stories liable to change according to their specific oral or written destination and contemporary politics.[53] Therefore it might be risky to reconstruct abstract story patterns without first having analyzed each single literary version with regard to its intentions and meaning.

The foundation story is obviously momentous for the relations between *mētropolis* and colony.[54] Many sources state what the word *mētropolis* implies: these relations have a natural model in the one between parents and sons.[55] But departure from home is not the common destiny of a son who can trust in his father's patrimony. The very fact of leaving for a colonial adventure somehow questions the natural ties. Why had colonists to leave? Did citizens and colonists act as fathers and sons?

The fourth-century Cyrene decree for the Theraeans (*SEG* IX 3) shows how the foundation story was recalled when ties of blood had to be renewed. The Cyrenaeans gave the *isopoliteia* ('reciprocity of civic rights') the Theraeans were asking for. In the version of the foundation story which the fourth-century decree recalls, every detail is devised to establish good relations. Not only does the supposed seventh century foundation decree which it cites grant to the Theraeans the very rights they are asking for; it also provides severe conditions regarding the right to return. Colonists have to stay abroad five years (ll. 33–7). Departure, and respect for this trial period, are enforced through death penalties and obscure menacing oaths. Theraeans helping infringers are liable to death, whereby stress is significantly laid on family ties:

> ὁ δὲ ἀποδεκόμενος ἢ ἀδήιζων ἢ πατὴρ υἱὸν ἢ ἀδελφεὸς ἀδελφεὸν παισεῖται ἅπερ ὁ μὴ λέων πλὲν (ll. 38–40) – i.e. θανά[σι]μος τένται καὶ τὰ χρήματα ἔστω αὐτοῦ δαμόσια (l. 37 f.).
>
> 'And he who receives or protects another, even if it be a father his son or brother his brother, shall suffer the same penalty as the man unwilling to sail' – i.e. he 'shall be liable to punishment by death and his goods shall be confiscated' (transl. Graham 1983, 225)

In this way the decree excuses precisely what actually happened (or what the Cyrenaeans believed had happened): colonists sailing back to Thera were repelled by stones (Hdt. 4.156.3).[56]

We imagine that the colonists' departure (or rather the reasons that forced them to leave) might sometimes weaken good relations with the mother city, but to find out we have to examine stories which are sometimes aimed at restoring these very relations. A difficult task, indeed! We know now that Greeks were able to get over old rifts by telling foundation stories. It does not necessarily follow that these stories reflect the historical development of the *mētropolis*–colony relations.

In fact, as a rule, we are not able to read the foundation stories as they were told by the citizen *élite*. Cyrene or Magnesia on the Maeander[57] are lucky, well-known, epigraphical exceptions. Sometimes Greek historians enquired at the colonies and mother cities about foundations,[58] but not all the narratives reflect the content and purposes of local tradition. In literary texts foundation stories reflect – as a rule – the views of other cities and of alien writers. Those writers did not often have any acquaintance with local tradition, or a special interest in respecting its viewpoint. Myron of Priene included in his *Messēniaka* the version of the foundation of Taras which we read in Diodorus (VIII 21), whose main purpose is to put the hated Spartans (and the Tarentines as their relatives) in a bad light.[59]

What about the two main accounts of the foundation of Taras, of Antiochus and Ephorus (*FGrH* 555 F 13; 70 F 216 ap. Strabo 6.3.2–3)? The two narratives share a general outline but suggest diametrically opposed ethical and social judgements on the protagonists.

According to Antiochus, the Partheniae were children of people who refused to take up arms against the Messenians and who for that reason were made helots.[60] The implied cowardice of the fathers is to be found in their sons. When their sacrilegious revolt during the Amyclaean *agōn* is foiled, they flee to the altars. The oracular order they receive from Delphi is to be 'the scourge of the Iapygians': they come to Italy and settle down among the barbarians placidly.[61] Far better the brave Spartans: they behave cleverly, generously and piously too, as they respect the suppliants of Apollo. Nota bene: between the present-day Spartiates and Tarentines there is no tie of blood; the Tarentines are related to the helots.[62]

According to Ephorus, the strange case of the Partheniae arose during the Second Messenian War. In the interest of the polis an indiscriminate union of the cream of the Spartan youth with the city's *parthenoi* ('unmarried girls') was authorized. Their birth gives no hope to the Partheniae: each of them has many fathers, but not one who could acknowledge him. They have – as another source explains – no hope for inheritance.[63] So the courageous and brotherly united Partheniae plan a revolt. The Spartans recognize the danger and an agreement is reached through *their fathers*' good offices. Accordingly, Partheniae have to leave, but, if they return, they will receive a fifth of Messenia – a liberality beyond comparison. The detail implies Spartans' goodwill and stresses the virtues of the Partheniae, because they will neglect the opportunity, support the Achaeans' fights against the barbarians and conquer their land in Italy. In contrast to Antiochus' account, Ephorus' story implies blood ties of the Tarentines with the Spartans who stayed home and their descendants.

Relations between these two accounts and the local tradition are hard to define. Antiochus' *peri Italiās* was probably written between the peace of Gela and Athens' Great Sicilian Expedition (424–415 BC),[64] while Ephorus wrote under the impression of Archytas' government (*c.* 361) and Taras' leading power in the Italiote League.[65] One can imagine that the Tarentine ambassadors asking Sparta for help in about 345 could have made use of a foundation story not too much different from Ephorus' version. But I cannot believe that Sparta and Taras co-operated in the Peloponnesian war on the basis of the foundation story narrated by Antiochus. One would like to know which kind of foundation story grounded, in the sixth or fifth century, the relations between Sparta and Taras.

The first Tarentine coins, of the late sixth century BC, depict a running boy with lyre and flower; in the next series he is joined, on the obverse, by the dolphin-rider. According to the most probable interpretation, the two figures are Hyacinthus and Phalanthus.[66] We cannot be sure that the pair are linked by a narrative connection, but certainly Phalanthus and Hyacinthus were pivotal to the Spartan identity of Taras. Therefore a foundation story involving Phalanthus was told at least from the late sixth century BC: we are left to imagine its literary form; there were maybe already many occasions for performance and more than one version: likely poems to be recited or sung at the Hyacinthia or at the oikist's sanctuary.[67] This leads to a question that I intend to deal with, even though I have already advised caution in using foundation stories: the actual fact of the colonization of Taras and the light it throws on the history of Sparta.[68]

We can, I think, safely suppose that the more archaic stories centered on the Partheniae and Phalanthus. Also the connection with the Messenian wars (a standard feature in the narratives we possess) is likely to be a pattern our later stories derive from their archaic models. Anyway, these models, while asserting Taras' historical identity, were also designed to make a symbolic statement about the nature of the community. They connected Taras to Sparta and maybe created different political and social *status* within the Tarentine *polis* (one may suppose that the first settlers' descendants formed a privileged group).[69] The fictitious character of these narratives is shown by the very image of Phalanthus riding on the dolphin: according to an ancient tradition Phalanthus was shipwrecked before reaching Italy, and was brought ashore by a dolphin.[70] Of course we cannot use inner verisimilitudes as a criterion, and our evidence does not allow us to check what is fictive and what is metaphor or, conversely, what is historical in the foundation of Taras.[71]

We can take as fact the departure of some settlers from Sparta, but this only makes the chronological problem more urgent. We cannot be sure that the traditional connection with the first Messenian war is historically well grounded. Antiochus (admittedly not referring to the first war) and Ephorus show how this context could be used either as a test of personal virtues or as a dramatic setting of extreme stress for the polis which, with no blame to them or to the *dēmos*,[72] engenders the marginal condition of the Partheniae. The Eusebian foundation date (706 BC: *Chron.* p. 91 Helm) depends on the foundation stories. On the other hand, the traditional chronology cannot be disproved by documentary evidence. The earliest Tarentine tombs date between the end of the eighth and the beginning of the seventh century BC, thereby suggesting a date for the foundation of the city,[73] which is not impossible to relate to the First Messenian War.[74] I think we could also argue for the connection through the Great Rhetra. The connection between the First Messenian war and the Great Rhetra, rests in my view on Tyrtaeus and is very strong. As to the further link with Taras' *apoikia*, there is room for doubt, but it seems to me that the departure of the colonists can be best placed in this historical context. This is what we might expect to find in a period in which Sparta was, as the Great Rhetra shows, formally as well as concretely defining its citizen body.[75]

Much more questionable seems to me the use of the circumstances of the foundation. The Partheniae have been envisaged as an age group, and their exclusion as a failed initiation, whose completion is reached by their successful arrival in Italy and their conquering of the new home.[76] The name of the Partheniae could indicate a group of young people of the same age, as it probably means 'sons of maidens' or 'of unmarried women'.[77] And a good place in the picture is also to be found for Phalanthus. The myth of the oikist saved by the dolphin is a clear metaphor of a promotional process – not only personal (to the status of hero), but a collective one as well (to the status of citizens of a new polis). But there is still more. Phalanthus' name means bald; and Antiochus says – in a somewhat puzzling connection – that Spartan full citizens grow their hair long. Pausanias has a good story about Phalanthus' hair. Delphi foretold that he would conquer a city, only when 'rain will fall under a blue sky'. In fact, says Pausanias, Phalanthus conquered a city when his wife Aethra (the blue sky) wept (rained).[78] The specification that, when she wept, she was removing lice from his head, seems superfluous. In fact the theme of weeping and removing lice is widely known in folklore.[79] But are lice on a bald head not 'rain under a blue sky'?[80] The impossible was thus already accomplished; Aethra's name and weeping – and maybe her character itself – is a later addition to a story no longer understood.[81] Thus Phalanthus is the long-haired bald one. We all remember the Spartan warriors with Leonidas, dressing their hair before the fight (Hdt. 7.208–9), and we know also that wearing long hair in Sparta was connected to transitions between age-groups.[82] So, Phalanthus' name and physical appearance are in paradoxical contrast, which metaphorically embodied the Partheniae's vicissitudes, from exclusion to the status of warriors and adult citizens. Also Apollo Hyacinthus' importance can be viewed in this context – in any case as a Spartan, not as a Pre-dorian or Amyclaean deity – not only because of the related juvenile rituals, but also because of the myth-historical memories of the conquest of Laconia which were bound to his sanctuary.[83] By giving importance to this cult, the colonists emphasized their military virtue, which the conquest of their new home had shown not inferior to that of their parents and ancestors.[84] The two sanctuaries may be viewed as monuments of the conquering of the land.

F. de Polignac sees in the initiatory feature of the tale the reflection of the actual use of ritual devices as a means of facing the dangers of the civil strife from which the colonial enterprise stems.[85] I totally agree with him on the reconciling function of the events narrated in the foundation story. But, from what I have said, it is clear that in the narrative of the misfortunes of the valorous Partheniae I would rather see a fiction devoted *inter alia* to the promotion of good relationships between metropolis and colony. In fact the whole story of the sons of the *parthenoi* seems to me to be a metaphor, a variation on the theme 'fathers and sons'. Departure in this case was to be expected: exposure is a common feature of stories of unmarried girls made pregnant by gods.[86] On the other hand, the young people will be of citizen descent, unless one proposes a biased and forced interpretation, as Antiochus did. Such a story fabricates concrete blood relations with the *mētropolis*, as we saw when commenting on Ephorus' account. These ties are less guaranteed when settlers are, for instance, an entire *genos* (clan) or a *morion* (section of the polis) forced to emigrate by civil strife (the colonies Plato had in mind in *Leg*. 4.708b).

Supposing, therefore, that the characters and the plot of our story are fictive, to what extent does the foundation story refer to Spartan social institutions? A story of young people with their initiatory duties, might seem a very Spartan one. But maybe it is just an archaic Greek story. I have interpreted Phalanthus' character as referring to Spartan use: in fact, a reference to Tarentine customs – hard to find – would have been more appropriate, since the story was created in a Tarentine, not in a Spartan, context. In any case, Apollo Hyacinthus' cult in Taras was certainly a Spartan offspring, and I think we can say that these stories were formulated in a context which not only bore a strong Spartan imprint, but also reflected its Laconian origins.

To sum up, information about customs of Spartan origin within the colony may lead us through cautious reasoning to formulate hypotheses regarding Sparta's culture and its political and religious institutions at the time of the colonists' departure. But there can be no conclusion that might be transformed into an established *communis opinio*. Taras' foundation story is full of hints for understanding how ancient people pictured both the colonial phenomenon and the relationship between metropolis and colony. However, the narratives only give us rather general information about the Spartan society at the relevant time.

After having insisted so much upon the limitations of the evidence at hand, I feel that it is not over-confident to remember certain deductions that appear more solid and more meaningful. Under this heading I would list the role of Dionysus and wine consumption in Spartan society in the eighth century, the connection between the conquest of the two cities' territories and the cult of Apollo Hyacinthus, and the relationship that we can postulate between the ousting of the Partheniae, the conquest of Messenia, the Great Rhetra and the definition of the civic body. We can hope that further investigation and discoveries concerning Taras will continue to advance our understanding of the archaic society of Sparta.

Notes

[1] Cf. Wuilleumier 1939, 229 ff.; Lomas 1993, 13 ff.

[2] Pfeiffer 1949, 419 f.

[3] Cf. below.

[4] Stibbe 1975; Nafissi 1991, 273–6. On Cnidus and its Spartan origins cf. Malkin 1997, 35.

[5] Cf. below.

[6] Graham 1983, 3, notes how difficult it is to follow the relationship between a colony and its metropolis over the years. Cf. Seibert 1963, 99–103.

[7] Cf. e.g. the Naupactus foundation decree (Meiggs-Lewis, no. 20); the Brea decree (*IG* I^3 46 = Meiggs-Lewis, no. 49); the Miletus–Olbia decree (Tod II, no. 195 = Schmitt 1969, no. 408) and the Locrian decree which was read by Timaeus (*FGrH* 566 F 12).

[8] *Ktisis* of Heraclea: Antiochus *FGrH* 555 F 11; Diod. 12.36.4. Political changes in Thurii: Diod. 12.35.1–3.

[9] Cf. below.

[10] Thuc. 8.91.2 with Meiggs-Lewis, no. 82.

[11] On the importance of the relationship between mother city and colony on the occasion of Archidamos' expedition cf. Diod., 16.62.4 f. Graham (1983, 145 f.) is very cautious here, but his parallel with the provision of the Syracusan decree in honour of Timoleon, to use a Corinthian general in future foreign wars (Plut. *Tim.* 38.4), is certainly apt. Diodorus (19.70.8), explicitly attributes the influence that Acrotatus had on the Tarentines to the *syngeneia* bonds. On Taras and the *condottieri* see now Urso 1998.

[12] Musti 1995, p. 358.

[13] Stob. *Ecl.* 4.1.138, p. 82 f. Hense = Thesleff 1965, 34. Date: Mele 1981, 73.

[14] Taras' calendar is totally unknown to us. Of Heraclea we only know the months of Panamos and Apellaios; they may have been in the Spartan calendar as well, but there is no proof: cf. Samuel 1980, 93, 138.

[15] I list just the most important sources.

Athena: Paus. 3.12.5; Leonidas XCI Gow-Page (*Anth.Pal.* VI 120) and coins; cf. Lippolis-Garraffo-Nafissi 1995, especially 140–1 ('excepting Heracles, Athena is the deity most frequently depicted on Tarentine coinage, from the second half of the fourth century BC onwards'); 177–8; 312; 333.

Apollo Hyacinthus and Apollo Carneus: Polyb. 8.28.2–4; silver diobols, Ravel 1947, no. 1357 and the well-known crater from Ceglie del Campo, Taranto, Museo Archeologico Nazionale 8269; cf. Lippolis-Garraffo-Nafissi 1995, 139; 173 f.; on the crater from Ceglie: Trendall 1967, 55; D'Amicis 1991, 132–7.

Dioscuri, depicted as horsemen on votive *pinakes* and coins; *IG* XIV 2406, 108; cf. Lippolis-Garraffo-Nafissi 1995, 55 f., 91, 114 f., 117 f., 142, 226–8, fig. XIV, XXIII, 1.

Gaia: votive inscriptions; Lippolis-Garraffo-Nafissi 1995, 188–90; fig. LVII 1–2.

Aphrodite Basilis: Hesych. s.v. βασιλίνδα; Jeffery 1990, 463, fig. 78; cf. Lippolis-Garraffo-Nafissi 1995, 170–2, 178 f. (also for the text of the inscription) and Osanna 1990 (for the evidence on her cult in Sparta: it is worth noting that this evidence had been overlooked, and is correctly brought out through the colonial case).

Artemis Corythalia: Hesych. s.v. κυριττοί; cf. Lippolis-Garraffo-Nafissi 1995, 203.

Artemis Agrotera: *SEG* XXXVIII 1015, perhaps also 1014; cf. Lippolis-Garraffo-Nafissi 1995, 174–7 and now also Aversa 1995, who has shown that the so-called dedication to Artemide Hagratera (*sic*) is in reality an altar; as to *SEG* XXXVIII 1014, his considerations do not change my opinion that the objects in the list relate mainly to a sacrificial context.

[16] On the subject of toponomastic references and cult derivations, it might be worthwhile to remember the place-name Messapeae in Laconia and the related cult of Zeus Messapeus (the relationship itself is evident and should not be under discussion). It has been considered 'an interesting example of reverse cultural transmission – from a colonized area to the corresponding

Greek metropolis' (Catling-Shipley 1989, 195–7; quotation from 197): but cf. Lombardo 1992, 106–9.

[17] Poseidon, Taras' father: Arist. fr. 590 Rose[3]; Caelius Antipater, *hist.* 35; Paus. X 10, 8; Prob. Verg. *Georg.* 2.197 f.; Serv. *Aen.* 3.551; Serv. *Georg.* 4.125. Coins: Ravel 1947, no. 1; cf. Lippolis-Garraffo-Nafissi, 149 f. I have suggested that the statue of Athena in Sparta, which Pausanias states to be an offering of the colonists, could be connected to the fourth-century relationships between the two cities (Lippolis-Garraffo-Nafissi 1995, 312).

[18] Cf. below. Seibert 1963, 101 n. 1.

[19] Cf. Lippolis-Garraffo-Nafissi 1995, 312.

[20] Bilabel 1920; Hanell 1934, 111 ff.; Sakellariou 1958; Ehrhardt 1983; Loukopoulou 1989, 95–160; cf. Antonetti 1997, 135–44.

[21] Gould 1985, 7 f.

[22] De Juliis 1985, 563 = *SEG* XL 901. There cannot be certainty on the nature of the eponymous officials who probably sign the Tarentine coins, and who are claimed to be ephors on analogy with Heraclea (cf. Kraay 1976, 191 and see the following note).

[23] Besides the Heraclea tables (*IG* XIV 645, I 1, 95; II 1), eponymous ephors date manumission-texts (Ghinatti 1980, 137 ff. = *SEG* XXX 1162–70) and coins (certain through an issue of the age of Pyrrhus, Van Keuren 1994, 84 nr. 109 pl. 11).

[24] Thera: *IG* XII, 3 Suppl. 322, 18; 326, 55; 330 B.1, C.109, C.270; 336.1 (hellenistic age).

Cyrene: Heracl. Lemb., *Exc. Polit.* 18 Dilts = Arist. fr. 611,18 Rose; Ptolemy's diagramma, 5 ephors: *SEG* IX 1, 1. 33; dedication of a *horoscopion*, middle 2nd century BC, 6 ephors (as suggested by Gasperini): Fraser 1956–58, 108–11, no. 3 = *SEG* XVIII 739; dedications: Gasperini 1967, p. 170 f. nos. 23 and perhaps 24.

Laconia (Epidaurus Limera, Boeae, Cotyrta, Cythera, Geronthrae, Gytheum, Pyrrichum, Caenepolis, Oetylus, Cardamyle, Gerenia, Thuriae) see the *index* in *IG* V 1 and furthermore *SEG* XI 922, 13; 923, 28. 33; 948, 3. 13; 949, 5; 974, 25. 34; XXIII 199, 15.

Euesperides: Fraser 1951, 132–43 = *SEG* XVIII 772, 1.

Arsinoe (Taucheira before 246 BC): decree of the 1st century BC, Reynolds 1973–74, 622–30 = *SEG* XXVI 1817, cf. Laronde 1987, 472–8.

[25] Pareti 1920, 125 n. 2, Busolt-Swoboda 1920–6, I 683 f. n. 2; Wuilleumier, 1939, 176–9; Chamoux 1953, 214–16; Kiechle 1963, 95; Huxley 1962, 38 and n. 229; Drews 1983, 80 n. 7; Sherk 1993, pp. 273, 273; Malkin 1994a, 74, 132; Malkin 1997, 31. Ephorate as a sign of Taras' faithfulness to Spartan institutions: cf. also Carlier 1984, 471 n. 658.

[26] The foundation of Thera (*c.* 800: Coldstream 1977, 217, cf. Malkin 1997, 30) certainly took place before the dates proposed by the ancient chronographic tradition for the beginning of the ephorate (754/3 or 753/2, and maybe 768/7; cf. Plut., *Lyc.* 7,1 = Apollod. *FGrH* 244 F 335a); furthermore, even these dates are early compared to what I feel is a probable reconstruction of Sparta's institutional history (Nafissi 1991, 114 ff.).

[27] Besides Polyb. 4.4.2, 31.2 and *IG* V 1,1472,2, see now the treaty with

Lysimachus *SEG* XLI 322,23, cf. *Bull. Ep.* 1995, no. 263. It is worth remembering that the oligarchic Athenian *hetaireiai*, before the official appointment of the Thirty, instituted a college of five ephors (Lys. 12.43 ff., 46, 76). The poetic version of Critias' *Lakedaimoniōn politeia* was surely destined for their reunions at *symposia*. It has been hypothesized that many of their policies were of Spartan inspiration (Whitehead 1982–3, 105 ff.).

[28] Arist. *Pol.* 5.1303a2–6, cf. Hdt 7.170 and Diod. 11.52.1 ff. As for democracy and its models, Moretti's (1970, 34 ff.) discussion remains fundamental; his comparison between Plut. *Quaest. Graecae* 42 and the amendment to the *Rhetra* (Plut. *Lyc.* 6.8) is, however, misleading.

[29] Cf. e.g. the Musae, whose cult was rarely of primary standing in the Greek *poleis,* excepting Thespiae, but was of some importance in Pythagorean theology and political theory and practice. As a matter of fact they were honoured both in Sparta (Paus. 3.17.5; Plut. *Lyc.* 21.7) and in Taras (Polyb. 8.25.11, 27.1). In Sparta their sanctuary was located on the *acropolis*, and their cult had a strong military tone (Plut. *loc. cit.*); in Taras there was a Mouseion by the *agora*: it was probably a recent foundation of Pythagorean leaning, more connected with civic concord (cf. Lippolis-Garraffo-Nafissi 1995, 204–6).

[30] Nafissi 1992; Lippolis-Garraffo-Nafissi 1995, 219 f. for details and sources.

[31] Strabo VI 3.4.

[32] Note that the Galaesus was *also* called Eurotas.

[33] Parker 1989, 99–101. For a different viewpoint, Stibbe 1991, 31 ff.

[34] Cf. e.g. Ael. *VH* XII 30.

[35] Fisher 1989; Nafissi 1991, 173–226; Lavrencic 1993; Fornis-Casillas 1997.

[36] Nafissi forthcoming[2].

[37] On the κρατὴρ Λακωνικός, cf. Stibbe 1989.

[38] On the subject, see now Powell 1998.

[39] Lippolis-Garraffo-Nafissi 1995, 180–8, cf. 38 f.

[40] Antiochus, *FGrH* 555 F 13 (on his foundation story see below); the Diodoran oracle (VIII 21) refers to Satyrion with the enigma of the τράγος (he-goat) who embraces the sea wetting the tip of his beard (image of the promontory where the acropolis was laid and of the harbour of Mar Piccolo): cf. Lippolis-Garraffo-Nafissi 1995, 301. Satyrion is usually identified with the present-day Saturo (e.g. Malkin 1994a, 121 n. 30).

[41] During the Hay-on-Wye conference, I showed a white ground *lēkythos* of the Beldam painter from Eretria, now in the National Museum of Athens (1129 CC 961), depicting Satyrs torturing a black woman (cf. Beazley 1956, 586 f.; Beazley 1971, 293 f.; Carpenter 1989, 139; Torelli 1994). We might take this as the image the Greeks of the second quarter of the fifth century had of the Satyrs' behaviour in a barbarian country. I think we can use it, with some caution, to better understand the sense of the name given to Satyrion, as the place where the colonists were going to have plenty of feasts and unrestrained revelling after their victory over the barbarians.

[42] Cic. *Verr.* 2.4.135.

[43] Iacobone 1988; Lippolis-Garraffo-Nafissi 1995, especially 51–3, 107–21, tables VII–XI.

[44] In the case of the burial customs, precisely with the intra-mural

depositions, these diverging developments gave birth to 'false friends': cf. Lippolis-Garraffo-Nafissi 1995, 303 f.

[45] According to Herodotean usage of the terms *tyrannos* and *basileus* (cf. Ferrill 1978, 385 ff.) he should be a 'traditional' king; for differing opinions see Drews 1983, 36 ff.; Carlier 1984, 471 f.; Cassola 1985, 26 f.; Luraghi 1994, 76 f.

[46] Carlier 1984, 298 ff.

[47] Even though this does not allow for risky speculation, such as the deductions concerning the historical evolution of the mother country based on the *nomima* encountered in colonies founded at different periods (Ehrhardt 1983, 246 ff.: cf. Brillante 1985, 330–6, Graham, 1987, 124–9, as well as the preface to the second edition of Ehrhardt, p. III f.). Ehrhardt seriously deals with the topic of takeover, which he contemplates, but considers a minor factor in institutional relationships between mother city and colony (214–6, 218 f., 238, 249). Cf. already Bilabel 1920, 128.

[48] Cf. Lippolis-Garraffo-Nafissi 1995, 263–90, 292–99, with the *testimonia* on the *ktisis* and the relevant bibliography; Nafissi, forthcoming[1].

[49] Calame 1996, 54.

[50] It is impossible to give an exhaustive bibliography here; I merely recall some important recent works here and in the following note: Sourvinou-Inwood 1974; Veyne 1983; Weiss 1984; Leschhorn 1984; Spawforth-Walker 1986; Malkin 1987, 1994a, 1994b, 1995, 1997; Scheer 1993; Buxton 1994, 182–93; Calame 1996. This part of my paper is in part a reaction to the brilliant and very stimulating paper F. de Polignac gave at the XXXVI Convegno di Studi sulla Magna Grecia, Taranto 1996. Many very useful suggestions on the topic were offered by L. Robert.

[51] Jan Assmann's 'Heisse Erinnerung' (Assmann 1998, 39 sgg.).

[52] Dougherty 1993a, spec. 31–44; Dougherty 1993b; McGlew 1993, 157–73; Ogden 1997, whose systematic reduction of foundation stories to a mere scheme (*loimos* and *pharmakos*) leaves me perplexed.

[53] On the topic of history, myth and politics see Gehrke 1994.

[54] Cf. Graham 1983, p. 7, for the same problem from the viewpoint of a scholar who believes in the kernel of truth of our *ktiseis*.

[55] Cf. Pind. *Paian* 2.28 f.; Hdt. 7.51, 7.22, 8.19, 7.150; Polyb. 12.9.3; Thuc. 1.38.3 (implicit in the verb στέργομαι) Plat. *Leg.* 754a–c; Diod. 10.34.3: παῖδες μὲν οὖν ἀδικούμενοι πρὸς πατέρας καταφεύγουσι, πόλεις δὲ πρὸς τοὺς ἀποικίσαντας δήμους ('children, when they are being ill-treated, turn for aid to their parents, cities turn to the communities who once sent them settling abroad'); Polyb. 21.24.10; *Inschr. Lampsakos* 4.26, cf. Curty 1995, no. 39; *IGR* I no. 861 = *IOSPE* I^2 no. 362 and *IOSPE* I^2 no. 357; *TAM* II no. 174 = Chaniotis 1988, T 19, V 10 cf. Curty 1995, no. 79. On this topic cf., e.g., Robert 1935, 497–9; Robert 1960, 519 f.; Seibert 1963, 76 f.; Musti 1963, 233 n. 15, 236; Werner 1971, 36.

[56] The best treatment of the document is Gawantka's (1975, 98–111); quite pertinent is the Corcyreans' statement: ' πᾶσα ἀποικία εὖ μὲν πάσχουσα τιμᾷ τὴν μητρόπολιν, ἀδικουμένη δὲ ἀλλοτριοῦται· οὐ γὰρ ἐπὶ τῷ δοῦλοι, ἀλλ' ἐπὶ τῷ ὁμοῖοι τοῖς λειπομένοις εἶναι ἐκπέμπονται ' (Thuc. I 34,1: 'every colony honours the mother city when it is well treated, but when it is injured it is made an

enemy; because colonists are not sent out to be slaves, but to be equals to those left behind').

[57] Kern 1900, no. 17.

[58] Herodotus gathers information on the foundation of Thera at Sparta and Thera, for the foundation of Cyrene at Thera and Cyrene (4.145 ff.). As for Locri, Timaeus gets his information from the Epizephyrian Locrian Echecrates and in mainland Locrides (Polyb. 12.9–10).

[59] Nafissi 1991, 43–9. There I have also attempted to demonstrate how the story of the *epeunaktoi*, originally connected with the war of Tyrtaeus, was only later introduced into the tradition on the first Messenian war.

[60] The relevant lines (10–12 in Jacoby's text) have also been otherwise understood (cf., e.g., Leschhorn 1984, 31 and Ogden 1997, 73: Partheniae were 'children born during the absence of the men in the Messenian War'), however on very questionable grounds (humanistic conjecture ὅσοι and the influence of Ephorus' account).

[61] Cf. Lippolis-Garraffo-Nafissi 1995, 299 f. I. Malkin has well perceived the contrast in Antiochus' narrative and envisages his hostility toward the Tarentines as an explanation. He uses this contrast to demonstrate the authenticity of the oracle (Malkin 1994a, 118–21) – a question, however, not at issue here.

[62] As to the relevance of this point for the actual relationships between colony and mother city, recall simply the Epidamnian aristocrats' gaining the support of their mother city by pointing at their ancestors' tombs in Corcyra (Thuc. 1.26.3).

[63] Justin 3.4.8.

[64] For an enlightening account of Antiochus' work on Italy, see Prontera 1992, 109 ff.

[65] Chronology of Ephorus: Momigliano 1935; although the date of Archytas' political activity is now questioned (cf. Urso 1998, 4 n. 16), I do not feel that there are compelling reasons to deviate from the date suggested by his relations with Plato.

[66] As to the identification of Hyacinthus, there is little room for doubt; the question concerning the dolphin-rider is not settled (many favour Taras): I have stated elsewhere my reasons for recognising Phalanthus in this type. See Lippolis-Garraffo-Nafissi 1995, 147–9, 293–8; cf. Caruso 1980, 228 ff.

[67] Cf. in general Dougherty 1994.

[68] Regarding the foundation of Taras and the development of Sparta's society and institutions, there are opposing approaches today: some use details that I find rather questionable, others leave aside the very fact of the *apoikia* (cf. Malkin 1994b and Thommen 1996, 15 f.).

[69] Cf., e.g., Arist. *Pol.* 4.1290b7–14 for Apollonia and Tera; one might also recall the Sybarites' claims at the time of the re-foundation of their city: Diod. 12.11. On Tarentine aristocracy between the 6th and the beginning of the 5th century, see Lippolis 1997, 3–17.

[70] Paus. 10.13.10.

[71] Veyne 1983.

[72] From this point of view, it seems to me, the Partheniae story resembles

the adventures of unintentional murders and the ones of bastard sons characterized as young men of value unjustly mistreated. For the same reasons these two kinds of stories are very important in the relationship between colony and mother city. The case of Tlepolemus, narrated in the *Catalogue of the Ships* (*Iliad* 2.653–70) might indicate, however, that they fulfil the primary need of self-representation (cf. McGlew 1993, 157–73) and that these old narrative patterns (how old depends on opinions on the *Catalogue of the Ships*) acquired new significance in the archaic-classical age, when the relationship between metropolis and colony grew in importance.

[73] Boschung 1994, 177; Neeft 1994, 185 f., 198.

[74] I am not convinced by recent attempts to deny the connection (Parker 1991, 28 ff.).

[75] Cf. Nafissi 1991, 35–81; Malkin 1994b and 1997; on the date of the Great Rhetra see also Liberman 1997, 204–7. Cf. also Musti 1996 and Hans van Wees' paper in this volume.

[76] Corsano 1979, Qviller 1996, de Polignac forthcoming. Lupi 1997, 115–20, also relates the story of the Partheniae to the Spartan system of the age-classes, adducing an impressive parallel, a tradition of the East-African Turkana (cf. Müller-Dempf 1989, 137–9; Müller-Dempf 1994, 80 f.). According to him, a Spartan generational custom declared the children born by fathers under age (thirty years) illegitimate. The narrative represents and paradigmatically founds, in his view, this custom. The former point seems to me well argued, but I am not convinced by the latter one. Relating Taras' foundation story to an exclusively Spartan context puzzles me. Furthermore, Ephorus' version accounts otherwise for the illegitimacy of the Partheniae.

[77] Corsano (1979, 127–9) suggested that Partheniae means 'garçon-fille'. Qviller 1996 connects the name with virginal customs which he supposes in early Spartan history were strictly enforced on the young Spartans under 20. Philippides 1979 argued for a special connection with a goddess *parthenos* or with Hyacinthus: according to him *parthenias* meant 'dedicated to, under the protection of, the *parthenos*'. On the suffix -ιας, see Chantraine 1933, 92–6: it is used for many semantic groups, such as other nicknames (designating 'un personnage par un trait caractéristique') and names of small and despised animals. Since the primary historical facts we have to recover are stories, and not events, I find it a very questionable procedure to replace the explanations given by Ephorus with modern explanations. The former is admittedly late in date, but authoritative if, and in as far as, he depends on the Tarentine tradition.

[78] Recent studies on the story: Goegebeur 1990 and 1994, Dougherty 1992, Ogden 1997, 76 f. For other opinions about the strange case of the lice on 'the bald head', see Goegebeur 1994, 68 n. 23. Removing lice does not mean or imply shearing the hair (as suggested by Ogden 1997, 76).

[79] Cf. Frazer 1898, V 269–70; Goegebeur 1994, 66.

[80] Cf. the saying for the hair shorn to baldness: 'to be shorn to the louse' (Pollux 2.29 and Photius *Lexikon* s.v. πρὸς φθεῖρα κείρασθαι = Eubulus F 31 Kassel-Austin).

[81] Easier, because of the wide diffusion of the folklore motif of weeping and removing lice. We should remember that the presence of women is a very

unusual feature in the *ktiseis*. Goegebeur 1994, 78 f. has also shown the mythological context (Aethra, Oceanus' daughter, is the mother of the weeping Hyadae) which in my view favoured the explanatory insertion of Aethra's character in the story of Phalanthus' lice.

[82] On all this see David 1992, 11–21. See also Ogden 1997, 75–9.

[83] See Arist. fr. 532 Rose; add Sosibius *FGrH* 595 F 25 and the *loci similes* collected by Jacoby, if we accept, as I would, the identification of Apollo Tetracheir with Apollo Hyacinthus: but against it see Kennell 1995, 162 f. For a recent review of the initiatory character of the cult see Pettersson 1992.

[84] They clearly share the mentality of the conquerors, which is founded on the Heracleid and Dorian historical identity of the Spartans. Such an identity was probably already in force before Tyrtaeus first witnessed it (fr. 1[a], 12 ff. Gentili-Prato: cf. Malkin 1994a, 33–43 and *passim*). The idea of the young men surpassing their fathers and ancestors can be devoid of animosity: cf. the well-known τριχορία, Plut. *Lyc.* 21.2–3 with, among others, Sosyb. *FGrH* 595 F 8 and Poll. IV 107.

[85] de Polignac, forthcoming.

[86] Binder 1964, Huys 1995; cf. McGlew 1993, 166 f.

Bibliography

Antonetti, C.

1997 'Megara e le sue colonie: un'unità storico-culturale?', in C. Antonetti, (ed.) *Il dinamismo della colonizzazione greca*, Naples, 135–44.

Assmann, J.

1992 *Das kulturelle Gedächtnis. Schrift, Erinnerung und politische Identität in frühen Hochkulturen*, Munich (Italian trans., Turin 1997).

Aversa, F.

1995 'Contributo agli studi sulle epigrafi arcaiche da Torricella (Taranto)', *Studi di Antichità* 8, 1, 35–54.

Beazley, J.D.

1956 *Attic Black-Figure Vase-Painters*, Oxford.

1971 *Paralipomena. Additions to* Attic Black-Figure Vase Painters *and to* Attic Red-Figure Vase-Painters, 2nd edn, Oxford.

Bilabel, F.

1920 *Die ionische Kolonisation*, *Philologus* Supplb. XIV.1, Leipzig.

Binder, G.

1964 *Die Aussetzung des Königskindes Kyros und Romulus*, Meisenheim a. Glan.

Boschung, D.

1994 'Die archaischen Nekropolen von Tarent', in *Catalogo del Museo Nazionale Archeologico di Taranto* III 1, *Taranto. La necropoli: aspetti e problemi della documentazione archeologica dal VII al I sec. a.C.*, Taranto, 176–82.

Brillante, C.

1985 rev. Ehrhardt 1983, *Rivista di Filologia e d'Istruzione Classica* 113, 330–6.

Busolt, G. and Swoboda, H.
1920–6 *Griechische Staatskunde* I–II^3, Munich.
Buxton, R.
1994 *Imaginary Greece. The contexts of mythology*, Cambridge.
Calame, C.
1996 *Mythe et histoire dans l'antiquité grecque*, Lausanne.
Carlier, P.
1984 *La royauté en Grèce avant Alexandre*, Strasbourg.
Carpenter, Th.H.
1989 Beazley Addenda. Additional references to ABV, ARV2 and *Paralipomena*, 2nd edn, Oxford.
Caruso, T.
1980 'I tipi monetari greci e la loro comune interpretazione', *Archeologia Classica* 32, 229–33.
Cassola, F.
1985 'Erodoto e la tirannide', in F. Broilo (ed.) *Xenia, Scritti in onore di P. Treves* , Rome, 25–35.
Catling, R.W.V. and Shipley, D.G.J.
1989 'Messapian Zeus: an early sixth-century inscribed cup from Lakonia', *Annual of the British School at Athens* 84, 187–200.
Chamoux, F.
1953 *Cyrène sous la monarchie des Battiades*, Paris.
Chaniotis, A.
1988 *Historie und Historiker in den griechischen Inschriften*, Stuttgart.
Chantraine, P.
1933 *La formation des noms en Grec ancien*, Paris.
Coldstream, J.N.
1977 *Geometric Greece*, London.
Corsano, M.
1979 'Sparte et Tarente: le mythe de fondation d'une colonie', *Revue de l'Histoire des Religions* 196, 113–40.
D'Amicis, A.
1991 'Ceglie del Campo, Crateri protoitalioti a figure rosse', in A. D'Amicis-A. Dell'Aglio-E. Lippolis,*Vecchi Scavi. Nuovi restauri*, Catalogo della mostra, Taranto, Taranto, 131–45.
David, E.
1992 'Sparta's social hair', *Eranos* 90, 11–21.
De Juliis, E.M.
1985 *L'attività archeologica in Puglia nel 1984*, in *Magna Grecia Epiro e Macedonia*, Atti del XXIV Convegno di Studi sulla Magna Grecia (Taranto 1984), Taranto, 559–81.
de Polignac, F.
forthcoming 'Mythes et modèles culturels de la colonisation grecque archaïque', in *Mito e storia in Magna Grecia*, Atti del XXXVI Convegno di Studi sulla Magna Grecia (Taranto 1996).
Dittenberger, W.
1915–1924 *Sylloge Inscriptionum Graecarum*, 3rd edn, Leipzig.

Dougherty, C.
1992 'When rain falls from the clear blue sky: riddles and colonization oracles', in *Classical Antiquity* 11, 28–44.
1993a *The Poetics of Colonization: from city to text in archaic Greece*, New York.
1993b 'It's a murder to found a colony', in C. Dougherty-L. Kurke (eds) *Cultural Poetics in Archaic Greece*, Cambridge, 178–98.
1994 'Archaic Greek foundation poetry, questions of genre and occasion', *Journal of Hellenic Studies* 114, 35–46.

Drews,R.
1983 *Basileus: the evidence for kingship in Geometric Greece*New Haven.

Ehrhardt, N.
1983 *Milet und seine Kolonien. Vergleichende Untersuchung der kultischen und politischen Einrichtungen*, Frankfurt am Mein (2. Aufl., Frankfurt am Mein 1988).

Ferrill, A.
1978 'Herodotus on tyranny', *Historia* 27, 385–98.

Fisher, N.R.E.
1989 'Drink, hybris and the promotion of harmony in classical Sparta', in A. Powell (ed.) *Classical Sparta*, London, 26–50.

Fornis, C. and Casillas, J.M.
1997 'An appreciation of the social function of the Spartan *syssitia*', *The Ancient History Bulletin* 11, 37–46.

Fraser, P.M.
1956–58 'Inscriptions from Cyrene', *Berytus* 12, 101–28.

Frazer, J.G
1898 *Pausanias's Description of Greece* I–VI, London.

Gasperini, L.
1967 'Le epigrafi', in S. Stucchi (ed.) *Cirene 1957–1966. Un decennio di attività della missione archeologica italiana a Cirene*, Quaderni dell' istituto italiano di cultura di Tripoli, Tripoli, 3, 165–80.

Gawantka, W.
Isopolitie. Ein Beitrag zur Geschichte der zwischenstaatlichen Beziehungen in der griechischen Antiken, Munich.

Gehrke, H.-J.
1994 'Mythos, Geschichte, Politik – antik und modern'*Saeculum* 45, 239–64.

Ghinatti, F.
1980 'Nuovi efori in epigrafi di Eraclea Lucana', in F. Krinzinger, B. Otto, E. Walde-Psenner (eds.) *Forschungen und Funde, Festschrift B. Neutsch*, Innsbruck, 137–43.

Goegebeur, W.
1990 'Myskellos, Aithra et Phalanthos: concordance entre les traditions de fondation de Tarente et de Crotone?', in R. De Smet, H. Melaerts, C. Saerens (eds.) *Studia varia Bruxellensia* II, Leuven, 83–99.

Goegebeur, W.
1994 'Aithra et Phalanthos: poux et pleurs, pluie et ciel bleu', in H. Melaerts, R. De Smet, C. Saerens (eds.) *Studia varia Bruxellensia* III, Leuven, 63–81.

Gould, J.
1985 'On making sense of Greek religion', in P.E. Easterling and J.V. Muir (eds.) *Greek Religion and Society*, Cambridge, 1–33.

Graham, A.J.
1983 *Colony and Mother City in Ancient Greece*, 2nd edn, Chicago. (1st edn Manchester 1964.)
1987 Rev. Ehrhardt 1983, *Gnomon* 59, 124–9.
1992 'Abdera and Teos', *Journal of Hellenic Studies* 112, 44–73.

Hanell, K.
1934 *Megarische Studien*, Lund.

Hodkinson, S.
1997 L.G. Mitchell and P.J. Rhodes (eds.) *The Development of the Polis in Archaic Greece*, London, 83–102.

Huxley, G.L.
1962 *Early Sparta*, London.

Huys, M.
1995 *The Tale of the Hero who was exposed at Birth in Euripidean Tragedy. A study of motifs*, Leuven.

Iacobone, C.
1988 *Le stipi votive di Taranto*, Rome.

Jeffery, L.H.
1990 *The Local Scripts of Archaic Greece*, 2nd edn, rev. suppl. A.W. Johnston, Oxford.

Kennel, N.M.
1995 *The Gymnasium of Virtue. Education and culture in ancient Sparta*, Chapel Hill and London.

Kern, O.
1900 *Die Inschriften von Magnesia am Maeander*, Berlin.

Kiechle, F.
1963 *Lakonien und Sparta. Untersuchungen zur ethnischen Struktur und zur politischen Entwicklung Lakoniens und Spartas bis zum Ende der archaischen Zeit*, Munich.

Kraay, C.M.
1976 *Archaic and Classical Greek Coins*, 1976.

Laronde, A.
1987 *Cyrène et la Libye hellénistique*, Paris 1987.

Lavrencic, M.
1993 *Spartanische Küche. Das Gemeinschaftsmal der Männer in Sparta*, Vienna.

Leschhorn, W.
1984 *'Gründer der Stadt.' Studien zu einem politisch-religiösen Phänomen der griechischen Geschichte*, *Palingenesia* XX, Stuttgart.

Liberman, G.
1997 'Plutarque et la "Grande Rhétra" ', *Athenaeum* 65, 204–7.

Lippolis, E., Garraffo, S. and Nafissi, M.
1995 *Taranto, Culti Greci in Occidente* I, Taranto.

Lippolis, E.
1997 'Aristocrazia e società in età arcaica', in *Catalogo del Museo Nazionale archeologico di Taranto,* I, 3 *Atleti e guerrieri. Tradizioni aristocratiche a Taranto tra VI e V sec. a.C.*, Taranto, 3–17.

Lomas, K.
1993 *Rome and the Western Greeks 350 BC – AD 200*, London.

Lombardo, M.
1992 'I Messapi: aspetti della problematica storica', in *I Messapi*, Atti XXX Convegno Studi Magna Grecia, Taranto 1991, 35–109.

Loukopoulou, L.D.
1989 *Contribution à l'histoire de la Thrace propontique*, Athens.

Lupi, M.
1997 *L'ordine delle generazioni. Classi di età e costumi matrimoniali a Sparta.* Doctoral thesis, Naples.

Luraghi, N.
1994 *Tirannidi arcaiche in Sicilia e Magna Grecia*, Florence.

Malkin, I.
1987 *Religion and Colonization in Ancient Greece*, Leiden.
1994a *Myth and Territory in the Spartan Mediterranean*, Cambridge.
1994b 'Inside and Outside: colonization and the formation of the mother city', *Annali dell'Istituto universitario orientale di Napoli. Seminario di studi del mondo classico. Sezione di archeologia e storia antica (Apoikia. Studi in onore di G. Buchner)*, n.s. 1, 1–9.
1997 'Categories of early Greek colonization: the case of the Dorian Aegean', in C. Antonetti (ed.) *Il dinamismo della colonizzazione greca*, Atti tavola rotonda Venezia 10–11 Nov. 95, Naples, 25–38.

McGlew, J.F.
1993 *Tyranny and Political Culture in Ancient Greece*, Ithaca.

Meiggs, R. and Lewis, D. (eds.)
1988 *A Selection of Greek Historical Inscriptions*, 2nd edn, Oxford.

Mele, A.
1981 'Il pitagorismo e le popolazioni anelleniche d'Italia', *Annali dell' Istituto universitario orientale di Napoli. Seminario di studi del mondo classico. Sezione di archeologia e storia antica* 3, 61–96.

Momigliano, A.
1935 'La storia di Eforo e le Elleniche di Teopompo', *Rivista di Filologia e d'Istruzione Classica* n.s. 13, 180–204 = in *Quinto contributo alla storia degli studi classici e del mondo antico*,II, Rome 1975, 683–706.

Moretti, L.
1971 'Problemi di storia tarantina', in *Taranto nella civiltà della Magna Grecia*, Atti Taranto X, 1970, Napoli, 21–65.

Müller-Dempf, H.K.
1989 *Changing Generations: Dynamics of generation and age-sets in south-eastern Sudan (Toposa) and north-western Kenya (Turkana)*, Saarbrücken.
1994 'Chevauchement de l'âge et de la génération en Afrique orientale (Toposa et Turkana)', in C. Attias-Donfut and L. Rosemayr, *Viellir en Afrique*, Paris, 69–86.

Musti, D.
1963 'Sull'idea di συγγένεια in iscrizioni greche', *Annali della Scuola Normale Superiore di Pisa, Cl. di lettere e filosofia* s. II, 32, 224–39.
1995 *Città di Magna Grecia tra Italici e Roma,* in *L'incidenza dell'antico, Studi in memoria di E. Lepore*, Naples.
1996 *Regole politiche a Sparta: Tirteo e la* Grande Rhetra, *Rivista di Filologia e d'Istruzione Classica* 124, 257–81.
Nafissi, M.
1991 *La nascita del* kosmos, Napoli.
forthcoming[1] 'Rapporti fra le poleis e dinamiche interne nelle tradizioni mitico-storiche: Siri-Eraclea e Taranto', in *Mito e storia in Magna Grecia*, XXXVI Convegno di Studi sulla Magna Grecia (Taranto 1996).
forthcoming[2] 'I sissizi spartani', in A. Perez Jimenez (ed.)*Dieta Mediterránea. Comidas y habitos alimenticios desde la Antigüedad al Renacimiento,* X curso-seminario de la Universidad de Málaga, septiembre 1997.
Neeft, C.W.
1994 'Tarantine graves containing Corinthian pottery', in *Catalogo del Museo Nazionale Archeologico di Taranto* III 1, *Taranto. La necropoli: aspetti e problemi della documentazione archeologica dal VII al I sec. a.C.*, Taranto, 184–237.
Ogden, D.
1997 *The Crooked Kings of Ancient Greece*, London.
Osanna, M.
1990 'Sui culti arcaici di Sparta e Taranto: Afrodite Basilis', *La Parola del Passato* 45, 81–94.
Pareti, F.
1920 *Storia di Sparta arcaica* I, Firenze.
Parke, H.W. and Wormell, D.E.W.
1956 *The Delphic Oracle*, 2nd edn, Oxford.
Parker, R.
1988 'Demeter, Dionysos and the Spartan Pantheon', in R. Hägg, N. Marinatos, G.C. Nordquist (eds.)*Early Greek Cult Practice,* Stockholm, 99–103.
Parker, V.
1991 'The Dates of the Messenian Wars', *Chiron* 21, 25–47.
Pettersson, M.
1992 *Cults of Apollo at Sparta*, Stockholm.
Pfeiffer, R.
1949 *Callimachus* I, Oxford.
Philippides, M.
1979 'The Partheniai and the foundation of Taras'*Ancient World* 2.3, 79–82.
Powell, A.
1998 'Sixth-century Lakonian vase-painting. Continuities and discontinuities with the 'Lykourgan' ethos', in N. Fisher and H. van Wees (eds.) *Archaic Greece. New approaches and new evidence,* London, 119–46.

Prontera, F.
1992 'Antioco di Siracusa e la preistoria dell'idea etnico-geografica di Italia', *Geographia Antiqua* 1, 109–35.

Qviller, B.
1996 'Reconstructing the Spartan Partheniai. Many guesses and a few facts', *Symbolae Osloenses* 71, 1996, 34–41.

Ravel, O.E.
1947 *Descriptive Catalogue of the Collection of Tarentine Coins formed by M.P. Vlasto*, London.

Reynolds, J.M.
1973–74 'A civic decree from Tocra in Cyrenaica', *Archeologia Classica* 25–26, 622–30.

Robert, L.
1935 'Inscription hellénistique de Dalmatie', *Bulletin de Correspondance Hellénique* 59, 489–513 = *Opera Minora Selecta* I, Amsterdam 1969, pp. 302–26.
1960 'Inscription hellénistique de Dalmatie', in *Hellenica XI–XII*, Paris, 505–41.

Sakellariou, M.
1958 *La migration grecque en Ionie*, Athènes.

Samuel, A.E.
1972 *Greek and Roman Chronology. Calendars and years in classical antiquity*, Munich.

Schmitt, H.H.
1969 *Die Verträge der griechisch-römischen Welt von 338 bis 200 v. Chr.*, Munich.

Seibert, J.
1963 *Metropolis und Apoikie. Historische Beiträge zur Geschichte ihrer gegenseitigen Beziehungen*, Diss. Würzburg.

Sherk, R.K.
1993 'The eponymous officials of Greek cities V',*Zeitschrift für Papyrologie und Epigraphik* 96, 267–95

Sourvinou-Inwood, C.
1974 'The votum of 477/6 and the foundation legend of Locri Epizephyrii', *Classical Quarterly* n.s. 24, 186–98.

Spawforth, A.J. and Walker, S.
1986 'The world of the Panhellenion. II. Three Dorian cities',*Journal of Roman Studies* 76, 88–105.

Stibbe, C.M.
1975 'Sparta und Tarent',*Mededeelingen van het Nederlandsch historischInstitut te Rome* 37, 27–46.
1989 *Laconian Mixing Bowls*, Amsterdam.
1991 'Dionysos in Sparta', *Bulletin Antieke Beschaving* 66, 1–44.

Thesleff, H.
1965 *The Pythagorean Texts of the Hellenistic Period*, Åbo.

Thommen, L.
1996 *Lakedaimonion Politeia*, Stuttgart.

Tod, M.N. (ed.)
1946 *A Selection of Greek Historical Inscriptions* I–II, 2nd edn, Oxford.
Torelli, M.
1994 'L'immaginario greco dell'oltremare. La lekythos eponima del Pittore della Megera, Pausania I 23,5–6 e Pitecusa', *Annali dell' Istituto universitario orientale di Napoli. Seminario di studi del mondo classico. Sezione di archeologia e storia antica* (*Apoikia, Scritti in onore di G. Buchner*) n.s. 1, 117–25.
Trendall, A.D.
1967 *The Red-Figured Vases of Lucania, Campania and Sicily*, Oxford.
Urso, G.
1998 *Taranto e gli* xenikoi strategoi, Rome.
Van Keuren, F.
1994 *The Coinage of Heraclea Lucaniae*, Rome.
Veyne, P.
1983 *Les Grecs ont-ils cru à leurs mythes?*, Paris.
Weiss, P.
1984 'Lebendiger Mythos, Gründerheroen und städtische Gründungstraditionen im griechisch-römischen Osten' *Würzburger Jahrbücher für die Altertumswissenschaft* 10, 180–208.
Werner, R.R.
1971 'Probleme der Rechtsbeziehungen zwischen Metropolis und Apoikie', *Chiron* 1, 19–73.
Whitehead, E.
1982–3 'Sparta and the Thirty Tyrants', *Ancient Society* 13/14, 105–130.
Wuilleumier, P.
1939 *Tarente des origines à la conquête romaine*, Paris.

Chapter 10

OLYMPIAD CHRONOGRAPHY AND 'EARLY' SPARTAN HISTORY

P.-J. Shaw

If we accept the absolute dating conventionally assigned to archaic Greek history, we are committed to accepting constituents of it that should, and sometimes do, strain our credulity. Some, such as conflicting dates for Lykourgos or Pheidon of Argos, are familiar; others are less so because they lie dormant in the sources – sources which, nonetheless, provide the basis of this absolute chronology, often in the form of numbered Olympiads. For example, according to Phlegon of Tralles and Eusebius, respectively, a philosopher named Thales of Miletos flourished during Olympiads 7 and 8 (*752–745* BC).[1] According to Eusebius, another philosopher named Thales of Miletos flourished in Olympiads 48 – 50 (*588–577* BC). The 'earlier' Thales was (also according to Phlegon) an exact contemporary of the first Olympic victor to be crowned with wild olive – the Messenian *Daikles*. Although the fact that Pheidon of Argos is also assigned to each of these periods has prompted historians to conclude that there must have been two Pheidons, no-one would seriously believe that there had been two philosophers called Thales of Miletos, living 170 years apart, nor yet that *the* Thales was active during the eighth century BC.[2] Thus Phlegon's testimony confronts us with a synchronism between Thales and a Messenian Olympic victor – *whereas conventional chronology sets the Lakedaimonians' subjugation of the Messenian state at least a century earlier than the accepted date for Thales.*

While the cases of Pheidon and Lykourgos receive scholarly attention from time to time, those of Thales and many others are seldom noticed by any but chronographers. Those that *are* detected are either interpreted at face value, if they are sufficiently remote not to disrupt conventional chronology, or are attributed to error or conflation, if they conflict with the more recent sequence derived from continuous written record. Most historians can live with the chronological discrepancies present in Pausanias' account of the Messenian wars, but if these were to be found in a more 'recent' context they might be judged unacceptably grave and numerous. This begs two questions. How do we reach the definition 'remote' or 'recent'? Such definitions depend on the absolute 'dates' assigned to given events, but the way in which such 'dates' have been established is seldom examined. How do we identify 'error'? It is only when we are certain of the validity of a chronological model that we are justified in classifying as 'mistaken' or 'anomalous', statements from ancient authors that appear not to fit that model. For the chronology of archaic Greece, we can claim no such certainty.

The title of this paper signals an attempt to examine ways in which Olympiad chronography has influenced the historical model for early Sparta and the Peloponnese. The scope is vast, and this paper must be short. The first part is devoted to presenting some results of an investigation of Olympiad chronography prompted by chronological discrepancies occurring in Pausanias' account of the Messenian wars; these results provide serious grounds for a radical revision not only of the chronology of those wars but also of the way in which numbered Olympiads are assigned chronological values. The second part consists of a test-case, in which Pausanias' account of, and Olympiad notice for, an event outside his Messenian narrative – the Battle of Hysiai – is re-examined in the light of my conclusions about Olympiad reckoning, and a proposal made, primarily on chronographic grounds, that the date of this battle should also be radically revised.

First, though, I appeal for the reader's patience. Examining chronology involves working at right-angles to everyone else, cutting across every field of ancient history. Since the system of Olympiad reckoning was planted deep in the soil of Greek chronology, during hellenistic antiquity, it follows that to question chronology based on that system of reckoning will provoke objections in almost every one of those fields. For example, the poets are crucial to the understanding of archaic Greece, as Rosalind Thomas has rightly stressed,[3] but the conventional dates of many of them are derived from numbered Olympiads, often recorded in late sources such as Eusebius' *Chronicle*, or the *Suda*. Therefore, if those Olympiads are called in question, not only do the poets' dates come under fire, but the value of the testimony their poetry contains, at least for the purposes of chronology, can only be realised if absolute dates can be established for those poets independently of those Olympiads. Problems such as these should surely not preclude the questioning of chronology, if it appears that there are otherwise good grounds for it; but since the problems *are* legion, they cannot all be tackled at once. Of those identified in this paper, but which lie outside its scope, most can be no more than acknowledged for the time being; some are already the subjects of further study.

Olympiad discrepancies

There is a well-known discrepancy in the closing section of Pausanias' narrative of the Second Messenian War. Following the fall of Hira, ostensibly two years after Hysiai, in the second year of the 28th Olympiad, many of the Messenians fled to Anaxilas, tyrant of Rhegion, at his invitation, and during the subsequent Olympiad (29) they assisted Anaxilas in the conquest of Zankle which was thereafter named Messena-on-the-Strait.[4] By conventional reckoning, then, Hira fell in 667 BC and Zankle was conquered by Anaxilas in the period 664–661BC.

Herodotos and Thucydides apparently give a much later date for Anaxilas' conquest, however. Herodotos sets Anaxilas' dealings with Zankle after the fall of Miletos and refers to the change of name in his account of Kadmos, whom Gelon later sent to Delphi in the year of Salamis. Thucydides records that Samians and Ionians, having fled from the Persians, seized Zankle and were themselves expelled shortly afterwards by Anaxilas, who colonised the city with mixed races, and named it 'Messena', after his own homeland. Thus the *terminus post quem* for Anaxilas' conquest is provided by the Ionian revolt, an event which would be assigned to the period of Olympiad 70 (*500–497* BC).[5]

In 1946, E.S. Robinson combined numismatic evidence with Thucydides' statement – that Samians had settled in Zankle before being expelled by Anaxilas – to establish a date for the conquest. He showed that, in Zankle, there had been five annual issues of Samian coinage, of Euboic-Attic weight, starting in *494/3* BC; these had been followed by issues of Anaxilas' own coinage, of Euboic-Khalkidic weight; thus Robinson dated Anaxilas' conquest of Zankle to *489* BC (the period of Olympiad 72). This is the date for the conquest still accepted by scholars.[6] Lack of space precludes discussion here of the responses of historians faced with the anomalous Olympiad for Anaxilas' conquest; however, the theory that there was a Messenian revolt in progress at the period of Marathon needs no rehearsing in a volume devoted to the study of Sparta.[7]

Historians rightly advocate cautious treatment of numbered Olympiads assigned to events before the mid-fifth century BC.[8] Here is such a one, in which there resides a discrepancy of about 170 years. To invert the usual procedure whereby the Olympiad number dictates the 'date' of the event, so that – instead – the event dictates the 'date' to be expressed by the number, might be judged over-reaction if Pausanias' notice for Olympiad 29 contained no more than one discrepancy. There is reason, however, to suspect the presence of others. In his notice for the conquest of Zankle Pausanias includes the name of the *stade* victor of Olympiad 29, the Lakonian Chionis. Chionis may have won at four consecutive festivals, Olympiads 28 to 31, although Pausanias records only the first three (the third appears in the context of the Lakedaimonians' capture of Phigalia).[9] When writing the Messenian narrative Pausanias appears not to have noticed a discrepancy between the date suggested by the Olympiad numeral '29' and the 'date' of Anaxilas' conquest. When he reached Olympia, however, and was confronted by the Olympiads recorded for Chionis' victories – 28–30 – he scoffed at the naïveté of those who informed him about Chionis' dedication. The first thing they told him was that Chionis had made the dedication himself – yet the accompanying inscription mentioned the fact that the Race in Armour *had not yet been instituted* and since the Eleans had only instituted it in Olympiad 65 (*520* BC), how could Chionis, victor in Olympiads 28–31, have known about it?[10] Pausanias thought his informants' second statement an even better joke; they said that the statue was a portrait – yet it was made by Myron of Athens. Myron was active in the period following the Persian wars; although Pausanias did not include an Olympiad 'date' for him, he clearly had a reason to think that Myron and Chionis were separated by too great an interval of time for the one to have made a portrait of the other.

Why did Pausanias reject this information about Chionis when, in the Messenian narrative, he saw nothing anomalous in the synchronising of Chionis' Olympic victory with Anaxilas' conquest of Zankle? In a recent discussion of Pausanias' handling of the past, Arafat has suggested that he probably used handbooks about painters and sculptors, whose *akmai* may have been assigned to Olympiads – as they were by the Elder Pliny.[11] Pausanias may have had such a handbook with him at Olympia, and at Olympia he had also acquired information about when the Race in Armour had been instituted. When discussing Chionis at Olympia, he appears not to have connected him with the Messenian reference to Anaxilas' conquest, nor does he mention the discrepancy in his other allusions to Chionis – the description of the athlete's statue in Sparta, and the Olympiad notice for the fall of Phigalia.[12] It was only when Pausanias, who assumed only one system of Olympiad reckoning, was confronted by the *numerical* conflict between the Olympiads assigned respectively to Chionis, to the Race in Armour, and to Myron, that he was driven to conclude that someone was mistaken about Chionis' dedication.

There may be another reason for Pausanias's failure to perceive anything anomalous in the Olympiad number '29' for Anaxilas' conquest. The next Messenian event in his narrative – the revolt that followed the great earthquake and culminated in the resettlement of Messenians at Naupaktos – was assigned by him to the Olympiad when Xenophon of Korinth won the *stade*, and Archimedes was archon in Athens. In the manuscript the number is 'twenty nine', but it was emended to 'seventy nine' (*464* BC) by Meursius a century after the printing of the *editio princeps* of 'Pausanias' in 1516. This *editio princeps* was made from apographs derived from the only manuscript of Pausanias to survive the Middle Ages – the Niccoli *codex*. The emendation was probably made on the grounds that Diodoros set the victory of Xenophon of Korinth in Olympiad 79, although he recorded a different name for the archon (Archedemides) and assigned the earthquake and revolt to Olympiad 77/4 (*469* BC).[13] It is rarely acknowledged in editions of Pausanias, and in six volumes of commentary Frazer does not mention it, but if the number 'twenty nine' had been allowed to stand, scholars would have encountered an interval of only one Olympiad – rather than 51 – between the fall of Hira (Ol. 28) and the great earthquake (Ol. 29). They might then have formed very different conclusions about the chronology of the Messenian wars, and might seriously have wondered whether there existed more than one formula for assigning a 'date' to a numbered Olympiad.

The presence, in this notice of Olympiad 29, of three traditions – that Anaxilas conquered Zankle, that an allusion to the Olympic Race in Armour was made in the lifetime of the victor of Olympiad 29, and that that victor was a contemporary of Myron of Athens – traditions which are mutually compatible, chronologically, and only rendered anomalous by the chronological value of the Olympiad numeral, led me to conduct the following experiment. If the dates of Anaxilas' conquest and the details concerning Chionis' dedication were allowed to govern the date of Chionis' second victory, rather than *vice versa*, then Olympiad '29' might be interpreted as the period in which Anaxilas' conquest was effected, a period usually designated Olympiad '72' i.e. *492–89* BC. A re-calibration, from this *datum*, of Olympiad 'dates' for events in Pausanias' Messenian narrative yields some interesting results (see Chart, pp. 280–1). The central column does double duty: (1) as conventional dates for events in the right-hand column

(Olympiads 44 onward), and (2) as dates re-calibrated from the *datum* of Anaxilas' conquest Ol. 29/72, for events in the left-hand column (Olympiads 1–43). I accept Mosshammer's argument that the source for the Olympiad notices of the first Messenian war was not Apollodoros but Sosibios,[14] and since Pausanias rationalises the chronological sequence of his own narrative and uses, throughout, a particular chronographic formula – one which he also uses for Hysiai – I treat his narrative of the two wars as a whole.

Working forwards, briefly, from *489* BC: Phigalia, to whose king, Tharyx, the Messenian hero Aristomenes gave his sister in marriage, would fall to the Lakedaimonians in *487* BC, a few years after the battle of Sepeia; an exodus of Messenians from Lakedaimon, set by Eusebius in year 4 of Olympiad 35, would occur in *465* BC.[15] Working backwards: Hira would fall in *495* BC, approximately the period to which Jeffery assigned the Lakedaimonian dedication made at Olympia to mark victory over the Messenians.[16] The institution of the *Gymnopaidiai* in Lakedaimon, dated by Eusebius, probably from Sosibios, would occur sometime between *498* and *493* BC (see Appendix).[17] Olympiad 27, treated in detail below, would fall in *500* BC, and thus Hysiai in *497* BC; the Second Messenian War would break out in *513* BC.[18]

The First Messenian war would end in *551* BC; according to each chronology, an 'Anaxandridas' would be king in Sparta. This revision might reconcile conflicting traditions about the institution of the Ephorate.[19] *550* BC is roughly the period of Chilon and of the Lakonian bronzesmith Gitiades, credited with casting the two older tripods raised at Amyklai to mark victory over the Messenians.[20] Herodotos records how at this time Kroisos learnt that the Lakedaimonians, who had been victorious in *all their wars* except those waged against the Tegeates, had now *recovered from grave misfortunes*.[21]

Outside Pausanias' Messenian narrative, Sosibios supplies, through Eusebius, a further Olympiad 'date', for a war between Lakedaimonians and Argives over Thyrea, which he assigns to the 2nd year of Olympiad 15; recalibrated, this becomes *547* BC, the conventional period of a war between Lakedaimonians and Argives over Thyrea: Herodotos' Battle of the Champions.[22] Plutarch has been thought mistaken in ascribing to the Agiad King Polydoros a long comment about this battle; in Pausanias' narrative, Polydoros was alive at the end of the First Messenian War. Returning to Pausanias' Messenian narrative, Ampheia was captured in the 3rd year of Olympiad 9; this would become *570* BC. Hostilities opened when the Eleans held their 4th Games, *c. 592* BC.[23]

Between Olympiads 4 and 9, in the 2nd year of Olympiad 8, Eusebius enters the notice to which I referred at the beginning of this paper: *Thales Milesius physicus philosophicus agnoscitur.* The *akme* of Thales is usually associated with the archonship, in Athens, of Damasias, whose name is scattered through the early archon-list, though not at any period conventionally reckoned the 8th Olympiad. 21½ Olympiads before Anaxilas' conquest, however, would set him in *575* BC. Thales' prediction of the eclipse that ended a war involving Alyattes, is set in the 4th year of Ol. 48 (*585* BC), and Eusebius has an entry for him in the 3rd year of Olympiad 49, (*582* BC) and for the recognition of the Seven Sages (of whom Thales was one) in the 2nd year of Olympiad 50 (*579* BC). Since Phlegon of Tralles stated that Thales was already known by Olympiad 7, he may be Eusebius' source for this ascription to Olympiad 8, and it was Phlegon, a crucial source for Olympic history and Olympiad notices, who ascribed to Iphitos the introduction of the crown of wild olive, also in the 7th Olympiad, when Daikles the Messenian was victor.[24] These first 'crowned', or stephanitic, Olympic Games would, according to Phlegon's chronography and to my proposed revision, be contemporary also with the first stephanitic *Pythian* games (*582* BC), and with the appointment in Olympiad 50 (*580* BC) of two Elean *Hellēnodikai* whose names, according to Phlegon, were inscribed on a *diskos*.[25] Pausanias assigns to Olympiad 8 the Olympic *coup* of Pheidon of Argos who, in the Herodotean sequence, was contemporary with Thales.[26] Unlike Pheidon, though, Thales is too well-documented an historical figure to be awarded a *Doppelgänger* 170 years earlier than himself; perhaps this is why even Mosshammer offers no comment on this Eusebian entry for him.

This is not the proper occasion for discussion of how these apparent anomalies may have been generated; in any case the problem is far more complex than that of a single source of discrepancy requiring simple re-calibration. But they prompt reflection on three sobering points. (a) The Olympiad system consists of disinterested numbers and thus acts like an algebraic expression of the tradition to which it was applied – often *post eventum* – by chronographers whose sources may themselves have been innocent of the instinct for absolute chronology. (b) Olympiad numbers are, even so, always interpreted by modern scholars at face value and – being numbers – fall into sequence by themselves. Therefore (c), once such a number – whatever its origin – is placed in sequence, anything anomalous about it will seem to vanish and may only be re-exposed if it conflicts with other evidence associated with that Olympiad notice. As a rule, however, when this

CHART showing effects of re-calibrating Olympiads from datum: Ol. 29 = 492–89 BC (Anaxilas) until mid-fifth century BC/Ol. 80. The central column does double duty: (1) as conventional dates for events in the right-hand column (Olympiads 44 onward), and (2) as re-calibrated dates for events in the left-hand column (Olympiads 1–43).

BC	*Ol./yr.*	*Events/Personalities*	BC	*Ol./yr.*	*Events/Personalities*
776	1	Victor: Koroibos of Elis (Apollod.).	**604**	44	
764	4	Victor: Polychares. **Mess./Lak. hostilities flare**.	**592**	47	
760	5		**588**	48	
757	5/4	1st Ephor (Euseb. (Hieron.) 87b (H)).	**585**	48/4	**Thales' eclipse**.
756	6	Oracle to Iphitos re: Olympic olive crown.	**584**	49	
754	6/3		**582**	49/3	1st crowned Pythian Games (*Mar.Par.* A38).
752	7	*fl.* **Thales** (Phlegon). 1st crowned victor: Daikles.	**580**	50	Two Elean *hellenodikai* established.
750	7/3		**579**	50/2	Seven Sages incl. **Thales**; **archon**: **Damasias**.
748	8	**Pheidon's** Anolympiad.	**576**	51	
747	8/2	**Thales'** *akme*.	**575**	51/2	
744	9		**572**	52	chariot victory: Kleisthenes of Sikyon.
743	9/2	**Ampheia captured**.	**571**	52/2	**Pheidon's son, suitor for Agariste**.
742	9/3	Alyattes, K. of Lydia (Euseb. (Hieron.) 89b (H)).			
728	13		**556**	56	Chilon, Ephor.
724	14	*Diaulos* introduced (1st recorded Games (Kallim.)).	**552**	57	...**reign of Anaxandridas**...
723	14/2	**1st War ends**; **tripods**; **Anaxandridas** (Hdt. only).	**551**	57/2	*fl.* **Gitiades (tripods)**.
720	15	Victor: Orsippos of Megara; dedication late 6th cent.	**548**	58	Death of Thales.
719	15/2	...**reign of Polydoros**. **Battle of Thyrea**...	**547**	58/2	**Champions (Polydoros' apophthegm)**.
716	16		**544**	59	
714	16/3	Accession of Numa who knew Pythagoras.*	**542**	59/3	
712	17		**540**	60	*fl.* **Hipponax** (Plin. *HN* 36.11).
708	18		**536**	61	
706	18/3	Founding of Taras (Euseb. (Hieron.) 91b (H)).	**533**	61/3*	...Pythagoras (akme); archon: Therikles.
696	21		**524**	64	**archon: Miltiades**.
693	21/4		**521**	64/4	?**archon: Peisistratos**.
692	22		**520**	65	Race in Armour.

688	23	*fl.* **Hipponax** (Euseb. (Hieron.) 93e (H)).	**516**	66	
685	23/4	**2nd Mess. War breaks out**.	**513**	66/4	
684	24	Victor in dolichos: Phanas, killed at...	**512**	67	Victor: Phanas of Pellene.
683	24/2	...Battle of Great Trench.	**511**	67/2	
680	25		**508**	68	
676	26	Pisatan Anolympiad; Terpander, 1st Karneia.	**504**	69	(?) Demaratos' **state chariot** victory.
672	27	Victors: *stade*: Eurybates (Ath); **state chariot**: Elis. **archon**: **Leostratos.** *fl.* Alkman (*Suda* s.v. Alkman, 1.117).	**500**	70	**Peisistratos'** dedic. to Pyth. Apollo, ?early-5th-cent. lettering.
669	27/4	**Battle of Hysiai**: **archon**: **Peisistratos**.	**497**	70/4	
668	28	Victor: Chionis I (Paus)/Charmis (Euseb.) Lakonian.	**496**	71	**archon: Hipparchos**.
667	28/2	**Fall of Hira**; archon: Autosthenes.	**495**	71/2	(approx.) ?Laked. vict. dedicatn. at Olympia.
667 or 665	28/2 or 28/4	**1st gymnopaidiai**. **Leotychidas** in 2nd Mess. War; (king only in Hdt.'s list).	**495–3**	71/2 or /4	
			494	71/3	(approx.): Battle of Sepeia.
664	29	Victor: Chionis, Lakonian II(I) =	**492**	72	(?) Demaratos deposed. **Leotychidas**.
664–1	29	**archon**: **Miltiades**; *fl.* Simonides and Archilochos	**490**	72/3	Marathon. **Miltiades**.
		Anaxilas conquers Zankle =	**489**	72/4	***Anaxilas conquers Zankle.***
660	30	Victor: Chionis, Lakonian III(II).	**488**	73	*fl.* Simonides.
659	30/2	Fall of Phigalia; **archon**: **Miltiades**.	**487**	73/2	
658	30/3	*fl.* Alkman (Euseb. (Hieron.) 94b.25 (H)).			
656	31	(approx.) Chionis' dedication (?) portrait by Myron.	**484**	74	**archon: Leostratos**.
652	32		**480**	75	
648	33		**476**	76	
644	34	Anolympiad; Pisa and allies incl. Makistos destroyed.	**472**	77	Games re-ordered; Zeus' temple fr. Pisatan spoils.
640	35		**468**	78	?Makistos destroyed in Hdt.'s lifetime.
639	35/2	**Thales'** ***akme***; **archon**: **Damasias**.	**467**	78/2	Period of **Myron.**
637	35/4	**Messenians leave Lakedaimon**.	**465**	78/4	**Tyrtaios** post-Marathon (Lyk. *in Leoc.* 105).
636	36	*fl.* **Tyrtaios** (Euseb. (Hieron.) 96b (H)).	**464**	79	(emend. fr. 29) **Messenians leave Lakedaimon**.
632	37		**460**	80	
628	38		**456**	81	e.g. pankratiast Timanthes' statue by **Myron**.
612	42	(approx.) *fl.* Alkman (Euseb. (Hieron.) 98b.12 (H)).	**440**	85	

happens, it is the 'other evidence', or the number as written in the manuscript, that scholars typically challenge or emend, not the system of reckoning itself. Sources on the establishment of the Olympic Games indicate that, even in antiquity, there were differing opinions as to which Olympiad should be designated 'No. 1' *for the purposes of dating*,[27] but even though the numbering of Olympiads assigned to events before the mid-fifth century BC (when continuous written record begins) may have been influenced by these different definitions, they are always interpreted as the products of a single system – as if, at a *Bureau de Change*, a given figure were always accorded the same monetary value regardless of the currency.

Pausanias' notice for the battle of Hysiai

Pausanias records the date of the battle of Hysiai as the 4th year of the Olympiad in which 'Eurybotas' of Athens won the *stade*, when Peisistratos was archon in Athens. The Olympiad number may not have been present in the Niccoli *codex* of Pausanias,[28] and Hitzig proposed the restoration ἑβδόμης καὶ εἰκοστῆς, 'twenty seven', relying on Dionysios of Halikarnassos who recorded 'Eurybates' as victor for the 27th Olympiad, and gave 'Leostratos' as Athenian archon for the 2nd year of that Olympiad.[29] The situation is thus comparable with that of Pausanias 4.24.5, discussed above, except that the number is restored, not emended. Whether or not Pausanias, or his source, supplied the number,[30] the term 'Olympiad' is used, and the year, the victor, and the Athenian archon, are supplied, so this notice may be grouped with 15 others formulated thus in his text (see below). The Athenian archon included in Pausanias' notice for Hysiai is 'Peisistratos'. The name is also associated with political activity in the late sixth and early fifth century, as well as the mid-sixth century, in Athens. This is also the case for two other names – 'Miltiades', found as archon in Olympiads 29 and 30, but also in Ol. 64 (*524* BC) and in the context of Marathon, and 'Leostratos', archon in Olympiad 27 but also in Olympiad 74.[31] The odds on there being three named co-evals politically active in Athens at two distinct periods separated by 170 years are long, to put it mildly.[32]

This battle may, then, have been fought two Olympiads before Anaxilas' conquest of Zankle, and 12½ after a battle of Thyrea between Lakedaimonians and Argives, and if the notice were re-calibrated according to the terms outlined in the previous section, this would yield a date of *497* BC. Is there any justification for treating the Hysiai notice in the same way as those in the Messenian narrative? I think there is, on three counts. (1) The number '27' precedes, immediately, the numbers for the closing events of the Second Messenian War, and follows by only 4 that given for its outbreak, '23'; another Sosibian date is that of Olympiad '26' for the first *Karneia*.[33] (2) The formula (Olympiad, year, victor and archon) is the same as that used for the Messenian notices; it is familiar chiefly from Diodoros[34] and may originate with Timaios. Of the 15 instances where Pausanias employs the formula, 7 are associated with Messenian/Lakedaimonian conflict;[35] the contexts of all 15 are subjects treated by one of Pausanias' principal sources, Plutarch, and many of them, earlier, by Kallisthenes.[36] (3) All of Pausanias' apparently 'early' Olympiads expressed in this formula refer to events concerning the Lakedaimonians.

The conventional context of the battle: 'Pheidon'

Most scholars who accept the historicity of the battle of Hysiai[37] nonetheless find it difficult to accommodate at the conventional date, *669* BC. On the other hand, they cannot ignore it because of its association with an Olympiad notice; it may be for this reason that Hall considers the importance of the battle exaggerated.[38] In order to account for the defeat of the Lakedaimonians, historians such as Wade-Gery posited a powerful Argive army, and that meant the tyrant Pheidon.[39] If Pheidon had been responsible for this Argive victory, one might expect it to be recorded with his other deeds, but no source associates him with Hysiai,[40] nor with any conflict in the Second Messenian War, which was apparently being brought to its conclusion at this very period (Hira fell in Ol. 28). Pausanias relates, in a section of his narrative not drawn from Rhianos of Bene, how Argives as well as Messenians and Arkadians were ready to revolt in Olympiad 23. The *P.Oxy.* 3316 fragment attributed to Tyrtaios also contains an allusion to Argives in a battle context.[41] This raises the separate question of Tyrtaios' date; Eusebius sets his *floruit* in Olympiad 36 (*636* BC), but the only testimony independent of numbered Olympiads is Tyrtaios' own reference to Theopompos' action against Messene two generations before his own.[42] This in turn raises the familiar problem of the genealogy of Leotykhidas and the Eurypontid king-list, too large and complex an issue to be dealt with here.[43] Allusions, in *P.Oxy.* 3316, to a trench and wall have led some scholars to associate the poem with the Battle of the Great Trench, but I do not think that these references can be treated as topographically specific; Aristotle implies that a trench is a not uncommon tactical feature in battle, when he declares inferior the courage that stems from being unable to flee because the commander has dug a trench behind his army against such temptation. Homer refers to a trench and a wall as constituents of the Akhaian defences before Troy.[44]

To bring Pheidon into the picture depends on a proposal, made in Falconer's and Weisserborn's 1807 edition of Strabo, that Pausanias' numeral '8' for Pheidon's Olympic *coup* should be emended to that of '28' given by Eusebius for a Pisatan celebration of the Games. This emendation has gained sufficient scholarly acceptance for Pheidon to become associated in many minds with Hysiai.[45] Although no ancient source implicates Pheidon in this Pisatan Olympic celebration, most modern scholars connect him with it – but only by virtue of Falconer's emendation. Pausanias' text is not corrupt here, however, and the 28th Olympic festival, according to Philostratos and Eusebius, was not the occasion of a Pisatan *coup* as such; rather, the Pisatans held the Games because the Eleans were occupied in a war with the Dymaians. Also, the only victors recorded for Olympiad 28 (in the *stade* and *pentathlon*) were Lakonians, which would be surprising if Pheidon were holding the Games having just defeated them, unless – that is – they were from other parts of Lakonia not involved in the conflict and which might later have been described as *perioikic*.[46] Pheidon should not be forced into association with Hysiai and, if the date of the battle were revised as I suggest, he does not need to be, for a plausible context may be found in the period immediately preceding the Persian wars.

Before considering this revised context, however, I think it worthwhile to survey what can be learnt about the position of Hysiai, its relationship with the Argive and Lakedaimonian combatants, and the *casus belli*. It is difficult, if not impossible, to discover the nature of territorial control, or to draw an ethnic and political map of the Peloponnese, before the mid-fifth century BC. Herodotos' use of the term 'Argive' may only reflect the situation, or opinions, of his own time, and Pausanias' identification of Hysiai as an 'Argive' *polis* could refer to a period later than the battle; he or his source may simply have been following Thucydides' statement that Hysiai was an 'Argive' town when it was razed by the Lakedaimonians in a context of Argive *stasis* (civil strife) a year before the Athenian expedition against Melos. Hysiai may only have become Argive after the Persian wars for, according to Stephanus, Pherekydes identified it as 'Αρκαδίας πόλις in the early fifth century BC,[47] and while Pausanias alludes to the synoikism of Hysiai, Mycenae, Tiryns (MAP, 4c), Midea and Orneai with Argos (MAP, 4a) as part of a strategy to contain the strength of

Sparta after the Persian wars, the synoikists were not all originally Argive. Pausanias qualifies as 'the sole Argives' those Mycenaeans listed on the victory dedication raised at Olympia after the battle of Plataia; since Tirynthians were also on the list, it follows that they were *not* Argives at the time of the dedication.[48] Pausanias' references to Hysiai indicate that it lay near modern Achladokampos (MAP, 1a) and there are also traces of a sizeable settlement at Belanidia (MAP, 1b). Both lie south of the R. Erasinos (MAP, 2), between Mts. Pontinos/Ktenias (MAP, 5a/b) and Mts. Zavitsa/Parthenios (MAP, 6a/b).[49] It was at the Erasinos that Kleomenes I performed his fruitless *diabatēria* (frontier sacrifice) before the Battle of Sepeia (MAP, ?4b), conventionally dated to *496–4* BC,[50] which would mean that his adversaries' territory at that time extended only 6 km south of Argos itself and did not include Hysiai. Hysiai would have shared its western frontier with the Tegeates who, according to Herodotos, were a force to be reckoned with and hostile to the Lakedaimonians until shortly before the fall of Kroisos and the Battle of the Champions.[51] Sparta is separated from Hysiai by Mts. Parthenios/Zavitsa, by Tegeatis, and by Karyatis (MAP, 8c) which, at the time of the battle of Mantineia (*418* BC), was its north-eastern border.[52]

According to Herodotos, 'Argives' had possessed Thyrea (MAP, 7b, 7c or 7d) until just before Kroisos approached the Lakedaimonians in his search for allies against Kyros.[53] His term 'Argive' may or may not refer to the population whose southern boundary, a few decades later, was the Erasinos, but if Argives had once inhabited Hysiai, did they lose it, along with Thyrea, at the battle of the Champions, so that their frontier receded to the Erasinos? If so, who then gained possession? The fact that Hysiai participated in an *Argive* synoikism a generation after Sepeia suggests that it was not the Lakedaimonians. From this it may also be inferred that Hysiai was distinct from Thyrea, which *was* still in Lakedaimonian hands at the beginning of the Peloponnesian war.[54] If the Erasinos was the Argives' southern frontier at the time of Sepeia, and if Hysiai could nevertheless be synoikised with *Argos* soon afterwards, it would appear that, until then, Hysiai was neither Argive nor Lakedaimonian nor Thyrean, and that, in his time, Pherekydes was probably right in designating it Arkadian. Thus the combatants would not have been fighting on their own soil, nor would they have shared a frontier over which to wrangle.

The *casus belli*

There is nothing in Pausanias' reference to Hysiai to indicate what

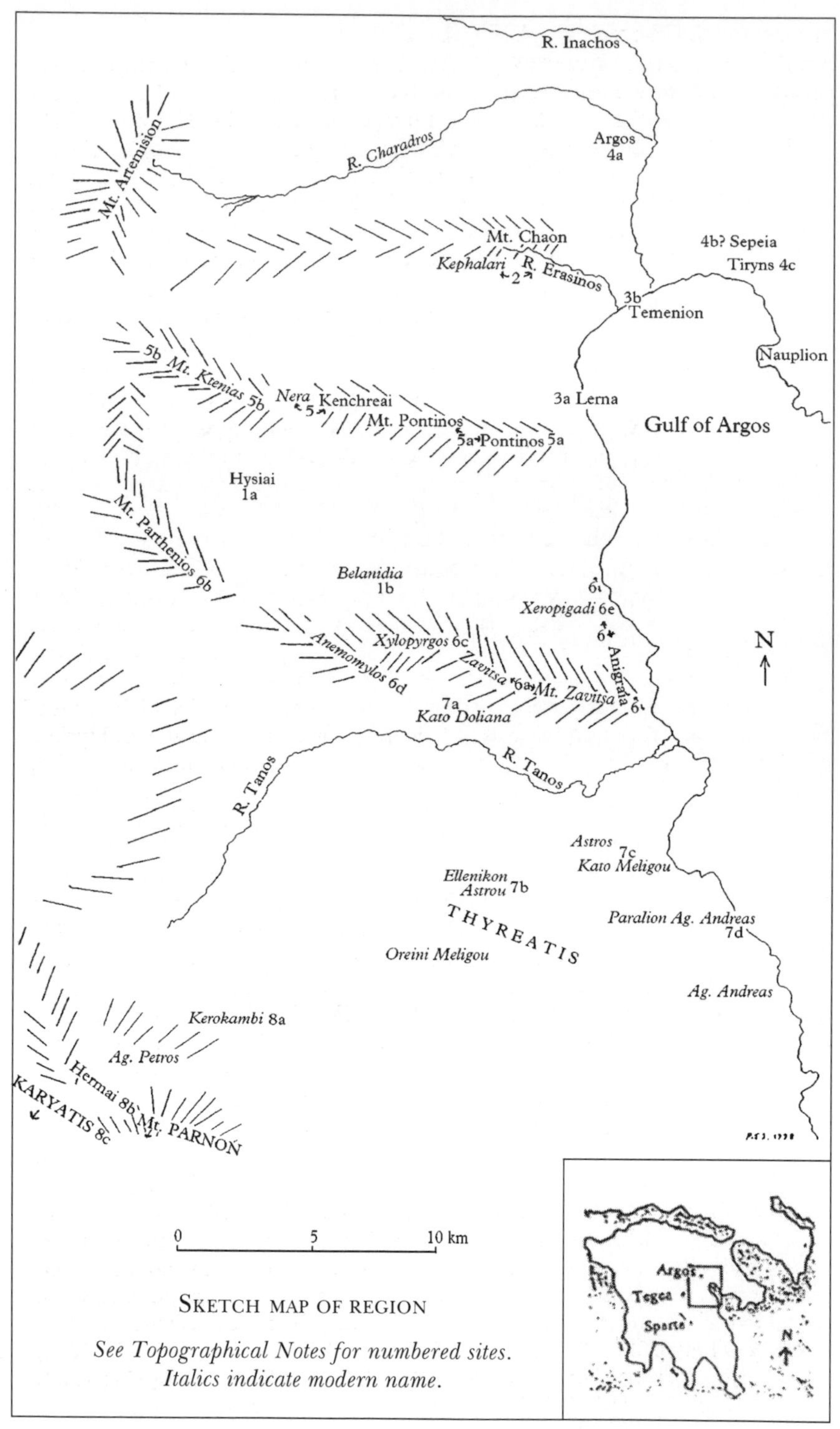

SKETCH MAP OF REGION

See Topographical Notes for numbered sites.
Italics indicate modern name.

Topographical Notes for Map

Hysiai (1a): Paus. 2.24.7; 8.6.4, 54.7; must be near Achladokampos. Approached via Argive Kenchreai , or via Mt. Parthenios **(6b)**, or from E near Lerna. (Frazer 1898, vol. 3, 214; Παπαχάζης 1963, 12–13, map, 309. Tomlinson 1972, 37. Pritchett 1995, 223 ff.). *Classification*: Pherekydes (*FGrH* I.3 F 5): Ἀρκαδίας πόλις. Pausanias: πόλις. Strabo C376: τόπος γνώριμος τῆς Ἀργολικῆς; Strabo C404, Steph.Byz. s.v. Ὑσία Ethnika 291: κώμη. Thuc. 5.83.2 and D.S. 12.81.1: χωρίον. Several pyramidal structures in Peloponnese e.g. nr. Erasinos **(2)** and 18 km NE of Tiryns (Paus. 2.25.7; Tomlinson 1972, 61; Fracchia 1985, 683–9; Λάζος 1995, 19–44.). In 1997 I saw another, newly discovered, *c*. 200 m NW of walled promontory E of Achladokampos. Promontory may be 'akropolis' of Hysiai; Pritchett (1995, 209–10, 223) thinks it a place of refuge. Ancient remains 10 km to SE at **Belanidia (1b)**. **Kenchreai (5)**: Strabo C376; Paus. 2.24.8; *polyandria* for Argives who died at Hysiai. ?Modern Nera; springs; dressed marble; remains of ?temple and warriors' graves (Frazer 1898, vol. 3, 212; Pritchett 1980, 62–3, citing refs., and 1995, 210); ancient route from **Argos (4a)** over Pontinos/Ktenias via Kenchreai and Hysiai to Tegea (Pritchett 1980, 54 f. and 1995, 227; Πίκουλας 1989, 296–7). **R. Erasinos (2)**: Hdt. 6.76, Paus. 2.24.6, 2.36.6–7; issues from mountain at **Kephalari (2)**. Pausanias describes as first feature on road to **Lerna (3a)** from **Argos (4a)**, but records that it fell into (unidentified) R. Phrixos which reached sea between **Lerna** and **Temenion (3b)**. If so, its course was short; this might suggest that Kleomenes came via **Kenchreai** not Thyrea. **Sepeia (4b?)**: Hdt. 6.77. Not identified; ?near **Tiryns (4c)**. *Classification*: Hdt.6.77: χῶρος. **Mt. Pontinos (5a)**: Paus. 2.36.8, 2.37.1–2, S of Lerna; S limit of Argive plain; massif extends W, as **Mt. Ktenias (5b)**, ?ancient Kreopolos (Strabo C376) N of Hysiai.

Mt. Zavitsa (6a): = ?**Mt. Parparos** (Plin. *HN* 4.17; Christien and Σπυρόπουλος 1985, 457; Christien 1992, 164–6). Paus. 2.38.4 refers to **?Anigraia (6)**: narrow route S of Kiverion over E extremity, *or* across saddle, of Zavitsa. Roads over Zavitsa: Pritchett 1980, 105–6, pls. 56–66, 1982, 42, and 1991, 177, fig. 10; Καλίτσης, 1967, 10–18. ?Cenotaph (*SEG* 13.266) found on Zavitsa route from **Belanidia (1a)** to **Kato Doliana (7a)**; Lakonian watch-towers: **Xylopyrgos (6c)**, **Anemomylos (6d)**, **Xeropigadi (6e)**; Πίκουλας 1990–91, 248. **Thyrea**: Hdt. 1.82; Thuc. 2.27, 4.56–7, 5.14, 5.41, 6.95; Xen. *Hell.* 2.2.9; Isoc. *Arch.* 99; Paus. 2.29.5, 2.38.5, 3.7.5, 8.35.8, 8.54.4; Plut. *Mor.* 306b; (Καλίτσης, 1964, 219–35; Pritchett 1995, 236); *Classification*: Hdt. 1.82: χῶρος; Thuc.: πόλις/Θυρεάτιδος γῆς; Xen.: πόλις; Plut.: χώρα. Poss. locations: **Ellenikon Astrou (7b)** (Φακλάρης 1990, 232, though (1987, 101–19) he set 'Champions' at **Xerokambi (8a)**); **Kato Meligou (7c)** (Christien and Σπυρόπουλος 1985, 457); **Paralion Ag. Andreas (7d)** (Goester 1993, 107; Pritchett 1995, 236). Pritchett (1980, 120) sets 'Champions' near **Xylopyrgos (6c)**. Pausanias has *polyandria* of 'Champions' inland from fertile region S of **?Anigraia (6)**. **Anthana**: Thuc. 5.41; Paus. 2.38.6; Steph.Byz. s.v. *Anthana* (Griffiths 1989, 64). *Classification*: Thuc.: πόλις; Paus.: κώμη. Pausanias describes location '...as you go from the *polyandria*...', identifies as 'site re-settled by Aiginetans'. Poss. locations: above **Kato Doliana (7a)** on S slope of Zavitsa, fortified by Lakonians (Christien and Σπυρόπουλος 1985, 457; Christien 1992, 164–6; Pritchett 1995, 247); **Kato Meligou (7c)** (Cartledge 1979, 189); **Paralion Ag. Andreas (7c)** (Φακλάρης 1990, 233, pls. 7–9; Παπαχάζης 1963, 300, pls. 337–8). Pausanias' *Korinthiaka* ends at the **Hermai (8b)** (Paus. 2.38.7).

might have led Argives and Lakedaimonians to fight each other there. Cartledge, who thought the battle of Hysiai probably authentic, though he suspended trading on its date, made the important observation that the battle site pointed to Spartan, rather than Argive, aggression, but he did not examine the question of motive.[55] Hall concedes that occasional clashes could have occurred between Argives and Lakedaimonians over Thyrea during the seventh century BC, though he does not enlarge on the nature of such conflicts, but whereas the issue at the Battle of the Champions was probably territorial, and smouldered throughout the fifth century BC,[56] it seems unlikely, from the available evidence, that Hysiai reflected that kind of dispute – whether a formal frontier battle or an attempt at annexation.[57] The engagement was probably tactical and the *casus belli* should be sought elsewhere, perhaps in a context of *stasis*, or the obligations attendant on an alliance or *xenia* relationship; it may have been a punitive expedition. No record survives of such circumstances in the seventh century, but a plausible context may be found at the revised date that I propose: *c. 497* BC.

The revised context of the battle

Both sides must have had commanders, though none are mentioned by Pausanias. While Herodotos' account of Lakedaimonian affairs before the Persian wars may provide clues, few Argive records have survived to complement it, and little is known of named individuals in the late archaic Argolid who might have instigated the attack or led the defence. Pausanias and Diodoros mention a handful of kings and tyrants who, with the exception of Pheidon, failed to enter the mainstream of history. They include Damokratidas who expelled the Naupliotes; Meltas, the last Temenid who was deposed by the Argive *dēmos*; his father, Pheidon's son, Lakedas, who was a suitor for Agariste of Sikyon, daughter of the tyrant Kleisthenes; Perilaos, son of Alkenor, one of the surviving Champions, who allegedly killed the sole Lakedaimonian survivor of that battle, Othryades; he destroyed the bronze tomb of Akrisios' daughter *while he was tyrant*, and won the wrestling at the Nemean Games. A fifth is the king who, after a defeat by the Lakedaimonians, was expelled by the *dēmos*, and fled to Tegea, when he refused to distribute among them the ancestral lands on which he had settled certain Arkadian exiles. The last is the tyrant Laphaes who was also expelled by the *dēmos* and sought to reinstate himself with Lakedaimonian help – but without success.[58] If the Argive synoikism had yet to be effected, as seems likely, more than one dynasty may be represented among these elusive figures. There was still an Argive βασιλεύς at the time of Xerxes' invasion, though whether hereditary or magisterial it is beyond the scope of this paper to discuss.[59] Hall concludes that at this period Argos was experiencing conflict between two groups; this is also suggested by the allusions of Herodotos, Aristotle, Diodoros and Plutarch, to expulsions, and extensions of citizenship.[60] Hall's theories, that early fifth-century Argos was still culturally distinct from other Argolic settlements, and her territory not yet extensive, are gaining recognition.[61]

Only a single Lakedaimonian king might be expected to command an army at this period, if Herodotos' account of the attempt to reinstate Isagoras in Athens, and our understanding of the chronology, are correct.[62] The response to Kleomenes I which Herodotos puts into the mouth of Krios, leader of the Aeginetans who had medised in the year before Marathon, might suggest that it was then still customary for both Lakedaimonian kings to command the army, although Carlier has argued that Krios was incited to protest by a Demaratos driven more by personal political motives than by zeal for constitutional propriety.[63] The chronology of Athenian/Aeginetan hostilities is beset with difficulties but, at all events, Herodotos indicates that Demaratos and Kleomenes were both still reigning when Dareios despatched envoys to demand the tokens of earth and water. What does emerge from Herodotos' account of the Lakedaimonians in the generation after Anaxandridas' reign is that they were active in the affairs of cities and populations other than their own – Athens, Aegina, possibly Plataia, Arkadia, Samos and Thessaly – and that during the decade before Marathon there was at least one hostile campaign against the Argives, which culminated in the battle of Sepeia; although Herodotos describes only Kleomenes' role in the Sepeia campaign, Plutarch received a tale in which Demaratos was also involved.[64]

If Hysiai were fought *c. 497* BC and Sepeia *c. 496–4*, it would be more likely than not that the battles were connected. In Herodotos' account the campaign of Sepeia comes out of the blue, but the issue does not seem to have been territorial there, either, for the victorious Lakedaimonians did not take Argos despite effectively destroying its male population – the Argives claimed to have lost 6000 men as a result of the hostilities.[65] Among several *apophthegms* concerning the Argives which Plutarch attributes to Kleomenes I was one in which Kleomenes justified his violation of the seven-day truce before Sepeia thus: ὅ τι ἂν κακόν τις ποιῇ τοὺς πολεμίους, τοῦτο καὶ παρὰ θεοῖς καὶ παρὰ ἀνθρώποις δίκης ὑπέρτερον νομίζεσθαι ('whatever ill one can do to one's enemies is regarded, among both gods and men, as something higher than justice.').[66] Also, Herodotos relates how Kleomenes, thwarted by the outcome of his *diabatēria* at the Erasinos before Sepeia, remarked that ἄγασθαι μὲν ἔφη τοῦ Ἐρασίνου οὐ προδιδόντος τοὺς πολιήτας, Ἀργείους μέντοι οὐδ' ὣς χαιρήσειν. ('he honoured the Erasinos for protecting its people, *but the Argives would not get away with it.*').[67] Kleomenes seems to allude here to some injury for which satisfaction was required. I suggest that he brought a force against Argos to settle a score – which is why he inflicted so many casualties but claimed to think the oracle fulfilled without his actually taking the city, – and that that score was the Lakedaimonian defeat and casualties at Hysiai.[68]

If one allows the revised date, then Hysiai might account for Sepeia, but this still would not account for Hysiai. It is possible that it represented an earlier phase of the Sepeia campaign, signified by Kleomenes' venomous remark and his unsuccessful *diabatēria* and withdrawal from the Erasinos, itself only 10 km north of Kenchreai (Map, 5). Pausanias gives no clues; he merely mentions the location of Kenchreai and the common graves of the victorious Argives, gives the 'date' of the battle, and reports on the outcome for the Lakedaimonians, which he describes as πταῖσμα – as much a blunder as a defeat.[69] In the absence of any other acknowledged source, only conjecture is left; when Pausanias is near the grave of Perseus' daughter Gorgophone, in the *agora* of Argos, he gives the following report:

> In front of the grave is a trophy of stone made to commemorate a victory over an Argive, Laphaes. When this man was tyrant – I write what the Argives themselves say concerning themselves – the people rose up against him and cast him out. He fled to Sparta, and the Lakedaimonians tried to restore him to power, *but were defeated by the Argives, who killed the greater part of them* and Laphaes as well. [70]

Although no-one specifically connects this monument with the battle of Hysiai, the accompanying report fits the description of the battle rather well; it might even be called a πταῖσμα. Pausanias is non-committal about his source for Hysiai, but the story of Laphaes he draws from Argive tradition; and the affair, or something like it, would make a plausible *casus belli* for Hysiai. The issue is not territorial, but political. No Argive commander is mentioned; Laphaes was expelled, and perished anyway, and it was the *dēmos* who repulsed him and his Lakedaimonian allies when he tried to make a come-back; if they were led by Meltas, who was also (subsequently?) expelled, he too might have been edited out of the Argive record.[71] No Lakedaimonian record of the battle survived nor was their commander mentioned (which would not be surprising if it were a heavy defeat), but before the Persian wars they were involved in Athenian affairs, in attempts to expel the Peisistratids and the rival Alkmaionids, and also to restore Isagoras. Likewise, a battle at Hysiai, well away from Argos, might be explained in terms of heading-off an opposing faction. Also, Herodotos relates that before the Battle of Sepeia Kleomenes' force included αὐτομόλους ἄνδρας, deserters or men who were acting on their own account.[72] Lastly, neither side would have been fighting on a territorial issue; but the Lakedaimonians would indeed have been the aggressors.

To propose bringing this battle into the beginning of the fifth century BC may seem radical, but since scholars already doubt either the historicity of the battle, or the sacrosanctity of its date, and since nothing else is known about it, then the magnitude of the revision proposed is not the significant issue. The battle of Hysiai has never really been at home in the early seventh century, dragging Pheidon into almost the only remaining period to which no chronographer has ever assigned him. I suggest that a Lakedaimonian intervention in late archaic Argive *stasis* may provide a more comfortable context for this mysterious passage of arms.

Appendix

Gymnopaidiai

Given the chronological revision I have suggested, the earliest allusion to the *Gymnopaidiai* is of critical importance. Herodotos supplies it, in the context of Demaratos' deposition,but as Dillery has recently noted, he did *not* refer to it in his account of the Battle of the Champions *c. 546* BC.[73] This may be mere Herodotean silence, but it is particularly surprising that he should mention neither this ritual nor the*Thyreatikoi,* Thyreatic wreaths, (if these were indeed worn at the same festival, as Sosibios states), in a narrative explaining the origins of hair-styles; surprising, that is, unless the *Gymnopaidiai* had yet to be instituted in Lakedaimon, as the revision proposed in this paper would imply. It should be stressed that Eusebius' Olympiad notice refers only to the institution of this ritual 'in Lakedaimon', and that Sosibios says of the *Thyreatikoi* only that this was the Lakedaimonians' name for the wreaths and that they were worn by choruses who performed at the festival where the *Gymnopaidiai* were held.[74] The three choruses to which Sosibios refers performed music by Dionysodotos, whose date is unknown, and by Alkman and Thaletas, whose dates are only expressed as Olympiads by Eusebius and the *Suda*, so that these poets provide for the *Gymnopaidiai* no *terminus ante quem* independent of Olympiads. The choruses may have been the *Trichoria*, the institution of which Pollux ascribed to Tyrtaios; but Tyrtaios' date begs the Olympiad question again, and at least one source, Lykourgos, implies that Tyrtaios was alive after the Persian wars. The *Trichoria* are nowhere explicitly associated with the *Gymnopaidiai*, nor the *Gymnopaidiai* with Tyrtaios.[75]

Hysiai, Gymnopaidiai, *and* Parparōnia

The article in which Bölte argued for the Thyreatic character of the *Parparōnia* (itself epigraphically attested for the late archaic era), and rightly distinguished between it and the *Gymnopaidiai*, drew a response from Wade-Gery which has exerted a potent influence on debate concerning the institution of the ritual.[76] Most scholars, *pace* Den Boer, and Billot, now associate the *Gymnopaidiai* with the Battle of Hysiai, and accept Wade-Gery's argument that the *Thyreatikoi* were a later addition, whereas Bölte had argued that the *Gymnopaidiai* and Thyreatic ritual were only linked after Leuktra, when the Lakedaimonians lost Thyrea and thus could no longer hold the *Parparōnia* there.[77]

The numerical relationship between the respective Olympiads assigned to Hysiai (27) and to the institution of the *Gymnopaidiai* in Lakedaimon (28) is not altered by the revision I propose, although the *real* chronological relationship between the two events cannot be proven. Wade-Gery's argument that the *Thyreatikoi* were a later addition to the *Gymnopaidiai* requires two assumptions that are not valid. One is that there existed a single, coherent chronological structure, in which the relationship between Eusebius' 'Olympiad 28' and Herodotos' context for the battle of the Champions is unequivocal. Similarly, the evidence with which Wade-Gery supports his argument concerning the 'early' use of Feather crowns at Sparta – Alkman's epithet for a girl in a chorus as φιλόψιλος, and depictions of Feather crowns on Tarentine vases – requires, for poet and colony, firm dates enjoying chronological coherence with the date of the Champions.[78] The second invalid assumption concerns the geographical affinities of the *Gymnopaidiai*; these lie chiefly with Thyrea,[79] but Wade-Gery assumed that Thyrea comprehended Hysiai – whereas the evidence suggests the contrary – and from this he drew two historical conclusions: (a) that the battle of Hysiai was fought at the end of Theopompos' reign, for which he cited only Pausanias' statement that Theopompos was still reigning when the so-called *Thyreatic* war occurred; and (b) that it was the victory at *Hysiai* that gave Thyrea to the Argives for over a century, and the Lakedaimonians' victory at Thyrea – commemorated (so he reasoned) by the addition of the *Thyreatikoi* to the *Gymnopaidiai* – that reversed this situation; neither the identity of the 'Argives' nor the political map of the Argolid before the Persian wars is sufficiently well defined to provide support for this argument.[80] I reiterate that Pherekydes identified Hysiai not as Lakonian or Argive, but as Arkadian; since he is the only source to give such an opinion, and was active before the main period of Argive synoikism, it is unlikely that Stephanus invented this.[81]

Parparos

Parparos is associated with Thyreatic ritual in the *Anecdota Graeca*, and with choruses and an *agōn* by Hesychius.[82] The elder Pliny calls Parparos a mountain of Argolis, and Christien and Spyropoulos identify it with Mt. Zavitsa. Pausanias clearly traversed Zavitsa, but gave it no name.[83] Phaklaris, reasoning from the discovery of a sixth-century bronze bull, inscribed ΗΕΛΙΚΙΣ ΑΝΕΘΕΚΕ ΠΑΡΠΑΟ, at Xerokambi (MAP, 8a) west of Oreini Meligou on a hill below Mt. Parnon, sets the Champions' battle there; thus Parparos may have been that hill. However, not all scholars accept his reading of the dedication.[84] Near Xerokambi stood the *Hermai* (MAP, 8b) marking the triple frontier of Argolis, Arkadia and Lakonia – a plausible location for frontier disputes except that, in Pausanias' account, it is separated from the Champions' battle-ground by several other sites.[85]

Late archaic wreathed bronze figures

It might be argued that the sixth-century date assigned to bronze statuettes of wreathed youths found at Amyklai, Olympia, and Mt. Lykaion, which have sometimes been linked with the *Gymnopaidiai* because they are wreathed apparently with palm-leaves, feathers, or reeds, would militate against setting the institution of that ritual in Lakedaimon as late as *495* BC.[86] However, as Pipili noted, none of the figures was found at a site associated with the *Gymnopaidiai*, and none is explicitly tied to it by, for example, an inscription. Pausanias records that palm-wreaths were the most common at festivals, and they were an acknowledged symbol of victory; Pausanias also says that Dionysos surnamed *Psilax* (?feathered) was worshipped at Amyklai, where one of the bronzes was discovered.[87]

To treat these figures as a single group may be misleading, for they might reflect different practices, some of which may have been not

Lakedaimonian but Arkadian. Two of the youths have long hair and two have short (one of each from Olympia, long from Lykaion, short from Amyklai), a distinction recalling Herodotos' remarks about hairstyles in his account of the Champions. Also, the wreaths on the bronzes are not all alike. Some may be of *kalamoi*, reeds, like those which Sosibios says were worn at the *Promakhia*. The occasion of this festival is unknown, though it might have celebrated the Champions' victory in Thyrea. However, the wreaths were worn not by young Spartiates who had undergone the *agōgē*, but by the boys ἀπὸ τῆς χώρας ('from the country'), who also wore metal tiaras called *stlengides*.[88] In the *Anabasis*, Xenophon not only refers to Arkadian practices concerning dancing as a form of martial training, but he also recounts how the Arkadian Xenias offered gold *stlengides* as prizes in the Games he organised to honour Zeus Lykaios. One of the wreathed bronze statuettes was found on Mt. Lykaion, Pausanias lists Thyraios as one of Lykaion's sons, and the Elder Pliny records that: *'ludos gymnicos in Arcadia Lycaon (instituit)'*.[89] Polybios gives a similar picture, Ephoros refers to Mantineian martial arts, and Hermippos attributes the institution of these to the Mantineian Demonax whom the Lakedaimonians sent to establish order in Kyrene.[90] Ephoros sets the original *Hoplomachia* at Mantineia, while the Mantineian Dance may form part of the *Mōleia* festival to commemorate the duel between Lykourgos and Areithous.[91] Thus, martial dancing and musical training-in-arms are not practices peculiar to the Spartiates, and the institution of the *Gymnopaidiai* 'in Lakedaimon' could have been relatively late, i.e. in the early fifth century. This would sit well with the theory (now starting to gain acceptance) that Spartan austerity should really be set at the end of the archaic era. In summary, I can find nothing that militates against a date of *c. 495* BC for the institution of the *Gymnopaidiai* in Lakedaimon.

Acknowledgements

Earlier versions of this chapter were read at the *UWICAH* Conference, 'Sparta: New Perspectives', at Hay-on-Wye in September 1997, and, by invitation of Dr Andrew Laird, at a Research Seminar at Warwick University in January 1998. On both occasions, the discussions that ensued, and the comments of those present, were of great value to me. I also acknowledge, with profound gratitude, the encouragement and constructive criticism I have received from Professor W.K. Pritchett, Dr Paul Cartledge, Dr Anton Powell, Dr Stephen Hodkinson, Dr Hans van Wees; my supervisor, Dr Nick Fisher; my son Benedict and, above all, my husband, Dr Stephen Shaw.

Notes

[1] See n. 24. I italicise calendar dates to emphasise that they, too, are merely symbols employed in a system of chronological reckoning.

[2] See n. 26.

[3] Thomas 1995, 104; Morris 1996, 21, 25 ff.

[4] Paus. 4.23.9–10, and 4.23.4 for fall of Hira.

[5] Herodotos 6.23, 7.164; Thuc. 6.4–5. Diodoros (= D.S.) 11.48, reports that in Ol. 76/1 (*476* BC) Anaxilas tyrant of Rhegion and *Zankle* died after 18 years' reign, and Mikythos became regent; in Ol. 78/2 (*467* BC) Hieron told the sons of Anaxilas to demand an account from Mikythos and assume control of Zankle. In Ol. 79/4 (*460* BC) Zanklians and Rhegians expelled Anaxilas' sons (D.S. 11.76); their land was later divided among the Geloans. Pausanias (4.24.6) described Anaxilas as third in line from Alkidamidas who migrated to Rhegion after Aristodemos' death and the fall of Ithome.

[6] Robinson 1946, 13–21; Shero 1938, 529; Williams 1972, 2; Kraay 1969, 22–47, pl. vi, 6; Kraay and Hirmer 1966, pls. 182.613, 16.50; Barron 1966, 45; Carradice 1995, 27, 29, 34–5; Howgego 1995, 6, 63, illustr. 13, 14.

[7] Jeffery 1949, 27; Wallace 1954, 32–5.

[8] Samuel 1972, 190; Mosshammer 1979, 85–6, 93.

[9] Paus. 8.39.3.

[10] Race in Armour: *IG* ii^2.2326; victor: Damaretos of Heraia, Paus. 5.8.10, 6.10.4, but Philostratos, *Gymn.* 144.11, sets first Race in Armour during a war between *Eleans* and *Dymaians*, in Ol. 28; how many historians would accept that it was instituted in *668* BC? Moretti (132), 74.

[11] Arafat 1996, 16–17, 63, 75.

[12] Elsewhere (5.25.7), however, he makes use of the tradition that Anaxilas changed the name 'Zankle' to 'Messena', in order to date the sculptor, Aristokles of Kydonia, who executed a commission for Euagoras of Zankle. Pausanias (5.24.6—5.26.2–7) also describes dedications made at Olympia by Anaxilas' regent, Mikythos, who describes himself, in the accompanying inscription, '...of Rhegion and Messena' (Schwyzer 1923, 794). Hdt. 7.170. Arafat 1996, 61–3, 66. Also Shero, 1938, 505 ff., 512 ff., 520–26, 530–31. Chionis at Olympia: Paus. 6.13.2; at Sparta: Paus. 3.14.3. Hyde 1921, 32, and no. 362. Moretti (40, 42–7), 63–4. Raschke 1988, 40–1. See n. 9.

[13] Paus. 4.24.5; D.S. 11.70.1. Emendation of εἰκοστήν to ἑβδομηκοστήν, attributed to Meursius: Hitzig (ed.) 1901–4, 64 nn. 13, 14; Rocha-Pereira (ed.) 1989, 327. Frazer 1898, Vol. 3, 418. Hammond 1955, 374 n. 2. Diller 1957, 185. Gomme Vol. 1. 298, at Thuc. 1.101.2, which he places before the surrender of Thasos; Hornblower vol. 1. 157–8. Gomme vol. 1. 302, at Thuc. 1.103.1, for the problematic δεκάτῳ ἔτει, which he places before the accession of Megara to Athens; McNeal, 1970, 313 ff. retains '10th'; Gomme argues for '6th'; Hornblower vol. 1. 160–1, at Thuc. 1.103.1, suggests '5th', but does not press it. Discussing Thucydides' account of the Messenian revolt, Gomme vol. 1. 403, comments: 'Pausanias...in his account of Messenia *carefully dates* the earthquake and revolt to *the 79th Olympiad.*' D.S. (11.63–4) sets this in Ol. 77/4 (*469* BC), and states that it was followed by a 10-year siege of Ithome; he mentions (15.66) how, after these events, Messenians settled in Sicilian

Messena which was ἀπ᾽ ἐκείνων ὀνομασθεῖσαν; he is usually understood to mean that it was *they* who re-named Zankle. Pausanias' archon for Ol. 79 is *Archimedes*, emended to *Archidemides* by Palmerius (in the 17th cent.) so as to harmonise Pausanias with D.S. Tauchnitz, 1829, vol. 2, 72, allows neither emendation. Gomme (loc. cit.). *Nike* monument dedicated by Μεσσάνοι καὶ Ναυπάκτιοι at Olympia: *Inschr. von Ol.* 259 = *IGA* 348 = *ML* 74. Xenophon, and Thessalos, Pind. *Ol.* 13. Moretti (249–50), 94, and (154), 79.

[14] Sosibian dates: Mosshammer 1979, 205; Pearson 1962, 416, believed Myron of Priene knew the Olympiads. That the dates are not Apollodoran: Huxley 1962, 130, n. 384.

[15] Paus. 8.39.3, 4.24.1. Miltiades: Hdt. 6.133–6; according to Stesimbrotos *FGrH* 107 F 2 *ap*. Plut. *Them*. 4, Miltiades was still alive when silver was struck at Laureion. Ol. 35/4: *Messena a Lacedaemoniorum societate discedit:* Euseb. (Hieron.) 169 Fotheringham (= F) 96b Helm (= H); cf. Thuc. 1.101–3.

[16] Fall of Hira: Paus. 4.23.4. *IG* v.1.1962. Jeffery 1949, 28, and *LSAG*, 196.

[17] *Gymnopaidiai*: Hdt. 6.67; Xen. *Hell*. 6.4.16. Ol. 27/3: Euseb. (Hieron.) 87d Schöne (= S) and (Arm.) 86d (S). Ol. 28/2: Euseb. (Hieron.) 94b (H)/165 (F). Ol. 28/4: Euseb. (Arm.) 184 Karst (= K); Synkellos 401.20.

[18] Outbreak of 2nd war: Paus. 4.15.1; victor: Ikaros of Hyperesia cf. Phlegon *FGrH* 257 F 5 *ap*. Steph.Byz. s.v. Ὑπερασία; Moretti (28), 63.

[19] End of 1st war, Ol. 14/2: Paus. 4.13.7; victor: Dasmon of Korinth; Moretti (14), 61. Herodotos: (7.204) Anaxandridas, son of Leon, father of Leonidas; (8.131) in Leotykhidas' genealogy, Anaxandridas follows Theopompos. Pausanias: (3.7.5) has Theopompos succeeded by grandson, Zeuxidamos whose father, Archidamos, pre-deceased him; he records only *Agiad* Anaxandridas, and *one* Leotykhidas. Chilon as 1st Ephor: D.Laert. 1.68; year of office: archonship of Euthydemos: *Mar.Par. FGrH* 239 A41 year 292 (*556* BC). Chilon's year of office: Ol. 56 (*556* BC): Euseb. (Hieron.) 102b (H)/181(F). Elatos as 1st Ephor, and office established by Lykourgos: Plut. *Lyk*. 7; office established by Theopompos: Arist. *Pol*. 1313a26–8. Theopompos made Ephors associates of kings: Plut. *Mor*. 779E. Office established in Ol. 5/4: Euseb. (Hieron.) 87b (H)/151 (F).

[20] Tripods: Paus. 4.14.2–3, 3.18.7–8. Frazer 1898, Vol. 3, 350; Jeffery 1949, 27, and *LSAG* 196; Lippold 1950, 32; Cartledge 1979, 91–2; Haynes 1992, 20, n. 6. Signature of Kalon, who cast the 3rd Amyklaian tripod marking victory over the Messenians: *IG* ii.501, *c. 500* BC; Morgan 1990, 102 and nn. 97–8 does not discuss the discrepancy.

[21] Herodotos: (1.65 ff.) sets this in the reigns of Ariston and Anaxandridas.

[22] Battle of Thyrea Ol. 15/2: Euseb. (Hieron) 157 (F); 90b (H), (Arm.) 183 (K). Victor in Ol. 15: Orsippos (Orhippos) of Megara (or Ol. 32: *Etym.Mag.* s.v. γυμνάσια); epigram: *IG* vii.52; O. allegedly first to run naked, a recent innovation (Thuc. 1.6 and *Schol.*) but attrib. by D.H. (7.72) to Lakonian Akanthos. *Testimonia*: Moretti (16), 61–2. Champions: Hdt. 1.82; Chrysermos *ap*. Plut. *Mor*. 306a–b, *FGrH* 287 F 2; *Anth.Pal*. 7.431 (?Simonides) and 7.721 (Chairemon); Ovid *Fasti* 2. 663–6. Plut. *Mor*. 864. *Apophthegm* attributed to Polydoros: Plut. *Mor*. 231E; Alkman's ref. to Polydoros (and Leotykhidas?): *P.Oxy*. 2390 fr. 2, col. ii.18; Lobel 1957; Page 1962, 23; Harvey 1967, 67–8;

West 1965, 190–1, but 1992, 4, for revised view.

23 Paus. 4.5.10.

24 Thales: Hdt. 1.170. Birth: Ol. 35; death: Ol. 58: Apollodoros *FGrH* 244 F 28 *ap* D.L. 1.37. *akmē*: Ol. 7: Phlegon *FGrH* 257 F 33 *ap. Suda* s.v. Θαλῆς, and F 11 for Messenian Daikles, 1st crowned victor. Ol. 8/2: Euseb. (Hieron.) 88b (H)/152.18 (F); (Arm) 81h (S); Synkellos 402.16. Bodleian MS facsimile (ed. Fotheringham), fol. 74 qviiii 3; *Cod. Ox. Bod. Auct.* T.II.26; Bod. microfilm: *SFW* 204. Ol. 35/2: Euseb. (Hieron) 96a (H).* Eclipse: Xenophanes fr. 19 (Diels); Hdt. 1.74; Arist. *Met.* A3983^{b} 20; Ol. 48/4: Apollod. *ap.* Plin. *HN* 2.53. Ol. 49: Euseb. (Hieron.) 100f (H). Seven Sages: Plato *Protag.* 343A; in archonship of Damasias: Dem. Phal. *FGrH* 228 F 1 *ap.* D.L. 1.22. Ol. 50/2: Euseb. (Hieron.) 101b (H)/179 (F); (Arm) 187 (K). *Mar.Par. FGrH* 239 A38 (year 318 = *582/1* BC). Archonship of Damasias: *vid. sup.* and * Ol. 35/2 : D.H. 3.36.1.

25 As was Lykourgos' name, according to Aristotle *ap.* Plut. *Lyk.* 1.

26 Pheidon's dates: late seventh century–early sixth century. Herodotos (6.127) states that Pheidon regulated measures, held Olympic Games, and was father of Lakedas, suitor for Agariste, daughter of Kleisthenes of Sikyon (whose Olympic chariot win Moretti (96), 69–70, sets in Ol. 51 or 52, (576/*572* BC). Thus Herodotos (1.74; 1.170) synchronises Pheidon with Thales – a coeval of Alyattes and Harpagos. *Terminus ante quem* provided by Xenophanes fr. 4. (Diels) *ap.* Pollux 9.83. Mid-eighth century (10th from Temenos): Ephoros, *FGrH* 70 F 115 *ap.* Strabo: C358. Anolympiad in Ol. 8 (*748* BC): Paus. 6.22.2. Early 9th cent. (6th from Temenos): Theopompos *FGrH* 115 F 393 *ap.* D.S. 7.17; also *Mar.Par. FGrH* 239 A30 year 631 (*895–3* BC). Andrewes 1949, 74–7 and 1951, 44–5. Hall 1995, 586–7. Lenschau 1936, 395. Kelly 1976, ch. 6.

27 Lack of space precludes discussion of these sources here, but fragments from Phlegon provide the important indication that *he* assigned the number '28' to the Olympic victory of Koroibos of Elis, though by convention it is always numbered '1'.

28 e.g. Tauchnitz 1829, vol. 1, 202, has: ...τετάρτῳ δὲ ἔτει τῆς ὀλυμπιάδος, ἣν Εὐρύβοτος Ἀθηναῖος ἐνίκα στάδιον.

29 Or 'Eurybotos' or 'Eurybatos', according to the MSS derived from the Niccoli *codex*. Paus. 2.24.7; D.H. 3.1.3. Africanus gives 'Eurybos'; Euseb. *Chron.* I (Arm.) 197 (S); Moretti, (36) 63. A Lakonian Eurybates was 1st victor in wrestling in Ol. 18 (*708* BC): Paus. 5.8.7; Philostr. 142.22. Moretti, (22) 62, cf. *IG.* V.2.93. In the Hysiai notice the *Athenian* Eurybotas won the *stade.* A 'Eurybates' was the Argive pentathlete who independently led 1000 men to help the Aeginetans against Athens; he was killed by Sophanes of Dekeleia after winning μονομαχίαι against three other Athenians (Hdt. 6.92, 9.73–4). Thus he was active in the period before Marathon; he is not listed as an *Olympic* victor. Aristotle *fr.* 84 R. Pritchett 1971, *GSAW*, 121–6. Forrest 1960, 225. Ephoros (*FGrH* 70 F 58) and D.S (9.32) refer to 'Eurybates', an Ephesian mercenary in Kroisos' pay, who defected to Kyros and became a byword for perfidy. For Ol. 27 Phlegon records a surprisingly early state chariot-victory of Eleans of Dyspontium; Moretti, (39), 63. D.S. 8.1, for the establishment of

a settled way of life among the Eleans before Xerxes' invasion, and 11.54 for synoikism of Elis in Ol. 77/2 (*471* BC).

[30] An Olympiad could be identified by the victor long before any system of numeration was devised, e.g. Thuc. 3.8 and 5.49.1, although in both cases he names the victor in the *pankration* rather than the *stade*.

[31] Discussion of the archonship of the younger Peisistratos is not appropriate here, but the inscription, *IG* 1.ii.761, on the altar he dedicated to Pythian Apollo *during his archonship*, continues to puzzle historians and epigraphists, since it includes letter-forms normally assigned to the early fifth century BC, too late for the accepted date of that archonship, Ol. 64/3 (*522–21* BC). See Arnush 1995, *esp*. 147, 154.

[32] Miltiades in Ol. 29: Paus. 4.23.9–10, and in Ol. 30: Paus. 8.39.3. Leostratos in Ol. 27: D.H. 3.1.3, and in Ol. 74: D.H. 8.77.1.

[33] Institution of *Karneia*: Sosibios, *FGrH* 595 F 3, 1st victor, Terpander: Hellanikos, *FGrH* 1 F 129, both *ap*. Ath. 635E–F.

[34] And from Dionysios, who usually omits the Olympiad year, as Pausanias does for Olympiads 29/79.

[35] All refs to Pausanias: 4.5.9: 1st Lakedaimonian attack on Messenians, Ol. 9/2. 4.13.7: end of '1st' Messenian war, Ol. 14/1. 4.15.1: '2nd' Messenian war, or 'revolt', broke out, Ol. 23/4. 4.23.4: fall of Hira, Ol. 28/1. 4.27.9: restoration of Messenia, Ol. 102/3. 6.5.3: Alexander of Pherai captured Skotoussa, and 8.27.8, founding of Megalopolis, both Ol. 102/2. 6.9.5: Gelon occupied Syracuse (ref. to his Olympic dedication), Ol. 72/2. 7.25.2: Helike destroyed by tidal wave, Ol. 101/3. 8.39.3: Lakedaimonians took Phigalia, Ol. 30/2. 8.45.4: archaic temple of Athene Alea,Tegea, burnt, Ol. 96/2. 10.2.2: Phokians occupied Delphi, 2nd Sacred War, Ol. 105/4. 10.3.1: Philip ended 2nd Sacred War, Ol. 108/1. 10.5.5: 4th temple of Apollo, Delphi, burnt, Ol. 58/2. 10.23.9: Celtic expedition against Hellenes, Ol. 125/3 and Celts crossed into Asia the following year. *Olympiad/victor/archon, year unspecified*: 4.23.10: Anaxilas conquered Zankle, Ol. 29. 4.24.5: revolt after violation of Tainaron: Ol. 29 (emend. to 79). 7.16.7: end of Roman war, Ol. 160. *Olympiad notices, lacking one or more of standard details*: 4.4.5: Eleians held 4th Olympiad when Messenian Polychares won the only event – the *stade*. 5.23.4: 30 years' Peace between Lakonians and Athenians, after 2nd conquest of Euboia, Ol. 83/2. 6.19.13: Megarians dedicated Olympian treasury from Korinthian spoils, before Eleans kept records of Games; life-archon: Phorbas. 10.7.3–4: prize for flute, flute-singing, and athletic contests, introduced at Pythian Games, Ol. 48/3.

[36] Plutarch is cited by Habicht 1985, 96–116, as one of Pausanias' principal sources, and his catalogue includes two lost works, *Lives* of Epaminondas and Aristomenes, figures associated with Messenian struggles for independence. Plutarch's sources included Aristotle, Kallisthenes, Sosibios, Timaios, Demetrios of Phaleron and Philostephanos of Kyrene.

[37] Kelly doubted it, 1970b, 30.

[38] Hall 1995b, 591.

[39] e.g. Wade-Gery 1949, 81.

[40] No commander is recorded for either side.

[41] *P.Oxy*. 3316.15 (= Tyrt. fr.23aW), Coles and Haslam 1980, 5. Arkadians

and Argives as Messenian allies: Paus. 4.15.1, 7.

42 *Myrtaeus* (*sic*) Ol. 36/3 (*634* BC): Euseb. (Hieron.) 169 (F), 96b (H); Tyrtaios' ref. to Theopompos: fr. 5W *ap*. Paus. 4.6.5, Schol. Plat. *Leg*. 629a; Strabo C279 and C362.

43 Hdt. 8.131.

44 *P.Oxy*. 3316.16 and 19 (= Tyrt. fr. 23aW), Coles and Haslam 1980, 3; Ducat 1983, 200; Great Trench: Paus. 4.17.2; Arist*EN* 1116b.1; Hom. *Il*. 12. 3–5.

45 Wade-Gery 1949, 81, n. 3; Andrewes 1949, 77 and 1951, 44; Kelly 1970b, 32, 37, and 1976, 94, 97–100, nn. 11–15.

46 Ol. 28: Philostr. 142.12; Victors: *Stade*: Χάρμις Λάκων (Euseb. Lib. Chron. I (Arm) 198.6–10 (S)) or Χίονις Λάκων (see nn. 4 and 9; Eusebius (Lib. Chron. I (Arm) 198.12–18 (S)) lists Χίονις as *stade* victor for Ols. 29–31; *Pentathlon*: Φιλόμβροτος Λάκων Euseb. (Arm) 198 (S). Moretti, (40–42), 63–4.

47 Pherekydes *FGrH* 1 F 5 *ap*. Steph.Byz. s.v. Ὑσία. Destruction of Hysiai: Thuc. 5.83.

48 Synoikism: Paus. 8.27.1. Mycenae: D.S. 11.65; Paus. 2.16.4; 7.25.3. Tiryns: Paus. 2. 25.8; a Tirynthian won the boys' boxing in Ol. 78 (*468* BC), *P.Oxy*. 222; Moretti (244), 93. Plataia dedication: Paus. 5.23.1–3. Andrewes 1952, 5. Willetts 1959, 499–500. Tomlinson 1972, 101–9. Kelly 1976, 45–6, 64–7, 88–9. Demand 1990, 59–61, 64.

49 Sites are numbered on the map, in the text, and in the Topographical Notes. Paus. 8.27.1. Strabo C373.

50 Hdt. 7.202, 9.28; Pritchett 1995, 209.

51 Hdt. 1.65 ff.

52 Karyai as Lakedaimonian frontier: Thuc. 5.55. The Lakedaimonians need not have crossed the Tegean Plain, or entered Thyreatis, to reach Hysiai; Tausend 1989, 142, and Pritchett 1995, 223–4, both believe that a route may have traversed the hills from Hysiai to Karyatis, SW of Agios Petros (MAP, 8c).

53 Hdt. 1.82, 8.73.

54 Thuc. 5.14 and 41.

55 Cartledge 1979, 125–6. His view was recently endorsed by Osborne (1996, 184, 289).

56 Paus. 2.20.1–2, and 2.38.5. See nn. 22, 53.

57 e.g. Mitchell 1996 in Lloyd (ed.), 95.

58 Damokratidas: Paus. 4.35.2; Meltas: D.S. fr. 7.13.2. Wade-Gery 1966, 298. Lakedas: Hdt. 6.126. Andrewes 1951, 44–5. Kelly 1976, 108 f. Griffin 1982, 55, (that Meltas was Lakedas' uncle). Carlier 1984, 393. Perilaos: Hdt. 1.82; Paus. 2.23.7; 2.21.1, 7. Laphaes: Paus. 2.21.8. Paus. 2.19.2. 'Argive' king-list: *IG* iv.614 = *SEG* 11.336.

59 Hdt. 7.149. 'Melanta' was *basileus* in a mid-fifth century inscription *re*. Argive arbitration between Knossos and Tylisos, *SIG*[3] 56.43–5 = *SEG* 11.316: *GHI* 42; *LSAG*, 165. No Argive βασιλεύς in treaty of *420* BC (Thuc. 5.47.8). Plutarch's Eagle King was chosen (Plut. *Mor*. 340C *and* 396C). In a late-fifth-century inscription from Argos, *probasileus* preceded *mantis*, *stratagos* and *hiareus*; Κρίτζας 1979, 217. Carlier 1984, 382–3. Drews 1983, 61, argued that Pheidon's *basileia* was magisterial.

[60] Hdt. 6.83; Arist. *Pol.* 1303a7–11; Plut. *Mor.* 245C–F; D.S. 10.26; Paus.2.20.9. Forrest 1960, 230–31. Willetts 1959, 496 f.

[61] Hall 1995, 587, and 1997, 70–2. *Anth.Pal.* 14.73. Sixth-century legislative (?) body at Tiryns: *SEG* 30.380.4; Βερδελῆς *et al.* 1975, 192–3; Hansen 1984, 162–3.

[62] Hdt. 5.70–2, 74.

[63] Hdt. 6.49–50. Carlier 1984, 279–80, 291–2; Boedeker 1987, 20. I am grateful to Stephen Hodkinson for his gentle insistence on this point.

[64] Hdt. 5.64, 70, 75, 90; 6.49–50, 70, 74–81; Plut. *Mor.* 223C, 245D–E. Cawkwell 1993, 507, 519, 522.

[65] Hdt. 7.148.

[66] Plut. *Mor.* 223B.

[67] Hdt. 6.76; Krios warned Kleomenes in similar words (Hdt. 6.50). Willetts 1959, 503–5.

[68] Philostephanos of Kyrene *ap.* Steph.Byz. s.v. Ἀνθάνα, for Kleomenes' flaying of Anthes at Anthana (MAP, 7a, 7c, 7d). Griffiths 1989, 62–7 concludes that Kleomenes may have visited Anthana before Sepeia. Καλίτσες 1964, 231–2. Inscription, *c. 500* BC, found near Xylopyrgos (MAP, 6c) on old road over Zavitsa (*SEG* 13.266; Ῥωμαίος, 1950, 237; Κρίτζας 1985, 710; Goester 1993, 88). Pritchett 1980, 109, and 1995, 252, identifies it as a cenotaph; Christien 1992, 158 disagrees.

[69] πταῖσμα also used by Argives of their misfortune at Sepeia; Herodotos (1.65) uses προσέπταιον to convey Lakedaimonians' failure to overcome the Tegeates.

[70] Paus. 2.21.8.

[71] Carlier 1984, 393, thinks Ephoros' source for the king who fled to Tegea was not Argive.

[72] Hdt. 6.79.

[73] Parker 1989, 144 and n. 39. Demaratos' deposition: Hdt. 6.67.3. Dillery 1996, 233. Battle of Champions: Hdt. 1.82.

[74] Sosibios, *FGrH* 595 F 5 *ap.* Ath. 678C. *Anec.Graec.* 32.18 (Bekker): Γυμνοπαιδία are paeans honouring those who fought at Thyrea. See n. 79.

[75] Alkman, whose music was sung by the *Trichoria*, is dated to Ol. 42 (*609* BC) by Eusebius, but in *Suda* to Olympiad 27 (*672* BC). *Trichoria*: Pollux 4.107; did he mean Tyrtaios of Mantineia (Plut. *Mor.* 1137F)? Plut. *Lyk.* 21.3. Lyk. *in Leoc.* 106.

[76] Bölte 1929, 131–2. *IG* v.i.213, lines 44–9, 62–4; *LSAG*, 196, 201, Lakonia no. 52; Wade-Gery 1949, 79–81.

[77] Den Boer 1954, 221–7; Billot 1989–90, 93.

[78] *PMG* 32. *Suda* s.v. ψιλεύς. Wade-Gery 1949, 80, cf. Kelly 1970b, 40.

[79] *Pace* ref. in *Etym. Magn.* s.v. γυμνοπαιδία to paeans honouring those περὶ Πυλαίαν* πεσόντας. (*Usually emended to Θυρέαν.).

[80] Paus. 3.7.5. Wade-Gery 1949, 80. See pp. 284–5.

[81] Since Wade-Gery wrote his article, the watch-towers (MAP, 6c, 6d, 6e) located at Xylopyrgos, Anemomylos and Xeropigadi, and thus south of Hysiai, have been investigated; they yielded artefacts which post-date the conventional period of the Champions and are only of Lakonian type.

Pritchett 1980, 118–19; Φακλάρης 1990, 238; Goester 1993, 91, 98. Πίκουλας 1990–91, 248.

82 *Anec.Graec.* 1408 s.v. Πάρπαρος (Bekker); Hesychius s.v. Πάρπαρος.

83 Plin. *HN* 4.17. Christien and Σπυρόπουλος 1985, 456.

84 Προτονοτάριου-Δεΐλακη 1971, 84, pl. 70 β; Φακλάρης 1987, 101–19; Christien and Σπυρόπουλος 1985, 459; Φακλάρης 1990, 226–8; Κρίτζας 1985, 714–15; Dubois 1987, 416. Pritchett 1995, 260. Parallels from Lykosoura and Perachora: Κουρουνιώτης 1912, 160, fig. 41; Payne 136, pl. 43 nos. 5–7. Κρίτζας argued that the bull was dedicated *by* 'Paos'. Bull of similar style and date from the sanctuary of the Kabeiroi at Thebes (now in National Museum, Athens (NM 10545)), inscribed from *Paon* to *Kabiro*. Kleomenes sacrificed a bull to Poseidon at Thyrea before embarking for Tiryns (Map, 4c) and Sepeia (Hdt. 6.76).

85 *Hermai*: Paus. 2.38.7. 'Ρωμαίος 1905, 137 f.

86 Refs. in Pipili 1987, 78–9.

87 Palm wreaths: Paus. 8.48.2–3; victory symbol: Arist. *M.M.* 1196a 36; Plut. *Mor.* 723–4; Dionysos *Psilax*: Paus. 3.19.6. Ψίλοι or ψιλῆται can mean light-armed troops. Herodotos (9.28) refers to ψίλοι τῶν εἰλώτων; Eustathius (1222.53). Pollux (3.83) uses οἱ γυμνῆτες to mean Argive serfs. Christien 1992, 168, parallels respective Argive and Lakedaimonian institutions of γυμνῆτες and εἵλωτες.

88 Sosibios *FGrH* 595 F 4 *ap.* Ath. 674–B; Xen. *Anab.* 1.2.10; cf. Ath. 128E.

89 Paus. 8.35.7; Plin. *HN* 7.205; Xen. *Anab.* 6.1.11 ff. Poursat 1968, 550–3.

90 Polyb. 4.20.12. Ephoros *FGrH* 70 F 54 and Hermipp. fr. 82 Wehrli, both *ap.* Ath. 154D; Demonax: Hdt. 4.161; D.S. 8.30.2.

91 *Hoplomachia*: Ephoros *FGrH* 70 F 104–6. *Mōleia*: Ariaithos of Tegea *FGrH* 316 F 7. Mantineian martial arts: Wheeler 1982, 223–33. See n. 75.

Bibliography

Abadie, C. and Σπυρόπουλος, Θ.

1985 'Fouilles à Helleniko (Eua de Thyréatide)', *BCH* 109, 385–454.

Andrewes, A.

1949 'The Corinthian Actaeon and Pheidon of Argos', *CQ* 43, 70–8.

1951 'Ephoros Book 1 and the Kings of Argos', *CQ* 45, 39–45.

1952 'Sparta and Arcadia in the early 5th century', *Phoenix* 6, 1–5.

Arafat, K.W.

1996 *Pausanias' Greece*, Cambridge.

Arnush, M.F.

1995 'The career of Peisistratos son of Hippias', *Hesperia* 64, 135–62.

Badian, E. (ed.)

1966 *Ancient Society and Institutions: Studies presented to V. Ehrenberg on his 75th birthday*, Oxford.

Baladié, R.

1980 *Le Péloponnèse de Strabon. Etude de géographie historique*, Paris.

Barron, J.

1961 *The Silver Coins of Samos*, London.

Βερδελῆς, N., Jameson, M., Παπαχριστοδούλου, I.
1975 ‘ Αρχαικαὶ επιγραφαὶ εκ Τίρυνθος ’, *ArchEph.*, 150–205.
Billot, M–F.
1989–90 ‘Apollo Pythéen et l’Argolide archaïque: histoire et mythes’, *Archaiognosia* 6, 35–100.
Boedeker, D.
1987 ‘The two faces of Demaratus’, *Arethusa* 20, 185–201.
Bölte, F.
1929 ‘Zu lakonischen Festen’, *RhMus* 78, 124–43.
Bowra, C.M.
1938 ‘Xenophanes and the Olympic Games’, *AJPh* 59, 257–79.
1941 ‘Xenophanes. Fragment 3’. *CQ* 32, 89–102.
Cadoux, T.J.
1948 ‘The Athenian archons from Kreon to Hypsichides’, *JHS* 68, 70–123.
Carlier, P.
1977 ‘La vie politique à Sparte sous le regne de Cleomène 1er’, *Ktema* 2, 65–84.
1984 *La Royauté en Grèce avant Alexandre*, Strasbourg.
Carradice, I.
1995 *Greek Coins*, British Museum Press.
Cartledge, P.A.
1977 ‘Hoplites and heroes. Sparta’s contribution to the technique of ancient warfare’, *JHS* 97, 11–27.
1979 *Sparta and Lakonia. A regional history 1300–362* BC, London.
Cawkwell, G.
1993 ‘Cleomenes’, *Mnemosyne* 46 no. 4, 506–27.
1995 ‘Early Greek tyranny and the people’, *CQ* n.s. 45, 73–86.
Charbonneaux, J., Martin, R., Villard, F.
1971 *Archaic Greek Art 620–480* BC, London.
Christien, J. and Σπυρόπουλος, Θ.
1985 ‘Eua et La Thyréatide. Topographie et histoire’, *BCH* 109, 456–61.
Christien, J.
1992 ‘De Sparte à la côte orientale du Péloponnèse’, *Polydipsion Argos, BCH Suppl.* 22, 157–72.
Coles, R.A. and Haslam, M.W. (eds.)
1980 ‘Oxyrhynchus Papyri’vol. 47, no. 3316, Egyptian Exploration Society.
Connor, W.R.
1988 ‘Early Greek land warfare as symbolic expression’, *Past & Present* 119, 3–29.
Cook, R.M.
1989 ‘The Francis-Vickers chronology’, *JHS* 109, 65–70.
Crowther, N.B.
1984/5 ‘Studies in Greek Athletics’, *CW* 78, 497–558.
Demand, N.
1990 *Urban Re-location in Archaic and Classical Greece*, Bristol.
Den Boer, W.
1954 *Laconian Studies*, Amsterdam.

Detienne, M.

1968 'La Phalange', in Vernant (ed.) *Problèmes...*, 119–47.

Diller, A.

1956 'Pausanias in the Middle Ages', *TAPA* 87, 84–97.

1957 'The manuscripts of Pausanias', *TAPA* 88, 169–88.

Dillery, J.

1996 'Re-configuring the past: Thyrea, Thermopylae, and narrative patterns in Herodotus', *AJPh* 117 no. 2, 217–54.

Dillon, M.P.J.

1995 'The Lakedaimonian dedication to Olympian Zeus: the date of Meiggs/Lewis 22 (*SEG* 11 1203A)', *ZPE* 107, 60–8.

Drachmann, A.B. (ed.)

1903 *Scholia vetera in Pindari carmina*, Leipzig.

Drews, R.

1983 Basileus*: the Evidence for Kingship in Geometric Greece*, New Haven and London.

Dubois, L.

1971 'Bulletin Epigraphique: Arcadie, no. 621', *REG* 100, 416.

Ducat, J.

1962 'L'Archaïsme à la recherche de points de repère chronologiques', *BCH* 86, 165–84.

1971 *Les Kouroi du Ptoion*, Paris.

1983 'Bulletin de bibliographie thématique. Histoire: Sparte archaïque et classique. Structures économiques, sociales, politiques', *REG* 96, 194–225.

Fitzhardinge, L.F.

1986 *The Spartans*, London.

Forrest, W.G.

1960 'Themistocles and Argos', *CQ* n.s.10, 221–40.

1983[3] *A History of Sparta*, London.

Fotheringham, J.K. (ed.)

1905 *The Bodleian Manuscript of Jerome's Version of the Chronicle of Eusebius Reproduced in Collotype*, Oxford.

1923 *Eusebii Pamphili Chronici Canones: Latine vertit adauxit, ad sua tempora produxit S.Eusebius Hieronymus*, London.

Fracchia, H.

1985 'The Peloponnesian pyramids re-considered', *AJA* 89, 683–9.

Frazer, J.G.

1898 *Pausanias. Guide to Greece*, London.

French, A.

1987 *Sixth Century Athens. The Sources*, Sydney.

Fuqua, C.

1981 'Tyrtaeus and the cult of heroes', *GRBS* 22, 215–24.

Goester,Y.C.

1993 'The plain of Astros. A survey', *Pharos* 1, 39–112.

Gow, A.S.F. and Page, D.L. (eds.)

1965 *The Greek Anthology: Hellenistic Epigrams*, Oxford.

Griffin, A.
1982 *Sikyon*, Oxford.
Griffiths, A.
1989 'Was Kleomenes mad?' in Powell (ed.) *Classical Sparta*, 51–78.
Habicht, C.
1985 *Pausanias' Guide to Ancient Greece*, Berkeley.
Hall, J.M.
1995a 'Approaches to ethnicity in the Early Iron Age of Greece', in Spencer (ed.) *Time, Tradition and Society*, 6–17.
1995b 'How Argive was the Argive Heraion?' *AJA* 99, 577–613.
1997 *Ethnic Identity in Greek Antiquity*, Cambridge.
Hammond, N.G.L.
1955 'Studies in Greek chronology of the sixth and fifth centuries BC.' *Historia* 4, 371–411.
Hansen, O.
1984 'Some evidence for an amphictyony in Tiryns', *AAA* 17, 162–3.
Hansen, W. (trans.)
1996 *Phlegon of Tralles' Book of Marvels*, Exeter.
Hanson, V.D. (ed.)
1991 *Hoplites: The classical Greek battle experience*, London.
Harvey, F.D.
1967 '*Oxyrhynchus Papyrus* 2390 and early Spartan history', *JHS* 87, 62–73.
Haynes, D.
1992 *The Techniques of Greek Bronze Statuary*, Mainz/Rhein.
Helm, R. (ed.)
1956[2] *Die Chronik des Hieronymus, Eusebius Werke VII*, Berlin.
Hitzig, M. (ed.)
1901–4 *Pausaniae Graeciae Descriptio*, Leipzig.
Hooker, J.T.
1980 *The Ancient Spartans*, London.
Howgego, C.
1995 *Ancient History from Coins*, London.
Huxley, G.L.
1958 'Argos et les derniers Tèménides', *BCH* 82, 588–601.
1962 *Early Sparta*, London.
1975 'A problem in the Spartan king-list', Λακωνικαί Σπουδαί 2, 110–14.
Hyde, W.W.
1921 *Olympic Victor Monuments and Greek Athletic Art*, Washington.
Jacoby, F.
1941 'The date of Archilochus', *CQ* 35, 97–109.
1949 *Atthis*, Oxford.
Jeffery, L.H.
1949 'Comments on some archaic Greek inscriptions', *JHS* 69, 25–38.
1961 *The Local Scripts of Archaic Greece*, Oxford, = *LSAG*.
1966 'Two inscriptions from Iria', *ArchDelt.* 21A, 18–25.
1976 *Archaic Greece. The City-States c. 700–500* BC, London.

Καλίτσης, K.I.
1964 'Θυραία κατὰ τοὺς ἀρχαίους συγγραφεῖς καὶ τὸ ἔτυμον αὐτῆς', ΠΛΑΤΩΝ 31/32, 219–35.
Kelly, T.
1970a 'The traditional enmity between Sparta and Argos: the birth and development of a myth', *Amer.Hist.Rev.* 75, 971–1003.
1970b 'Did the Argives defeat the Spartans at Hysiai in 669 BC?' *AJPh* 91, 31–42.
1976 *A History of Argos to 500* BC, Minneapolis.
Kiechle, F.
1963 *Lakonien und Sparta*, Vestigia 5, Munich.
Κουρουνιώτης, K.
1912 'τὸ ἐν Λυκοσούρα Μέγαρον τῆς Δεσποίνης', *ArchEph.*, 160.
Kraay, C.M. and Hirmer, M.
1966 *Greek Coins*, London.
Kraay, C.M.
1969 *Greek Coins and History*, London.
1976 *Archaic and Classical Greek Coins*, London.
Κρίτζας, X.
1979 'ΑΡΓΟΛΙΚΟΚΟΡΙΝΘΙΑ', *ArchDelt.* 29, 211–49.
1985 'Remarques sur trois inscriptions de Cynourie', *BCH* 109, 709–16.
Lamb, W.
1925–6 'Arcadian bronze statuettes', *ABSA* 27, 133–48.
Lazenby, J.F.
1991 'The killing zone', in Hanson (ed.) *Hoplites*, 87–109.
Λάζος, X.Δ.
1995 Πυραμίδες στην Ελλάδα, Athens.
Leahy, D.M.
1958 'The Spartan defeat at Orchomenos', *Phoenix* 12, 141–65.
Lenschau, Th.
1936 'Forschungen zur griechischen Geschichte des VII. und VI. Jahrhunderts v. Chr.', *Philologus* 91, 385–411.
Lewis, D.M.
1962 'The archon of 497/6 BC', *CR* 12, 201.
Lewis, R.G.
1997 'Themistokles and Ephialtes', *CQ* 47, 358–62.
Lippold, G.
1950 *Die Griechische Plastik*, Munich.
Lloyd, Alan B. (ed.)
1996 *Battle in Antiquity*, London.
Lobel, E. (ed.)
1957 'Oxyrhynchus Papyri', vol. 24, no. 2390, Egyptian Exploration Society.
Lord, L.E.
1938 'The pyramids of Argolis', *Hesperia* 7, 481–527.
1939 'Watchtowers and fortresses in the Argolid', *AJA* 43, 78–84.
1941 'Blockhouses in the Argolid', *Hesperia* 10, 93–112.

Loring, W.
1895 'Some ancient routes in the Peloponnese', *JHS* 15, 25–89.
Mahaffy, J.P.
1881 'On the authenticity of the Olympic Register', *JHS* 2, 164–78.
Malkin, I.
1994 *Myth and Territory in the Spartan Mediterranean*, Cambridge.
Mallwitz, A.
1988 'Cult and competition locations at Olympia', in Raschke (ed.) *The Archaeology of the Olympics*, 79–109.
McNeal, R.A.
1970 'Historical methods and Thucydides 1.103.1', *Historia* 19, 308–25.
Meiggs, R.
1966 'The dating of fifth century Attic inscriptions', *JHS* 86, 86–98.
Meiggs, R. and Lewis, D.M. (eds.)
1975[2] *A Selection of Greek Historical Inscriptions to the end of the 5th Century* BC, Oxford.
Merritt, B.D.
1939 *Greek Inscriptions*, Hesperia Suppl. 8, 59–65.
Miller, M.
1959 'The early Persian dates in Herodotus', *Klio* 37, 49–52.
Mitchell, S.
1996 'Hoplite warfare in ancient Greece', in A.B. Lloyd (ed.) *Battle in Antiquity*, 87–105.
Moretti, L.
1959 'Olympionikai; i vincitori negli antichi agoni olimpici', *Atti della Accademia Nazionale dei Lincei*, Ser. 8, Vol. 8. Rome.
1970 'Supplemento al Catalogo degli Olympionikai', *Klio* 52, 295–303.
Morgan, C.
1990 *Athletes and Oracles*, Cambridge.
Morgan, C. and Whitelaw, T.
1991 'Pots and politics: ceramic evidence for the rise of the Argive State', *AJA* 95, 79–108.
Morris, I.
1996 'The strong principle of equality', in Ober and Hedrick (eds.) *Demokratia*, 19–48.
Mosshammer, A.A.
1979 *The* Chronicle *of Eusebius, and Greek Chronographic Tradition*, Lewisburg.
Murray, O.
1993 *Early Greece*, London.
Ober, J. and Hedrick, C. (eds.)
1996 *Demokratia*, Princeton.
Osborne, R.
1996 *Greece in the Making 1200–479* BC, London.
Page, D.L. (ed.)
1962 *Poetae Melici Graeci*, Oxford.
1981 *Further Greek Epigrams*, Cambridge.

Παπαχάζης, N.
1963 Παυσανίου Ἑλλάδος Περιήγησις, Ἐκδοτική Ἀθηνῶν.
Parke, H.W. and Wormell, D.E.W.
1956 *The Delphic Oracle*, vol. 2, Oxford.
Parker, R.
1989 'Spartan Religion', in Powell (ed.) *Classical Sparta*, 142–72.
Parker, V.
1991 'The dates of the Messenian Wars', *Chiron* 21, 25–43.
1993 'Some dates in early Spartan history', *Klio* 75, 45–60.
Pearson, L.
1962 'The pseudo-history of Messenia and its authors'*Historia* 11, 410–26.
Peiser, B.
1990 'The crime of Hippias of Elis: zur Kontroverse um die Olympionikenliste', *Stadion* 16, 37–65.
Φακλάρης, Π.Β.
1987 'Η Μάχη τῆς Θυρέας (546 π.χ.), *Horos* 5, 101–19.
1990 'Αρχαιά Κυνουρία, Athens.
Πίκουλας, Γ.
1989 Πρακτικά τοῦ Β' Τοπικού Συνεδρίου 'Αργολικῶν Σπουδῶν, Athens.
1990–91 ' Πύργοι: Δίκτυοι, χρήση, ἀπορίες καὶ ἐρωτήματα ', *Horos* 8–9, 247–57.
Pipili, M.
1987 *Laconian Iconography of the Sixth Century* BC, Oxford.
Plommer, R.
1969 'The tyranny of the Archon-List', *CR* 19, 126–9.
Polignac, F. de (trans. Lloyd)
1995 *Cults, Territory, and the Origins of the Greek City-State*, Chicago.
Poursat, J.C.
1968 'La representation de Danse Armée dans la céramique attique', *BCH* 92, 550–615.
Powell, A. (ed.)
1989 *Classical Sparta. Techniques behind her success*, London.
1995 *The Greek World*, London.
Pritchett, W.K.
1965–89 *Studies in Ancient Greek Topography*, vols. 1–6, Berkeley.
1990–91 *Studies in Ancient Greek Topography*, vols. 7–8 Amsterdam, = *SAGT*.
Pritchett, W.K.
1971, 79, 85 *The Greek State at War*, vols. 1, 3, and 4, Berkeley, = *GSAW*.
1995 *Thucydides'* Pentekontaetia, Amsterdam.
Προτονοτάριου-Δεΐλακη, Ε.
1971 ' ΤΥΧΑΙΑ ΕΥΡΗΜΑΤΑ ', *ArchDelt.* 28B', 84.
Raschke, W.J. (ed.)
1988 *The Archaeology of the Olympics*, Wisconsin.
Raubitschek, A.E.
1949 *Dedications from the Athenian Acropolis*, Cambridge, Mass.

Robinson, E.S.G.
1946 'Rhegion, Zankle, Messana and the Samians', *JHS* 66, 13–21.
Rocha-Pereira, M-H. (ed.)
1989 *Pausaniae Graeciae Descriptio*, Leipzig.
'Ρωμαίος, Κ.
1905 'Laconia. The *Hermai* on the NE Frontier', *ABSA* 11, 137 f.
1950 ' 'Ερευνητική περιοδεία εἰς Κυνουρίαν ', *PAE*, 235–40.
Roy, J.
1972a 'An Arcadian League in the earlier 5th century BC?' *Phoenix* 26, 334–41.
1972b 'Arcadian nationality as seen in Xenophon's *Anabasis*', *Mnemosyne* 25, 129–36.
Σακελλαρίου, Μ.Β.
1981 'Contributions à la histoire archaïque de Sparte et d'Argos', *Archaiognosia* 2, 83–93.
Samuel, A.E.
1972 *Greek and Roman Chronology*, Munich.
Schneider, J.
1985 'La chronologie d'Alcman', *REG* 98, 1–64.
Schöne, A. (ed.)
1875 *Eusebii Chronicorum Libri Duo. Vol. I. Eusebii Chronicorum. Liber Prior*, Berlin.
Schwyzer, E (ed.)
1923 *Dialectorum Graecorum Exempla Epigraphica Potiora*, Leipzig.
Shero, L.R.
1938 'Aristomenes the Messenian', *TAPA* 69, 500–31.
Spencer, N. (ed.)
1995 *Time, Tradition and Society in Greek Archaeology. Bridging the Great Divide*, London.
Tarkow, Th.A.
1983 'Tyrtaeus 9D. The role of poetry in the new Sparta', *Ant.Class* 52, 48–69.
Tauchnitz, C. (ed.)
1829 *Pausaniae Graeciae Descriptio*, Leipzig.
Tausend, K.
1989 'Zur Historizität der Schlacht von Hysiai', *RSA* 19, 137–46.
Theocaris, P.S., Liritzis, I., Galloway, R.B.
1997 'Dating of two Hellenic pyramids by a novel application of thermoluminescence', *JAS* 24 no. 5, 399–405.
Thomas, R.
1995 'The place of the poet in archaic society', in Powell (ed.) *The Greek World*, 104–29.
Tomlinson, R.A.
1972 *Argos and the Argolid*, London.
Van Wees, H.
1995 'Politics and the battlefield', in Powell (ed.)*The Greek World*, 153–78.

Vernant, J.-P. (ed.)
1968 *Problèmes de la Guerre en Grèce Ancienne*, Paris.
Vian, F.
1952 *La Guerre des Géants*, Paris.
Wade-Gery, H.J.
1949 'A note on the origin of the Spartan *gymnopaidiai*', *CQ* 43, 79–81.
1966 'The *Rhianos*-Hypothesis', in Badian (ed.) *Ancient Society*, 289–302.
Waisglass, A.A.I.
1956 'Demonax ΒΑΣΙΛΕΥΣ ΜΑΝΤΙΝΕΩΝ', *AJPh* 77, 167–76.
Wallace, W.P.
1954 'Kleomenes, Marathon, the helots and Arcadia', *JHS* 74, 32–5.
West, M.L.
1965 'Alcmanica I. The Date of Alcman', *CQ* n.s 15, 188–202.
1992 'Alcman and the Spartan Royalty', *ZPE* 91, 1–5.
Wheeler, E.L.
1982 '*Hoplomachia* and Greek dances in arms', *GRBS* 23, 223–33.
Wilamowitz-Moellendorf, U. von
1922 *Pindaros*, Berlin.
Willetts, R.F.
1959 'The servile interregnum at Argos', *Hermes* 87, 495–506.

Chapter 11

THE SOCRATICS' SPARTA AND ROUSSEAU'S

Paul Cartledge

The majority praise [the Spartans] in moderate terms, but some speak of them as if the demigods ran the state there (Isocrates)[1]

I

We are all democrats now, and democracy was invented some 2500 years ago, in Greece, where it flourished until oligarchs and imperialists from Rome stamped it out in the second century BCE. Stamped out it remained thereafter, both as a fact and as an idea, until the eighteenth century of our era, when Rousseau did as much as anyone, and much more than most, to reinvigorate the idea of democracy in preparation for its restoration in fact by the French Revolution.

That, in consciously crude outline, is one popular modern story, or myth, of democracy's historic trajectory. But at least among classicists and ancient historians it is no secret that in antiquity democracy did not by any means triumph altogether over oligarchy, aristocracy, kingship or tyranny, and that both in antiquity and from antiquity to the modern era the dominant intellectual-political tradition was not only anti-democratic, but also, and often precisely because of that bias, pro-Spartan. As for Rousseau, he not only was of, but also in crucial ways was against, the Enlightenment, and it was typical of the paradox of the man that he managed to be both pro(to)-democratic, unlike most Enlightened thinkers, and, like most of them, pro-Spartan. A fair amount, therefore, of our western political-theoretical and practical-political heritage can be seen to hang on what Elizabeth Rawson (1969) called the 'Spartan tradition in European thought', and on Rousseau's place within that tradition.

It is that perspective on Sparta's 'shadow' that this paper aims to explore or re-explore by comparing and contrasting Rousseau's take on Sparta with that of the two most prominent and influential 'laconists' of antiquity. The upshot, in short, is on the face of it paradoxical: whereas Plato and Xenophon as anti-democratic Athenians might have been expected to evince strong sympathy for Sparta, and Rousseau as a proto-democrat to denounce her, in fact Plato and Xenophon offer far more devastating criticisms than any Rousseau could manage to contrive. The explanation, it will be suggested, lies within the specific political and intellectual conjunctures of their respective, broadly utopian projects.

The paper's strategy will be, first, to outline what is at stake in evaluating the tradition about ancient Sparta (section II), and especially in distinguishing within that tradition the various senses of 'laconism' (III); then, to ask who were 'the Socratics', and decide which of them will count as such for present purposes (IV); next, to ask who Rousseau was, or rather who did he like to think he was or to present himself as (V). That will lead into discussion of the various and varying laconism(s) of my chosen Socratics (VI–VIII) and of Rousseau (IX). Finally, by way of a prospect more than a conclusion, I shall open the essay out into a broader discussion of utopianism and utopiography (X)[2].

II

It was François Ollier (1933–43) who coined the usefully vivid phrase 'le mirage spartiate'. By 'mirage' he meant the series of more or less distorted, more or less invented images through which Sparta has been reflected and refracted in the extant literature by non-Spartans, beginning in the late fifth century BCE with Critias of Athens, pupil of Socrates, relative of Plato, and leading light (or prince of darkness) of the so-called Thirty Tyrants (of whom more anon).[3]

For historians of 'how it actually was' in ancient Sparta and Spartan society, the mirage poses a major historiographical problem. Since practically all our detailed evidence for what they were 'really' like comes from within the mirage, how can we be sure that any one alleged detail, let alone the totality, is not just a figment of the writer's or writers' imaginative projection? In fact, the problem is even more intractable than that. The mirage in its written form began to take shape at just the same time as – and, in part, precisely because of – an enormous crisis that was coming to a head in Spartan polity and society. To put it very simply, Sparta's prolonged involvement and eventual victory in the Peloponnesian War during the last third of the fifth century either brought about, or at any rate hastened, the downfall of the model military state.[4]

For historians of ancient Greek political thought, and of its post-classical reception, on the other hand, the situation is not of course anything like as bad – at first sight, anyhow. The mirage or myth is precisely the evidence that is required by them, since it offers up Sparta as a political model or paradigm, an imaginative or imaginary representation of political virtue in living actuality.

Yet, all the same, for historians like myself who want to study not the mirage as such, but the possible links between it and the political-philosophical projects of the Socratics and Rousseau, the mirage effect remains problematic. Apart from such purely factual questions as whether or not, and, if so, how, the Socratics and Rousseau were directly influenced by Sparta, or rather their idea of Sparta, there is the further interpretative question: how historically authentic, and therefore how realistic or pragmatic, were any of their supposedly Sparta-based political prescriptions intended to be?

III

Before grappling with such issues in detail, we may distinguish for expository purposes three principal modes or forms of 'laconism' in classical Greece; three different ways, that is, of appealing to or appropriating Sparta for different political and/or philosophical ends. There is, first, what I shall call descriptively social laconism or, pejoratively, laconomania. This was a matter largely of outward show – as exhibited in choice of ragged clothing, the growing of facial and other head hair, and the embrace of an ostentatiously unwashed or emaciated style of life. Such laconomania was largely confined, at Athens anyhow, to upper-class, but not seriously educated, characters, whose praise of Sparta was based essentially on snobbish social prejudice. Socrates, as we shall see, was implicated with such people, in Aristophanic comedy, though whether or not he was fairly so implicated is another matter.

Second, there is pragmatic-political laconism. This was the sort espoused by those who, as Aristotle bluntly put it, want to 'get rid of existing *politeiai*, praising the Spartan or some other' (*Pol.* 1288b39–40). We are dealing, in other words, with a notionally realistic programme put forward by would-be revolutionary politicians who found Sparta a suitable alternative model either for consciousness-raising propaganda purposes or as a desirable practical goal. The Thirty Tyrants, as we shall see, fit the bill as pragmatic-political laconisers very nicely.

Then, third, there is political-theoretical laconism, including not only public attitudes held or struck (e.g., Cynic praise of Spartan austerity: Fisher 1994, n. 46) but also theoretical expressions of political laconism addressed to private philosophical schools or cliques and not to mass audiences. This variety of laconism might or might not overlap with Type 2 laconism in having a directly practical political aim, whether – to borrow Michael Walzer's language (1988; cf. Ober 1998, 48–9) – 'immanent' (reformist) or 'rejectionist' (revolutionary).

The question we might want to consider at the outset, therefore, is whether the Socratics were merely social laconisers, or did they rather take what they understood Sparta to be like as a model for political change, at the limit as the goal for counter-revolutionary change, in their own city or cities? But first we must complete our definition of terms by introducing our cast of thinking and acting characters: who were the Socratics, and who was Rousseau – or who did he want to be thought of as?

IV

The adjective *Sōkratikos* makes its debut in Aristotle's *Poetics* (1447b11), though his *Sōkratikoi logoi* are a broader literary genre than just the dialogues and other discourses composed by Plato and other associates of Socrates. But the idea of the Socratics as a recognised group of Socrates's followers goes back at least to the parade of *homilētai* or disciples to be found in Xenophon's *Memoirs of Socrates* (1.1–2, esp. 1.2.12, 48).[5] Granted, then, that 'the Socratics' were a recognisable if ill-defined ancient intellectual group, in our present context of laconism just two of them, Plato and Xenophon, demand detailed consideration – unless of course Socrates was from this point of view the original Socratic (see further below). In each case, what we are interested in is what they made of Sparta: that is, not just what they thought Sparta was like but how they used their understandings or constructions of Sparta to inform or further their own political theories, projects and (if such be the right word) programmes, in so far as those can be recovered.

V

Rousseau, it has been claimed without too much obvious exaggeration, was eccentric or marginal in practically everything. He was also a bundle of paradoxes: a supporter of the Ancients in their quarrel with the Moderns, yet also a master of modern sensibility; a *philosophe* who cast himself as a latter-day Socrates in opposition to the Sophists but used 'philosophesque' as an insult; a theorist who denied the Enlightenment's fundamental commitment to the individual and publicly favoured a communitarian, proto-democratic ideal while himself withdrawing as a solitary dreamer to an inner world of self-absorption, a pose that his erstwhile intellectual and political comrades-in-arms found contemptible.

Here, surely, is a case of the 'Do as I say, not as I do' syndrome, and this is one reason why Rousseau is so hard to read – even once, let alone the twice he recommends in the Second Discourse.[6] But it is by no means the only reason. The differences of occasion of Rousseau's publications (and in some cases their non-publication), compounded by the development (or vagaries) of his thought over time, gave rise to several major inconsistencies in his *oeuvre* as a whole. Against such a background of eccentricity, paradox, and inconsistency, if not self-contradiction, those issues on which Rousseau did *not* change his mind stand out in high relief. Signally, if unpredictably, the latter included ancient Sparta. Rousseau himself one might reasonably have thought to be as un-Spartan in crucial respects as could possibly be imagined, and yet he remained consistently a devoted laconiser. The paradox to end all paradoxes? First, let us consider the Socratics' Sparta(s).

VI

Karl Marx is supposed once to have remarked, on reading his self-styled disciples' deformation of his thought, that at least he was not a 'Marxist'. In the same sense, we might begin by asking – in the context of our restricted agenda, namely attitudes to and uses of Sparta – whether Socrates was a 'Socratic'. Speaking generally, it might be thought surprising that any Greek intellectual should really have loved a people such as the Spartans who were, in the words of a fourth-century *rhētōr, hēkista philologoi* – that is, minimally or not at all devoted to reasoned, especially written, intellectual discourse.[7] Yet Spartan non- or minimal literacy could be turned, as Rousseau was to show, to Sparta's advantage, on the grounds that it exhibited a proper preference for substance over mere form, and Socrates notoriously did not actually write down his philosophy.

More specifically, there are, first, the representations of Socrates and his followers by Aristophanes. To his *Birds* we owe the freshly minted verbs *Sōkratein*, 'to Socratise', and *lakōnomanein*, 'to go Sparta-crazy':

> they aped the manners of Sparta, let their hair grow long, went hungry, refused to wash, 'Socratised', and carried walking sticks (1281–2).

At first blush, that may look more like Aristophanic humour than Socratic reality: just as in *Clouds* Aristophanes could deliberately confuse Socrates with a tabloid version of the supposedly typical Sophist, so here in *Birds* he appears deliberately to have confused Socrates with the laconomanes, the better to smear his target.[8] And yet, it was also characteristic of Aristophanes' absurd humour to blend fantasy with fact, or rather to take off into fantasy from a basis of perceived fact. So the basis of the *Birds* joke may be that in 414, a time of anti-oligarchic witchhunt, Socrates was associated in the highly suspicious mind of the Athenian democratic public not with merely 'social', lifestyle laconism but with one or both of the other sorts, the 'pragmatic-political' and/or the 'political-theoretical'.[9]

At all events, whatever we may think or believe of Aristophanes's humour, Socrates (or 'Socrates') was indeed consistently portrayed elsewhere as admiring of Sparta's *politeia*, or more exactly its *eunomia*; by which was meant not the excellence of the Spartans' laws but their orderly and unquestioning obedience to their *nomoi*, 'unwritten' in the twofold sense that they were not committed to writing and were (therefore) deemed to be universally and without exception binding.[10] But was there more to Socrates's attitude to Sparta than a vague and general admiration from afar? Nothing like proof is available, but in light of the recent attempts to recuperate Socrates as a good, indeed much better than the average, Athenian democrat, it may be useful, not to restate yet again the evidential basis of an opposite but necessarily inconclusive reading of his political outlook, but to suggest a possible scenario for the sorts of considerations, emotional as well as narrowly rational, that could have influenced it.[11]

Suppose, for the sake of argument, that like his best pupil Plato – or at any rate the 'Plato' of the *Seventh Letter* – Socrates too had looked forward to and welcomed the installation at Athens in 404 of the regime of the Thirty (not yet 'Tyrants'), led as it was by another of his former pupils, Critias, a relative of Plato. Suppose further that the Thirty, at least in their softening-up propaganda, had argued along something like the following lines: once the (Peloponnesian) War is over and we Athenians have unconditionally surrendered, the Spartans will certainly want a change of political regime here, an end to the democracy they despise. But they will not necessarily want to rule us directly. At any rate, they might not want to if the new regime we introduce should prove acceptable to them.

As things turned out, the known constitutional aspect of the Spartans' peace terms included nothing more specific than a requirement that the Athenians restore the 'ancestral constitution', meaning some sort of oligarchy. For domestic consumption, the Thirty's own cant word was apparently *epanorthōsis*, 'rectification', of the *politeia* (*Ath.Pol.* 35.2): that is to say, not a *tabula rasa* and *ex nihilo* (re)construction from the ground up, but some kind of 'reformist' remodelling.[12] For external, principally Spartan consumption, however, Critias gave out that he personally considered Sparta's to be the *kallistē politeia* (Xen. *Hell.* 2.3.34) and consistently with that propaganda claim gave the 'rectification' of Athens's *politeia* a decidedly laconising aspect. Thus, the Thirty themselves corresponded in number to Sparta's governing Gerousia, a senate of thirty members including the two kings; a body of five Ephors makes a shadowy appearance under the Thirty, a copy surely of the Spartans' five-man Ephorate; and the new, that is oligarchically determined, Athenian citizen body of 3000 corresponded roughly in size to the existing Spartan citizen body.[13] The regime was, anyhow, considered sufficiently laconising, or sufficiently worth backing on other grounds, for Sparta to be willing to grant the Thirty a Spartan garrison when domestic opposition began to make itself seriously felt.

In light of this plausible scenario, Socrates's conduct under the Thirty can, I submit, be usefully reviewed in its proper political perspective. First of all, his decision to remain in the city in 404 under the Thirty was not a matter merely of geography or of his allegedly incorrigible urbanism. 'The men of the City', as they were habitually referred to in shorthand, stood for the new, oligarchic Athens as opposed to 'the men in the Peiraieus', who represented what was left of Athenian democracy. When, therefore, Socrates was enrolled as one of Critias's 3000 citizens, as he must surely have been, he was knowingly throwing in his lot with a counter-revolutionary – both antidemocratic and laconising – oligarchy.

Thereafter, we can well imagine that Socrates, like the author of the Platonic *Seventh Letter*, was thoroughly disgusted by the behaviour of the Thirty, as of course were other prominent citizens among the 3000, not to mention those wealthy metics like Lysias and Polemarchos, sons of the Kephalos in whose house the *Republic* is set, who were specifically targeted by Critias and his henchmen. That disgust did not, however, drive Socrates to leave Athens nor, even if it had, would it detract from my main contention that Socrates had, arguably, once valued Spartan-style *eunomia* as a potentially practicable model for a renewed or remade virtuous Athens. If that contention holds good, Socrates must be adjudged a laconiser of both the pragmatic-political and the political-theoretical kinds. The persuasive – if not wholly accurate – claim made by Aeschines in court half a century later, that the Athenians had killed Socrates the Sophist for having taught Critias, might then be extended and emended to read 'for teaching Critias – the laconiser'.[14]

VII

What of Socrates's intellectual followers? The standard view of Xenophon, probably, is that he was a reflective man, with ambitions to write edifying literature, but not all that impressive a thinker, at least not as judged by the highest standards of philosophical originality. The opposed view has been championed by among others W.E. Higgins, for whom Xenophon is not only heroic but subtle. Higgins' case, in brief, is that Xenophon, so far from being a (mere) laconiser, was ever the 'simple and restrained Socratic'.[15]

On our suggested reading of the historical Socrates, of course, that might not have been so very different, especially to a follower like Xenophon who represented himself somewhat implausibly (Nehamas 1998, 94–5 and nn. 91–5) as a disciple of the great man: above all in the *Apology*, in which he makes Socrates respond to the impiety charge in a most unsubtly literalist way, and in the *Memorabilia* or *Memoirs of Socrates*. There are several references to Sparta in the latter, of which I select for discussion here just two passages, since they lead in neatly to discussion of the most obviously relevant of his works, the so-called *Constitution of the Spartans* (or *Lac.Pol.*).

First, a mini-dialogue between Socrates and the younger Pericles (son of Pericles and Aspasia, one of the generals executed in 406), on the relative merits of Athens and Sparta (*Mem.* 3.5). 'I can't understand, Socrates, how it was that our country ever deteriorated.'[16] The explanation, Socrates rejoins, is that the Athenians abandoned 'their ancestors' way of life'; but, supposing they were to rediscover it and to follow it as well as the ancestors did, 'they would prove to be just as good men as they were'. Or alternatively, Socrates suggests, the Athenians might choose to copy the way of life of the Spartans – which, if they applied themselves with more assiduity even than the Spartans, they might not merely emulate but actually surpass. Pericles (junior) remains very far from convinced, and (however implausibly as historical fact) he produces what we may guess had become by the time of writing (the 370s?) some of the standard laconist tropes: respect for their elders; development of their bodies; obedience to authority; unanimity or concord; and co-operation for the common good – in all these ways, Pericles opines, the Athenians have no chance of equalling let alone surpassing the Spartans. But Xenophon's patriotic Socrates is not to be gainsaid: 'do not despair of the Athenians as being disorderly', he counsels; for with expert leadership, especially expert generalship, they can at the least do very much better than they are doing at present. That turn in the dialogue could perhaps be interpreted to mean that Xenophon himself (if 'Socrates' was his mouthpiece) was not a diehard laconiser, less so anyhow than his 'Pericles' character. But it could also be read as grist to the overall political strategy of the *Memorabilia*, which was to continue and develop the *Apology*'s defence of Socrates by covering up or removing any taint of disloyalty to his native city.

The second passage comes from a dialogue staged between Socrates and Hippias of Elis, one of the four so-called 'ancient Sophists' (*Mem.* 4.4). The *leitmotif* of this exchange is Xenophon's introductory claim – a faint echo of Plato's *Crito* – that Socrates 'chose to abide by the law of Athens and die, rather than break it and live'. In the longest utterance by far Socrates bombards Hippias with a whole battery of questions that are not meant to be merely rhetorical. The first two go as follows: 'Are you aware...that Lycurgus the Spartan would have made Sparta no better than any other city if he had not inculcated in it the greatest *obedience to the laws*? Don't you know that the best leaders are those who are the most efficient in making the people *obey the laws,* and that a city in which the people are most *obedient to the laws* has the best life in time of peace and is irresistible in war?' (my emphases). Socrates then turns to praise 'concord' and, using a specifically Spartan term (Gerousia), rams home the necessity for a compact between the Gerousia and aristocracy, on the one hand, and the ordinary citizens, on the other, to ensure that the latter do *obey the laws.* The barrage concludes with a volley of praises for the 'law-abiding man'.

This is all thoroughly Xenophontic, especially the almost overdone emphasis on *peitharchia*,[17] and the connection with the earlier Pericles dialogue is palpable. Yet 'Socrates' has here made a crucial further move. Before, he had held out patriotically for at least the possibility of a better Athens, better even, indeed, than Sparta. Now he presents Sparta, or rather Lycurgan Sparta, as simply better than any other city, and without demur from Hippias. Conspicuously, however, there is no discussion of the merits of the laws themselves. What is praised is Sparta's Lycurgus-inspired law-abidingness, or *eunomia*. For an account of the laws on their own terms we must turn to the *Lac.Pol.* attributed to Xenophon, and it is on our reading of this work above all else that any estimate of Xenophon's laconism must finally rest.

I stress that the *Lac.Pol.* is 'attributed to' Xenophon. For the unanimous ancient attribution has in modern times been questioned, on various and variously persuasive grounds. Some fans of Xenophon, for example, have been keen to dissociate him from it, because it seems to them to make such a botched job of its purported aim – that is, holding up Sparta, the ideal Sparta of Lycurgan virtue, as a model for imitation by other Greek cities. Nevertheless, the standard modern view holds, rightly in my judgement, that it is indeed Xenophon's and that it is fundamentally a pro-Spartan tract, imperfect though it may be as such. The one discordant chapter, which points out how and how far the contemporary reality of Sparta marks a declension from the supposedly Lycurgan ideals, can on this cogent view be read as confirming the essentially pro-Spartan, model-building message of the other fourteen.[18]

Leo Strauss (1939), however, and his follower Higgins, while accepting the essay's Xenophontic attribution, have read the *Lac.Pol.* otherwise, very much so. Their claim – a standard sort of Straussian claim (cf. Mitchell 1993, 208–9 n. 102) – is that the tract, when read attentively, can be shown to mean the opposite of what it has usually been taken to mean. The rogue chapter of explicit criticism is thus for them 'only the most blunt and visible part of an integrated conception of the Spartan system' (Higgins 1977, 67), and the anomalies that they claim to detect throughout the work indicate to them that the pamphlet as a whole, so far from being designed as a sincere praise of the Spartan way of life, was intended rather as its contrary.

Doubtless, Xenophon could be gently subtle, but in my view – and that of almost every other modern reader – he was never quite that devilishly subtle. The *Lac.Pol.* should probably therefore continue to be understood more straightforwardly. What Xenophon saw, most admired and held up to other Greeks for imitation in 'Lycurgan' Sparta were, above all, the following five traits: a comprehensive state educational system (the *agōgē*); discipline, especially of a military kind; a refusal or even outright legal prohibition of *khrēmatismos* (commercial moneymaking); a simple and austere *diaita* or way of life; and, fifthly and finally, obedience to the laws and to those empowered to enforce them (*peitharchia*).

One sentence in the work seems most fully to capture its essence: '(Sparta) alone makes the development of moral excellence (*kalokagathia*) a public duty' (10.4).[19] This highest of high praise is then confirmed in reverse by the opening of the discordantly negative chapter: 'Were anyone to ask me whether I think the laws of Lycurgus still remain in force unchanged even at the present time, by Zeus, no, I would not have the confidence to make that claim today' (14.1). Just exactly when 'today' was, is one of the many unresolvable problems surrounding Xenophon's literary biography. But the circumstantial and other evidence that points to Xenophon's having been a participant observer of Spartan society, from a vantage point at the very top of the Spartan political elite, is compelling. Xenophon's laconism, in other words, was not just of the armchair variety. For much of his adult life, too, his actions seem to have been congruent with his words. Exiled from Athens, he resided for many years on an estate near Olympia granted him by the Spartans (*Anab.* 5.3), and he repaid his benefactors in full, as good friends properly should, in words (*Mem.* 4.4). Not only in and with the *Lac.Pol.* and *Memorabilia*, but also in the *Agesilaos*, his encomiastic moral biography of that Spartan king and personal patron, in several vignettes in his general history of Greece, and in certain, important details of his moral-political quasi-novel, the *Cyropaedia*, Xenophon presented Spartans and Spartan institutions as models good not merely to think with but to emulate in deed.[20] At any rate, in so far as the Spartans themselves preserved the ideals attributed to Lycurgus by Xenophon, behind whose picture of the mythical lawgiver there possibly lay his image of the historical Socrates. When, however, they failed to do so, then Xenophon could be deeply critical, in sorrow more than in anger.

VIII

Altogether more zestful, complex, and influential an ancient Athenian exponent of Socratic laconism was Plato, the 'Socratic' *par excellence*. In considering his contribution to the Spartan tradition, two main questions must be kept uppermost in our mind. First, how deeply was Plato's political project imbued with a laconist dye – or, to put that the other way round, how far was his Sparta a Platonist confection? Second, did Plato intend his Platonist Sparta, or his laconising ideal cities of Kallipolis (*Republic*) and Magnesia (*Laws*), as blueprints to be acted upon? I shall use as my guide Tigerstedt's still unsurpassed investigation of the 'legend of Sparta in classical antiquity'.[21]

The Swedish scholar's three principal conclusions were that: first, Plato was not a laconiser in the sense of being an Athenian partisan of Sparta; second, although there are many important points of similarity or identity between his ideal state(s) and Sparta (1965, 254–62), there are more fundamental differences (1965, 262–76), and anyhow it cannot be shown that on the important points of similarity or identity he was inspired by Sparta (1965, 274); and, third, Plato never let up on his practical endeavour to reshape the present and the future.

I concur unreservedly with the first, as practically everyone does, and shall say little more on that score.[22] I am much less certain about the third, though willing to give it the benefit of the doubt. But on

Tigerstedt's second conclusion I shall hope to show good reason at least to suspend judgement. Apart from simply recalling that in the *Crito* (52e) Plato makes his Socrates praise Sparta (but also 'Crete') for its *eunomia*, I shall concentrate on the *Republic* and the *Laws*, which may – or may not – be two sides of the same coin.

First, then, Tigerstedt's contention that in more fundamental ways Plato did *not* model his ideal state or states on Sparta. The cornerstone of his negative case is the radical, unbridgeable gulf between Plato's ideal state(s) and all actually existing Greek states. For Plato had great contempt for all existing constitutions, 'degenerate' or otherwise, and was thus no conventional oligarch.[23] Next, he adduces the almost as yawningly wide gulf between Sparta's lack of, or hostility to, intellectual culture (*amousia* and *apaideusis*) and Plato's belief that the true muse was reason plus philosophy or *logos mousikēi kekramenos* (*Rep.* 548e–549b). Then, those two gulfs are reinforced, as Tigerstedt sees it, by the slashing attack in *Republic* book VIII on the timarchic character – competitive, ambitious, mercenary – which is explicitly identified as Spartan (545a), and by the only slightly less slashing attack in the *Laws* on Sparta's one-sided concentration on military virtue at the expense of a balanced approach. Both these attacks, moreover, Tigerstedt would stress, are on the pristine 'Lycurgan' Sparta, not some degenerate version of it. Finally, Tigerstedt adds in some important formal differences between the real Sparta and the ideal states of both the *Republic* and (especially) the *Laws*: Sparta's tripartite social stratification was not the prototype for the division of labour in Kallipolis; unlike the society laboriously prescribed in the *Laws*, Sparta lacked private property and written laws (the model for which was the Athenian *patrios politeia* rather than Spartan *eunomia*), did not use the lot for appointing some officials, and did not place a ban on active pederasty.

On the other side – to which in all fairness Tigerstedt gives a very decent hearing – one might begin by noting the relative un-decadence of timarchic Sparta in the *Republic*, only one stage of corruption down from the happy state of Kallipolis; and the Athenian Stranger's acknowledgement in the *Laws* (692c) that legislatively Sparta could serve as a *paradeigma gegonos*, an ideal model of the historical past. Then, there are a dozen or more formal similarities to Sparta in the ideal states of both the *Republic* and the *Laws*, including some of unarguably central importance: the irreversible hierarchy of rulers over ruled; equality of lifestyle; freedoms for women; state education of the youth; moral and political order; and constant surveillance of the citizens. Finally, besides, and over and above, all those I – *pace*

Tigerstedt – would want to adduce the *Republic*'s notion or dogma of one person/one class:one function (*prattein ta heautou* or *oikeiopragia*), literally the governing idea of Kallipolis – apart of course from the metaphysics of knowledge revealed only to the Philosopher Rulers, for which *ex hypothesi* there could be no counterpart in Sparta or indeed any other hitherto existent polity.

Tigerstedt is, however, formally correct that the correspondence of Kallipolis's three classes or castes with the stratification of Spartan society is not exact: the rulers of Sparta, the citizen elite, correspond not to the Philosopher Rulers but to the Warrior Guards of the *Republic*. On the other hand, it was, I would argue, the legislated exemption and abstention of all Spartan citizens from productive labour (apart from warfare) that gave Plato the key clue to the practical side of Kallipolis's arrangements.[24]

How, then, would I explain or explain away Plato's slashing attacks on Sparta, which were not confined, as were those of Xenophon (above), to an allegedly corrupt present Sparta but extended also to the pristine 'Lycurgan' Sparta? Partly, as a consequence of his irreconcilably different epistemology: on that basis, no actual polity, living or once living, could possibly begin to match up to his ideal state. But partly also as a smokescreen: precisely because Sparta or an image of Sparta had so deeply imbued his own political ideals, especially perhaps his youthful ideals before the disillusionment induced by the regime of the Thirty set in, he simply had to distance his mature, philosophically grounded ideals from any real – contemporary or past – Spartan polity.

Before leaving Plato's laconism, we must touch briefly upon its practicability. Few today, or probably in fourth-century BCE or later antiquity, have considered that the ideal cities of either the *Republic* or the *Laws* were especially practicable. But that is not by itself a good reason for supposing that Plato himself did not believe them to be practicable and intend them to be so taken.[25] One reason why he might have believed they could be is the very same one that I shall suggest animated the laconism of Rousseau, despite all the differences between these extraordinary thinkers.[26]

IX

The self-styled 'citizen of Geneva' was by no means hostile to Plato, indeed was powerfully influenced by him.[27] But Rousseau was also, as Plato never could be, a friend in principle to democracy – direct, participatory democracy, ancient-style, not any newfangled eighteenth-century variety of representative democracy.[28] Consistent with that preference was his fundamental difference of political epistemology. Against Plato's objectively verifiable scientific truths, absolutes denoted by a transcendent natural or divine order, accessible only to the very very privileged and very very few, Rousseau pitted the virtues of mass opinion, the general will, involving democratic knowledge, and a democratic regime of truth. [29]

Not that we, like certain over-enthusiastic French Revolutionaries, should rush to co-opt Rousseau as a democrat *pur sang*. Awareness of his fervent laconism (below) should be sufficient on its own to save us from making that error. Rather, it is the peculiar combination of that backwards-looking laconism with the most progressive form of political thinking then available that requires our explication and, if possible, explanation. Arguably, 'no writing on the ancient city has ever been innocent of the burning issues of the day'.[30] Certainly, that was the case, incandescently so, with Rousseau's Sparta – a weapon to be wielded in any number of battles, fought as much against those whom one might have thought Rousseau would have considered his friends as against his more obvious foes.[31]

Rousseau's own education had been extremely un-Spartan: he was an autodidact, and he read voraciously from an early age (not least in ancient Greek and Roman history). It may indeed be precisely because he was not well educated in the formal sense that his attitude to Sparta, especially when compared to that of the classically educated Voltaire, was conservative, not to say reactionary. The main sources for his knowledge of – or beliefs about – how it actually was in ancient Sparta were, to begin with, the stirring moral biographies of Plutarch, which he read with passion (in Amyot's sixteenth-century translation) from the age of seven.[32] His other main ancient Greek source, not only for his Sparta but for his political theory more generally, was Plato, whom he read in Latin as well as French but not Greek (he confessed that he had tried but failed to learn that language).[33] No doubt, Rousseau's dominant historiographical method remained frankly speculative, rather than empirical and inferential.[34] Yet it is important not to underestimate the extensiveness and accuracy of Rousseau's familiarity with the primary sources – even if only in translation.

Rousseau's favourable view of Sparta was formed in the course of a raging polemic on luxury during the years 1749–53. That was a period when he was 'entre Socrate et Caton', between the Greek sage, the better philosopher, and the Roman republican philosopher in arms, the better citizen.[35] In his prizewinning First Discourse

(*Discours sur les sciences et les arts*, 1749–50) there occurs his celebrated description of Sparta as a city as famous for its 'heureuse ignorance' as for the 'sagesse de ses lois'; in short, as 'a republic of demi-gods', a phrase which – whether he knew it or not – was a calque of Isocrates (see our epigraph).[36] Then came the fragments of 1751–3, which include not only a parallel between Sparta and the Roman Republic but also, more remarkably, the beginnings of a history of Sparta (in which, perhaps thankfully, he did not get very far).[37] Thereafter, in all the major works of his mature political philosophy, from the Second Discourse of 1755 (*Discours sur l'origine et les fondemens de l'inégalité parmi les hommes*) onwards,[38] Sparta and its legislator turn up for honourable, if rarely extended, mention.

Rousseau's ideal state, in brief, was a very small, compact entity conceived on the lines of the (ideal) Greek *polis*: a perfectly balanced republic, where men were free because they ruled themselves, and in which every citizen should feel personally involved. But why, granted that Rousseau proclaimed himself emphatically an Ancient not a Modern political thinker and reformer, should he have placed himself equally firmly in the camp of 'the partisans of Sparta' (Grell 1995, 785), and not those of Athens? Four main reasons may be suggested.

First, Rousseau was obsessed with corruption and the necessity for moral regeneration or rebirth, and full of hope for a new or renewed innocence. He therefore resisted 'bourgeois' economic modernization in the luxury debate and always associated aesthetic cultivation with moral decadence. Sparta, though civilised, was not cultivated: in the First Discourse, as we saw, Rousseau lauded her 'happy ignorance', and he counterposed that precisely to the 'vain learning' of Athens. Apostrophising Sparta (in the 'tu' mode), he praised her extravagantly – and not entirely accurately – for chasing away from her walls (!) 'the Arts and Artists, the Scientists and the "Savans" ' (the ancient counterparts of his contemporary bugbears, the *philosophes*). Of course, Sparta did unfortunately represent men in society, and not in the – for Rousseau – intrinsically superior state of nature. But Sparta's austere, simple and uniform lifestyle placed her closer than most to the ideally true or pure natural state, which in any case could not in Rousseau's view be recuperated.[39]

Second, Sparta stood for civic morality, patriotism, and devotion to the collectivity, realising the time-honoured dream of an integration of the individual and the collective, and displaying 'satisfying habits, a sturdy group spirit, an inclination to do right by one's fellows'.[40] Here, with a vengeance, the *moi humain* was crushed in the *moi commun*, especially through public education and within the framework of the citizen-army.[41]

Third, Rousseau ideally wished not only to dissolve the individual in the collective but also to restrict the private arena in favour of the public.[42] Rousseau's Sparta had done likewise. Moreover, although Rousseau suspected a universal tendency for men to be governed by women, unnaturally, in the private realm, at least the women of Sparta had had the decency to rule their men chastely for the glory of the state and the happiness of the public.[43]

Finally, and not least, Rousseau iconised Sparta because of Lycurgus 'the legislator' or 'lawgiver'. To such semi-divine beings he assigned a 'mission salvatrice' (Grell 1995, 500), endowing them with the capacity to restore desperate situations, and to bring about the division and equilibrium of powers, thereby ensuring political order, stability, and durability.[44] This Rousseauian fixation received one of its sharpest formulations in the *Considérations sur le Gouvernement de Pologne* of 1772: against mere 'lawmakers' Rousseau here counterposed the three ancient 'lawgivers', that is, Moses, Lycurgus, and Numa; and of Lycurgus he wrote, approvingly, that he fixed 'an iron yoke' and tied the Spartans to it by filling up every moment of their lives. This ceaseless constraint was, in Rousseau's thought, ennobled by the purpose it served, that of patriotism, which was constantly presented to the Spartans in their laws, games, homes, mating, and feasts.[45] That passage in turn recalls Rousseau's earlier (1758) *Lettre à d'Alembert*, where, citing Plutarch, Rousseau had applauded Sparta's festivals for being conducted 'without pomp, without luxury, without show', and for exhibiting 'the secret charm of patriotism' and 'a certain national spirit', without 'sensuality or perversion'.[46]

In most respects, then, Rousseau's Sparta not merely was superior to Athens but matched up to his own ideal republic. Not that he was unaware of or unwilling to acknowledge Spartan failings; indeed, in a footnote to the *Social Contract* he even anticipated my remark (above, section II) that the mirage came into being just as the real Sparta hit serious internal crisis: 'A people becomes famous only once its legislation begins to decline. No one knows how many centuries the institution of Lycurgus made for the Spartans' happiness before the rest of Greece took notice of them.'[47] But by and large it was very much the positive that he chose firmly to accentuate.

X

To sum up so far, in a thoroughly Plutarchan manner, with a brief *sunkrisis* of Xenophon's, Plato's and Rousseau's laconisms: all three saw some bad as well as good in Sparta, but Plato and even Xenophon, each for his own reasons (Plato more metaphysical-philosophical, Xenophon more moral-political), detected or admitted far more bad than did Rousseau. Therein lies a paradox. For whereas Plato and Xenophon, as anti-democrats, needed to cling on to the idea of a 'good' Sparta that was both aristocratic-oligarchic and consistently anti-democratic, Rousseau, as a proto-democrat (if no more), did not. At least three possible reasons might be suggested to account for this stance.

First, Athens was not yet available to him as the model of democratic (as opposed to high-cultural) virtue that it was to become in the nineteenth century.[48] In any case, Rousseau was not as much responsible for the transvaluation of democracy in the later eighteenth century as has sometimes been claimed.[49]

Second, Rousseau was not in any event a radical egalitarian democrat. A deeply revealing note added by himself to the Second Discourse shows that he was aware of, and approved, the ancient Greek notion of 'geometric' or proportional equality (for which he interestingly cites neither Plato nor Aristotle, but Isocrates), and that notion was unequivocally oligarchic as opposed to democratic.[50] He has been dubbed, perhaps with some anachronism, 'the champion of a middle-class property owning democracy'; certainly, he advocated a community which knew neither great wealth nor deep poverty, not one in which wealth was equally distributed.[51] Concretely, freedom mattered more to him than equality – if freedom of Rousseau's peculiar kind, involving the dissolution of self by participation in the citizen community.

Third, and above all, Rousseau needed a really virtuous Sparta, not a virtual Sparta, because he insisted, sincerely I think, that he took men as they really are and that his projects were therefore practicable.[52] That claim does, however, require some amplification and justification, for there is no doubt that on one level for Rousseau, as for Mably and Turpin, Sparta was 'un mythe historico-politique', which he used both as 'a critical model for judging the present situation' (Grell 1995, 500) and to demonstrate that good *moeurs* are an essential condition of the greatness (and therefore prosperity) of states, so that morality must be the foundation of politics.[53] Not that Rousseau invented the myth of Sparta, of course, but he did refashion and refurbish it, thereby indeed restoring to it a power it had lost.[54]

However, to claim further, as does Grell (1995, 500), that a good deal of the success of his refashioned model Sparta lay in its mythic, that is 'inaccessible, oneiric, utopian', character seems to me only partially right. For Rousseau's Sparta, not least as seen by him, was not only nor most importantly a made-up myth. Even with all the benefit of nineteenth-century *Quellenkritik* behind them, such acute critics as George Grote and J.S. Mill could still view Lycurgus's alleged legislation as the first major event in Greek history to be reliably attested. No wonder, therefore, that its historicity had gone unquestioned by Rousseau. As for the alleged utopianism of Rousseau's Sparta, Rousseau himself remained to the very end keen to stress the practical realism of his own writing, distancing it sharply from 'the land of chimeras...the Republic of Plato, Utopia, and the Sévinambes'.[55] Rousseau therefore, in short, needed Sparta – or rather his Sparta, as read through Plutarch (and Plato) rather than through Xenophon – as the most perfect instantiation of fundamental tenets of his own political philosophy, such as the general will (instantiated in Lycurgus's legislation) and republican citizenship.[56] As he put it in the *Social Contract*, 'Let us consider what can be done in the light of what has been done... The inference from what is to what is possible seems to me sound.'[57]

But ought Rousseau to be allowed to get away with that disavowal of utopianism? In *The Soul of Man under Socialism* Oscar Wilde opined that a map of the world without 'Utopia' marked on it was not worth consulting. What I should like to conclude by observing is that a literary map of utopianism without 'Sparta' marked on it would be likewise supererogatory. For Sparta, by way of the mirage, was the *fons et origo* of the whole Western tradition of political utopiography. Ancient Athenian theorists of a Socratic tendency found Sparta a suitably different and distant place on which to project their longings for radical political change at home, and many subsequent thinkers followed suit, Rousseau by no means the least among them.[58]

The relevance of that observation, finally, seems to me to be this: that all political thought, all serious political thought, anyhow, which is seriously concerned with altering as well as understanding or explaining the world as it is, is necessarily, in some way or other, more or less utopian: 'Unless we admit that the very notion is senseless, it demands at least an ounce of utopianism even to consider [political] justice...'[59] Conversely, to compose a utopia in writing, as Plato did more than once, with decisive impact not least on Rousseau's political thought, is 'to ask whether and to what extent it is possible for us, who live in our world, to rearrange the categories that we typically use to understand and navigate that world'.[60]

It seems most appropriate, however, to close with a quotation from the French. This one applies in context to Rousseau, but it has, I should like to think, a quite general application: 'la référence antique, en effet, a pour fonction fondamentale de tourner la pensée vers l'avenir'. [61] That, surely, is the only way to go.

Acknowledgements

Besides its presentation at Hay, earlier versions of this paper have been delivered in Cambridge (Faculty of Classics) and London (Institute of Historical Research); I am most grateful for criticism and guidance to my various hosts and interlocutors, especially Josh Ober and Malcolm Schofield (Cambridge), Janet Coleman, John Hope Mason and Robert Wokler (London), and not least the editors of this volume. A tidied-up state of the London version is available on e-mail through the IHR's *Electronic Seminars in History*.

Notes

[1] Isocrates 12 (*Panath.*) 41, trans. N. Fisher in Powell and Hodkinson 1994, 348; the present essay might well be read in conjunction with the latter collection. For the Spartan 'shadow' or 'mirage', see further below, text and n. 3.

[2] To avoid any possible misunderstanding, I must emphasise at the outset this essay's deliberately restricted focus. For example, it is in no way intended to do anything like justice to Plato's or Rousseau's thought as a whole.

[3] Tigerstedt 1965–78 covered the same ground as Ollier, in enormously greater detail, paying as much attention to the modern as to the ancient bibliography; see further below. Rawson 1969 is an elegant and incisive résumé and continuation of Ollier and Tigerstedt, taking the story down to the mid-twentieth century; see also Christ 1986.

[4] Cartledge 1987, *passim*.

[5] Nevertheless, this listing manages to exclude the two major literary Socratics, Plato and of course Xenophon himself. So too does the standard modern edition of Giannantoni (1990), which amasses the fragments of some seventy others. Aristotle, though treated as a 'Socratic' by Wood and Wood 1978, was emphatically not a laconiser of any sort: Schütrumpf 1994. Modern discussion of the term 'Socratics': Vander Waerdt 1994, 1–19.

[6] *Discours sur l'origine et les fondemens de l'inégalité parmi les hommes* (1755), trans. Cranston 1984, 48. See further below, text and n. 38.

[7] Alcidamas, *ap.* Aristotle *Rhet.* 1398b14. On Alcidamas, see briefly Gagarin and Woodruff 1995, 276–89.

[8] For 'laconomania', see also *Wasps* 475–7; cf. Plato *Protag.* 342bc; *Grg.* 515e; Dem. 54. 33–4; with Carter 1986, 71 ff.; Fisher 1994, 358 and n. 40.

[9] On the 414 witchhunt, see Cartledge 1990.

[10] Socrates and Sparta: Montuori 1974, 286–93; note also Fréret 1981 (originally 1736). Spartan *eunomia*: Andrewes 1938. Unwritten laws: Ostwald 1986, 130.

[11] The case *for* a democratic Socrates: Vlastos 1994a, Euben 1997; *contra*:

Wood and Wood 1986; my review of Euben 1997 in *CR* 49 (1999) 156–7.

[12] Schütrumpf in Eder 1995, 273.

[13] The genuineness of the Thirty's laconising makeover may justly be doubted: Cartledge 1987, 282.

[14] Aesch. 1.173. The literature on the trial of Socrates is too huge to cite or even to cite representatively from, but there are many pointers in Nehamas 1998.

[15] Higgins 1977, 66. More recent literature on Xenophon's political views: Vander Waerdt 1994, Cartledge in Waterfield and Cartledge 1997. On his laconism specifically, see Proietti 1987; *contra*: Tuplin 1993, 1994; neither Proietti not Tuplin seems to me to get quite right the balance between Xenophon's devotion to and criticism of Sparta. See further below, n. 20.

[16] Translations from Robin Waterfield's Penguin Classics Xenophon, *Conversations of Socrates* (Harmondsworth, 1990).

[17] Dillon 1995.

[18] Translation and brief commentary: Rebenich 1998; a full commentary (the last was Ollier's of 1934) is forthcoming from M. Lipka.

[19] Translations from R. Talbert (ed.) *Plutarch on Sparta* (Harmondsworth, 1988) 166–84.

[20] Of course, Xenophon could also be critical of Sparta, even devastatingly so, as at *Hell.* 5.4.1; but these are criticisms of Spartan practice rather than Spartan theory or ideals, and they resonate as those of a disappointed true believer, not an unsympathetic and never convinced opponent. For a nuanced view of Xenophon's laconism, see now Noreen Humble's adroit essay (this volume).

[21] Ollier (1933, 217–93) was unfortunately not at his best on Plato: see Tigerstedt 1965, 544–5 n. 202. Rawson (1969, esp. 62–72) gives a characteristically elegant and erudite synopsis, but inevitably no more. Dawson (1992, esp. 78–93, 166) is excellent in some ways, but tends to rush to judgement. The essays in Powell and Hodkinson 1994 are up-to-date and very useful (esp. Hodkinson 1994, 201–7, and Powell 1994), but it is hard, for example, to think of anyone other than Tigerstedt who could have made such profitable use of a 1794 German dissertation (1965, 544–5 n. 202, 560 n. 366).

[22] For the record, it is perhaps just worth mentioning that a pupil of Aristotle, Dikaiarchos (fr. 41 Wehrli), stressed Plato's sympathy for Sparta, and that Plutarch (*Lyc.* 31.2) stated flatly that Plato borrowed his ideal state (but which one?) from Lycurgus.

[23] This, I agree, is a relevant point, because Tigerstedt believes, as I do (Cartledge 1978), that the constitution of the real Sparta represented some form of oligarchy. But that remains an open question: see recently e.g. Rahe 1992, Book I, ch. 5; Dawson 1992, 49 n. 36.

[24] Wilamowitz (cited by Tigerstedt 1965, 537 n. 145) thought the idea was mediated to Plato by way of his relative Critias, who wrote not one but two accounts of the Spartan social regimen; but that surely is not a necessary hypothesis, especially as Critias's unbecoming conduct as leader of the Thirty Tyrants would appear to have disgusted him.

[25] Whether they were intended also, as Wood and Wood 1978 have argued, as an activating charter for counter-revolution in existing democratic states

and for maintenance of the status quo in oligarchic states, is a rather different question.

[26] On Rousseau's political thought and writings generally (Rousseau 1962, 1964) see e.g. Derathé 1950, Shklar 1985, Wokler 1995, Gourevitch 1997a, ix–xli; for their context, Wokler 1996. Rousseau's Rome (e.g. 1964b; cf. Thom 1995, 58–85) would require a separate study, but it is perhaps worth adding here that in the mirage the political systems of Sparta and Republican Rome were sometimes assimilated to the point of Rome's being considered not merely influenced politically by but directly or indirectly descended, genetically, from Sparta: Rawson 1969, 99, 101–6.

[27] See below text and n. 33.

[28] Held 1994 among much else compares and contrasts the ancient and modern 'models'; cf. Nippel 1994, 1996; Roberts 1994.

[29] Miller 1984, Wokler 1994. Thomson 1969, 105 fathers on him 'the democratic doctrine of the Sovereignty of the People, which for the last two hundred years has dominated world history'.

[30] Thom 1995, 89.

[31] Guerci 1979, 47.

[32] Pire 1958; Wokler 1980, 273–4 n. 10.

[33] Silverthorne 1973, Quantin 1988.

[34] This is insisted upon by Grell 1995, 498–9; my debt to her 1335-page *thèse pour le doctorat-ès-lettres* (originally completed in 1990) will readily become apparent, even – or especially – when I do not completely agree with it.

[35] Pichois and Pintard 1972.

[36] Gourevitch 1997a, 1–110 translates not only the Discourse itself (1–28) but also a number of related texts; cf. Wokler 1980, Hope Mason 1987.

[37] Rousseau 1964a, 1964b.

[38] Gourevitch 1997a, 111–88 (Discourse, including Dedicatory Epistle and Preface), 189–222 (author's own Notes), 223–31 (Replies). See also Cranston 1984, a most useful edited translation.

[39] Cranston 1984, 105.

[40] Miller 1984, 198; cf. Grell 1995, 783.

[41] Shklar 1985, 15 (in a section on 'The Spartan Model', 12–21); Hope Mason 1989; Vidal-Naquet 1996, 116. Rousseau and Spartan education: Legagneux 1972, 143–5.

[42] Viroli 1987, 173.

[43] Dedicatory Epistle to Second Discourse = Gourevitch 1997a, 122.

[44] On the figure of the 'legislator' in general see *Du Contrat social ou Principes du droit politique* (1762) Bk II ch. 7, with Quantin 1989; on order, Viroli 1987, 1988; and Nippel 1996, 231; on durability, Miller 1984, 196.

[45] Gourevitch 1997b, 181. There is also a translation of the *Considérations* by Kendall (1972).

[46] Vernes 1978, 63–132; Hope Mason 1992; cf. Grell 1995, 569.

[47] Bk II ch. 7: Gourevitch 1997b, 69*. See also Melzer 1990, 63.

[48] Besides, Rousseau did not consider Athens a true democracy: *Encyclopédie* article 'Economie politique' (1755) = Gourevitch 1997b, 3–38, at 8. For the (largely) antidemocratic tradition of western political thought since antiquity,

see Roberts 1994 (esp. 163–8, for Rousseau); for the 'embourgeoisement' of Athens, Vidal-Naquet and Loraux 1995.

[49] Exaggerated claims by Miller 1984; cf. Dawson, S. 1995.

[50] Gourevitch 1997a, 222; cf. Charvet 1974, 137; Shklar 1978. For further references to and discussion of ancient constructions of equality see Cartledge 1996.

[51] Thomson 1969, 104, 105. Unlike the Chevalier de Jaucourt, author of 'Lacédémone' in the *Encyclopédie*, Rousseau did not buy the ancient (cf. Dawson 1992) as well as modern myth of the equality of Spartan landholding: see Grell 1995, 480.

[52] See the opening of the *Social Contract*: Gourevitch 1997b, 41.

[53] Miller 1984, 102 cites *Laws* 903b (where Plato's Athenian Stranger remarks that myths are needed for the 'enchantment of the soul') and comments that mythic cities of classical antiquity 'enchanted Rousseau himself'.

[54] Grell 1995, 468; citing Guerci 1979, chs 1–2. See also Rawson 1969, 231–42, Borghero 1973, Leduc-Fayette 1974, Leigh 1979.

[55] From the posthumous *Lettre de la Montagne* VI, as cited by Miller 1984, 234 n. 52.

[56] Mat-Hasquin 1981, 240.

[57] *Social Contract* Book III, ch. 12 = Gourevitch 1997b, 110.

[58] Cartledge 1987, 414–16; cf. Iacono 1996.

[59] Shklar 1957, 272.

[60] I am grateful to Danielle Allen for allowing me to quote this from her unpublished paper 'Plato's *Republic*: Utopian How?'.

[61] Touchefeu 1989, 188 n. 50.

Bibliography

Andrewes, A.

1938 'Eunomia', *CQ* 32, 89–102.

Bolgar, R.R. (ed.)

1979 *Classical Influences on Western Thought AD 1650–1870*, Cambridge.

Borghero, S.

1973 'Sparta tra storia e utopia. Il significato e la funzione del mito di Sparta nel pensiero di Jean-Jacques Rousseau', in G. Solinas (ed.) *Saggi sull'illuminismo*, 253–318, Cagliari.

Carter, L.B.

1986 *The Quiet Athenian*, Oxford.

Cartledge. P.A.

1978 'Literacy in the Spartan oligarchy', *JHS* 98, 25–37.

1987 *Agesilaos and the Crisis of Sparta*, London and Baltimore.

1990 'A curious lawsuit in classical Athens (Antiphon frr. 57–59 Thalheim)', in Cartledge, Millett and Todd *NOMOS*, 41–60.

1996 'Comparatively equal' in J. Ober and C. Hedrick (eds.) *Demokratia. A conversation on democracies, ancient and modern*, 175–85, Princeton.

Cartledge. P.A. , Millett, P. and Todd, S.C. (eds.)

1990 *NOMOS. Essays in Athenian law, politics and society*, Cambridge.

Charvet, J.
1974 *The Social Problem in the Philosophy of Rousseau*, Cambridge.
Christ, K.
1986 'Spartaforschung und Spartabild' in K. Christ (ed.) *Sparta*, 1–72, Darmstadt. Repr. 1996 in his *Griechische Geschichte und Wissenschafts-geschichte*, Hist. Einzelschr. 106, Stuttgart.
Cranston, M. (ed. and tr.)
1984. *Rousseau. Discourse on Inequality*, Harmondsworth.
Dawson, D.
1992 *Cities of the Gods. Communist Utopias in Greek thought*, N.Y.
Dawson, S.
1995 'Rousseau and Athens in the democratic imagination', *Political Theory Newsletter* 7, 1–6.
Derathé, R.
1950 *Rousseau et la science politique de son temps*, Paris.
Dillery, J.
1995 *Xenophon and the History of his Times*, London and N.Y.
Eder, W. (ed.)
1995 *Die athenische Demokratie im 4. Jahrhundert v. Chr.*, Stuttgart.
Euben, J.P.
1997 *Corrupting Youth. Political education, democratic culture, and political theory*, Princeton.
Fisher, N.
1994 'Sparta re(de)valued', in Powell and Hodkinson (eds.) *The Shadow of Sparta*, 347–400.
Fontana, B. (ed.)
1994 *The Invention of the Modern Republic*, Cambridge.
Fréret, N.
1981 'De la condamnation de Socrate' (1736, publ. 1809) in Montuori, *De Socrate Iuste Damnato*, 31–59.
Gagarin, M. and Woodruff, P.
1995 *Early Greek Political Thought. From Homer to the Sophists*, Cambridge.
Giannantoni, G. (ed.)
1990 *Socratis et Socraticorum Reliquiae*, 2nd edn, Naples.
Gourevitch, V. (ed.)
1997a *Rousseau. The Discourses and other early political writings*, Cambridge.
1997b *The Social Contract and other later political writings*, Cambridge.
Grell, C.
1995 *Le Dix-huitième siècle et l'antiquité*, 2 vols, Oxford.
Grell, C. and Michel, C. (eds.)
1989 *Primitivisme et Mythes des Origines dans la France des Lumières 1680–1820. Colloque tenue en Sorbonne les 24 et 25 mai 1988*, Paris.
Guerci, L.
1979 *Libertà degli Antichi e Libertà degli Moderni? Sparta, Atene e i "philosophes" nella Francia del Settecento*, Naples.
Held, D.
1994 *Models of Democracy*, 2nd edn, Oxford.

Higgins, W.E.
1977 *Xenophon the Athenian. The problem of the individual and the society of the polis*, Albany, N.Y.

Hodkinson, S.
1994 ' "Blind Ploutos"? Contemporary images of the role of wealth in classical Sparta', in Powell and Hodkinson (eds.) *The Shadow of Sparta*, 183–222.

Hope Mason, J.
1987 'Reading Rousseau's First Discourse', *Studies on Voltaire and the Eighteenth Century* 249, Oxford, 251–66.
1989 'Individuals in society: Rousseau's republican vision'*HPT* 10, 89–112.
1992 'The *Lettre à d'Alembert* and its place in Rousseau's thought', in *Rousseau and the Eighteenth Century*, 251–69, Oxford.

Iacono, A.M.
1996 'L'utopia e i Greci', in Settis (ed.) *I Greci I*, 883–900.

Kendall, W. (ed.)
1972 *Rousseau. The Government of Poland*, Indianapolis and N.Y.

Leduc-Fayette, D.
1974 *Jean-Jacques Rousseau et le mythe de l'Antiquité*, Paris.

Legagneux, M.
1972 'Rollin et le "mirage spartiate" de l'éducation spartiate' in J. Proust (ed.) *Recherches nouvelles sur quelques écrivains des Lumières*, 111–62, Geneva.

Leigh, R.A.
1979 'Jean-Jacques Rousseau and the myth of Antiquity in the XVIIIth century', in Bolgar (ed.) *Classical Influences*, 155–68.

Lévêque, P. and Vidal-Naquet, P.
1996 *Cleisthenes the Athenian. An essay on the representation of space and time in Greek political thought from the end of the sixth century to the death of Plato*, ed. D.A. Curtis, Atlantic Highlands, N.J.

Mat-Hasquin, M.
1981 *Voltaire et l'Antiquité Grecque* (*SVEC*), Oxford.

Melzer, A.
1990 *The Natural Goodness of Man. On the system of Rousseau's thought*, Chicago and London.

Miller, J.
1984 *Rousseau: Dreamer of Democracy*, New Haven.

Mitchell, J.
1993 *Not By Reason Alone. Religion, history and identity in early modern political thought*, Chicago.

Montuori, M.
1974 *Socrate. Fisiologia di un mito*, Florence. Eng. trs., Chicago, 1981.
1981 *De Socrate Iuste Damnato. The rise of the Socratic problem in the eighteenth century*, Amsterdam.

Morrow, G.R.
1960 *Plato's Cretan City*, Princeton.

Nehamas, A.
1998 *The Art of Living. Socratic Reflections from Plato to Foucault*, Berkeley, Los Angeles and London.

Nippel, W.
1994 'Ancient and modern republicanism', in Fontana (ed.) *The Invention of the Modern Republic*, 6–26.
1996 'Republik, Kleinstaat, Bürgergemeinde. Der antike Stadtstaat in der neuzeitlichen Theorie', in P. Blickle (ed.) *Theorien kommunaler Ordnung in Europa*, Munich, 225–47.

Ober, J.
1998 *Political Dissent in Democratic Athens. Intellectual critics of popular rule*, Princeton.

Ollier, F.
1933–43 *Le mirage spartiate. Etude sur l'idéalisation de Sparte dans l'antiquité grecque de l'origine jusqu'aux Cyniques*, 2 vols, Paris. Repr. in 1 vol., 1973, N.Y.

Ostwald, M.
1986 *From Popular Sovereignty to the Sovereignty of Law. Law, society, and politics in fifth-century Athens*, Berkeley.

Pagden, A. (ed.)
1987 *The Languages of Political Theory in Early-Modern Europe*, Cambridge.

Pichois, C. and Pintard, R. (eds.)
1972 *Jean-Jacques entre Socrate et Caton. Textes inédits de Rousseau 1750–1753*, Paris

Pire, G.
1958 'Du bon Plutarque au Citoyen de Genève', *Rev. de litt. comparée* 32, 510–47.

Powell, A.
1994 'Plato and Sparta: modes of rule and of non-rational persuasion in the *Laws*', in Powell and Hodkinson (eds.) *The Shadow of Sparta*, 273–321.

Powell, A. and Hodkinson, S. (eds.)
1994 *The Shadow of Sparta*, London.

Proietti, G.
1987 *Xenophon's Sparta. An introduction*, Leiden.

Quantin, J-L.
1988 'Traduire Plutarque d'Amyot à Ricard. Contribution à l'étude du mythe de Sparte au XVIIIème siècle', *Histoire, Economie et Société* 7, 243–59.
1989 'Le mythe du législateur au XVIIIe siècle: état de recherches' in Grell and Michel (eds.) *Primitivisme et Mythes*, 153–64.

Rahe, P.
1992 *Republics Ancient and Modern. Classical Republicanism and the American Revolution*, Chapel Hill and London.

Rawson, E.
1969 *The Spartan Tradition in European Thought*, Oxford. Repr. pbk, 1991.

Rebenich, S. (ed. and tr.)
1998 *Xenophon. Die Verfassung der Spartaner*, Darmstadt.

Roberts, J.T.
1994 *Athens on Trial. The antidemocratic tradition in western thought*, Princeton.

Rousseau, J-J.
1962 *Political Writings*, ed. C. Vaughan, 2 vols. Oxford. (Originally 1915.)
1964 *Oeuvres Complètes de Jean-Jacques Rousseau*, vol. III. *Ecrits politiques*, Paris.
1964a 'Histoire de Lacédémone' (1751–3), in *Oeuvres Complètes*, 128–30.
1964b 'Parallèle entre les deux républiques de Sparte et de Rome' (1751–3), in *Oeuvres Complètes*, 125–7.

Schütrumpf, E.
1994 'Aristotle on Sparta' in Powell and Hodkinson (eds.) *The Shadow of Sparta*, 323–45.
1995 'Politische Reformmodelle im vierten Jahrhundert. Grundsätzliche Annahmen politischer Theorie und Versuche konkreter Lösungen', in Eder (ed.) *Die athenische Demokratie*, 271–300.

Settis, S. (ed.)
1996 *I Greci I. Noi e I Greci*, Turin.

Shklar, J.
1957 *After Utopia. The decline of political faith*, Princeton.
1978 'Jean-Jacques Rousseau and equality', *Daedalus* 107.3, 3–25.
1985 *Men and Citizens: a study of Rousseau's social theory*, 2nd edn, Cambridge.

Silverthorne, M.
1973 'Rousseau's Plato', *SVEC* 116, 235–49.

Strauss, L.
1939 'The spirit of Sparta and the taste of Xenophon', *Social Research* 6, 502–36.

Thom, M.
1995 *Republics, Nations and Tribes*, London.

Thomson, D.
1969 'Rousseau and the general will', in D. Thomson (ed.) *Political Ideas*, 95–106, Harmondsworth.

Tigerstedt, E.N.
1965, 1974, 1978 *The Legend of Sparta in Classical Antiquity*, 2 vols + Index vol., Stockholm, Göteborg and Uppsala.

Touchefeu, Y.
1989 'Le sauvage et le citoyen: le mythe des origines dans le système de Rousseau', in Grell and Michel (eds.) *Primitivisme et Mythes*, 177–91.

Tuplin, C.J.
1993 *The Failings of Empire. A reading of Xenophon,* Hellenica *2.3.11–7.5.27*, Stuttgart.
1994 'Xenophon, Sparta and the *Cyropaedia*', in Powell and Hodkinson (eds.) *The Shadow of Sparta*, 127–81.

Vander Waerdt, P. (ed.)
1994 *The Socratic Movement*, Ithaca and London.
Vernes, P.
1978 *La Ville, la fête, la démocratie: Rousseau et les illusions de la communauté*, Paris.
Vidal-Naquet, P.
1996 'Democracy: a Greek invention', in Lévêque and Vidal-Naquet, *Cleisthenes the Athenian*, 102–18.
Vidal-Naquet, P. and Loraux, N.
1995 'The formation of Bourgeois Athens' (1979), in Vidal-Naquet, *Politics Ancient & Modern*, 82–140, Cambridge.
Viroli, M.
1987 'The concept of *ordre* and the language of classical republicanism in Jean-Jacques Rousseau', in Pagden (ed.) *The Languages of Political Theory*, 159–78.
1988 *Jean-Jacques Rousseau and the 'Well-ordered Society'*, Cambridge.
Vlastos, G.
1994 *Socratic Studies*, ed. M. Burnyeat, Cambridge.
1994a 'The historical Socrates and Athenian democracy' (1983), in *Socratic Studies*, 87–108.
Walzer, M.
1988 *The Company of Critics. Social Criticism and political commitment in the twentieth century*, New York.
Waterfield, R. and Cartledge. P.A.
1997 *Xenophon: Hiero the Tyrant and other Treatises*, Penguin Classics, London.
Wokler, R.
1980 'The *Discours sur les sciences et les arts* and its offspring: Rousseau in reply to his critics', in Harvey, S. et al. (eds.) *Reappraisals of Rousseau. Studies in honour of R.A. Leigh*, 250–78, Manchester.
1994 'Democracy's mythical ordeals: the Procrustean and Promethean paths to popular self-rule', in G. Parry and M. Moran (eds.) *Democracy and Democratization*, 21–46, London and N.Y.
1995 *Rousseau*, 'Past Masters' series, Oxford.
1996 'The Enlightenment and the French Revolutionary birth pangs of Modernity', *Sociology of the Sciences Yearbook* 20, 22–47.
Wood, N. and Wood, E.M.
1978 *Class Ideology and Ancient Political Theory: Socrates, Plato, and Aristotle in social context*, Oxford.
1986 'Socrates and democracy: a reply to Gregory Vlastos', *Political Theory* 14.1, 55–82.

Chapter 12

SŌPHROSYNĒ AND THE SPARTANS IN XENOPHON

Noreen Humble

I

A representative example of the standard scholarly view that classical writers associated *sōphrosynē* with Sparta is found in H. North's book *Sophrosyne*:[1]

> Another development [in the fourth century], on the frontier between politics and philosophy, singled out sophrosyne as the characteristic virtue of Sparta, making it the basis of her envied stability, moral conservatism, and military discipline. This tendency, already strong in the fifth century, was intensified in the fourth, particularly in the semi-historical, semi-philosophical writing of which Xenophon's *Constitution of the Lacedaemonians* affords a fair sample.

North's statement contains three separate generalisations: (i) that there was a strong tendency in the fifth century to assign *sōphrosynē* as the characteristic virtue of the Spartans, (ii) that in the fourth century this singling out of *sōphrosynē* as the Spartan virtue became more prominent, and (iii) that Xenophon in particular provides a strong example of this tendency. There are problems with each of these points but it is specifically the mistaken view that Xenophon singled out *sōphrosynē* as the characteristic Spartan virtue that I shall address in this paper, commenting briefly at the end on the other two broader generalisations.

In support of this general statement North further remarks that in the *Constitution of the Lacedaemonians* (henceforth referred to as *Lak.Pol.*), during the discussion of the education of male citizens, the youngest boys are taught obedience, *sōphrosynē* and *aidōs*, and the next age group are taught *sōphrosynē* and *aidōs*. She also notes that, regarding the instillation of *sōphrosynē*, the Spartan system is comparable to the Persian system which Xenophon puts forth in the *Cyropaedia*.[2] The problem with her interpretation is that in the *Lak.Pol.* there is no mention at all of *sōphrosynē* in the section dealing with the education of the youngest boys. In fact, there are only two uses of cognates in the whole work (*Lak.Pol.* 3.4, 13.5). Though the first of these occurs in the discussion of the second age group, it can hardly be asserted on the basis of two references that Xenophon singled out *sōphrosynē* as the characteristic virtue of the Spartans in the *Lak.Pol.*

However, North is able to make her observation by assuming that when Xenophon uses the term *enkrateia* he means *sōphrosynē*. It is certainly true that, in general terms, there is some overlap in meaning between *sōphrosynē* and *enkrateia*: both can be used to refer to physical control over pleasures and pains, such as hunger, thirst and lust, and so can be and are translated as self-control or self-restraint. Plato, for example, at one point in the *Republic* (430e) defines *sōphrosynē* as *enkrateia hēdonōn* and Aristotle in the *Nicomachean Ethics* defines *enkrateia* as simply a lesser form of *sōphrosynē* in which control over pleasures is obtained but there still remains a desire for the pleasures.[3] However, the two terms are not entirely interchangeable. The meaning of *enkrateia* does not stretch beyond physical self-control whereas *sōphrosynē* encompasses a much wider range of meanings; hence the variety of possible English translations in addition to the two previously mentioned: moderation, prudence, modesty, chastity, wisdom, discipline, soundness of mind, discretion, good sense, sanity, temperance, etc.[4] To make the distinction more clear, *sōphrosynē* can be used in a general moral sense to refer to self-control in matters of diet, pain and the like, i.e. as equivalent to *enkrateia*, but *enkrateia* cannot be used in the wider intellectual/prudential sense, i.e. to mean prudence, good sense, wisdom,[5] or even knowledge itself (a definition of *sōphrosynē* which Plato reaches in the *Charmides*).[6] *Enkrateia* is not, in other words, an absolute synonym of *sōphrosynē*. In addition, not only does *sōphrosynē* have a wider range of application, it is not always used exclusively in the same sense by one author, as the two Platonic examples cited above show, and its meaning is, on the whole, very much dependent on context.[7] Indeed, Xenophon differs in no way from his predecessors and contemporaries in this regard; he makes wide use of *sōphrosynē* and its cognates throughout his works, in both the moral and intellectual sense.[8]

It can, however, be demonstrated through a comparison with the education system in the very work with which North closely links the *Lak.Pol.*, the *Cyropaedia*, that Xenophon does not intend his audience to infer *sōphrosynē* when he mentions *enkrateia* in the *Lak.Pol.* and so does not single out *sōphrosynē* as the characteristic virtue of Spartans in that work.[9] Further, a more general look at the characters to whom he attributes the virtue throughout his whole corpus shows that, with one explicable exception, he does not portray Spartans as possessors of *sōphrosynē*, and so cannot be said in any regard to single out *sōphrosynē* as *the* Spartan virtue.

II

Although there is little hope of discovering the relative chronology of the *Lak.Pol.* and *Cyropaedia*, there are sufficient internal and external indications that Xenophon himself linked these works. The verbal similarities between the openings of the two works are striking (*Lak.Pol.* 1.1; *Cyr.* 1.1.1, 3): in both Xenophon marvels at a certain phenomenon – in the one, Spartan power and renown, in the other, Cyrus' ability to govern men. In both there is a comparison with other states, in both a discussion of the education system for citizen males divided by age groups and in both sections expressing outright criticism and disillusionment at (*Cyr.* 8.8) or near (*Lak.Pol.* 14) the end. Such are these general similarities and so widespread is the view that Xenophon is blindly pro-Spartan that many consider Xenophon's Persians to be thinly-disguised Spartans.[10] However, Xenophon is not blindly pro-Spartan and the similarities in structure and substance between the *Cyropaedia* and *Lak.Pol.*, particularly in the discussions of the education systems, are surely intended to draw attention to the differences between the Spartans and Persians.[11]

In the Spartan education system young boys aged 7–14 are placed under the direction of a *paidonomos* whose task it is to deal out physical punishment when conduct is lax in order to instil *aidōs* and obedience (*Lak.Pol.* 2.2). Further, the boys are not allowed shoes so as to toughen their feet (2.3), allowed only one cloak so as to deal better with heat and cold (2.4) and allowed only a modest diet so as to cope better with hunger and to be more healthy (2.5–6). Stealing is permitted in order to supplement their diet since it encourages development of skills useful in war (2.6–7). Stealing itself is not a crime, stealing badly is (2.8–9). Such training is meant to make boys more obedient (*eupeithesteroi*), more respectful (*aidēmonesteroi*) and more self-restrained (*enkratesteroi*) than any other Greek education (2.10). *Sōphrosynē* is not cited as an aim at this stage of the education; rather the three areas of importance are obedience, *aidōs* and *enkrateia* and these are all instilled through fear of punishment.

Youths aged 14–20 are kept under even stricter watch in the recognition that this is a difficult time of life; thus they are kept busy, with unspecified tasks, so that they do not succumb to base desires (3.1–2). Shirkers are punished by being excluded from participating in the normal activities of Spartan male citizens (3.3). To instil *aidōs* further they walk around in silence with their hands under their cloaks and their eyes firmly on the ground with the result, Xenophon remarks, that it has become clear that males are stronger than females with respect to *to sōphronein* (3.4). Here, then, is the first use of a term linguistically related to *sōphrosynē* in the *Lak.Pol.* and there is no avoiding the fact that Xenophon is using the concept to describe the behaviour of Spartan youths. Yet, as always, context needs to be taken into account and I will come back to this passage below, noting here only that one mention of the concept in the description of the age groups' activities hardly amounts to wholesale attribution of the virtue to the Spartans. In fact, the quality of prime importance in the Spartan system appears to be *aidōs*.

In the *Cyropaedia*, Xenophon's Persians also have a public education in which children progress through age groups. In the first stage (*Cyr.* 1.2.6–8) boys to the age of 16/17 learn justice (cf. *Cyr.* 1.3.16–17), *sōphrosynē* (cf. *An.* 1.9.3), obedience and *enkrateia* as well as how to shoot arrows and throw spears. Justice is taught through judging standards of right and wrong and observing trials; *sōphrosynē*, obedience and *enkrateia* are taught through lessons and by observing and imitating elders who possess these qualities.[12] Persian boys are punished if they commit crimes of theft, robbery, deceit, violence, or slander, or if they accuse each other falsely or fail to return a favour when they are very clearly capable of doing so because ingratitude is said to lead to shameful things (*aischra*, *Cyr.* 1.2.7). Three important points of contrast with the first stage of Spartan education can be seen: in Persia there is a clear distinction between *sōphrosynē* and *enkrateia*, physical punishment is not cited as a means of instilling virtue, and stealing is most definitely a crime.

In the next age group (*Cyr.* 1.2.9–12) young men aged *c.* 16–26 guard the city by night in order to increase further their *sōphrosynē* (*Cyr.* 1.2.9). Again it is noted, as it was with regard to Spartan youths, that this is a difficult time of life when most care needs to be taken. During the day they do whatever the state requires, including, for example, hunting with the king which, like the practice of stealing in the Spartan system, trains the young men for war.[13]

In short, then, in the Spartan system during the first stage of education the qualities of importance are *aidōs*, obedience and *enkrateia*; in the second stage, though all three are clearly implied, only *aidōs* is specifically mentioned as an aim. In the Persian system during the first stage justice, *sōphrosynē*, obedience and *enkrateia* are the qualities of importance; in the second stage, again though all four are implied, the only one mentioned as an aim is *sōphrosynē*.

The inclusion of both *enkrateia* and *sōphrosynē* in the Persian system quite clearly highlights the absence of *sōphrosynē* in the Spartan system. In fact, following the above schema, rather than assume that Xenophon identified *enkrateia* with *sōphrosynē*, a more plausible interpretation would have been that Xenophon equated *sōphrosynē* with *aidōs* since in the Spartan system *aidōs* appears, just as *sōphrosynē* in the Persian system, in both the first and second stages and is the only virtue mentioned in the second stage. Certainly there is a close association between these two qualities also.[14] Since *aidōs* encompasses the English concepts of 'shame, respect, sense of honour and modesty',[15] like *sōphrosynē* it 'tend[s] to inhibit free indulgence in passion of any kind'.[16] Also, the two concepts are particularly associated with youths and with women, especially with regard to modesty and chastity.[17] Indeed, the first of the two references to cognates of *sōphrosynē* in the *Lak.Pol.* (3.4, as noted above) involves a comparison between the *sōphrosynē* of males and females:[18] to instil *aidōs* Spartan youths were required to walk silently with their eyes on the ground[19] and their hands under their cloaks, resulting in the male sex being more in possession of *sōphrosynē* than the female.[20] Here, the two concepts do seem to be virtually equated in the sense 'modesty'.[21] This equation of *aidōs* and *sōphrosynē*, however, is not sustained nor is it meant to be applied more widely, for example, to the younger age group where *aidōs* is most definitely to be taken in the sense 'shame' or 'respect' (cf. *Lak.Pol.* 2.2, 2.10). Further, it is specifically *aidōs* which is the aim of the silent, eye-lowered walking, not *sōphrosynē* which is mentioned in a virtual aside, in a comparison between males and females, not, as is the pattern throughout the work, in a comparison between Spartans and other Greeks.[22]

Most importantly, in the *Cyropaedia*, the acquisition of *aidōs* is shown to be concomitant with the acquisition of *sōphrosynē*. After the Persian education is set out, how Cyrus fared in it is recounted. It is noted how he acquires *aidōs* (modesty/bashfulness) as he turns from a boy to a youth (*c.* 12–15 years old, *Cyr.* 1.4.4) and this is seen as a natural consequence, i.e. Persian children educated in *sōphrosynē* will develop *aidōs* as a matter of course. Later on in the *Cyropaedia* (8.1.31) is found an explicit expression of the difference between *aidōs* and *sōphrosynē*: those in possession of *aidōs* avoid doing shameful deeds only in public; those in possession of *sōphrosynē* avoid doing shameful deeds even in private.[23] The distinction is, by and in itself, a forced one as *aidōs* can certainly inhibit private wrong-doing.[24] However, this stated difference between the two concepts does in fact succinctly characterise Xenophon's views on the difference between the Persian and Spartan education systems, the latter of which concentrates solely on public virtue:[25] in the Persian system where *sōphrosynē* (along with justice)[26] is taught by persuasion and example, boys and youths learn to behave the same way both in private and in public; hence stealing is a crime. In the Spartan system where *aidōs* is taught by compulsion, boys and youths learn only how they must behave in public so as to escape punishment; hence stealing is not considered a crime.[27]

Apart from the comparison between Spartan males and females, there is one other use of a cognate of *sōphrosynē* in the *Lak.Pol.* It occurs outside the discussion of the age-groups: at sacrifices on campaign – the circumstances are highly specific – ephors watch what each person does and 'chastise/bring to their senses' all as fitting (*sōphronizousin*, *Lak.Pol.* 13.5). The sense here is prudential but general (see n. 29 below) and hardly can be stretched to support an argument suggesting Xenophon attributed *sōphrosynē* to the Spartans. In addition, then, to the fact that the word and its cognates rarely appear in the *Lak.Pol.*, a comparison between the Persian and Spartan education systems reveals that there is no justification for equating *enkrateia* with *sōphrosynē* – quite the contrary, in fact, since Xenophon clearly distinguishes between the two in the similarly presented Persian system.

III

Objections could possibly be raised if in his other works Xenophon quite clearly attributed *sōphrosynē*, in any sense, to Spartans. There are, however, certainly no outright examples in either the *Hellenica* or *Anabasis*, the two other works in which Spartans figure prominently. In general most Spartans in these works are hardly ever portrayed, even implicitly, behaving prudentially.[28] Certainly the verb *sōphroneō* is in common use throughout both works but usually just in a general prudential sense, in the formulaic phrase 'if you are sensible (*ean sōphronēte*), you will follow some course of action' and this expression is used by a wide variety of characters with no evident pattern.[29] In two instances in the *Hellenica* there is a slight possibility that with such a general phrase Xenophon is playing on a tradition of associating *sōphrosynē* with the Spartans without endorsing the view himself. In the first Xenophon reports a speech of Critias in which Critias heaps praise upon the Spartan constitution and then proceeds to say 'if you are sensible, you will not spare Theramenes' (*HG* 2.3.34). If this use of the phrase *ean sōphronēte* is meant to be pointed, given Critias' own definite attribution of *sōphrosynē* to the Spartans,[30] and is meant to be understood as 'if you are sensible *like the Spartans are*', it can only be meant as ironic given that Xenophon does not like or approve of Critias.[31] The second example also involves a rather general statement with possible overtones given the context (*HG* 6.3.5): the Athenian Callias on a peace embassy to the Spartans and their allies remarks that 'it is the characteristic of sensible men (*sōphronōn*) not to undertake war…'; he is not made to attribute *sōphrosynē* directly to the Spartans, yet it might be argued that he is appealing to them as supposed possessors of *sōphrosynē*, particularly considering that he is the Spartan *proxenos*. However, as in the case of Critias, Xenophon's treatment of Callias is not entirely flattering.[32] These two examples, therefore, of a general formulaic use of *sōphrosynē* are hardly sufficient to argue that Xenophon singled out *sōphrosynē* as the characteristic virtue of the Spartans, particularly given the large number of Spartans who appear in the *Hellenica* and *Anabasis*. Neither example is explicitly applied to Spartans and neither is directly attributable to Xenophon himself; rather, both are placed in the mouths of interlocutors whom he does not regard highly.

In the *Memorabilia* there is only one instance where *sōphrosynē* is linked with Spartans. In a conversation with the younger Pericles (*Mem.* 3.5) Socrates suggests that the degenerate Athenians can be brought back to their former superior state by practising to be like their noble ancestors or, failing that, to imitate those currently pre-eminent. Pericles takes up this point enthusiastically, noting all the ways in which Sparta surpasses Athens. Socrates retorts by saying that in Athens discipline and order are found among sailors and choristers. Pericles counters by pointing out that the army lacks *sōphrosynē* (*Mem.* 3.5.21) and good order and obedience. Socrates suggests that this situation might not be the soldiers' fault but the fault of their leaders, sparking another of the discussions on good leadership found in the *Memorabilia*. Again, it might be argued that this is a reference to the supposedly famous Spartan *sōphrosynē*[33] but if so, it is the only example in the work and is not presented as Xenophon's own opinion but is placed in the mouth of an interlocutor who is on the losing end of an argument.[34] It is, in fact, Socrates himself who is held up as the paradigm of *sōphrosynē* in the *Memorabilia*,[35] not the Spartans, and Socrates whom Xenophon defends as instilling – teaching by example – *sōphrosynē* in those who associated with him.[36]

Where *sōphrosynē* and its cognates are used to describe a Spartan is in Xenophon's encomium of Agesilaus. Here, very definitely, Agesilaus is credited with the virtue (*Ages.* 5.4, 7 and 11.10; indirectly at 10.2), and at one point is said to advance with his army like the most *sōphrōn* maiden (*sōphronestatē*, 6.7).[37] The appearance of the concept in this work, however, can be explained on generic grounds. Though there are only a few surviving encomia which are earlier than the *Agesilaus* and though only one of these is a prose encomium about an actual rather than mythological person (Isocrates' *Evagoras*), *sōphrosynē* belongs to the canon of virtues ascribed to the subjects of these works,[38] a canon which Aristotle's rhetorical handbook (which just postdates Xenophon's encomium) also advises those composing encomia to follow.[39] It would, therefore, have been peculiar if Xenophon did not attribute *sōphrosynē* to Agesilaus in the encomium.[40] Certainly Agesilaus is not described by Xenophon as *sōphrōn* elsewhere;[41] he is *sōphrōn* in his encomiastic incarnation as an ideal man, not in his capacity as a Spartan.

IV

It is clear, then, that Xenophon does not single out *sōphrosynē* as the characteristic virtue of Spartans in his corpus in general – the only exception, the encomium references, being explicable in terms of generic convention – and certainly not in the*Lak.Pol.* where the temptation to equate *enkrateia* with *sōphrosynē* cannot be justified in view of the obvious comparison with the substantially more sophisticated Persian education system in which both *sōphrosynē* and *enkrateia* are considered separate, teachable virtues. It is, on the other hand, equally clear that Xenophon considers *sōphrosynē* an important and worthy virtue, as seen by his attribution of it, along with *enkrateia*, to Socrates and to Cyrus[42] and also by the discussions of the concept found in varying degrees of depth in both the *Memorabilia* and *Cyropaedia*.[43] Though Xenophon did sometimes portray individual Spartans behaving with good sense,[44] that he did not see *sōphrosynē* as a goal of the Spartan way of life complements his generally sober treatment of Spartans in the *Hellenica*[45] and should make us wary of reading any part of the *Lak.Pol.* as an idealisation of the Spartan way of life[46] or as encomiastic.[47]

Finally, there is the wider question of whether or not Xenophon stands alone in resisting the apparently – if North is correct – contemporary cliché of *sōphrosynē* being the pre-eminent Spartan virtue. I think there is something striking in Xenophon's attitude, though the evidence is much less clear cut than North would have us believe. References to *sōphrosynē* in the fourth century refer back as often to ancestral Athens as to Sparta and though they certainly indicate a conservative, anti-democratic sentiment, it is less clear how far such references necessarily are meant to conjure up images of Sparta.[48] In the fifth century the only two authors who can be shown in any way to attribute *sōphrosynē* to the Spartans are Thucydides and Critias.[49] Still, if the attribution of *sōphrosynē* to the Spartans was common in oligarchical circles of the late fifth century, Xenophon is certainly showing independence of thought and greater subtlety and philosophical insight than he is generally credited with. In short, the *Lak.Pol.* is an exceedingly important document for anyone interested in both the reality of the Spartan way of life and in the accompanying Spartan mirage and so it is vital to read and evaluate what Xenophon actually says, not what we think he might or should have said.

Acknowledgements

Earlier versions of this paper were presented at the CAC meeting at Memorial University in Newfoundland, June 1997, and at the Manchester Ancient History Seminar in April 1998; I am grateful to the audiences on both occasions for comments and suggestions. Roger Brock and Douglas Cairns merit particular thanks each for casting a critical eye over the paper. Thanks are also due to the editors of this volume for graciously accepting this paper for inclusion and for their generous advice. Responsibility for the views presented and for any errors or omissions rests fully with myself.

Notes

1 North 1966, 122. Cf. also Cornford 1912, 258 on *sōphrosynē* in the *Lak.Pol.*; and, more generally, on *sōphrosynē* as the characteristic virtue of the Spartans see Rawson 1969, 20–2, Fisher 1994, 375 and Hodkinson 1984, 195.

2 North 1966, 131 n. 24 and 133.

3 On Aristotle's analysis see North 1966, 200–3, Young 1991, 107–25 and Cairns 1993, 419–20. On the Platonic passage see Guthrie 1975, 156.

4 North 1966, *passim*. See Guthrie 1975, 157 and n. 2 there, and Young 1991, 121 n. 1 on the difficulty of translating *sōphrosynē*.

5 Cf. *Mem.* 3.9.4 where Xenophon says Socrates equated wisdom with *sōphrosynē* and Guthrie 1975, 156 n. 5 for further references in Plato.

6 See North 1966, 153–8, Guthrie 1975, 155–74 and Watt 1987, 165–74 on the *Charmides* in general. On the distinction between the popular/moral meaning of *sōphrosynē* and the intellectual/prudential meaning see Guthrie 1975, 156–7, North 1966, *passim*, Nill 1985, 44 and 101 n. 106 and Carey 1989, 70.

7 See, for example, North 1966, 69–70 on Euripides' exploitation of the varied meanings of *sōphrosynē*.

8 As acknowledged by North herself 1966, 123–32.

9 There is still some discussion about the authorship of the *Lak.Pol.* Lana 1992, 17–26, uses correspondence analysis to argue that Diogenes Laertius

(2.57) was correct in stating that Xenophon wrote neither the *Athenaiōn Politeia* nor the *Lak.Pol.*; however, Lana's statistical analysis compares these two works only with the *Hellenica*, ignoring too substantial a portion of Xenophon's literary output; see also Dover 1981, 443–4 for a discussion of the problems inherent in statistical analysis of Xenophon's works. I believe firmly that the *Lak.Pol.* is from Xenophon's hand, and that there is nothing in the work which does not fit with his pattern of thought elsewhere (as noted long ago by Ollier 1933, 378).

[10] See, for example, Tigerstedt 1965, 178–9, Rawson 1969, 50, Gera 1993, 70 n. 145 and Kennell 1995, 133.

[11] Cf. Tuplin 1994, *passim* for a demonstration that Xenophon's Persians are not carbon copies of his Spartans.

[12] Cf. *Cyr.* 8.1.21–33 where Cyrus is said to teach virtuous behaviour, including *sōphrosynē* and *enkrateia*, by example.

[13] Cf. *Cyr.* 8.1.34–6 and also *Cyn.* 12.1–9 for Xenophon's praise of hunting as the best training for war, and particularly 12.7 where he says that hunting makes youths *sōphronas* and *dikaious*.

[14] Though they are not synonymous, on which see North 1966, 7 and Cairns 1993, 104.

[15] Cairns 1993, 455 gives these translations as an *aide-mémoire* only. On the general difficulty of translating *aidōs* see Cairns 1993, 1–4.

[16] North 1966, 7.

[17] Cairns 1997, 54 ff. Note that in the *Symposium* Xenophon describes Autolycus as possessing both *aidōs* and *sōphrosynē* (*Symp.* 1.8); the latter virtue is ascribed again to Autolycus at *Symp.* 8.8. For youths and *aidōs* in general see Cairns 1993, General Index s.v. *aidos*: and young people; for women and *aidōs*, ibid., General Index s.v. women.

[18] It is on this point alone that Cornford 1912, 258 says 'insistence on the *Sōphrosynē* of the *meirakion* was a special feature of Spartan training'.

[19] On the connection between lowering one's eyes and *aidōs* see Williams 1993, 198 and Cairns 1993, General Index s.v. *aidōs*: and the eyes.

[20] Being quiet and walking in a slow and orderly manner with hands under cloaks is elsewhere linked to *sōphrosynē*, sometimes in a setting presupposing a strong connection with Spartan behaviour but just as often not; therefore it cannot be argued to be a specifically Spartan feature. Cf. for example the sayings ascribed to Chilon, the 6th century Spartan ephor (D–K vol. 1, 63; but see Burn 1968, 207–9 on the difficulty of assigning any particular phrase to a particular Sage); Plato *Charmides* 159b where quietness in walking and talking is the first definition given of *sōphrosynē* (see North 1966, 156 on this as a popular conception of the term); Aristophanes in the *Clouds* (961–4) where it is said that in the old education *sōphrosynē* was cultivated through silence and walking orderly in the streets (on which see Guthrie 1975, 165); Isocrates *Areopagiticus* 48 where he recounts how young men in the past had avoided the market-place or passed through it with *aidōs* and *sōphrosynē*; Aeschines 1.25–6 on men of old, including Solon, being so *sōphrōn* that they kept their arms under their cloaks while speaking. On *sōphrosynē* and the Athens of Solon, see also n. 48 below.

[21] See Tuplin 1994, 156. Perhaps also 'chastity' is implied, given the prior discussion of the edict to forbid sexual relations between males (*Lak.Pol.* 2.13) and the following comment on youths being more modest (*aidēmonesterous*, *Lak.Pol.* 3.5) than maidens in the bridal chamber.

[22] The comparison itself, as Tuplin 1994, 156, suggests, seems more likely to be a comment 'calculated to draw attention to common criticisms of Spartan women'.

[23] North 1966, 92, comments on this distinction recalling 'sophistic discussions of offenses committed with and without witnesses'. For an examination of such 'sophistic discussions' see Cairns 1993, 360–70.

[24] As Xenophon himself knew. He did not believe that Spartans could not internalize *aidōs*, simply that *aidōs* would be more likely to be internalized where the methods of education were gentler and the curriculum wider. In general on the internalization of *aidōs* see Cairns 1993, *passim*, particularly 360–70.

[25] See particularly *Lak.Pol.* 10; on this see Strauss 1939, 517 and Humble 1997, 218 ff.

[26] Though the focus of this paper is on *sōphrosynē*, it is important to note that an education in justice is also lacking in the Spartan system.

[27] See Tuplin 1994, 157–8 on the emphasis in the Persian system on truth (an element of Persian education which occurs in all accounts, not just Xenophon's; ibid. 172 n. 43 for further references) and positive approaches to education versus the emphasis in the Spartan system on deception and negative approaches to education.

[28] The nearest to an outright example occurs when Agesilaus' army is said to be following a Thessalian army *sōphronōs* (*HG* 4.3.6). Whose policy it was to follow the enemy in such a manner is not revealed but Agesilaus decides the policy is mistaken, urges swift attack and defeats the Thessalians (*HG* 4.3.6–8; cf. *Ages.* 3–4).

[29] North 1966, 124 comments on the prudential sense of *sōphrosynē* in the *Anabasis* and *Hellenica*. The following list of references expands on hers. Examples of the type *ean sōphronēte*: Xenophon to the mercenaries (*An.* 5.8.24 *bis*), Achaeans and Arcadians about themselves (*An.* 6.2.11), Heracleides to guests of Seuthes (*An.* 7.3.17) and to Seuthes (*An.* 7.6.42), Polycrates to the mercenaries (*An.* 7.6.41), Critias to the Athenians (*HG* 2.3.34), Callias to Spartans and their allies (*HG* 6.3.5), Lycomedes to Arcadians (*HG* 7.1.24). Examples using the verb *sōphronizō* ('bring to one's senses'): Xenophon about himself (*An.* 6.1.28) and to Seuthes (*An.* 7.7.24), ephors about the Eleans (*HG* 2.2.23). Using some form of the adjective *sōphrōn*: Xenophon's judgement of an action of Iphicrates (*HG* 6.2.39) and a general observation about wise men by the Thebans (*HG* 7.3.5).

[30] Critias D–K 88b6.

[31] Cf. *HG* 2.3.2–56, 2.4.8–9; *Mem.* 1.2.12.

[32] On Xenophon's satirical treatment of Callias in the *Hellenica* see Humphreys 1983, 26–7 and Tuplin 1993, 104–5 (his n. 10 gives references to other ancient works satirizing Callias) and endnote 6 on the similar presentation in Xenophon's *Symposium*.

[33] See Rawson 1969, 42.

[34] See Gray 1998, 141 on Socrates' 'patriotic fervour' here.

[35] *Sōphrosynē* is directly attributed to Socrates at *Mem.* 1.2.15, 1.2.20, 1.2.28; cf. also *Ap.* 14.

[36] Passages concerned with Socrates teaching *sōphrosynē* include *Mem.* 1.1.16, 1.2.17–18, 1.2.26, 4.3.1–2, 4.3.17–18; cf. *Ap.* 19.

[37] This passage is surely a conscious echo, or vice versa depending on dating, of *Lak.Pol.* 3.4.

[38] Cf. Isocrates *Evag.* 22; also see Agathon's encomium of Eros in Plato's *Symposium* 194e4–197e8 in which Eros is attributed with justice, *sōphrosynē*, courage and wisdom (see Dover 1984, 11–12, 122 ff. on similarities with the *Agesilaus*); the adherence to generic considerations is even more striking here as *sōphrosynē* is not an obvious virtue to attribute to Eros. See also Isocrates' mini-encomium of Theseus (*Helen* 18–37, especially 31) and on virtues in encomia in general see Dover 1974, 66–7.

[39] Aristotle (after pointing out that virtue and what is noble are the aims of one who praises) describes the components of virtue (*Rhetorica* 1366b1–3): μέρη δὲ ἀρετῆς δικαιοσύνη, ἀνδρία, σωφροσύνη, μεγαλοπρέπεια, μεγαλοψυχία, ἐλευθεριότης, πραότης, φρόνησις, σοφία ('the parts of virtue are justice, courage, *sōphrosynē*, magnificence, greatness of soul, liberality, gentleness, practical wisdom and intelligence'); cf. 1366b13–15 for elaboration, including a limiting of *sōphrosynē* to its moral/encratic sense.

[40] It is noteworthy too that in the most extended passage describing Agesilaus' *sōphrosynē* in the encomium (*Ages.* 5) Xenophon limits *sōphrosynē* to its moral, not intellectual sense; i.e. he equates it with *enkrateia* (see North 1966, 125 and Dover 1974, 208 and 213; note too the correspondence with Aristotle's *Rhetorica* in this regard, n. 39 above). The only certain attribution of intellectual *sōphrosynē* to Agesilaus in the work is at 10.2. 11.10 is ambiguous; at 7.3 and 7.6 are found cognates used in a general prudential way.

[41] *HG* 4.3.6 is ambiguous (see n. 28 above).

[42] For Socrates and *sōphrosynē* see nn. 35 and 36 above. He is said to possess *enkrateia* at *Mem.* 1.2.1, 1.2.14, 1.3.7, 1.5.6, 4.8.11 and instructs others in it at 1.5.1–5, 2.1.1–2 and 4.5.1–12. For *sōphrosynē* attributed to Cyrus see 6.1.47, 8.1.30, 8.1.37; for *enkrateia* explicitly attributed to Cyrus see *Cyr.* 8.1.32 (for implicit attribution see Due 1989, 170–81); for his believing *enkrateia* a worthy virtue to possess and instructing others in it see 1.5.9, 7.5.75–6, 8.1.36.

[43] Discussions of *sōphrosynē* in the *Memorabilia* include 1.2.19–23, 1.2.26–7, 1.3.8–9 and 3.9.4 (and nn. 35 and 36 above); in the *Cyropaedia* see 2.2.14, 3.1.16–22 (on which see Gera 1993, 95), 7.5.75–6 (which passage distinguishes between *sōphrosynē* and *enkrateia*), 8.1.30–1, 8.4.14 and 8.6.10 (and n. 42 above).

[44] e.g. Lysander at Notium (*HG* 1.5.10–15) though Xenophon does not explicitly call his actions *sōphrōn*.

[45] See particularly Tuplin 1993.

[46] Compare Plutarch's idealisation of Spartan life in his *Life of Lycurgus* in which *sōphrosynē* is regularly noted as a goal of the Spartan way of life and as a characteristic of Spartans in general (e.g. 5.10, 11.7, 12.6, 14.2, 15.10, 15.13, 17.2, 26.2, 31.1).

[47] The most common views; see for example Ollier 1934, Delebecque 1957, Tigerstedt 1965, Breitenbach 1967, Moore 1983, Luppino Manes 1988, Rebenich 1998. For alternative interpretations see Strauss 1939, Higgins 1971, Proietti 1987 and Humble 1997, Chapter 5; Tuplin 1994 is also useful though his point is not specifically to examine the purpose of the *Lak.Pol.*

[48] For different views see Tuplin 1994, 156, Thomas 1994, 119–33 and Too 1995, 99–102; on fourth-century appeals to Sparta, particularly in oratory, see Fisher 1994.

[49] See, for example, Thucydides 1.68.1, 1.79.2, 1.84.1, 1.84.3 and Critias D–K 88b6. Herodotus, a notable fifth-century source on Spartan affairs, does not fall into this category.

Bibliography

Breitenbach, H.R.

1967 *RE* 9A s.v. Xenophon (6), 1569–2052.

Burn, A.R.

1968 *The Lyric Age of Greece*, London.

Cairns, D.L.

1993 *Aidos*, Oxford.

1997 'The meadow of Artemis and the character of the Euripidean Hippolytus', *Quaderni Urbinati di Cultura Classica* 57, 51–75.

Carey, C. (ed.)

1989 *Lysias: Selected Speeches*, Cambridge.

Cornford, F.M.

1912 'Psychology and social structure in the *Republic* of Plato', *CQ* 6, 246–65.

Delebecque, E.

1957 *Essai sur la vie de Xénophon*, Paris.

Dover, K.J.

1974 *Greek Popular Morality*, London.

1981 *A Historical Commentary on Thucydides*, vol. 5, Oxford.

Dover, K.J. (ed.)

1984 *Plato: Symposium*, Cambridge.

Due, B.

1989 *The Cyropaedia*, Aarhus.

Fisher, N.R.E.

1994 'Sparta re(de)valued: some Athenian public attitudes to Sparta between Leuctra and the Lamian War', in A. Powell and S. Hodkinson (eds.) *The Shadow of Sparta*, London, 347–400.

Gera, D.L.

1993 *Xenophon's Cyropaedia*, Oxford.

Gray, V.J.

1998 *The Framing of Socrates*, Stuttgart.

Guthrie, W.K.C.

1975, 1978, 1981 *A History of Greek Philosophy*, vols 4, 5 and 6, Cambridge.

Higgins, W.E.
1972 *Xenophon the Athenian*, Albany.
Hodkinson, S.
1994 ' "Blind Ploutos"? Contemporary images of the role of wealth in classical Sparta', in A. Powell and S. Hodkinson (eds.) *The Shadow of Sparta*, London, 183–222.
Humble, N.
1997 'Xenophon's view of Sparta', Diss., McMaster University, Hamilton.
Humphreys, S.
1983 *The Family, Women and Death*, London.
Kennell, N.M.
1995 *The Gymnasium of Virtue*, Chapel Hill.
Lana, M.
1992 'Xenophon's *Athenaion Politeia*: a study by correspondence analysis', *Literary and Linguistic Computing* 7.1, 17–26.
Luppino Manes, E.
1988 *Un progetto di riforma per Sparta*, Milan.
Moore, J.M.
1983 *Aristotle and Xenophon on Democracy and Oligarchy*, London.
Nill, M.
1985 *Morality and Self-interest in Protagoras, Antiphon and Democritus*, Leiden.
North, H.
1966 *Sōphrosynē*, Ithaca.
Ollier, F.
1933 *Le mirage spartiate*, Paris
1934 *Xénophon. La République des Lacédémoniens*, Paris.
Proietti, G.
1987 *Xenophon's Sparta*, Leiden.
Rawson, E.
1969 *The Spartan Tradition in European Thought*, Oxford.
Rebenich, S.
1998 *Xenophon. Die Verfassung der Spartaner*, Darmstadt.
Strauss, L.
1939 'The Spirit of Sparta or the Taste of Xenophon', *Social Research* 6, 502–36.
Thomas, R.
1994 'Law and the lawgiver in the Athenian democracy', in R. Osborne and S. Hornblower (eds.) *Ritual, Finance, Politics*, Oxford.
Tigerstedt, E.N.
1965 *The Legend of Sparta in Classical Antiquity*, vol. 1, Stockholm.
Too, Y.L.
1995 *The Rhetoric of Identity in Isocrates*, Cambridge.
Tuplin, C.
1993 *The Failings of Empire*, Stuttgart.
1994 'Xenophon, Sparta and the *Cyropaedia*', in A. Powell and S. Hodkinson (eds) *The Shadow of Sparta*, London, 127–81.

Watt, D.
1987 'Introduction to *Charmides*' in T.J. Saunders (ed.) *Plato. Early Socratic Dialogues*, Harmondsworth, 165–74.

Williams, B.
1993 *Shame and Necessity*, Berkeley.

Young, C.M.
1991 'Aristotle on Temperance', in J.P. Anton and A. Preuss (eds.) *Essays in Ancient Greek Philosophy IV. Aristotle's Ethics* New York, 107–25.

Chapter 13

ATHENIAN IDEOLOGY AND THE EMPOWERED SPARTAN WOMAN

Ellen Millender

In recent years, scholars have begun to examine more closely the complex relationship between representations of Sparta and Spartan reality. While several studies have reassessed popular images of classical Sparta and have helped to cut through the 'Spartan mirage' that has shaped and distorted both ancient and modern conceptions of Sparta, one stereotype seems to have escaped the benefit of this scholarly breath of fresh air – that of the empowered Spartan woman. Even those recent works which have attempted to provide more nuanced treatments of Spartan women have continued to portray them as unusually liberated, independent, and powerful in relation to other Greek women, particularly those of Athens.[1] Most of these studies, however, share a number of weaknesses which seriously undercut their value, the most important being their general lack of interest in the provenance of information on Spartan women and the possible bias and prejudice inhering in such evidence, particularly Athenian-based material. Almost all of the information we have concerning Spartan women comes from non-Spartan sources. More importantly, the image of the sexually and politically powerful Spartan woman which figures so largely in fourth-century and later sources first seriously developed in Athens in the latter half of the fifth century.[2] The *topos* of the empowered Spartan female, consequently, must be understood in the context of fifth-century Athenian political, social, and cultural discourse as well as of Athens' long and bitter rivalry with Sparta for hegemony in the Aegean.

This essay examines fifth-century representations of Spartan women and considers two intertwined issues: (1) the role which sexuality and gender played in Athenian self-definition and definition of others in the context of this conflict and (2) the effect which Athens' antagonistic relationship with Sparta had on contemporary depictions of Spartan sexual mores and gender roles. As a number of ethnographically-based works have argued, sexuality and gender form an important ideational area of contact between societies and tend to operate as key indicators of difference in inter-cultural contact.[3] Greek authors, for example, often conceptualized their enemies in terms of variant sexual practices and gender systems. Cultural differentiation in sexual and gendered terms occurs with particular clarity and frequency in Herodotus' *Histories* and repeatedly underlies tragic characterizations of non-Greeks, such as the Egyptian maidens who refuse to submit to marriage with their cousins in Aeschylus' *Supplices* of *c.* 463 and Euripides' Medea, whose unhealthy obsession with her *lechos* ('marriage-bed') ultimately forces her to subordinate her maternal instincts to her own sexuality.[4]

In this essay I argue that gender and sexuality performed a similar function in fifth-century Athenian constructions of Spartan 'otherness'. Authors of this period repeatedly defined and reaffirmed Athenian norms of monogamous marriage and patriarchal authority through treatments of Sparta as a society in which both of these configurations were replaced by their inversions – female promiscuity and gynecocracy. The empowered Spartan female, accordingly, came to occupy the same conceptual framework that earlier created and housed the sexually and politically powerful barbarian woman. The first section of this essay examines Athenian-based constructions of Spartan female power and licentiousness. In the second and third sections, I consider the validity of these representations and situate them in the context of Athenian democratic ideology and views on sexual relations and the proper role of women.

I. Sex and the Spartan woman: inversion, license, and gynecocracy

Several fifth-century Athenian-based authors reveal a fascination with Spartan women, portraying them as abnormally independent, sexually promiscuous, and both economically and politically powerful. This interest in Spartan women runs through Herodotus' *Histories*, which provides detailed descriptions of many powerful barbarian women but devotes far less attention to the women of Hellas and even more rarely presents examples of influential Greek women. Herodotus, however, refers to Spartan women with greater frequency and detail than all other Greek women.[5] In four separate instances he also depicts Spartan females who parallel many non-Greek women in the *Histories* by displaying unusual intelligence and initiative, playing an active role in the political sphere, and outsmarting the male leadership of their *polis*.

In his account of the adventures of the Minyae in Lacedaemon, Herodotus describes how the imprisoned Minyae avoid death through the machinations of their Spartan wives, who trade clothing with their husbands and effect their escape (4.146). Through both their adoption of male dress and their ability to hoodwink their fathers, these clever women temporarily overturn male order. Herodotus introduces a similarly crafty Spartan woman in his portrayal of Argeia, the mother of the twin founders of the Agiad and Eurypontid houses, whose cleverness and desire that both of her sons be made kings are ultimately responsible for the institution of the dyarchy (6.52.2–7). The other Spartan female whose initiative and influence twice merits Herodotus' particular attention is Gorgo, the daughter of Cleomenes I and wife of Leonidas I. In the first of these accounts, the eight-year-old Gorgo assumes the role of wise adviser for her father in his dealings with the Milesian despot, Aristagoras (5.51.2–3), and thereby joins a select group of females in the *Histories* who perform a similar function in the courts of both Greek and non-Greek dynasts, such as Polycrates' daughter (2.124) and the Persian queen Atossa (3.134).[6] Later, as the wife of Leonidas, Gorgo alone discovers the secret of the message sent by the exiled Spartan king, Demaratus, to the Lacedaemonians concerning Xerxes' plan to attack Hellas (7.239.4).

In his accounts of Spartan history and customs, Herodotus also twice alludes to Spartan female sexual freedom. His use of the term σύμμιγα to describe the cooperation of both sexes in the Spartan royal funeral arguably lends a tone of impropriety to the ceremony and semantically associates the intermingling of the mourners with sexual promiscuity (6.58.3).[7] When the soon-to-be-exiled King Demaratus later questions his mother about the malicious rumor that she had conceived him by means of a tryst with an ass-keeper, he claims that if she has committed such an act, she is not the only Spartan woman to have done so but is in good company (6.68.2–3). His mother defends her wifely virtue against these rumors, but both the rumors themselves and Demaratus' slur insinuate that not all Spartan wives remained as true to their vows.

Although the scanty nature of the evidence does not permit any firm conclusions, fifth-century Athenian comedy appears to exhibit a similar attitude toward Spartan women. A tantalizing unattributed fragment of Eupolis (fr. 385) contains a brief dialogue between the Athenian Alcibiades and an unknown interlocutor, who seems to refer to Alcibiades' illicit intercourse with many – probably Spartan – women.[8] Aristophanes' *Lysistrata* of 411 further reveals Athenian interest in the figure of the empowered Spartan woman. In this comedy he introduces the Spartan Lampito, whose beautiful skin, firm breasts, and muscular physique earn Lysistrata's admiration and whose revealing clothing induces her Athenian counterparts to study her body with both ease and wonder (78–84). While Lampito provides an example of Sparta's legendary reputation for beautiful women (cf. Hom. *Od.* 13.412), her ability to throttle an ox with her bare hands (81) would appear to exceed the customary bounds of feminine beauty. Calonice's rather unseemly reaction to Lampito's breasts and her use of the term τὸ χρῆμα to describe them further suggest the extraordinary nature of the Spartan woman's loveliness (83).[9] It is also noteworthy that Aristophanes uses the term τιτθός to refer to a woman's breasts only in Calonice's praise of Lampito and in the vivid scene in his *Thesmophoriazusae,* where the women expose Mnesilochus' manhood and remark on the odd nature of this female impersonator's 'breasts' (640).[10] Lampito's comeliness, moreover, is not simply the product of nature but rather of exercise in the open air, an example of which she offers in her performance of a dance in which she kicks her buttocks (82). Lampito represents feminine sexuality gone awry. Her virile beauty subverts heterosexual expectations and accords with the Spartan penchant for anal/homosexual intercourse mocked by Aristophanes throughout the comedy (cf., esp., 1148, 1157, 1162–3, 1174).[11]

Euripides furnishes the most explicit evidence of Athenian fascination with Spartan women in a number of tragedies which represent them as subverting sexually the natural order and transgressing their socially authorized role. In his extant tragedies, especially those which recount the Trojan War and its aftermath, two particular women come to embody Spartan female licentiousness: the infamous Helen and her daughter, Hermione.[12] Euripides offers a striking characterization of Helen which departs radically from Homer's Argive Helen, the semi-divine offspring of Zeus and Leda, who becomes the unwitting victim of the gods and Paris and passive cause of the Trojan War.[13] In Euripides' hands, Helen repeatedly assumes the more 'human'[14] role of the adulterous Spartan female whose unbridled lust ultimately wrought untold destruction among Greeks and Trojans alike.[15] Euripides also heavily emphasizes her Spartan origin, another note-worthy departure from earlier authors.[16] Although Lacedaemon/Sparta serves as the home of Menelaus and Helen in the *Iliad* and the *Odyssey,* it receives little attention in Homer's account of Telemachus' visit to the reunited couple in the *Odyssey,* and Helen is primarily described as 'Argive' in both works.[17] References to Helen's Spartan origin occur in other early works and several fifth-century texts, but in our extant sources Spartan provenance only becomes a defining characteristic of Helen in Euripidean tragedy.[18]

Euripides' characterization of Helen as a sexually-driven and destructive Spartan adulteress appears most vividly in his *Troades* of 415. This treatment is particularly apparent in the *agōn* between Helen and her erstwhile 'mother-in-law', Hecuba, which takes place in the presence of Helen's cuckolded husband, Menelaus (914–1032). In an attempt to convince Menelaus to put his wife to death, Hecuba launches into a lengthy diatribe against Helen, in which she repeatedly calls attention to the latter's Spartan origin (986, 994, 999) and portrays the Spartan queen as a woman driven by a voracious appetite for both sex and wealth (983–97):

> You claim – this really makes me laugh – that Aphrodite
> came along with my son to the house of Menelaus.
> Could she not have carried you together with the very city of Amyclae
> to Ilium, without leaving the quiet of heaven?
> My son was remarkably handsome,
> and looking at him your mind was transformed into Cypris.
> For among human beings all acts of folly are Aphrodite,
> and rightly does the name of the goddess begin with the word for folly.
> Beholding him in the barbaric splendor of his robes,
> gleaming with gold, you went out of your mind.
> Dwelling in Argos in little luxury, you hoped
> that once you got rid of Sparta for the Phrygian city
> streaming with gold, you could indulge in
> extravagance. No longer was Menelaus' house
> sufficient to allow you to revel in luxuries.[19]

The reversal in characterization which has taken place on stage between Greek and non-Greek is particularly noteworthy. It is the Greek Helen who has deviated from normal sexual behavior and who has also become infatuated with the East, its riches, and its barbaric customs.[20] As the Trojan Hecuba later points out, Helen could not bear to leave Priam's court, where she ran riot and exulted in the barbarian custom of *proskynēsis* (1020–2), a practice long associated with Persian despotism and abhorred by the Greeks (cf. Aesch. *Pers.* 152, 588–9; Hdt. 7.136.1).[21] This 'barbarized' Helen appears in several Euripidean tragedies, especially the *Orestes* of 408, which provides the Spartan queen with a makeshift Oriental court staffed by Phrygian eunuchs (1110–14, 1367–1526).[22]

Euripides offers an even more explicit and vehement attack on Spartan women in his earlier *Andromache* of *c.* 425. From the moment he brings her onto the stage, Euripides portrays the Spartan Hermione as a woman who has completely overstepped her proper bounds and who behaves in a manner contrary to normal, civilized Greek custom.

The sumptuously garbed Hermione at once boasts about her independent wealth and describes her paternal inheritance in terms which emphasize both her Laconian nationality and her unusually powerful position in her household (147–53):[23]

> Hither I come, with my head decked in costly gold ornaments
> and my body clothed in this raiment of broidered robes –
> not offerings from the house of Achilles or Peleus,
> but from the Laconian land of Sparta
> my father Menelaus gave me these things
> along with many wedding gifts,
> so that I should have freedom of speech.[24]

As in his characterization of her mother, Euripides underscores Hermione's 'barbarism' through both his depiction of her luxurious attire and the vivid scene in which the Trojan Andromache castigates the Greek Hermione for exhibiting behavior improper for a wife (205–31), particularly sexual incontinence (215–21, 229–31; cf. 236, 240, 242, 244).[25] According to Andromache, Hermione's husband has good cause to hate his Spartan wife: she constantly complains about her lot, lords her independent wealth and superior lineage over him, and manifests a sexual possessiveness which is both excessive and destructive (209–19). Hermione's socially and sexually transgressive behavior later leads her to run off with her cousin Orestes (987–1008; cf. 922–3) and implicitly refers the audience to her mother, whose intemperate fondness for the opposite sex (229–31) and abandonment of hearth and husband similarly violated the Greek norms of male ascendancy and monogamous marriage (cf. 619–23).

The single Spartan male in both plays, Menelaus, reveals the flipside of Spartan feminine power and transgression in his masculine weakness and susceptibility to manipulation by his wife and daughter. The latter failing, according to the Trojan Andromache, has repeatedly led him to commit murder and other outrages for the sake of a woman (*Andr.* 361–3). The aged Peleus in the *Andromache* similarly claims that the sexual control exerted by the wanton Helen led Menelaus to commence the deadly war with the Trojans (605–18) and later even induced him to bid his brother Agamemnon to sacrifice Iphigenia (624–6).[26] As Peleus next points out in a vivid description of the Spartan couple's later reunion, Menelaus' immoderate physical desire for his wife also, ironically, forced him to spare her life. At the very sight of Helen's breasts, Menelaus supposedly became overpowered with desire, threw away his sword, and proceeded to kiss and fondle the 'traitorous bitch' (627–31).[27]

Helen's sexual domination of her husband also figures prominently in the *Troades*, particularly in Euripides' portrayal of Menelaus' judgment of Helen.[28] While offering arguments in favor of Helen's execution, Hecuba repeatedly reveals her concern that the uxorious Menelaus' passion will never allow him to slay his wife (890–4, 1049, 1051). Menelaus himself indicates this lack of resolve when he makes the odd wish that Helen should go and find those who will stone her to death, thereby implicitly absolving himself of all responsibility for her punishment (1039–41).[29] The chorus of Trojan women's later description of the couple's return to Sparta seems to support Hecuba's fear and suggests that Menelaus already lost his resolve to kill her before their departure (1100–17).[30] Euripides' portrait of a happily reunited Menelaus and Helen in the later *Orestes* fully demonstrates the cogency of Hecuba's fears concerning Helen's ability to control, weaken, and corrupt her husband's character (cf. 737, 742).

Euripides' *Andromache* portrays an equally dysfunctional relationship between Menelaus and Hermione, whose powerful manipulation of her father impels him to take up arms yet again, this time against a defenseless woman and child (326–8; cf. 370–3). Menelaus clearly appears to be just as incapable of exerting any influence over Hermione's behavior as he was earlier unable to keep her mother, Helen, at home (590–5, 602–4; cf. *Tro.* 943–4). The Spartan king's inability to control the females in his family leads several Euripidean characters to challenge his masculinity (cf. *Andr.* 353–4, 590 ff.; *IA* 945), which again comes into question in Euripides' *Orestes* of 408. In this tragedy Menelaus enters the stage πολλῇ ἁβροσύνῃ (349) – a term which links him with the luxurious and effeminate East – and is later described disdainfully by his nephew, Orestes, as 'priding himself on his shoulder-length blond curls' (1532).[31]

Although Euripides' *Helen* of 412 presents far more positive treatments of both Helen and Menelaus, a good deal of gender role reversal occurs in this utopian drama as well. At the very beginning of the play, Euripides sharply contrasts Helen and Menelaus in terms of their ability to deal with adversity. Compared to the long-suffering Helen, who bravely endures her undeserved reputation as a traitress and attempts to remain true to her husband (1–67), Menelaus appears pathetic, weak, and comical. Desperately clinging to his fame in the Trojan War and indulging in self-pity, he fears losing face among the local inhabitants because of his present state of misfortune and weeps like a baby when the old woman at Theoclymenus' gate utterly deflates his oversized ego by showing no interest in his triumph at Troy (386–458).

His lack of resolution in the face of the portress closely parallels his weakness before Hermione and Peleus in the *Andromache*, Helen in the *Troades*, and Tyndareus in the *Orestes*.[32]

Even later in the play, when Euripides portrays Menelaus more seriously as a faithful husband willing to kill or be killed for the sake of his wife (806–54), he still depicts the victor of Troy negatively in comparison with his wife. When the two ponder their options against Theoclymenus, it is Helen who supplies the plan which eventually leads to their rescue (813 ff.). Menelaus, on the other hand, continues to rely on and boast about his now empty triumph at Troy (806, 808, 845–50, 948–9) and can only envision a rescue involving brute force and murder rather than a stratagem (809–14). While it is true that they make use of both guile and physical force in order to effect their escape (1526–1613), Menelaus' prowess appears at once ridiculous and pathetic next to Helen's superior cleverness.[33]

The figures of Helen, Hermione, and Menelaus together present a picture of Sparta as a society characterized by an inverted gender hierarchy, in which both women and men demonstrate excessive and destructive sexual desire and an attraction to the barbarian East. In Euripides' hands the Spartan royal house comes to exemplify the topsy-turvy gender system which the Athenians had long associated with the barbarian world, a repository of 'abnormal' sexual practices and conceptual space inhabited by transgressive females and emasculated males. The confused state of the Spartans' sexual mores and gender relations receives particular attention in a diatribe on Spartan practices delivered by Peleus in the *Andromache*. In this tendentious speech, Peleus not only casts aspersions on Menelaus' manhood but also indulges in a tirade against Spartan female liberation and license in general (590–604):

> You call yourself a man, coward of cowards bred?
> What right have you to be reckoned as a man?
> You, who lost your wife to a Phrygian,
> having left your house and hearth unlocked and unattended,
> as if you had a modest wife at home
> instead of the most wanton of women. Even if she wanted,
> no Spartan girl could be modest.
> They leave their homes empty,
> and with their thighs bared and robes ungirt,
> they share the race-courses and the wrestling grounds with the young men[34]
> – things which I find intolerable! Is there any need to wonder then
> if you do not train your women to be self-controlled?
> You should ask Helen, who abandoned your bonds of love

and went rampaging out of the house
with her young man to a foreign land.[35]

Scholars have generally viewed these representations as negative Athenian responses to the freer lifestyle and looser sexual mores of contemporary Spartan women.[36] This assessment accords with the typical modern belief that Spartan women exhibited an extraordinary degree of sexual license, economic activity, and personal independence among Greek women of both the archaic and classical periods. Although we should not discount the possibility that some truth lies behind the image of the empowered Spartan female, an investigation of the literary and archaeological evidence – with primary consideration given to contemporary or near-contemporary sources – suggests that both the reality behind the stereotype and the above authors' reactions to Spartan sexual mores and gender roles are far more complex than earlier studies have suggested.

II. The empowered Spartan woman: fact or fiction?

Scholars working on Spartan women and the connected issues of Spartan sexual mores and gender roles face a relative dearth of information from the fifth century. Although Herodotus is the only extant fifth-century author besides Euripides who deals extensively with this sphere of Spartan life, he provides useful information concerning Spartan marital practices, particularly in connection with the two royal families. Herodotus' two allusions to Spartan female promiscuity (6.58.3, 68.3) appear to support Euripides' more obviously biased portraits of Spartan women. However, the other evidence he furnishes on Spartan marital customs suggests that the Spartan woman displayed no more independence in these matters than her counterpart in Athens. According to Herodotus, the Spartan kings of his day had jurisdiction over the allocation of every *patrouchos* ('unwedded heiress') whose father had not made arrangements for her marriage before his death (6.57.4). This piece of information, along with Herodotus' description of Leotychidas II's 'giving' (δόντος) of his daughter in marriage to his grandson, Archidamus II (6.71.2), suggests that the responsibility for betrothal, in normal circumstances, belonged not to the daughter, but rather to the Spartan father.[37] Euripides lends support for this practice in his *Andromache*, despite this tragedy's generally tendentious depiction of Spartan women. When her cousin Orestes responds positively to Hermione's plea to take her from Phthia and talks of their marriage, the otherwise uncontrollable Hermione reminds him that her marriage is her father's responsibility

(987–8). Aristotle (*Pol.* 1270a26–9) offers further support for the existence of the *kyrieia*, the legal guardianship of a female by her nearest male relation, usually her father or his closest male heir before her marriage and then her husband. According to Aristotle, if the father did not betroth his heiress, that right fell to the *klēronomos*, most probably her male next-of-kin.[38]

The only piece of evidence which possibly argues against this type of marital procedure occurs in Herodotus' account of King Demaratus' *harpagē* ('seizure') of Percalos, the intended bride of his relative (and later royal successor), Leotychidas, before the latter had consummated his marriage (6.65.2). It makes better sense, however, to view Demaratus' rape of his kinsman's bride as an aberrant and infamous example of a symbolic 'marriage by capture' (cf. Plut. *Lyc.* 15.4–9) which likely occurred after the arrangement of the marriage between the bride's *kyrios* and the bridegroom.[39] For our purposes, it is important to note that the Spartan woman plays an entirely passive role in both stages of the marital process. Female passivity in matrimonial matters is similarly suggested by Herodotus' accounts of the marriages contracted by kings Anaxandridas II (5.39–40) and Ariston (6.62–63.1).

Although the above accounts of Spartan marital customs fail to demonstrate Spartan female sexual independence, scholars continue to argue that Spartan women were long allowed sexual freedoms unknown elsewhere in Greece. These claims are invariably based on later evidence, particularly Xenophon's work on the Spartan constitution and the relevant information provided by Polybius and Plutarch.[40] According to Xenophon, the Spartan lawgiver, Lycurgus, instituted various forms of wife-sharing, ostensibly in order to maximize the child-bearing potential of healthy, young Spartiate women (*Lac.Pol.* 1.7–8). One type made it legal for an elderly husband to introduce into his house a younger man, whose physique and character he admired, for the sake of producing children with his wife. Another offered a solution to the man who did not wish to marry but desired children. This form of wife-sharing legally allowed such a man to produce children with another man's wife, provided that he had previously gained the husband's permission. Xenophon claims that Lycurgus sanctioned many similar arrangements, and his description suggests that these, too, involved some form of wife-sharing. He implies that by means of such practices, women could take charge of two households, and men could produce for their sons brothers who would share in the family and its influence but have no claim to the family's wealth (*Lac.Pol.* 1.9).

Polybius, writing in the second century BCE, states that it had long been the custom at Sparta for three, four, or even more brothers to share one woman and for their offspring to be counted as the property of all in common.[41] He adds that when a Spartan male had produced a sufficient number of children, it was honorable and customary for him to pass his wife on to a friend (12.6b.8). Plutarch, writing *c.* 100 CE, claims in his *Life of Lycurgus* that Lycurgus attempted to free the Spartans from jealousy and possessiveness in their sexual relations by making it honorable for all worthy men to share in the production of offspring (15.11; cf. *Comp. Lyc.-Num.* 3.1). He then describes, with slight variations, the two wife-sharing schemes mentioned by Xenophon (15.12–13).[42] Unlike his predecessors, however, Plutarch defends these arrangements as attempts to produce children of the best stock possible. He refers to Spartan women's reputation for wantonness but twice states that licentiousness played no part in Lycurgus' provisions (15.11, 16) and even claims that *moicheia* ('adultery') was wholly unknown in Lycurgan Sparta (15.16–18; cf. *Mor.* 228b–c).

Although we cannot entirely dismiss the evidence from these sources, we must approach it with the greatest of caution. Of the three, Xenophon commonly inspires the most faith because of his long and close association with Agesilaos II, his brief residence in Sparta, and his opportunity to gain an unusual familiarity with Lacedaemonian customs and institutions during the first half of the fourth century. The authorship of the *Lacedaemoniōn Politeia*, however, remains contested, and scholars have suggested dates for its composition ranging from *c.* 395 to the period of Cleomenes III (*c.* 260–219).[43] Even if we were to believe that Xenophon composed this essay, we cannot be sure that the social conditions he describes in the fourth century existed earlier. Xenophon's tendency both to moralize and to idealize Sparta further undermines his worth as a source on Spartan women and sexual mores in general. Polybius has the added disadvantage of increased distance from fifth-century historical, political, and social conditions. Plutarch poses his own set of problems: an even greater distance from the period under discussion, a marked tendency toward moralization, and a dependence on earlier sources, which are not necessarily trustworthy in themselves.

Scholars, nevertheless, have generally accepted the notion that the Spartans practiced some form of wife-sharing, if not outright polyandry, and have supplied numerous explanations for this phenomenon.[44] Most today believe that these customs must have arisen in response to the ever-pressing need to keep up the number of Spartan *homoioi*.[45] If the need to increase citizen numbers promoted these practices, they may parallel the type of marital arrangement sanctioned by a late fifth-century Athenian decree which supposedly attempted to address the chronic shortage of men during the Peloponnesian War by temporarily suspending the rule requiring that a child's parents be formally married. According to a number of sources, this decree allowed citizens to marry one woman and breed legitimate children with another.[46] In his detailed studies of Spartan inheritance and land tenure, Stephen Hodkinson admits that wife-borrowing may have originated for the purpose of increasing the population but sees a more important link between Spartan sexual and marital practices and a system of universal female inheritance. He classes wife-borrowing and polyandry along with other marriage customs which aimed at both the limitation of legitimate children and the preservation of family wealth and power.[47] According to Hodkinson, the severe economic and social stratification which would have encouraged such marriage practices developed in Sparta in the mid-fifth century.[48]

Several factors, however, suggest caution in attributing wife-borrowing and polyandry to fifth-century Sparta. The only extant evidence concerning these practices comes from fourth-century and later sources, and the date of their origin must remain conjectural. We also lack the prosopographical information on Spartan marriages which would allow us to assess how common such marital arrangements were in any period of Spartan history.[49] Even if one were to argue for their existence in fifth-century Sparta – whether for population control or expansion – these practices, similar to the matrimonial rites mentioned by Herodotus, cast women in a passive role. The descriptions of these wife-sharing schemes outlined above, particularly Xenophon's (*Lac.Pol.* 1.8) and Plutarch's (*Lyc.* 15.3; cf. *Mor.* 242b) claims that permission had to be sought from the husbands of the females involved, not only place men in full control of the exchange of women between households but also provide further support for the existence of the *kyrieia*.[50] Instead of supporting fifth-century Athenian portraits of the sexually licentious and powerful Spartan woman, these accounts underline both her role as her husband's possession and her primary importance as a producer of children for a male-dominated society.

Scholars who posit the existence of the empowered Spartan woman focus not only on the practices of wife-borrowing and polyandry but also on evidence concerning Spartan women's supposed penchant for exercise and for wearing revealing clothing.[51] The ancient literary and archaeological evidence, however, presents a more complex picture of both Spartan female athletics as well as the semi-nudity or nudity which both ancient and modern writers have incorrectly associated with the average Spartiate woman's daily dress.[52] While the Euripidean Peleus links Spartan girls' participation in athletic events with Spartan female licentiousness in general (*Andr.* 595–601), other contemporary sources which refer to Spartan women's physical exercise rather stress its eugenic aim. Aristophanes' portrayal of Lampito in the *Lysistrata*, for example, offers an exaggerated and absurd picture of the type of woman fostered by the Spartans' interest in producing strong, healthy mothers (78–84, 117–18) without making any allusion to Spartan female sexual license. More explicit and laudatory treatments of the Spartan interest in eugenics are furnished briefly by Critias in his work on the Spartan *politeia*, written *c.* 425–403 (DK[6] 88, fr. 32), and in more detail in Xenophon's study of the Spartan constitution (1.3–4). Xenophon makes Lycurgus responsible for instituting a regimen of physical fitness for women which included contests of running and strength and which was calculated to produce strong mothers of vigorous offspring. Plutarch (*Lyc.* 14.3 and *Mor.* 227d), who expands these earlier descriptions of racing and wrestling contests into a full athletic program to which he adds the throwing of the discus and the javelin, similarly attributes female athletics to the Spartans' desire to produce healthy children.

Although none of these sources places Spartan female athletics in a ritual context, it is likely that at least some of the sporting events described by these authors – particularly the foot races – had a ritual significance.[53] Alcman's *Partheneion*, written toward the end of the seventh century, for example, provides several references to a race (1.39 ff., 3.8–9) which most likely occurred in the context of the cult of the Spartan Helen, served as one of the rites of passage which introduced Spartan girls into the community as adult women, and paralleled the type of race among Laconian maidens described much later by Pausanias (3.13.7).[54] Aristophanes later alludes to this cult practice at the conclusion of his *Lysistrata*, where the Spartan ambassador sings of girls sporting like colts along the banks of the Eurotas, led by the maiden-goddess Helen (1307–15).[55]

The semi-nudity and nudity which several ancient sources associate with Spartan women's participation in athletic events offers further indication of the intermingled eugenic and ritual character of Spartan female exercise.[56] Although the Euripidean Peleus sees signs of sexual license in Spartan girls' wrestling and racing with their thighs bared and robes ungirt (*Andr.* 595–601), other contemporary sources rather emphasize the eugenic aspect of athletic nudity. Aristophanes' unnaturally healthy Lampito, for example, seems to exemplify the benefits arising from exercise in the nude (*Lys.* 82), and Critias explicitly refers to female athletic nudity in his praise of the Spartans' methods of producing strong children (DK^{6} 88, fr. 32). Plutarch's later discussion of Lycurgus' institution of a female sports program highlights the ritual aspect of athletic nudity and Spartan female exercise in general. According to Plutarch, Lycurgus freed Spartan girls from softness, delicacy, and effeminacy by accustoming naked maidens to take part in processions and to dance and sing at certain festivals when the young men were present as spectators (*Lyc.* 14.4–6; cf. *Mor.* 227e). Plutarch defines these activities as 'incitements toward marriage', among which he includes Spartan maidens' *apoduseis* ('undressing') and participation in athletic contests (*Lyc.* 15.1). Like the processions and dances performed by Spartan maidens, female athletic contests and athletic nudity played a significant role in Spartan girls' transition to marriage and adult life.

Although Plutarch is a late source and seems to be alone in his suggestion that Spartan girls participated in these events totally nude, both his account of female ritual nudity and ancient references to Spartan female semi-nudity[57] accord with the archaeological evidence provided by a series of bronze mirror handles and freestanding figurines most likely produced or influenced by Laconian workshops between *c.* 570 and *c.* 470 BCE. These bronzes, most recently collected and discussed by Andrew Stewart, include five archaic statuettes depicting running girls dressed in *chitōniskoi* and approximately twenty-eight handles displaying fully naked girls.[58] The identification, function, and ritual context of these female statuettes remain debated. However, their generally underdeveloped physiques and various accoutrements suggest that they represent girls and young women involved in the cycle of initiation rites marking the progression toward marriage, like the Spartan females participating in the processions, dances, and athletic contests described by Plutarch and others.[59]

Through their inclusion of cultic nudity and athleticism, Spartan female rites of passage paralleled a number of initiation ceremonies observed in other parts of Greece. Ritual vessels discovered in the sanctuary of Artemis at Brauron and several other locations in Attica, for example, suggest that nudity and physical exercise also served a religious and socializing function in the Athenian celebration of the Brauronian Arcteia or 'Bear Festival.' These vases, dating from the late sixth to the late fifth centuries, depict girls, both naked and clothed in short chitons, running races in honor of Artemis.[60] Similar to the majority of the bronze mirror attachments and statues from archaic Sparta, most of the females on the vases found at Brauron have undeveloped, prepubescent bodies.[61] Literary and archaeological evidence connected with the Brauronia, in addition, indicates that there may have been an element of exhibitionism in the ritual nudity and semi-nudity of the participants in the Arcteia paralleling that of the Spartan prenuptial ritual described by Plutarch. In his *Peace* of 421, Aristophanes suggests that men were present at one penteteric procession from Athens to Brauron (872–6), and in this passage he further implies that they may have witnessed girls in the short chitons worn during the festival.[62] A fragment of a crater representing the Brauronian ritual also appears to depict a male figure and may point to male involvement in the festivities.[63]

The Athenian Brauronia and Spartan prenuptial rituals clearly differed in a number of respects. The Brauronia was apparently an exclusive affair which took place far from Athens and involved prepubescent girls aged five to ten.[64] Spartan female prenuptial rites, on the contrary, took place in front of the whole community and likely included both prepubescent and post-pubescent girls, since Spartan girls supposedly married relatively late, around eighteen to twenty years of age.[65] Nevertheless, both rituals demonstrate the central role which athletics and nudity performed in the preparation of adolescent girls for marriage and adulthood. In Sparta, however, exercise and semi-nudity or nudity belonged to a state-organized system of education and initiation rites for Spartan girls. This comprehensive process of socialization corresponded to the renowned 'upbringing' of Spartan boys and was intricately bound up with the Spartans' practice of eugenics. The Spartans' emphasis on the cultivation of vigorous mothers of Spartiate warriors and their complex cycle of girls' initiation ceremonies most likely made athletics a more common feature of female life in Sparta than in Athens and produced physically fit Spartan women accustomed to both outdoor activity and interaction with males. The Spartans' elaborate initiatory system also gave adolescent females a prominent role in the *polis'* cults and festivals, and their concerns regarding procreation clearly placed a high value on women's roles in childbearing and rearing.[66] Both Spartan female athletics and athletic/cultic nudity, nevertheless, ultimately served the interests of the male-dominated community and its promotion of marriage and healthy offspring.

While there seems to be little reality behind either ancient or modern assertions that Spartan women enjoyed an unusual degree of sexual freedom and indulged in sexually-empowering athletic practices, Spartan women appear to have exercised a greater degree of economic power than their Athenian sisters. Herodotus provides the earliest evidence concerning Spartan female economic activity in his discussion of the Spartan kings' jurisdiction over the allocation of every unmarried *patrouchos* not betrothed by her father (6.57.4). This term probably corresponds to the *patroiokos* of the nearly contemporaneous Gortynian law code, a daughter with no father or brother from the same father (8.40–2) who inherited her father's estate, explicitly controlled her patrimony, and only had to relinquish a portion of it to the next-of-kin she was expected to marry in the event that she refused him (cf. 7.35–8.12).[67] The Gortynian heiress's control over her property conforms to other provisions in the code which make it clear that at Gortyn women could own and deal with property in their own right and bequeath property to their children, and daughters inherited a share of the family estate even in the presence of sons.[68] The paucity of evidence of the dowry at Gortyn, in addition, suggests that the portion of the family estate which Gortynian daughters received as marriage settlements functioned as a form of pre-mortem inheritance.[69]

Herodotus stresses the Spartan *patrouchos'* lack of independence in marital matters and does not state whether she legally controlled her patrimony like her Cretan namesake. However, several sources suggest that Spartiate females possessed and managed property in their own right.[70] Beneath its biased and hostile portrayal of Spartan women, Euripides' *Andromache* provides an important kernel of information concerning the economic position of Spartan women. When she first enters the stage, Hermione draws attention to her costly ornaments and clothes, possessions which she claims to have acquired from her father along with her wedding gifts (147–53; cf. 873–4). Hermione's assertion that these gifts were meant to secure her freedom of speech (153), her later reference to her possession of great wealth (940), and Andromache's criticism of Hermione's lording her wealth over her husband (211) together suggest that the property which the Spartan princess had received as a marriage-settlement remained under her control instead of passing under the supervision of her husband. Two fourth-century females, Agesilaus II's sister, Cynisca, and Euryleonis, who both owned sufficient land and commanded the financial resources necessary to breed and maintain the horses with which they won victories in Olympic chariot races, provide explicit evidence for Spartan women's possession of property.[71] Aristotle later criticizes Spartiate females' ownership of approximately two-fifths of the land, which he holds partly responsible for Sparta's ultimate decline as a military power and attributes to both the high number of heiresses and the practice of giving large dowries (*Pol.* 1270a11–34).

Although Euripides describes Hermione's independent wealth in terms which usually refer to a dowry (ἕδνον, φερνή),[72] and Aristotle emphasizes the size of dowries (προῖκας), the powerful position of women in fourth-century Spartan land tenure suggests that Spartiate daughters did not simply receive voluntary bridal gifts of extraordinary proportions. It is more likely that they, similar to Gortynian daughters, actually inherited part of the family estate in the form of a marriage-settlement. [73] As Hodkinson's studies of Spartan land ownership and inheritance have shown, Spartan females from at least the mid-sixth century possessed rights of inheritance enjoyed by their counterparts in fifth-century Gortyn. Under this system of inheritance – which Hodkinson has termed 'universal female inheritance' – Spartan daughters inherited even in the presence of male siblings, their portion being half that of a son.[74]

Did Spartiate women's control over property, however, translate into an unusual degree of female independence and power in the Spartan state, as Aristotle seems to imply in his lengthy diatribe against their license, wealth and influence (*Pol.* 1269b12–1270a34, esp. 1269b23–5, 31–4)? Although modern scholars have followed Aristotle and made this very argument concerning Spartan women, their insistence on viewing Spartan women in monolithic terms necessarily undercuts the validity of their conclusions.[75] Aristotle's criticism of Spartan female land ownership likely applies only to wealthy Spartiate women and does not provide a generalized picture of the female Spartan population.[76]

Spartan women's ability to inherit, possess, and use wealth in their own right throughout the classical period, however, had important repercussions on their position in Sparta. Since the Spartiate male's status and privileges as a citizen rested upon his mess dues and ultimately his possession of sufficient agriculturally productive property to make these contributions, the Spartan female's ownership of property made her a valuable commodity in the marriage market. By means of economically advantageous marriages, families could maintain or increase their holdings and ensure their sons' inheritance of citizen status.[77] The acquisition and preservation of wealth would also have safeguarded such families' preeminent position and influence in the Spartan community.[78] Aristotle's criticism of Spartan female land ownership and its contribution to Spartan *oliganthrōpia* demonstrates just how important women had become in the fierce competition which Spartan *oikoi* ('households') waged in their struggle to maintain or improve their land-holdings and status.

Spartan women's relative economic independence also likely gave them a certain degree of leverage in familial matters and allowed them to function as more than pawns in inter-familial economic strife.[79] Although we possess no fifth-century evidence on this issue aside from Euripides' portrayal of the rich and powerful Hermione, contemporary evidence from Athens reveals that rich heiresses and well-dowered Athenian women were capable of exercising influence over the economic affairs of their families, despite their ostensible lack of control over their property.[80] It is probable that Spartan women, given their relative economic independence, demonstrated this type of influence with both greater frequency and efficacy.[81]

A number of scholars have argued that along with female possession of property, the Spartan husband's continued absence from the household empowered the Spartan woman and enabled her to exercise control over domestic concerns.[82] The Spartiate male's days were occupied by hunting, exercising, training for warfare, and performing other compulsory duties as a citizen and as a soldier, and he took his meals at the common messes. Until the age of thirty, he lived in barracks with other males, only occasionally making furtive visits to his wife under cover of darkness (cf. Xen. *Lac.Pol.* 1.5; Plut. *Lyc.* 15.7–10). The Spartans' frequent campaigns would also have kept men away from home for prolonged periods. All of these factors, taken together, make it likely that the average Spartiate husband spent less time at home than other Greek males. Although the Spartan male spent the majority of his time engaged in public activities, he must have taken an interest in the economic health of his *oikos,* on which his retention of citizenship, his status within the community, and the future of his descendants depended. Contemporary evidence from Athens suggests that the Athenian male also tended to have little involvement in household management and left control over domestic matters to the women of the house (cf. Lys. 1.6–7; Xen. *Oec.* 7.3–10.13). Scholars, however, have generally not assumed that the prominent place of women in the Athenian *oikos* either empowered them or diminished the Athenian male's interest in and ultimate control over his household.

As the above examination demonstrates, Spartan women enjoyed a lifestyle which allowed them to play an important role in Spartan society but which hardly conforms to fifth-century Athenian representations of Lacedaemonian females as unnaturally liberated, licentious and powerful. Similar to most other Greek women, they entered marriage under the direction of their fathers or closest male relatives and devoted their lives to procreation and the supervision of their households. While their comparatively late age of marriage supposedly placed them more on a par with their husbands,[83] it ultimately served a eugenic purpose, and the less tendentious accounts of Spartan marital practices stress male dominance in conjugal relationships. At times in Spartan history, their husbands may have involved them in wife-sharing schemes or polyandrous marital arrangements, but these customs ultimately reveal less about Spartan women's sexual independence and power than about their primary value as child-bearers and owners of property.[84] Spartiate females may also have engaged in athletic exercise more than other Greek women, but this practice, too, underscores their importance as wives and mothers. Only in the economic sphere do they reveal power and independence in their legal ownership of property.

Nevertheless, several Athenian-based authors portray Spartiate females as sexually intemperate and represent Sparta as a veritable gynecocracy, a construction which gained in force in the works of Aristotle (cf. *Pol.* 1269b12–1270a8) and later authors and has found support in many modern studies.[85] While one could possibly attribute such depictions to either repugnance toward or miscomprehension of a variant gender system, the fact that these writers transmuted cultural differences into dichotomies and furnished Sparta with a fully inverted sexual hierarchy points rather to their configuration of Lacedaemon as antithetical in sexual and gendered terms. These representations, accordingly, must be examined in the context of the sexual expectations and values which informed Athenian conceptions of self and other.

III. Spartan women and Athenian ideology

In order to elucidate the set of norms against which Spartan women were implicitly measured, we must return to Euripides, who provides useful information concerning Athenian attitudes toward the proper behavior and role of women in a number of his tragedies, particularly the *Troades*. In this tragedy, which morally opposes 'barbarized' Spartans and hellenized – or 'Athenianized' – Trojans, the Trojan Andromache ironically defines the type of conduct deemed appropriate for a 'Greek' wife. While bemoaning her fate, Andromache claims that she acquired her good reputation and brought honor to her husband's house by remaining at home and giving no one cause to speak ill of her (643–55). This ideal of feminine seclusion and modesty permeated almost all areas of literary production in classical Athens and receives its clearest expression in Thucydides' account of the funeral oration delivered by Pericles over the Athenian war-dead in 431/0.[86] After addressing the families of the dead, he concludes his speech with a word of advice to those widowed in the first year of the Peloponnesian War, which sheds light on the cultural expectations pertaining to the women of Athens. Similar to Andromache in Euripides' *Troades*, he suggests that a woman's proper place is within the home, where she would avoid gossip for good or ill and preserve her good repute (2.45.2).

This powerful ideology regarding feminine behavior not only permeated almost all areas of literary production but also influenced the iconography of contemporary vase-painting. The second half of the fifth century witnessed a dramatic increase in the number of illustrations of women, the majority of which have a domestic and private orientation and likely depict scenes from the gyneceum. Women are characteristically shown indoors, often accompanied by other women and performing the tasks Xenophon's Ischomachus ordains as the customary duties of a wife – spinning wool, weaving, and rearing children (cf. *Oec.* 7.3–10.13).[87] Even though many of these scenes decorate smaller vessels used by women, they were painted, marketed and purchased by men and likely reflect male fantasies and concerns regarding women's place in Athenian society.[88] The fact that women owned and probably received such vases as presents, however, suggests that the scenes on these vessels were also pleasing to them and reflect their own aspirations and values as well as those of their menfolk.[89]

Although a number of scholars have argued that female seclusion and quiescence were not just normative ideals but rather the reality for Athenian women, common sense and a judicious use of both literary and archaeological evidence lead to the conclusion that many Athenian women did not experience the type of sheltered life described by Euripides' Andromache. Athenian females of citizen status were not an undifferentiated mass, and it is likely that women on the upper and lower ends of the age spectrum enjoyed greater freedom than those in the full bloom of their sexuality.[90] Differences in economic and social status also shaped the experiences, conduct, treatment, and cultural expectations of women in ancient Athens. Only wealthy families which owned enough slaves to allow their women to remain confined at home could have adhered to this norm. Contemporary sources and vase-paintings demonstrate that many, if not most, Athenian families could not live up to this ideal and needed their women to fetch water, help with agricultural work, and perform other tasks which would take them out of the house.[91] Numerous references in fifth-century Athenian works also indicate that financial straits forced many citizen women to hold jobs outside the household and further explain Aristotle's claim that it was impossible to prevent poor women from going out-of-doors (*Pol.* 1300a6–7).[92]

Although only the well-to-do could translate the ideal of feminine seclusion into practice, this gender expectation remained dominant in Athens throughout much of the fifth century and most of the fourth. Explanations for both its power and endurance must be sought in the important position which women of citizen status occupied in both the individual household and the democratic Athenian *polis* as a whole. Athenian women served as vital links in the ties of kinship and religion which united separate households and bound together the closed community of Athenian citizens through two important mechanisms. First, they produced legitimate sons and heirs for their husbands' *oikoi*. Second, they transmitted wealth, along with ancestral religious rites and duties, both within and among *oikoi*. Although Athens' democratization entirely excluded them from the political process, Athenian women nevertheless played a fundamental role in the social organization and political structure of the Athenian *polis*. They perpetuated the *oikoi* whose aggregate comprised the citizen body and transmitted citizenship and all of its perquisites to their sons.[93] After the enactment of Pericles' citizenship law of 451/0, the male Athenian's citizenship became dependent upon his birth from two Athenian parents of citizen status (Arist. *Ath.Pol.* 26.4). By excluding the offspring of ethnically-mixed unions from citizenship, this law limited the number of males entitled to the highly prized economic privileges and political power which Athens' democratic constitution conferred upon its civic body.[94]

The Athenian female's crucial role in both the production of male citizens and legitimation of their political rights and status made her sexuality a matter of public and private importance. Her possible seduction and adultery endangered not only the normal perpetuation of ancestral cults and the transmission of the rights of inheritance but also the very continuity of the *oikos*. More importantly, female sexual license threatened to breach the jealously guarded boundary wall which surrounded the democracy's exclusive 'male citizens' club.' Male control and order in the *polis*, accordingly, were contingent upon male control and containment of female sexuality in the *oikos*.[95] Both the Athenian female's responsibility for male political privilege and the growing anxiety over the threat posed by the sexually transgressive female to the stability of the civic order led to a preoccupation with feminine fidelity which pervaded Athenian society.[96] This concern lay behind the increasing frequency of references in Athenian works of fiction to men's fears of adultery, women's infidelity, and the dangers of such behavior.[97] It also informed the law which defined adultery as grounds for justifiable homicide.[98]

Athenian democratic ideology resolved the tension surrounding the role of women in the democratic *polis* by constructing Athenian women as secluded and quiescent and by conceptually negating the very existence of the sexually and politically threatening female in Athens. The woman who transgressed the limits which society imposed upon her existed in the imaginary terrain of tragedy, where negative models served to question, criticize, and ultimately reaffirm the Athenian polity's self-image, political and social structures, and system of values. She likewise commonly figured in the fantasy world of Aristophanic comedy, where the inversion of the normal societal order freed women from social constraints and enabled their exercise of both sexual and political power. As several fifth-century Athenian tragedies amply demonstrate, the transgressive female also inhabited the conceptual realm of the barbarian and, more specifically, belonged in the non-democratic world. Aeschylus provides an early example of this association in his *Persae* of 472, in which the Persian queen Atossa's control and domination of the action until Xerxes' return (159–852) suggest her dominion over the Persian royal court in his absence.[99]

Herodotus' depictions of the courts of both Greek and non-Greek autocrats similarly posit a connection between undisciplined, dominating women and despotism, which Aristotle later explicitly formulates in his *Politics* (1313b32–9, 1314b25–7, 1319b27–9).[100] With only one exception, all of the powerful and influential barbarian women who inhabit Herodotus' *Histories* are connected to various royal courts.[101] His treatment of Greek women reveals a similar picture. Apart from a number of priestesses and the Spartan wives of the Minyae (4.146.3–4), the only Greek women whose independent power or influence over powerful men merit Herodotus' particular notice are members of Greek tyrants' families, members of the ruling house of Cyrene, and members of the two royal dynasties of Sparta.[102] This conceptual link between gynecocracy and autocracy may explain his carefully considered inclusion of the anecdotes concerning both Argeia and Gorgo.

Herodotus' treatment of the Persian royal house particularly reflects the association in the Athenian imagination between sexually powerful women and despotism. Herodotus at several points in the *Histories* portrays the Persian court as a natural breeding ground for female transgression, a place where a woman could use her sexuality to gain access to power. Herodotus provides a clear example of this type of situation in his description of the circumstances surrounding the Greek physician Democedes' return to Greece (3.133–5).[103] Although Democedes stands in excellent favor with Darius, he desires nothing more than to return home and only obtains his wish by a fortuitous set of events which give him leverage over Darius' consort, Atossa. In return for curing a lump on Atossa's breast, he asks her to encourage Darius to consider leading an expedition against Hellas, a plan which would require Democedes' aid and allow him to return to his homeland. According to Herodotus, Atossa manages to coerce her husband into considering such a campaign by means of both a traditionally sexually manipulative argument, equating might and manliness with conquest (3.134.1–3),[104] and a simple command (3.134.5). Despite the highly dubious nature of Herodotus' knowledge of the Persian royal family's bedroom secrets, this account nevertheless reflects fifth-century Athenian notions concerning the power which royal females wielded.

By portraying Sparta as a society characterized by topsy-turvy sexual mores and gender roles, fifth-century authors relegated it to the imaginary realm hitherto occupied only by the royal courts of the East in Athenian thought. Both the shifting focus of Athenian hostility from Persia to the Peloponnesus in the mid-fifth century and the increase in tensions surrounding the place of women in the democratic *polis* after 451/0 created the conditions in which the image of the powerful Spartan woman developed. As Athens' new foil, Sparta inevitably inherited much of the conceptual baggage which had accompanied and would continue to figure in Athenian representations of the barbarian world, including the association of gynecocracy and autocracy. Sparta's hereditary dyarchy and the tangible differences which existed between Spartan female roles and privileges and those of contemporary Athenian women, in turn, helped to strengthen the linkage being forged between Sparta's gender system and that of Athens' non-Greek enemies.

In the Athenian imagination, the transgressive female who had no place in the democratic *polis* could and did belong to those societies which posed a threat to Athenian hegemony and whose ostensibly inferior social and political structures made them both less capable and less worthy of exercising leadership. As several fifth-century Athenian-based writers suggest, when women are in a position to dominate men, sexually or politically, men inevitably assume the position of women, with dire consequences for both the health of the state itself and its position vis-à-vis other powers. Herodotus underlines the dangerous consequences of feminine domination in his account of Xerxes' entanglement in the struggles among the females of the royal family (9.108–114). This *logos* both connects Xerxes' weakness with the threat of rebellion and the extermination of his brother's family and juxtaposes the enervated, female-dominated Persian court with the wholly masculine and increasingly powerful Athenian forces in the Hellespont (9.114). Euripides, too, emphasizes the dangers of female domination in the *Andromache* through his portrayal of the uxorious Menelaus' inability to control his own household and exert his influence over Phthia. For the Athenians, male rule over the female not only guaranteed the normal functioning of the democracy but also became a precondition for rule over others. By linking female sexual independence, gynecocracy, and despotism in their representations of the enemy, Athenian authors not only validated their *polis'* democratic structures but also bolstered Athens' claims to hegemony in the Aegean.

Notes

[1] See, e.g., Bradford 1986, 13–18; Kunstler 1987, 31–48; Zweig 1993, 32–53; Fantham et al. 1994, 56–66.

[2] It is also possible that this image occurred in earlier sources which are no longer extant. Although the sixth-century lyric poet Ibycus seems to refer to scantily clad Spartan women (fr. 58 Page/Campbell = Plut. *Comp.Lyc.-Num.* 3.6), numerous problems impede the interpretation of this attenuated fragment. Since Plutarch reveals nothing concerning the context of Ibycus' remark, we can make no definite conclusions concerning Ibycus' interest in or attitude toward Spartan women. The scholiast to Anacreon (fr. 99 Page/Campbell) claims that his suggestion that girls 'go Dorian' involves the stripping off of their clothes. While Stewart (1997, 30, 108) uses this fragment of *c.* 500 BCE to argue that Spartan girls went about naked at this time, it is not clear that Anacreon is referring to Spartans, and both the context and Anacreon's attitude toward this practice remain unclear.

[3] See, e.g., Said 1978, 6, 103, 167, 186–90, 309, 311–16; Colley 1992, 250–3.

[4] On Herodotus' use of sexual and marital mores as cultural indicators, see, esp., Pembroke 1967, 1–35; Rosellini and Saïd 1978, 949–1005.

[5] Hdt. 4.145.5, 146.3–4; 5.39–41, 48, 51.2–3; 6.52.2–7, 58, 61–63.1, 65.2, 67.3–69, 71.2; 7.205.1, 239.4.

[6] See also Periander's daughter (3.53.2–5), Artemisia (7.99.3; 8.68–9, 101–3, 107.1), and Sesostris' wife (2.107).

[7] Although there are many non-sexual uses of συμμίσγω and the related term μίσγομαι in Herodotus' text (cf., e.g., 1.123.2; 2.116.4; 4.23.3, 114.1; 6.138.2; 7.129.1, 3, 203.2; 8.38, 58.1, 77.2; 9.19.2), the abundance of sexual uses of these terms, particularly μίσγομαι, strongly suggests that Herodotus' statement at 6.58.3 has sexual connotations. See Hdt. 1.198, 199.1, 3–4, 216.1; 2.46.4, 64.1, 66.1, 89.2, 131.1, 181.2–4; 3.118.1–2; 4.9.2, 114.1, 172.2, 176, 180.5; 5.20.1, 92η3; 8.33; 9.116.3. This usage is striking, since sexual promiscuity was viewed as not only characteristic of barbarian societies but also anathema to classical Greek society in general, and Athens in particular. For examples of barbarian promiscuity in the *Histories*, see Hdt. 1.93.4, 199, 203.2, 216.1; 3.101; 4.104, 172.2, 176, 180.5; 5.6.1. See Hartog 1988, 153. By drawing attention to women and men mixing promiscuously at Spartan royal funerals, Herodotus further emphasizes the 'barbaric' quality of these funeral rites (cf. Hdt. 6.58.2–3). For a full discussion of the links Herodotus forges between the Spartans and various barbarian peoples in both his treatment of the Spartan royal funeral ceremony and other sections of his text, see Millender 1996, chapter 3.

[8] Eup. fr. 385 (Kassel and Austin): (Αλκ.) μισῶ λακωνίζειν, ταγηνίζειν δὲ κἂν πριαίμην. | (Β.) πολλὰς δ' οἶμαι νῦν βεβινῆσθαι... See also fr. 148 (Kassel and Austin) of Eupolis' lost *Helots*, in which he has either a character or the chorus discuss poetry and express approval of a certain Gnesippus, who owes his popularity to his invention of night-time songs for μοιχοί to summon forth women. Although Edmonds (1957, 369) has translated these songs as 'lover's serenades', the term μοιχός means 'adulterer' rather than 'lover', which makes this passage assume a much racier aspect. Although we cannot be sure whether the fragment's lost context refers to Sparta, it could be another reference to the Spartans' supposedly looser sexual mores.

[9] Cf. Aristophanes' use of this term at *Lys.* 1031, 1085; *Ach.* 150. See Henderson 1987, 77–8.

[10] According to Henderson (1987, 78) τιτθίον is the *vox propria* in comedy. Both Henderson (1987) and Sommerstein (1990) read τῶν τιτθῶν in *Lys.* 83. As Jeffrey Henderson has kindly pointed out to me, the retention of the article is more idiomatic, and τιτθῶν is likelier to have been corrupted into the usual τιτθίων than vice versa.

[11] Both in this passage and at the conclusion of the play (1306–15), however, Aristophanes reveals admiration for Spartan female beauty and celebrates sexuality in general as part of his case in favor of peace between Athens and Sparta. For detailed discussions of Aristophanes' attitude towards Sparta, see Harvey 1994, 35–58 and Millender 1996, chapter 4.

[12] In addition to the plays discussed below, see Eur. *El.* 1027–9, 1065; *Cyc.* 179–86; *IA* 68–71, 75, 583–6.

[13] Although characters in the Homeric corpus occasionally blame Helen for the war and its destruction (cf. *Od.* 11.438, 14.68), both the *Iliad* and *Odyssey* tend to portray Helen with a good deal of sympathy. Consider, for example, the descriptions of her passivity and sadness at her fate at *Il.* 3.170–80, 399–412. Cf. Ath. 5.188a–c, 13.560b.

[14] Euripides continues to refer to Helen as the semi-divine daughter of Zeus

and Leda throughout his corpus: *Andr.* 145; *Tro.* 441, 767, 770, 943, 1109; *Hel.* 19, 81, 134, 470, 489, 490, 616, 638, 1144–6, 1641–85; *Or.* 1387, 1439, 1629–43, 1673–4, 1683–90; *IA* 686, 781, 795–7. However, he repeatedly reminds his audience of Helen's mortal role as the daughter of Tyndareus. See *Andr.* 898–9; *Hec.* 269; *Tro.* 34–5, 766; *Hel.* 17, 137, 472, 494, 568, 614, 1179, 1497, 1546; *Or.* 1154, 1423, 1512, 1689; *IA* 55, 61, 67, 78, 1335. Consider also the questioning of Helen's semi-divine origin at *Tro.* 766–71 and *IA* 793–800. On Euripides' humanization and debasing of Helen, see, esp., Ghali-Kahil 1955, 128–41. See also Dale 1981, vii–viii.

[15] Early sources occasionally paint Helen in negative terms (cf. *Anth. Graec.* 7.218.14, 9.166.3), and Aeschylus further accentuates her culpability in his *Agamemnon* (60–7, 403–55, 681–98, 1455–61, 1464–7). This image of the destructive Helen, however, occurs with far greater frequency, consistency, and harshness in the Euripidean corpus, the only apparent extant exceptions being Euripides' *Helen* of 412 and *El.* 1280–3. See *Andr.* 248, 605–15; *Hec.* 265–6; *Tro.* 442–3, 767–73, 881, 892–4, 969–1021, 1037–41, 1044–5, 1214–15; *El.* 213–14; *IT* 356, 439–45, 522, 526; *Or.* 1131–42, 1153–4, 1305–10, 1363–5, 1515, 1584; *IA* 1253–4. See Ghali-Kahil 1955, 139–40, at 139 n. 4; Dale 1981, vii–viii.

[16] Cf. *Andr.* 592–631; *Hec.* 441–2; *Tro.* 34–5, 133, 210–11, 250, 869, 944, 986, 994, 999, 1110–13; *IT* 521–4; *Or.* 65, 457, 537, 626, 1438; *IA* 73, 179, 1205; fr. 722 (Nauck^2); fr. pap. 130 (Austin). Euripides' close linkage between Helen and Sparta spills over into his far more positive presentation of her character in his *Helen* (17, 30, 58, 115, 124, 162, 210, 227, 235, 245, 350, 472, 474, 492–3, 495, 929, 1119, 1473–4, 1492, 1671). Although the loss of earlier material makes it impossible to prove the uniqueness of Euripides' treatment of Helen, the extant sources suggest that his continuous reference to Helen as Spartan is unusual. See Ghali-Kahil 1955, 140, who notes this particular aspect of Euripides' characterization of Helen but fails to develop or investigate this theme.

[17] For Homeric references to Helen's Spartan origins, see *Il.* 2.581–6; 3.387, 443; *Od.* 1.93, 285; 2.214, 327, 359; 3.326; 4.1, 10, 313, 702; 5.20; 11.460; 13.412, 414, 440; 15.1; 17.121. See also *Od.* 21.13. While the Homeric account in the *Odyssey* sets Telemachus' visit with Menelaus and Helen in Lacedaemon, Helen is still referred to as 'Argive Helen' in this section of the work (*Od.* 4.184, 296; 17.118; 23.218). For other Homeric references to Argive Helen, see Hom. *Il.* 2.161, 177; 4.19, 174; 6.323; 7.350; 9.140, 282. See also Hes. fr. 200.2, 204.43, 55, 62 (Merkelbach and West); *Anth. Graec.* 16.149.1. Euripides occasionally refers to Argos as Helen's home and destination after the war (cf. *Tro.* 875, 993, 1002, 1055, 1087; *Hel.* 124), but he never has characters refer to her Argive provenance in their attacks on her behavior and reserves Sparta for this role.

[18] For other references to Helen's Spartan origin, see Ath. 5.191a, 13.556d (Homer); Hes. fr. 199.2 (Merkelbach and West); Hdt. 2.113.1, 117 (Cyprian poems); 7.169.2; 9.73; Soph. fr. 176 (Radt); Ar. *Lys.* 1314–15, cf. 155–6; *Thesm.* 859–62; Cratinus fr. pap. 70 (Austin).

[19] Eur. *Tro.* 983–97: Κύπριν δ' ἔλεξας (ταῦτα γὰρ γέλως πολύς) | ἐλθεῖν ἐμῶι

ξὺν παιδὶ Μενέλεω δόμους. | οὐκ ἂν μένουσ' ἂν ἥσυχός σ' ἐν οὐρανῶι | αὐταῖς 'Αμύκλαις ἤγαγεν πρὸς Ἴλιον; | ἦν οὑμὸς υἱὸς κάλλος ἐκπρεπέστατος, | ὁ σὸς δ' ἰδών νιν νοῦς ἐποιήθη Κύπρις· | τὰ μῶρα γὰρ πάντ' ἐστὶν 'Αφροδίτη βροτοῖς, | καὶ τοὔνομ' ὀρθῶς ἀφροσύνης ἄρχει θεᾶς· | ὃν εἰσιδοῦσα βαρβάροις ἐσθήμασιν | χρυσῶι τε λαμπρὸν ἐξεμαργώθης φρένας. | ἐν μὲν γὰρ Ἄργει σμίκρ' ἔχουσ' ἀνεστρέφου, | Σπάρτης δ' ἀπαλλαχθεῖσα τὴν Φρυγῶν πόλιν | χρυσῶι ῥέουσαν ἤλπισας κατακλύσειν | δαπάναισιν· οὐδ' ἦν ἱκανά σοι τὰ Μενέλεω | μέλαθρα ταῖς σαῖς ἐγκαθυβρίζειν τρυφαῖς.

[20] Euripides also emphasizes Helen's unnatural and excessive greed and attraction to the wealth of the East at *Tro.* 1022–3, 1107. On Euripides' 'barbarized' Helen, see Ghali-Kahil 1955, 131, 138; Scodel 1980, 113. See also Hall 1989, 209–10, on Sophocles' and Euripides' use of vocabulary and themes connected with representations of barbarians in their portrayals of decadent Greeks.

[21] Compare Hermione's treatment of the captive Andromache at*Andr.* 164–5 and the fawning behavior of Helen's Phrygian slaves at *Or.* 1507–8. On the practice of*proskynēsis* (low bowing or prostration before social superiors) and its role in Greek tragic portrayals of barbarians, see Hall 1989, 96–7.

[22] See also Eur. *IA* 71–5 and *Cyc.* 182–5.

[23] Euripides also refers to Hermione's independent wealth at *Andr.* 211, 873–4, 940 and again stresses her abnormal control over her household at *Andr.* 940. He likewise reminds his audience of both Hermione's and Menelaus' Spartan nationality throughout the play at *Andr.* 29, 41, 194, 209–10, 437, 446–63, 486–7, 582, 595–641, 725, 734, 889, 916.

[24] Eur. *Andr.* 147–53: κόσμον μὲν ἀμφὶ κρατὶ χρυσέας χλιδῆς | στολμόν τε χρωτὸς τόνδε ποικίλων πέπλων | οὐ τῶν 'Αχιλλέως οὐδὲ Πηλέως ἀπὸ | δόμων ἀπαρχὰς δεῦρ' ἔχουσ' ἀφικόμην, | ἀλλ' ἐκ Λακαίνης Σπαρτιάτιδος χθονὸς | Μενέλαος ἡμῖν ταῦτα δωρεῖται πατὴρ | πολλοῖς σὺν ἕδνοις, ὥστ' ἐλευθεροστομεῖν.

[25] His depiction of her adornment echoes the barbarian Andromache's earlier description of herself as an Asiatic bride (*Andr.* 1–2). On this echo, see Stevens 1971, 115. Euripides' description of her rich attire also strikingly parallels his later representation of the Trojan Paris in the*Cyclops* (182–4) and the *Iphigenia at Aulis* (73–4) in terms of both vocabulary and imagery.

[26] Euripides frequently underlines the folly of Menelaus' expedition to Troy and waste of Greek life for the sake of a wanton woman. See, e.g.,*Tro.* 368–73; *Or.* 521–2, 647–50; *Cyc.* 283–4; *IA* 389–90. Even Menelaus himself hints at the other Greeks' disdain for his leading an expedition to Troy for Helen's sake (*Tro.* 863–6). For Menelaus' shameful and selfish request that Agamemnonslay his own child, see also Eur. *IA* 97–8, 358–75, 397–401, 404–14. As Stevens (1971, 172) points out, Aeschylus offers a markedly different characterization of Menelaus in the *Agamemnon* and does not represent Menelaus as attempting to influence Agamemnon's decision (205–17).

[27] Eur. *Andr.* 627–31: ἑλὼν δὲ Τροίαν (εἶμι γὰρ κἀνταῦθά σοι) | οὐκ ἔκτανες γυναῖκα χειρίαν λαβών, | ἀλλ', ὡς ἐσεῖδες μαστόν, ἐκβαλὼν ξίφος | φίλημ' ἐδέξω, προδότιν αἰκάλλων κύνα, | ἥσσων πεφυκὼς Κύπριδος, ὦ κάκιστε σύ. This scene, which is first attested in the *Little Iliad* (fr. 19 Davies), became a familiar motif in later art and literature (cf. Ibycus fr. 296 (Page/Campbell) and Ar.*Lys.* 155–

6). See Stevens 1971, 172, who offers an interesting commentary on the language at *Andr.* 630.

[28] See also *IA* 385–7.

[29] See Barlow 1986, 213.

[30] For a useful discussion of this scene in the *Troades* and Euripides' interest in presenting Menelaus' sexual weakness, see Ghali-Kahil 1955, 132–6, who also examines fifth-century artistic treatments of this theme. Ghali-Kahil rightly argues (132) that while the Trojan cycle already presented Menelaus' inability to punish his wife, Euripides makes this aspect of the legend a central element in his portrayal of Menelaus. See also Craik 1990, 8–9.

[31] See Hall 1989, 81, 83, 99, 126–9, 209–10 for an exhaustive discussion of the term ἁβρός (as well as cognates and compounds) and its role in fifth-century dramatic representations of barbarians. On Menelaus' 'barbarization', see also Hall 1989, 209–10.

[32] Fear also plays an important role in the Spartan king's plan to flee to his wrecked ship if Theoclymenus should prove to be savage-minded (506–7). On Euripides' comical deflation of Menelaus, see, esp., Blaiklock 1952, 87– 93; Poole 1994, 21–2, 24–5.

[33] As Anton Powell has kindly pointed out, this treatment of Helen as a more competent figure than her husband goes back to the *Odyssey* in the scene depicting Helen's entrance to meet Telemachus at Sparta. While Menelaus wonders how to address Telemachus, Helen directly asks the young man about his identity. It is later her idea to drug the wine during the meal in order to banish temporarily all painful memories of the Trojan War and its aftermath (*Od.* 4.116–234). Euripides, however, repeatedly emphasizes Helen's mental superiority over Menelaus and helps to reinforce the image of the clever Spartan female which recurs in Herodotus' *Histories*.

[34] Although Peleus only claims that the girls shared the same exercise facilities as the young men and does not explicitly state that males and females competed together, the vitriolic nature of the speech supports this interpretation of the Greek. Cf. Cartledge 1981, 91; Scanlon 1988, 190.

[35] Eur. *Andr.* 590–604: σὺ γὰρ μετ' ἀνδρῶν, ὦ κάκιστε κἀκ κακῶν; | σοὶ ποῦ μέτεστιν ὡς ἐν ἀνδράσιν λόγου; | ὅστις πρὸς ἀνδρὸς Φρυγὸς ἀπηλλάγης λέχους, | ἄκληιστ' ἄδουλα δώμαθ' ἑστίας λιπών, | ὡς δὴ γυναῖκα σώφρον' ἐν δόμοις ἔχων | πασῶν κακίστην. οὐδ' ἂν εἰ βούλοιτό τις | σώφρων γένοιτο Σπαρτιατίδων κόρη· | αἳ ξὺν νέοισιν ἐξερημοῦσαι δόμους | γυμνοῖσι μηροῖς καὶ πέπλοις ἀνειμένοις | δρόμους παλαίστρας τ' οὐκ ἀνασχετῶς ἐμοὶ | κοινὰς ἔχουσι. κᾆιτα θαυμάζειν χρεὼν | εἰ μὴ γυναῖκας σώφρονας παιδεύετε; | Ἑλένην ἐρέσθαι χρὴ τάδ', ἥτις ἐκ δόμων | τὸν σὸν λιποῦσα Φίλιον ἐξεκώμασεν | νεανίου μετ' ἀνδρὸς εἰς ἄλλην χθόνα.

[36] See, e.g., Cantarella 1987, 42; Sealey 1990, 82; Poole 1994, 9–10.

[37] See Cartledge 1981, 100; Hodkinson 1989, 90–1; Sealey 1990, 85–6, 88. On Hdt. 6.71.2, see MacDowell 1986, 77.

[38] Cartledge 1981, 99; Hodkinson 1986, 396–8 and 1989, 90–1.

[39] Den Boer 1954, 215; Hodkinson 1989, 91.

[40] See, e.g., Kunstler 1987, 38.

[41] My reading of this passage follows that offered by Lane Fox (1985, 222

n. 68), who argues that ἀδέλφους ὄντας should be taken with all the preceding accusatives. I thank Stephen Hodkinson for this reference.

[42] Cf. Plut. *Comp.Lyc.–Num.* 3.3; *Mor.* 242b. See also Nic. Dam. *FGrH* 90 F 103z.

[43] On this work's authorship, see, most recently, Proietti 1987, 44 n. 1; Flower 1991, 90 n. 68. For a date *c.* 395, see Chrimes 1948, 17–22. Wüst (1959, 53–60), dates this work to the time of King Cleomenes III.

[44] However, not all scholars who accept the evidence for wife-sharing and polyandry interpret these sexual practices as freedoms. See, e.g., Hodkinson (1986, 392–404 and 1989, 79–121), who views such sexual mores as social practices of advantage to the *oikos*, both male and female members.

[45] See, e.g., Cartledge 1979, 310–11 and 1981, 103–4; MacDowell 1986, 85.

[46] Dem. 23.53, Gell. 15.20.6, Ath. 13.556a–b, Diog. Laert. 2.26.

[47] Hodkinson 1986, 392–404, esp. 404, and 1989, 79–121, esp. 90–3.

[48] Hodkinson 1989, 95–114, esp. 105–9.

[49] See Hodkinson 1989, 93.

[50] See Cartledge 1981, 102–3 and nn. 112, 117.

[51] For the connection between Spartan female exercise and libertine sexual habits, see Cantarella 1987, 42. Kunstler (1987, 36–7), links Spartan female athletic practices with Spartan female power and 'intra-sexual solidarity'. See also Redfield 1977–78, 148. For the connection between Spartan female dress and licentiousness, see, e.g., Cartledge 1981, 91–92; Blundell 1995, 155.

[52] See, esp., Poll. 2.187, 7.54–5; Clem. Al. 2.10.114.1; Plut. *Comp.Lyc.-Num.* 3.6–8. For the modern view that Spartan women regularly wore a short, revealing garment, see, e.g., Ollier 1933, 1.34; Oliva 1971, 32.

[53] See Cartledge 1981, 91; Scanlon 1988, 197–202.

[54] Cf. Hesychius, s.v. *Dionysiades*. Hesychius, s.v. *en Drionas,* discusses another ritual race performed by Spartan girls. See Scanlon 1988, 214 n. 63. A similar type of race seems to take place in Theoc. *Id.* 18, which describes Helen and her age-mates racing along the Eurotas (ll. 22–3) and uses equestrian imagery in comparing Helen to a Thessalian horse (l. 30). See Calame 1977, 1.335–9, 2.123–5; Scanlon 1988, 197; Hamilton 1989, 468. One may also compare Alcman's race to Pausanias' later description of the race held at the Olympian *Heraea* (5.16.2–3), which Scanlon (1988, 186, 201), believes was originally a prenuptial initiation rite. On Alcman's references to some form of female race, see, esp., Calame 1977, 2.70–2; Hamilton 1989, 467–8. For interpretations of these races as prenuptial rituals, see Scanlon 1988, 197–202. See also Calame 1977, 1, *passim,* esp. 350–7; 2, *passim,* esp. 11–12, 41–2, 137–45, who (2.121 ff.) assigns the rite described by Alcman to the cult of Helen.

[55] Cf. Eur. *Hel.* 1465 ff. See Calame 1977, 1.308, 334–5, 339–40; 2.122–4 and n. 148.

[56] Cf. Scanlon 1988, 189–90.

[57] See, e.g., Ibycus fr. 58 (Page/Campbell) = Plut. *Comp.Lyc.-Num.* 3.6; Soph. fr. 788 (Radt) = Plut. *Comp.Lyc.-Num.* 3.8; Eur. *Hec.* 933 f.

[58] Stewart 1997, 30, 108–16, 249–51. See also Scanlon 1988, 191–200, 203, 209–14 nn. 30–65.

[59] See Scanlon 1988, 191 ff.; Stewart 1997, 108–16.

[60] Naked girls appear, for example, on a fragmentary crater of *c.* 430–420. See Ghali-Kahil 1965, pl. 10, 6–7 and 1977, fig. B, pl. 19.

[61] For those few examples of females with well-developed figures, see Scanlon 1990, appendix, nos. 18, 25.

[62] On the possible 'element of exhibitionism' in the Arcteia, see Perlman 1983, 126–7.

[63] For this fragment, see Ghali-Kahil 1963, pl. 14.3 and 1965, fig. 8.8; Sourvinou-Inwood 1988, pl. 3.8.

[64] Although scholars have offered a variety of arguments concerning both the eligibility and age of the girls participating in this festival, most scholars agree that only a select few participated in each Arcteia and ranged in age from five to ten years. See, e.g., Sourvinou-Inwood 1988, 24, 111–18.

[65] For the probability that Spartan girls appeared scantily clad or nude after puberty, see Calame's reconstruction of the Spartan female's prenuptial ritual cycle (1977, 1.251–357, esp. 350–7). See also Cartledge 1981, 92, and Stewart 1997, 110, 115–16, who discusses the archaeological evidence. On the age of Spartan girls at marriage, see Xen. *Lac.Pol.* 1.6, Plut. *Lyc.* 15.4, and Cartledge 1981, 94–5.

[66] For this complex system of rites of passage, see Calame 1977, 1, *passim,* esp. 350–7; 2, *passim,* esp. 11–12, 41–2, 137–45. On adolescents' important role in Sparta's cults and festivals, see Jeanmaire 1939, chapter 7, esp. 524–40; Brelich 1969, 113–207; Calame 1977, 1.251–357, esp. 350–7.

[67] On the correspondence between the two terms, see Cartledge 1981, 98; Hodkinson 1986, 395, and 1989, 82. On the Gortynian *patroiokos,* see Schaps 1979, 44–7, 128–9 nn. 119–39.

[68] Women owning their own property: *Lex. Gort.* 2.45–50; 3.17–37, 40–3; 4.23–7; 5.1–9, 17–22; 6.9–46; 7.35–8.30; 8.47–50; 9.1–21. Maternal bequests: *Lex. Gort.* 4.43–6; 6.31–46; 11.42–5. The Gortynian heiress's ability to inherit half of the portion due to a son: *Lex. Gort.* 4.37–5.9.

[69] See Cartledge 1981, 98; Hodkinson 1986, 399. Ephorus alone talks of the female share as a 'dowry' (*FGrH* 70 F 149, *ap.* Strabo 10.4.20).

[70] For arguments favoring the Spartan woman's control over her property, see, esp., Hodkinson 1986, 394–406 and 1989, 79–121.

[71] Cynisca: *IG* V.i.1564a; *Anth. Graec.* 13.16; Xen. *Ages.* 9.6; Plut. *Ages.* 20.1; Paus. 3.8.1, 15.1; 5.12.5; 6.1.6. For her chariot races, likely won in 396 and 392, see Moretti 1957, nos. 373, 381. On Euryleonis, who won the two-horse chariot race in 368(?), see Moretti 1957, no. 418. See also Paus. 3.8.1, 17.6. One should also consider Agis IV's mother and grandmother, women Plutarch portrays as both exceptionally rich and influential in his *Lives of Agis and Cleomenes* (4.1, 6.7, 7.1–4, 18.8). For a fuller discussion of both Agesistrata and Archidamia, see Anton Powell's chapter in this volume.

[72] On the meanings of the terms used by Euripides in the *Andromache* (cf. 2, 153, 873, 1282), see Stevens 1971, 86–7, 115.

[73] See Cartledge 1981, 98; Hodkinson 1986, 398–9, 403–4, and 1989, 82.

[74] Hodkinson 1986, 398–406 and 1989, 79–121. See also Hodkinson 1992, 25–38.

[75] See, e.g., Bradford 1986, 13–18, esp. 18; Kunstler 1987, 42.

[76] Cartledge 1981, 105.

[77] See Redfield 1977–78, 160; Figueira 1986, 187; Hodkinson 1986, 405 and 1989, 79–121, esp. 105–9.

[78] Although the Spartiate male's observance of the Spartan codes of bravery and military *aretē* had an important effect on both his status in the society and the prestige of his household, the growing esteem for wealth from the mid-fifth century onward gradually made it an increasingly important determinant of status. See, esp., Hodkinson 1983, 254, 261–5, 281; 1989, 95–100, 110, 112–13; and 1993, 146–76.

[79] See Redfield 1977–78, 146–61, esp. 160; Hodkinson 1986, 405–6 and 1989, 112.

[80] Cf., e.g., Eur. fr. 775 (Nauck[2]); Lys. 32.11–18; Pl. *Leg*. 774c; Aeschin. 1.170; Dem. 30.12; 36.14; 40.10; 41; 45.27; 47.57. See Foxhall 1989, 22–44.

[81] Hodkinson 1989, 112.

[82] See, esp., Kunstler 1987, 31–3.

[83] See Hodkinson 1989, 111.

[84] See Cartledge 1981, 105.

[85] Cf. Plut. *Lyc*. 14.2; *Comp.Lyc.-Num*. 3.9. See also Plut. *Agis* 6.7, 7.4; *Mor*. 240 ff.; Ael. *VH* 12.21. For modern discussions of a Spartan gynecocracy, see Bradford 1986, 13–18. See also Kunstler 1987, 31–48; Fantham et al. 1994, 64–5.

[86] Cf. Eur. *Andr*. 876–8; *El*. 341–4; *Med*. 214 ff., 244–9; *Heracl*. 474–6; *Phoen*. 88–96, 192–5; Soph. *El*. 516–18; Xen. *Oec*. 7.3–10.13; Lys. 3.6; Isae. 3.13–14; Lyc. *Leoc*. 40; Dem. 47.38, 52–61.

[87] See, e.g., London E 773 = *ARV*[2] 805 (89). For other examples, see Webster 1972, 235–41.

[88] See Sutton 1981, 46, 464; Keuls 1985, 214–15.

[89] On the active role of women in the pottery market, see, esp., Bérard 1989, 89–90.

[90] Just 1989, 112.

[91] Women fetching water: Eur. *El*. 109–11, 140 f., 309; Ar. *Lys*. 327–31. Cf. Electra carrying water on the pelike by the Jena Painter, *ARV*[2] 1516.80. Women performing agricultural work: Ar. *Pax* 536; Dem. 57.45. For vase-scenes depicting agricultural work, see the crater by the Orchard Painter, New York 07.286.74 = *ARV*[2] 523.1 and Harvey 1988, 244–5, who believes that it depicts a ritual activity. The pyxis London E 772 = *ARV*[2] 806 (90) shows women both picking fruit and fetching water from a fountain. See Lissarague 1992, 196–7. Although Hannestad (1984, 252–5) concludes that free women are represented on these vases, her argument that women ceased to fetch their own water in the fifth century ignores fifth-century literary evidence and the existence of economic stratification in fifth-century Athens. There has been much debate on the identity of female figures on vases and whether those portrayed in more public settings are free, citizen women or rather slaves and hetaerae. See, esp., Bazant 1981, 14–20; Williams 1983, 93–106; Harvey 1988, 242–54. There is clearly a danger in using the traditional belief in Athenian female seclusion to interpret scenes in which women appear in public contexts, such as the fountain-house (cf. Williams 1983, 103).

Unless other elements of the scene's iconography suggest that they are slaves (such as cropped hair and ethnic characteristics like tattoos) or hetaerae (such as money pouches or sexually suggestive behavior or clothing), there is no reason to assume that the women pictured cannot be free Athenian women.

92 See, e.g., Ar. *Vesp.* 497, 1388–1414; *Lys.* 457–8, 562–4; *Ran.* 857–8; *Thesm.* 446–58; Dem. 54.30–1, 34–5.

93 For discussions of the links between the Athenian woman's important roles in the *oikos* and the *polis*, see, esp., Just 1989, *passim*, esp. 23–5, 39, 55, 98–9; Patterson 1991, 48–72, esp. 59–60.

94 On this law, see also Plut. *Per.* 37.3; Ael. *VH* 6.10, 13.24, fr. 68 = Suid. (Δ 451) δημοποίητος.

95 On the *polis* and *oikos* as mutually defining and necessary oppositions in fifth-century Athenian democratic ideology, see Foley 1982, 3. See also Humphreys 1983, 69.

96 Although concerns about female fidelity pre-dated Athens' democratization, the female's key function in the production and legitimation of Athenian citizens under the democracy necessarily increased the importance of the issue of adultery. See Foley 1981, 150–1.

97 While the greater number of extant sources in the second half of the fifth century may also have contributed to the increasing number of such allusions, the frequency of references to uncontrolled female sexuality and adultery cannot be explained by this factor alone. See, e.g., Eur. *Hipp.* 407–25; Ar. *Pax* 979–85; *Lys.* 107, 404–19; *Eccl.* 225, 325, 350, 520–6; *Thesm.* 340–5, 395–404, 414–17, 476–501, 519, 783, 812–13. Other references to adultery occur at Ar. *Nub.* 1076–1100; *Plut.* 168. See Gardner 1989, 51–62.

98 See Cohen 1991, 98–132, who provides a particularly cogent discussion of the treatment of adultery in classical Athens.

99 See Sancisi-Weerdenburg 1983, 24, who concludes that Atossa's conduct in the tragedy is more dependent on dramatic necessities than on real historical data. See also Hall 1989, 95, on Aeschylus' failure to make any mention of the fact that Xerxes left Artabanus in control of the empire in 480 (cf. Hdt. 7.52).

100 Although Greek authors repeatedly link autocracy and feminine power, we should not assume that these associations had no basis in reality. I hope to investigate this topic in the future.

101 The one exception seems to be his account of the Issedones (4.26.2). Although their political structure remains unclear, it was most probably royal like the others in the region (cf. Hdt. 4.119).

102 Tyrant families: Periander's daughter (3.53.2–5) and wife Melissa (5.92η1–4), Polycrates' daughter (3.124). Royal house of Cyrene: Eryxo (4.160.4) and Pheretime (4.162.2–5, 165, 167, 200.1, 202, 205). Royal houses of Sparta: Gorgo (5.51.2–3; 7.239.4) and Argeia (6.52.2–7).

103 See Brosius 1996, 48–51, 105–9, who questions the historical validity of Herodotus' portrayal of Atossa in her detailed study of women in ancient Persia.

104 Lateiner 1985, 94.

Bibliography

Barlow, S.A. (ed.)
1986 *Euripides' Trojan Women*, Warminster.

Bazant, J.
1981 *Studies on the Use and Decoration of Athenian Vases*, Prague.

Bérard, C.
1989 'The Order of Women', in C. Bérard et al. (eds.) *A City of Images: Iconography and society in ancient Greece*, trans. D. Lyons, 89–109, Princeton.

Blaiklock, E.M.
1952 *The Male Characters of Euripides*, Wellington, New Zealand.

Blundell, S.
1995 *Women in Ancient Greece*, Cambridge, Mass.

Bradford, A. S.
1986 'Gynaikokratoumenoi: did Spartan women rule Spartan men?' *AW* 14, 13–18.

Brelich, A.
1969 *Paides e parthenoi*, Rome.

Brosius, M.
1996 *Women in Ancient Persia* 559–331 BC, Oxford.

Calame, C.
1977 *Les choeurs de jeunes filles en Grèce archaïque*, 2 vols., Rome.

Cantarella, E.
1987 *Pandora's Daughters: The role and status of women in Greek and Roman Antiquity*, trans. M.B. Fant, Baltimore.

Cartledge. P.A.
1979 *Sparta and Lakonia: A regional history 1300–362 BC*, London.
1981 'Spartan Wives: liberation or license?' *CQ* n.s. 31, 84–105.

Chrimes, K.M.T.
1948 *The* Respublica Lacedaemoniorum *ascribed to Xenophon*, Manchester.

Colley, L.
1992 *Britons: Forging the nation 1701–1837*, New Haven and London.

Craik, E.
1990 'Sexual imagery and innuendo in Troades', in A. Powell (ed.) *Euripides, Women, and Sexuality*, 1–15, London and New York.

Dale, A.M. (ed.)
1981 *Euripides'* Helen, repr. Bristol.

Den Boer, W.
1954 *Laconian Studies*, Amsterdam.

Edmonds, J.M.
1957–61 *The Fragments of Attic Comedy after Meineke, Bergk and Kock*, 3 vols., Leiden.

Fantham, E., et al.
1994 *Women in the Classical World: Image and text*, Oxford and New York.

Figueira, T.
1986 'Population patterns in late archaic and classical Sparta', *TAPA* 116, 165–213.

Flower, M.

1991 'Revolutionary agitation and social change in classical Sparta', in *Georgica: Greek studies in honor of George Cawkwell*, *BICS* 58, 78–97.

Foley, H.P.

1981 'The conception of woman in Athenian drama', in H.P. Foley (ed.) *Reflections of Women in Antiquity*, 127–68, New York.

1982 'The female intruder reconsidered: women in Aristophanes *Lysistrata* and *Ecclesiazusae*', *CP* 77, 1–21.

Foxhall, L.

1989 'Household, gender and property in classical Athens', *CQ* n.s. 39, 22–44.

Gardner, J.F.

1989 'Aristophanes and male anxiety – the defence of the *oikos*', *G&R* 36, 51–62.

Ghali-Kahil, L.

1955 *Les enlèvements et le retour d' Hélène dans les textes et les documents figurés*, Ecole Française d'Athènes, travaux et mémoires 10, Paris.

1963 'Quelques vases du sanctuaire d'Artémis à Brauron', *AK* 1, 5–29.

1965 'Autour de l'Artémis attique', *AK* 8, 20–33.

1977 'L'Artémis de Brauron: rites et mystère', *AK* 20, 86–98.

Hall, E.

1989 *Inventing the Barbarian: Greek self-definition through tragedy*, Oxford.

Hamilton, R.

1989 'Alkman and the Athenian Arkteia', *Hesperia* 58, 449–72.

Hannestad, L.

1984 'Slaves and the fountain house theme,' in H.A.G. Brijder (ed.) *Ancient Greek and Related Pottery: Proceedings of the International Vase Symposium in Amsterdam, 12–15 April, 1984*, Allard Pierson Series, vol. 5, 252–5, Amsterdam.

Hartog, F.

1988 *The Mirror of Herodotus: The representation of the other in the writing of history*, trans. J. Lloyd, Berkeley.

Harvey, F.D.

1988 'Painted ladies, fact, fiction and fantasy', in J. Christiansen and T. Melander (eds.) *Ancient Greek and Related Pottery: Proceedings of the 3rd Symposium, Copenhagen, August 31–September 4, 1987*, 242–57, Copenhagen.

1994 'Lacomica: Aristophanes and the Spartans,' in A. Powell and S. Hodkinson (eds.) *The Shadow of Sparta*, 35–58, London and New York.

Henderson, J. (ed.)

1987 *Aristophanes'* Lysistrata, Oxford.

Hodkinson, S.

1983 'Social order and the conflict of values in classical Sparta', *Chiron* 13, 239–81.

1986 'Land tenure and inheritance in classical Sparta' *CQ* n.s. 36, 378–406.

1989 'Inheritance, marriage and demography: perspectives upon the success and decline of classical Sparta', in A. Powell (ed.) *Classical Sparta: Techniques behind her success*, 79–121, London.

1992 'Modelling the Spartan crisis: computer simulation of the impact of inheritance systems upon the distribution of landed property', *Bulletin of the John Rylands Library* 74.3, 25–38.

1993 'Warfare, wealth, and the crisis of Spartiate society', in G. Shipley and J. Rich (eds.) *War and Society in the Greek World*, 146–76, London.

Humphreys, S.

1983 *The Family, Women, and Death*, London.

Jeanmaire, H.

1939 *Couroi et Courètes. Essai sur l'éducation spartiate et sur les rites d'adolescence dans l'antiquité hellénique*, Lille.

Just, R.

1989 *Women in Athenian Law and Life*, New York.

Keuls, E.C.

1985 *The Reign of the Phallus*, New York.

Kunstler, B.L.

1987 'Family dynamics and female power in ancient Sparta', in M.B. Skinner (ed.) *Rescuing Creusa: New methodological approaches to women in antiquity*, *Helios*, n.s. 13/2, 31–48.

Lane-Fox, R.

1985 'Aspects of inheritance in the Greek world', in P.A. Cartledge and F.D. Harvey (eds.) *Crux: Essays in Greek history presented to G.E.M. de Ste. Croix*, 208–32, Exeter.

Lateiner, D.

1985 'Limit, propriety, and transgression in the Histories of Herodotus', in M.H. Jameson (ed.) *The Greek Historians: Literature and history. Papers presented to A.E. Raubitschek*, 87–100, Saratoga.

Lissarrague, F.

1992 'Figures of women', in P.S. Pantel (ed.) *A History of Women in the West*. Vol. I: *From Ancient Goddesses to Christian Saints*, 139–229, Cambridge, Mass. and London.

MacDowell, D.M.

1986 *Spartan Law*, Edinburgh.

Millender, E.

1996 '"The teacher of Hellas": Athenian democratic ideology and the "Barbarization" of Sparta in fifth-century Greek thought,' Diss., University of Pennsylvania.

Moretti, L.

1957 *Olympionikai, i vincitori negli antichi agoni olimpici = Atti Accad. Naz. Lincei, cl. sci. mor., stor. e filol.* 8 8.2, 53–198, Rome.

Oliva, P.

1971 *Sparta and her Social Problems*, Amsterdam and Prague.

Ollier, F.

1933–43 *Le mirage spartiate. Étude sur l'idéalisation de Sparte dans l'antiquité grecque*, 2 vols., Paris.

Patterson, C.B.
1991 'Marriage and the married woman in Athenian law', in S.B. Pomeroy (ed.) *Women's History and Ancient History*, 48–72, Chapel Hill and London.
Pembroke, S.
1967 'Women in charge: the function of alternatives in early Greek tradition and the ancient idea of matriarchy', *JWI* 30, 1–35.
Perlman, P.
1983 'Plato *Laws* 833C–834D and the Bears of Brauron',*GRBS* 24, 115–30.
Poole, W.
1994 'Euripides and Sparta', in A. Powell and S. Hodkinson (eds.) *The Shadow of Sparta*, 1–33, London and New York.
Proietti, G.
1987 *Xenophon's Sparta: An introduction*, Leiden and New York.
Redfield, J.
1977–8 'The women of Sparta', *CJ* 73, 146–61.
Rosellini, M. and S. Saïd
1978 'Usages des femmes et autres nomoi chez les 'sauvages' d'Herodote', *ASNP* series 3, 8, 949–1005.
Said, E.
1978 *Orientalism*, London.
Sancisi-Weerdenburg, H.
1983 'Exit Atossa: Images of women in Greek historiography on Persia', in A. Cameron and A. Kuhrt (eds.) *Images of Women in Antiquity*, 20–33, Detroit.
Scanlon,T.F.
1988 'Virgineum Gymnasium: Spartan females and early Greek athletics', in W. Raschke (ed.) *The Archaeology of the Olympics*, 185–216, Madison.
1990 'Race or chase at the Arkteia of Attica?' *Nikephoros* 3, 73–120.
Schaps, D.
1979 *The Economic Rights of Women in Ancient Greece*, Edinburgh.
Scodel, R.
1980 *The Trojan Trilogy of Euripides*, Göttingen.
Sealey, R.
1990 *Women and Law in Classical Greece*, Chapel Hill.
Shimron, B.
1964 'Polybius and the reform of Cleomenes III', *Historia* 13, 147–55.
Sommerstein, A.
1990 *The Comedies of Aristophanes. Vol. 7: Lysistrata*, Warminster.
Sourvinou-Inwood, C.
1988 *Studies in Girls' Transitions: Aspects of the Arkteia and age representations in Attic iconography*, Athens.
Stevens, P.T. (ed.)
1971 *Euripides'* Andromache, Oxford.
Stewart, A.F.
1997 *Art, Desire, and the Body in Ancient Greece*, Cambridge.

Sutton, R.
1981 'The interaction between men and women portrayed on Attic red-figure pottery,' Diss. North Carolina.

Walbank, F.W.
1957 *A Historical Commentary on Polybius*, vol. 1, Oxford.

Webster, T.B.L.
1972 *Potter and Patron in Classical Athens*, London.

Williams, D.
1983 'Women on Athenian vases: problems of interpretation', in A. Cameron and A. Kuhrt (eds.) *Images of Women in Antiquity*, 92–106, Detroit.

Wüst, F.R.
1959 'Laconica', *Klio* 37, 53–62.

Zweig, B.
1993 'The only women who give birth to men: a gynocentric, cross-cultural view of women in ancient Sparta', in M. De Forest (ed.) *Essays on Classical Antiquity in Honor of Joy K. King*, 32–53, Wauconda, Ill.

Chapter 14

SPARTAN WOMEN ASSERTIVE IN POLITICS?
Plutarch's Lives of Agis and Kleomenes

Anton Powell

Most unusually for Greek texts, these two linked Spartan Lives claim to give factual detail about a series of named women active in the high politics of Greece. This detail has not yet penetrated into the mainstream of scholarship.[1] It may seem triply marginal. It comes to us from Plutarch rather than directly from an early source; it concerns the hellenistic, not the classical, period; and it relates to Sparta rather than Athens. Also, the sheer colour and drama of Plutarch's detail may make it suspect. His Spartan heroines may seem to have more to do with fiction than with history. This detail about individual women is quite unlike our information from classical Athens; Athenian women tend to be identified as 'so-and-so's wife' or 'so-and-so's sister', following the formulation of speech-writers who chose to keep them nameless. Perikles seemingly talked about the need for Athenian women to have no reputation at all among men.[2] Yet here in Plutarch we are told that Arkhidamia was 'the most distinguished of the female citizens' of Sparta (*Ag*. 20.3; ἐν ἀξιώματι μεγίστωι τῶν πολιτίδων).[3]

In this chapter I shall first lay out some of the narrative involving the Spartan women, and then explore how much it may reveal about reality in Sparta. Something like an archaeological approach will be used, identifying layers in the source material. It will be argued that at base may lie revealing material from within female Sparta.

In chapter 4 of the *Agis* Plutarch begins his detailed account of the young reformer, king Agis IV. (Agis reigned *c*. 244–41, at a time when Sparta's power had shrivelled, and the big powers in the Greek world were mainly of Macedonian origin.) In the first sentence it is stated that Agis was brought up 'amid the riches and luxury of women, his mother Agesistrata and his grandmother Arkhidamia, the richest individuals among the Spartans'. Not the richest among Spartan women, we note, but the richest among 'the Spartans'. However, the young Agis resists soft living, and resolves to reform Sparta in the direction of austerity. He lobbies his mother with the aid of a male relative of hers (*Ag*. 6.7). The roles are unfamiliar: the male as intercessor approaches the powerful female. The mother is here described as 'very influential in the *polis*, by virtue of her host of dependants (πλήθει...πελατῶν), friends and debtors, and well used to dealing with public affairs'. The mother and also, it seems, the grandmother are persuaded (μετέπεσον ταῖς γνώμαις αἱ γυναῖκες; *Ag*. 7.3 f.); they urge Agis on and approach both their male friends and other women to promote the cause,[4]

> knowing that the Spartan men were always subject to their womenfolk (κατηκόους ὄντας ἀεὶ τῶν γυναικῶν) and allowed them to meddle (or 'intervene', πολυπραγμονεῖν)[5] more in public affairs than they themselves did in private ones. At the time the majority of Spartan riches belonged to women, and it was this which made Agis' work difficult and onerous to accomplish. For the women opposed him, from fear of losing not just their luxury...but the high status and influence which they derived from their riches... (*Ag*. 7.4–6).

These conservative women invite Sparta's other king, Leonidas, to help their opposition (*Ag*. 7.7).[6]

For a time Agis' scheme of pooling wealth goes forward. He contributes his own vast property, the cash element of which came to 600 talents. The same is done by 'the mothers' (τὰς μητέρας, i.e. Agesistrata and Arkhidamia) and their friends and relatives, 'the richest of the Spartans' (*Ag*. 9.5 f.). King Leonidas is deposed and threatened; to his aid comes his daughter, Khilonis. Although she is the wife of Kleombrotos, the man who will shortly, in Agis' interest, supplant Leonidas as king, she leaves her husband and joins her father in sanctuary (*Ag*. 11.7–9). After a military setback for Agis, the tide turns politically and Kleombrotos himself flees to sanctuary for protection against the resurgent Leonidas (*Ag*.16). In a long and graphic passage, Khilonis is described as now joining her husband in his plight, 'with her arms thrown around him, and her little children at her feet, one on each side'. She makes a speech of self-assertion as well as of self-pity, referring to herself as standing by her men in adversity but with criticism of both of them; she threatens suicide (*Ag*. 17.5–10). She eventually goes into exile by her husband's side, the wife and the husband each bearing one child in their arms (*Ag*.18.3). As often with stories about Sparta this is highly visual, a statue in words. King Agis himself flees to sanctuary, but is lured out and hanged. His mother and grandmother, who have come to the prison doors in an attempt to save him, are lured in. The grandmother, Arkhidamia, is then hanged.

The mother, Agesistrata, is able to make decent provision for her mother's body then goes to her own death, saying 'I hope only that all this will be for the good of Sparta' (μόνον συνενέγκαι ταῦτα τῆι Σπάρτηι) (*Ag*. 19–20).

The Life of Kleomenes continues the narrative. Agis left a young widow, Agiatis, rich, virtuous and 'far more beautiful than any other Greek woman'. King Leonidas, the conservative, has her married to his young son, Kleomenes. We are told that she resisted the forced marriage at first, but then became a good wife to Kleomenes. The new husband listened attentively while Agiatis expounded to him her former husband's radical political thought (*Kl*. 1.2–3). On succeeding to the kingship (?235 BC), Kleomenes III is himself ambitious for radical reform and shows sustained, enthusiastic, interest in the policies of Agis (*Kl*. 3.2–4). Later he cultivates many potential Spartan allies for his reforms through the agency of his mother, Kratesikleia, who 'provided with him unstinting subsidies and shared his ambition' (ἀφειδῶς συγχορηγούσης καὶ συμφιλοτιμουμένης) (*Kl*. 6.2). Kratesikleia, a widow, was said to have been 'in no need of marriage', but now, to help her son's career, she makes a political marriage. By means of violence against the ephors king Kleomenes brings in a scheme of land redistribution and of austerity similar to Agis' (autumn 227). Like Agis before him, Kleomenes gives his private wealth to the pool (*Kl*. 11.1). When Agiatis dies, young, we are told again of her great beauty and virtue and of Kleomenes' passion for her, which caused him often to take leave from military campaigns to visit her (*Kl*. 22.1 f.) – a practice, we should note, far from the spirit of austere classical Sparta.

Kleomenes sets about a vigorous restoration of Spartan military power in the Peloponnese. Financial help is offered to him by king Ptolemy III of Egypt – on condition that Kleomenes sends his mother and children to Egypt as hostages. Kleomenes is for long ashamed to ask his mother, but when he does raise the subject she eagerly volunteers to go 'wherever you think this body of mine will be of most use to Sparta' (ὅπου ποτὲ τῆι Σπάρτηι νομίζεις τὸ σῶμα τοῦτο χρησιμώτατον ἔσεσθαι) (*Kl*. 22.5). Later, from Egypt she urges Kleomenes to make policy in disregard of her, in keeping with Spartan standards and in Sparta's interest (τὰ τῆι Σπάρτηι πρέποντα καὶ συμφέροντα πράττειν) (*Kl*. 22.9). But Kleomenes' great military alliance is crushed by the Macedonian Antigonos Doson, at the battle of Sellasia (222 BC). Of 6,000 Spartan citizens present, all but 200 were killed – reportedly (*Kl*. 28.8). In the aftermath Kleomenes flees, stopping briefly at Sparta en route to exile in Egypt. Spartan wives emerge to attend to the survivors. But

Kleomenes himself, though inside his own house, stands in heroic pose – graphically described: exhausted but still wearing his breastplate, he leans against a pillar, head on forearm. Far from relaxing, he will not accept even a drink from 'the free woman of Megalopolis whom he kept after his wife's death' (*Kl.* 29.3). In Egypt he is faced with the death of his patron Ptolemy III; the successor, Ptolemy IV, allows the kingdom to fall into 'self-indulgence, drunkenness and rule by women [or 'a womanish atmosphere'; γυναικοκρατίαν, MSS γυναικοκρασίαν]'; 'the highest matters of state were administered by the king's mistress Agathokleia and her mother the whore-keeper Oinanthe' (*Kl.* 33.1 f.).

Kleomenes loses favour under the new regime, and is reported as making an unfortunate remark about the new Ptolemy's attachment to female musicians and to catamites. Kleomenes is put under house arrest but escapes captivity. He attempts a coup in Alexandria, fails, and arranges a group suicide of his small Spartan band. It falls to the distinguished Spartan warrior Panteus to supervise, and check that all are indeed dead before killing himself (*Kl.* 34–7). Ptolemy's vengeance then falls upon the Spartan women hostages, including Kleomenes' mother, Kratesikleia. She is attended at the last by the (unnamed) wife of Panteus; we are told of her earlier escape from Sparta to join Panteus, against her parents' wishes, of her great beauty and of the intense passion between the (newly) married pair. Kratesikleia facing death shows concern for her doomed young grandchildren before herself. Panteus' wife nobly attends the execution of Kratesikleia and her women, covering their corpses, then goes to her own death arranging that any attendant nudity shall be seen by as few as possible (*Kl.* 38). The final chapter of the work begins: 'Sparta played out these events with the role of the women a match for that of the men...' ('Η...Λακεδαίμων ἐφαμίλλως ἀγωνισαμένη τῶι γυναικείωι δράματι πρὸς τὸ ἀνδρεῖον...) (*Kl.* 39.1).

The structure of both Spartan Lives is contrived to highlight women. Each biography ends with a female Spartan going to her death courageously and dutifully, attending to another Spartan woman who has herself died. In each case the last woman to die shows concern for propriety in the matter of covering female flesh. The dying women expire in parallel with eminent male relatives; with Agis die 'the mothers', in parallel with Kleomenes dies Kratesikleia, and with Panteus his wife. The cases of Panteus and his wife involve the further parallel in that both, man and wife, independently and nobly perform the task of surviving, briefly, to watch over the deaths of companions. Both biographies begin with prominent reference to female relatives of the eponymous male. The young Kleomenes listens sympathetically to his wife's account of Agis' ideals; it is easily inferred that his wife was a main cause of Kleomenes' political development. In the case of Agis himself, 'the mothers' attend his juvenile years with their luxury; there is no explicit suggestion that the mothers induced his conversion to austerity, even by reaction (let alone by precept or example). The point of the reference to early female influence on the central male is therefore quite different in the *Agis*. Even in the case of Kleomenes, female influence is not *explicitly* recorded. So it may be that what connects these parallel notices of women in the two biographies is not (so much) feminine influence on the eponymous male as female assertiveness for its own sake. In both biographies the central male is aided in his policy by a wealthy mother who mobilises male support on his behalf. Each of the central males has a supportive wife – indeed the same woman – Agiatis.

Most prominent of the other women is Khilonis, who supports two male relatives, one on each side of the *stasis* involving Agis. The sympathy of the reader, in both Lives, is regularly directed towards the reforming central male rather than towards his Spartan opponents. Consistently with this, in the case of Khilonis it is her noble stand in defence of her husband, Agis' ally, which receives the evocative and detailed description, and not her earlier loyalty to her conservative father, Leonidas, the enemy of Agis. Nevertheless, her character is depicted as transcending male factions. An interest in female assertiveness, in loyalty to one male relative though in defiance of another, is shown also by the depiction of Panteus' wife, who disobeys her parents and follows her husband to Egypt. Finally, we are given more detail than we might have expected of the young woman from Megalopolis whose physical comfort after a battle the defeated Kleomenes impressively refused.

Now who created this picture of colourful women? There are, at least at first glance, three possible sources for moral embroidery, or full-scale myth-making.

Plutarch

The biographer's interest in virtuous females is well known, not least from his essay on the subject (= *Mor.* 242e–263c). Women more colourful than virtuous were also of much interest to him, as can be seen from his insertion into the *Perikles* of elaborate material on Aspasia. Blomqvist (1997, 84), in a recent study of women in politics in Plutarch, observes that of the honourable wives, mothers and grandmothers 'the majority' are Roman matrons or 'spirited Spartan ladies'. I shall look in a moment at why there should be the bias towards Sparta, when our written evidence for Greek culture is in other respects greatly biased towards Athens.

As a historical source Plutarch has well-known imperfections, but it is not commonly argued that he invented whole episodes: in the words of Christopher Pelling (1990, 36), 'the big invention is not in his style'. Close comparison of Plutarch with his sources, where those are extant, suggests rather a fairly faithful paraphrase or précis:[7] thus a very large part of the *Nikias* has been judged to follow straightforwardly the account of Thucydides.[8] There is some consensus among scholars over the forms which Plutarch's inventions tend to take. Most importantly for us, Plutarch creates minor dramatic detail, including, in the ancient way, words used in conversation or speech-making.[9] He also creates parallels, and not only between the paired Greek and Roman principals of his Parallel Lives.[10] It is difficult or impossible to prove whether Plutarch invented whole episodes. Even if we found many episodes in Plutarch which jarred with external and better evidence, it would always be possible that Plutarch did not invent them but derived them from sources now lost (cf. Pelling 1980, 129–30). But I suspect that if Plutarch had practised large-scale fiction, he would have left clear traces of it. In his moralising Plutarch leaves 'signatures' in the form of repetitive comment on a few themes, occurring in Life after Life. Russell (1995, 93) delicately refers to these as Plutarch's 'special interests'. (Examples are the gentleness and self-control, πραότης, of his heroes: Kimon,[11] Perikles,[12] Agis,[13] even Lykourgos,[14] and – Russell 1995, 80 – the danger in empowering crowds of ordinary people.) If the dogged consistency of Plutarch's moralising had been anything like matched by a consistency in inventing extended narrative, we should have found many episodes which, while being suspect for other reasons, such as lack of fit with external sources, contained material plainly close to Plutarch's heart.

Some details on women in the *Agis and Kleomenes* reflect Plutarch's taste as evidenced elsewhere. He was fond of scenes of death, and in particular of the death of women. In both our Spartan Lives the death of the male hero is somewhat overshadowed by the dramatic demise of associated females. Compare Plutarch's *Antony*, where the hero all but drops out of the narrative; the last 10 chapters are concerned instead with the colourful end of Cleopatra.[15] Agesistrata, in her death-scene in the *Agis* (20.5), is made to refer to τὸ πρᾶον, one of Plutarch's special interests. Plutarch begins his collection of stories, the *Virtues of Women*, with the claim that 'the virtue of man and of woman is one and the same' (μίαν...καὶ τὴν αὐτὴν ἀνδρός τε καὶ γυναικὸς ἀρετήν; 242f–243a). In summarising at the end of the *Kleomenes*, he writes similarly: 'Sparta played out these events with the role of the women a match for that of the men; Sparta thus showed that in these ultimate moments virtue cannot be trampled underfoot by fortune' (39.1; the similarity is noted by Blomqvist 1997, 90 n. 11). These words immediately follow his account of the noble deaths suffered by Kratesikleia, mother of Kleomenes, and by her attendant the wife of Panteus. Shortly before came the deaths of the two women's male kin, Kleomenes and Panteus; Plutarch's moral about the equivalence of the sexes in virtue comes now most conveniently. Plutarch in other Lives is suspected of freehand embroidery especially at dramatic moments; in the *Agis and Kleomenes* narrative of women's actions is at times highly dramatic. Not only do outstanding female virtue, and female participation in politics, form prominent and recurrent themes within the Spartan narrative of these two Lives; there is a similar motif prominent in the two Roman Lives which Plutarch has paralleled with them, of Tiberius and Caius Gracchus. There are, then, several reasons for a preliminary suspicion that Plutarch may have performed minor elements of fiction or distortion in connection with the Spartan women of *Agis and Kleomenes*.

It is helpful to compare, briefly, the portrayal of women in the Lives of the Gracchi. Two women receive significant attention: Licinia, the wife of Caius Gracchus and a member of the *gens* of the Licinii Crassi, and Cornelia, mother of the Gracchi and daughter of Scipio Africanus. As Caius leaves home for his last, fatal, day in politics, Licinia pleads with him to desist. Grasping her husband with one hand, and holding their small child with the other, she utters highly rhetorical expressions on the futility and danger of his course of action. Gently Caius moves away from her; she collapses and is carried to her brother (*GG* 15.2–5). Cornelia, the mother, is a far more prominent, indeed recurrent, figure in Plutarch's account. Introduced at the start of the work, her success – as a widow (courted in vain by a Ptolemaic dynast) – in educating the two brothers is said by Plutarch to have contributed more even than their innate qualities to the virtues of the pair (*TG* 1.4–7). She is reported by Plutarch as, according to some, a cause of her son Tiberius' embarking upon dangerous reform; on this account she had scolded her sons for being less eminent than her son-in-law (*TG* 8.7). While not explicitly rejecting this version, Plutarch does not endorse it. He similarly distances himself from the report which he carries that Cornelia helped to organise the recruitment of mercenary supporters for Caius (*GG* 13.2). The longest set of references to Cornelia comes at the very end of the *Gracchi*. Her later years are described: much visited by learned men and still the object of respect from foreign potentates, she looks back on her murdered sons with warmth but serenity. Plutarch rebuts the idea that she was callous or senile; rather, he asserts, she demonstrated how virtue can triumph over chance affliction (*GG* 19).

There are apparent here elements of circular composition and of cross-reference between the Spartan and the Roman Lives. Cornelia, in her nobility, begins and ends Plutarch's story of the Gracchi. Like the womenfolk of Agis and of Kleomenes, her role in the upbringing of the central males is given prominence. Like the Spartan women, she provides the occasion for Plutarch's concluding sermon on the supremacy of virtue over fortune. There may even be a conscious comparison involving Egypt: the Spartan women die at the order of a Ptolemy, but gain a moral victory; Cornelia is able to turn down a later Ptolemy's offer of marriage. Has the creation by Plutarch of parallelism or other pattern caused serious distortion to the account of the Spartan women? With the Roman Licinia contrast the Spartan Khilonis. Each woman is shown pleading dramatically to save the life of a male relative; each is described in memorable pose with her offspring. But Licinia fails, whereas Khilonis succeeds first in supporting her father then in defending her husband; twice she asserts herself successfully against the ruling males of the state. Contrast the Roman Cornelia with the Spartan mothers. In shaping the character of her offspring, Cornelia's efforts are of major consequence; she is a better educator than Agis' mother had been (though perhaps Agiatis, Agis' widow and Kleomenes' wife, matched Cornelia in influence). But twice Plutarch refuses the opportunity – provided by his sources – of asserting that Cornelia was responsible for particular moves within her sons' careers. Kratesikleia is shown intervening much more in the policy of her son, Kleomenes. It has been argued persuasively – by Blomqvist (1997) – that in general Plutarch approves of female assertiveness in politics only where that is altruistic, aimed at enhancing not replacing male domination. He makes Cornelia a model of moral success; if anything, he seems to have played down, rather than worked up, evidence from his sources of Cornelia's political role, in accordance with a preference for female subordination. There is, perhaps, no reason to think that a desire for parallelism with the *Gracchi* has led Plutarch to magnify the roles of the Spartan women as active in politics. Blomqvist has argued that Plutarch's heroines 'are essentially

Roman matrons, strong and virtuous, even when dressed in the traditional Greek peplos'.[16] I suggest that, in the present context, this may mislead. The Spartan women are distinct; in assertiveness they outdo their Roman counterparts in these Lives.

Phylarchus

That influential women formed an attractive theme for Plutarch is clear enough. But because Plutarch was probably unwilling to invent detail on a large scale, the question now arises: where did he get his information? Scholars are agreed, I think rightly, that the narratives of the *Agis and Kleomenes* are drawn overwhelmingly from the third-century historian Phylarchus (of Athens, or perhaps of Naukratis).[17] Phylarchus is known to have covered the period; he is cited by Plutarch in four passages of these Lives;[18] no other source has such prominence here. Much of the material is in Phylarchus' distinctive manner, as we shall shortly see. And in the one area of these Spartan Lives where we can be virtually certain, from external evidence, what Phylarchus wrote, we see that it corresponds strikingly in substance and vocabulary with what Plutarch wrote (Athen. 141f–142f; Plut. *Kl.* 13.4–7).

So, again the blunt question: how much of the detail about Spartan women may Phylarchus have made up? Polybius wrote a lively attack on Phylarchus' historical method (2.56; cf. 58.11–15, 59.2 f.). Phylarchus, he suggested, composed like a tragedian (2.56.10–12). (Plutarch himself, in one passage, says something very similar about Phylarchus: *Themist.* 32.4; cf. *Mor.* 345e, 362bc.)[19] Polybius suggests that Phylarchus composed speeches and described events on the basis of what was conceivable under the circumstances; he was not governed by knowledge of what had actually happened (2.56.10, cf. 3). True history, implies Polybius, was often mundane. Phylarchus, in contrast, went for the visual and shocking and sensational (πρὸ ὀφθαλμῶν τιθέναι τὰ δεινά), to evoke pity and other emotion. He brought in 'clinging women, dishevelled hair and the thrusting out of women's breasts' (περιπλοκὰς γυναικῶν καὶ κόμας διερριμμένας καὶ μαστῶν ἐκβολάς; 2.56.7 f.). Such phrases may suggest straightforward male eroticism. Perhaps Polybius intended that, as a secondary meaning; Phylarchus is very interested in the erotic, as we shall see. But Polybius meant here primarily the tragic, the desperate actions of women in crises – where they might bare their bodies in an appeal for mercy, as Klytaimnestra showed her breast to Orestes when he came to kill her (A. *Choeph.* 896–8).[20] Polybius accuses Phylarchus of composing material which was ignoble and womanly (γυναικῶδες; 2.56.9). This last point, about the womanly, may be more significant than Polybius himself realised.[21]

Polybius had an intimate loathing of Phylarchus; he himself, when decrying Phylarchus, is a very biased witness. Phylarchus had written with favour about the Spartan attempt to dominate the Peloponnese in the third century and about Kleomenes, leader of that attempt and sacker of Megalopolis. Polybius – of Megalopolis – was in the next century a leading official of the Achaian League, a body which Sparta and Kleomenes had opposed. (See, further, Gabba 1957, 13.) But even Polybius did not write Phylarchus off – in practice. He borrowed a passage of Phylarchus, and a highly characteristic passage too, in describing Kleomenes' tragic end in Egypt.[22] (Elsewhere Polybius even records a Greek woman in Egypt displaying her breasts in an attempt to escape death; 15.31.13.) We think of Plutarch himself, mistrusting Phylarchus in some places, relying on him extensively as a source in others.[23]

Phylarchus' use of female undress helps us understand his treatment of Sparta. When Agis' mother and grandmother are hanged, the mother – before she dies – ensures that the dead grandmother is decently covered. In the death scene of Kleomenes' mother, Panteus' wife has a similar role and is also most proper, before she dies, in ensuring that no one but the executioner sees her own naked flesh. This on its own would look like the imitation of tragedy. Polyxena in Euripides dies under the sacrificial knife, ensuring – even as she falls – that men should not see anything improper (E. *Hekab*. 568–70). But when we find that Phylarchus – probably[24] – described how the women and girls of Sparta earlier in the third century dug a defensive trench wearing very little and tucking up their clothes (Plut. *Pyrrh*. 27.6), his interest recalls salacious tabloid journalism. Educated Greek males are likely to have been well used to female nudity – in slaves and courtesans. In contrast the sight of flesh of female citizens was – in most cities – stolen fruit. Phylarchus' references to nakedness at women's death appealed to him, or he hoped would appeal to his male readers, partly for erotic reasons; there is no doubt an element of fiction. Sparta's citizen females in the classical period were famed for the amount of bare flesh they showed in the presence of men.[25] Phylarchus' women diggers with their bare legs may be authentically Spartan; the anxiety about nudity-after-death is less persuasive.

The death of women occurs again and again in Phylarchus, even though what is demonstrably left of Phylarchus' works – apart from the wholesale borrowings in Plutarch – only accounts for some 27 pages in Jacoby's Fragments (*FGrH* IIA, pp. 162–89). We should consider briefly Phylarchan passages from elsewhere than Plutarch's *Agis and Kleomenes*. A courtesan, Danae, is put to death for saving her lover in defiance of her mistress, queen Laodice. Phylarchus, the dramatic historian, knows what she said just before she was pushed over a cliff: impressively philosophic words (Ath. 593bd). Khilonis – another young Spartan lady of that name – is described, very probably by Phylarchus. (The details about her come shortly before, and shortly after, Plutarch's citation of Phylarchus concerning the defensive trench at Sparta.) Khilonis' elderly husband, Kleonymos, is in exile, and she – a beauty, we are told – is having an affair with a heroic young Spartan, Akrotatos, son of king Areus. When the husband comes with a foreign army to invade Sparta, she withdraws with a rope around her neck, ready to die, should Sparta fall. (As it turned out, the invasion was defeated; Khilonis' lover fought valiantly and senior Spartans urged him to go and take Khilonis: 'Just be sure you make good sons for Sparta'; Plut. *Pyrrh.* 26.17–19, 27.10, 28.5 f. Adultery approved – not a common thing in Greek literature. But in classical Sparta breaches of monogamy for purposes of breeding had been permitted, and Kleonymos, the husband, was a traitor in arms.) Another woman with a noose in Phylarchus is the mythical Euopis, who does hang herself, in circumstances reminiscent of Phaidra (Parthen. *Narr.Am.* 31). There is a perverse sexuality in some men concerning the hanging of beautiful women; Thomas Hardy was prey to it, and his Tess of the Durbervilles ends that way. For Greek readers there was a special twist. When Plutarch, probably following Phylarchus (see below), writes of a 'very beautiful' virgin 'taking off her girdle and rigging up a noose' (*Mor.* 253d), he is using words, λύσασα τὴν ζώνην, reminiscent of women about to have sex (LSJ s.v. ζώνη, Ia).

Phylarchus emphasises often the sheer beauty of his female characters. Agiatis, Kleomenes' wife, is the most beautiful woman in Greece.[26] The unnamed wife of Panteus is similarly lovely; the (non-Spartan) Timosa excelled all women in beauty (Ath. 609ab) – the list goes on.[27] Did Phylarchus do a survey, perhaps touring the festivals of Greece, one of the few occasions when comely female aristocrats as well as courtesans would be predictably seen out of doors? No; he is writing part-fiction, to keep the interest of male readers. (Compare journalists who, until recently, were encouraged to apply the adjective 'attractive' to women, wherever possible.)

Phylarchus' taste, as we see, was not for beautiful dollies. His heroines in other surviving fragments are often assertive, active and resourceful – like Mysta, lover of Seleukos II, who saw what was likely to happen to her at the end of a lost battle. She put on rags so that the enemy would not detect her identity or her status. Accordingly she was sold routinely into slavery rather than kept for exorbitant ransom, then she revealed her identity and got back to Seleukos (Ath. 593e). Phylarchus, probably, described the death of king Pyrrhus, hit in street fighting by a missile thrown by an elderly woman (Plut. *Pyrrh.* 34.1 f.). The elderly woman had been 'watching the battle like the other women, from the roof', but intervened with a tile when she saw her son in danger. When a pro-Macedonian tyrant of the late 270s, Aristotimos in Elis, was overthrown after a brief rule noted for the violent ill-treatment of many women, and his own female relatives had to die, a brave and merciful woman on the victorious side, Megisto, intervened. She brought it about that the tyrant's young daughters were allowed the right to kill themselves, by hanging, records – probably – Phylarchus (Plut. *Mul.Virt.* 15 = *Mor.* 250f–253e).[28] The story, told by Plutarch, of women under Aristotimos seems highly Phylarchan, and in several ways recalls, with its stress on female assertiveness as well as with its pathos and frustrated hedonism, the tale of the Spartan women in Alexandria. Women and children are abused by an autocrat as hostages, their lives under threat (*Mor.* 252a); the autocrat threatens to kill the small child of Megisto, leader of the women, before her eyes (*ib.* 252c). In face of the imminent death of herself and her child, Megisto makes a defiant speech. When fortunes are dramatically reversed, and Megisto attends the killing of Aristotimos' daughters, we are told that the latter are 'still virgins, very beautiful to look at and ripe for marriage' (*ib.* 253c). The elder daughter makes a virtuous speech, before hanging herself (*ib.* 253de). Also, like Agis' mother and like Panteus' wife, before dying she makes arrangements for the corpses of her female companion and of herself to be laid out decently. Phylarchus is very interested in what women could do successfully when in danger, whether on the battlefield or in intrigues in high places. Because I shall be arguing in a moment that women helped to shape these stories, it should be re-emphasised now that the stories also have heated male finger-prints over them, in a pattern somewhat familiar today.[29]

There is an anti-Macedonian pattern to much of Phylarchus' work. Rulers of Macedonian origin are shown colourfully degraded: Antiochus II by drunkenness (Ath. 438cd), Ptolemy II by gout (Ath. 536de), Ptolemy IV by base women. Since Sparta under Kleomenes took the lead in opposing direct Macedonian rule, Phylarchus may surely have inflated the virtue of the Spartan king and his female associates to further an anti-Macedonian case. Phylarchus' portraits of noble Spartan women contrast with his depictions of the low women in high places under Ptolemy IV.[30] The heroic deaths of the Spartan women in Alexandria reflect on the Ptolemy who ordered them; the nobler the women, the more hateful he was. Here is another reason to fear we are dealing with partisan fiction.

Phylarchus dwells on luxury, notably in matters of food and drink.[31] The word τρυφή occurs repeatedly in the fragments, albeit with the aid of a bias in the preservation; Athenaeus who preserved these references to luxury selected them for record because of his own interest in the subject.[32] Like a popular journalist condemning immorality, Phylarchus goes into intimate detail about the thing he abhors, as on the excess which supposedly preceded the fall of Sybaris.[33] Perhaps the largest concentrations of wealth ever known by Greeks in historical times belonged to the conquerors of the Persian empire, the Macedonians and their successors. Phylarchus, via Plutarch, has Agis say that his own fortune – no doubt one of the greatest private fortunes in Greece – was small compared with the wealth even of the underlings of a Ptolemy or a Seleukos (7.2). An idealist who wished to construct in fantasy an antithesis to hellenistic extremes, a community where wealth was widely shared if not quite levelled, especially in matters of food and drink, would be likeliest to hit on Sparta.[34] Sparta in classical times had been the inspiration of communitarian intellectuals, such as Plato. If Spartan rulers in Phylarchus' lifetime tried to level wealth, to the extent of giving away their private fortunes, that would have presented a huge intellectual temptation to an opponent of luxury such as Phylarchus. Those rulers might well be shown as profoundly virtuous, and their women with them.

Finally on the negative side of Phylarchus, there is the unlikelihood, on first principles, that he had a good source for much of the female nobility that he describes. Who was present at the deaths of Agis, his mother and grandmother? Probably only Agis' enemies and people those enemies trusted. Would they faithfully report noble dying words of Agesistrata, when any nobility would tell against themselves, her killers? When Agiatis talked to her impressionable husband Kleomenes about Agis' noble policies, those policies had been officially condemned and were not safe to mention (*Kl.* 2.1). Presumably such conversation is understood as having occurred in privacy at home. Who was there to become, later, a reliable witness? Agiatis and Kleomenes might both tell, but each would have reason to invent. Who reported Kleomenes' manly pose in his house after Sellasia? In the striking death scene of the Spartan women in Alexandria, who would survive to pass on the noble details? Ptolemy's execution party? In some, or all, of these cases we are surely dealing with fiction.

Here, then, in the *Agis and Kleomenes* are stories of passionate attachments between men and women; stories of women asserting themselves in public affairs, the world of men; stories of women dying interestingly. We have reason to suspect that all three categories of story were much to Phylarchus' taste. It is certain that he has lovingly embroidered, at the very least, the tales about Sparta. He may have invented them. But Phylarchus in other respects has much plausible detail about Sparta. For example, he makes Spartan revolutionaries appeal to divination (*Ag.* 9.1–4, 11.3–6, cf. *Kl.* 7.3 f.) and to bogus argument from political precedent (*Ag.* 12.2 f., *Kl.* 10.1–10) in a way which fits our evidence for classical Sparta;[35] compare his testimony on Spartan matters otherwise unknown to us, the existence of a shrine of Fear (*Kl.* 8.3–9.7; though cf. David 1989, 2), and the name of the place of execution, the Δεχάς (*Ag.* 19.8). Did Phylarchus, like some historical novelists of today, splice romantic fictions of his own into well-researched background material? Or was he perhaps drawn to a body of stories already existing, and generated by Sparta itself? This kind of process is also familiar today, as historians and especially biographers choose subjects which already, in pre-existing forms, correspond with their own temperaments, then proceed to slant or embroider, to make the material even more personally congenial.

Would the Sparta of the late third century have valued such tales? What manner of society had Sparta become?[36] We are short of literary sources for hellenistic Sparta – apart from these very stories of Plutarch and Phylarchus. A source independent of our authors is coinage. King Areus I of Sparta in the early third century broke the centuries-old 'Lykourgan' ban and issued silver tetradrachms. The types recall Alexander the Great; the pre-eminence of Areus in other respects has suggested that elements of hellenistic, autocratic, kingship had taken root in Sparta (Cartledge and Spawforth 1989, 35–7). Kleomenes III was to follow Areus' example; the designs of Kleomenes' tetradrachms echoed Seleucid and Ptolemaic usage (*id.*, 55). Plutarch writes of hellenistic courtly influence upon Sparta, and represents it as a subject of political debate there. Leonidas II, opponent of the reforming king Agis, is described as having imported to Sparta grand and alien courtly ways acquired during his long sojourn in Asia; Agis in debate taunts him with foreignness and with ignorance of Spartan practice (*Ag*. 3.9, 10.4). Plutarch elsewhere (*Pyrrh*. 26.21), again very likely using Phylarchus, suggests that the traditional education-system of Sparta was believed by king Pyrrhus of Epirus to exist still in his own day (273 BC). However, the impression given in Plutarch's Lives of Agis and Kleomenes is that austere Spartan culture had in other respects been allowed to lapse (e.g. *Ag*. 3.1, *Kl*. 2.1). This, we know, was the view of Phylarchus; a long fragment of his work (Ath. 141f–142f) refers to the pursuit of 'courtly indulgence' (αὐλικὴν ἐξουσίαν) at Sparta by kings Areus I and (his son and successor) Akrotatos. Some private individuals at Sparta, according to Phylarchus, far outdid in their spending even these two kings (Ath. 142b). It may be that Plutarch, like Phylarchus, found it convenient to over-emphasise how far the Sparta of Agis and Kleomenes had fallen from its old ideals, so as to enhance the contrast with the two reformers. (There is an explicit, stark contrast between Kleomenes and other rulers at *Kl*. 13. Similarly Phylarchus paints contrasting pictures, on the one hand of Kleomenes' dining arrangements, on the other of the Spartan luxury under Areus and Akrotatos; Ath. 141f–142b.) For an external check upon the Lives of Agis and Kleomenes, our best resource is comparison with classical Sparta, made in the light of general developments in hellenistic Greece.

Sparta in the classical period generated evocative and visually detailed stories.[37] Herodotus knows how Sparta's king Leotykhidas was caught with a foreign bribe: sitting on a (distinctively Persian) sleeve stuffed with silver (VI.72).[38] Thucydides, who could be impressively agnostic about detail concerning even the recent past,[39] passes on – albeit with reserve (λέγεται, 1.134.1) – an adventure tale from bygone Sparta. When the Spartan ephors came to arrest their wayward regent Pausanias, one ephor used a discreet head movement to warn Pausanias, who had been trapped in the first place by official eaves-droppers behind a screen (I.133–134.1). Such memorable, visual tales usually served the official ethos, and justified government decisions at Sparta. They probably came from Sparta. The creation of moralising story was seemingly a political fact of Spartan life. Perhaps such stories had in Sparta something like the position that tragedy had in Athens: entertaining, dealing with spectacular moral error and death, evoking *Schadenfreude*, integrative, cementing the community's values.

Some of these Spartan stories show how sexual attachment served the official order, by motivating a brave death. For example, a Spartan officer of the fourth century, Anaxibios, is reported by Xenophon as refusing to run away in an impossible military position; he dies fighting like a good Spartan and his boyfriend – *paidika* – stays loyally at his side (*Hell.* 4.8.38 f.).[40] The latter is identified not by his name but only in terms of his erotic relation to Anaxibios.

Famously the Spartans seem to have generated tales of good death, of what Nicole Loraux called *la 'belle mort' spartiate*.[41] The greatest of all was of the small force which at Thermopylai in 480 waited obediently to engage an uncountable host of the Persians. Herodotus has graphic details; the little band was observed beforehand by a Persian spy, doing gymnastics and combing their hair (7.208 f.). When, in 425, some 120 Spartans in a better-documented despair did capitulate, there was astonishment through Greece; Spartans had actually surrendered (Thuc. 4.40.1). So much had the Thermopylai tale achieved in public relations.

It may seem that the tales from Plutarch and Phylarchus are in a Spartan tradition, with their suspiciously graphic details, their heroism and their politically useful sexual liaisons. But there are some differences between the classical pattern of story and that in Plutarch/ Phylarchus. And the main differences concern the role of women.

Sexuality first. From Xenophon in the late classical period we have stories celebrating the benign power of homosexual links among Spartiates. In the account of Plutarch/Phylarchus, homosexuality still counts; Panteus, who dies loyally by Kleomenes' corpse, had been Kleomenes' lover in younger days (*Kl.* 37.14). We are told that, after embracing the king's corpse, he killed himself over it (*ib.* 37.16). But now, unlike the classical period, tales also of passionate heterosexual couples serve the Spartan ideal. Women join male partners in the stories. Panteus acts worthily of his male ex-lover, and his (passionately beloved) wife acts worthily of him. Kleomenes, in his passion for his beautiful wife, drinks in the revolutionary ideas which may have inspired him to patriotic reform. Could such tales come from within Sparta, or are they close relatives of the romantic Greek novel, where heroines were loving, assertive, courageous and given to travel – especially in Egypt?[42]

At the end of the classical period Aristotle writes something which historians of Sparta have not found easy to digest: that the Spartan men – during their empire (of the early fourth century) – were by Greek standards remarkably under the thumb of their sexual partners. But these partners were not, suggests Aristotle, predominantly homosexual – unlike those other noted warriors, the Celts. Spartan men were mainly in thrall to women (*Pol.* 1269b). Was Aristotle right?

On first principles, it should not surprise us if the commendation of homoerotic links in Xenophon's stories of classical Sparta did not perfectly reflect the prevailing Spartan practice. The commendation of one form of behaviour may be an implicit admission that its opposite may occur. We must concede that the shift from a couple of stories (in Xenophon) implicitly commending homosexuality in the classical period to a couple more (from Plutarch) implicitly commending heterosexuality in the hellenistic does not supply a compelling statistical basis. But it does prompt a question: whether the community of females at Sparta had, by hellenistic times, changed from a rather separate society, paralleling men in such matters as athletics,[43] to something more closely integrated with men. If the influence of female sexual partners over men, recognised by an outsider in late classical times, could now be admitted and implicitly commended in Spartan patriotic story, does that reflect a further increase – even as compared with Aristotle's day – in the standing of Spartan women?

Thomas Africa (1961, 43 f.) wrote that 'Women are far more prominent in Phylarchus' work than they were in the world in which it was composed.' Is this correct? With the hellenistic courts of Macedonian origin came influential women in the form of royalty and courtiers.[44] Renewed autocracy elsewhere in the Greek world no doubt brought other women to prominence, as it had centuries earlier in the age of the tyrants (Ar. *Pol.* 1314b). But women as politicians at Sparta? The tale in Herodotus (5.51), of the little girl Gorgo reminding her royal father Kleomenes I of his political duty, may have been inspired more by hostility towards Kleomenes than by observation of his daughter; the point may have been that *even* a child, *even* a girl, could put Kleomenes right.[45] The stereotype of the fierce Spartan mother, who tells her adult son to come home from war either with credit or dead, is recorded only from post-classical times. There is, however, some tantalising detail from a contemporary, Theopompos, of Spartiate women taken all too seriously as political influences in the early fourth century.[46] The fragmentary passage, from Athenaeus (609b), should be quoted in full:

> Theopompos in Book 56 of the *Histories* [writes that] Xenopeitheia, the mother of Lysandridas [Lysanoridas?], had been more beautiful than all the other women of the Peloponnese. The Spartans put her to death along with her sister Khryse, at the time when Lysandridas himself, the enemy of king Agesilaos, had been defeated by Agesilaos in civil strife and when Agesilaos had procured his exile by the Spartans.

'Lysandridas' is probably the Lysanoridas recorded elsewhere as having gone into exile in circumstances in which Agesilaos would have been intensely interested, following Sparta's loss of Thebes (379), where Lysanoridas had been a senior commander.[47] On the strength of the passage quoted, which is all the evidence we have for Xenopeitheia and Khryse, it seems that the two women were, in the prevailing view, too formidable to be left alive as a source of agitation in Lysanoridas' cause. The importance of Lysanoridas' post, in the age-oriented culture of Sparta, means that his mother was almost certainly in her fifties or older when she died, formidable now as a politician rather than a *femme fatale*.

Further speculation on this case is probably unjustified. In the two cases recounted above, of the lynching of women – the 'mothers' of Agis and the daughters of the Elean Aristotimos – the murdered women were associated with regimes which themselves had been oppressive to women. In the Elean case, women in numbers had suffered, and Megisto is shown moving from being arch-victim to presiding over the killing of Aristotimos' daughters. In the case of Agis' 'mothers', we know that women of the wealthy and, at the time of the killings, dominant class had themselves felt threatened by the reforms of Agis' group. There is a promising coherence in Phylarchus' unusual stories of lynched women; each case may have involved the unusual event that the sufferings of other women had removed the normal Greek inhibition against killing females. This inhibition was almost certainly derived in part from the opinions of women themselves, the generality of women of the citizen class.

We should be very wary of insisting that many of the private events described by Plutarch and Phylarchus and involving Spartan women, actually happened. But the deaths of Arkhidamia and Agesistrata form an exceptional case. They surely were events of such interest that, in outline, they were unlikely to be falsified. The detail, as with the death of Princess Diana, might immediately flourish out of control. But the bare fact of violent death is all but secure. If the 'mothers' both died at the same time as each other and as king Agis, that must mean political killing. And that in turn means that the mothers were widely seen as important political players. (Their case has also a significant difference from that of the daughters of Aristotimos. The daughters were reportedly of marriageable age; they might through marriage have perpetuated the tyrant's line and faction. In contrast, Agis' grandmother certainly, and his mother probably, were beyond the age of childbearing, as probably were the mother and aunt of Lysanoridas in the other Spartan case of the political killing of women.) If Agesistrata and

Arkhidamia had been seen by most contemporary Spartans as harmless ladies, one of them middle-aged the other elderly and with a distinguished patriotic history, to kill them would have been an appalling blunder – likely to create a backlash of sympathy. For appalling read 'unlikely'.

Aristotle's remark about the power of sexually-based affections among soldierly men may prompt speculation as to whether Spartan athleticism conduced to an unusual level of sexual energy and to an unusually high value put on sexual charm in a partner. There is, however, a more prosaic element to weigh in any account of female influence among Spartans: the wealth of some Spartiate women. Dowries were large, according to Aristotle (*Pol.* 1270a); Cartledge (1981a, 98) suggests that these were, rather, marriage settlements: that is, wealth which remained under the legal control of the wives. In the same passage, Aristotle states that heiresses were numerous. Cartledge and Hodkinson have argued that, among Spartans, women may have inherited on very different terms as compared with the best-known Greek community, Athens.[48] A Spartan daughter without brothers could, it seems, inherit as a πατροῦχος (cf. Hdt. 6.57.4) and retain, for life, legal ownership of her late father's wealth.

A daughter may have inherited a significant, if lesser, share of paternal wealth even when she had a surviving brother. Hodkinson has shown reason to believe that, in the circumstances of the classical period, the distribution of Spartan wealth through inheritance tended – albeit in the long term – to impoverish many families and thereby, under the 'Lykourgan' rules, to exclude from citizenship Spartans unable to contribute their share of provisions for the messes.[49] While that process conduced to the shrinking of the Spartiate population, a few families would become very rich indeed as daughters with significant landed wealth tended to marry men with great wealth of their own (cf. Aristotle, *ibid.*). Such marriages would often produce heiresses with even greater wealth. For the later classical period we have Aristotle's general remark, that women own (present tense) nearly two fifths of Spartan land, and that Spartan men in the period of their empire had themselves been subject to the power of women in administrative (not domestic) matters (*Pol.* 1269b–1270a). To be the bearer of inherited wealth does not on its own make a person influential. For example, if a woman is compelled by family to marry, and to stay married to, a certain man, her wealth may not enable her (as distinct from her family) to bargain with that man. We do not know whether a Spartan woman could – on her own initiative or that of others – divorce her husband. Nor is there much evidence for Spartan women having a say in choice of men to marry. However, in Plutarch's *Kleomenes* the king's (widowed) mother, Kratesikleia, seems to be represented as in control of her own marital status. It is reported (guardedly: λέγεται) that she had no need to marry, but that for her son's sake she married a man pre-eminent in reputation and power (6.2).

The stories of political women from Plutarch and Phylarchus make sense as a development from the Sparta Aristotle knew. The evidence for strong and repeated revolutionary pressures in third-century Sparta suggests that polarisation of wealth had continued since Aristotle's day. Plutarch (*Ag.* 5.6 f.) has a picture of Sparta with 'not more than 700' male citizens; of these only 'perhaps 100' owned much landed wealth, while the rest 'lacked wealth and status'. With that figure of 'perhaps 100' for the reign of Agis, compare the congruent number given for those expelled from Sparta by Kleomenes at the time of his land reform: 80 (*Kl.* 10.1). The 80 were presumably seen as the most wealthy and conservative, and likely to resist redistribution of land. A growth in the resources associated with women of the elite would make it likely (though not certain) that there was further growth in the influence of those women. That wealthy women were numerous would encourage them to assert themselves; there may have been no shortage of role-models, or of companions, to inhibit them. The picture of Kratesikleia in control of her own marital status matches the picture of her spending large sums in pursuit of her own political ends.

Aristotle, looking back to the Theban invasion of Spartan territory (370–369 BC), describes the women of Sparta as misbehaving, creating more noise and confusion than the enemy (*Pol.* 1269b); Xenophon, more sympathetic to Sparta, agrees that the women lost their self-control (*Hell.* VI.5.28).[50] In contrast, when king Pyrrhus of Epirus attacked Sparta a century later, we hear that Spartan women were prominently involved in the resistance, headed by Arkhidamia, the future grandmother of king Agis (Plut. *Pyrrh.* 27.4, 6–9). Indignant at a plan to send the women away to Crete, she invaded – as other Greeks would have seen it – the male sphere, by coming to the *gerousia* and demanding a particular course of action. She is described, in what we can now see as both Spartan and Phylarchan mode, as bearing a sword and uttering brief, challenging, patriotic words (Plut. *Pyrrh.* 27.4). The prolonged absence of men on military service may have helped to build up a tradition of political and administrative activity among Spartan women. And if social distances were indeed increasing within the shrinking citizen body, it may have become more attractive to departing Spartiates of the elite to delegate control to female relatives than to male citizens whose loyalties and political attitudes had grown less dependable. Spartiates often fought abroad as mercenaries in the fourth and third centuries. Plutarch writes (*Pyrrh*. 27.2) that the self-assertion of Spartan women during Pyrrhus' invasion happened in the absence of king Areus who had gone away to Crete, no doubt taking other Spartans with him. As has recently been observed of Sparta's wealthy women, 'the demonstrable weakness of their once invincible menfolk will have given them their opportunity to intervene publicly at the highest political level' (Cartledge and Spawforth 1989, 34).

We have seen that at the battle of Sellasia out of 6000 Spartan male citizens all but 200 were reportedly killed (Plut. *Kl*. 28.8, cf. Polyb. II.69.10; contrast Justin 28.4). A little band of survivors returned to Sparta, only for its leader, Kleomenes, and his entourage to take off promptly – and permanently – into exile. From that point, for many years, the citizen body of Sparta would be overwhelmingly female, if Plutarch and Phylarchus are even approximately right. Among the social elite, the class of Kleomenes and no doubt many of his lieutenants who had most personally to fear from Macedonian vengeance, exile may have produced a shortage of males even more marked than among the Spartiates generally. Since we are told by Aristotle that Sparta had, earlier, a history of *gynaikokratia*, we might reckon on very great female influence now. The administration of Sparta after Sellasia may have been substantially feminised.

Spartan input into the accounts of Phylarchus and Plutarch? A speculation

Two important propositions may be related: (1) for no state of the Greek mainland, at any period, do we have sober, generalising evidence for much political influence of women – except for Sparta in the late classical period, the evidence being Aristotle's; (2) for no state of the Greek mainland, at any period, do we have such a volume of detailed anecdotal evidence for the role of women in politics as we do for hellenistic Sparta.

The closeness of these propositions is unlikely to be accidental. It is worth speculating whether much of the feminine component of our Lives is a product, direct or indirect, of the dominance of Spartan women, especially after Sellasia. Two scenarios, not mutually exclusive, suggest themselves. The first involves ideological initiatives taken by women themselves. Did some women conclude that, since the state was now to a considerable extent theirs, so should ideology be? That since men in story were assigned glorious patriotic deaths, so should women be? The second scenario involves male Spartiates' recognising the greatly increased political activity of women and seeking to channel that activity by creating images of women in patriotic and self-sacrificing roles. Classical Sparta had known, and so hellenistic Sparta surely remembered, how to turn a military disaster into a moral victory, a psychological weapon for future war and politics. Kleomenes and his men, his mother and her women, died in Egypt in wretched circumstances, if not exactly as our authors describe. The women died in parallel with their men. Plutarch, at least, while loving parallels was probably too honest to invent one here. It may be that it was invented by Spartan women, or by men seeking to influence them. Was Alexandria to be the women's Thermopylai?

Finally, there is a fact awkward at first sight. Most of the women who star in these Lives live, or die, as loyal supporters of the reform faction at Sparta. But most Spartan women, initially under king Agis, opposed the reforms; so Plutarch reports, no doubt reflecting the opinion of wealthy women above all. Of these conservative women he says no more. But did their views cease to matter? Agis failed; his revolution, and his female family, came to grief. Kleomenes' revolution after a promising run came to grief – to utter disaster for Sparta, probably the greatest disaster in Sparta's history. A further speculative scenario may be sketched. There were some 20 years from Agis' reforms to Kleomenes' debacle: time perhaps for female opinion to change, and partly to swing behind the reform faction as it became the established authority under Kleomenes. But did the opinion of rich, conservative, influential women entirely disappear? Wealthy women were probably much aggrieved by Kleomenes' expulsion of 80 (presumably rich and conservative) men, to many of whom they would be closely related. Differences between women are likely to have been entrenched by this exiling of key men.

After Sellasia, when the exiles very likely returned, might female conservatism not have come into its own, sadly but firmly vindicated by events? The reformers had failed. Some of their best-known women had come to unpleasant ends. Sparta itself had come to the brink of annihilation; after Sellasia Sparta's enemies could, at will, have wiped the place off the map. We hear from Plutarch that influential women disagreed with each other on high policy under Agis; some conservativesorganised, through men, to obstruct reform. Surely there were tensions within the female citizenry after Sellasia. Conservative women could then have seen the fate of their female rivals-in-policy as a symptom of their political error. The unpleasant and unhappy ends of the royal women might well seem self-inflicted. Reformist women might therefore need to reply with stories that vindicated Arkhidamia, Agesistrata, Kratesikleia and the rest. The dying words of Agesistrata in the prison, 'I only hope that all this will be for the good of Sparta', and Kratesikleia's similar patriotic slogan about her going to Egypt for Sparta's sake, could have been designed by a partisan storyteller to answer criticism: these women acted for their country, not for selfish and destructive family ambition. Alternatively, storytellers might have sought to heal dissension, in the aftermath of disaster. Khilonis in this respect is especially interesting; although Phylarchus, the opponent of luxury and of Macedon, would no doubt have liked to show her as firmly for the reform party, and may have slanted his account that way, she is still left as a blameless defender of two male relatives, one from each faction. Was this image of Khilonis evolved as an emollient answer to those at Sparta who claimed that women's intervention in high politics involved family-chauvinism, destructive of Sparta's common interests? We see, in the societies we know best, how advanced feminist theory can co-exist with powerful conservative practice by women. One woman's feistiness is another woman's pushiness. In fact, modern female conservatism probably fuels the female radicalism. The idealisation of the Spartan women in Plutarch and Phylarchus, if it originated with women themselves, may have been part of a dialogue, for which the original intended audience was not Greek male readers but the people whose opinions Spartan women cared about most – other Spartan women.[51] And if we do indeed have, surviving in these Lives of Plutarch, elements of a dialogue between ancient Greek women, we have a great rarity.

Notes

1 A preliminary study is Mossé 1991.

2 Thuc. 2.45.2.

3 In general on Spartan women, Cartledge 1981. On public references to women by men at Athens, Schaps 1977.

4 The Greek leaves it possible that Agis' female relatives used men as go-betweens in their sollicitation of other women; παρακαλεῖν may be understood as governing διαλέγεσθαι (see LSJ s.v. παρακαλέω III.1).

5 Not necessarily a pejorative term here. Compare its use at Plut. *Pyrrh.* 29.12, where, as in the *Agis,* the biographer is probably following Phylarchus.

6 These female conservatives are overlooked in the generally very valuable study of Pédech (1989, 477–8).

7 Cf. Pelling 1979, 84 f., 91, and esp. 1990, 36 on reluctance to fabricate;

though contrast Bosworth 1992, 62 f., 70. For debate about whether Plutarch fabricated extensively concerning Athenian reactions to the building of the Parthenon, Stadter 1989, 149, Powell 1995; cf. Andrewes 1978.

[8] Pelling 1992, esp. p. 12.

[9] Cf. Pelling 1980.

[10] Carney 1960, 26 f. Further on Plutarch's tendencies as a biographer: he imputes emotional, rather than calculating and political, motives to his heroes (Russell 1995, 87). He mistakenly tidies, or ignores, chronology and where he found evidence of complex, paradoxical motives he tends to be reductive, to produce simplicity (Pelling 1980, 127 f.; 1988, 265–7; Bosworth 1992). He inserts moral lectures. He surrenders to the biographic vortex, whereby the actions and words of others are ascribed instead to the hero (Pelling 1979, 79; 1980, 129; Russell 1995, 87).

[11] *Kimon* 16.3.

[12] *Kimon* 14.5.

[13] *Agis* 20.5, 21.5.

[14] *Lykourgos* 28.13.

[15] Pelling 1980, 138.

[16] 1997, 90.

[17] Bux 1925; Gabba 1957, 28f.; Jacoby *FGrH* IIC 133 f.; Africa 1961, 3; Pédech 1989, 403.

[18] *Ag.* 9.3 (myth of Daphne); *Kl.* 5.3 (death of Arkhidamos); 28.2 (treachery at Sellasia); 30.3 (death of Doson).

[19] In his treatment of sources, scholars have found Plutarch markedly inconsistent; e.g. Pelling 1980, 139. In the first chapter of the *Lykourgos,* for example, he gives an impressively sceptical summary of the contradictory source material, then swiftly proceeds to reproduce naive and almost transparent myth (as, e.g., on Lykourgos' having father and grandfather named, respectively, Eunomos and Prytanis). In the *Aratos* (38.12), Plutarch emphatically suggests that Phylarchus is so invalidated by bias in favour of Kleomenes that his words should not be trusted, save where confirmed by Polybius; cf. Pelling 1990, 22. In the *Agis and Kleomenes,* Plutarch is plainly not so sceptical, and himself takes a strongly pro-Kleomenes line. Where Plutarch does name Phylarchus in our two Lives, it is with no sign of disrespect.

[20] Cf. Justin 16.1. The use of the bared breast to evoke pity for a mother is different from its display as sexual invitation by endangered Celtic women, as when faced with Julius Caesar's genocidal army: Caes. *BG* 7.47.5 f.

[21] Cf. Pédech 1989, 477.

[22] F.W. Walbank, *A Historical Commentary on Polybius,* vol. 1 (Oxford 1957), 565 f.

[23] See above, n. 19.

[24] Phylarchus is named by Plutarch as a source for the dimensions of the trench; *Pyrr.* 27.8.

[25] e.g. Eur. *Androm.* 595–600, cf. Ibycus ap. Plut. *Comp. Lyc. et Num.* 3 and Cartledge 1981, 91 f.

[26] For references to the reputation of Spartan women for beauty, see Cartledge 1981, 93 n. 58.

[27] Cf. Phylarchus on Pantika; Ath. 609bc.

[28] Stadter 1965, 86 f.

[29] With Phylarchus' scenarios of female beauty and partial nudity in a context of violence we are not far away from the perfect rock video, as defined by the comic character Butthead: 'Chicks in bikinis – and explosions'.

[30] If the text at *Kleom.* 33.1 should indeed be read as γυναικοκρατίαν, it is interesting that this pejorative term should be used of Ptolemy's women while nowhere in these Lives is it applied to the influential women of Sparta, to whom Aristotle referred with his memorable γυναικοκρατούμενοι (*Pol.* 1269b).

[31] Cf. Pédech 1989, 448–52. His chapter 3 is interesting and important on tragic structures, traceable to Phylarchus, in the *Agis and Kleomenes*.

[32] Ath. 141f–142f, 521be, 526a, (528c), 536de, 539b–540a. For other Phylarchan references to luxury, in the form of food or drink, Ath. 150df, 334ab, 412f, 438cd, 442c.

[33] Phyl. ap. Ath. 521be, cf. 526ac.

[34] Cf. Pédech 1989, 449, 468.

[35] Parker 1989, 154–63 (divination); Powell 1988, 217 f. (precedent).

[36] On this see especially Cartledge and Spawforth 1989, chs. 3–4. Kennell (1995) is also valuable, though should be read with caution concerning the survival or otherwise, and the recreation, of the traditional education system in the third century.

[37] Powell 1989.

[38] On the Persian sleeve (χειρίς), Xen. *Hell.* 2.1.8, *Cyrop.* 8.3.14.

[39] On the agnosticism, Thuc.I.1.3 with Powell 1988, 2 f.

[40] See also the tale of the attachment between king Agesilaos' son, Arkhidamos, and the extremely good-looking young Spartiate Kleonymos: Xen. *Hell.* 5.4.25–33. In general on Sparta's use of pederasty, Cartledge 1981b.

[41] Loraux 1977.

[42] On Egypt and the near east as standard settings for romantic adventure, E.L. Bowie, *OCD*[3] 1050 (entry on 'Novel, Greek').

[43] On women and athletics see now the papers of Hodkinson and Millender in this volume.

[44] See especially the material collected in Ogden (1999).

[45] On anti-Kleomenes tradition, see e.g. Griffiths 1989. Further on Spartan women in Herodotus, Millender (this volume) 357.

[46] I owe this point to Paul Cartledge.

[47] Plut. *Pelop.* 13.3, *Mor.* 576a; cf. Xen. *Hell.* 5.4.13, D.S. 15.27.3.

[48] Cartledge 1981a, 86–9 and esp. 97–9; Hodkinson 1986, 394, 399–404.

[49] Hodkinson 1989.

[50] Steve Hodkinson kindly points out to me that the women reportedly reacted to the sight of smoke from burning properties, and that wealthy women who owned such might have taken this especially badly.

[51] Cf. the words given to Khilonis on her status among women (*Ag.* 17.8).

Bibliography

Africa, T.W.

1961 *Phylarchus and the Spartan Revolution,* Berkeley.

Andrewes, A.

1978 'The opposition to Perikles', *JHS* 98, 1–8.

Blomqvist, K.

1997 'From Olympias to Aretaphila: women in politics in Plutarch', in J. Mossman (ed.) *Plutarch and his Intellectual World,*London, 73–97.

Bosworth, A.B.

1992 'History and artifice in Plutarch's *Eumenes*', in P.A. Stadter (ed.) *Plutarch and the Historical Tradition,* London and New York, 56–89.

Bux, E.

1925 'Zwei sozialistische Novellen bei Plutarch', *Klio* 19, 413–31.

Carney, T.F.

1960 'Plutarch's style in the *Marius*', *JHS* 80, 24–31.

Cartledge, P.A.

1981a 'Spartan wives: liberation or licence?', *CQ* 31, 84–105.

1981b 'The politics of Spartan pederasty', *PCPhS* 30, 17–36.

1987 *Agesilaos and the Crisis of Sparta,* London.

Cartledge, P.A. and Spawforth, A.

1989 *Hellenistic and Roman Sparta: a Tale of Two Cities,* London.

David, E.

1989 'Laughter in Spartan society', in A. Powell (ed.) *Classical Sparta,* London, 1–25.

Gabba, E.

1957 'Studi su Filarco. Le biographie plutarchee di Agide e di Cleomene', *Athenaeum* 35, 3–55, 193–239.

Griffiths, A.

1989 'Was Kleomenes mad?', in A. Powell (ed.) *Classical Sparta,* London, 51–78.

Hodkinson, S.

1986 'Land tenure and inheritance in classical Sparta', *CQ* 36, 378–406.

1989 'Inheritance, marriage and demography: perspectives upon the success and decline of classical Sparta' in A. Powell (ed.) *Classical Sparta,* London, 79–121.

Kennell, N.M.

1995 *The Gymnasium of Virtue: Education and culture in ancient Sparta,* Chapel Hill and London.

Loraux, N.

1977 'La "belle mort" spartiate', *Ktema* 2, 105–20.

Mossé, C.

1991 'Women in the Spartan revolutions of the third century BC', in S. Pomeroy (ed.) *Women's History and Ancient History,* Chapel Hill and London, 138–53.

Ogden, D.

1999 *Polygamy, Prostitutes and Death*, London.

Parker, R.
1989 'Spartan religion', in A. Powell (ed.) *Classical Sparta*, 142–72.
Pédech, P.
1989 *Trois historiens méconnus: Théopompe, Duris, Phylarque*, Paris.
Pelling, C.B.R.
1979 'Plutarch's method of work in the Roman Lives', *JHS* 99, 74–96.
1980 'Plutarch's adaptation of his source material', *JHS* 100, 127–40.
1988 'Aspects of Plutarch's characterisation', *Illinois Classical Studies* 13, 257–74.
1990 'Truth and fiction in Plutarch's Lives', in D.A. Russell (ed.) *Antonine Literature,* Oxford, 19–52.
1992 'Plutarch and Thucydides', in Stadter (ed.) *Plutarch and the Historical Tradition,* 10–40.
Pomeroy, S.
1997 *Families in Classical and Hellenistic Greece,* Oxford.
Powell, A.
1988 *Athens and Sparta,* London.
1989 'Mendacity and Sparta's use of the visual', in A. Powell (ed.) *Classical Sparta,* London, 173–92.
1995 'Athens' pretty face: anti-feminine rhetoric and fifth-century controversy over the Parthenon', in *idem* (ed.) *The Greek World,* London, 245–70.
Russell, D.A.
1995 'On reading Plutarch's Lives', in B. Scardigli (ed.) *Essays on Plutarch's Lives,* Oxford, 75–94.
Schaps, D.
1977 'The woman least mentioned: etiquette and women's names', *CQ* 27, 323–30.
Stadter, P.A.
1965 *Plutarch's Historical Methods: An analysis of the* Mulierum Virtutes, Cambridge, Mass.
1989 *A Commentary on Plutarch's* Pericles, Chapel Hill and London.
Stadter, P.A. (ed.)
1992 *Plutarch and the Historical Tradition*, London and New York.
Walbank, F.W.
1955 'Tragic history. A reconsideration', *BICS* 2, 4–14 [on Phylarchus].

INDEX

Greek names have been hellenised wherever possible: thus 'Khilon', 'Kyrene', 'Lykourgos', 'Tyrtaios', but 'Aeschylus'.